Chicago's Pride

CHICAGO'S PRIDE

The Stockyards, Packingtown, and Environs in the Nineteenth Century

Louise Carroll Wade

UNIVERSITY OF ILLINOIS PRESS
Urbana and Chicago

First paperback edition, 2003

This book is printed on acid-free paper.

Library of Congress Cataloging-in-Publication Data
Wade, Louise Carroll, 1928–
Chicago's pride : the stockyards, Packingtown, and environs in the nineteenth century / Louise Carroll Wade
p. cm.
Includes bibliographical references (p.) and index.
ISBN 0-252-07132-8 (pbk. : alk. paper)
1. Meat industry and trade—Illinois—Chicago—History.
2. Pork industry and trade—Illinois—Chicago—History.
3. Stockyards—Illinois—Chicago—History.
4. Packing-house workers—Illinois—Chicago—History.
5. Chicago (Ill.)—Social conditions.
I. Title.
II. Title: Packingtown.
HD9418.C4W33 2003
338.4'76649029'0977311 85-16525

Contents

Diagram and Maps

Acknowledgments

During the lengthy research and writing of this book, the author has accumulated many more personal obligations than can be acknowledged in a short space. However, I do wish to thank archivist Archie Motley, Grant Dean, and Larry Viskochil of the Chicago Historical Society; Rev. M. J. Madaj, archivist at St. Mary of the Lake Seminary; and the staff of the Joseph Regenstein Library, University of Chicago. Permission to use the Town of Lake records in the early 1970s was granted by Deputy County Clerk John H. Walsh. The maps were prepared by Jim Akerman of the Map Room, Newberry Library, and Tim Basaldua of Publication Design, Chicago. Moreover, I am grateful to those who read all or parts of the manuscript in its various stages: Mark Haller, Blake McKelvey, Archie Motley, Richard Maxwell Brown, Herbert Gutman, and especially Arthur Mann. Their comments strengthened it, though of course none can be held accountable for its shortcomings. Enid R. Scofield helped with the typing, and Patricia Hollahan, University of Illinois Press, deserves credit for the final editing.

My largest debt is to three friends whose long-sustained interest in the project helped transform it from an idea to a reality. The encouragement of Heinie Bush Wade and Sylvia B. and Arthur Mann is an essential ingredient of *Chicago's Pride* and one which the author deeply appreciates.

Abbreviations

BAI	Bureau of Animal Industry, U.S. Department of Agriculture.
CFLPS	Chicago Foreign Language Press Survey
JISHS	Journal of the Illinois State Historical Society
MVHR	Mississippi Valley Historical Review
Nat. Prov.	National Provisioner
Sun	Stockyards Sun
Times	Chicago Times
Trib.	Chicago Tribune
USYTC	Union Stock Yard and Transit Company

Chicago omitted from Board of Trade, Department of Health, etc. The annual reports of these organizations were published in Chicago.

Introduction

The square mile of land which contained the Stockyards and Packingtown and made Chicago "Hog Butcher for the World" is now an industrial park, and the 1879 Stone Gate which once marked the official entrance to the yards is now an historical landmark. The animal pens, the maze of railroad tracks, the huge packinghouses with their high chimneys, the livestock, the buyers and sellers, the butchers, the medley of sounds, the pungent smells, and the endless swirl of activity have long since disappeared. However, Chicagoans still refer to the surrounding residential areas as "the Stockyards neighborhood" and "Back of the Yards." Many of them take pride in tracing their family roots to this community even though its twentieth-century reputation was stained by Upton Sinclair's unflattering portrait in *The Jungle* (1906). Scholars in recent decades have provided more accurate accounts of the community, the workers' unions and strikes, the Back of the Yards Neighborhood Council, and the imperatives under which Sinclair produced his novel.[1] Two economic historians have studied the development of the packing industry and weighed Chicago's contributions.[2]

Curiously, however, no one has focused on the growth of the Stockyards, Packingtown, and the "instant suburb" in which they were located. In 1875, when the stockyard was only ten years old, a Chicago editor asserted that visitors would as soon think of leaving the city without having seen the yards and packinghouses as "the traveler would of visiting Egypt, and not the pyramids; Rome, and not the Coliseum; Pisa, and not the Leaning-Tower." Chicagoans kept an eye on the "marvelous growth" of the suburb as its population soared from three thousand in 1870 to eighty-five thousand by 1889. They celebrated the annexation of the thirty-six-square-mile township of Lake because its mushroom growth and the fame of the Stockyards and Packingtown enhanced their own image.

Historical records for studying the township were available. Chicago newspapers routinely reported on its "progress," and at the Stockyards Harvey Goodall published the *Drovers Journal* and a first-rate community paper, the Stockyards *Sun*. Terence Powderly's account of the 1886 strikes could be tested against the Knights of Labor Papers, while church and voluntary association records revealed the interaction of old-timers and newcomers. Fortunately, I was able to locate in the vaults of Chicago's City Hall the Town of Lake official records, undisturbed and apparently forgotten after the 1889 annexation.

It seemed to me that there was a need for such a study. When I began my research, E. P. Thompson, Herbert G. Gutman, David Brody, and Stephan Thernstrom had examined workers, trade unions, employers, and their impact on community from challenging new angles. Robert H. Wiebe had explored the consequences of late-nineteenth-century "pell-mell expansion" in our industrial cities, and Samuel P. Hays was calling for closer scrutiny of the process of change within specific communities.[3] The Town of Lake offered a unique opportunity to study the rise of a major industry, the sudden transformation of a rural township, the accommodation of "Americans," Irish, Germans, Bohemians, and Poles within that community, and the actions of stockyard and packinghouse employes as workers and as residents. The rich harvest of labor, ethnic, and community studies during the past decade greatly enriched my understanding of the broad themes I was handling. This book owes a good deal to scholars whose work has shaped my perspective on industrialism, labor relations, government regulations, ethnicity, and community.[4]

Chicago's Pride seeks to provide as full a picture as possible of this unusual township. Historical evidence, not models or theories, determined the conceptual framework: this is an account of what *did* happen, not what *ought* to have happened. All groups contributed to the success of the township, and thus no single group stands in the limelight or receives favored treatment. I consider the book's multiple themes—growth of the livestock trade and meat-packing, air and water pollution, expansion of the packinghouse work force and the status of those employes, changes in the burgeoning neighborhoods, the role of voluntary associations in forging the community, and the process of self-governance—to be of relatively equal importance. I have not published articles on these themes because I wanted the reader to see in the completed manuscript the interrelationships between the themes and the connections among employers, employes, foreign-born, native-born, Protestants, Catholics, officeholders, voters, commuting "colonels," and wage earners. This is inclusive not exclusive history.

Part One covers the earliest packing operations on the branches of the river, the scattered livestock sales yards, and Chicago's acquisition of the title "Porkopolis" during the Civil War. The price of this honor was pollution of the South Branch and chronic traffic jams between bipeds and quadrupeds fighting for the right-of-way on city streets. Railroad managers, livestock dealers, and packers solved the latter problem by devising a novel centralized stockyard beyond the urban boundaries. In 1865 they built the Union Stock Yard in the township of Lake where it was accessible to all railroads and to the packers. A few pork packers abandoned their South Branch location for land due west of the new facility. By the end of the 1860s, the construction workers' encampment east of Halsted Street had grown into the "Stockyards neighborhood." Several miles south and a world away was the Englewood commuters' enclave at the railroad junction. The township's largest landowners dominated local government and no doubt considered both settlements intrusive.

It was impossible to slow the invasion, as Part Two demonstrates. New rail lines quadrupled livestock receipts during the 1870s, and the Stockyards company hired Daniel Burnham and John Root to commemorate the achievement with the Stone Gate and several new buildings. Construction of many more modern packing plants in the western half of Town of Lake's industrial square mile and the development of canned meats and packinghouse by-products enabled packers to quadruple the value of their output. Livestock dealer Gustavus Swift and pork packer Philip Armour came to Mecca in 1875, and the thousands of new workers started settlements south and west of the packinghouses. The population of the Stockyards neighborhood shot up; and the Rock Island Railroad brought other newcomers to the vicinity around its carshops. After the Chicago fire well-heeled refugees heeded Englewood's advertisement of its suburban advantages and close proximity to Cook County Normal School. The township's elected supervisors were Protestants from either the carshops neighborhood or Englewood, but their nonpartisan political coalitions slated Stockyards Irish Catholics for "end spots" on the ticket.

Pell-mell expansion characterized both the industry and the community in the years between 1880 and the Columbian Exposition. Part Three examines the changes which made the livestock trade and packing industry Siamese twins and the repercussions for workers. Thanks to settlement of the plains and extension of Chicago's rail network, thirteen million cattle, sheep, and hogs arrived at the Stockyards in 1892. The company had upgraded its facilities and installed electric lights to permit unloading of stock trains before dawn and after dusk. The packers were using an ever larger proportion of the livestock; their shift from natural to artificial refrigeration in the plants and their purchase of refrigerated railroad cars enabled them to dominate the national market for chilled fresh meat. And the relentless pursuit of new packinghouse by-products enabled some of them to abide by Chicago's regulations against polluting the South Branch or its South Fork. The importance of chilled beef increased the number and elevated the status of cattle butchers in Packingtown. These skilled "knife men" led the campaign for shorter hours in 1886 and, in the wake of Haymarket, organized a Knights of Labor assembly to preserve the eight-hour day. The packers signed a contract with the beef workers prior to returning the pork houses to ten hours. Neither Powderly nor the local Knights of Labor leaders were prepared for the resulting walkout or the participation of some beef workers in that first strike. A much larger strike in November failed because the state militia arrived, confidence in Powderly waned, and the gulf between skilled and unskilled workers widened. The union disintegrated, but strikers and even strike leaders got their jobs back.

In an era when urban progress was equated with growth, the Town of Lake had reason to be proud, as Part Four reveals. The surge of newcomers touched off a building boom in working-class cottages, stores, fraternal halls, commercial blocks, churches, and schools. Horsecar lines paced the expansion and eroded the 1870s neighborhood boundaries. The various ethnic groups within the township strengthened their own voluntary associations and engaged in constant comparison with others. They vied for influence on the school boards and patronage from the town board. The rapid population changes produced "political cyclones" every few years. A Protestant livestock dealer from the north end of town toppled the Englewood "ring" but then fell victim to a new coalition headed by the Irish police chief. He lavished too much patronage on the Irish and was defeated by a combination of "Americans," Germans, Scandinavians, and Bohemians. A law and order spokesman satisfied the electorate in 1887 and 1888, but the Irish bounced back in the township's final election. In contrast to the volatile politics, improvements in streets, water distribution, and the fire and police departments were steady and predictable. Town of Lake surpassed the other suburbs in sewer construction, and its drainage plan was closely coordinated with Chicago's.

When the first annexation referendum came up in the fall of 1887, residents felt that their town board was doing a good job. Two-thirds of the voters said "no thanks" to the metropolis. By 1889 Chicago was promising the suburbs exemption from its building code, preservation of their local option districts, and the right to elect their own assessors. The city also pressed its "right" to collect the suburbs before the 1890 census and before Congress decided the site of the international exposition. Town of Lake, with a population nearly as large as Denver's and an "instant city" in its own right,[5] was just barely convinced by the advocates of merger.

The township as an independent entity died in 1889, but Chicago continued to sing the praises of the Stockyards and Packingtown. They were "the eighth wonder of the world," and thus it was only natural that well over one million people paid a visit during the year of the fair. Guided tours of the yards and packinghouses were "as popular as a ride in the Ferris wheel and far more interesting," said one person. Without a doubt, contemporaries thought that the economic miracles performed in that one square mile redounded to Chicago's credit and illustrated America's industrial prowess.

Historians, Mr. Dooley once observed, are like doctors, "always lookin' f'r symptoms. Those iv them that writes about their own times examines th' tongue an' feels th' pulse an' makes a wrong dygnosis. Th' other kind iv histhry is a post-mortem examination. It tells ye what a counthry died iv. But I'd like to know what it lived iv."[6] It is my hope that readers will understand what this unusual nineteenth-century community lived of and why it was Chicago's pride.

NOTES

1. David Brody, *The Butcher Workmen: A Study of Unionization* (Cambridge, Mass., 1964); James R. Barrett, "Work and Community in 'The Jungle': Chicago's Packing House Workers, 1894–1922" (Ph.D. diss., University of Pittsburgh, 1981); Robert Allen Slayton, "'Our Own Destiny': The Development of Community in Back of the Yards" (Ph.D. diss., Northwestern University, 1982); Christine Scriabine, "Upton Sinclair and the Writing of *The Jungle*," *Chicago History,* 10 (Spring, 1981), 26–37.

2. Margaret Walsh, *The Rise of the Midwestern Meat Packing Industry* (Lexington, Ky., 1982); Mary Yeager, *Competition and Regulation: The Development of Oligopoly in the Meat Packing Industry* (Greenwich, Conn., 1981).

3. E. P. Thompson, *The Making of the English Working Class* (New York, 1966); Herbert G. Gutman, "Class, Status, and Community Power in Nineteenth Century American Industrial Cities—Paterson, New Jersey: A Case Study," in *The Age of Industrialism in America: Essays in Social Structure and Cultural Values* (New York, 1968); Herbert G. Gutman, "The Reality of the Rags-to-Riches 'Myth'; The Case of the Paterson, New Jersey Locomotive, Iron, and Machinery Manufacturers, 1830–1880," in Stephan Thernstrom and Richard Sennett, eds., *Nineteenth Century Cities, Essays in the New Urban History* (New Haven, Conn., 1969); Herbert G. Gutman, "Work, Culture, and Society in Industrializing America, 1815–1919," *American Historical Review,* 78 (June, 1973), 531–88; Brody, *Butcher Workmen;* Stephan Thernstrom, *Poverty and Progress: Social Mobility in a Nineteenth Century City* (Cambridge, Mass., 1964); Robert H. Wiebe, *The Search for Order, 1877–1920* (New York, 1967); Samuel P. Hays, "A Systematic Social History," in George Billias and Gerald Grob, eds., *American History: Retrospect and Prospect* (New York, 1971); Samuel P. Hays, "The Changing Political Structure of the City in Industrial America," *Journal of Urban History,* 1 (Nov., 1974), 6–38.

4. Chapter notes and the essay on sources acknowledge the full debt, but I would like to mention David Montgomery, "Workers' Control of Machine Production in the Nineteenth Century," *Labor History,* 17 (Fall, 1976), 485–509 and "Immigrant Workers and Managerial Reform," in Richard L. Ehrlich, ed., *Immigrants in Industrial America, 1850–1920* (Charlottesville, Va., 1977); Alan Dawley, *Class and Community: The Industrial Revolution in Lynn* (Cambridge, Mass., 1976); Daniel Nelson, *Managers and Workers: Origins of the New Factory System in the United States, 1880–1920* (Madison, Wis., 1975); Daniel J. Walkowitz, *Worker City, Company Town: Iron and Cotton-Worker Protest in Troy and Cohoes, New York, 1855–84* (Urbana, Ill., 1978); Kathleen Neils Conzen, "Immigrants, Immigrant Neighborhoods, and Ethnic Identity: Historical Issues," *Journal of American History,* 66 (Dec., 1979), 603–15; Olivier J. Zunz, *The Changing Face of Inequality: Urbanization, Industrial Development, and Immigrants in Detroit, 1880–1920* (Chicago, 1982); Don Harrison Doyle, *The Social Order of a Frontier Community: Jacksonville, Illinois, 1825–70* (Urbana, Ill., 1978); and Thomas Bender, *Community and Social Change in America* (New Brunswick, N.J., 1978).

5. Gunther Barth, *Instant Cities: Urbanization and the Rise of San Francisco and Denver* (New York, 1975).

6. Finley Peter Dunne, *Mr. Dooley on Ivrything and Ivrybody,* selected by Robert Hutchinson (New York, 1963), 208.

PART ONE—1830S TO 1870

CHAPTER 1

In the Beginning

Chicago's early settlers pegged their hopes for a thriving community on the Illinois and Michigan Canal. Expectation of what that internal improvement would do for their economy explains the presence of some twenty-five thousand residents in 1848 when the project was finished. During the twelve years of waiting for the canal, purveyors of meat met growing local demand, fed the construction crews, and even ventured into exports to eastern cities and to Britain. Their meat products constituted 10 percent of the total value of the city's exports in 1848. It was the railroad, however, that would shape Chicago's destiny. In the 1850s the lucky town became the center of a forty-seven-hundred-mile network of tracks reaching north, west, south, and east. Population quadrupled and new industries, many of them dependent upon iron horses for hauling supplies and distributing goods, sprang to life. Thanks to the railroads and the rapid settlement of territory traversed by the "iron bands of commerce," Chicago's meat packers would have a chance to catch up with their midwestern rivals. Meanwhile, the city's startling growth necessitated readjusting urban boundaries. In the process, Bridgeport, the rural hamlet where canal construction commenced in 1836, was swallowed up. The outlying township of Lake was still sparsely populated on the eve of the Civil War, but savvy investors were buying land along its railroads and plank roads.

Butchers, Drovers, and Packers

In 1833 Chicago's first newspaper confidently announced that the ragged little settlement in the shadow of Fort Dearborn would soon become the "natural depot and market place" that God and Nature intended it to be. An Indian evacuation treaty, designation as the seat of Cook County, and a military road to Fort Detroit plus more primitive routes to Peoria on the Illinois River and Danville and Vincennes in the Wabash River valley were the most obvious assets, but Chicagoans dreamed of a canal linking their river with the Illinois and thus with the mighty Mississippi. The federal government approved the project and gave the state alternate sections of land along the proposed route in the 1820s. However, it was not until 1836 that the legislature finally authorized construction and the town experienced its first boom.[1]

In four years the population soared from less than two hundred to nearly four thousand. Harriet Martineau visited Chicago during the height of the frenzy and was amazed to see men paying more for "wild land on the banks of a canal, not yet marked out," than one needed to purchase "well improved" land along the Erie Canal. Emigrant families waited in covered wagons and tents until they could secure dwellings. Food was scarce and prices so high that the *Democrat* pleaded with farmers in the Illinois and Wabash valleys to send produce, cattle, and hogs: "our stock of edibles is almost exhausted." None of these inconveniences discouraged the "buoyant" residents or cramped the style of "land traders and gentlemen speculators." Indeed, future prospects looked so bright that Chicagoans secured a city charter and elected one of the speculators mayor in 1837. So rapidly had the town expanded that William B. Ogden presided over Illinois' largest incorporated community.[2]

Fortunately for the town dwellers, there were butchers in their midst and enough farmers in the surrounding countryside to provide an adequate meat supply. Farmers let cattle graze on prairie grass and hogs forage in oak groves; they slaughtered in late fall, rendered lard and tallow in large iron kettles over open fires, and preserved their meat by drying, smoking, or curing in a brine solution. The right combination of salt, cold weather, and good luck usually kept the "pickled" meat edible. Extra cattle and hogs were fattened on corn before being driven to Peoria, Danville, or Chicago; some farmers slaughtered the cantankerous "razorback" hogs in the winter and teamed the frozen carcasses to market as weather permitted. Although townspeople usually knew how to slaughter and cure meat and some continued to do it, most found it more convenient to patronize a butcher shop.[3]

Archibald Clybourn was Chicago's first commercial butcher. Arriving from Virginia in 1823, he farmed with his father and brothers on the North Branch of the river until 1827, when he built a slaughtering shed and an enclosure for the livestock he brought from the Illinois and Wabash valleys. Clybourn sold to Chicagoans and the Fort Dearborn garrison and was well enough known to be elected Cook County treasurer. Nonetheless, he advertised his butchering services as soon as Chicago acquired a newspaper. "A. Clybourn," said an 1833 notice, butchers hogs and sells "cheap for Cash, at wholesale, at his Butchers Shop two miles from Chicago"; he stocks pork and beef, "both fresh and salt . . . at his market in Chicago." Expanding his slaughtering and market facilities as the town grew, Clybourn was able to afford a twenty-room brick mansion by 1836. Sharing in his prosperity was a North Branch neighbor, Daniel Elston, who used the tallow to supply Chicagoans with soap and candles.[4]

Gurdon S. Hubbard of Danville had raised hogs for the Chicago market and traded with the Indians until 1833. When settlement of the upper Wabash valley ruined his Indian trade, he moved to Chicago, purchased land, started a slaughterhouse, and then a mercantile store. At the end of his first year in Chicago he informed a brother-in-law in Danville, "so far I have no regret for having moved to the smaller town." By the end of the decade he had a slaughtering and packing house on the bank of the Chicago River and his commission firm, G. S. Hubbard and Company, handled the sale of beef and pork from a brick warehouse on Kinzie Street. Hubbard had served as a town trustee and an Illinois and Michigan Canal commissioner, and he was building an enviable reputation as a land speculator.[5]

Sylvester Marsh, a meat-market owner, supplied Hubbard with cattle from the Wabash district. Until 1833 Marsh had packed meat in Ashtabula, Ohio, and shipped it east over the Erie Canal. He started in Chicago with a meat market, added the cattle supply business, and in 1836 constructed a packinghouse on the river. But it was George W. Dole, not Marsh, who apparently made the first shipment of meat from Chicago. In 1832 Dole contracted with Oliver Newberry in Detroit to send both beef and pork, and these two subsequently became partners in the commission firm of Newberry and Dole and owners of a slaughterhouse on the South Branch of the Chicago River. From time to time they purchased stock from Clybourn. An 1833 contract specified that Clybourn provide one hundred "good, fat, merchantable beef cattle" and two hundred hogs "cut up ready for salting and packing." It was "distinctly understood," however, that Newberry and Dole got "all the hides and tallow and one-half the tongues coming from said cattle."[6]

These early purveyors of meat benefited, of course, from construction of the Illinois and Michigan Canal. Work on that project commenced in 1836 at the juncture of the Chicago River's South Branch and its South Fork. An access road, later called the Archer Road, followed the south side of the South Branch to Bridgeport, a tiny hamlet of German farmers at the juncture. In spite of the 1837 financial panic, work continued until the winter of 1840–41. The commissioners then agreed to cut costs by revising the plans. Instead of digging a six-foot-deep channel, navigable by steamboats, they settled for a four-foot depth which restricted traffic to canal boats only. It also meant that water would not flow from the Chicago River into the canal during dry periods or when the lake level was low, but engineers remedied this by adding a pumping station at Bridgeport. The first canal boats passed through the locks in April, 1848, and Chicagoans turned out in large numbers to cheer. After twelve years of waiting for this internal improvement, they anticipated economic miracles from "the wedding of the Father of Rivers to our inland seas."[7]

Those who traveled to Bridgeport to inspect the turning basin were fascinated by the huge hydraulic pumps and steam engines capable of generating power "equal to 200 horses." Bridgeport surprised them too. It had three hundred residents, many of them former canal laborers of Irish extraction, and the Archer Road was alive with taverns and mercantile and provision stores. A *Gem of the Prairie* reporter thought Bridgeport had a future "aside from the business of the canal." The extra hydraulic pump could provide power for mills and factories, while the canal and South Branch offered inexpensive transport for raw materials and finished goods. Bridgeport, he decided, "is a most capital point for manufacturing purposes. . . . Very soon it will be only a suburb" of Chicago.[8]

Chicago, meantime, with a population exceeding twenty-five thousand in the late 1840s, was a capital market for beef and pork. Its earliest butcher-packers had expanded their operations; several new firms had entered the business; and drovers were delivering close to thirty thousand cattle and hogs per year to Chicago. Innovations in livestock delivery, plant construction, and marketing facilitated the growth of meat-packing in the 1840s.

The earliest packers had either done their own droving or hired young men to bring the stock to their slaughterhouses. Sylvester Marsh, for example, took on the Hough brothers, Rosell and Oramel, as drovers after he opened his own packinghouse. But there were many opportunities for free-lance drovers. Sometimes they paid the farmers before departing with the animals; more often they operated on credit and squared accounts when they returned for more livestock. One drover with two assistants could handle seventy-five to one hundred cattle or several hundred hogs. They let the animals graze along the way, and drovers put up at night with farmers who had a fenced enclosure and earned extra money boarding travelers. The drovers generally sold their animals the same day they reached Chicago and then hitched a ride back with farmers. Occasionally they stayed on in Chicago to help slaughter and pack. John Stephen Wright encountered these drovers in Beaubien's boarding house. "The 'Hoosiers,'" he later recalled, "were never too busy with killing, and never wasted time with washing, to keep them behind at meal times. Mrs. Beaubien . . . tried her best to get some of the 'slap-jacks' to me, but the hog-killers were so on the alert, that two weeks' fighting for my living, impressed upon my memory pretty effectually the early days of Chicago pork-packing."[9]

Peddling livestock in the city had its drawbacks. One newspaper complained in 1839 that Chicago's foremost nuisance was "swine—streets full of them." Willard F. Myrick hit upon a better solution. In 1837 he had purchased a farmers' boardinghouse on the lakefront plus adjacent property between Twenty-sixth and Thirty-first streets. There were only two distant neighbors on the shore and no settlers to the west until "the shanties of Bridgeport." When Myrick reopened the boardinghouse and found many more drovers than farmers, he fenced an area for their livestock and "cut all the hay I needed off the land just back of me." Within a few years he enlarged these "yards" and purchased the city's first platform scale for weighing cattle. Since buyers drove their purchases into the city on Cottage Grove, Myrick eventually moved his hotel-tavern to that road. He was operating a race track as early as 1840, and the mix of drovers, livestock purchasers, sporting fans, and "city ladies for partners" made "Mr. Myrick's tavern" a well-known gathering place.[10]

Both the delivery of livestock and the packing process were seasonal operations. Drovers brought the cattle to market shortly after the first frost ended grazing; hogs were rounded up and fattened on corn before being sold in December. The packers began slaughtering cattle as soon as the weather was cool enough to chill the carcass, usually October, and they continued packing hogs until late February or early March. The packing season could be interrupted by unexpectedly warm weather, shortages of salt or barrels, and a dearth of livestock or workers. Unheated plants had to be closed in extremely cold weather because workmen could not safely expose their hands. Between March and October packinghouse employees sought jobs in lumber- and brickyards and on construction projects and Great Lakes vessels.

Until 1841 most of Chicago's beef and pork was purchased locally or by canal contractors. Although canal work was temporarily halted in the early 1840s, packers did not cut back on production. They shipped some fifteen hundred barrels of pork and eight hundred barrels of beef to eastern markets in 1842 and a reporter, worried about recession, said: "The wheat business did much for us, but the pork will certainly enable us to save our bacon. We are literally going the whole hog." Five years later, despite resumption of canal work and larger local demand, the packers exported nearly forty-nine thousand barrels of pork and beef, some of it to England and Canada.[11]

More livestock and new packing plants made this possible. Archibald Clybourn built on the site of his original slaughtering shed in the early 1840s. He could handle between two and three thousand cattle per year in this facility, and for a time he packed on consignment to William Felt of New York. Sylvester Marsh and George W. Dole formed a partnership in 1839 with Dole handling sales and Marsh managing a new packing plant on the South Branch. They rented the old Newberry and Dole house to newcomer Eri Reynolds. Even though Gurdon Hubbard built a second plant, he needed still more space and in 1848 purchased land about one mile up the North Branch and constructed Chicago's largest slaughtering and packing house. Here he remained until 1870 when fire destroyed the plant and Hubbard retired from the packing business.[12]

The outstanding new firm in the 1840s was formed by provision merchants John P. Chapin, Julius W. Wadsworth, and Thomas Dyer. Aware of the successful sale of Chicago meat in Boston and New York during 1842–43, Chapin rented the Newberry and Dole house in 1844 and put Thomas Dyer in charge. Julius Wadsworth joined them the following year with the capital to build a large plant on the South Branch outside the city limits. Chapin dropped out of the partnership in 1846, the year he was elected mayor of Chicago, but Wadsworth and Dyer did very well on their own. They packed two thousand cattle and nearly eleven thousand hogs in the winter of 1845–46 and were the first Chicago packers to ship beef to England and to secure a contract with the United States Navy. These transactions convinced the *Democrat* that Chicago was "destined to be the greatest beef market in the U.S. if not in the world."[13]

By 1848 Wadsworth, Dyer, and Company had seventy-five to eighty employes handling an average of 150 cattle per day. The firm had developed a technique for preserving, or pickling, beef in a solution of salt and water with smaller amounts of brown sugar, saltpeter, and saleratus. (Only Turk's Island or St. Ubes salt went into the wooden tierces of beef for the English market because it kept longer.) John Stephen Wright visited the South Branch plant and described the packing operations in *Prairie Farmer.* After the steer was skinned and eviscerated, the "beef is slit in halves and hangs for a time to dry. It then goes into the cutting and packing room, where it is . . . divided into 8 pound pieces. A skillful cutter soon learns to cut without varying two ounces from the required weight." Next, the beef went into larger wooden tubs filled with the pickle solution, and every twenty-four hours it was moved to another tub with fresh pickle. After six days of soaking, the meat was packed, exactly thirty-eight pieces to a tierce with "the best Turk's Island salt only." These three-hundred-pound tierces left the plant on canal boats and were placed aboard Great Lakes vessels in the Chicago harbor.[14]

The lifting and moving of carcasses and tierces was done by hand, and reporters often described packinghouse butchers and laborers as "stalwart" or "robust." Wright noticed one laborsaving device: the pickle solution in the tubs passed by pipes into a cauldron where it was heated, skimmed, and pumped back into the tubs. "This carrying of the brine was formerly done by hand; a terrible process." Wright was impressed by the "economies" at Wadsworth, Dyer, and Company. Instead of throwing away the necks and shanks, they trimmed the meat, salted and dried it, and then shipped it to the West Indies where it brought 3¢ a pound as "jerked beef." The trimmed necks, shanks, and bones, as well as entrails and heads, went into a cauldron to be boiled down for tallow. Some fifty barrels of tallow were produced daily and sold to soap- and candlemakers, yielding a profit of $2,000 a year. Beef tongues, removed at the time of slaughter, were cured and sold in New York. Hides were dried at the plant and sold either in Chicago or eastern markets. Hoofs and horns went for 10¢ a set in Chicago. As a further economy, the firm made its own oak tierces and barrels. In addition to the eighty butchers, there were about one hundred men employed in these ancillary tasks. Wright had a few suggestions. The "boiled shreds of meat, cast forth as waste, after the tallow is obtained, . . . might be fed to swine with advantage." And the bones, blood, and manure "ought to find their way back to the land. There are hundreds of loads of this, for which there is no demand." Well in advance of Armour and Swift, Wright concluded, "Perfection will only be reached when nothing is lost."[15]

There are no comparable descriptions of pork-packing in Chicago in the 1840s, but newspaper articles outlined the general process. The hog was driven into an enclosure where one man struck it over the head, a second slit its throat, and a third man dragged it into a cauldron of scalding water to loosen the bristles. It is uncertain how the carcass was removed from the cauldron, but once it was out of the water, scrapers removed the bristles. The carcass was then cut open, eviscerated, and pushed out of the way—"piled up"—until it had cooled. In the packing section, men lifted each carcass onto a six-foot square cutting block. Three men worked at each block, one severing the head with a cleaver and the other two using knives to separate hams, shoulders, ribs, and fat. In the center of the room were scales and large boxes or vats for each of these cuts, and the butchers apparently threw the pieces from the block to the boxes. Others weighed the cuts and placed them in a pickle solution of water, rock salt, molasses, and saltpeter to soak for several weeks. The pork was then packed in wooden barrels with a heavy mallet before the barrel was sealed. Reporters admired the speed and skill of the "robust" butchers but considered their jobs "exceedingly unpleasant" because they stood in "gore" and were "saturated with it from head to foot."[16]

Pork- and beef-packing stimulated auxilliary industries. The larger houses rendered their own fat into lard and boiled heads and entrails to produce tallow, but small packers and many market butchers sold their "wastes" to Charles Cleaver, who dominated the tallow, lard, soap, and candle business in the 1840s. For several years after his arrival from England in 1833, Cleaver had difficulty securing raw materials. By the early 1840s, however, "it was coming in faster than I could melt it by the old process." Cleaver consulted the owner of the Eagle Steam Foundry, Philetus W. Gates, who designed a steam boiler that rendered animal fat much faster than iron cauldrons over wood-burning fires. Cleaver's steam rendering tank gave him an edge over competitors, but he realized that it was only a matter of time until the packers installed similar equipment. Hides from the local packers were purchased by Chicago's five tanneries. Walter S. Gurnee's operation at the fork of the Chicago River was the largest and employed fifty men. Still, by 1845 the packinghouses were producing more hides than tanners could process and Chicago began exporting hides.[17]

Tanners, renderers, slaughterers, and packers deliberately positioned themselves on the banks of the Chicago River or its branches. The city had neither a water distribution nor sewerage system, so these manufacturers drew water from the river and discharged into it. "Packing Houses, as they are called," explained a reporter, "are generally located on the side of a river" because they need large quantities of water for "constant cleansing" and a place to get rid of blood, shreds of meat, floor sweepings, and manure. City fathers tried without much success in the 1830s and '40s to defend the Chicago River. In May, 1837, the newly organized city council gave slaughterers a choice—either "destroy the offal . . . and other offensive and useless parts" or else "convey the same into some place . . . not . . . injurious or offensive to the inhabitants." Packinghouse waste material went into the river in an ever-increasing volume, so the council passed a more specific ordinance in May, 1843. It prohibited the deposit of "offal, or other putrid or unwholesome substance" in Lake Michigan or on its shores, or in the Chicago River or either of its branches within the city limits. The penalty was a $25 fine, half of which went to the informant. This ordinance may have influenced Wadsworth, Dyer, and Company to build outside the city limits, but it did not deter packers from using the river as their sewer. The problem of packinghouse waste disposal had been identified, but in the absence of any solution John Lewis Peyton, a Virginian visiting Chicago in 1848, found the river repulsive—"a sluggish, slimy stream, too lazy to clean itself."[18]

Pre-Civil War statistics on the packing industry in Chicago and the Midwest are unreliable and incomplete. But it would appear that by 1848 Chicago's six packing firms were employing about three hundred men to slaughter, cure, and pack their beef and pork and another three hundred as drovers, teamsters, coopers, and laborers. The value of Chicago's meat shipments came to about $1,000,000 in 1848. This constituted one-tenth of the city's total exports. Eighteen forty-eight was the first year that Chicago's exports exceeded her imports and, significantly, the year in which the Chicago Board of Trade was established. Thomas Dyer, the innovative leader at Wadsworth, Dyer, and Company, was instrumental in founding this organization, and he was the first president of the Chicago Board of Trade. Yet not even Dyer expected meat-packing to become as important an industry in Chicago as it already was in Cincinnati. Chicago's twenty thousand hogs put her ahead of all other Illinois packing centers except Beardstown, but the operation was tiny compared to Cincinnati's 350,000 hogs in 1848. The Ohio River city was the nation's "Porkopolis, the grand emporium of hogs."[19]

The Advent of Railroads

Chicagoans were so fascinated by the first navigation season on the Illinois and Michigan Canal that they paid scant attention to three other developments in 1848—installation of the first telegraph line, completion of the first plank road, and a trial run on the first ten miles of railroad track. Local boosters were more perceptive. Judge Jesse B. Thomas promised that the new "arteries of trade" would "at once, and by magic, change the condition and prospects of our City." The editor of the *Democrat* predicted "untold riches" now that we have "reached out our arms to the country around us—in the canal, the railroad and the plank roads."[20]

The success of plank roads in New York State prompted Illinois to try them. Constructed by private companies and maintained by tolls, these elevated eight-foot-wide wooden roadways enabled teams to travel ten miles an hour. That was faster and safer than the newfangled railroads, noted one reporter. Chicago's first plank road went southwest to the Des Plaines River (Ogden Avenue today) and was later extended to Naperville. A Western Plank Road Company built out to Elgin; the Northwestern Road (Milwaukee Avenue today) tied Chicago to Wheeling; and a ten-mile section of State Street south of the city limits became the Southern Plank Road. The last and finest was Blue Island Plank Road, constructed in 1854. It ran southwest to the fork in the South Branch and then straight south to the settlement of Blue Island (Blue Island and Western Avenues today). Since it was wider and better drained than the other plank roads, realtors pushed ten- and twenty-acre farms along the route as ideal locations for growing vegetables and fattening livestock for the city market. And the small settlement of Brighton at the intersection of Archer Road and the Blue Island Plank Road soon acquired a drovers' hotel and stockyard.[21]

Chicago packers, aware of the drovers' difficulties on the "notoriously bad" Vincennes road, informed the *Democrat* in 1834 that "common sense suggests . . . a rail-road." Gurdon Hubbard, George Dole, and others secured a charter the following year but failed to raise the necessary money to build a Chicago and Vincennes Railroad. So Chicago's first railroad was the Galena and Chicago Union. The panic and depression played havoc with construction schedules, but packer Thomas Dyer helped them complete the ten-mile stretch to the Des Plaines River. It opened late in 1848,

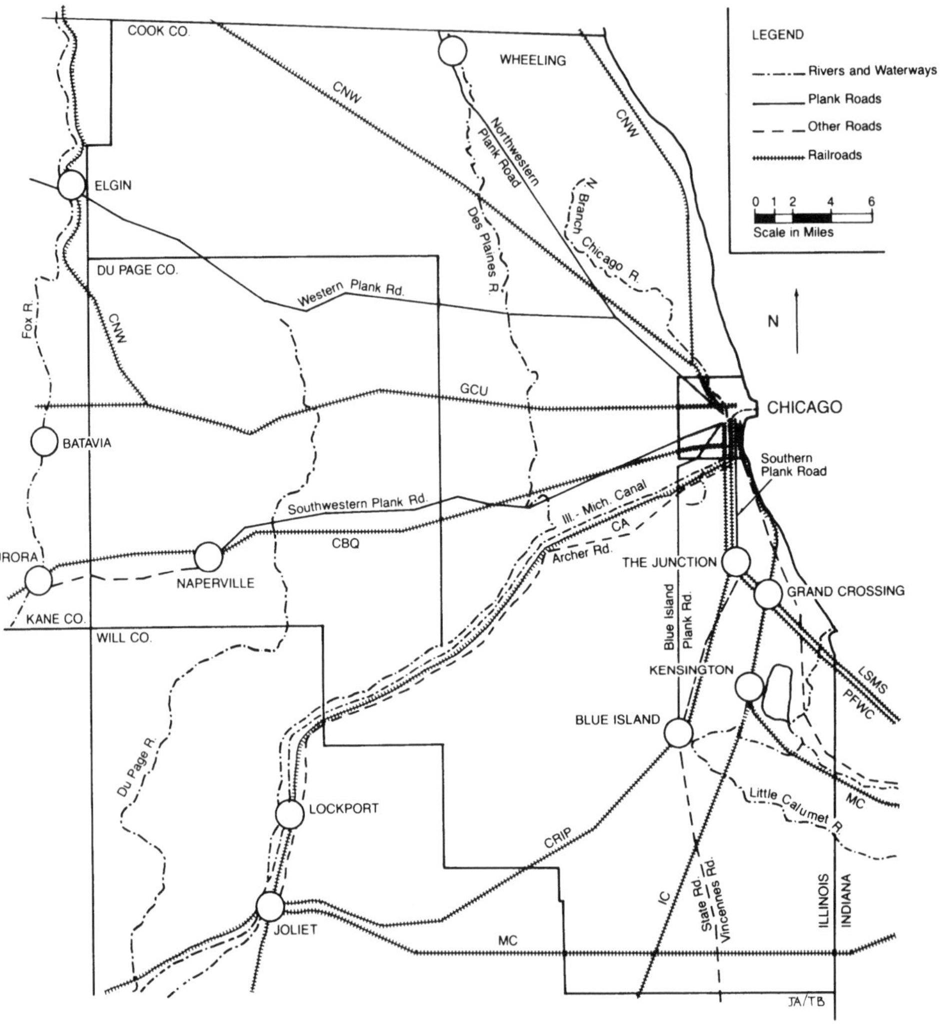

KEY TO RAILROAD ABBREVIATIONS

CA – Chicago and Alton
CBQ – Chicago, Burlington and Quincy
CNW – Chicago and Northwestern
CRIP – Chicago, Rock Island, and Pacific
GCU – Galena and Chicago Union
IC – Illinois Central
LSMS – Lake Shore and Michigan Southern
MC – Michigan Central
PFWC – Pittsburgh, Ft. Wayne, and Chicago

Map 1. Chicago area plank roads and railroads, 1860

reached Elgin in 1850, and terminated five years later at Fulton on the Mississippi, having bypassed the fading town of Galena. Farmers were quick to take advantage of the railroad to ship hogs to Chicago. Observing the arrival of more than one thousand hogs at the Galena and Chicago Union freight depot on a December day in 1852, a *Tribune* reporter commented, "What a waste of time, labor and capital would have been expended, had these been brought to the city by teams. How can we overestimate the value of railroads?"[22]

In short order Chicago acquired seven other lines and found itself at the center of a veritable spiderweb of "iron bands of commercial intercourse." The Chicago and Rock Island paralleled the canal and Illinois River to Peru and then reached the Mississippi in 1854. Two years later it had a railroad bridge between Rock Island and Davenport, and its sights were set on Council Bluffs. Hide manufacturer Walter S. Gurnee built a line from Chicago to Milwaukee, while William B. Ogden was consolidating small lines in Wisconsin into the Chicago and North Western Railway. By 1865 the North Western network included the Milwaukee road and the pioneer Galena line and was ready to press across the Mississippi River into Iowa.[23]

After promising to build a north-south trunk line from Chicago to the Gulf of Mexico, the Illinois Central in 1850 snagged the first federal land grant to finance railroad construction. The company hired Roswell B. Mason from the New York and New Haven Railroad, and he devised a Y-shaped route with Cairo at the southern tip and Chicago and Galena the northern termini. Construction started simultaneously at Chicago and Cairo, and Illinois Central trains traversed the state by 1856. This important seven-hundred-mile artery spurred settlement in central Illinois, brought grain, produce, and livestock to Chicago, and opened new markets for city merchants and manufacturers. Hogs formerly delivered to Terre Haute or Cincinnati now came to Chicago, and packers utilized the railroad to explore southern markets. A New Orleans newspaper reported in December, 1856, that a commission house in that city was awaiting a shipment of pork, lard, and hams from Chicago. The goods would travel by rail to Cairo and thence by steamboat. "This is the first shipment of the kind that has ever been made from Chicago to this port and is intended as an experiment to be followed up by others in case it pays a remunerative profit." Trade was so profitable that the Illinois Central developed its own packet line from Cairo to New Orleans with stops at St. Louis, Memphis, and Vicksburg.[24]

The Chicago and Alton Railroad also tapped the Mississippi River trade. While track was being laid from Alton to Joliet, one of Roswell Mason's surveyors, Timothy B. Blackstone, built the first railroad along the South Branch of the Chicago River and the southern bank of the Illinois and Michigan Canal. Mason had recommended this route into Chicago to the

Illinois Central, arguing that its potential freight traffic outweighed the advantages of a lakefront track. Overruled by his superiors, Mason encouraged Blackstone and backers of the Joliet and Chicago Railroad to go ahead and build. Their line ultimately merged with the Alton line and by the early 1860s, when Blackstone became president of the Chicago and Alton, livestock from the lower Illinois and Mississippi River valleys routinely came to Chicago rather than Beardstown or Alton.[25]

The Michigan Central and the Michigan Southern (later the Lake Shore and Michigan Southern) were Chicago's first lines to the East. Their completion in May, 1852, broke the monopoly of Great Lakes vessels and provided "iron bands" to Detroit and Toledo and connections to Cleveland, Buffalo, Albany, Boston, and New York. Eager for Chicago's trade and already thinking about the territory beyond, the two railroads were fierce rivals. The Michigan Central was incorporated in 1846 with Boston financier John Murray Forbes as president, but the railroad was the creation of James Frederick Joy, a Dartmouth and Harvard Law School graduate who was practicing law in Detroit, and his friend, civil engineer John Woods Brooks. The new company merged several small lines between Detroit and Kalamazoo before building across the state to Michigan City. Joy, Brooks, and Forbes were determined to beat the New York-backed Michigan Southern Railroad into Chicago. "These are times when bold action is the only safe action," wrote Joy. The Michigan Southern will "cripple us irreparably unless we act in self-defense." Neither group hesitated to use the courts or legislatures of Indiana and Illinois to frustrate the other's construction plans and approach to Chicago. Each sought allies. Rock Island interests sided with the Michigan Southern, while financial backers of the Illinois Central aided the Michigan Central. John Wentworth, former Chicago congressman, owner of the *Democrat*, and Dartmouth classmate of Joy, threw his support to the Forbes coalition. The Michigan Central shared the Illinois Central's right-of-way into Chicago and sent its first train on May 21, 1852. The following day a Michigan Southern train arrived on tracks laid by that railroad.[26]

Even before the Michigan Central won this race, its backers were looking for western routes out of the city. Their first acquisition was the Aurora Branch Railway which shared the Galena tracks into Chicago. Under Joy's leadership from 1853 until 1857, this road pushed west to the Mississippi and established a ferry to Burlington, Iowa. Since it also had a line to Quincy, Illinois, the state legislature in 1855 authorized the road to change its name to Chicago, Burlington and Quincy Railroad. Spurred by the progress of the Michigan Southern-Rock Island combination in Iowa, the Chicago, Burlington and Quincy group acquired control of the Burlington and Missouri River Railroad and resumed building west. They had tracks out to Ottumwa, Iowa, by the end of the decade. Meantime, Forbes had taken over the Hannibal and St. Joseph Railroad and constructed a line across Missouri to Kansas City. This meant heavy expenditures in a district that was sparsely settled, but a Burlington agent assured company officials in 1858 that "the Western part of your road must become *a great cattle raising region* . . . [and, because] of the *peculiar adaptation of the soil to corn* and the large quantities *of Mast, a hog growing region*—thus making it a great stock freightage for the whole length of your road." Just one year later, the Burlington delivered more cattle and hogs to Chicago than any other railroad. A connecting track along Sixteenth Street facilitated transfer of livestock and freight to the Michigan Central's lakefront tracks.[27]

Chicago had a third route to the East Coast—the Pittsburgh, Fort Wayne and Chicago Railroad. An amalgam of shorter lines whose construction had been delayed by the 1857 panic, this company sent its first train into Chicago on Christmas Day, 1858. Its connections beyond Pittsburgh to Philadelphia, Baltimore, and Washington helped Chicago shippers, and this line constituted an alternate route to the important New York market.[28]

A decade after the trial run on the Galena and Chicago Union track, most of Chicago's 100,000 residents understood the importance of the iron horse. Railroads delivered over two-thirds of the city's imports and carried approximately three-quarters of its shipments to other markets in 1860. The Illinois and Michigan Canal, taunted by railroads along its banks, handled an insignificant 2 percent of the value of Chicago's exports. Merchants and manufacturers, including the purveyors of meat, had schemed to make their city a major rail junction, and they had invested their own money in the forty-seven-hundred-mile network. But the strategic location of Chicago and its reputation as a "comer" among midwestern cities enabled it to acquire railroads without spending a penny of public money. While boosters looked ahead to "a great national railroad" from Chicago to the West Coast, rival cities grudgingly acknowleged the fait accompli. "The city of Chicago has built herself up," said the *Detroit Advertiser* in 1853, "doubled her trade, doubled her manufactures, trebled the value of her real estate and rendered it saleable by a single act of policy—that of making herself a railroad center."[29]

Bridgeport and the Town of Lake

It was inevitable that railroads and plank roads would stimulate growth in Chicago and Cook County, yet the 1860 census figures surprised many people. In just ten years, city population climbed from 29,000 to 109,000 and the number of county residents outside city limits increased from 13,000 to 36,000. Since contemporaries measured urban progress in terms

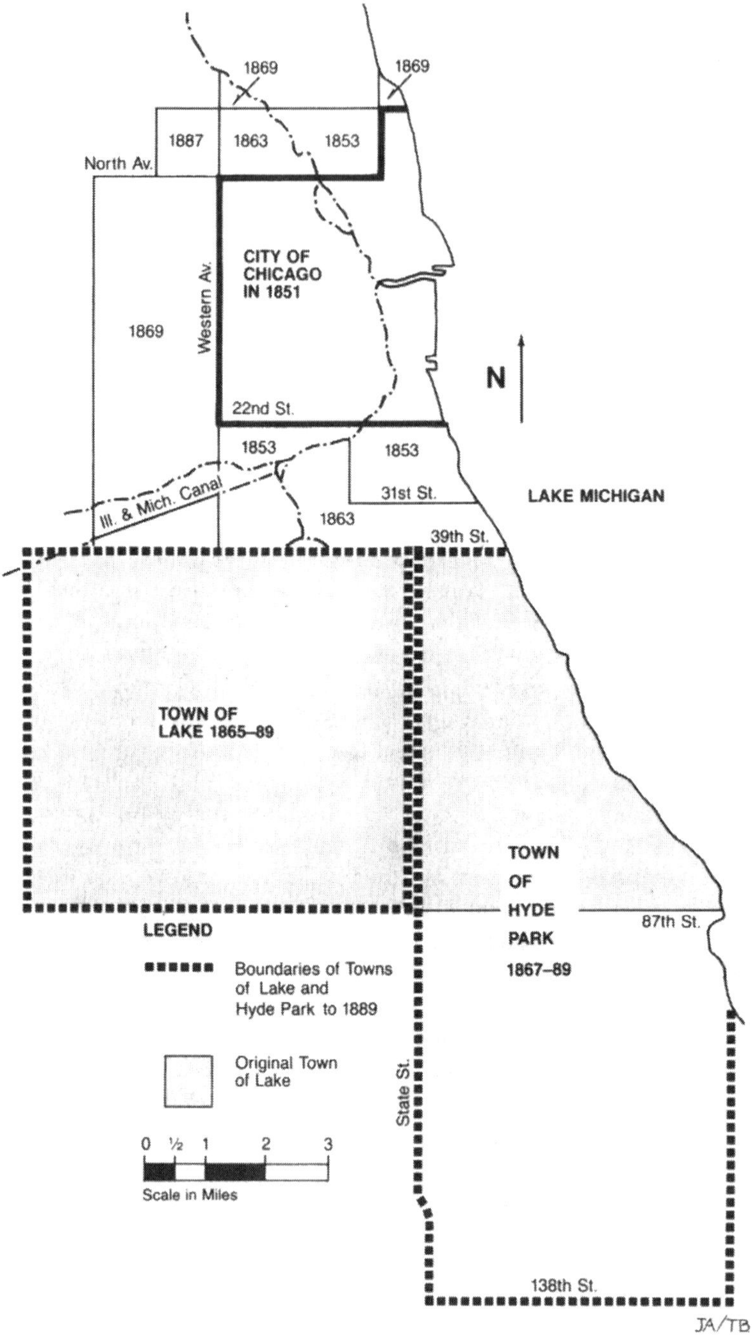

Map 2. Chicago annexations, 1853, 1863, and boundaries of townships of Lake and Hyde Park

of new settlers, dwellings, stores, factories, and expanding boundaries, Chicago editors had reason to be cocky about the "rapidity [with which] the city is extending itself." Western Avenue became a boundary in 1851, and the southern limit went from Twenty-second Street to Thirty-first Street in 1853.[30] A decade later it was moved to Thirty-ninth Street, and the promising "suburb" of Bridgeport found itself part of the city of Chicago. Lying along the South Branch between Halsted Street and Ashland Avenue, Bridgeport was one of the fastest growing areas in the 1850s. The canal and the river plus Archer Avenue and the Chicago and Alton Railroad were magnets for new industries. Packing plants and a glue factory provided winter employment for men who worked on the canal and Great Lakes during the navigation season. In addition, there were foundries, lumberyards, furniture factories, and planing mills. Bridgeport's largest employer in the 1860s was the Union Rolling Mill whose sprawling plant at Ashland and Thirty-first Street fronted on the Chicago and Alton tracks, the canal, and the South Branch.[31]

Irish canal workers and their families laid claim to the southwestern end of Bridgeport's thoroughfare, Archer Avenue, and they soon outnumbered German residents. The two best-known figures were Michael Scanlon, an immigrant laborer turned saloon-keeper, and Robert Healy, formerly a stone-quarry worker who acquired enough Bridgeport land to have his name attached to the largest slough. Scanlon and Healy started St. Bridget's parish in 1850 and were staunch supporters of the church, school, and industrial training center on Archer. These St. Bridget's buildings and the Union Rolling Mill were the anchors of Irish Bridgeport. The northeastern sector of Bridgeport was predominantly German, and Archer, from Halsted to its origin at Nineteenth and State, passed through a neighborhood called Hamburg. John Raber's Prussian parents had settled in the original Bridgeport hamlet alongside other German farmers, but he resented the Irish "invasion" and moved into the section annexed to Chicago in 1853. His hotel-restaurant-tavern on Archer was a popular German gathering place, and Raber used it to recruit for the new Republican party and eventually get himself elected Fifth Ward alderman.[32]

Cook County outside Chicago was organized into townships in 1850, and the unit immediately south of Chicago was the township of Lake. Thirty-ninth Street was its northern boundary and what would become Eighty-seventh Street its southern limit. It stretched from the lakefront—thus the designation Town of Lake—to the Town of Lyons with the future Cicero Avenue as the dividing line between the two townships. That census enumerators found 349 people in Town of Lake in 1850 and 1,755 a decade later was due in large part to the new arteries of transportation. Five railroads—Illinois Central, Michigan Central, Lake Shore and Michigan Southern, Rock Island, and the Pittsburgh, Fort Wayne—laid tracks through the township in the 1850s. In addition, the Southern Plank Road and the Blue Island Plank Road became north-south highways lacing the township to the city. Farmers settled close to these roads and along the extensions of Ashland and Halsted. Albert Colvin, for example, owned land near the Blue Island Road in the southwestern part of Town of Lake, while Hugh Chittick was on Ashland and John Gerber had access to Halsted. Daniel Burckey cultivated a small farm near Sixty-third and State and operated a hostelry on the Southern Plank Road. At the north end of the township Cyremus Beers was farming canal lots along a small stream leading into the South Fork of the South Branch. His property was valued at $9,500, making him the wealthiest resident in 1850. Railroad construction and maintenance workers constituted a second element in the Town of Lake population. They lived in modest frame houses around the intersection of the Michigan Southern and the Rock Island lines. Their settlement, known as The Junction, expanded when the Pittsburgh, Fort Wayne and Chicago came through at the end of the decade.[33]

During the 1850s commuters became an important third element in the population. Lawyer Ira J. Nichols built a fine home at The Junction, and on the lakefront Paul Cornell purchased three hundred acres and staked out lots between Fifty-first and Fifty-sixth streets. He donated sixty acres to the Illinois Central on the condition that its trains stop for commuters at his village of Hyde Park. This service started June 1, 1856, and was so successful that the railroad opened another commuter station at Kenwood in 1859. At least one Chicago editor worried about the appeal of these suburbs: "*Urbs in Horto* . . . is still on our municipal seal, but the din of business and the rise of block after block of iron, marble and brick stores, warehouses, mills and manufactories are fast . . . driving our garden afar from the dusty streets." Soon "our solid men . . . will seek their homes . . . in quiet suburban retreats." The 1860 census proved that a number of substantial citizens had already found their way to Town of Lake. A score of lawyers, doctors, and bankers in Hyde Park and Kenwood, as well as Nichols at The Junction, owned houses and lots valued at $40,000 or more.[34]

Since Paul Cornell's settlement was the largest nucleus of population and the one that anticipated the most rapid growth, the "solid men" on the lakefront decided to sever ties with the farmers and railroad workers in the western half of Lake. In 1861 the legislature agreed to charter the new Town of Hyde Park, and residents promptly elected their founding father to the post of township supervisor. Despite the loss of the lakefront, the people living west of State Street stubbornly insisted upon keeping the name Lake. In 1862, at Nichols's prodding, they built a four-room brick structure at The Junction to serve as schoolhouse, nondenominational church, and polling place. It was the revamped township's one symbol of community.[35]

The Hyde Park secession did not dampen interest in land acquisition in the Town of Lake. Investors kept buying large tracts along the railroads and plank roads, even in the southern end of the township. Resumption of canal land sales in 1848 disposed of most of those lots north of Forty-seventh Street. Section 5 in Town of Lake—the square mile bounded by Thirty-ninth, Halsted, Forty-seventh, and Ashland that would become the site of the famous stockyard and packinghouses—was sold by canal commissioners in 1852. Cyremus Beers picked up forty acres in the northwest corner of the section. The entire eastern half of Section 5 went to John Wentworth and his father-in-law, Riley Loomis. Wentworth had been schooled in railroads, urban growth, and land values by his friends James Frederick Joy and Stephen A. Douglas. As congressman and owner of the *Democrat*, he preached the importance of railroads, and he began acquiring land in Chicago in the 1840s. His first purchase in Town of Lake was a parcel along the proposed route of the Blue Island Plank Road. In 1852 Wentworth and Loomis paid $7,400 for their 320 acres in Section 5. A scant thirteen years later they would sell that land to the Union Stock Yard and Transit Company for $100,000.[36]

Chicago owed its sudden transformation from an unprepossessing village to a dynamic city of over one hundred thousand people to a number of factors—new modes of transportation, rapid settlement of the hinterland, and the steady influx of newcomers. Butchers, drovers, and meat packers were an integral part of the growth process. In the 1830s they kept pace with increasing local demand, in the 1840s they began exporting beef and pork, and in the 1850s they positioned themselves to take full advantage of railroad delivery of livestock and railroad distribution of meat products to new markets. Understandably, the packers shared the boosters' "rambunctious pride" in Chicago.[37] Although their practice of dumping wastes in the Chicago River had come to the attention of municipal authorities, the packers and most of their contemporaries were more interested in catching up with the older, larger packing center on the banks of the Ohio River.

NOTES

1. *Weekly Chicago Democrat*, Nov. 26, 1833; Alfred T. Andreas, *History of Cook County, Illinois* (Chicago, 1884), 73–80, 107–28; Bessie Louise Pierce, *A History of Chicago*, vol. 1, *The Beginning of a City, 1673–1848*

(New York, 1937), 34–45, 317–27; Robert P. Howard, *Illinois: A History of the Prairie State* (Grand Rapids, Mich., 1972), 154–65; James W. Putnam, *The Illinois and Michigan Canal: A Study in Economic History* (Chicago, 1918), 34–37, 92–95; George P. Brown, *Drainage Channel and Waterway: A History of the Effort to Secure . . . Disposal of the Sewage of the City of Chicago* (Chicago, 1894), 141–86.

2. Quoted in Bessie Louise Pierce, ed., *As Others See Chicago: Impressions of Visitors, 1673–1933* (Chicago, 1933), 84; *Chicago Democrat,* June 3, 1835; *Chicago American,* Dec. 31, 1836; Pierce, *Chicago,* 1:317–24.

3. R. Carlyle Buley, *The Old Northwest: Pioneer Period, 1815–1840,* 2 vols. (Bloomington, Ind., 1951), 1:187–89, 213–16; Rudolf A. Clemen, *The American Livestock and Meat Industry* (New York, 1923), 40–46, 52–54, 58–59.

4. *Trib.,* Aug. 5, 1863; Feb. 20, 1887; John Drury, *Rare and Well Done: Some Historical Notes on Meats and Meatmen* (Chicago, 1966), 111–13; "Archibald Clybourn: Pioneer Packer," *Chicago History,* 7 (Fall, 1963), 25–27; Andreas, *Cook County,* 101–4; *Weekly Chicago Democrat,* Dec. 3, 1833; June 29, 1836; *Inland Architect,* 1 (1883), 17, 36.

5. C. Emma Cheney, "Gurdon Saltonstall Hubbard," *Evangelical Episcopalian,* 15 (Oct., 1903), 286–92; Clint Clay Tilton, "Gurdon Saltonstall Hubbard and Some of His Friends," *Illinois State Historical Library Publication,* no. 40 (Springfield, 1933), 89–139, 142–65; Gurdon Saltonstall Hubbard, *The Autobiography of Gurdon Saltonstall Hubbard* (Chicago, 1911), 178–79; "Chicago Provision Trade: Its Rise, Progress, and Present Position," in Chicago Tribune, *Fifteenth Annual Review of the Trade and Commerce of the City of Chicago* (Chicago, 1864), 14.

6. *Nat. Prov.,* 5 (Aug. 13, 1892), 24; *Trib.,* Dec. 31, 1884; Feb. 20, 1887; Edwin O. Gale, *Reminiscences of Early Chicago and Vicinity* (Chicago, 1902), 47; Elmer A. Riley, *The Development of Chicago and Vicinity as a Manufacturing Center Prior to 1880* (Chicago, 1911), 38; Josiah Seymour Currey, *Manufacturing and Wholesale Industries of Chicago,* 3 vols. (Chicago, 1918), 1:89–91; Newberry and Dole, *Cash Book, January, 1832–August, 1833* (Chicago Historical Society).

7. Putnam, *Illinois and Michigan Canal,* 38–62; George P. Brown, *Drainage Channel and Waterway,* 196–204; John H. Krenkel, *Illinois Internal Improvements, 1818–1848* (Cedar Rapids, Iowa, 1958), 42–43, 99–100; Andreas, *Cook County,* 151–54; *Chicago Journal,* Apr. 17, 1848; *Chicago Daily Democrat,* Apr. 11, 1848.

8. "Bridgeport," *Trib.,* Feb. 25, 1900; John Drury, "Old Chicago Neighborhoods, Bridgeport," *Landlord's Guide,* 40 (Dec., 1949), 14; W. V. Pooley, *The Settlement of Illinois, 1830 to 1850* (Madison, Wis., 1908), 383–91, 499–501; "Steam Power at Bridgeport," *Gem of the Prairie,* Feb. 19, 1848.

9. Buley, *Old Northwest,* 1:478–81; Milo M. Quaife, *Chicago's Highways Old and New* (Chicago, 1923), 149–50; *Prairie Farmer,* 9 (Oct., 1849), 305–6; *Griffiths Annual Review of the Live Stock Trade at Chicago, 1878* (Chicago, 1879), 13–14; John S. Wright, *Chicago: Past, Present, Future* (Chicago, 1868), 208n.

10. Weston A. Goodspeed and Daniel D. Healy, eds., *History of Cook County, Illinois,* 2 vols. (Chicago, 1909), 1:146; *Trib.* Feb. 20, 1887; *Drovers Journal,* Jan. 28, 1889; *Griffiths Annual Review, 1878,* 14–15; Pierce, *Chicago,* 1:138, 207.

11. Clemen, *Livestock and Meat Industry,* 110–12; Andreas, *Cook County,* 324–25; Pierce, *Chicago,* 1:138–39; James W. Norris, *General Directory and Business Advertiser of the City of Chicago for the Year 1844* (Chicago, 1844), 77; *Weekly Chicago Democrat,* Oct. 19, 1847.

12. "Chicago Business Directory," *The Laws and Ordinances of the City of Chicago* (Chicago, 1839), 44; "Chicago's Chief Glory," *Trib.,* Feb. 20, 1887; Charles Cleaver, *Early-Chicago Reminiscences* (Chicago, 1882), 48–49; *Times,* May 31, 1870.

13. Riley, *Development of Chicago,* 59; James W. Norris, *Business Directory and Statistics of the City of Chicago for 1846* (Chicago, 1846), 15; *Trib.,* June 24, 1864; Feb. 20, May 30, 1887; *Weekly Chicago Democrat,* Oct. 21, 1845.

14. *Chicago Daily Democrat,* Sept. 26, Oct. 31, 1848; *Weekly Chicago Democrat,* Dec. 21, 1847; "Beef Packing in Chicago by Wadsworth, Dyer & Co.," *Prairie Farmer,* 8 (Nov., 1848), 336.

15. *Weekly Chicago Democrat,* Oct. 18, 1847; *Prairie Farmer,* 8 (Nov., 1848), 336–37; Patrick E. McLear, "John Stephen Wright and Urban and Regional Promotion in the Nineteenth Century," *JISHS,* 68 (Nov., 1975), 412.

16. *Weekly Chicago Democrat,* Dec. 21, 1847; "Hog Killing and Pork Packing," *Chicago Daily Tribune,* Dec. 1, 1852.

17. Riley, *Development of Chicago,* 39, 63–64, I. D. Guyer, *History of Chicago; Its Commercial and Manufacturing Interests and Industry* (Chicago, 1862), 81, 182; Charles Cleaver, *History of Chicago from 1833 to 1892* (Chicago, 1892), 42–43; Cleaver, *Reminiscences,* 50.

18. *Chicago Daily Tribune,* Dec. 1, 1852; *Weekly Chicago Democrat,* Nov. 26, 1833; *The Laws and Ordinances of the City of Chicago* (Chicago, 1837), 15; *Amendments . . . Laws and Ordinances . . . in Force December 1, 1843* (n.p., n.d.), 5–6; John Lewis Peyton, *Over the Alleghanies and across the Prairies* (London, 1869), 325.

19. Norris, *Business Directory for 1846,* 7; *Chicago Democrat,* Mar. 15, 1849; Howard C. Hill, "The Development of Chicago as a Center of the Meat Packing Industry," *MVHR,* 10 (Dec., 1923), 254–58; Charles Henry Taylor, ed., *History of the Board of Trade of the City of Chicago,* 3 vols.

(Chicago, 1917), 1:157, 176; Charles Cist, *Sketches and Statistics of Cincinnati in 1851* (Cincinnati, 1851), 276, 278–79, 285–86; Margaret Walsh, *The Rise of the Midwestern Meat Packing Industry* (Lexington, Ky., 1982), 11–37.

20. Jesse B. Thomas, *Report of Jesse B. Thomas, as a Member of . . . the Chicago Harbor and River Convention, of the Statistics concerning the City of Chicago* (Chicago, 1847), 26; "Prospects of Chicago," *Chicago Daily Democrat,* Feb. 19, 1850.

21. Quaife, *Chicago's Highways,* 122–37; *Chicago Daily Tribune,* Dec. 28, 1850; Daily Democratic Press, *The Railroads, History and Commerce of Chicago* (Chicago, 1854), 50–53; Judson Fiske Lee, "Transportation—A Factor in the Development of Illinois Previous to 1860," *JISHS,* 10 (Apr., 1917), 29–36; William Bross, *History of Chicago, Historical and Commercial Statistics, Sketches, Facts and Figures* (Chicago, 1876), 49.

22. *Weekly Chicago Democrat,* June 18, 1834; Pierce, *Chicago,* 1:114–18; Andreas, *Cook County,* 167–68; 178–79; *Chicago Daily Tribune,* Dec. 18, 1852.

23. Bessie Louise Pierce, *A History of Chicago,* vol. 2, *From Town to City, 1848–1871* (New York, 1940), 40–43, 51–53, 483; Andreas, *Cook County,* 179–80; Lee, "Transportation," 37–56; William E. Hayes, *Iron Road to Empire: The History . . . of the Rock Island Lines* (New York, 1953), 19–26.

24. Carlton J. Corliss, *Main Line of Mid-America: The Story of the Illinois Central* (New York, 1950), 29–68; Paul Wallace Gates, *The Illinois Central Railroad and Its Colonization Work* (Cambridge, Mass., 1934), 41–42, 84–98; Andreas, *Cook County,* 168, 173–78; quoted in Howard G. Bronson, *History of the Illinois Central Railroad to 1870* (Urbana, Ill., 1915), 100.

25. D. W. Hungmeyer, "An Excursion into the Early History of the Chicago and Alton Railroad," *JISHS,* 38 (Mar., 1945), 7–37; Andreas, *Cook County,* 181; Pierce, *Chicago,* 2:49–50; Henry L. Schroeder and C. W. Forbrich, *Men Who Have Made the Fifth Ward* (Chicago, 1895), 41–42; Corliss, *Main Line of Mid-America,* 46–48.

26. John Lauritz Larson, *Bonds of Enterprise: John Murray Forbes and Western Development in America's Railway Age* (Cambridge, Mass., 1984), 33–46; Richard C. Overton, *Burlington Route: A History of the Burlington Lines* (New York, 1965), 26–32; Richard C. Overton, *Burlington West: A Colonization History of the Burlington Railroad* (Cambridge, Mass., 1941), 25–30; Gates, *Illinois Central,* 40–45; Thomas C. Cochran, *Railroad Leaders, 1845–1890: The Business Mind in Action* (New York, 1965), 34–41, 365; F. E. Cary, *Lake Shore and Michigan Southern, History of Its Development* (Chicago, 1900), chap. 4; Henry Greenleaf Pearson, *An American Railroad Builder, John Murray Forbes* (Boston, 1911),

49–55; Arthur M. Johnson and Barry E. Supple, *Boston Capitalists and Western Railroads: A Study in the Nineteenth Century Railroad Investment Process* (Cambridge, Mass., 1967), chaps. 6–9.

27. Larson, *Bonds of Enterprise,* 48–82; Overton, *Burlington Route,* 3–9, 14, 38; Overton, *Burlington West,* 40–48; Pierce, *Chicago,* 2:50, 493; Harold M. Mayer, "The Railway Pattern of Metropolitan Chicago" (Ph.D. diss., University of Chicago, 1943), 55–56.

28. George H. Burgess and Miles C. Kennedy, *Centennial History of the Pennsylvania Railroad Company, 1846–1946* (Philadelphia, 1949), 177–78; Andreas, *Cook County,* 183–84.

29. Carl Abbott, *Boosters and Businessmen: Popular Economic Thought and Urban Growth in the Antebellum Middle West* (Westport, Conn., 1981), 131–38; Board of Trade, *First Annual Statement of the Trade and Commerce of Chicago, for the Year Ending December 31, 1858,* 6; "Chicago and Her Railroads," *Daily Democratic Press,* Jan. 31, 1854; *Detroit Advertiser,* quoted in Goodspeed and Healy, *Cook County,* 1:243–44.

30. *Eighth Census, 1860,* "Population," 102; *Chicago Democrat,* Nov. 4, 1848; Andreas, *Cook County,* 341; Pierce, *Chicago,* 2:306.

31. *Trib.,* Dec. 3, 1864; May 14, 1894; Goodspeed and Healy, *Cook County,* 1:271; S. S. Schoff, *The Glory of Chicago, Her Manufactories. The Industrial Interests of Chicago . . .* (Chicago, 1873), 9, 11, 22, 180.

32. Goodspeed and Healy, *Cook County,* 1:289–90; "Bridgeport," *Trib.,* Feb. 25, 1900; Schroeder and Forbrich, *Men Who Have Made the Fifth Ward,* 14, 41–45; *Times,* Nov. 28, 1857; Joseph James Thompson, ed., *The Archdiocese of Chicago, Antecedents and Development* (Des Plaines, Ill., 1920), 271, 273.

33. *Seventh Census, 1850,* Manuscript Schedule, Lake Township, 6–7; *Eighth Census, 1860,* "Population," 90; Goodspeed and Healy, *Cook County,* 1:523–37, 312–31; Illinois and Michigan Canal Records, IM–L17 Lands, 1848–55, Certificates nos. 608, 1307 (Illinois State Archives, Springfield).

34. Andreas, *Cook County,* 391, 521, 528, 562; quoted in Goodspeed and Healy, *Cook County,* 1:279; *Eighth Census, 1860,* Manuscript Schedule, Town of Lake, 441, 443–51.

35. Ann Durkin Keating, "Governing the New Metropolis: The Development of Urban and Suburban Governments in Cook County, Illinois, 1831 to 1902" (Ph.D. diss., University of Chicago, 1984), 143; Laura Willard, "Local Government in Illinois as Illustrated by the Municipal Development of Hyde Park" (M.A. thesis, University of Chicago, 1895), 17, 23–24; Gerald E. Sullivan, ed., *The Story of Englewood, 1835–1923* (Chicago, 1924), 1–23; Jean F. Block, *Hyde Park Houses: An Informal History, 1856–1910* (Chicago, 1978), 6, 8.

36. Arthur Charles Cole, *The Era of the Civil War,* vol. 3 of *Centennial*

History of Illinois (Springfield, Ill., 1919), 87–88; Don E. Fehrenbacher, *Chicago Giant: A Biography of "Long John" Wentworth* (Madison, Wis., 1957), 15, 112–14; Illinois and Michigan Canal Records, IM–L17 Lands 1848–55, Certificates nos. 34, 608, 1269–74, 1307, 1308, 1466. Wentworth purchased 120 acres and Loomis 200 acres in the May and September canal land sales in 1852.

37. Carl Abbot, "Civic Pride in Chicago, 1844–1860," *JISHS*, 63 (1970), 421.

CHAPTER 2

Chicago Becomes Porkopolis

Chicago's livestock and packing statistics provide one measure of the dramatic changes wrought by the railroads. From approximately 30,000 animals delivered in 1848, the number rose to 450,000 by 1860 and then quadrupled during the peak season of 1862–63. Packinghouse products and livestock shipments accounted for one-third of the city's trade on the eve of the Civil War. By 1865 nearly everyone in the country knew that the brash young city on the shores of Lake Michigan had become the new Porkopolis. Behind these figures lie interesting changes in the way livestock was sold and transshipped and an impressive growth in the number and size of Chicago's packing plants. The leaders in the industry were active members of the urban establishment, serving as mayors and presidents of the Board of Trade and Chamber of Commerce. But the packers' economic triumph contributed to a pollution crisis in the South Branch of the Chicago River. The city resolved the matter by pressing ahead with two massive projects—deepening the Illinois and Michigan Canal and building a water tunnel into Lake Michigan. New city and state regulations on rendering, slaughtering, and packing convinced Chicagoans that they had control over the "inconveniences" which accompanied the thriving industry.

The Impact of the Railroad

It was not until 1859 that the Board of Trade attempted its first compilation of livestock trade and meat-packing figures. The reason for the delay, the secretary confessed, was the inability of the railroads and packers "to furnish them." Constant change in the volume of animals delivered and the way they were sold to packers contributed to the confusion. So too did the practice of transshipment; for the first time, railroads made it feasible to send cattle and hogs to eastern markets. The scope of the revolution in the livestock trade can be gauged by the fact that Chicago's 20,000 hogs and 10,000 cattle arrived "on the hoof" in 1848. By 1860, three-quarters of the

450,000 animals arrived by rail and 200,000 of these traveled on by rail to eastern livestock markets.[1]

Cattle raisers in Illinois pioneered the changes in the livestock trade. Drawn by the richness of the prairie, the presence of the Illinois Central Railroad, and the expanding Chicago market, they conducted breeding experiments and developed new techniques for fattening stock. As a result, the average weight of a steer rose to about 1,000 pounds and "razorbacks" gave way to hogs of 250 pounds or more. Benjamin Franklin Harris's huge steers caused a sensation in Chicago in 1856 because Archibald Clybourn paraded a dozen of them through the city preceded by a band and followed by butchers on horseback. John Wentworth experimented with Durham cattle and Suffolk hogs on his farm near Summit and published reports in his own newspaper and in John Stephen Wright's *Prairie Farmer*. Both Wentworth and Wright were active in the Illinois State Agricultural Society, founded in 1853.[2]

Two other Illinois cattle raisers, John B. Sherman and Samuel W. Allerton, operated on a smaller scale but would shift the focus of their activities to the Chicago livestock trade. Both were sons of Dutchess County, New York, farmers and cattle growers who turned to dairying when railroads delivered cheaper western produce and livestock. Sherman, born in 1825, accompanied his father on cattle drives to New York City, staying at the Bull's Head Inn on the outskirts of town near the slaughterhouses. He chased gold in California until the early 1850s, when he bought land in the Fox River valley of Illinois and began farming and fattening cattle for the Chicago market. Samuel W. Allerton, born a few years after Sherman, tried raising livestock in upstate New York and selling in the Buffalo market before he too decided to settle in Illinois. He invested his $5,000 savings in a Piatt County farm close by the Illinois Central mainline to Chicago.[3]

Railroad managers and the drovers using plank roads needed some type of enclosure where they could sell to packers and butchers. Recognizing the potential of the proposed Southwestern Plank Road and the Galena and Chicago Union Railroad, realtor Matthew Laflin purchased one hundred acres near the juncture of the plank road with Ashland Avenue and Madison Street, due west of the center of Chicago. When the plank road opened, Laflin had a fenced enclosure ready. In 1849 he persuaded the railroad to make a stop nearby so that cattle and hogs could jump from low-slung cars onto a sand pile. Sales were so brisk that Laflin built Bull's Head, a three-story frame hotel and tavern, on the east side of Ashland. To make his hotel, stockyard, and real estate subdivisions more accessible to city dwellers, Laflin started Chicago's first horse-drawn omnibus in 1851. Then, eager to invest in new projects, he sold the hotel and stockyard to Horace Hopkins in 1852.[4]

Sherman sold his livestock at Bull's Head and occasionally boarded at the hotel, and in 1854 he decided to lease the facility. Two brothers left Dutchess County to help run it, Charles taking charge of the yard and I. N. Walter Sherman managing the hotel and tavern. Business increased so rapidly that Sherman added a clerk, George T. Williams, and together they prepared weekly summaries of the sales at Bull's Head. Distributed to buyers, sellers, and city newspapers, these accounts were among the earliest livestock reports. By 1856 they needed more space to accommodate country drovers, the Galena and Chicago Union, and the Chicago, Burlington and Quincy railroads. But the omnibus line had encouraged settlement at the western end of Madison Street and expansion was impossible. When the railroads unveiled plans for the east-west connecting track along Sixteenth Street, Sherman realized that a lakefront location would enable him to make both Chicago sales and shipments east. So he signed a ten-year lease on Myrick's property in 1856 and sent Charles Sherman to supervise the Illinois Central and Michigan Central livestock business there. The following year Walter Sherman, with the assistance of yet another brother, eighteen-year-old William, built a new hotel at Twenty-eighth and State. John Sherman closed Bull's Head as soon as the so-called Illinois Central Crossing track was finished. Fully ensconced on the lakefront by 1858, Sherman quickly developed thirty-two acres of pens capable of holding five thousand cattle and thirty thousand hogs.[5]

One of Sherman's employes was a teenager named Nelson Morris. Born in 1838 in Heckingen, Germany, near the Black Forest, Morris was the son of a Jewish cattle-dealer whose trade was ruined in 1848. The lad sold copper, skins, and rags with his father until a relative paid for his transportation to the United States in 1852. Unable to speak English when he arrived, Morris accepted odd jobs and peddled for two years. He made his way west with the help of Erie Canal boat and lake vessel employment, walking the final stretch from Michigan City into Chicago. There he took a stockyard job cleaning animal pens. In later years, Morris said this was at the Myrick yards, but since his employer was John B. Sherman and he landed the job in 1854, he probably started at Bull's Head. As a common laborer he received $5 a month plus room and board; he earned a few extra dollars watching hogs on winter nights to make sure they did not huddle and suffocate. By the time Morris moved to the lakefront with the Shermans, he was a feedmaster receiving $14 per month.[6]

Sherman's Lake Shore Yards served three railroads—the Illinois Central, the Michigan Central, and the Burlington. The rival east-west railroad combination, the Michigan Southern and Rock Island, established its own stockyard in 1852. Called the Southern Yards, this twenty-five-acre enclosure was located along the tracks near Twenty-second Street. John R. Hoxie, an upstate New York livestock dealer familiar with the Michigan

Southern trade, came to Chicago in the late 1850s as the railroad's livestock agent. The Chicago and Alton used the Brighton Yards. When the Pittsburgh, Fort Wayne line reached Chicago, it built a small enclosure west of the South Branch and just north of the Illinois Central Crossing. Unable to expand during the war years though pressed by heavy shipments of hogs, the enterprising manager of the Fort Wayne yards double-decked his hog pens.[7]

Unless a shipper consigned his stock to a certain packer, the stockyard manager handled the sale. As volume increased, some railroads appointed full-time livestock agents. But in the mid-1850s, people familiar with raising and selling livestock presented themselves as middlemen. They paid cash for the animals in the countryside, met the cost of transportation by rail to Chicago, and then sold to the highest bidder. First designated cattle or hog dealers, these men were also known as brokers. In the 1860s, individuals pooled their capital in partnerships known as livestock commission firms. Most of them charged a fee for their services, but stock growers seldom objected because they were paid in cash when the animals left their premises.[8]

Chicago's first full-time livestock broker was Solomon P. Hopkins. A Dutchess County friend of Sherman's, Hopkins had tried his luck at steamboating, farming, running a provision firm in California, and organizing for the Republican party before settling in Chicago in 1856. At first he handled cattle shipments for the Michigan Southern and Michigan Central, being paid by the railroads for each shipment he lined up. Soon he was buying and selling hogs and cattle on a commission basis in all of the Chicago stockyards. Samuel Allerton shipped on the Illinois Central and sold in Sherman's yard, so he had an opportunity to watch Sol Hopkins. The work appealed to him and so did Chicago, the only place, he said, "where the world turned around every twenty-four hours." In 1859 he moved to the city and established himself as a livestock dealer. Meantime, Nelson Morris had been purchasing crippled and smothered hogs which he sold to renderers and then cattle from farmers in Blue Island which he sold at the Lake Shore Yards. When he was ready to try full-time cattle dealing, John Sherman gave him encouragement, advice, and the money to get started. In 1859 Morris and Isaac Waixel, a recent German immigrant who knew about hogs, formed a partnership and this was the first livestock commission firm in Chicago.[9]

The railroads brought comparable changes to the packing industry. By increasing the supply of livestock and carrying barreled meat and lard to distant markets, the iron horses were responsible for more packinghouse and allied jobs and for larger exports. Whereas six houses in 1848 had handled thirty thousand animals, thirty firms in 1860 needed two hundred thousand cattle and hogs. To the annoyance of some townspeople, drovers used city streets to get the animals from the railroad stockyards to the packing plants, and reporters accused packers of turning the upper stretches of the South Branch into "a stream of effluvia . . . which might be cut with a knife, it is so thick and so powerful." Most of the new plants built in the 1850s were further out the South Branch where land was cheaper, population sparser, and city regulations inapplicable.[10]

The new ordinances of 1849 and 1851 coincided with a cholera epidemic and the widespread belief that filthy streets and impure drinking water were connected with the disease. "The great mass of the deaths . . . in our own city are clearly attributable to butchering within the city limits!" asserted the *Democrat* in June, 1849. "How much longer is this nuisance to be tolerated?" The council created a new Board of Health to see that streets, alleys, and public markets were kept clean and that no offal and dung went into the lake, the river, or its branches. In December, 1849, the council prohibited the erection of new slaughterhouses within the city limits and banned conversion of existing buildings for that purpose. When cholera reappeared in the summer of 1850, there was talk of banning all slaughtering and rendering within the city.[11]

Gem of the Prairie came to the defense of the "enterprising packers," and hide manufacturer Walter Gurnee won the mayoralty race in 1851 on a platform calling for "judicious measures" to correct "the evil complained of, without depriving the city of . . . hundreds of thousands of dollars, and the employment [of] . . . a large number of our citizens." Gurnee blamed the cholera epidemic on the city's failure to create a water distribution and sewerage system. Noting that the Illinois legislature had authorized Chicago to establish a Board of Water Commissioners, he hoped the council would hire a "competent engineer" and settle for additional regulation of packers and renderers, not an outright ban. Chicago's Slaughtering House Ordinance of September, 1851, required packers and slaughterers to post bonds and secure permits; keep blood, bones, and offal out of the lake and the river and its branches; and remove these waste materials from their premises every twenty-four hours between May and November and every forty-eight hours the rest of the year. The council instructed them to collect the wastes in tubs or vats and either bury them at least twenty rods from the river or cart them four miles beyond the city limits where they could be "deposited" on the prairie or in the lake. Health officers could inspect slaughtering and packing plants, and owners in violation of the ordinance could be fined $100 and deprived of their operating permit. The aldermen did impose a ban on rendering within the city if it created "any offensive smell," but they did not define "offensive smell."[12]

Gurnee won reelection the following year, and in 1853 Chicago moved its southern boundary from Twenty-second to Thirty-first Street. Enforcement of the 1849 and 1851 ordinances slackened and the Board of Health ceased functioning because cholera disappeared. Nonetheless, lard manufacturers, renderers of offal into fertilizer, and those using animal parts to make glue and soap knew that their plants emitted offensive odors. They were the first to relocate. Charles Cleaver chose land on the lakefront, two miles south of the city. He remembered being "laughed at, and asked with a smile if I ever expected Chicago to reach as far south as that." Obviously he did, for he platted a subdivision and persuaded the Illinois Central to stop at Cleaverville. His first buildings were a brick rendering plant and a slaughterhouse for city butchers. The latter preferred to drive their animals from the lakefront stockyard to their shops and take their chances slaughtering in the city. And the new packinghouses installed their own "melting apparatus" to make lard. So Cleaver quit the rendering business in 1857. Chicago's first glue factory was established in 1854 near the intersection of Archer, Thirty-first, Ashland, and the South Fork of the South Branch, safely outside city limits. The managers were Louis and Christian Wahl, young German immigrants whose father had a Milwaukee glue factory. Aware that railroads were making Chicago a major source of animal heads and hooves, the family soon migrated. The Wahls started with glue, but by the end of the decade they had a second factory turning bones and dried offal into fertilizer.[13]

The packing fraternity moved farther down the South Branch in the 1850s because it was outside city limits, closer to the lakefront stockyard, and land was available for new plants, warehouses, smokehouses, separate buildings for rendering, and railroad spurs. The five largest packing plants had a capital investment of $155,000 exclusive of land by 1860. Steam-powered machinery to mix and circulate brine was routine; steam hoists to raise an unconscious steer into position for slaughter were new, as were steam rendering tanks. Owners of these new packing plants could market their own tallow and lard and some sold "tankings"—remnants of boiled heads and offal—to farmers like Cyremus Beers for fertilizer. They still had no use for animal blood, "the only real loss," thought Wright. "Can it not be made available for sugar refining or dying or something else?"[14]

The largest packing plant in 1860 was New York-owned Cragin and Company. Its four-and-one-half-acre facility on the South Branch was run by John L. Hancock, formerly a beef packer in Maine who sold to the New York provision firm. The company sent Hancock to Chicago in 1854 and spent $45,000 on a plant that included a separate smoke house, rendering facility, and copper shop. Hancock soon needed the assistance of his nephews, Arthur Albion Libby and Charles Perly Libby. The Chicago house was so profitable that Cragin and Company doubled the size with a main building stretching 214 feet along the South Branch and 110 feet deep. Capable of handling four thousand hogs and four hundred cattle per day, Cragin and Company accounted for one-sixth of Chicago's hog pack and one-half of its cattle in 1860.[15]

Hancock's closest competitor in hog-packing was the firm established in 1850 by Oramel and Rosell Hough, former drovers for Sylvester Marsh. Oramel Hough was the superintendent at Wadsworth, Dyer when he resigned to go into business with his brother. They purchased land near Bridgeport and, short of capital, put up a frame plant without steam power. Fortunately, however, a sample of their preserved beef won a prize at the Crystal Palace Industrial Exhibition in London in 1851, and they secured a contract from the British government and a market for their meat in England. When fire destroyed their original plant, they rebuilt on a much larger scale, using stone and brick and installing steam-powered machinery. By 1860 the Hough brothers were packing as many hogs as Cragin and Company, though their cattle kill was much smaller. Marsh kept slaughtering in an old-fashioned plant on the lakefront near the mouth of the river. By operating at night he managed to elude city officials, but he knew his future was cloudy. When the New Hampshire legislature gave him a charter to build a railroad to the top of Mount Washington, the pioneer packer departed.[16]

Several small firms started in the 1850s would evolve into leading firms in the future. Orville Tobey ran a rendering plant for Marsh before forming a partnership with Heman Booth in 1850. Within two years they could build on the South Branch and specialize in pork-packing for the European market. Charles Culbertson and Daniel Jones sold their small Iowa packinghouse and came to Chicago in 1858. They soon were employing one hundred men and packing fifteen thousand hogs annually. Albert Emmett Kent gave up a Connecticut law practice to establish with his brother Sidney a commission firm selling grain and hides. The Kents rented a porkhouse in 1858 and did well enough to afford a $50,000 plant in the early 1860s.[17]

Although Chicago had a longer winter packing season than did Cincinnati, her packers showed a keener interest in extending the period by means of artificial cooling. The use of ice to chill small, insulated boxes was well known by the 1840s and widely applied to storage of butter and fresh produce. John C. Schooley of Cincinnati perfected a method of cooling a larger unit, comparable to a refrigerator, and securing adequate ventilation. In 1854 he constructed an icehouse adjacent to a Cincinnati porkpacking plant, connected the basements of the two buildings, and thus had a cool, well-ventilated area to chill hog carcasses in warm weather. Schooley's experimental unit apparently worked well during the summer of 1854, but the Cincinnati pork packers paid little attention and the next year his "refrigerator" was used for fruit storage. Two Chicago packers, who either saw Schooley's unit or read his book, experimented with the arrangement in the summer of 1858. That firm did not last long, but Tobey and Booth tried the same thing in 1859 and became the city's first year-round pork house. They could cure meat in mid-summer, marveled an observer, "with the Thermometer at 100 degrees, by means of their Ice Houses."[18]

Thanks to the railroad and the new packing facilities, Chicagoans killed more cattle than any other city in the West by 1860, and they had increased their hog pack eightfold since 1848. The city's 160,000 hogs in 1860 put her well ahead of all other towns in Illinois as well as competitors like Terre Haute, Milwaukee, and St. Louis. Upon compiling still "imperfect" commercial statistics for the year 1860, the *Tribune* estimated that Chicago's exports had jumped from approximately $10,700,000 in 1848 to $33,800,000. The newspaper valued livestock shipments at $4,411,000; beef and pork at $3,277,000; lard and tallow at $1,295,000; and hides at $1,161,000. Thus, on the eve of the Civil War, the livestock trade, meatpacking, and allied industries accounted for nearly one-third of Chicago's exports.[19]

The Civil War Opportunity

The "most sanguine of our citizens," said the *Tribune*, "did not dream of taking from Cincinnati the title of Porkopolis, at least for ten years to come." That was reasonable on the eve of the Civil War, for Chicago packed only one-third as many hogs as the Queen City. Yet it was clear that the economic advantages of the Ohio River packing center were eroding. Livestock production in its hinterland could not match the supply potentially available to Chicago packers, thanks to their railroad network. Cincinnati leaders thought steamboats and river transport invincible; they were slow, almost lethargic, about acquiring railroads. The Civil War was a crippling blow because they lost Confederate supplies and markets and Mississippi River navigation was interrupted. Only government orders for pork and unexpectedly large sales in Europe saved the Cincinnati packers from disaster. Their hog kill peaked at 600,000 in the winter of 1862–63, then declined to 350,000 at the end of the war, the same number packed in the early 1850s.[20]

By contrast, the Civil War was a blessing for Chicago's livestock dealers and meat packers. The city's railroads were vital to the transport of western foodstuffs, and wartime demands for grain and livestock stimulated an already flourishing trade. Within three years, cattle receipts tripled and hog receipts more than quadrupled. Livestock shipments out of Chicago increased from 250,000 animals in 1860 to about 920,000 during 1863.

Many of the cattle and hogs went to the Union army, which preferred to feed its soldiers fresh meat whenever possible. Chicago benefited from government use of the Illinois Central as the supply route to its armies in Kentucky and Tennessee. The "cracker" trains, traveling over temporary tracks south of Cairo, delivered barrels of pork and crates of bacon and dried beef prepared in Chicago. Moreover, many farmers who had marketed their corn down the Mississippi prior to the war now acquired and bred hogs, fed the corn to them, and shipped the hogs to Chicago. This was so prevalent by 1863 that a speaker at the ship-canal convention in Chicago praised the hog's "benevolent and efficient aid. . . . The hog eats the corn and Europe eats the hog. Corn thus becomes incarnate; for what is a hog but fifteen or twenty bushels of corn on four legs?"[21]

Chicago packers stepped up production in order to fill government contracts and requests from eastern provision firms for western beef and pork. It was the pork packers who achieved the most spectacular results. They handled 272,000 hogs in the winter of 1860–61 and a staggering 970,000 in the peak season of 1862–63. The number declined to 750,000 in the final winter of the war. Chicago officially became "Porkopolis" at the close of the 1861–62 season when it was clear that her pork packers had dispatched about 30,000 more hogs than their rivals in Cincinnati. Chicago widened the margin in the next two years and ended the 1864–65 season with a two-to-one lead over Cincinnati. "Chicago *is the greatest Pork Packing point in the United States and in the world!*" crowed the *Tribune*. "The high position held by Cincinnati . . . is now occupied by her younger sister."[22]

The well-publicized opportunities to make money in the livestock trade and meat-packing drew newcomers to Chicago and tempted residents. Typical of the newcomers were Herbert and Henry Mallory, who left railroad stockyard jobs in Michigan to start a livestock firm in 1863. English-born John Adams was a hog buyer in Milwaukee before he came to the more promising city. Benjamin F. Murphy sold a provision firm and packinghouse in Newcastle, Indiana, to finance his entry. John and Thomas Nash set up shop near Healy Slough and made it clear that only Irish butchers need apply for jobs. Successful grain merchant Benjamin Peters Hutchinson tried pork-packing as a sideline; by the end of the war Burt, Hutchinson and Snow was one of Chicago's strongest firms.[23]

Chicago's packing facilities underwent vast changes during the war years. The number of establishments mushroomed to fifty-eight during the winter of 1863–64, forty-two of which were still functioning in the spring of 1865. Established packers enlarged their plants, new houses were constructed, and vacant buildings were pressed into service as slaughtering and packing sheds. When the *Prairie Farmer* bragged in February, 1864, that "the packing houses now are among the wonders of this thriving city," the editor was thinking of the large modern plants, not the marginal operations. Albert and Sidney Kent startled Chicagoans when they spent $50,000 in 1862 to build the city's most modern packing plant at Twenty-second and the South Branch. This spurred Cragin and Company to enlarge its killing house and invest $12,000 in a new rendering plant. Tobey and Booth spent twice that amount to construct a second pork house, install eight steam rendering tanks, enlarge their South Branch dock, and lay more railroad track.[24] (See Fig. 1.)

The most interesting new plant and the first to fully exploit the gravity principle was built in 1863 by Jones and Culbertson. It was located in Bridgeport with the usual South Branch dock and connecting railroad spurs. The main building covered twenty-eight thousand square feet of ground and was three stories high, "a landmark . . . attracting special attention from its immensity and solid appearance." Instead of placing the stock pens outside the house, Jones and Culbertson put them on the flat roof of the building. The hogs were driven up an inclined plane and allowed a day of rest before slaughter. They were killed in the usual manner by a blow on the head and their throats were slit on the floor of the killing pen. But this floor pitched toward a large central drain which conveyed the blood through a downspout to tanks outside the building. The carcass went down an inclined plane into the scalding tubs, thereby eliminating the task of lifting the dead hog into the steam bath. The carcass was scraped of bristles, cooled, and cut on the third floor. Near the cutting tables "conveniently constructed chutes" carried the various cuts of meat to the second floor where they were pickled, cured, and packed. The first-floor warehouse had "several acres of sides, hams and shoulders," according to one visitor. Adjacent to the main building was a "lard house" with rendering tanks made of heavy boiler iron, six feet in diameter and twelve feet high. After the lard was drawn off, the tanks were emptied by shoveling out the solid waste and draining off the liquids. The latter substance, said an admiring reporter, just "disappears into the sewer, and is soon mingled with the Chicago river."[25]

Reporters did not bother with the numerous marginal pork operations, but they must have offered a striking contrast. Most were located far out on the South Branch or Healy Slough, and they were either cheap new frame structures or crudely converted factories, warehouses, or stores. The secretary of the Board of Trade, summarizing Chicago's progress in pork-packing during 1862, referred to the "large number of smaller structures, of more or less permanence; all of which, with the temporary occupation of stores, out-houses, etc., give great additional facilities." All the marginal pork packer needed was a place to slaughter, pickle the meat, pack the barrels, and dump his wastes. He did not worry about city ordinances or the quality of his product. The leading packers did. Men like Hancock, Hough, Hubbard, Culbertson, Tobey, Booth, and the Kents, all of whom had substantial investments in their plants, knew that "shoddy" packers could ruin the reputation of Chicago meat in the competitive postwar market. They were aware of the Chicago Board of Trade's inspection rules for grain and flour and of the employers' associations recently formed by foundrymen, mine owners, and others. While most of those trade associations combated wage demands, that seems not to have been a problem in Chicago. When the beef and pork packers organized in 1863 it was "for the mutual protection and the advancement of the packing interests."[26]

As the war drew to a close, the Chicago Pork Packers' Association decided to do something about "the irregularity of packing and absence of accepted rules." A committee headed by Rosell Hough drew up specifications for cuts of beef and pork and defined standards for packing and labeling barrels and tierces. The Pork Packers' Association gave approval in March, 1865, and the Board of Trade then endorsed these rules and regulations. The packers also devised a system of voluntary inspection of samples. In order to be certified as "standard," meat products had to comply with the new specifications. If the samples did not pass inspection, the barrel or tierce would be stamped "rusty," "sour," or "tainted." Orville Tobey, respected for his high quality pork, was chosen as the first inspector. *Directions for Cutting, Packing, and Curing Pork and Beef, and Rules Regulating Sale of Same* came off the press in 1865 and was the first manual of its kind in the United States.[27]

In Chicago, as in other midwestern centers, economic success opened doors to political and civic leadership in the mid-nineteenth century, and the men developing the livestock trade and meat-packing took advantage of these openings. Hide manufacturer Walter Gurnee served two terms as mayor, and packer Thomas Dyer won that office in 1856. Benjamin P. Hutchinson and Samuel W. Allerton were founders of the influential First National Bank of Chicago, while Clybourn, Hubbard, Hough, Hancock, and Solomon Hopkins played important roles in the Republican party. During the war, Rosell Hough was colonel of an Illinois regiment and John L. Hancock held the same rank in the Chicago city guards. The business community honored these patriots and economic leaders by electing Hancock president of the Board of Trade and choosing Hough in 1865 to head the new Chamber of Commerce. Colonel Hough had the additional honor of presiding over Chicago's impressive memorial ceremonies for the slain President Lincoln. Chicagoans admired the driving energy and dedication, as well as the economic prowess, of their business leaders, and they were proud of what had been accomplished. Visitors, noted Mrs. Rayne in 1865, are always taken to one of the new pork houses and shown "our extensive and perfect arrangements for supplying the whole country with bacon!"[28]

Grappling with Pollution

The new Porkopolis paid a price for its victory. In 1860 the Prince of Wales and civic dignitaries had toured the pumping station in Bridgeport and inspected the South Branch without finding anything offensive. Two packing seasons later, Chicago's water supply was threatened by South Branch pollution. Panicky officials ordered both pumps into round-the-clock action to force the filthy water into the canal. The *Tribune* jauntily advised all those "desirous of taking a parting sniff of the Chicago river perfume . . . to visit Bridgeport today." The pumps were making such progress that the vile stuff "will in a few days be on its way to the rebels. If the latter can stand it, it will be of no use to bombard them any longer."[29]

There was little doubt that the crisis stemmed from lax enforcement of Chicago's 1843, 1849, and 1851 ordinances and the predilection of packers to locate outside city jurisdiction. In the 1850s, when packing plants "were not considered a nuisance, there was no objection . . . to running the offal

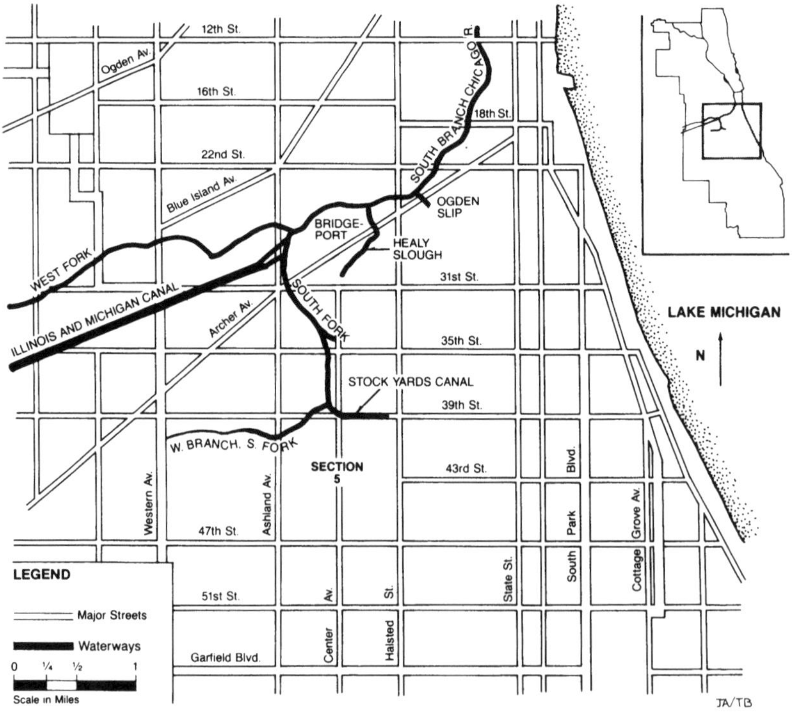

Map 3. The South Fork of the South Branch of the Chicago River

of the hog or the steer into the Chicago River," admitted the *Tribune*. "Indeed, it was one of the leading inducements held out . . . to the packers," and realtors invariably advertised the "convenience" of river property. Moreover, marginal packers in the early years of the war often chose South Branch sites below Thirty-first Street to escape "the supervision of the City Fathers." In the summer of 1863 a *Times* reporter found vacant fields covered with entrails, tankings, and embryotic animals, rotting in the sun, emitting dreadful odors, and covered with "innumerable rats" and "countless millions of flies." Hoping to cure the so-called Bridgeport nuisance, Chicago extended its southern boundary from Thirty-first Street to Thirty-ninth Street in 1863. Prisoners of war were set to work cleaning up the South Branch debris, burying it in pits, and covering the excavations with lime and clay. All slaughterers, packers, and renderers on the South Branch and Healy Slough were warned of the city's intention to enforce its ordinances. Thirty-three companies promptly signed contracts to sell offal to the Wahls, who had just installed new drying equipment in their fertilizer factory. These actions, it was hoped, would solve the crisis.[30]

But one month into the packing season of 1863–64 the South Branch was "thick as mud, black as ink," and "sickening" to smell. All the slaughtering houses were obeying the law, said the *Times*, "yet in some occult way [the offal] does move, notwithstanding, down the bed of the Chicago River." This time officials tried reversing the Bridgeport pumps and sending canal water coursing through the South Branch. It cleansed the river by flushing the filth and stench into Lake Michigan, the source of Chicago's drinking water. Dr. Edmund Andrews of Rush Medical College issued a thunderous warning: "No city can be bathed in putrid air with impunity, and if Chicago shall neglect to make a thorough removal of its filth, it will be infallibly scourged with these pestilences which through all time have smitten cities that commit sins against cleanliness and pure air."[31]

Ironically, Chicago's progress in water distribution and sewer construction aggravated the condition of the river. The private water companies of the 1840s had served only one-fifth of the population, and in 1851 the city appointed a Board of Water Commissioners and assumed this responsibility. One-half mile north of the mouth of the Chicago River the commissioners built a pumping station and intake pipe, and they delivered the first municipal water in 1854. At the time, the city had only a half-dozen storm sewers, all of them emptying into the river. Human wastes went into privy vaults, roadside drainage ditches, or under plank sidewalks where nature and hogs took care of it. In Chicago as in other cities piped water led to an increase in the number of water closets, and this meant overflowing vaults, standing groundwater, and pressure to convert storm sewers into outlets for human waste material. This problem was handed to a Board of Sewer Commissioners in 1855, and the board hired Ellis Sylvester Chesbrough as its engineer. A former railroad construction engineer, Chesbrough helped build the Boston water distribution system and was later appointed city engineer. He was familiar with Boston's storm sewers and its experiments with the water-carriage system of removing household wastes. Developed by English sanitarians, "arterial sewerage" used small pipes comparable to water mains for removal. The system worked well in Boston and New York, where all sewage went into the ocean and thus could not contaminate the water supply.[32]

Chesbrough came to Chicago in 1855 determined to introduce arterial sewers and effective storm sewers. He soon learned that low-lying land, clay subsoil, and a slow-moving river contributed to the sanitary "abominations." He rejected the options of letting sewers drain into Lake Michigan or into artificial reservoirs, and he knew that the city could not finance a deeper Illinois and Michigan Canal channel which would force the river to reverse its flow. So he settled for the Chicago River as the outlet and recommended raising the grade of the city to facilitate gravity flow in the new sewers. Should the North or South Branches become polluted, conduits to the lake would give relief, Chesbrough insisted. The water commissioners had no objections to Chesbrough's plans because they thought their Chicago Avenue pumping station and intake was a safe distance from the mouth of the river. Worried about costs, not pollution, the sewer commissioners sent Chesbrough to Europe to inspect other municipal sewerage systems. His report reaffirmed the wisdom of his master plan for Chicago, and so the city proceeded to elevate its main streets and construct approximately fifty-four miles of combined household and storm sewers by 1861. In that year the water and sewer commissions were combined in a new Board of Public Works, and chief engineer Chesbrough took charge of water, sewers, and the condition of the Chicago River.[33]

His first annual report revealed his game plan. Spring thaws would "scour the river very thoroughly" and "remove its offensive character for the time being," while filters over the water intake would effectively screen out fish and solid debris. The latter was not sewage; it was "refuse from the slaughter and packing houses, . . . besides distilleries, glue factories, [and] establishments for rendering offal." In 1863 and again in 1864 the Board of Public Works asked the city for money to build a South Branch cleansing conduit to the lake. The city council refused, so Chesbrough joined other Chicagoans seeking federal funds for a steamship channel in the Illinois and Michigan canal. Speakers at the ship-canal convention in Chicago in June, 1863, argued that it was essential for national defense and commerce. Congress preferred a transcontinental railroad and adroitly sidestepped Chicago's drainage and water supply problems. Chesbrough then suggested that the city build a tunnel extending far enough into Lake

Michigan to tap pure water. Scoffed at originally, the unprecedented scheme finally won council approval because the Chicago River was deteriorating so rapidly. In the spring of 1864 construction started on a two-mile underground tunnel and intake crib, an innovative and ambitious project for its day.[34]

The South Branch, meanwhile, had become "a staple of conversation," "rivaling even . . . the weather." Advocates of strict enforcement of the city's ordinances, and this included the large packers, found themselves pitted against a coalition of South Branch employers and employees. An anonymous Bridgeport workingman reminded reformers that the packing houses and "grease factories" on "Cologne Creek . . . add largely to the life of our city." Louis Wahl claimed that packers and renderers in Cincinnati and St. Louis dumped in their rivers without ever being criticized. In the fall of 1864 the Wahls' glue and fertilizer factories were destroyed by a spectacular $150,000 fire, perhaps of incendiary origin. Packers were stuck with their offal that season and so much went into the South Branch that lawyer Edwin C. Larned dispatched an angry letter to the *Tribune:* "It is extraordinary that . . . a city of nearly two hundred thousand inhabitants . . . should quietly permit a river running through its entire limits to be converted into a gigantic sewer. . . . Is it possible that the mechanics and laboring men of this city . . . are going to . . . permit a few wealthy men to corrupt the air and the water, which are the common property of all?" The *Tribune* replied editorially that Chicago could "better afford to bring its drinking water from Evanston than to drive the packing houses to St. Louis." The Chicago River was "the natural 'main' of our sewerage system" and Lake Michigan "large enough to receive it all." But the newspaper endorsed Larned's idea of an investigation and public meeting to discuss pollution of the river.[35]

The city council and the Board of Trade appointed a joint committee which reported in January, 1865, to a public meeting chaired by Edwin Larned. The report was presented by Colonel Rosell Hough and contained two recommendations: licensing all businesses located on the river and deepening the Illinois and Michigan Canal. There was no mention of the fact that Chicago had added sixty-five miles of sewers in the preceding three years. Committee members, backed by the council, Board of Trade, large packers, newspapers, and public opinion, took their proposals to the state. In February, 1865, the legislature gave Chicago permission to build the original deep-cut, or steamship channel, in the canal. Lowering the summit level, as Chesbrough was quick to point out, would enable lake water to pass through the Chicago River, into the canal, and thus into the Illinois and Mississippi Rivers. The city sold bonds in the summer and started construction in the fall of 1865. Chicagoans hoped to have a new sewerage route by 1868, but in the meantime the Bridgeport pumps could keep the river tolerable only if "especial vigilance were exercised to keep out deleterious substances."[36]

This meant, of course, cracking down on polluters. Enforcement of the nuisance and sanitary ordinances had been in the hands of the police since 1860 when the Board of Health was abolished, and reformers knew that the police were not paying attention. So they turned to the state legislature and in February, 1865, secured "An Act to Provide Sanitary Measures and Health Regulations for the City of Chicago." The law required Chicago to appoint a health officer and appropriate funds for enforcement of its ordinances. Packers and renderers within Chicago or four miles of its limits must remove "animal matter" and "dead, undressed, unslaughtered" animals every twenty-four hours and dispose of the material beyond the four-mile limit. Chicago was forbidden to license renderers who handled "decayed, putrid or unsound animal matter" or operated within four miles of the city limits. Violators could be taken to court by either the health officer or the sheriff of Cook County, fined a maximum of $500, and enjoined from continuing their business. Similar punishment could be dealt out to lard, tallow, and soap manufacturers.[37]

Prodded by the legislature and reformers and faced with the opening of another packing season, Chicago aldermen passed a tougher licensing ordinance in November, 1865. It required distillers, slaughterers, packers, and renderers to post bond and secure licenses from the council. They could not allow offensive matter to get into "the Chicago River, or into either of the branches thereof, or any of the canals or slips connected therewith," or Lake Michigan. The blood, bones, offal, and distillery-slops had to be removed every twenty-four hours in summer, forty-eight hours in winter, and buried at least forty rods from the river, its branches, the lake, and any dwellings. The offensive material had to be in tightly covered boxes, "as the Health Officer may direct, and shall then be buried and covered with a layer of earth at least twelve inches in depth." Renderers could not "taint the air" within the city limits or two miles outside. And there was a comprehensive caveat to the "distiller, tanner, brewer, butcher, pork and beef packer, soap boiler, tallow chandler, dyer, [and] livery-stable keeper" to keep "offal, manure, rubbish, filth," and "nauseous liquor" out of the river and lake and off the shore, river banks, streets, alleys, and vacant lots. The council set maximum fines at $100 and agreed to split that sum with informants.[38]

Chicago's leading packers, especially Colonel Hough and Board of Trade president John Hancock, played important roles in securing the 1865 restrictions. Their own well-equipped houses set fine examples. Inquiring about "offensive matter" at Cragin and Company and the Houghs' plant, Mrs. Rayne found "not an ounce of it being run into the river." Tobey and Booth in the densely populated district at the Eighteenth Street bridge was so clean that it would be "an agreeable halting place for the Aldermanic smelling committees, when next they make their rounds among the slaughtering establishments of the South Branch." Yet the broad scope of the ordinance made enforcement difficult, and renderers and packers who wanted to ignore its provisions were usually able to do so. A *Times* reporter found the South Branch "impregnated" as usual, and he thought the new state law was "almost a dead letter." Convincing evidence, however, that some packers tried to comply with the regulations came to light half a century later. While excavating the foundation for a new packing plant west of the Union Stock Yards, workmen were stymied by a large mass of gummy material. The substance turned out to be thousands of hogs' heads buried in an unmarked Town of Lake grave during the Civil War era.[39]

Chicago's railroad network enlarged the animal supply, created a livestock trade with eastern cities, and enabled packers to expand production. The twenty thousand hogs dispatched on the eve of the railroad era soared to nearly one million the year Chicago officially became Porkopolis. In the interim, the "model" plants acquired rendering machinery, steam hoists, and ice-cooling apparatus to extend the packing season. Inefficient, marginal pork houses, often located outside city limits, dumped their waste material into the South Branch and contributed to the pollution crisis of the 1860s. The responsible packers, many of whom were also civic leaders, formed a trade association to regulate the quality of Chicago meat products. And they gave strong support to the 1865 state and city regulations on packing, slaughtering, and rendering. These tough laws, plus the two-mile water tunnel and the plan to deepen the canal and reverse the flow of the river, made Chicagoans sanguine about their future. Livestock dealers and packers, however, still fretted over the chronic competition between pedestrians and cattle and hogs for the right-of-way on city streets.

NOTES

1. Board of Trade, *Annual Report, 1859*, 54, 56, 57–59; *1860*, 37, 38; *1864, and Supplement to Mar. 31, 1863*, 46, 52; Bessie Louise Pierce, *A History of Chicago*, vol. 2, *From Town to City, 1848–1871* (New York, 1940), 493–94; Charles Leavitt, "Transportation and the Livestock Industry of the Middle West to 1860," *Agricultural History*, 8 (Jan., 1934), 20–33.

2. James W. Whitaker, *Feedlot Empire: Beef Cattle Feeding in Illinois and Iowa, 1840–1900* (Ames, Iowa, 1975), 18–41; Paul Wallace Gates, "Cattle Kings in the Prairies," *MVHR*, 35 (Dec., 1948), 379–412; M. V.

Harris, ed., "The Autobiography of Benjamin Franklin Harris," Illinois State Historical Society, *Transactions*, 30 (1923), 89–93; *Chicago Democratic Press*, Mar. 25, 1856; Don E. Fehrenbacher, *Chicago Giant: A Biography of "Long John" Wentworth* (Madison, Wis., 1957), 115–16; Lloyd Lewis, *John S. Wright, Prophet of the Prairie* (Chicago, 1941), 149–51.

3. John Drury, *Rare and Well Done: Some Historical Notes on Meats and Meatmen* (Chicago, 1966), 107; [Frank Gilbert], *A History of the City of Chicago, Its Men and Institutions* (Chicago, 1900), 190–91; John Joseph Flinn, *The Hand-Book of Chicago Biography* (Chicago, 1893), 25–26; Edward N. Wentworth, *A Biographical Catalog of the Portrait Gallery of the Saddle and Sirloin Club* (Chicago, 1920), 167–72.

4. *Drovers Journal*, Dec. 14, 1885; June 28, 1939; *Encyclopedia of Biography of Illinois* (Chicago, 1894), 2:128–33; *Trib.*, Jan. 30, 1887; Drury, *Rare and Well Done*, 148–49; M. S. Parkhurst, *History of the Yards, 1865–1953* (Chicago, 1953), 8; *Inland Architect*, 1 (Apr., 1883), 36.

5. *Trib.*, Jan. 30, Feb. 20, 1887; *Drovers Journal*, Dec. 14, 1885; Aug. 24, 1889; May 17, 1890; *Times*, Dec. 12, 1865; *Sun*, Oct. 24, 1891; *Land-Owner*, 6 (Jan., 1874), 9; *Griffiths Annual Review of the Live Stock Trade at Chicago*, (Chicago, 1879), 15–16; Alfred T. Andreas. *History of Cook County, Illinois* (Chicago, 1884), 685.

6. Wentworth, *Portrait Gallery*, 182; Nelson Morris, "Personal Reminiscences of the Chicago Market," *Breeder's Gazette*, 46 (Dec. 2, 1904), 1156; *Sun*, Oct. 24, 1891; Ira Nelson Morris, *Heritage from My Father: An Autobiography* (New York, 1947), 2–4.

7. Richard C. Overton, *Burlington Route: A History of the Burlington Lines* (New York, 1965), 16–17; *Times*, Dec. 12, 1865; *Trib.*, Feb. 20, 1887; Andreas, *Cook County*, 679; Elias Colbert, *Chicago, Historical and Statistical Sketch of the Garden City* (Chicago, 1868), 59.

8. D. B. Cooke and Company, *Directory of Chicago for the Year 1858* (Chicago, 1858), 341; Smith and Dumoulin, *Chicago City Directory for the Year Ending May 1, 1860* (Chicago, 1860), 463; *Prairie Farmer*, 24 (Dec. 19, 1861), 407; Drury, *Rare and Well Done*, 106–8; Rudolf A. Clemen, *The American Livestock and Meat Industry* (New York, 1923), 87–89.

9. *Drovers Journal*, Oct. 3, 1890; Harris, "Autobiography of Benjamin Franklin Harris," 93; Andreas, *Cook County*, 679; *Trib.*, Jan. 7, 1883; Mar. 14, 1886; Wentworth, *Portrait Gallery*, 170, 182; Flinn, *Hand-Book of Chicago Biography*, 25–26; Nelson Morris, "Personal Reminiscences," 1156; David Ward Wood, ed., *Chicago and Its Distinguished Citizens, or the Progress of Forty Years* (Chicago, 1881), 367–68.

10. Board of Trade, *Annual Report, 1860*, 37, 38; Daily Democratic Press, *The Railroads, History and Commerce of Chicago* (Chicago, 1854), 56; *Chicago Daily Democrat*, Nov. 15, 23, 1849.

11. Charles E. Rosenberg, *The Cholera Years: The United States in 1832, 1849, and 1866* (Chicago, 1962), 165–72; Weston A. Goodspeed and Daniel D. Healy, eds., *History of Cook County, Illinois*, 2 vols. (Chicago, 1909), 1:212–14; Pierce, *Chicago*, 2:334, 336; *Chicago Daily Democrat*, June 28, Dec. 11, 18, 1849; Oct. 30, 1850; *Charter of the City of Chicago and Amendments with Rules of Council and Ordinances* (Chicago, 1849), 9, 194.

12. *Gem of the Prairie*, Nov. 16, 1850; *Chicago Daily Journal*, Mar. 11, 1851; *Private Laws of the State of Illinois, 1851* (Springfield, 1851), 143–44; George Manierre, comp., *The Revised Charter and Ordinances of the City of Chicago* (Chicago, 1851), 214–16; Faith Fitzgerald, "Growth of Municipal Activities in Chicago, 1833–1875" (M.A. thesis, University of Chicago, 1933), 130–35.

13. Department of Health, *Report of the Board of Health for 1867, 1868 and 1869; and a Sanitary History of Chicago from 1833 to 1870*, 20; *Trib.*, Dec. 14, 1852; Apr. 19, 1891; Apr. 26, 1892; Oct. 29, 1893; Charles Cleaver, *Early-Chicago Reminiscences* (Chicago, 1882), 50–51; Charles Cleaver, *History of Chicago from 1833 to 1892* (Chicago, 1892), 95–103; S. S. Schoff, *The Glory of Chicago, Her Manufactories. The Industrial Interests of Chicago . . .* (Chicago, 1873), 184–85.

14. Margaret Walsh, "From Pork Merchant to Meat Packer: The Midwestern Meat Industry in the Mid-Nineteenth Century," *Agricultural History*, 56 (Jan., 1982), 127–37; *Eighth Census, 1860*, "Manufactures," 87; *Gem of the Prairie*, Nov. 16, 1850; *Prairie Farmer*, 10 (Dec., 1850), 382; Board of Trade, *Annual Report, 1860*, 36, 37; Daily Democratic Press, *Railroads, History and Commerce of Chicago*, 62–63.

15. Chicago Tribune, *Fifteenth Annual Review of the Trade and Commerce of the City of Chicago* (Chicago, 1864), 15; Board of Trade, *Annual Report, 1860*, 36–38; Cleaver, *Reminiscences*, 49; Louisa Libby Burrows, comp., *Arthur Albion Libby* (n.p., [1953]), 5–6.

16. Board of Trade, *Annual Report, 1860*, 36–38; *Prairie Farmer*, 10 (Dec., 1850), 382; *Gem of the Prairie*, Nov. 16, 1850; *Times*, Dec. 12, 1865; *Trib.*, Dec. 28, 1850; Dec. 31, 1884; Feb. 20, 1887; Mar. 9, 1892.

17. Board of Trade, *Annual Report, 1860*, 36, 37; *Prairie Farmer*, 10 (Dec., 1850), 382; Chicago Tribune, *Fifteenth Annual Review*, 15; George Upton, *Biographical Sketches of the Leading Men of Chicago* (Chicago, 1876), 129; "Sidney Albert Kent," in Thomas W. Goodspeed, *The University of Chicago Biographical Sketches*, 2 vols. (Chicago, 1922), 1:83–87; Elizabeth T. Kent, "William Kent, Independent: A Biography" (typescript, 1950, Chicago Historical Society), 8–13.

18. Oscar E. Anderson, Jr., *Refrigeration in America: A History of a New Technology and Its Impact* (Princeton, N.J., 1953), 23–26, 34; John C. Schooley, *A Process of Obtaining a Dry Cold Current of Air from Ice,*

and Its Different Applications (Cincinnati, 1855), 1–5; Board of Trade, *Annual Report, 1860,* 36; Margaret Walsh, "Pork Packing as a Leading Edge of Midwestern Industry, 1835–1875," *Agricultural History,* 51 (1977), 712–13.

19. Margaret Walsh, *The Rise of the Midwestern Meat Packing Industry* (Lexington, Ky., 1982), 50–54; Howard C. Hill, "The Development of Chicago as a Center of the Meat Packing Industry," *MVHR,* 10 (Dec., 1923), 258–63; Chicago Tribune, *Annual Review of Trade and Commerce for 1860* (Chicago, 1861), 38.

20. *Trib.*, Apr. 10, 1862; Carl Abbott, *Boosters and Businessmen: Popular Economic Thought and Urban Growth in the Antebellum Middle West* (Westport, Conn., 1981), chap. 6; Hill, "Chicago as a Center of the Meat Packing Industry," 262–63; E. Merton Coulter, "Effects of Secession upon the Commerce of the Mississippi Valley," *MVHR,* 3 (Dec. 1916), 281–84; Walsh, "Pork Packing," 715–16; Chicago Tribune, *Annual Review of Trade, Business and Growth of Chicago during 1865* (Chicago, 1866), 32.

21. John S. Wright, *Chicago: Past, Present, Future* (Chicago, 1868), 164, 165, quoted 213; Elmer A. Riley, *The Development of Chicago and Vicinity as a Manufacturing Center Prior to 1880* (Chicago, 1911), 126–27; Pierce, *Chicago,* 2:46–47; Board of Trade, *Annual Report, 1862,* 32; *1865,* 43; Emerson D. Fite, *Social and Industrial Conditions in the North during the Civil War* (New York, 1910), 44–54, 76–80; Thomas Weber, *The Northern Railroads in the Civil War, 1861–1865* (New York, 1952), 83–93.

22. Board of Trade, *Annual Report, 1864,* 46, 52; *1865,* 37; *1871,* 44; *Trib.*, Apr. 10, 1862; Mar. 13, 1864. Trying to comprehend Chicago's hog pack of 1863–64, James Parton said: "Walking in single file, close together, that number of hogs would form a line reaching from Chicago to New York." [Parton], "Chicago," *Atlantic Monthly,* 19 (Mar., 1867), 332.

23. *Drovers Journal,* Nov. 4, 1887; *Sun,* Oct. 31, Nov. 2, 1889; Andreas, *Cook County,* 682; *Trib.*, Mar. 13, 1864; Apr. 16, 1883; Mar. 17, 1899; Wentworth, *Portrait Gallery,* 166; William Ferris, "Old Hutch—The Wheat King," *JISHS,* 41 (Sept., 1948), 231–33.

24. Board of Trade, *Annual Report, 1860,* 37, 38; *1864,* 47, 53; *Prairie Farmer,* 29 (Feb. 20, 1864), 116; *Trib.*, Mar. 13, 1864; Mar. 9, 1892; Kent, "William Kent," 8–13; Chicago Tribune, *Fifteenth Annual Review,* 17–20; M. L. Rayne, *Chicago and One Hundred Miles Around: Being a Complete Hand-Book and Guide* (Chicago, 1865), 92–95; Walsh, *Midwestern Meat Packing,* 60–63.

25. Rayne, *Chicago and One Hundred Miles Around,* 91–92; *Prairie Farmer,* 29 (Feb. 20, 1864), 116–17. The first plant in the Cincinnati area to combine slaughtering and packing was built across the Ohio River in

Covington and had killing pens on the top floor. William Chambers described it in *Things as They Are in America* (Edinburgh, 1854), 156.

26. Board of Trade, *Annual Report, 1862*, 32; Clarence E. Bonnett, *History of Employers' Associations in the United States* (New York, 1956), 66–90; Chicago Tribune, *Annual Review of Trade, 1865*, 32; *Trib.*, Mar. 20, 1865.

27. J. C. W. Bailey, *Chicago City Directory for the Year 1865–66* (Chicago, 1865), 822–23; *Trib.*, Mar. 20, 1865; Jan. 1, 1866; *Times*, Mar. 28, 1865; Chicago Pork Packers' Association, *Directions for Cutting, Packing, and Curing Pork and Beef, and Rules Regulating Sale of Same* (Chicago, 1865); Board of Trade, *Annual Report, 1866*, 5, 16–21; Chicago Pork Packers' Association, *Annual Report of the Packing of the West* (Chicago, 1876), 7.

28. Frederic Cople Jaher, *The Urban Establishment: Upper Strata in Boston, New York, Charleston, Chicago, and Los Angeles* (Urbana, Ill., 1982), 453–63; Goodspeed and Healy, *Cook County*, 1:366–67, 437, 456, 471, 484, 487, 498; *Trib.*, May 2, 3, 1865; Mar. 9, 1892; Abbott, *Boosters and Businessmen*, 3–4, 119–30; Rayne, *Chicago and One Hundred Miles Around*, 89.

29. *Trib.*, Sept. 24, 1860; May 30, 1862.

30. Chicago Tribune, *Fifteenth Annual Review*, 12; "A Visit to Bridgeport," *Times*, July 16, 1863; *Trib.*, Feb. 21, June 17, Dec. 23, 1863; Dec. 3, 1864.

31. *Trib.*, Nov. 12, 1863; *Times*, Oct. 30, Dec. 4, 1863; George P. Brown, *Drainage Channel and Waterway: A History of the Effort to Secure . . . Disposal of the Sewage of the City of Chicago* (Chicago, 1894), 307; Department of Health, *Report . . . and Sanitary History*, 68–69.

32. Martin V. Melosi, ed., *Pollution and Reform in American Cities, 1870–1930* (Austin, 1980), 59–64; Louis P. Cain, *Sanitation Strategy for a Lakefront Metropolis: The Case of Chicago* (DeKalb, Ill., 1978), 20–23, 38–43; James C. O'Connell, "Technology and Pollution: Chicago's Water Policy, 1833–1930" (Ph.D. diss., University of Chicago, 1980), chaps. 2, 3; C. D. Hill, "The Sewerage System of Chicago," *Journal of the Western Society of Engineers*, 16 (Sept., 1911), 548–49; Louis P. Cain, "Raising and Watering a City, Chesbrough and Chicago's First Sanitary System," *Technology and Culture*, 13 (July, 1972), 353–69.

33. Cain, *Sanitation Strategy*, 24–35; Andreas, *Chicago*, 2:65–66; Ellis S. Chesbrough, *Chicago Sewerage, Report of the Results of Examinations Made in Relation to Sewerage in Several European Cities* (Chicago, 1858), 88–89; George P. Brown, *Drainage Channel and Waterway*, 30–33, 49–58, 65.

34. Board of Public Works, *First Annual Report for the Year Ending Jan.*

1, 1862, 40–41, 48; George P. Brown, *Drainage Channel and Waterway,* 65–71, 235–57; [Jack Wing], *The Great Chicago Lake Tunnel* (Chicago, 1867), 10–11; Thomas D. Garry, "History of Chicago Sewers" (typescript, 1941, Chicago Historical Society), 1–12; Cain, *Sanitation Strategy,* 43–48; O'Connell, "Technology and Pollution," 42–44.

35. *Trib.*, June 25, July 28, Nov. 4, 5, 30, 1864; letter to editor, ibid., Jan. 3, 1864; Wahl Bros. and Lighthall to editor, ibid., Dec. 22, 1864; E. C. L. to editor, ibid., Dec. 18, 1864; "Chicago River," ibid., Dec. 19, 1864; *In Memory of Edwin Channing Larned* (Chicago, 1886), 15–16.

36. *Trib.*, Jan. 4, 6, 16, 18, 1865; George P. Brown, *Drainage Channel and Waterway,* 72–84; James W. Putnam, *The Illinois and Michigan Canal: A Study in Economic History* (Chicago, 1918), 143; Cain, *Sanitation Strategy,* 59–63.

37. Joseph E. Gary, comp., *Laws and Ordinances Covering the City of Chicago, Jan. 1, 1866* (Chicago, 1866), 518–19, 200–205; Department of Health, *Report . . . and Sanitary History,* 313–15; act of Feb. 16, 1865, Illinois, *Private Laws, 1865*, 1:590–91.

38. Gary, *Laws and Ordinances,* 290–95; Department of Health, *Report . . . and Sanitary History,* 86–87, 321–24; Fitzgerald, "Municipal Activities," 138–47.

39. Rayne, *Chicago and One Hundred Miles Around,* 93–94; Chicago Tribune, *Fifteenth Annual Review,* 16–20; *Times,* June 14, 1865; *Nat. Prov.*, 52 (Jan. 16, 1915), 17.

CHAPTER 3

The Creation of a Chicago Stockyard

The widely scattered railroad stock enclosures brought an annoying increase in the number of hogs and cattle driven through city streets, and pedestrians, carriage drivers, city officials, railroad managers, packers, and livestock dealers cast about for a more efficient solution. They found it in one large, consolidated stockyard located outside the city yet accessible to the railroads and the packers. Constructed in the Town of Lake during the latter half of 1865, the novel Union Stock Yard was ready for business at the end of December. It worked so well that railroads delivered over three million animals to Chicago during 1870. James Parton called national attention to "the great bovine city" on Chicago's outskirts in an 1867 *Atlantic Monthly* article, and he credited the experiment with lifting the livestock trade "out of the mire" and making it "clean, easy, respectable, and pleasant."[1]

The Need

Nobody was happy with the arrangements for buying, selling, or distributing livestock in Chicago during the war. The distances between the various yards made it difficult to compare quality, volume, or price. Since newspaper livestock reports were incomplete, buyers wrestled with "conflicting rumors and quotations." Drovers tangled with pedestrians and vehicles, and these encounters led to arguments, traffic jams, and sometimes accidents. In November, 1863, an impatient drover ignored the warning bell and took his cattle onto the Rush Street bridge when it was about to open. As the span began moving, cattle stampeded to one end, blocking the only escape route for pedestrians and causing the iron bridge to twist and break. Fifty cattle and a dozen people went into the Chicago River, and taxpayers were set back $10,000. Similarly the railroads disliked the existing system because their stockyards were hemmed in by factories, stores, and residences and they could not expand. John Sherman managed to add fifteen more acres to the Lake Shore Yards, but the Chicago, Burlington and Quincy, the leading livestock carrier, announced plans to develop its own facility along Western Avenue. President John Van Nortwick wanted the Burlington yard in operation for the 1864–65 packing season.[2]

While this would help one railroad, it would complicate matters for livestock dealers, packers, and drovers, to say nothing of city traffic. Early in 1864 Samuel Allerton and John Sherman began advocating one large stockyard, accessible to all the railroads, not too distant from the South Branch packing plants, and "somewhere out on the prairie, beyond the line ever to be reached by the expanding city." Packers Hancock, Hough, Tobey, Hubbard, and Culbertson gave enthusiastic approval to the scheme, but a few small packers and livestock dealers thought a consolidated stockyard could lead to monopoly. Despite this fear, the Pork Packers' Association unanimously proposed on June 28 that the various stockyards around Chicago be consolidated and run "by a joint stock company, the stock of which should be accessible to all." The packers preferred a location near the southern city limits.[3]

In July Rosell Hough and John Hancock talked with railroad officials. Michigan Central president John W. Brooks wanted a "common centre" because the "scattered market" was "expensive and inconvenient"; moreover, it was "so embarrassing the streets that we shall be in great trouble about it." Brooks and James F. Joy thought that the new connecting tracks to the proposed facility should be "built at the joint and equal expense of all the parties." The packers then pledged $50,000 provided all the railroads participated. Van Nortwick still wanted a Burlington facility for the coming season, and directors authorized him to go ahead but to spend no more than was "absolutely necessary." They wanted the Burlington to be part of the larger project, for the advantages of a consolidated yard "are too obvious to require discussion," as Brooks put it to Joy.[4]

In the fall of 1864 nine railroads issued a prospectus of "The Union Stock Yard and Transit Company"; the incorporators were eleven railroad men and eight packers.* Chicago lawyer Frederick H. Winston drafted the

* The sponsoring railroads were the Burlington; Chicago and North Western; Chicago and Milwaukee; Rock Island; Chicago and Alton; Michigan Southern; Michigan Central; Illinois Central; and Pittsburgh, Fort Wayne and Chicago.

The railroad representatives were William D. Judson, president of the Chicago and Great Eastern Railway, which was awaiting incorporation; George W. Cass, president of the Pittsburgh, Fort Wayne; Timothy B. Blackstone, president of the Chicago and Alton; John F. Tracy, soon to become president of the Rock Island; James F. Joy of the Burlington and Michigan Central group; Martin L. Sykes, representing the Chicago and North Western and the Chicago and Milwaukee lines; Burton C. Cook and John S. Barry, both connected with the Michigan Southern; Homer E. Sargent, Chicago agent for the Michigan Central; Joseph H. Moore, Chicago agent for the Pittsburgh, Fort Wayne; John B. Drake, popular manager of the Tremont House, friend of all these men, and a director of the Chicago and Alton.

The packers, all of whom belonged to the Chicago Pork Packers' Association, charter, and newly elected state representative Solomon P. Hopkins sponsored the request for incorporation in the state legislature. On February 13, 1865, the governor signed a measure authorizing the incorporators to erect "the necessary yards, inclosures, buildings, structures, and railway lines, tracks, switches and turnouts" plus connecting railroad tracks which might cross "any street or highway . . . consistent with the use of said track so laid." The charter prohibited special agreements between the company and any of the railroads as well as bans on any roads seeking to do business at the stockyard. Furthermore, the charter forbade company interference with the right of shippers to consign their stock to other yards. The new arrangement, admitted the wary editor of *Prairie Farmer,* "should prove an advantage . . . provided it does not terminate in a giant monopoly." To secure the necessary capital, the incorporators issued ten thousand shares of stock, and in short order the nine railroads subscribed $925,000, the packers $50,000, and the public $25,000.[5]

Early in March the incorporators elected nine directors and officers to serve until the first annual meeting in January, 1866. The board members were packers Hancock, Hough, Culbertson, and Turpin, and five railroad men—Joy, Blackstone, and representatives of the Rock Island, Michigan Southern, and Pittsburgh, Fort Wayne. These directors named Chicagoan Timothy B. Blackstone president and Frederick Winston secretary. A private banking firm, Solomon Sturges' Sons, was designated treasurer. The incorporators had already settled on John Wentworth's half-section of land in Town of Lake as the preferred site. Its location midway between the lakefront tracks and the western trunk lines was ideal, and it was convenient for South Branch packers. James F. Joy thought a smaller parcel of about one hundred acres would suffice, but John B. Sherman persuaded the incorporators to take the entire 320 acres. Hemmed in at Bull's Head and cramped at the Lake Shore Yards, Sherman urged them to develop what they needed and hold the rest for expansion or sale at a later date and higher price. Thus the Union Stock Yard and Transit Company purchased the entire eastern half of Section 5 for $100,000.[6]

The next question was what to do about the Burlington yard and an adjacent facility, the Western Union Drovers' Yard, that would serve the North Western and the Chicago and Milwaukee. Van Nortwick spent over $200,000 on his project and refused the Union Stock Yard company's offer to buy his equipment at cost. Clearly, however, stockyards ranged along Western Avenue would perpetuate all the disadvantages and jeopardize the Town of Lake project. So Forbes, Brooks, and Joy overruled Van Nortwick, and the Burlington settled for $125,000 worth of Union Stock Yard

---

were John L. Hancock, Virginius A. Turpin, Rosell M. Hough, Sidney A. Kent, Charles M. Culbertson, David Kreigh, Joseph Sherwin, and Lyman Blair.

stock. Van Nortwick resigned, and James F. Joy became the Burlington president in July, 1865. Sponsors of the Drovers' Yard held out until summer when it was crystal clear that they could not compete with the new facility.[7]

Building the Union Stock Yard

There were no precedents for a consolidated railroad stockyard, and none of the incorporators felt competent to design such a structure. So they invited railroad and civil engineers to submit plans and promised that the winner would be appointed chief engineer. Octave Chanute, a railroad engineer who would later turn to aerial navigation and coach the Wright brothers, won this competition. Born in Paris in 1832 and raised in New Orleans and New York City where he studied civil engineering, Chanute came west in the 1850s to supervise railroad construction in Illinois and Indiana. By 1863 he was chief engineer of the Chicago and Alton and, undoubtedly, familiar with the bottlenecks in Chicago's livestock trade. Chanute informed his New York friend, W. H. Civer, in May that he was preparing estimates for the "Union Cattle Yard Co." and expected "to go on at once with the building of the Roads and Yards." He did so with the assistance of Civer, who was named resident engineer, and under the general direction of Rosell Hough, superintendent of construction.[8]

Chanute's original plan called for forty acres of animal pens, an office building and a hotel, and railroad tracks leading east and west of the new stockyard. Located in the northern half of the company's land, these improvements would cost $1,007,600. When the board learned that the three railroads using the Western Avenue yards would join, it authorized another $400,000 to enlarge the plan. Chanute recommended double connecting tracks to the lakefront and a single track to Western Avenue and then north to Sixteenth Street; he thought a sixty-six-foot-wide right-of-way advisable. "Relief from the annoyance of municipal regulations, and from the care of ballasting, repairing and draining the streets, would counterbalance the increased cost." The board of directors accepted the wide right-of-way, asked for double tracks on both approaches, and purchased another twenty-five acres northwest of their property to allow for easier railroad access from the west. Although these connecting tracks cost about $180,000, the company agreed to let the railroads use them without charge. This gentlemen's agreement lasted from 1865 until 1894.[9]

Drainage of the low-lying land was a challenge, and some skeptics said it could not be done. But Chanute laid thirty miles of sewers and drains which emptied into two discharge sewers, one paralleling Halsted Street to the South Branch and the other following Thirty-ninth Street to the

South Fork. Groundbreaking for the box sewer near Halsted took place June 1, 1865, and marked the official start of construction. Chanute's drains transformed the once swampy tract and convinced one reporter that in the matter of drainage the "bovine city will be far ahead of the human city which it adjoins." Construction materials for the yards came in by horse and wagon until the railroad tracks went down. Then three trains per day delivered lumber for the pens, platforms, and fencing. Chanute wanted to surface the pens with broken stones and a fireproof "impervious coat of Asphaltum." It would cost the same as wooden planking—$600,000—but the company felt it could not spare the time to get the necessary machinery to the site. So Chanute used traditional pine planks laid "like the floor of a house."[10]

Chanute's streets formed a grid, the only deviations being caused by curves in the railroad tracks. Two main thoroughfares divided the 160 acres into quarters. The north-south route, called Avenue E, was an extension of Laurel Street, which originated in Bridgeport. Chanute probably envisioned this roadway as the main approach for workmen; certainly he expected it to be the route for livestock departures to the South Branch packing houses. It was seventy-five feet wide and divided into three lanes so that drovers could take animals north and south in the outside sections, leaving the center lane for pedestrians, men on horseback, and the emergency "passing" of herds. Avenue E was paved with Nicholson blocks made from the unused ends of pine planks, and it had a slightly raised center to assure prompt drainage. "There is not a finer or smoother drive in Chicago," said one surprised visitor. Chanute's major east-west street was located at approximately Forty-first. It was sixty-six feet wide, planked and well-drained, with a raised sidewalk on the south side. This thoroughfare started at Halsted where the hotel was placed, passed through a wooden gate at the entrance to the yards, then by the office and bank building and on to Center Avenue. Artisans working on the hotel and exchange building christened it Broadway and this was its name for about a decade. Since the flow of biped traffic in the yards turned out to be east-west rather than north-south, Broadway became Central Avenue in the 1880s. The inevitable confusion with Center was resolved by changing the name once more—to Exchange Avenue.[11]

The yards were divided into four parts, three for receiving livestock and the fourth for shipments east. Division B at the north end served the three eastern roads, while Division A belonged to the Illinois Central and the Rock Island whose trains came in over the eastern connecting track. On the western side of the yards were Division C, assigned to the Burlington and the Chicago and Alton, and Division D for the Chicago and North Western. There were approximately fifteen miles of track within the Union Stock Yard, plus switches, turntables, water tanks and woodyards for the

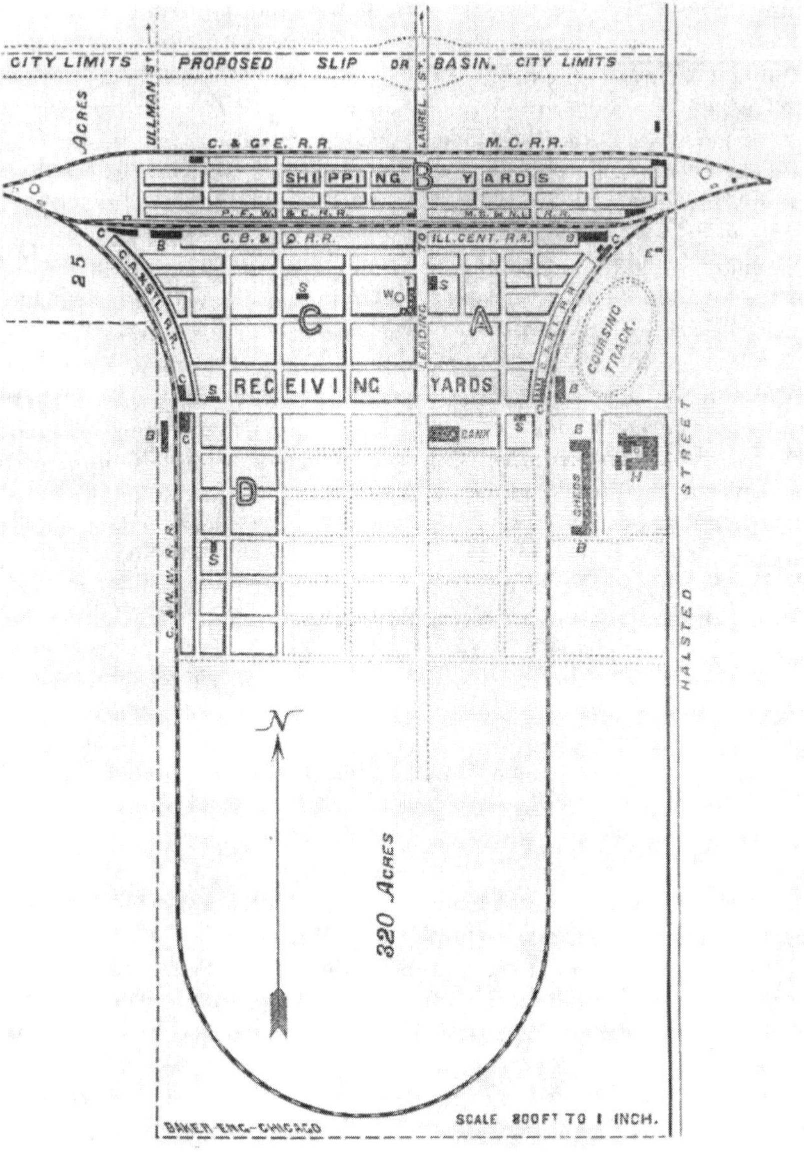

"Diagram of the Union Stock Yard," prepared by W. H. Civer, Resident Engineer. Frontispiece in Jack Wing, *The Great Union Stock Yards of Chicago* (Chicago, 1865). Courtesy, Chicago Historical Society.

engines, and "everything that is required at a great depot, which these yards, in fact, are." Each railroad had one thousand feet of unloading track within its division and platforms, chutes, and pens. The five hundred animal pens varied in size, and gates could be opened to turn two or more into one large enclosure. Some unloading platforms had two levels of chutes to accommodate those railroads using double-deck hog cars. Chanute's sixty acres of pens could hold fourteen thousand cattle and fifty thousand hogs.[12]

Water for the stockyard came from the west branch of the South Fork. It was "quite pure" because it was safely upstream from the sewer outlet into the South Fork. Chanute built a stone dam across this stream, created a large water reservoir, and used a wooden pipe to convey the water a distance of one mile to a deep well in the stockyard. Ranged around the well were five water tanks on raised platforms. A steam pump kept these tanks full and serviced a sixth one on the eastern edge of the yards for the locomotives. Six miles of water pipe led from the tanks to the animal pens, each of which had a water hydrant and trough. Chanute's water system delivered five hundred thousand gallons per day, and he assured the directors that it "worked very satisfactorily."[13]

The exchange and office building and the hotel were "accessory" structures as far as Chanute was concerned. He wanted the hotel on Halsted and the office building at the intersection of Broadway and Avenue E. Rosell Hough probably selected the architects, Frederick Baumann and Edward Burling, for they designed the new Chamber of Commerce building while Hough was president of that organization. Their Exchange building, of white Illinois brick, had two stories and a gabled attic. On the first floor were company offices, a bank, and the spacious sixty- by eighty-foot exchange with tables and chairs, a bar, and an "eating counter." On the second floor were ten large rooms to accommodate dealers and commission firms and an impressive telegraph headquarters.[14]

The showplace of the Union Stock Yard, however, was the hotel. Named Hough House for the popular colonel, it had a 130-foot frontage on Halsted, two long wings, and wide verandas and porches. Built of the same brick as the Exchange, the hotel was six stories high and its mansard roof sported a cupola topped with a weather vane. In the courtyard between the wings was an artesian well, one of the earliest in the Chicago area, and behind the structure was an elegantly appointed stable. Hough House, thought one observer, might well become a popular "suburban retreat." Guests could view the "boundless prairie" in one direction and in the other, from the cupola, "both branches of the river . . . with their long lines of masts. The city lies seemingly at your feet, wrapped in a thick cloud of smoke, as if you were standing above the clouds."[15] (See Figs. 2 and 3.)

Since the stockyard was about five miles from the center of Chicago and one mile from Bridgeport, laborers, craftsmen, and foremen had trouble reaching the construction site. The total number employed by the Union Stock Yard and Transit Company is unknown, but Chanute reported as many as one thousand men engaged in planking. Since the railroads did not carry passengers until the yards opened, it is likely that supervisory personnel traveled on horseback or in carriages while workmen walked down Halsted or Laurel. A few people put up shanties near Halsted and Thirty-ninth, "primitive" structures, sniffed a reporter, which "do not add much to the scene in an artistic point of view." He anticipated company housing in the future, but this never materialized because employes and livestock dealers acted first. In December of 1865 a *Times* reporter commented on the brisk sale of lots along Halsted south of Thirty-first Street and the appearance of frame cottages and newly planted trees. "Already something of a village has grown up around the yards, and the smoke of scores of chimneys may be seen rising from the vicinity." Several stores and groceries were doing a good business, and tavern-keepers occupied "a row of temporary buildings . . . arranged promiscuously . . .[and] embellished with elaborate signs." There was no doubt in his mind that the change "wrought upon this marshy prairie, in less than six months, is marvelous."[16]

Attention shifted to the west side of Halsted after the company announced that the "yards and hotel . . . will be opened for business on Monday the 25th instant." Two railroads advertised "dummy" service to the Union Stock Yard, both charging twenty cents for the thirty-minute ride. Nothing happened on Christmas, but the following day the Burlington brought in the first stock train, John Hancock made the first purchase for Cragin and Company, and drovers for the Hough brothers took the first lot of hogs to a packing plant. When close to twenty thousand animals had arrived by the end of the first week, even the suspicious "*habitues* of the old yards" bestowed their praises on the new enterprise. Sponsors and friends of the Union Stock Yard gathered at the hotel on New Year's Day to celebrate their achievement and thank the conscientious superintendent of construction. Rosell Hough responded to the lavish compliments with a short, simple speech encapsulating the midwestern businessmen's creed: "Uneducated, my lot was cast in the great West. I never went to school a day after I was twelve years of age. I mixed with the business men of the West, and if I have done anything more than anybody else I do not know what it is." The following day the *Tribune* spoke for the boosters: "The great Union Stock Yards are now a reality . . . and, like the Chamber of Commerce building, the lake tunnel, the packing houses, and Crosby's Opera House, one of the 'lions' of which Chicago may justly 'brag' on."[17]

Successful Operation

The first five years were a resounding success, thanks to the railroads and John B. Sherman's managerial skills. The extension of Chicago's railroad network to 11,000 miles by 1870 pushed livestock receipts at the yards from one and a half million during the first full year of operation to more than three million in 1870. The Rock Island and the Chicago and North Western reached Council Bluffs by 1869; both had railroad bridges across the Mississippi and both were ready to tie into the Union Pacific at Omaha. The aggressive Burlington built two Mississippi bridges, and president James F. Joy employed Octave Chanute to design the first railroad span across the Missouri River. This Kansas City bridge allowed the Burlington to reach into Kansas and Nebraska and tap the transcontinental route. Little wonder, therefore, that the ceremony in Promontory, Utah, in May, 1869, convinced Chicagoans that the riches of the Orient would soon be pouring into their laps, "to be distributed to the Atlantic cities, and thence to the European markets."[18]

As word spread of Chicago's excellent facilities for selling livestock, farmers in Wisconsin, Iowa, Missouri, Kansas, and Nebraska needed little encouragement to raise hogs and cattle as well as grain. Most of their cattle were familiar "natives," but Texas longhorns were new to the Chicago market. Small, lean, bony animals with horns often six feet apart at the tips, they reminded old-timers around the stockyards of "razorback" hogs, an inferior version of the real thing. Detractors complained about their fierce disposition and coarse flesh, while defenders called the beef "teasingly tough" and pointed to the high prices paid for "Cherokee" hides. Construction of the Kansas Pacific Railroad focused the Texas cattle trade in "cow towns" like Abilene, where Joseph McCoy started a stockyard in 1869, and Kansas City followed suit when the Missouri River railroad bridge opened. Fearful that the longhorns harbored ticks and spread Spanish fever, a number of state legislatures including Illinois regulated the grazing and fattening of these controversial cattle. Yet attractive prices for longhorns kept them coming to the Union Stock Yard.[19]

The new facility quickly put the older Chicago yards out of business and drew livestock dealers into the Exchange, Solomon Hopkins, Nelson Morris, and Samuel Allerton being the first to move. The railroad companies were as pleased as the livestock brokers. The president of the Pittsburgh, Fort Wayne hailed the Union Stock Yard as "more complete than anything of the kind on this Continent." At the first annual meeting in January, 1866, the four packers surrendered their board seats to railroad men, and Peyton R. Chandler of the Chicago and Alton replaced Timothy Blackstone as president. A report on stock distribution showed that Joy held the largest block, 2,650 shares for the Burlington. The Michigan Southern and the Pittsburgh, Fort Wayne each had 1,500 shares; railroad lawyers like James M. Walker of the Michigan Central held smaller amounts; packers Hancock and Hough owned about 300 shares, as did John B. Sherman.[20]

The latter was the obvious candidate to manage the new yards, but railroad rivalries dictated the choice. The Chicago and Alton had no alliances with either the Michigan Central-Burlington group or the Michigan Southern-Rock Island faction, so the presidency went first to Blackstone and then to Chandler. Both felt that Sherman was too close to Joy and Walker and thus might favor the Burlington and Michigan Central. So the board of directors named F. J. Bryant supervisor and let Sherman return to Dutchess County. Bryant's performance left much to be desired. He wasted money on artesian wells before finally laying pipes to Lake Michigan to augment the supply of water at the yards. He ignored a "ring" of livestock dealers who withheld price quotations from the newspapers and provoked an Illinois stock growers' boycott. But his timely death in the spring of 1867 allowed the board to summon Sherman back to Chicago.[21]

The outgoing Sherman, with the help of the competent team he had assembled at the Lake Shore stockyard, quickly established a vigorous regime. He pleased stock growers by quashing all "secrecy" at the Union Stock Yard, and he named George T. Williams as his liaison with company secretary Winston. Sherman renamed the hotel Transit House and with manager William F. Tucker developed one of Chicago's finest restaurants at that elegant hostelry. He also opened Dexter Park racetrack on company property; used primarily by horse-racing buffs, it also served as a place to display blooded livestock. In the barn behind the hotel and race track, Sherman sheltered a six-legged hog and a "camel-backed" horse, the beginning of his famous menagerie. When livestock dealers pressed Sherman for a chartered bank which could meet their needs far more effectively than the private bank, he saw to it that a Union Stock Yard National Bank was established. Capitalized at $100,000, it opened in the Exchange in 1868 and flourished in tandem with the Union Stock Yard and Transit Company.[22]

Although denounced as a "mad scheme" when first proposed, Chicago's experiment with a consolidated railroad stockyard was an unparalleled success. Shippers liked the Union Stock Yard prices, and stockholders appreciated the company's average annual profits of $150,000. Visitors marveled at the efficient operation of the stockyard, and James Parton informed *Atlantic Monthly* readers that nothing could be "more simple and easy." While cattle and hogs were being unloaded, watered, and fed, buyers and sellers conferred in the Exchange with food, drink, clerical assistance, and a bank at their command. The busy telegraph office provided them with "the price of beef, pork, and mutton in two hemispheres" and sent back to "the cattle markets of mankind the condition of affairs in this, the great bovine city of the world."[23]

The scattered, separate stockyards of the Civil War years aggravated shippers, buyers, railroad managers, and city officials. The disadvantages of livestock traipsing through busy streets were obvious to all concerned, but the solution Chicago worked out was especially ingenious. It drew upon John Sherman's knowledge of stockyard management, Octave Chanute's engineering skills, and Rosell Hough's ability to coordinate the massive construction project. Their finished product was more than "the pride of the city." It was "a monument of Western traffic never before equalled and never to be excelled."[24] Inevitably, the successful Union Stock Yard would affect the South Branch packers and the township of Lake.

NOTES

1. [James Parton], "Chicago," *Atlantic Monthly,* 19 (Mar., 1867), 332–33.

2. *Griffiths Annual Review of the Live Stock Trade at Chicago, 1878* (Chicago, 1879), 18; *Harper's Weekly,* Nov. 21, 1863; *Times,* Nov. 5, 13, 1863; Dec. 12, 1865; *Trib.,* Nov. 9, 1863; *Chicago Republican,* Dec. 27, 1865; Chicago, Burlington and Quincy Railroad Company, *Annual Report, 1862,* 6, 15; *Annual Report, 1863,* 12, 32–33; *Annual Report, 1864,* 11–14; Richard C. Overton, *Burlington Route: A History of the Burlington Lines* (New York, 1965), 47, 65–66; Jack Wing, *The Great Union Stock Yards of Chicago* (Chicago, 1865), 10–11.

3. *Land-Owner,* 6 (Jan. 1874), 11; *Trib.,* June 29, 1864; *Chicago Evening Journal,* June 29, 1864; Chicago Tribune, *Annual Review of the Trade, Business and Growth of the City of Chicago, 1865* (Chicago, 1866), 32; Joseph G. Knapp, "A Review of Chicago Stock Yards History," *University [of Chicago] Journal of Business,* 2 (June, 1924), 333–35.

4. Michigan Central Railroad Company, *Annual Report, 1866,* 10; Overton, *Burlington Route,* 66–67; *Trib.,* July 31, 1864; James F. Joy to John Van Nortwick, July 25, 1864, and enclosures of letters by John W. Brooks, July 18, 1864; John W. Brooks and James F. Joy to John Van Nortwick, Aug. 11, 1864; John Van Nortwick to board of directors, Aug. 16, 1864; James F. Joy to John Van Nortwick, Sept. 22, 1864 (Van Nortwick Special File; Chicago, Burlington and Quincy Archives; Newberry Library, Chicago).

5. *Private Laws of the State of Illinois, 1865,* vol. 2 (Springfield, 1865), 678–83; "The Union Stock Yards of Chicago," Illinois State Agricultural

Society, *Transactions*, 6 (1865–66), 315; Paul M. Angle, "The Union Stockyards, December 25, 1865," *Chicago History*, 7 (Winter, 1965–66), 293–94; *Prairie Farmer*, 31 (Jan. 21, 1865), 41.

6. "Union Stock Yards," Illinois State Agricultural Society, *Transactions*, 315; Wing, *Union Stock Yards*, 12; M. S. Parkhurst, *History of the Yards, 1865–1953* (Chicago, 1953), 15–16; Don E. Fehrenbacher, *Chicago Giant: A Biography of "Long John" Wentworth* (Madison, Wis., 1957), 15, 114; *Drovers Journal*, Dec. 14, 1885; Chicago, Burlington and Quincy, *Annual Report, 1865*, 31–32.

7. Chicago, Burlington and Quincy, *Annual Report, 1865*, 5–6, 13, 31–32; *Annual Report, 1866*, 13–14; Overton, *Burlington Route*, 66, 85; Chicago, Burlington and Quincy, Minutes of board of directors' meeting, Dec. 27, 1864; George L. Dunlap (General Superintendent, Chicago and North Western Railroad Company) to John Van Nortwick, Mar. 28, 1865; James F. Joy to John Van Nortwick, Apr. 15, 1865 (Van Nortwick Special File; Chicago, Burlington and Quincy Archives); *Griffiths Annual Review, 1878*, 18; Wing, *Union Stock Yards*, 10; *Trib.*, Jan. 26, 1865; Union Stock Yard and Transit Company (USYTC), *Minute Book*, July 28, 1865 (Chicago Historical Society, Chicago).

8. "In Memoriam—Octave Chanute," *Journal of the Western Society of Engineers*, 16 (May, 1911), 439–40; "Biographical Material" (Octave Chanute Papers, Box 18, Library of Congress); Octave Chanute to W. H. Civer, May 11, 1865 (Chanute Papers, Box 19).

9. Octave Chanute to the president and board of directors, May 15, 1865 (Chanute Papers, Box 17); Jan. 16, 1866 (Chanute Papers, Box 17); Parkhurst, *History of the Yards*, 15; *Drovers Journal*, Sept. 11, 1894; Harold M. Mayer, "The Railway Pattern of Metropolitan Chicago" (Ph.D. diss., University of Chicago, 1943), 97–98.

10. "The Great Stock-Yards of Chicago," *Times*, Dec. 12, 1865; Wing, *Union Stock Yards*, 13–15; Octave Chanute to president and board of directors, Jan. 16, 1866 (Chanute Papers, Box 17).

11. *Times*, Dec. 12, 1865; *Chicago As It Is . . . A Strangers' and Tourists' Guide to the City of Chicago* (Chicago, 1866), 60–61.

12. *Trib.*, Jan. 2, 1866; Wing, *Union Stock Yards*, 17–20; *Chicago As It Is*, 61–62; Octave Chanute to president and board of directors, Jan. 16, 1866 (Chanute Papers, Box 17).

13. *Times*, Dec. 12, 1865; *Trib.*, Jan. 2, 1866; *Chicago As It Is*, 62–63; Octave Chanute to the president and board of directors, Jan. 16, 1866 (Chanute Papers, Box 17).

14. Thomas E. Tallmadge, *Architecture in Old Chicago* (Chicago, 1941), 55, 89–90; *Inland Architect and Builder*, 5 (Feb., 1885), 11; *Times*, Dec. 12, 1865; *Trib.*, Jan. 2, 1866; Wing, *Union Stock Yards*, 27–28.

15. *Chicago As It Is,* 60, 64; Wing, *Union Stock Yards,* 23–24; *Times,* Dec. 12, 1865. Lithographers Hevne and Almini featured Hough House in *Chicago Illustrated* as an example of "the very best style of modern hotel architecture." James W. Sheahan and Hevne and Almini, *Chicago Illustrated* (Chicago, 1867), n.p.

16. Chanute to the president and board of directors, Jan. 16, 1866 (Chanute Papers, Box 17); Francis F. Cook, *Bygone Days in Chicago* (Chicago, 1910), 368; Wing, *Union Stock Yards,* 28–29; *Trib.,* Jan. 2, 1866; *Times,* Dec. 12, 1865.

17. Overton, *Burlington Route,* 67; *Chicago Republican,* Dec. 23, 26, 27, 28, 1865; Jan. 2, 1866; *Times,* Dec. 27, 28, 1865; Jan. 4, 1866; *Trib.,* Jan. 2, 1866.

18. Board of Trade, *Annual Report, 1871,* 143; William E. Hayes, *Iron Road to Empire: The History . . . of the Rock Island Lines* (New York, 1953), 54–56, 86; [Chicago and North Western Railway Company], *Yesterday and Today: A History of the Chicago and North Western Railway System* (Chicago, 1910), 55–75; Howard Gray Brownson, *The History of the Illinois Central Railroad to 1870* (Urbana, Ill., 1915), 138–40; Overton, *Burlington Route,* 90–98; "In Memoriam—Octave Chanute," 440–42; *Trib.,* May 10, 11, 1869.

19. Rudolf A. Clemen, *The American Livestock and Meat Industry* (New York, 1923), 174–77, 204–10; Ernest Staples Osgood, *The Day of the Cattleman* (1929; rpt. Chicago, 1970), 21–37; Edward Everett Dale, *The Range Cattle Industry* (Norman, Okla., 1930), 54–55; Robert Dykstra, *The Cattle Towns* (New York, 1974), 11–73; "Where the Beef Comes From," *Lippincott's Magazine,* 24 (Nov., 1879), 573; Department of Agriculture, *Report of the Commissioner, 1870,* "The Texas Cattle Trade," 346–52; Joseph G. McCoy, *Historic Sketches of the Cattle Trade of the West and Southwest* (Kansas City, Mo., 1874), 6, 53; *Times,* Aug. 21, 23, 31, Dec. 8, 1868.

20. *Chicago Republican,* Aug. 31, 1867; Dec. 14, 1866; John S. Wright, *Chicago: Past, Present, Future* (Chicago, 1868), 148–49; Pittsburgh, Fort Wayne and Chicago Railroad, *Annual Report, 1865,* 13–14; *Times,* Jan. 18, 1866.

21. Edward N. Wentworth, *A Biographical Catalog of the Portrait Gallery of the Saddle and Sirloin Club* (Chicago, 1920), 167–68; *Trib.,* Oct. 17, 1882; *Drovers Journal,* Dec. 14, 1885; USYTC, *Minute Book,* Dec. 1, 1865; Jan. 17, 1866; *Griffiths Annual Review of the Live Stock Trade at Chicago, 1871* (Chicago, 1872), 9–10; *Times,* Oct. 30, Nov. 13, 1866; *Chicago Republican,* Oct. 24, 1866; *Prairie Farmer,* n.s. 34 (Dec. 1, 1866), 353.

22. Alfred T. Andreas, *History of Cook County, Illinois* (Chicago, 1884), 669, 674; *Drovers Journal,* Jan. 30, 1888; June 28, Sept. 14, 1886; *Times,*

July 1, 1869; July 27, 1870; Sept. 20, 22, 1871; F. Cyril James, *The Growth of Chicago Banks*, 2 vols. (New York, 1938), 1:368, 440; *Trib.*, Feb. 20, Mar. 1, Apr. 7, 1868.

23. USYTC, *Minute Book*, Jan. 16, 1867; Jan. 15, 1869; Jan. 19, 1870; USYTC, *Third Annual Report, Jan. 15, 1869*, 5–6; [Parton], "Chicago," 332–33.

24. *Chicago Republican*, Jan. 11, 1868; Wing, *Union Stock Yards*, 29.

CHAPTER 4

Changes in the Fifth Ward and Town of Lake

The Union Stock Yard was a catalyst for change in the packinghouses, in the South Branch ward where most of them were located, and in the township of Lake. The increasing supply of livestock encouraged packers to invent and install time- and laborsaving machinery. Even so, the number of men working in the plants exceeded two thousand by 1870, a tenfold increase in one decade. Most of them lived in the Fifth Ward, which, after the 1863 annexation, embraced Bridgeport. Meat-packing and its allied enterprises were mainstays of the Fifth Ward economy, but they also contributed to the Bridgeport "stinks." Neither a brief experiment with a compulsory city slaughterhouse nor the creation of a Board of Health could save Healy Slough and Ogden Slip from pollution, yet experts were hopeful that the Chicago River would cleanse itself once it began carrying lake water into the Illinois and Michigan Canal. South of the city boundary in the township of Lake, the arrival of new settlers at The Junction, establishment of new industries along its railroad tracks, and, most important, the Union Stock Yard stimulated growth in the late 1860s. One large packing concern moved from the South Branch to land immediately west of the stockyard, and fully one-third of the township's 3,360 residents in 1870 lived east of the yards between Halsted Street and Stewart Avenue. Significantly, they were known as "the Stockyards settlement."

Developments at the Packinghouses

Although Chicago packers had been in the spotlight during the Civil War, reporters paid them little heed once the Union Stock Yard opened. The big story was the soaring livestock trade. Virtually unnoticed, however, the value of Chicago's beef and pork climbed to $19 million by 1870 and packinghouse by-products added another $4 million. This far outstripped the $7 million value of lumber and wood products in 1870 and the $6 million in clothing, $5 million in iron and steel, $3 million in flour, and $2 million in agricultural implements. Chicago packers widened their lead over competitors in the late 1860s, and they kept generating new jobs as production increased. Packinghouses employed 2,129 people in 1870, more than the number employed during the peak war years. Yet it was not until the close of the 1870–71 packing season that the *Times* singled out the meat packers as Chicago's "most energetic" businessmen.[1]

The packers accomplished this without extensive rebuilding of their South Branch plants and without a marked increase in the number of firms. The Board of Trade listed forty-two companies at the end of the war and forty-six in 1870. The leading packers maintained their dominant position in the export trade and oversaw enforcement of the Pork Packers' Association rules. All boxes, tierces, and barrels had to carry the packer's name and be inspected by Board of Trade agents in order to secure certification. If the goods passed inspection, buyers paid the fee; if not, the packer paid and usually lost the sale. These rules eliminated some marginal packers who had held on after 1865, but they had nothing to do with Clybourn's decision to bow out when the railroad stockyards closed or Hubbard's departure after fire destroyed his north side plant. The closing of these North Branch packinghouses and the merger of some small firms were balanced by the arrival of newcomers.[2]

Mechanical innovations—the overhead rail, the pig-hoist, and improved drying machinery and cooling units—helped packers increase production. Visitors to the South Branch plants in the late 1860s were struck by the speed of the packing operation. It was "perfectly astounding," said one, that a butcher could cleave and dissect nine hogs in three minutes. Louis Simonin's explanation was that hams could "salt . . . and stack themselves in barrels." More to the point, however, was the observation of an English traveler, Newman Hall, that the packinghouses were "semi-mechanical."[3]

It is uncertain where or when the overhead assembly line originated, but many Cincinnati and Chicago plants had them by the late 1850s. Parallel wooden tracks were attached to the ceiling; a gambrel stick inserted through the tendons of the hog's hind legs was then placed on these tracks; and workers used long wooden poles and muscle power to shove the carcass along the wooden track to the butchers and then into the cooling room. The wooden tracks gave way to steel rails and trolleys during the Civil War. A visitor to the Tobey and Booth plant said the hogs were "suspended on a rolling hook upon an elevated iron rail" and could be moved with a gentle push. By the end of 1866, a *Times* reporter referred to the overhead steel rail as "ordinary" and "common in all packing houses." Another time- and laborsaving device was a mechanism to lift hog carcasses out of the scalding tubs. It looked like a "rack of iron teeth, bent in the shape of fish-hooks," and all the worker had to do was move a lever to make the machine deposit the carcass on the scraping bench.[4] (See Figs. 5 and 6.)

Until the end of the Civil War, hogs were killed the "old-fashioned" way—stunned with a hammer, their throats slit in the killing pen, and then dragged to the scalding tubs. This was time-consuming, heavy work, and the horizontal, inert carcass retained blood. Chicago packers devised a solution in 1866. Windsor Leland of the small firm of Leland and Mixer invented a "slaughtering machine," as he called it. A steam-powered wheel raised the live hog by its hind leg and attached the animal to the elevated rail. This apparatus and similar versions of it were quickly dubbed "pig-hoists" or "hog elevators." Culbertson, Blair and Company installed one in the fall of 1866 and held a public demonstration for other packers, members of the Board of Trade, retail butchers, and reporters. The sponsors pointed out that killing a suspended hog facilitated bleeding and thus improved the quality of the meat. Reporters noted the time- and laborsaving aspects: hoisting, killing, scalding, scraping, and gutting takes no more than "two or three minutes, and during this time the lifting and moving of the hog is all done by machinery."[5]

The new method of slaughtering hogs impressed visitors for two other reasons. One was the spurting of blood caused by heart and muscular action during the dangling hog's death-struggle. It lasted only a minute or two but startled those who expected a slow gurgle. The other surprise was the noise. Prior to the introduction of the pig-hoist, hogs never made much noise on the killing floor. However, catching the live hog by a hind leg, clamping the pulley to that leg, and raising him to the overhead rail caused a shrill, piercing cry of alarm. By the late 1860s the frantic squealing of startled hogs was a common feature of the pork houses, and the phrase "squeal bloody murder" had entered the vocabulary.

Finding a use for animal blood was yet another innovation. A Bohemian immigrant chemist, Joseph Hirsch, developed a technique for turning it into albumen and dye and in 1867 persuaded his relatives, Solomon Stein and Morris Hirsch, to sell their clothing store and join him in the new venture. Four years later Stein, Hirsch and Company had commodious quarters on Archer Avenue, and Chicagoans were referring to their factory as a "sanitary institution" because it kept animal blood out of the South Branch.[6]

Technological improvements in drying machinery encouraged the Wahls to build a large fertilizer factory in Ainsworth, a tiny community twelve miles south of Chicago on the Michigan Southern and the Pittsburgh, Fort Wayne and Chicago railroads. They could handle dead and diseased animals as well as offal and tankings, and they collected these materials from packers and city scavengers at a depot on Twenty-sixth and Stewart. This business expanded so rapidly that the Wahls, who preferred their glue works in Bridgeport, sold out to the Northwestern Fertilizing

Company in 1868. By then, another firm, the Union Rendering Company, was also operating in Ainsworth.[7]

Although the records are sparse, it is clear that some Chicago packers were experimenting with refrigeration in the postwar years. Tobey and Booth had a ground-level icehouse and "swinging shutters" which cooled the cellar underneath. That basement room was about 40° F in summer and cool enough to chill a hog carcass before it spoiled. Hutchinson's plant at the Union Stock Yard probably had a large ice-cooled ground-level room for summer packing because twenty thousand hogs were slaughtered there in the 1870 off-season, March through October. Undoubtedly the packers were familiar with the sawdust-insulated cold storage warehouses used to hold fruit, fish, and poultry by the early 1860s. William Chandler's "iceboxes on wheels"—railroad freight cars cooled by ice bins—prompted the *Scientific American* to suggest in 1866 that they be used to deliver fresh western beef and pork to New York City. That would have been risky in a Chandler car because without any interior ventilation the meat would have spoiled.[8]

William Davis of Detroit secured a patent in 1868 for a "refrigerating" car capable of carrying carcasses suspended from ceiling hooks. His car did have rudimentary ventilation and vertical ice cylinders in the corners, which could be refilled from the roof. That same year Davis's friend, meat-market owner George Henry Hammond, and butcher Marcus M. Towle formed a new packing company in Detroit. The following spring they sent a Davis refrigerator car loaded with fresh beef to Boston. Its safe arrival prompted Hammond to secure exclusive rights to the Davis car and build a dressed beef plant in northern Indiana astride the Michigan Central tracks. Towle managed this plant, bought his cattle at the Union Stock Yard, and sent his first shipment of chilled fresh beef to Boston in September, 1869.[9] This omen for Chicago packers was little noticed at the time because they were still under the spell of what the new Union Stock Yard could do for them.

One thing it was doing was luring packers from other midwestern cities. The most important new firm was Armour and Company, the brainchild of Milwaukee packer Philip Danforth Armour. Born in 1832, the third of five brothers, Armour grew up on a farm near Stockbridge, New York, and while still a teenager accumulated $6,000 in the California gold fields by supplying the miners with water. When fire destroyed his Milwaukee soap factory, he joined a provision firm which shipped grain east and sold supplies to settlers heading west. Knowledgeable about meat products and a successful salesman, Armour came to the attention of Milwaukee's leading packer, John Plankinton. In 1862 the junior partner in Plankinton and Armour designed a new plant on the Menominee River so that the firm could handle government pork contracts. The following year Armour got permission to sell pork short while the price was $40 per barrel; he had to write his own contracts because the New York commission firms turned him down. When it came time to deliver, the price was $18 and it was believed that Plankinton and Armour cleared nearly $1,000,000. Some of the profits went into enlarging the existing plant, building a second packinghouse, and opening their own sales office in New York.[10]

Armour invested his share of the profits in a city which he felt had a brighter future than Milwaukee. He helped his younger brothers, Herman Ossian and Joseph Francis, start a provision firm in Chicago in 1863. Four years later, after the Union Stock Yard had proved itself, the firm rented a small packinghouse on the South Branch and handled twenty-five thousand hogs the first winter. Philip, Herman, and Joseph formed Armour and Company in 1868 and purchased a larger plant on Archer at the South Branch, a few blocks west of Halsted. Over the next three years they averaged annual net profits of about $70,000. During the winter of 1870–71, Armour and Company packed sixty-five thousand hogs and became Chicago's sixth largest pork house. Philip Armour was so impressed with the future of Chicago packing that he called his eldest brother, Simeon Brooks, from Stockbridge to assist Herman and Joseph.[11]

In its way, the departure of Benjamin Peters Hutchinson from the South Branch to the Town of Lake was as significant as the arrival of Armour and Company. The western half of Section 5 had been purchased in 1865 by two land syndicates, and the Union Stock Yard and Transit Company had guaranteed them free access to all railroad tracks. The northwestern quarter of the section was owned by John F. Tracy and Martin L. Sykes, incorporators of the Union Stock Yard and Transit Company, and attorney Henry H. Porter.* In the summer of 1868 these men put the land between Forty-first and Forty-third Streets on the market and called it the "Packers' Addition."[12]

Hutchinson was the first packer to take a chance on this location. He purchased land in September and started construction of a large packinghouse, smokehouse, brick warehouse, livestock pens, and a boardinghouse for the workmen. Meantime, he bought up several small firms and incorporated the Chicago Packing and Provision Company. Hutchinson packed sixty-seven thousand hogs during his last season on the South Branch; two years later the Chicago Packing and Provision Company handled nearly two hundred thousand hogs and was the leading firm. By that time, three small plants and several slaughtering sheds catering to local butch-

* Henry H. Walker, Briggs Swift, James D. Lehmer, and Nathan Powell held title to the southwestern quarter of Section 5.

ers had appeared in the Addition. Moreover, Nelson Morris and Samuel Allerton had purchased property, though neither would enter the packing industry until the 1870s. "Without being gifted with any prophetic powers," remarked a livestock reporter in 1870, "it may be anticipated that within a few years at the utmost, the entire packing trade of this city will be carried on in the immediate vicinity of the Union Stock Yard."[13]

The Impact on Bridgeport

The vast majority of the packinghouses in the late 1860s were located on the southern bank of the South Branch and they dominated life in Bridgeport. Served by the Chicago and Alton tracks and Archer Avenue as well as the river, packinghouses and lard, glue, soap, candle, brush, and hair factories stretched from Eighteenth Street to the head of the Illinois and Michigan Canal. Moreover, slaughtering houses patronized by Chicago meat-market owners lined Ogden Slip and Healy Slough, the meandering shallow waterway which left the South Branch in Bridgeport and gave up near Thirty-first Street. The large plants were "solid-looking brick and stone buildings, usually adorned with a tall chimney and surrounded by an acre or two of barrels and boxes," said one observer. All had "side-tracks running from the railroads to their very doors." When these packinghouses shut down for the summer, "with them closes the life and activity of Bridgeport. Nothing is doing."[14]

Packinghouse employment matched the looming physical presence of the plants. The 2,129 men holding these jobs worked in Chicago's Fifth Ward. It was established soon after the 1863 annexation and was bounded by the South Branch, Clark Street on the east, Thirty-ninth Street on the south, and Western Avenue. Coterminus with Bridgeport, this ward had nearly twenty thousand residents by the end of the decade.[15] Packinghouses were the major source of employment during nine months of the year, but those workers sought summer jobs on the canal, lake vessels, and construction projects. Other Bridgeport residents worked in the Union Rolling Mill, the lumberyards and furniture factories on the north side of the South Branch, and the Burlington or Pittsburgh, Fort Wayne railroad yards. There are few comparative wage statistics for these years, but according to the *Tribune* packinghouse workers did fairly well. Those in the pork plants earned from $2.50 to $5 per day, "proportionate to their skills," while cattle butchers commanded $4 to $5 depending upon their "expertness." Bricklayers in 1865 earned about $4.25 per day, blacksmiths $4, boilermakers $3.75, machinists and carpenters $3.50, sailors $3, tanners $2.75, and quarry workers only $2.25.[16]

Workingmen's cottages sprouted in the southeastern and western sections of the ward, thanks to horsecar service on State Street to the southern city limits and on Archer to Ashland. One realtor, for example, advertised a standard 25- by 125-foot lot and frame house containing a 10- by 12-foot parlor, two small bedrooms, kitchen, and pantry for $600 "at terms which place a home within the reach of all." While Halsted was still a dirt road below Thirty-first Street, its proximity to the Union Stock Yard attracted a nucleus of settlers. The Irish outnumbered other ethnic groups in the ward, as an 1868 Board of Health survey of the area around Healy Slough indicated. There were 1,468 Irish, 604 German, 381 American, 113 English, 30 French, 14 Swedish, 2 Danish, and 2 Bohemian residents. Reporters took a dim view of the rowdy Archer Avenue saloons, and when a headless, legless, eviscerated corpse, otherwise unbruised, turned up in the South Branch, the *Times* speculated that "professional" Bridgeport butchers committed the atrocity "in some slaughtering establishment." Residents of Bridgeport had a much higher opinion of themselves. One informed the *Tribune* that packinghouses and "grease factories" on the South Branch "add largely to the life of our city." Furthermore, Fifth Warders "represent many nations . . . and tongues" and they are "the bone and sinew of the city."[17]

South Branch wage earners took a lively interest in trade unions, the first of which appeared in Chicago in the 1850s. Seamen, coopers, bakers, bricklayers, and railroad engineers formed "protective" or "benevolent" associations during the Civil War, and the Brotherhood of Locomotive Engineers tried without success to strike all railroads entering Chicago in March, 1864. That same year the city's twenty-four trade unions established a General Trades Assembly and began campaigning for shorter hours. The Illinois legislature passed an eight-hour law in 1867, but it did not apply to workers hired by the hour, week, month, or year. Many employers announced plans to shift workers from the customary ten- or twelve-hour day to hourly employment when the law went into effect on May 1. Participating in the peaceful trade union parade on May 1, 1867, were the Chicago Butchers' Association, the German Butchers' Association, and the Ham-Sewers' Union. The butchers' associations were composed primarily of meat-market owners, while the ham-sewers were packinghouse workers who cut and stitched cloth coverings for hams. On May 2 and 3 "exciteable" groups of South Branch workers, armed with fence pickets and packinghouse gambrels, threatened employers who refused to shorten hours and workers who refused to join the walkout. Arrest of the ringleaders ended this protest.[18]

Relations between packinghouse butchers and meat-market owners were harmonious in the 1860s. Most proprietors knew how to slaughter an animal and dress a carcass, and some had formerly worked in packinghouses. James Peevy, for example, butchered in John Nash's plant before he opened a market and became an officer of the Chicago Butchers' Association. Market owners mingled with packinghouse butchers when they went to the plants to purchase cattle and hog carcasses, and the two groups talked about their common skill. In 1869 the Chicago Butchers' Association sponsored a contest at Reid and Sherwin's slaughterhouse to select the first national champion butcher. Two of the five contestants were Chicagoans, Charles Leyden and Thomas Mulrooney; the others came from St. Louis, Buffalo, and Toronto. Five hundred spectators paid $1 each to watch young Leyden slaughter and dress his steer in four minutes and forty-five seconds. The "knights of the cleaver" presented the proud victor with a silver and gold belt.[19]

The reappearance of cholera at the end of the Civil War rekindled Chicagoans' concern about packinghouse debris and the purity of their drinking water. Believing that either contaminated water or "portable" zymotic spores could spread the disease, they launched a municipal cleanliness campaign that included establishment of a compulsory municipal slaughterhouse, the first of its kind in the United States. Paris had found that enforcement of sanitary ordinances was easier in Hausmann's 1863 structure, and Chicago hoped that the reform would eliminate its many slaughtering sheds in the Fifth Ward. Late in 1865 the council signed a ten-year contract with John Reid and Joseph Sherwin, granting them "exclusive rights" to local slaughtering provided they built suitable facilities with adequate catch basins and drains. The proprietors could collect the "usual offal"—heads, feet, guts, and blood—but could charge no fees.[20]

Even before it opened in May, 1866, the Ogden Slip city slaughterhouse created controversy. There were cries of "monopoly" and objections to being told where one could or could not slaughter. Market butcher Louis Rumpft and packer James Turner brought a test case, and in 1868 the Illinois Supreme Court upheld their objections. Newspaper editors warned against a return to the old days of killing in "vile sheds . . . where the reek and filth shall imperil the homes of men." Most of the local slaughtering by 1870 was being done, not in vile sheds, but at Reid and Sherwin's, James Turner's, or the Schoenemann brothers' plants—Ogden Slip or Healy Slough. Meantime, New York, Boston, and New Orleans had emulated Chicago's ill-fated reform. Louisiana butchers sought protection under the new Fourteenth Amendment, but the United States Supreme Court in 1873 upheld the right of the state legislature to impose "restraint" upon the New Orleans butchers. Its definition of the Fourteenth Amendment in the Slaughter-House Cases encouraged state legislatures and municipal authorities to press ahead with regulation of the "nuisance" trades, and Chicago area packers, slaughterers, and market butchers would feel the effects of this decision in the 1870s.[21]

A second sanitary reform was a Board of Health modeled upon the one in New York City. Leading this campaign was Dr. John Henry Rauch, a convert to the public health movement during medical service in the Union Army. Such a board was established in March, 1867, with Dr. Rauch as sanitary superintendent. High on his agenda were Healy Slough and Ogden Slip, stagnant pockets of the South Branch clogged with "the decomposing remains of animal matter." He posted copies of the sanitary laws in all packinghouses and slaughtering and rendering establishments, and tried periodic inspections of the premises. Only the large packinghouses complied with all the regulations, including those calling for drains with catch basins and vapor-condensing machinery on all rendering tanks. After 1869 Mayor Roswell B. Mason often joined Dr. Rauch on tours of the slough, the slip, and the South Branch. Reporters called them "explorers on the Dead Sea of Chicago." When the Board of Public Works offered to fill in part of the slough, Healy insisted that he had a "navigable, natural waterway" despite its "perhaps two feet of animal matter." The city finally agreed to dredge the slough at taxpayers' expense, but the 1871 Chicago fire cancelled that plan. As a *Times* reporter said in 1866, the "renowned Healy Slough . . . is a shuttle-cock for timid politicians" and the game seems likely "to be prolonged *ad infinitum*."[22]

The sanitary problems caused by Bridgeport's major industry were put on the back burner for several reasons. Completion of the lake tunnel meant safe drinking water; cholera had disappeared; and everyone expected the South Branch to cleanse itself once the Chicago River began flowing toward the canal. Chicagoans had to wait six years for that $3 million project, but the longer they waited, the more certain they were of its sanitary benefits. In July, 1871, Mayor Mason, members of the Board of Health and Board of Public Works, alderman, and thousands of citizens lined the river banks and crowded onto the bridges to watch the change. One patriot insisted that the river traded "its black, greasy body for a bright, gray stream, with a decidedly perceptible current . . . bearing along with it, most refreshing whiffs of cold lake air!" An unbiased tourist saw only "great deeps of mud and slime and unimaginable filth" slowly breaking up. Straws moving on the surface of the water, "after some moments of indecision," were the only proof that the overburdened river was "sluggishly, sullenly" flowing away from the lake and toward the canal.[23]

New Settlements in the Town of Lake

The Union Stock Yard was directly responsible for much of the growth in Town of Lake during the latter half of the 1860s. The township prior to 1865 was "traversed by one or two lines of railroads, and . . . dotted here and there by a small house or shanty" but otherwise "all was desolate."

Halsted Street was only a farmers' trace, and in population Lake paled by comparison with Hyde Park. Yet by 1870 Town of Lake boasted 3,360 residents, only three hundred short of Hyde Park's total, and "thickly settled" Halsted was its "central thoroughfare" to the Fifth Ward and the city of Chicago.[24] (See Map 6, p. 150.)

The so-called Stockyards settlement east of Halsted claimed approximately one-third of the township residents. Owners of the eighty acres bounded by Halsted and Wallace, Thirty-ninth and Forty-third, refused to sell, but they did lease the lots facing Halsted and this strip became the first commercial district. Farnsworth House, a large frame low-cost hotel and restaurant, was directly across from the Transit House and nearby was Peter Caldwell's smaller hotel and saloon. Groceries and dry goods stores served the homeowners who had built on the south side of Forty-third Street and along the three streets paralleling Halsted—Emerald, Winter, and Lowe. Most of these people were livestock dealers or upper echelon employes of the Union Stock Yard company. Further east in more modest dwellings were bookkeepers and clerks, the tradesmen, shoemakers, carpenters, and construction workers. The 1870 census enumerator, for example, found brickmason James Corcoran and family sheltering Irish-born Matthew Fleming, a nephew, who helped operate a coal yard on Halsted. Laborers, usually young and often born in Ireland, filled the boarding houses and inexpensive hotels. This settlement east of the Union Stock Yard probably numbered about one thousand people by 1870, and it constituted "an immense change" from the "unbroken, wild prairie" of 1864.[25]

Peter Caldwell, an Irish immigrant and former Chicago saloonkeeper, was instrumental in securing the first school and the first parish for the Stockyards settlement. Cook County school districts did not necessarily coincide with township boundaries, and Lake had been divided at Center Avenue. School District No. 2 (eastern Lake and a narrow strip of Hyde Park) had only the one public school at The Junction when the Union Stock Yard opened. Following Caldwell's election to the school board, a small frame school was built on Forty-third Street just east of Wallace. Then Caldwell approached the pastor of St. Bridget's in Bridgeport for a "stockyards parish." Cognizant of the growing number of Irish families in the southern part of the Fifth Ward and around the stockyard, the priest purchased land at Thirty-fifth and Emerald and dispatched Father Michael Lyons in 1868. The latter boarded at Peter Caldwell's hotel and said mass in the Brown schoolhouse, Caldwell having secured permission from School District No. 2. When Lake and Fifth Ward parishioners disagreed about the location of a church, Father Lyons settled the argument by selecting property on the north side of Thirty-ninth Street between Halsted and Emerald. Peter Caldwell was bitterly disappointed, but he helped raise funds to purchase a former stable which was moved to the site, remodeled, and dedicated as Holy Angels' Church in April, 1868. As soon as Town of Lake parishioners outnumbered those from the Fifth Ward, they renamed the parish Nativity of Our Lord after the Town of Lake stable.[26]

The feisty, burgeoning Stockyards settlement looked very attractive to newspaper publisher Harvey L. Goodall. Though still in his thirties when he moved to Town of Lake, he had already been a seaman, toured Europe as treasurer of Seth Howes's circus, tried his hand at journalism and photography in New York, and published newspapers for the Union army. After the war, he stayed in Cairo, Illinois, expecting his *Daily Times* to become an influential state newspaper. By 1869, however, Cairo was fading and Goodall turned to Chicago. Lacking the financial resources to start a citywide newspaper, he scouted outlying areas and quickly decided that Town of Lake had the greatest potential. Goodall lived at the Transit House and rented space in the attic of the Exchange building for his publishing venture. There he installed his Washington handpress. The first issue of the weekly *Sun* was printed on November 29, 1869, and sold at the Exchange and Transit House and in stores on Halsted and State Street. Subscribers were assured of prompt delivery by carriers on horseback.[27]

The northeastern sector of Town of Lake attracted other industries because of its "three grand lines"—the Michigan Southern, the Rock Island, and the Pittsburgh, Fort Wayne and Chicago railroads. Running through the Fifth Ward and close by Stewart Avenue in the Town of Lake, these arteries of transport were "destined" to produce "manufactories and the dwellings of laborers," predicted a reporter in 1869. He was correct. The American Bridge Company built at Thirty-ninth and Stewart, and the Lake Shore and Michigan Southern opened a division shop between Forty-first and Forty-third streets. The Rock Island railroad decided in 1868 to move its carshops from Chicago to a Town of Lake site bounded by its Clark Street tracks and Wentworth, from Forty-seventh to Fifty-first. By the time the factories for building and repairing locomotives, freight, and passenger cars for the entire Rock Island system had been completed, there was a sizeable residential district west of Wentworth. The Bass foundry, which sold to both the Rock Island and Michigan Southern, expanded this industrial complex. While some workers in these industries settled east of State Street in Hyde Park, the majority chose the Town of Lake. The skilled mechanics, or "mechanical engineers" as they called themselves, held aloof from other workers in the railroad shops and ironwork factories, and because of the distance they had very little contact with the Stockyards settlement. In the residential district west of the Rock Island carshops, the census enumerator found that the blacksmiths, boilermakers, machinists, draftsmen, and woodworkers were usually American-born or immigrants from Canada, Scotland, England, Northern Ireland, Sweden, and Germany. The unskilled were primarily Irish Catholic immigrants living in boardinghouses on Forty-seventh Street, not in workingmen's cottages.[28]

Since the "three grand lines" converged near Sixty-third Street and also carried commuters, they stimulated growth at The Junction. During the 1860s that settlement spread both east and west of State Street, newcomers ignoring the boundary because the public school district reached over to South Park Avenue in Hyde Park. Henry B. Lewis, a prosperous dealer in wool, grain, and flour, moved to The Junction in 1867, and his wife persuaded neighbors to adopt the tonier name "Englewood." Lawyer Arthur B. Condit joined Ira J. Nichols in the wooded tract east of Sixty-third and Wentworth, and Dr. Alfred H. Champlin, a recent University of Michigan medical school graduate, arrived in 1869. The one grocery and dry goods store, located on State Street, was run by Patrick S. Fagan, formerly a Chicago grocer. A few small hotels on Halsted served farmers taking hay and corn to the Union Stock Yard or fresh produce to the Stockyards settlement. Aside from this traffic and the visibility of the "gigantic" Transit House on the horizon, residents of Englewood had few connections with Town of Lake's northern settlement.[29]

Three events in 1869 helped Englewood define its image. The post office officially recognized the name change from The Junction to Englewood. The Presbyterians collected enough money to begin construction of the community's first church, a handsome structure at Sixty-third and Yale streets. And Englewood won the Cook County Normal School. (See Fig. 4.) Its suburban setting and excellent transportation facilities were assets in the contest, but anxious residents left nothing to chance. They donated twenty acres of land just south of the railroad junction and raised $25,000, nominally a gift from the people in School District No. 2. The Cook County Board of Supervisors accepted the free land and cash gift and agreed to build the normal school at Sixty-eighth and Stewart. An 1869 suburban guide book correctly pointed out that Englewood's land values were shooting up in part because of the Cook County Normal School.[30]

Englewood also benefited from the decision in 1869 to establish a chain of parks and boulevards around Chicago. The city's few scruffy parks were an embarrassment compared to the country's model—Central Park in New York. So Chicago started out with a fine north side park named after the martyred President Lincoln. When realtor Paul Cornell then suggested a south side park outside city limits in Hyde Park, residents of the Fifth Ward objected. A satirical letter to the *Times* expressed their point of view: "Now, Mr. Editor, you have some influence with those voters out in Bridgeport who will be taxed to pay for this great park east of Michigan Avenue; and I want you to tell them it will promote their health to have this park; and please, sir, just tell them they won't be *taxed much,* and then they can take a nice walk on some pleasant Sunday afternoon or some evening, about four or five miles over to the park, have a little pic-nic, and then walk home again." Voters defeated the proposal in 1867, but newspaper editors and civic leaders, including the influential Dr. John Rauch, kept the idea alive.[31]

They soon developed a plan for a series of outlying parks, easily accessible from the city and linked to each other by broad boulevards. The South Park would lie within Hyde Park, but its western section would extend to Kankakee Avenue (renamed South Park). Fifty-fifth Street would become a boulevard from South Park through Town of Lake to Western Avenue, which would lead to Central Park (later Garfield Park), and north side boulevards would tie into Lincoln Park. The legislature passed this new measure early in 1869 and it went to the voters in March. The *Workingman's Advocate* assured its readers that horsecars and the Illinois Central could get them to the proposed South Park. It was "advantageously located for every employe in the immense establishment of the Rock Island Railroad Company." Moreover, approval of the measure would mean road construction jobs and opportunities for skilled artisans to build the "miles of dwellings" that would certainly line the boulevards. These arguments persuaded voters in Town of Lake but not in the Fifth Ward. Nonetheless, the park plan won approval—and property values went up around the edge of the proposed parks and along the boulevards. Fifty-fifth Street—renamed Pavilion Parkway and then Garfield Boulevard—became the northern limits of Englewood and something of a buffer zone between the commuter suburb to the south and the working-class settlements to the north.[32]

In 1870 the census taker listed people in the Town of Lake according to their post office address, either Union Stock Yard or Englewood. Without street names or house numbers, it is impossible to say how the 3,360 residents were distributed within the township. It is likely, however, that about 1,000 lived in the Stockyards settlement, another 800 or so between Stewart Avenue and State Street north of Fifty-first, and approximately 300 in Englewood. The others were farm families and agricultural laborers scattered over two-thirds of the land in Town of Lake. The wealthiest resident was gentleman-farmer James B. Colvin, whose property was valued at $50,000. The enumerator reported that 1,883 people had been born in the United States and 1,477 outside the country, but unfortunately he did not designate place of birth. Irish and German names were more prevalent than any other foreign group, the former usually listed at the Union Stock Yard post office, while the latter appear to have been farmers.[33]

These people governed themselves through an elected town board consisting of the supervisor, assessor, collector, and two trustees. An 1869 amendment to their charter allowed them to also elect a clerk, justice of the peace, and constable. Little is known about the early elections because reporters paid scant attention to Town of Lake politics and the Chicago fire destroyed county election returns in the courthouse. In the fall of 1868 there was a spirited contest for supervisor between Peter Caldwell of the Stockyards settlement and Englewood farmer John Gerber. The latter won but agreed to build a town hall at Halsted and Forty-second on land donated by the Union Stock Yard and Transit Company. The stockyard post office soon moved from the basement of the Transit House to its own small building beside the town hall, and four policemen were hired, apparently on Caldwell's recommendation since all were Irish and one of them, Thomas Gahan, had worked in Nash's packinghouse.[34]

Beginning in 1870, annual township elections were held in April. Supervisor Gerber bowed out, but assessor Albert Colvin (son of farmer James B. Colvin) and collector Daniel Burckey of Englewood were returned to their posts. As supervisor, township voters chose a man from the Rock Island carshop settlement. Zenas Colman had farmed and been a Baptist minister in Michigan and Illinois before settling in Town of Lake in 1867. There he sold lots to Rock Island employes and won election as a town trustee the following year. Colman was also a board member of School District No. 2 and Englewood appreciated his help in securing the Cook County Normal School. The combination of native birth, Protestant commitment, farming experience, business acumen, and interest in public education made him an attractive candidate. He pleased a sizeable majority of voters in 1870 and every year thereafter until he retired in 1875.[35]

In the short space of five years, the new Union Stock Yard generated important changes in the Fifth Ward and the Town of Lake. The South Branch packinghouses increased production to keep pace with growing livestock receipts at the yards. They did this with mechanical innovations and a larger work force. The packers, renderers, and slaughterers were major employers in the Fifth Ward, but at the same time they were major contributors to the Bridgeport "stinks." Chicago's new Board of Health tried to enforce existing regulations and residents expected deepening of the canal and reversing the flow of the Chicago River to cure the South Branch ailments. Meantime, the haphazard construction camp at the doorstep of the Union Stock Yard burgeoned into a bustling settlement of about one thousand residents. They constituted one-third of the township's 1870 population; another one-third lived along the railroad tracks in the northeastern sector and in Englewood; the remainder were farmers. "Let anyone ride to the Stock-yards," challenged a *Times* editor in 1869, and from the top of the Transit House gaze up Halsted. "This section, the greater portion of which is thickly settled, has all been built up within the last five years." And that growth was due in large part to the Union Stock Yard.[36]

NOTES

1. *Chicago Republican*, Dec. 11, 1866; Board of Trade, *Annual Report, 1871*, 143, 146–47; *Ninth Census, 1870*, vol. 3, "Industry and Wealth," 649; *Times*, Mar. 24, 1871.

2. *Trib.*, July 7, 8, 1870; *Times*, May 31, 1870; Board of Trade, *Act of Incorporation, Rules, Regulations and By-Laws . . . Also, Rules for the Inspection of Provisions. Adopted Sept. 19, 1871*, 37–39; Board of Trade, *Act of Incorporation, 1873*, 22–26; Board of Trade, *Annual Report, 1868*, 58; *1871*, 146; W. J. Jefferson, *Chicago Business Directory, for 1868–69* (Chicago, 1868), 143–44.

3. *Times*, Mar. 19, 1866; *Trib.*, Dec. 3, 9, 1864; Louis L. Simonin, *The Rocky Mountain West in 1867*, trans. Wilson O. Clough (Lincoln, Neb., 1966), 9, 10; Newman Hall, *From Liverpool to St. Louis* (London, 1870), 152.

4. *Chicago Republican*, Dec. 14, 1865; *Times*, Mar. 19, Dec. 11, 1866; Arthur Cushman, "The Packing Plant and Its Equipment," in *The Packing Industry* (Chicago, 1923), 110–11, 114; National Provisioner, *The "Significant Sixty": A Historical Report on the Progress and Development of the Meat Packing Industry, 1891–1951* (Chicago, 1952), 248.

5. *Times*, Dec. 11, 1866; *"Significant Sixty,"* 235; *Chicago Republican*, Dec. 11, 1866. In *Mechanization Takes Command* (New York, 1948), Siegfried Giedion refers to the elevated rail and the pig-hoist as the "apparatus for mass slaughtering." He dates the shift to mass production in meat-packing in the 1870s and cites as evidence the granting of some thirty patents for hog elevators between 1872 and 1874 and a widely publicized engraving of a Cincinnati pork house in 1873 which showed an elevated rail (see pp. 217, 229–33). Chicago plants had the apparatus for mass slaughtering by the mid-1860s.

6. John S. Wright, *Chicago: Past, Present, Future* (Chicago, 1868), 203–4; D. B. Cooke and Co., *Chicago City Directory for the Year 1860–61*, 171, 340; Edwards and Co., *Directory to City of Chicago for 1868–69*, 856; Lakeside, *Chicago City Directory, 1872–73*, 887; *Trib.*, May 3, 1920; Feb. 14, 1930; S. S. Schoff, *The Glory of Chicago, Her Manufactories. The Industrial Interests of Chicago . . .* (Chicago, 1873), 144–45.

7. *Griffiths Annual Review of the Live Stock Trade at Chicago, 1869* (Chicago, 1870), 84; Department of Health, *Report of the Board of Health for 1867, 1868, and 1869; and a Sanitary History of Chicago from 1833 to 1870*, 79–85, 97–98; *Trib.*, Jan. 11, 20, Feb. 2, 1873; *Times*, Feb. 4, 1869.

8. Board of Trade, *Annual Report, 1871*, 146; *Chicago Republican*, Dec. 14, 1865; Oscar Edward Anderson, Jr., *Refrigeration in America: A History of a New Technology and Its Impact* (Princeton, N.J., 1953), 45–48;

Charles Henry Taylor, ed., *History of the Board of Trade of the City of Chicago*, 3 vols. (Chicago, 1917), 1:369–70; "Transportation of Fresh Meats to Market," *Scientific American*, 15 (Nov. 10, 1866), 323; D. C. Brooks, "Chicago and Its Railways," *Lakeside Monthly*, 8 (Oct., 1872), 276–77.

9. Anderson, *Refrigeration in America*, 48–52; Rudolf A. Clemen, *George H. Hammond: Pioneer in Refrigeration Transportation, 1838–1886* (New York, 1946), 14–16; Rudolf A. Clemen, *The American Livestock and Meat Industry* (New York, 1923), 218–20, 31–32; "Transportation of Fresh Meats and Fruits, etc., through Long Distances—The Davis Refrigeration Car," *Scientific American*, 23 (Nov. 12, 1870), 312; *Trib.*, Apr. 9, 1882; Dec. 31, 1886; Jan. 16, 1892.

10. Harper Leech and John Charles Carroll, *Armour and His Times* (New York, 1938), 13–30; Edward N. Wentworth, *A Biographical Catalog of the Portrait Gallery of the Saddle and Sirloin Club* (Chicago, 1920), 178–81; *Trib.*, Jan. 3, 1886; Bayrd Still, *Milwaukee, the History of a City* (Madison, Wis., 1948), 186–87; Margaret Walsh, *The Manufacturing Frontier: Pioneer Industry in Antebellum Wisconsin, 1830–1860* (Madison, Wis., 1972), 191–95.

11. Leech and Carroll, *Armour*, 31–36, 102; John S. Wright, *Chicago*, 148; *Trib.*, Nov. 16, 1863; Cora Lillian Davenport, "The Rise of the Armours, an American Industrial Family" (M.A. thesis, University of Chicago, 1930), 37–40; Federal Trade Commission, *Report on the Meat-Packing Industry, 1919*, Part Five (Washington, 1919), 21–22; Board of Trade, *Annual Report, 1871*, 146.

12. Greeley, Carlson and Company, *Atlas of the Town of Lake* (Chicago, 1883), 5.

13. *Trib.*, Aug. 29, 1881; May 1, 1891; *Atlas of the Town of Lake*, 5; *Drovers Journal*, Apr. 16, 1883; Jan. 30, 1888; Board of Trade, *Annual Report, 1871*, 146; *Griffiths Annual Review of the Live Stock Trade at Chicago, 1870* (Chicago, 1871), 5.

14. *Times*, Mar. 19, 1866.

15. *Ninth Census, 1870*, vol. 1, "Population," 599. From 1869 to 1876 this ward was called the Sixth Ward. Since the boundaries remained the same and it recovered its original name in 1876, it will be called Fifth Ward even during the 1869–76 period.

16. Schoff, *Glory of Chicago*, 11, 22; Glen E. Holt and Dominic A. Pacyga, *Chicago: A Historical Guide to the Neighborhoods*, vol. 1, *The Loop and South Sides* (Chicago, 1979), 113–14; Chicago Tribune, *Annual Review of Trade, Business and Growth, 1865* (Chicago, 1866), 10–11. Sailors, stonecutters, and bricklayers were also seasonal workers.

17. *Times*, May 4, 1869; *Workingman's Advocate*, Nov. 9, 1867; *Statistical and Historical Review of Chicago: Rise and Value of Real Estate*

(Chicago, 1869), 65–77, 84; John S. Wright, *Chicago,* 264; Department of Health, *Report . . . and Sanitary History,* 171; *Times,* Mar. 28, 29, 1871; *Trib.,* Jan. 3, 1864.

18. Chicago Tribune, *Annual Review, 1865,* 12; Bessie Louise Pierce, *A History of Chicago,* vol. 2, *From Town to City, 1848–1871* (New York, 1940), 157–79; *Trib.,* Mar. 16–18, May 5, 1864; Jan. 1, Apr. 28, May 2–8, 11, 1867; *Times,* May 2, 3, 1867.

19. *Times,* May 16, 1869.

20. Charles E. Rosenberg, *The Cholera Years: The United States in 1832, 1849, and 1866* (Chicago, 1962), 175–210; George E. Shipman, *Cholera: Its Prevention and Cure* (Chicago, 1866); *Trib.,* Nov. 14, 1865; *Times,* Nov. 11, Dec. 21, 1865; *Chicago Republican,* May 12, 16, 1866; Giedion, *Mechanization Takes Command,* 209–10; Joseph E. Gary, comp., *Laws and Ordinances Governing the City of Chicago, Jan. 1, 1866* (Chicago, 1866), 519–22.

21. *Chicago Republican,* Feb. 25, 1868; *Times,* July 23, 1867; Feb. 21, 25, 1868; July 2, 1870; "Abattoir for New York," *Scientific American,* 15 (Aug. 18, 1866), 120; Charles V. Chapin, *Municipal Sanitation in the United States* (Providence, R.I., 1901), 205; Bernard Schwartz, *The Law in America* (New York, 1974), 124, 133.

22. Department of Health, *Report . . . and Sanitary History,* 118–23, 145–47, 170–71, 229; F. Garvin Davenport, "John Henry Rauch and Public Health in Illinois, 1877–1891," *JISHS,* 50 (Autumn, 1957), 278–79; *Trib.,* Feb. 28, 1873; *Times,* Aug. 7, 1869; Department of Health, *Report . . . and Sanitary History,* 84; *Times,* Dec. 14, 1865; Jan. 10, 1866; Aug. 7, 1869; Sept. 12, 1871.

23. *Trib.,* July 17, 26, 1871; Everett Chamberlin, *Chicago and Its Suburbs* (Chicago, 1874), 78; Grace Greenwood [Mrs. S. J. C. Lippincott], *New Life in New Lands: Notes of Travels* (New York, 1873), 18–19.

24. *Griffiths Annual Review, 1870,* 4–5; *Ninth Census, 1870,* vol. 1, "Population," 110.

25. *Times,* Dec. 12, 1865; Mar. 19, 1866; *Drovers Journal,* Mar. 19, 1885; Nov. 2, 1889; Apr. 26, 1890; Alfred T. Andreas, *History of Cook County, Illinois* (Chicago, 1884), 674, 676, 677, 679; *Chicago Republican,* Nov. 21, 1866; *Ninth Census, 1870,* Manuscript Schedule for Town of Lake, 28–31, 47–59; *Griffiths Annual Review, 1870,* 4.

26. *Sun,* Aug. 31, 1889; Cook County Superintendent of Schools, *First Annual Report . . . for the Year Ending Oct. 1, 1872* (Aurora, Ill., 1872), 2–4; "Exhibit of School District No. 2, Towns of Lake and Hyde Park" (pamphlet, n.d., Chicago Historical Society); Gilbert J. Garraghan, *The Catholic Church in Chicago, 1673–1871* (Chicago, 1921), 189–90, 200; Joseph James Thompson, ed., *The Archdiocese of Chicago, Antecedents and Development* (Des Plaines, Ill., 1920), 397, 399; Reverend Joseph M.

Cartan to Archbishop Quigley, June 6, 1905 (Nativity Parish Correspondence File, St. Mary of the Lake Seminary, Mundelein, Ill.); *Times,* Aug. 12, 1868.

27. The earliest extant copy of Goodall's paper, Oct. 10, 1871, is called the *Chicago Sun.* Later titles varied but always retained *Sun* and "published at the Union Stock-Yards." *Drovers Journal,* Sept. 28, 1889; Andreas, *Cook County,* 655.

28. *Times,* Dec. 12, 1869; Andreas, *Cook County,* 661; *Sun,* Jan. 27, 1894; Monte Calvert, *The Mechanical Engineer in America, 1830–1910: Professional Cultures in Conflict* (Baltimore, 1967), 13–15; *Ninth Census, 1870,* Manuscript Schedule for Town of Lake, 20–24.

29. Gerald E. Sullivan, ed., *The Story of Englewood, 1835–1923* (Chicago, 1924), 220–21 and chap. 2; Andreas, *Cook County,* 688, 696, 697, 700.

30. Andreas, *Cook County,* 689, 705; Sullivan, *Englewood,* chap. 8; Cook County Superintendent of Schools, *Annual Report, 1881,* 46; [James B. Runnion], *Out of Town. Being a Descriptive . . . Account of the Suburban Towns and Residences of Chicago* (Chicago, 1869), 41–42.

31. Lois Wille, *Forever Open, Clear and Free: The Historic Struggle for Chicago's Lakefront* (Chicago, 1972), 45–47; "John Smith, Jr." to editor, *Times,* Mar. 22, 1867; Apr. 18, 1867.

32. *Chicago Republican,* Feb. 28, 1868; John Henry Rauch, *Public Parks: Their Effects upon the Moral, Physical and Sanitary Condition of the Inhabitants of Large Cities, with Special Reference to the City of Chicago* (Chicago, 1869); *Workingman's Advocate,* Mar. 27, 1869; *Times,* Mar. 16, 24, Apr. 9, May 26, 1869.

33. *Ninth Census, 1870,* vol. 1, "Population," 110, 598; Manuscript Schedule for Town of Lake, 10.

34. *Sun,* Apr. 18, 1889; Andreas, *Cook County,* 654, 677.

35. Andreas, *Cook County,* 654, 663.

36. *Times,* May 4, 1869.

PART TWO—THE 1870S

CHAPTER 5

The Expanding Livestock Trade

Railroads were Chicago's lifeline to recovery after the 1871 fire, and they were the key to Union Stock Yard prosperity throughout the decade. The network more than doubled in size, reaching twenty-three thousand miles by 1880. Some fifteen thousand miles belonged to those lines which hauled nearly nine million cattle, sheep, and hogs to the Chicago Stockyards in 1880. In order to accommodate this threefold increase during the decade, Superintendent John B. Sherman upgraded existing facilities and added new ones. No matter how often the Exchange was enlarged, livestock dealers filled and then crowded the office space. The vast majority of shippers, dealers, and buyers liked the Chicago facility, but the Patrons of Husbandry considered it a monopoly and reformers kept a sharp eye for animal cruelty. An Illinois state investigating committee exonerated the Union Stock Yard and Transit Company of monopoly, and its report said the enterprise was something of which "the people of this state have just right to be proud." Chicagoans, established livestock dealers, newcomers to the trade, and all those tourists who passed through the Stone Gate at the Stockyards agreed.

Railroads and Livestock Receipts

In the fall of 1871 the railroads had a unique opportunity to prove that, just as they had built Chicago in the 1850s and '60s, they could rebuild the stricken city after the Great Fire. The *Times* editor had a premonition of disaster in 1869. Noting all the frame houses visible from the Transit House cupola, he warned that a fire and a wind from the southwest acting like "a huge and uncontrollable bellows" could cause "a serious calamity to the whole city." During two unforgettable days in October, flames did destroy three square miles, leave one-third of the population homeless, and ruin an estimated $200 million worth of property. Because city newspaper and telegraph offices were knocked out, the first description of the fire appeared in the October 10 Extra of the Stockyards *Sun*, and the earliest telegraph messages went out over Union Stock Yard wires.[1]

Chicago optimists found solace in the fact that most of the railroads, grain storage facilities, and lumberyards suffered little damage. The same was true of the rolling mills and foundries on the North and South Branches of the river and many west side factories. And, of course, the flames did not touch the South Branch packinghouses or the Union Stock Yard. In fact, just a few months after the conflagration, Mayor Roswell B. Mason and the aldermen escorted Grand Duke Alexis of Russia to the Stockyards to inspect the Exchange, animal pens, and Hutchinson's new packing plant before enjoying a champagne dinner at the Transit House. Chicagoans boasted of $40 million worth of new buildings on the first anniversary of the fire, and they marked the second anniversary with an Inter-State Industrial Exposition in a handsome glass and iron building located on a new lakefront park created out of fire debris.[2]

During the period of reconstruction the city tilted perceptibly to the southwest. Superb rail facilities attracted industrialists, they in turn created jobs, and workers took their chances on building wooden cottages despite new ordinances requiring fireproof materials. The fire prompted Samuel J. Walker to develop his fifteen-hundred-acre site on the southwest side into Chicago's "most desirable *Manufacturing* and *Dock Property*." One of his customers was Cyrus H. McCormick, who was looking for a place to rebuild the Reaper Works. McCormick's large new plant at Blue Island and Western avenues opened early in 1873. By the end of that year the so-called South Branch district had six factories supplying railroad equipment, four iron and steel companies, a furniture and a wagon factory, and thirty brickyards. A reporter exploring Ashland Avenue between Archer and Thirty-first Street was surprised to find men working the night shift in the iron and steel mills. The tall smokestacks of these factories sent "the light of their banners of flame far over the prairie." Bridgeport might always conjure up an "unpleasant odor," but at least it now had some "redeeming features."[3]

Undamaged by either the 1871 fire or the 1873 panic, the Stockyards and packinghouses steadily forged ahead. By 1880, livestock receipts stood at 8,800,000, nearly three times the number of animals arriving in 1870. Chicago area packers and slaughterers purchased more than six million of those animals in 1880. This was six times more than they had needed in 1870, and it meant that transshipments declined from 55 percent of the receipts to only 28 percent during the course of the decade. Since nearly all the cattle, sheep, and hogs traveled by rail and packinghouse products left the city in freight cars, no one questioned the critical role of the railroads in the prosperity of the two industries. Nor were there any doubts that the expansion of the rail network—from eleven thousand to twenty-three thousand miles of track during the 1870s—fed the continuous growth of both the livestock trade and meat-packing.[4] (See Map 7, p. 178).

The Union Stock Yard tapped the network in two ways—the participation of five new railroads and the expansion of those lines which had founded the enterprise in 1865. In the panic year the Chicago, Milwaukee, and St. Paul joined, and the following year the Baltimore and Ohio came in over the Illinois Central tracks. Between 1878 and 1880 three other railroads built through Town of Lake to reach the yards. The Canadian Grand Trunk ran east-west along Forty-ninth Street, while the Wabash, St. Louis and Pacific paralleled the Pittsburgh, Fort Wayne tracks. The Chicago and Western Indiana Railway was a twenty-eight-mile connecting line between downtown Chicago and the Illinois-Indiana state line, and it provided entry and egress for a number of smaller railroads. Throughout the 1870s, the Burlington carried the largest amount of livestock to the Chicago yards. The presidency of that line passed from James F. Joy to his friend James M. Walker in 1871 and the latter pressed construction of feeder lines in Missouri and Iowa and main lines through Kansas and Nebraska. By the end of the decade the Burlington had access via the Atchison, Topeka and Sante Fe to the southwest and it was ready to build its own line to Denver. Surveying the city's rail network in 1879 and thinking of the much-heralded "range cattle industry," the Board of Trade confidently announced that the supply of cattle was "constantly widening . . . as the railway lines are extended westward."[5]

Other midwestern packing centers hoping to benefit from that trade established "modern" facilities modeled on the Chicago yards. Those in Cincinnati, Louisville, Indianapolis, and Milwaukee were not serious threats, but Chicago worried about St. Louis and Kansas City. James M. Walker chaired the board of the Kansas City Stock Yards, and Samuel W. Allerton played a leading role in the establishment of the St. Louis National Stockyards on the east side of the Mississippi in East St. Louis. Because of its wider rail network and superior market for cattle and hogs, however, the Union Stock Yard stayed far ahead of its competitors. St. Louis understood why. Both cities had roughly equal population and railroad mileage in 1870, but Chicago, despite the fire, had a wide lead by 1880. "What wonders have ten years worked . . . in the construction of railroads," said a resigned St. Louis editor.[6]

The lines running east out of Chicago tied into the four trunk lines—New York Central, Erie, Pennsylvania, and Baltimore and Ohio. Carrying livestock was more profitable for these railroads than hauling barreled or boxed meats, and after the 1873 panic they lowered livestock rates to compete for business in Chicago, St. Louis, and Kansas City. During 1874 a group of Chicago livestock dealers suggested to the New York Central, Erie, and Pennsylvania that centering the trade in Chicago and "pooling" it from there to the East Coast would be more profitable. The three roads liked the idea of stabilizing their livestock business and excluding the new competitor, the Baltimore and Ohio. The following year an agreement was reached whereby the railroads charged a standard rate of $115 per car, rebated $15 to the Chicago shipper, and trusted the "Eveners" to balance the traffic. It was later charged that Allerton and Nelson Morris were among the instigators of this scheme and that its purpose was to stifle the growth of the St. Louis and Kansas City stockyards. Whatever its origin and purpose, small shippers in Chicago and livestock dealers in St. Louis and Kansas City were soon complaining about the "Cattle Pool." The House Agriculture Committee conducted hearings in the spring of 1878, one result of which was the separate publication of James F. Rusling's testimony, *The Railroads! The Stock-Yards! The Eveners! Expose of the Great Railroad Ring that Robs the Laborer of the West of $5,000,000 a Year.* This publicity embarrassed the railroads, if not the "Eveners." They attempted to extend the agreement to St. Louis and then backed away from any standard rates. The practice of pooling livestock shipments from Chicago did not die out until the early 1880s, and then it was simply abandoned because the railroads, livestock shippers, and dressed-meat men were embroiled in a far more serious controversy.[7]

Improvements in the Yards

Perhaps because everything at the Union Stock Yard came in multiples—animals, pens, and tourists—people began using the plural, "Stock Yards" or "Stockyards." They dropped "Union" completely. Guidebooks, which had featured the attraction since 1865, conformed to local usage by the mid-1870s, and most foreign visitors complied as well. Few of the latter were prepared for the vast scale of operations, the relentless motion of men and animals, or the noise. The proper Englishman W. G. Marshall was unnerved by the mingled shouts and bellows, but James MacDonald thought the "panoramic view" from the top floor of the Exchange compensated for the "medley sound." Such was the fame of the Stockyards that no traveler wanted to miss that Chicago landmark. On its tenth anniversary, the *Tribune* claimed that "strangers visiting the city would as soon think of quitting it without having seen them as the traveler would of visiting Egypt, and not the pyramids; Rome, and not the Coliseum; Pisa, and not the Leaning-Tower."[8]

The person who brought order out of what seemed to be chaotic motion at the Stockyards was John B. Sherman. Universally respected by those who transacted business there, the superintendent was, they said, a "straightforward and honorable" man. "His word always goes. His friends never have any difficulty in placing him." Sherman arrived on horseback at the yards promptly at 6:00 A.M. and usually worked until dark. Although neat and fastidious about his personal appearance, he positioned his cluttered desk in the center of the large Union Stock Yard and Transit Company office in the Exchange so that he was accessible to all callers. He liked interruptions, the bustle of clerks around him, the shouts from the Exchange trading room, and the sound of drovers, animals, and trains outside.[9]

Livestock growers shared Sherman's interest in breeding experiments, and some had visited his "laboratory," a farm near Washington Heights on the Rock Island line close by Blue Island. Sherman occasionally displayed his own fine cattle and hogs in the barn behind the Transit House and encouraged other breeders to do the same. He exchanged information with local livestock growers like Samuel Allerton, Nelson Morris, and John D. Gillett, and corresponded with western producers and eastern buyers of livestock. Convinced that interest in breeding was widespread enough to support a new journal, Sherman discussed the possibility with Harvey L. Goodall, publisher of the Stockyards *Sun*. In January, 1873, Goodall launched a second weekly, the *Drovers Journal*. It carried market reports from the Union Stock Yards, personal notes on men doing business at the yards, and information about breeding and stock raising. This publication was an instant success, and in 1877 Goodall started the *Daily Drovers Journal*, the first daily livestock newspaper in the country.[10]

Livestock dealers informed growers that the packers would pay higher prices for fat cattle and hogs. With Sherman's help, they persuaded the Union Stock Yard and Transit Company to sponsor a swine exhibition at Dexter Park in September, 1871. As interest in breeding grew, a larger show seemed feasible, and in 1878 the Stockyards company agreed to be the main financial backer if the Illinois State Board of Agriculture sponsored and held it in Chicago's lakefront Exposition Building. Unlike other livestock shows, this one would specialize in thoroughbred, well-fattened cattle, sheep, and hogs known in the trade as "blooded fat-stock." To the delight of its sponsors and those eager to establish Chicago's convention trade, this first Fat Stock Show drew livestock breeders and dealers from throughout the United States as well as Canada and England. Top award for the best animal in all categories went to a shorthorn bullock entered by John D. Gillett and nicknamed "Sherman." A reporter described this animal as a "very smooth thoroughbred . . . with good broad back and excellent loin . . . flesh solid, mellow, well-matured and evenly distributed . . . a beef that would cut to the best profit to the butcher." John B. Sherman purchased the prizewinner for $1,000 and used it for "Christmas beef" at the Transit House.[11]

The hotel, jointly managed by Sherman and William F. Tucker during the 1870s, enhanced its reputation for fine food and personal service. Affluent livestock growers always stayed at the Transit House, and they mingled with dealers, visitors, Chicagoans, and patrons of Dexter Park racetrack in the famous dining room of the hotel. The Union Stock Yard National Bank, with Tucker at the helm until 1878, did very well throughout the decade. It weathered the financial panic of 1873 when five of Chicago's nineteen national banks and the livestock banks in Cincinnati and St. Louis suspended operations. At no time did the Chicago bank have to deny funds to its regular customers, and this brought about "a perfect stampede" of cattle and hogs to the Union Stock Yards. Cultivating goodwill for the bank was vice-president John R. Hoxie, livestock breeder and dealer, Texas ranch owner, and friend of almost everyone who did business at the yards.[12]

Although the Union Stock Yard and Transit Company prospered throughout the decade, it suffered an embarrassment in 1872 when directors discovered that President Chandler, with the help of Secretary Winston, borrowed $75,000 of company money. A special board meeting replaced Chandler with James M. Walker and ruled that henceforth all checks must be signed by both the president and the superintendent. Since Walker was also president of the Burlington railroad until 1876 and head of the Kansas City Stock Yards, he relied heavily upon the advice and judgment of his friend John B. Sherman. Company directors expressed their appreciation of Sherman's services by raising his salary, naming him superintendent on a permanent basis, and electing his ally, George T. Williams, to the post of secretary. Railroad presidents and directors dominated the board throughout the decade, but the large blocks of stock owned by the railroads were gradually dispersed. Chicagoans, midwestern livestock growers, and eastern investors picked up shares. The company doubled its capital stock in 1873 and increased it to $4,400,000 just three years later. In spite of the Chandler loss, stockholders received 10 percent dividends during the depression decade and 15 percent in 1879.[13]

On Sherman's recommendation, the company spent approximately $1,000,000 in the 1870s to upgrade and enlarge its facilities. The Chicago fire inspired macadam paving of the main roads, cindering the alleys, and rebuilding hay barns and corn cribs with brick and iron. Additional pens, chutes, and scale houses were added to accommodate increased traffic. A costly but important improvement was ordered by Walker, whose Burlington railroad was replacing its original iron rails with steel ones. The latter proved so superior that he had thirty miles of Union Stock Yard connecting track replaced with steel rails. And the rickety frame gate to the yards, a Halsted Street eyesore, was demolished. One block west on Broadway the company erected a much larger entrance gate. It had a wooden central arch for drovers and livestock, two small pedestrian arches on either side, and a south-side office for company watchmen. Chanute's original plan had called for a canal paralleling Thirty-ninth Street from Halsted to the

South Fork and that was excavated in the early 1870s. Presumably the "Stock Yards Canal" would provide dockage for lake vessels and warehouses for heavy cargo. This never happened because the Stockyards slip had no current and quickly filled with sewer debris from the yards and packinghouses. By the end of the decade it was polluting the South Fork, a dilemma Chanute had not anticipated.[14]

The company had better luck with other parts of its building program. The original Exchange was crowded by 1872 with company offices, the Union Stock Yard National Bank, some forty livestock commission firms, and Goodall's press operation. In 1873, therefore, a new wing was constructed at right angles to the main building and all the coal stoves were replaced with steam heat. This doubled the amount of office space, and within a year a dozen more commission firms moved into the Exchange. The company also invested in a separate bank building. These two projects cost approximately $60,000 and were probably done by Baumann and Burling, architects of the 1865 structures.[15]

The closely related matters of water supply and fire protection required attention in the 1870s. Town of Lake and Hyde Park opened a jointly owned waterworks at the lakefront in 1874, and mains on Forty-seventh and Forty-first streets conveyed water to the Stockyards and tied into Chanute's grid of pipes. This arrangement worked well until the end of the decade, when the intake pipe at the lakefront began to clog with sand in the summer and ice in the winter. Meantime, the company replaced the original wooden water-storage tanks with huge stone reservoirs and installed larger mains leading into each division. New pumping machinery and a 100-foot-high standpipe guaranteed adequate pressure and steady delivery of water. Since the Town of Lake had only a small volunteer fire force whose members were difficult to contact and slow to assemble in daytime, the Union Stock Yard Company maintained its own volunteer fire-fighters recruited from the ranks of employes. In 1874, when connection was made with the public water system and relocation of the packinghouses was in full swing, the company established a full-time, professional fire brigade. It also built a fire station and paid $12,000 for a "first-class new Silsby fire steamer." Christened the "Liberty Engine," this famous machine and its smartly uniformed crew fought many a blaze in the yards, the packinghouse district to the west of the stockyard, and elsewhere in Lake and even Hyde Park. Its first major test came during the cold winter of 1879 when the waterworks was paralyzed by ice. Armour's warehouse caught fire and threatened the stockyard as well as other packing plants. By pumping from Armour's own water reservoir, the Liberty Engine put out the blaze and kept damage below $10,000. Town of Lake packers and Union Stock Yard officials begged the local government to replace the defective intake pipe; Lake officials were sympathetic, but Hyde Park trustees resisted. They "hate expenses as far as the Water-Works are concerned," noted a reporter.[16]

Recognizing the need for still more office space in the Exchange, the company shifted its architectural business at mid-decade to the new and as yet unrecognized firm of Daniel H. Burnham and John W. Root. John B. Sherman was responsible for this fortunate decision. He had engaged the two young architects to design and build a house for him on Prairie Avenue, and by 1874 Burnham had won the heart of young Margaret Sherman. The following year, the Union Stock Yard Company hired Burnham and Root to construct separate buildings on Halsted for the Stockyards post office and Goodall's publishing company. In 1878 the architects added a second wing to the Exchange. Then they persuaded the company to enclose the water standpipe in a brick tower and build a limestone base around the tower and pumping machinery. At the top of the water tower they designed a lookout for visitors and the watchman who kept a sharp eye for fires. By 1879 the approach to the yards was quite impressive. At Forty-first and Halsted stood the Transit House with its immaculate grounds and extensive gardens and the complex of smaller buildings sheltering the town hall, post office, and publishing company. Continuing west on what was being called "the Exchange street," one came to the railroad passenger depot and then the massive Exchange. Lawns and shrubbery around the Exchange and bank were carefully tended and a low iron picket fence enclosed these buildings.[17] (See Fig. 8).

The functional but unpretentious wooden gate marking the official entrance into the yards was clearly unsuitable for a company transacting $115 million worth of business, so the directors asked the architects for a gate worthy of their success. Burnham and Root retained the concept of three separate openings, but their structure was much larger, forty-six feet wide and forty-six feet high, and built of Lemont rough-faced limestone to match the base of the water tower. Above the center arch was a steep copper roof containing an iron grille that was lowered at night to lock the entrance. On either side were smaller pedestrian arches, each of which had an iron hinged gate. Carved into the limestone above the central arch were the words "Union Stock-Yard, Chartered 1865," and under the copper roof and projecting from the very top of the arch was the carved head of a shorthorn bullock. This was "Sherman," the prizewinner at the Fat Stock Show. Adjoining the gate on the south side was a two-story brick building shared by company security forces and agents of the Illinois Humane Society. The new entrance opened to the public in June of 1879, though it was not finished until August. The "Stone Gate," which became in effect the logo of the Union Stock Yard and Transit Company, had far greater symbolic value than its actual cost of $12,000.[18] (See Fig. 7).

Security was also a factor in the design of the Stone Gate. Prior to 1879 company employes kept keys to the livestock pens in their possession at all times, yet there was theft of healthy animals as well as of condemned cattle and hogs. The hog losses were so heavy in the winter of 1878–79 that Sherman called in Pinkerton detectives. They caught Michael Harty with keys to hundreds of pens and accused him of helping scalpers move the animals at night. Harty and two accomplices went to the penitentiary. Upon completion of the new gate, Melchior Hoerner, a company guard since 1865, became chief of a security force numbering sixty night and forty day watchmen. Each morning employes signed at the gatehouse for their keys, returned them at night, and filed reports on deliveries, sales, removals, and final counts of the animals in their pens. Night watchmen received these accounts and any losses were charged to them. The iron grille went up at 6:00 A.M. and down at 6:00 P.M. Anyone entering the yards thereafter needed permission and a pass from the gatehouse. Since 1879, noted the *Drovers Journal* a decade later, "not an animal has gone astray."[19]

Reformers, Critics, and Newcomers

It was fortunate for the company that Superintendent Sherman was a diplomat and skilled negotiator. He much preferred to welcome new livestock dealers to the Chicago yards, but he was always cordial to people who suspected monopoly and those on the lookout for cruelty to animals. He engaged in long discussions with both reformers and critics, sometimes acted upon their suggestions, and even in disagreement retained their respect.

The reformers belonged to the Illinois Humane Society for the Prevention of Cruelty to Animals, founded in 1870 by Edwin Lee Brown of Englewood and John C. Dore, whose Western Union Drovers' Yard lost out to the Union Stock Yard. The Illinois organization closely resembled those being promoted in other states by Henry Bergh and the American Society for the Prevention of Cruelty to Animals, but Dore also wanted to protect animals in transit. He secured an 1869 state law requiring that all livestock being transported by rail be unloaded, fed, and watered after twenty-eight hours of travel. Edwin Lee Brown, the first president of the Illinois Humane Society, and John B. Sherman, a member of the board of directors, were in full agreement with the intent of Dore's law. Most of the animals delivered to the Chicago Stockyards crossed state lines, however, and the reformers needed either additional state laws or a federal statute.[20]

George T. Angell's *Cattle Transportation in the United States* (1872) alarmed livestock shippers, roused public opinion, and greatly assisted the cause. Congress responded in 1873 with a twenty-eight-hour law modeled on the Illinois statute. The Illinois reformers urged other states to establish humane societies, and Edwin Lee Brown organized the American Humane Association in 1877. John B. Sherman helped the reformers stage a well-publicized conference at the Union Stock Yards in 1880, and he issued stern warnings to shippers and railroad managers. In addition, Chicago area packers vowed to penalize suppliers of animals with damaged hides or bruised flesh. The Illinois Humane Society's agent at the Chicago yards, John McDonald, kept a sharp watch for the illegal use of prods, whips, or pitchforks on animals and such abusive practices as withholding food and water or salting and overwatering before taking animals to the scales. Sherman welcomed McDonald's help, but some drovers took offense at his meddling. One man caught with a sharp-tipped prod made the mistake of assaulting McDonald, who polished him off "in about eight seconds . . . a la Marquis of Packingtown rules." The reformer sat on the unconscious drover and read out loud to the assembled crowd the rules and regulations of the society concerning the handling of livestock.[21]

Vigilance by the Illinois Humane Society and agitation by the American Humane Association brought great improvements in the transport and handling of livestock during the 1870s. Drovers were more circumspect in the use of whips and prods. Railroads added roofs to their open cattle cars and occasionally feed troughs. Slat floors in double-deck hog and sheep cars, which caused injuries to legs and allowed filth to fall on animals below, were replaced by solid floors. More important was the decision of the railroads to charge by weight rather than by the carload, for this eliminated the incentive to overcrowd. When Edwin Lee Brown took charge of the national organization in 1877, he was replaced on the state level by Chicagoan John G. Shortall. The Illinois organization shortened its name to Illinois Humane Society and found itself shouldering the care of "defenseless children." President Shortall assured members in 1881, however, that the work with children, which came to us "without our seeking it, . . . thus far has not lessened or impaired the efficiency of our animal protective service." Given these priorities, it was appropriate that the Illinois Humane Society's headquarters were at the Stone Gate of the Stockyards.[22]

The Patrons of Husbandry also kept close watch on the Chicago yards in the 1870s. Organized in the office of the *Prairie Farmer* in 1868, the Illinois Grange kept growing until 1873. Membership declined thereafter but many people still called themselves "grangers." They resented the railroads, and they disliked middlemen who sold them agricultural machinery and other supplies as well as middlemen who stored and sold their grain or received their livestock. As one rural politician put it, "We were all grangers. I never belonged to the order, but I was a granger just the same." At the demand of angry farmers, the 1870 Constitutional Convention contained an article authorizing the legislature to regulate private corporations engaged in businesses that affected the public interest. To the surprise of many conservatives, the 1871 legislature proceeded to exercise this authority. A series of laws set maximum railroad passenger rates, required the railroads to base freight rates on distance, and forced grain warehouses to secure state licenses, issue warehouse receipts, and abide by a maximum rate schedule. The legislature capped its work by creating a Board of Railroad and Warehouse Commissioners to carry out inspections and supervise enforcement of the 1871 laws.[23]

Even before the United States Supreme Court upheld these "granger" laws, Illinois farmers and livestock producers had broadened their attack on middlemen. They started cooperative stores to circumvent the "Harvester Ring" and the "Plow Ring," and grangers ran a cooperative livestock commission firm at the Union Stock Yards for a brief period. But they soon decided that the best way to even the score against middlemen was to place the Union Stock Yard and Transit Company under the jurisdiction of the Board of Railroad and Warehouse Commissioners. The commission could then regulate fees imposed by the stockyard and the commission firms. Bills to this effect were introduced in the 1873 session of the legislature, and the Senate appointed a special committee to investigate. This committee toured the Union Stock Yard in March and took testimony from James M. Walker, John B. Sherman, and many others. Its report commended the centralized stockyard where "now the seller meets face to face with the buyer" and is no longer, as "under the old system, . . . a prey to sharpers and tricksters." Charges for corn, hay and yardage—8¢ a day for hogs and sheep and 25¢ a day for cattle—were reasonable; the company provided free labor, free water, free use of its railroad tracks, and levied no yardage fees on animals in transit. The report mentioned filth in some hog pens, a condition company officials blamed on a sudden spring thaw. That was a mitigating circumstance, concluded the report, but in order to secure "clean dry pens" the Board of Commissioners should regulate all stockyards in Illinois. The state legislature read the report and ignored the regulatory bills.[24]

Failing to make the legislature take action, farmers tried in 1873 and again in 1878 to organize a voluntary movement to withhold hogs from market. This would destroy the "Stockyards Ring" and bring company officials, livestock dealers, and packers to heel. These "hold your hogs" campaigns had little effect on a market drawing most of its swine from outside Illinois. The hostility of Illinois "grangers" to the Union Stock Yards surfaced again in 1879 when they proposed bills to make the company divulge its earnings and thereby prove that yardage fees were exploitive. It was Solomon P. Hopkins, former livestock dealer and employe of the Union

Stock Yard company and a member of the legislature from 1873 until 1881, who battled the "Farmers' Ring" and defeated the punitive bills. A Hopkins speech, noted a Springfield reporter, "raises the hair of the Grangers." At the end of the decade, some Illinois farmers still believed the Stockyards was a "moneyed monopoly" controlled by slick urbanites. There were plenty of Chicagoans who contemptously dismissed rural critics of the Stockyards as jealous hayseeds.[25]

Livestock dealers firmly believed that they aided livestock growers and that steadily increasing receipts proved that shippers wanted to transact business at the Chicago yards. Dealers like Samuel Allerton, John Adams, and Texas cattle specialist Wilson Keenan doubled or tripled their sales in the 1870s. The Mallory brothers pressed their sons into partnership, while John and Samuel Wood called upon their two brothers to share the work load. Morris and Waixel transacted the largest volume, and their shipments to Britain convinced James MacDonald that Nelson Morris was "the most extensive cattle-dealer in the world." The shy, reserved Morris was often a lonely figure at the yards, but his unfailing courtesy and consideration to other dealers made him something of an "institution." In 1866, he hired James J. McCarthy, a Bridgeport school dropout who had been buying hogs for a packinghouse. McCarthy's subsequent entry into the livestock trade illustrates the opportunities for newcomers. Morris tutored him in the cattle trade and badgered him into attending night school, and in 1875 the twenty-eight year old "Buck" McCarthy started the firm of McCarthy and McGregor.[26]

The Chicago yards also drew "immigrants." Livestock dealers left Kansas City, St. Louis, and smaller centers to seek their fortunes at the Exchange. One of the newcomers was the Boston firm of Hathaway and Swift. Its junior partner, Gustavus Franklin Swift, grew up on Cape Cod, worked with an older brother who was a butcher, and tried his hand at cattle dealing in the Brighton stockyards outside Boston. By the early 1870s, Swift was running a large meat market in Clinton, Massachusetts, with a younger brother and purchasing cattle for D. M. Anthony, a slaughterer and wholesale meat dealer outside Fall River, and for James A. Hathaway, a Brighton cattle dealer who shipped to England. Realizing that the railroads were bringing superior cattle from the west, Swift moved his family to Albany, then investigated the Buffalo cattle market, and finally in late 1874 paid his first visit to the Union Stock Yards. It looked so promising that he brought his pregnant wife and five children to the Town of Lake in January, 1875.[27]

Although Swift was a small operator in the Chicago yards, he stood out immediately because of his New England accent, unusual height, and curious choice of a Texas pony to ride around the pens. Other cattle dealers took pride in their horses and scoffed at an animal that left Swift's long legs dangling in mud and manure. Always a stickler for saving time, Swift preferred the pony because he could open the gates without dismounting and was in a convenient position to feel cattle butts for excess fat, an unusual practice in Chicago. The Yankee explained, "Back where I ship these cattle to, they're bought that way. That's how I sell 'em, and how I buy 'em." Chicago dealers tolerated these eccentricities because Swift was such a shrewd buyer. In later years, Nelson Morris was fond of explaining why the New Englander came to the Union Stock Yards. Morris shipped a load of cattle from Chicago to Albany and heard from his agent that the cattle had been sold for four and a quarter cents a pound. "I was mad. They were good cattle—ought to have brought more. I wired the agent 'Cattle sold too cheap. Buy them back at a quarter of a cent profit.' . . . Well, he wired, 'Can't be done. Sold cattle to Swift. He knows a bargain as well as you do.'" Swift figured that "if cattle could be shipped from Chicago and sold in Albany for four and a quarter cents," then Chicago was "the place money could be made, right on the ground floor."[28]

The Chicago Stockyards flourished in the midst of the 1870s depression because the city's rail network penetrated a fertile crescent of stock growers, and they chose to sell their cattle and hogs in the country's most efficient market. To facilitate the growing volume of business, the capable John B. Sherman built more pens, upgraded the water system, established a fire brigade, and added two wings to the Exchange plus a commodious bank. By the end of the decade, when seventy-odd livestock firms were handling the delivery, sale, or transshipment of nearly nine million animals, it was only proper that the Union Stock Yard Company erect the Stone Gate to mark its achievement. Illinois's self-styled "grangers" and members of the Humane Society refused to stand in awe of the enterprise, but people engaged in the buying and selling of cattle and hogs knew that Chicago was the place to be. Another illustration of the Union Stock Yards' magnetic power was the steady migration in the 1870s of South Branch packers to the western half of Section 5 in the Town of Lake.

NOTES

1. *Times*, May 4, 1869; *Chicago Sun* [Union Stock-Yards], Oct. 10, 1871. The *Sun* Extra, the only extant copy of Goodall's paper before the 1880s, is in the Chicago Historical Society.

2. Bessie Louise Pierce, *A History of Chicago*, vol. 3, *The Rise of a Modern City, 1871–1893* (New York, 1957), chap. 1; Chicago Times, *New Chicago: A Full Review of the Work of Reconstruction* (Chicago, 1872); *Times*, Jan. 3, 1872.

3. Homer Hoyt, *One Hundred Years of Land Values in Chicago* (Chicago, 1933), 103–7; Raymond Fales and Leon Moses, "Land-Use Theory and the Structure of the Nineteenth-Century City," Regional Science Association, *Papers*, 28 (1972), 65–79; Everett Chamberlain, *Chicago and Its Suburbs* (Chicago, 1874), 138–40; William T. Hutchinson, *Cyrus Hall McCormick*, 2 vols. (New York, 1930, 1935), 2:495–502, 512–13; "City of Chicago," *Inland Monthly Magazine*, 10 (Mar., 1877), 1196–1207; S. S. Schoff, *The Glory of Chicago, Her Manufactories. The Industrial Interests of Chicago* . . . (Chicago, 1873), 9–12, 22, 25, 128–31; *Trib.*, Sept. 19, 1872.

4. Board of Trade, "Supplementary . . . on Packing and Provision Business," *Annual Report, 1871*, 143; Board of Trade, *Annual Report, 1880*, 34–35; Chicago Times, *Chicago and Its Resources Twenty Years After, 1871–1891* (Chicago, 1892), 140.

5. D. C. Brooks, "Chicago and Its Railways," *Lakeside Monthly*, 8 (Oct., 1872), 271–75; Alfred T. Andreas, *History of Chicago*, 3 vols. (Chicago, 1886), 3:200–228; Pei-lin Tan, "The Belt and Switching Railroads of Chicago Terminal Area" (Ph.D. diss., University of Chicago, 1931), 29–36; Pierce, *Chicago*, 3:522–23; Richard C. Overton, *Burlington Route: A History of the Burlington Lines* (New York, 1965), 120, 132–45; Board of Trade, *Annual Report, 1879*, 14.

6. Margaret Walsh, *The Rise of the Midwestern Meat Packing Industry* (Lexington, Ky., 1982), 74–75; Cuthbert Powell, *Twenty Years of Kansas City's Live Stock Trade and Traders* (Kansas City, Mo., 1893), 15–20; Wyatt W. Belcher, *The Economic Rivalry between St. Louis and Chicago: 1850–1880* (New York, 1947), 168–93, 205–6; Rudolf A. Clemen, *The American Livestock and Meat Industry* (New York, 1923), 203–6; BAI, *First Annual Report, 1884* (Washington, 1885), 247–48; "Chicago and St. Louis," *St. Louis Republican*, Aug. 27, 1881, rpt. in *Trib.*, Aug. 29, 1881.

7. Mary Yeager, *Competition and Regulation: The Development of Oligopoly in the Meat Packing Industry* (Greenwich, Conn., 1981), 30–41; *Railway Age*, 3 (Jan. 31, 1878), 67; *Trib.*, Dec. 11, 12, 17, 23, 1877; May 1, 1883; Treasury Department, *Report on the Internal Commerce of the United States, 1879* (Washington, 1879), 164–77; Algie Martin Simons, "Railroad Pools," Wisconsin Academy of Sciences, Arts and Letters, *Transactions*, 11 (1896–97), 72–73; Senate Select Committee, *Report . . . on Transportation and Sale of Meat Products* (Washington, 1890), 2–3, 16; and Senate Select Committee, *Testimony . . . on the Transportation and Sale of Meat Products* (Washington, 1889), 57–59, 232–33.

8. [J. M. Wing and Co.], *Seven Days in Chicago: A Complete Guide* (Chicago, 1876), 46–47; Walter Gore Marshall, *Through America: Nine Months in the United States* (London, 1882), 89; James MacDonald, *Food*

from the Far West, or American Agriculture with Special Reference to the Beef Production and Importation of Dead Meat from America to Great Britain (London, 1878), 185; *Trib.*, Dec. 23, 1875.

9. *Trib.*, May 10, 1882; *Chicago Herald*, Dec. 12, 13, 1885; *Drovers Journal*, Dec. 14, 1885.

10. Paul Wallace Gates, "Cattle Kings in the Prairies," *MVHR*, 35 (Dec., 1948), 383–405; *Drovers Journal*, Nov. 3, 1884; Nov. 3, 1888; Sept. 28, 1889.

11. *Griffiths Annual Review of the Live Stock Trade at Chicago, 1870* (Chicago, 1871), 42; *1871*, 52; *Trib.*, Dec. 3–7, 1878; *Drovers Journal*, Nov. 28, 1882; Illinois Department of Agriculture, *Transactions . . . for the Year 1878* (Springfield, 1880), 71.

12. *Times*, Apr. 26, 1874; *Drovers Journal*, June 28, Sept. 14, 1886; F. Cyril James, *The Growth of Chicago Banks*, 2 vols. (New York, 1938), 1:440, 445–58; *Land-Owner*, 5 (Dec., 1873), 219; *Griffiths Annual Review of the Live Stock Trade at Chicago, 1873* (Chicago, 1874), 8, 12–13; *Trib.*, Mar. 22, 1880.

13. "Report of Special Committee to Visit the Union Stock Yards, at Chicago, Mar., 1873," *Reports Made to the General Assembly of Illinois, 1873* (Springfield, 1874), 4:237, 242–44, 260–62; Federal Trade Commission, *Report on the Meat-Packing Industry* (Washington, 1919), part 3, 194–96; USYTC, *Minute Book*, June 27, 1872; Jan. 15, Sept. 1, 1873; Feb. 24, 1874; Mar. 20, 1875; May 31, 1876; Jan. 18, 1879 (Chicago Historical Society, Chicago).

14. *Griffiths Annual Review, 1873*, 7–8; *1874*, 9–12; *Wing's Illustrated Travellers' and Visitors' Hand-Book to the City of Chicago* (Chicago, 1874), 46; *Seven Days in Chicago*, 47; *Drovers Journal*, Aug. 17, 1889; *Times*, Apr. 22, 1869; *Trib.*, May 12, 1872; Dec. 23, 1875; Oct. 20, 1878; *Griffiths Annual Review, 1870*, 5–7; *1872*, 8; Andreas, *Chicago*, 3:334–35.

15. *Griffiths Annual Review, 1873*, 7–8; *1874*, 9–12; *Trib.*, Dec. 23, 1875; *Seven Days in Chicago*, 46–50.

16. Board of Public Works, *Annual Report, 1872–73*, 95; *Drovers Journal*, May 8, 1879; *Griffiths Annual Review of the Live Stock Trade at Chicago, 1874* (Chicago, 1875), 9; *Trib.*, Jan. 19, 26, Feb. 26, 1879; Jan. 1, 1880.

17. Louise C. Wade, "The Stockyards Connection of Burnham and Root," *Chicago History*, 4 (Fall, 1975), 139–41; *Trib.*, Dec. 23, 1875; Aug. 15, 1879; Jan. 1, 1880; *Drovers Journal*, May 8, 1879; June 1, 1889.

18. Wade, "Stockyards Connection of Burnham and Root," 142; M. S. Parkhurst, "Background of Stone Gate, June 25, 1954" (memorandum, Chicago Historical Society); Commission on Chicago Historical and Ar-

chitectural Landmarks, *Summary of Information on the Union Stock Yard Gate* (Chicago, 1971); *Trib.*, Aug. 15, 1879; Jan. 1, 1880; *The Graphic*, Mar. 6, 1886. In view of Burnham and Root's contribution to the Stockyards, Louis Sullivan's recollection of his first encounter with Daniel H. Burnham is revealing. The teenaged Sullivan was viewing the Sherman residence, still under construction in 1874, when Burnham appeared and confided, "I'm not going to stay satisfied with houses; my idea is to work up a big business, to handle big things, deal with big business men, and to build up a big organization." Added Sullivan, "he faltered not—his purpose was fixed." Louis H. Sullivan, *The Autobiography of an Idea* (New York, 1926), 285, 288.

19. *Trib.*, Aug. 15, 1879; Feb. 26, 1882; Feb. 6, Apr. 13, Sept. 9, 1883; *Drovers Journal*, Nov. 6, 1883; June 6, July 29, 1884; Jan. 30, 1888; June 1, 1889.

20. *Public Laws of the State of Illinois, 1869* (Springfield, 1869), 114–17; "An Appeal in Behalf of the Illinois Humane Society, Chicago, Mar. 1, 1871" (pamphlet, Chicago Historical Society); *Laws Relating to Prevention of Cruelty to Animals* (Chicago, 1872), 11–12; John Visher, *Hand-Book of Charities* (Chicago, 1897), 78–81; *Trib.*, Feb. 16, 1871.

21. *Trib.*, Feb. 27, 1875; May 14, 1879; Mar. 6, Apr. 30, May 2, 1880; Mar. 7, 1881; Illinois Humane Society, *Annual Report, 1880*, 6–7; "Remarks of Edwin Lee Brown of Chicago, President of the American Humane Association . . . Nov. 17, 1880" (pamphlet, Chicago Historical Society), 20–23; *Drovers Journal*, Feb. 17, 1888. The story about McDonald was recounted in the late 1880s when "Packingtown" was a familiar term. It was unknown in the 1870s.

22. Illinois Humane Society, *Annual Report, 1879*, 5–6; *Trib.*, Mar. 7, May 8, June 9, 1881; "Remarks of Edwin Lee Brown," 1–19; Visher, *Hand-book*, 78; Clemen, *Livestock and Meat Industry*, 195–98; Sydney H. Coleman, *Humane Society Leaders in America* (Albany, 1924), 149–52, 247–50.

23. Solon J. Buck, *The Agrarian Crusade: A Chronicle of the Farmer in Politics* (New Haven, Conn., 1920), 47–48; Solon J. Buck, *The Granger Movement: A Study of Agricultural Organization and Its Political, Economic, and Social Manifestations, 1870–1880* (Cambridge, Mass., 1913), 123–36; A. E. Paine, *The Granger Movement in Illinois* (Urbana, Ill., 1904), 3–24, 29.

24. "Report of Special Committee to Visit the Union Stock Yards, at Chicago, Mar., 1873," *Reports . . . 1873*, 4:238–41; *Trib.*, Mar. 22, 1873.

25. Jonathan Periam, *The Groundswell: A History of the Origin, Aims, and Progress of the Farmers' Movement* (Cincinnati, 1874), 361; Paine, *Granger Movement in Illinois*, 42–44; *Prairie Farmer*, Dec. 12, 1874;

Western Rural, 17 (Sept. 27, 1879), 308; *Trib.*, Sept. 11, 12, 1873; Feb. 28, 1879.

26. Joseph G. Knapp, "A Review of Chicago Stock Yards History," *University [of Chicago] Journal of Business,* 2 (June, 1924), 337; *Origin, Growth, and Usefulness of the Chicago Board of Trade: Its Leading Members, and Representative Business Men* (New York, 1886), 226, 328, 331; Alfred T. Andreas, *History of Cook County, Illinois* (Chicago, 1884), 672, 681, 687; *Trib.*, Nov. 29, 1874; Nov. 19, 1881; MacDonald, *Food from the Far West,* 186; George Upton, *Biographical Sketches of the Leading Men of Chicago* (Chicago, 1876), 216; Elizabeth T. Kent, "William Kent, Independent: A Biography" (typescript, 1950, Chicago Historical Society), 71–72.

27. Louis F. Swift and Arthur Van Vlissingen, *The Yankee of the Yards: The Biography of Gustavus Franklin Swift* (Chicago, 1927), 24–25, 49–52, 122–27; Thomas W. Goodspeed, "Gustavus Franklin Swift, 1839–1903," *University [of Chicago] Record,* 7 (Apr., 1921), 91–97; David C. Smith and Anne Bridges, "The Brighton Market: Feeding Nineteenth-Century Boston," *Agricultural History,* 56 (Jan., 1982), 20–21; Helen Swift, *My Father and My Mother* (Chicago, 1937), 27–28.

28. Swift and Vlissingen, *Yankee of the Yards,* 29, 58–59; Swift, *My Father and My Mother,* 27, 90.

CHAPTER 6

The "Pig-Killing Concerns"

In many respects, the increase in packinghouse production during the 1870s was more striking than the expansion of the livestock trade. Chicago packed over five million animals in 1880, and the annual value of beef and pork products climbed from $19 to $85 million in that decade. Among the ingredients in this success story were railroad delivery of cattle and hogs to the Stockyards, a much larger packinghouse labor force, and a growing number of urban Americans who wanted the packinghouse products. But Chicago area packers made a number of smart moves in the 1870s, starting with the construction of huge, modern plants in the western half of Section 5, Town of Lake. Large sums were invested in hog-scraping machinery, more efficient drying equipment, and the development of canned meats and margarine. Wider use of natural refrigeration by means of ice and brine extended the pork-packing season, and Gustavus Swift demonstrated that fresh, chilled beef could be shipped in refrigerated railroad cars to eastern cities and sold at a profit. Chicagoans, of course, bragged endlessly about their pacesetting "pork packeries." David Macrae of Scotland agreed that they were marvelous, but in his travel memoir he evened the score: "Chicago has the biggest saints, the biggest sinners, and the biggest pig-killing establishments in America. 'Yes, sir,' as one enthusiastic . . . gentleman declared, 'the biggest pig-killing concerns in God's creation!'"[1]

Relocation of the Packinghouses

Of the forty Chicago area packing firms at the end of the 1870s, about half were still operating on the South Branch or Ogden Slip and Healy Slough. The companies that slaughtered for the local market had good reason to stay where they were. Tobey and Booth had an efficient plant and no trouble abiding by city and state sanitary regulations, so they stayed. Some packers disliked uprooting themselves and their workers from the Fifth Ward, and others, like Culbertson, stuck it out on the South Branch until retirement. The larger packers, however, and those who wanted to expand in the future moved into the Packers' Addition. They would have instant access to cattle and hogs and freedom from Chicago's prohibition against driving cattle through city streets between 8:00 A.M. and 5:00 P.M. The township, moreover, did not frown on rendering plants. Purchasers of land in the western half of Section 5 had the right to use Union Stock Yard railroad tracks for deliveries and shipments, an important consideration. And at $80 per front foot for lots four hundred feet deep, the land was considerably cheaper than South Branch property and readily available.[2]

These advantages of the Packers' Addition, unmatched at the time by any other livestock center, lured packers from Bridgeport and farther afield. The lots went so rapidly that Tracy, Sykes, and Porter opened four more subdivisions, and James D. Lehmer's group started selling their property south of Forty-third Street. Some of the new firms in the Town of Lake were partnerships formed by small operators who sold their South Branch houses and pooled their resources. William Jones and Josiah Stiles did this in 1876. Moran and Healy was formed by Nash's bookkeeper and a Tobey and Booth superintendent. Samuel Allerton launched his career as a packer with an impressive new pork house in 1871–72; Nelson Morris started with a modest plant but enlarged it in 1877. Michener and Company left Philadelphia for the Packers' Addition, and George D. Baldwin said good-bye to Boston. The British firm of Davies, Atkinson and Company sold a plant in Canada in order to build near the Stockyards. The Fowler brothers, natives of northern Ireland and partners in an English commission firm, staked their future on meat-packing in Chicago. By 1879 their Anglo-American Packing and Provision Company occupied seven acres and employed eighteen hundred men. Even so, the five Fowlers were outdistanced by the Armour brothers.[3]

Philip Armour paid $100,000 in 1872 for twenty-one acres. Fresh from constructing a new plant with John Plankinton in Kansas City the year before, Armour first built an immense pork house, thereby quadrupling production and profits. Eager to continue packing pork in the summer, he asked architect Joseph T. Nicholson to build him a large storeroom surrounded by an icehouse. This 1874 structure is considered to be the first large chill room in an American packinghouse, and it worked so well that Armour and Plankinton built another in Kansas City. Then Joseph Armour, manager of the Chicago plant, fell ill with Bright's disease, which would claim his life in 1881. Even without Joseph's sickness, it is certain that Armour would have moved from Milwaukee to Chicago sometime during the 1870s. He came in 1875 with his family and his right-hand man, Michael Cudahy.[4]

Cudahy and his brothers John and Patrick grew up with the packing industry of Milwaukee. They came in 1849 from Kilkenny, Ireland, and Michael started working in slaughterhouses when he was fourteen. By

1869 he was the Plankinton and Armour plant superintendent and a one-eighth owner of the firm. The only reason Plankinton let him go with Armour was that Patrick Cudahy was ready to replace Michael. In Chicago, Cudahy managed the packing operation while Armour supervised finances and sales from an office near the Board of Trade. The Armour brothers made Cudahy a one-eighth owner in 1877.[5]

Armour and Company's original $160,000 investment in its South Branch plant had been parlayed to a net worth of $500,000 by 1875, the year Armour and Cudahy came down from Milwaukee. By continuing to reinvest four-fifths of the profits, the company was able to keep expanding. Under Cudahy's expert direction, a second pork house was built, then a beef house and extensive storage facilities. An experimental sausage kitchen evolved into a separate division with a staff of experienced German sausage-makers. The company ventured into canned meats in 1878, had a full line of these products on the market a year later, and added oleomargarine and butterine in 1880. By that time Armour's "village" covered twelve acres, the buildings laced together with company railroad tracks and protected by an Armour fire brigade and extensive fire alarm system. Net worth in 1879 was $2 million and net profit just over $700,000. Armour and Company not only led Chicago competitors but was considered to be the wealthiest packinghouse in the world.[6]

In the wake of the packinghouse migration to the Town of Lake came scores of managers and foremen who were as important to their companies as Cudahy was to Armour and Company. Robert Neill of Belfast opened the Fowler Brothers' plant, and machinist John Bouchard, a native of Quebec, was a Fowler employe until Cudahy made him an Armour engineer in 1879. Frank Bischoff's first job upon arrival from Germany was in a Fifth Ward gut-cleaning factory, but he became Armour's expert on casing, pickling, sausage making, and meat preservation. Some newcomers used their packinghouse skills as stepping-stones to different careers. Canadian carpenter Henry Wilmott was a construction engineer at Chicago Packing and Provision Company before turning to real estate and home building in the burgeoning Town of Lake. There were also, of course, some employes whose stay was brief. Two interesting examples are Illinois Republican William E. Lorimer who, as a fatherless teenager, worked in the packinghouses in the 1870s and Bavarian-born Oscar F. Mayer, who spent three years in Armour's sausage division before opening his own meat market on Chicago's north side.[7]

Although only half of the Chicago area firms were located in the Town of Lake at the end of the decade, those houses accounted for the dramatic increase in production. Nine hundred thousand hogs and 21,000 cattle had been packed in 1870. Ten years later, the figures were 4,700,000 hogs and 500,000 cattle, and the value of beef and pork products had quadrupled to $85 million in 1880. "Fabulous," proclaimed one visitor, while another calculated, "During the one hundred and one working days of the last season, fourteen hundred miles of hogs were converted into pork in the city. This was at the rate of a hog in less than three seconds—an average of 1,400 an hour." By mid-decade there were enough large packinghouses in the western half of Section 5 for the newspapers to lump them with the livestock trade and simply place both industries "at the Stockyards." On the tenth anniversary of the opening of the Union Stock Yard, the *Tribune* took stock of the changes that had occurred. The stockyard company, livestock firms, and railroads serving the yards employed about 1,500 workers. The South Branch and Town of Lake packers in 1875 kept 7,500 men year round and employed another 350 in the busy winter months. Close to 1,000 men worked as coopers, teamsters, and mechanics at the packinghouses or as operatives in glue, lard, and rendering plants. This meant, according to the *Tribune*, that nearly one-fifth of the Chicago area population was dependent upon the Stockyards and packinghouses. Little wonder the editor pronounced them "the greatest industry of the city."[8]

New Machinery and New Products

The Pork Packers' Association of Chicago opened its annual report for 1875–76 with the assertion that its business was "now conducted upon systematic principles in keeping with the enlightenment of the present age and progress of our country." They were thinking of steam hoists and overhead rails—"machines . . . touched with Chicago lightning" for David Macrae—but also the earliest experiments with automatic hog-scraping machinery. When Walter Marshall watched one of these at the Anglo-American plant in 1879, he described it as a "grid-iron, having a surface of steel blades . . . set in motion by machinery." This marvelous machine removed the hog bristles "far quicker than hand-labour," in fact, in "less than a quarter of a minute." The hog carcass "wriggled and tossed about on top of these moving blades like an india-rubber ball" before emerging "snow-white" and ready for the butchers.[9] (See Figs. 5 and 6.)

Hand-scraping bristles from steaming carcasses was arduous and unpleasant work for the six "scrapers," three on either side of the table. When John Plankinton saw the first Chicago hog elevator, he said it was a fine invention but "if you want to get up something big, make a steam hog-scraper." Two patents were granted in the early 1870s to eastern inventors who claimed to have workable machines. Neither contrivance, however, was effective. It was William W. Kincaid of Fowler Brothers who designed and patented the first successful hog-scraping machine in 1876. His apparatus had metal blades, some revolving vertically, some horizontally, but all held against the body of the hog by means of springs. As a windlass pulled the carcass through the machine in a horizontal position, the revolving reels scraped off hair and bristles. John Bouchard, Kincaid's friend and co-worker, experimented with metal spools and flexible steel scrapers. After Bouchard went to Armour's, Michael Cudahy helped him perfect a scraping machine that would adjust automatically to individual carcasses. They came up with an ingenious system of counterweights to hold the spools against the carcass, and Cudahy allowed Bouchard to secure the patent in December, 1880. Because of the flexible steel blades, movable bearings, and carcass control, the Cudahy-Bouchard hog-scraper was vastly superior to the Kincaid machine. However, since nine other hog-scraping machines were patented in the next six years, Bouchard won more fame than money.[10]

John Bouchard also developed an efficient method of drying blood and tankings, so that packers could sell them at a small profit to fertilizer manufacturers. James Turner, who stayed within the city limits and thus had to comply with the ordinance concerning rendering odors, devised a method of piping fumes and gases from a rendering tank back into the furnace and consuming them. When Turner added carbon to the mixture, he found that it could be used as fuel or illuminating gas. Dr. John Rauch was so impressed with Turner's patented rendering machine that he carried drawings of it to sanitary conventions and issued a Chicago Board of Health regulation forcing other renderers to burn their fumes and gases. Chemists entered the packinghouses in the 1870s. Louis and Christian Wahl employed them as consultants on several occasions in the 1870s to solve specific problems at their glue works, but it was lard manufacturer Nathaniel K. Fairbank who hired the first chemist full-time. In 1878 he added William B. Allbright, a Massachusetts Institute of Technology graduate in chemical engineering, to the staff of N. K. Fairbank Co. Asked to improve the lard product, Allbright hit on the use of fuller's earth, then devised the lard-cooling roll, and in the mid-1880s discovered how to blend cottonseed oil in shortening.[11]

New products, as well as new machinery, increased packinghouse profits. One of them was oleomargarine, an animal-fat substitute for butter. Discovered by Mège-Mouries during the Franco-Prussian War, it was approved by French health authorities in 1872 and quickly accepted on the market. The formula involved heating beef fat until the animal tissue and oleo oil separated, then churning the oil with milk, water, and a trace of coloring matter. Mège-Mouries called it oleomargarine from the oleic and margaric acids, and he secured English and American patents before French reports were released and translated in 1873. New York City had an Oleomargarine Manufacturing Company the following year, and a Chicago newspaper noted in 1876 that James Turner was using "the French process" to produce a "grease" that fortunately was marketed in England. Since oleomargarine cost only half as much as butter, it did well in the American market. In 1880 three Chicago firms, Turner, Armour, and Fairbank, produced $437,800 worth of margarine. Illinois dairy interests complained as early as 1877; David Ward Wood, the Englewood editor of the *Western Rural,* assailed the butter substitute as "exceedingly filthy" and full of dangerous "animalculae." "Next to the liquor traffic," he thought, the manufacture of margarine was "the most unworthy in which men engage." The Illinois legislature passed its first margarine law in 1879, a mild measure requiring manufacturers and sellers of butter substitutes to label their products with the "true and appropriate name."[12]

Canned meat was a more important packinghouse product. Fruits, vegetables, and fish had been preserved in glass jars or primitive tin cans prior to 1847, but the invention in that year of a tin-can-making machine and Gail Borden's subsequent success with canned condensed milk popularized the idea of buying food in a tin container. The sale of "canned goods" increased sixfold during the 1860s, and the United States Navy experimented with canned beef. Preserved meat, however, shriveled in the final cooking process, leaving a tasteless mixture of juice, grease, and tired meat. William J. Wilson produced the first appetizing canned meat. He and his brother had moved from a Chicago provision firm into meatpacking, discovering along the way that putting more meat in the can and cooking it faster produced a tastier product. They could not prepare it in large quantities, however, until steam-pressure autoclaves came on the market in the winter of 1873–74. With this machine to cook the meat and a modified pyramidal can that let the contents slide out, Wilson knew he had a superior product. He incorporated the Wilson Packing Company in 1874 and secured a patent on his "Original Corned Beef Can" the following year. Wholesale grocers showed no interest in the product until Wilson insisted that they put an open can on the counter for customers to sample. By the time *Frank Leslie's Illustrated Newspaper* featured Wilson's canned corned beef in 1878, the company had a large Chicago plant, sales offices in New York, and scores of competitors.[13]

One was the tiny Chicago firm of A. A. Libby and Company. Launched in 1868 by Hancock's nephews, Arthur and Charles Libby, and their friend Archibald McNeill, it packed beef and experimented with preservation of ox, beef, and pork tongues. When they secured Wilson's permission to use his pyramidal can, they formed Libby, McNeill and Libby and started marketing canned corned beef and roast beef. Sales soared in the United States and the products even penetrated the English market. By the end of the decade, the company had a large modern plant in Chicago, a thriving hotel and restaurant trade in fresh tenderloins, and a need for two hundred thousand cattle per year. Meantime, Allerton launched the St. Louis Beef Canning Company, Armour started canning in 1878, and Nelson Morris and Nathaniel K. Fairbank established a canning and beef-packing company in the Packers' Addition. Moreover, Anglo-American and Chicago Packing and Provision companies had followed Armour into canned beef, potted ham, and a variety of tongues. Everyone was using Wilson's pyramidal can, though only Libby, McNeill and Libby had a license to do so. Wilson brought suit, spent a large sum on legal fees before losing in the United States Supreme Court, but was still the leading meat canner in 1880. Neither the Board of Trade nor the Bureau of the Census separated canned meat from other packinghouse products, yet the *Tribune*'s financial editor knew that "from an insignificant beginning the canning of meats has grown during the past five years into a most important business."[14]

Wider Use of Natural Refrigeration

The growing proportion of Americans who lived in towns and cities in the 1870s and '80s created the expanding market for packinghouse products. Local butchers stocked packinghouse hams, preserved beef and pork, and the specialty canned meats because their customers asked for them. Like store-baked bread, these items were convenience foods, and town-dwellers saved time with ingenious combinations such as the luncheon sandwich made of specialty meats between two thick slices of bread. Yet the transition from rural to urban living did not affect their appetities for fresh meat; in the eyes of some, Americans were "too carnivorous," feeding too "exclusively on steaks of beef, chops of mutton, cutlets of veal, and joints of meat." So long as local slaughterers provided city butchers with fresh meat, the packers could not participate in that market. By trial and error in the 1870s, however, packers found a way to deliver fresh beef from western livestock centers to distant eastern markets.[15]

It all began with more extensive use of ice and brine to cool warehouses and packing plants. During the post-Civil War years, the proliferation of ice-cooled warehouses for fresh produce plus fish, poultry, and meat convinced wholesale butchers that cold storage actually improved the flavor of fresh pork and beef. So Andrew J. Chase of Boston designed for market butchers a "pure, dry, cold air refrigerator and conservatory." By 1873 Chase's coolers were being used in Faneuil Hall markets, the Swift market in Clinton, and also in New Bedford and Providence. Indianapolis packer Thomas Kingan had patented another type of cooling unit; it fanned air over crushed ice and salt into a storage room where beef and pork were suspended.[16]

Armour's cold-storage warehouse, the first of its kind in Chicago, set a precedent for other packers. Hutchinson promptly added an ice-cooled warehouse, and plants constructed after 1875 almost always had a large chill room. Since the packers closely guarded the design of their plants, no two houses were alike and the cold-storage structures varied. All of them, however, used ice as the cooling element and all were carefully insulated. Parallel brick walls, each eighteen inches thick, with a ten-inch air space between, was one method of insulating a chill room. Another was to construct an interior wooden wall and fill the space between it and the outside brick wall with wood shavings or sawdust. The success of the cooling operation depended upon an unfailing supply of ice, and thus the packers built huge icehouses on their premises. By the end of the 1870s, they were using about one-third of the ice sold in Cook County and worrying about the size of the winter ice harvest, since that raw material was as important as coal for the engine rooms and livestock for the slaughtering departments.[17]

Refrigeration altered the traditional November to March packing season. Livestock could be slaughtered at any time and carcasses held in cold storage until convenient to ship or cut, cure, pickle, or dry salt them. Packers with cold-storage facilities had greater freedom in marketing, and they could provide steadier employment. Since Chicago summers were shorter and seldom as hot or humid as those in Cincinnati, St. Louis, or Kansas City, it was less costly to pack year-round in Chicago. This gave the city one more advantage over its competitors. Statistics illustrate the increase in summer packing. Between March and November of 1870, Chicago packers handled fewer than 50,000 hogs and this was about 6 percent of the annual pork pack. In 1875 they killed over 700,000 hogs in the off-season. Four years later they dispatched 2,155,000 hogs between March and October, just about half the annual pack. The secretary of the Board of Trade explained that this miracle was performed "with the aid of ice. The meats being mostly dry salted, and handled with care, are esteemed as desirable as those packed in the colder weather."[18]

Chicago's cattle-kill doubled between 1870 and 1875, then increased tenfold in the latter half of the decade. Canners and traditional beef packers used most of these animals, but approximately one-quarter of the cattle left Chicago in 1880 as "dressed beef"—that is, chilled, quartered carcasses in refrigerated railroad cars.[19] Dressing beef required less labor than cutting, trimming, curing, preserving, and packing in tierces, barrels, boxes, cans, or jars. In fact, the beef quarter could travel on the same overhead hook through the killing bed, the cooler, the refrigerator car, and into the wholesaler's cold-storage warehouse. Refrigeration, of course, was the essential element in the dressed beef trade. Less than thirty miles from the stockyards, Hammond and Company had already demonstrated the feasibility of shipping fresh chilled beef to eastern markets. Yet it took a transplanted New Englander to launch the dressed-beef business in Chicago.

When Swift came to Chicago to buy cattle, he already knew about Hammond's regular shipments of dressed beef in refrigerator cars to Boston. He soon heard of Nelson Morris's attempts to send boxes of frozen beef to Boston in freight cars in the winters of 1874 and 1875, and there must have been discussion of the vagaries of Hammond's refrigerator cars and those being used by the Nofsinger packing company in Kansas City. Insufficient ventilation caused some loads of beef to sour, and if the meat touched the ice, it discolored and spoiled easily when warmed to room temperature. Carcasses hung from the ceiling could be set in motion by sharp curves in the track, and their pendulum action overturned cars. Most important for Swift, the refrigerator cars were expensive. Unable to buy or build a car, Swift's earliest attempts to ship beef instead of live cattle resembled those of Nelson Morris. In the winter of 1875–76 he sent beef in an ordinary railroad car with the door slightly ajar for ventilation, and thanks to continuous cold weather, the meat arrived in good condition at Anthony's warehouse in Fall River and the Swift market in Clinton. In 1876 he purchased William Moore's small slaughterhouse in the Packers' Addition and staffed it with six butchers dispatched to Chicago by D. M. Anthony. For the next two winters Swift continued his experiments, often rigging the carcasses in the cars himself, searching always for a reliable way to ship fresh beef in railroad freight cars without resorting to refrigerator cars.[20]

Swift's Fall River partner was willing to continue the experiments, but James A. Hathaway wanted Swift to abandon the meat shipments and concentrate on cattle buying. Hathaway came to Chicago in 1878, and, after a friendly discussion, the two men dissolved their partnership. Swift emerged with approximately $30,000 and promptly formed Swift Bros. and Co. Now able to afford the refrigerator cars, Swift tried shipping in the Wickes car and the Anderson and Zimmerman models, none of which satisfied him. In 1879 he turned to Andrew J. Chase, the Boston engineer who had installed the Clinton market cooler and just completed a cold-storage warehouse for Anthony and Swift in Fall River. Asked to design the perfect refrigerator car for shipping dressed beef, Chase utilized some features of cars already on the market. However, he placed the ice bunkers in the top of the car at both ends. This improved ventilation within the car and permitted workers to re-ice the bunkers from outside. Chase patented his railroad car in 1879 and his "Cold-Blast Refrigerator" in 1881. Meantime, the Michigan Central Railroad refused to build these cars for Swift, so he contracted with the Michigan Car Company in Detroit for ten Chase refrigerator cars, putting 15 percent down and promising the rest out of earnings from the cars. Hammond claimed patent infringement, but the court had ruled in Swift's favor by the time the cars were built.[21]

The Michigan Central and Lake Shore and Michigan Southern wanted livestock shipments from the Chicago Stockyards, and both railroads refused to haul Swift's meat cars. But the Chicago and Grand Trunk, a newcomer with a circuitous Canadian route to New England and not much livestock trade, agreed to carry them if Swift took responsibility for re-icing along the way. Swift built icehouses on the Grand Trunk line and also along the New York Central tracks east of Buffalo where some cars were transferred. The refrigerator cars soon delivered more meat than the Swift market and D. M. Anthony could distribute, so new dealers were sought. In Boston, wholesalers Hyde, Wheeler and Company sold Swift's meat in competition with Hammond's Indiana product. Another distributor was I. M. Lincoln of Providence, owner of one of the earliest Chase coolers. By the early 1880s, Swift's dressed beef was being marketed in Lowell, Fitchburg, Worcester, and Springfield, Massachusetts; New Haven and New Britain, Connecticut; and Buffalo, Rochester, and Albany, New York.[22]

Swift purchased more land in the Packers' Addition and in 1880 began construction of an immense cattle slaughtering house, 495 feet long and 150 feet deep, the only one of its kind at the Yards. The killing beds required much less space than the chill rooms, designed by Chase, and the necessary icehouse. The cellar was devoted to hides and tallow. Adding to the efficiency of this operation was a new fertilizer plant owned by Swift and his friend L. B. Darling, a fertilizer manufacturer in Pawtucket, Rhode Island. Since Swift's money was going into refrigerator cars and the new slaughterhouse, Darling financed the fertilizer factory and sent his son Ira to Chicago to manage it. When the Swift plant opened in 1881, the fertilizer factory was ready to turn the cattle offal into neatsfoot oil, glue, ground bones, and fertilizer. The scope of the operation attracted the attention of a newspaper reporter, who described Swift Bros. and Co. as "this celebrated firm of cattle and beef dealers" whose "extensive business . . . built up in four years . . . shows unmistakably the character of the men at the helm." Swift kept his distance from reporters, so several years would pass before they knew that G. F. Swift was at the helm or that the G. stood for Gustavus rather than George. Reporters were still confused in 1881, but Swift's Cape Cod family knew that "Stave's Wild West scheme" was a reality.[23]

Although Swift and Hammond shipped about thirty thousand tons of dressed beef from the Chicago area in 1880, neither had entered the export trade. Experimental shipments in the early 1870s, with frozen boxed beef lashed to an open deck, gave way in 1875 to shipments of chilled carcasses in refrigerator holds. Timothy C. Eastman of New York, who shipped livestock to Britain, persuaded the Anchor Line and White Star Line to build ice chests between decks and install a fan to keep the cool air circulating. Eastman sent his first large shipment in the fall of 1875, and other dealers entered the trade as soon as they learned that the beef arrived in excellent condition and commanded a high price. John Leng sailed on a White Star ship with one of these coolers. It was, he wrote, "a huge meat safe . . . coated all round with zinc, and the meat is hung . . . from hooks; a small steam engine above works a fan which causes a continual circulation of fresh air." Improvements in the steamship coolers and construction of cold-storage warehouses at American and British docks permitted the trade to expand. Less than fifty tons of fresh beef had been shipped in 1874, but forty-two thousand tons of dressed beef left New York, Philadelphia, and Boston in refrigerator holds during 1880.[24]

British livestock producers and meat dealers cried out against this American invasion. Imported dressed beef was called "dead meat" and compared unfavorably to time-honored English roast beef. The primary purpose of James MacDonald's 1877 trip to America was to investigate and report to *The Scotsman* on "dead meat from the Far West." That same year *Punch* reflected national concern with a cartoon showing a British butcher tossed high in the air by a longhorned Texas steer. In the meat capital of the "Far West," however, the mood was just the opposite. Jubilant over advances in meat canning and the dressed beef trade, a Chicago editor remarked, "The barrel has seen its best days." The future belongs to dressed beef: "There are few branches of American business enterprise that at this moment have so prosperous an outlook. . . . The stock-raisers, the drovers, those who prepare the cattle for the refrigerators, the transportation lines, as well as the ocean steamers, are all parties in interest."[25]

Since the combined value of dressed and canned beef at the end of the decade was less than one-tenth the value of pork, ham, bacon, and lard, the pork packers were annoyed at the publicity lavished on canners and "slaughterers," as they condescendingly referred to the dressed beef men. Throughout the decade, Chicago pork packers had been opening new markets in the South and aggressively pushing their products in Europe. Some stationed sales agents in England, France, and Germany, while others established branch houses to distribute their brands. The newspapers ignored these mercantile feats, but in 1878, during the presidency of Nathaniel K. Fairbank, the Chicago Board of Trade tried to placate the pork packers. It publicized the fact that pork packers operated summer as well as winter and said their export trade was growing at the rate of 40 percent annually, faster than any other industry in Chicago. The pork packers' "immense business," noted the Board of Trade "is but little seen or its extent appreciated by most of the people of the city, save by the occasional aroma which floats on the southern breeze."[26]

Nonetheless, the touchy pork packers nursed several grievances against the Board of Trade. Some of them bypassed the board's inspection system because fees were too high or because the board refused to certify summer pork prepared under refrigeration. In the rush to join the export trade, a few packers cut corners and avoided inspection because they knew they were marketing an inferior product. In 1878 the board reduced inspection fees and agreed to stamp "Regular" on all pork products that passed inspection regardless of when they had been prepared. However, the board required written inspection reports and placed a chief inspector in charge of warehouse receipts on beef and hog products. The old system, remarked the *Tribune,* was "chiefly remarkable" for what it "did not prohibit." The new regulations should force the packers to return to "a 'squarecut.'" Unfortunately, some improperly cured hams caused a furor in Belgium early in 1879, and the board blamed the commission firm rather than the packer and inspector. This controversy blinded everyone to a far more ominous development: the Italian government in February, 1879, banned all American hog products except lard. A European exclusion movement was underway.[27]

Despite the sluggish national economy in the 1870s, the packing industry like the livestock trade experienced steady growth. Demographic changes helped create new markets for packinghouse products, but the packers took steps to modernize their operation. Relocating their plants in the Town of Lake close by the Stockyards was an important change. Widespread use of hoists, overhead rails, hog-scraping machines, and new drying equipment increased plant efficiency. The development of margarine, canned meats, and an improved quality of lard augmented packinghouse products and profits. Refrigeration enabled many pork houses to operate year-round, and it tempted Gustavus Swift to find a practical way of shipping chilled, fresh beef to eastern urban markets. By 1880, Chicago's forward-looking packing industry accounted for one-third of the city's total value of manufactured goods.[28] There were two by-products of packinghouse progress in the 1870s that came as a surprise to these industrialists. Some of their employes demanded recognition (Chapter 7), and municipal authorities finally cracked down on polluters (Chapter 8).

NOTES

1. David Macrae, *The Americans at Home,* 2 vols. (Edinburgh, 1870), 1:xviii.

2. Board of Trade, *Annual Report, 1880,* 35–36; City of Chicago, *Health*

Ordinances and Sanitary Regulations of the City of Chicago, 1874 (Chicago, 1874), 6, 23, 24; *Wing's Illustrated Travellers' and Visitors' Hand-Book to the City of Chicago* (Chicago, 1874), 118, 120; *Trib.*, Dec. 13, 1871; Jan. 24, Feb. 6, 1875; Feb. 10, 1884; *Times*, Oct. 13, 1872.

3. Greeley, Carlson and Company, *Atlas of the Town of Lake* (Chicago, 1883), 5, 7; Mary Oona Marquardt, "Sources of Capital of Early Illinois Manufacturers, 1840–1880" (Ph.D. diss., University of Illinois, 1960), 441; [Frank Gilbert], *A History of the City of Chicago, Its Men and Institutions* (Chicago, 1900), 200–201; Alfred T. Andreas, *History of Cook County, Illinois* (Chicago, 1884), 670–71; *The Biographical Dictionary and Portrait Gallery of Representative Men of Chicago* (Chicago, 1892), 52, 55–56; *Times*, Jan. 1, 1880; *Trib.*, Sept. 8, 1872; Mar. 17, Aug. 10, 1879; Nov. 19, 1881; *Sun*, Oct. 19, 1889; July 10, 11, 1893.

4. "Sixtieth Anniversary Number," *Armour Magazine*, 16 (Apr., 1927), 7; Cora Lillian Davenport, "The Rise of the Armours, an American Industrial Family" (M.A. thesis, University of Chicago, 1930), 40–54; Board of Trade, *Annual Report, 1872*, 168; *1873*, 48; *Trib.*, Sept. 8, 1872; *Land-Owner*, 5 (Dec., 1873), 200–201; Harper Leech and John Charles Carroll, *Armour and His Times* (New York, 1938), 39.

5. Marquardt, "Sources of Capital," 326, 448–50; John Joseph Flinn, *The Hand-Book of Chicago Biography* (Chicago, 1893), 117; Charles Ffrench, ed., *Biographical History of the American Irish in Chicago* (Chicago, 1897), 176–81, 192–98; William Terence Kane, *The Education of Edward Cudahy* (Chicago, 1941), chaps. 1–3; *Trib.*, Nov. 27, 1910.

6. *Times*, Jan. 1, 1880; *Trib.*, Jan. 26, Mar. 12, 1879; *Armour Magazine*, 16 (Apr., 1927), 7, 32; "Developing Packinghouse By-Products," *Nat. Prov.*, 52 (Jan. 23, 1915), 41; Marquardt, "Sources of Capital," 329–30; Federal Trade Commission, *Report on the Meat-Packing Industry, 1919* (Washington, 1919), part Five, 21; Board of Trade, *Annual Report, 1880*, 36; Margaret Walsh, "From Pork Merchant to Meat Packer: The Midwestern Meat Industry in the Mid-Nineteenth Century," *Agricultural History*, 56 (Jan., 1982), 136–37.

7. Andreas, *Cook County*, 672, 673, 683, 687; *New World*, 3 (Nov. 3, 1894), n.p.; *Sun*, Oct. 19, 1889; Oscar Mayer and Company, *Link*, 4 (Sept.–Oct. 1963), 2–11; Joel A. Tarr, *A Study in Boss Politics: William Lorrimer of Chicago* (Urbana, Ill., 1971), 8.

8. "The Stock-Yards," *Trib.*, Dec. 23, 1875; David H. Mason, "The Chicago of the Manufacturer," *Lakeside Monthly*, 10 (Oct., 1873), 318; *Ninth Census, 1870*, vol. 3, "Industry and Wealth," 649; *Tenth Census, 1880*, vol. 2, "Manufactures," 393.

9. Pork Packers' Association of Chicago, *Annual Report of the Packing of the West* (Chicago, 1876), 7–8; Macrae, *Americans at Home*, 2:194;

Walter Gore Marshall, *Through America: Nine Months in the United States* (London, 1882), 91.

10. Arthur Cushman, "The Packing Plant and Its Equipment," in *The Packing Industry* (Chicago, 1923), 108–9; *Drovers Journal,* Feb. 22, 1886; Siegfried Giedion, *Mechanization Takes Command* (New York, 1948), 238–39.

11. "Developing Packinghouse By-Products," *Nat. Prov.,* 52 (Jan. 23, 1915), 17, 41; *Times,* Oct. 13, 1872; *Trib.,* Aug. 20, 1876; Rudolf A. Clemen, *The American Livestock and Meat Industry* (New York, 1923), 357–58, 364–65; National Provisioner, *The "Significant Sixty": A Historical Report on the Progress and Development of the Meat Packing Industry, 1891–1951* (Chicago, 1952), 318.

12. Katharine Snodgrass, *Margarine as a Butter Substitute* (Palo Alto, Calif., 1930), 125–33; Clemen, *Livestock and Meat Industry,* 358–60; *Trib.,* Aug. 20, 1876; Feb. 21, 1877; *Tenth Census,* vol. 2, "Manufactures," 393; David Ward Wood, ed., *Chicago and Its Distinguished Citizens, or the Progress of Forty Years* (Chicago, 1881), 157–58; *Laws of the State of Illinois, 1879* (Springfield, 1879), 116–17.

13. James H. Collins, *The Story of Canned Foods* (New York, 1924), chaps. 1–3; Richard J. Hooker, *Food and Drink in America: A History* (Indianapolis, 1981), 214–15; Daniel J. Boorstin, *The Americans: The Democratic Experience* (New York, 1973), chap. 35; *Nat. Prov.,* 24 (Jan. 5, 1901), 15–16; *Trib.,* Apr. 2, 1882; *Drovers Journal,* Nov. 28, 1885; Louisa Libby Burrows, comp., *Arthur Albion Libby* (n.p., [1953]), 8; *Frank Leslie's Illustrated Newspaper,* Oct. 12, 1878; Giedion, *Mechanization Takes Command,* 224–25.

14. Burrows, *Arthur Albion Libby,* 7–11; Department of Agriculture, Bureau of Animal Industry, *First Annual Report, 1884* (Washington, 1885), 262–63; *Trib.,* Feb. 5, 1878; Jan. 1, 1880; Feb. 10, 1884; *Times,* Oct. 13, 1872; *The International Provision Trade Directory, 1879* (Philadelphia, 1879), 265; *Tenth Census, 1880,* vol. 3, "Productions of Agriculture," 1109–10.

15. Susan Strasser, *Never Done: A History of American Housework* (New York, 1982), 22–23; Hooker, *Food and Drink,* 242, 220.

16. Oscar E. Anderson, Jr., *Refrigeration in America: A History of a New Technology and Its Impact* (Princeton, N.J., 1953), 26–36, 45–47; J. F. Nickerson, "The Development of Refrigeration in the United States," *Ice and Refrigeration,* 49 (Oct., 1915), 170–75; Edward A. Duddy, *The Cold Storage Industry in the United States* (Chicago, 1929), 6; Andrew J. Chase, *Lyman's Patent Pure, Dry, Cold Air Refrigerator and Conservatory* (Boston, 1873), 1–20.

17. *Griffiths Annual Review of the Live Stock Trade at Chicago, 1870*

(Chicago, 1871), 30, 41; Cushman, "Packing Plant and Its Equipment," 107–8; Anderson, *Refrigeration in America,* 53–56; *Trib.,* Mar. 10, 1877, Jan. 1, 1878; Jan. 21, 1881.

18. *Griffiths Annual Review of the Live Stock Trade at Chicago, 1877* (Chicago, 1878), 96; *Trib.,* Jan. 1, 1878; Board of Trade, *Annual Report, 1871,* "Supplementary," 146; Pork Packers' Association, *Report of the Packing of the West,* 20; Board of Trade, *Annual Report, 1880,* 36, 34; Margaret Walsh, *The Rise of the Midwestern Meat Packing Industry* (Lexington, Ky., 1982), 85, 92.

19. Board of Trade, *Annual Report, 1880,* 35.

20. F. C. Holder, Memorandum, 1941 (Swift and Company Archives, Chicago); Thomas W. Goodspeed, "Gustavus Franklin Swift, 1839–1903," *University [of Chicago] Record,* 7 (Apr., 1921), 100; Louis F. Swift and Arthur Van Vlissingen, *The Yankee of the Yards: The Biography of Gustavus Franklin Swift* (Chicago, 1927), 178–80, 85–86; Louis Unfer, "Swift and Company: The Development of the Packing Industry, 1875 to 1912" (Ph.D. diss., University of Illinois, 1951), 24–33, 53–54; BAI, *First Annual Report, 1884,* 265–67.

21. Swift and Vlissingen, *Yankee of the Yards,* 25, 188–89, 197–99; Unfer, *Swift and Company,* 55, 33–35; Anderson, *Refrigeration in America,* 49–52; Federal Trade Commission, *Food Investigation: Report . . . on Private Car Lines, 1919* (Washington, 1920), 25–29, 37–38.

22. *Nat. Prov.,* 39 (Nov. 7, 1908), 19; Unfer, *Swift and Company,* 36–46; Swift and Vlissingen, *Yankee of the Yards,* 184–85; Clemen, *Livestock and Meat Industry,* 233–36; Mary Yeager, *Competition and Regulation: The Development of Oligopoly in the Meat Packing Industry* (Greenwich, Conn., 1981), 59–61.

23. Swift and Vlissingen, *Yankee of the Yards,* 190, 199; Andreas, *Cook County,* 675; *Trib.,* Nov. 19, 1881; Goodspeed, "Swift," 110.

24. Albert S. Bolles, *Industrial History of the United States . . . Being a Complete Survey of American Industries* (Norwich, Conn., 1881), 122–24; Anderson, *Refrigeration in America,* 60–61; James T. Critchell and Joseph Raymond, *A History of the Frozen Meat Trade* (London, 1912), 164, 190–91, 246; John Leng, *America in 1876* (Dundee, 1877), 13–14; *Tenth Census, 1880,* vol. 3, "Productions of Agriculture," 1110; Richard Perren, "The North American Beef and Cattle Trade of Great Britain," *Economic History Review,* 20 (Aug., 1971), 430–35.

25. "Where the Beef Comes From," *Lippincott's Magazine,* 24 (Nov., 1879), 73–79; James MacDonald, *Food from the Far West, or American Agriculture with Special Reference to the Beef Production and Importation of Dead Meat from America to Great Britain* (London, 1878) vii; Yeager, *Competition and Regulation,* 55–57; *Punch,* 71 (Mar. 10, 1877), 103; *Trib.,* Jan. 1, 1878.

26. *Trib.*, Jan. 1, 1878; Jan. 1, 1879; Board of Trade, *Annual Report, 1878*, 15–16; *1879*, 32.
27. Charles Henry Taylor, ed., *History of the Board of Trade of the City of Chicago*, 3 vols. (Chicago, 1917), 1:551; Board of Trade, *Annual Report, 1878*, 16, 20–21; *International Provision Trade Directory, 1879*, 99–101; Board of Trade, *Act of Incorporation, Rules, By-Laws and Inspection Regulations . . . in Force Apr. 3, 1880*, 74–76; *Trib.*, Jan. 1, Mar. 13, 1879.
28. *Tenth Census, 1880*, vol. 2, "Manufactures," 391, 393.

CHAPTER 7

"The Union Is a New Thing"

Although Chicago area packers and their employes escaped the hardships of the 1870s depression, packinghouse workers were sensitive to the travails of other wage earners. They turned out to support striking railroad employes in 1877 and a small delegation even asked packers for a wage increase at that time. However, it was not until the country began to pull out of the depression and the cost of living rose sharply in 1879 that the packinghouse workers took concerted action on their own behalf. The immediate impetus was the desire of pork house knifemen to share the winter wage increase customarily granted only to the most highly skilled. Realizing that they needed the cooperation of laborers, union officials promised that their organization would defend unskilled as well as skilled workers. Large numbers signed up, and the Butchers' and Packing-House Men's Protective Union and Benevolent Association won a wage increase without a fight. Its subsequent demand for a closed shop met vehement opposition from the large packers. Strikers forced the plants to close for a short time in December, 1879, but they won no concessions and their organization soon disintegrated. Henry Botsford, owner of a small pork house, was ambivalent about the large packers' strategy and keenly aware that half of his employes joined the strike while the others were staunchly anti-union. Botsford inadvertently spoke for all the participants when he said, "The Union is a new thing for us, and we don't know how to treat it."[1]

Chicago Workers in the 1870s

Trapped in a prolonged depression, the country celebrated its one hundredth birthday with deep forboding. Bank failures and money shortages during the 1873 panic soon led to factory and business closings and fear that the American economy "will soon collapse under the dead weight of the paralysis." Since only four states collected labor statistics, historians cannot speak with precision about wage cuts or unemployment. It appears that skilled workers lost one-third of their predepression wages and unskilled workers one-half. Plausible estimates of the number of jobless adults in 1878 range from five hundred thousand to two million. The picture in Illinois and Chicago is blurred because the state did not establish a Bureau of Labor Statistics until 1879 when recovery was underway and Chicago factory inspection started in 1880. The newspapers make it clear, however, that construction workers who had come to rebuild Chicago after the fire were the first to find themselves stranded. Then the lumber- and brickyards felt the slowdown, and in time the South Branch industrial district and even the McCormick Reaper Works had to cut production, wages, and jobs. Some of the victims asked the state to become the employer of last resort, while others demanded immediate distribution of Relief and Aid Society funds to tide them over. The *Times* responded that government "owed" no one a job; workers should "economize . . . and make every available preparation for such hard times as may be before us."[2]

Worker opposition to wage cuts was sporadic and ineffective in Chicago. Railroad mechanics and repair crews on the two major lines leading east accepted a 10 percent cut in 1873 without comment. Coopers asked for more pay when they worked over ten hours but in the end settled for lower wages. Iron molders in Bridgeport objected to a cut in 1877 but reconsidered when employers locked them out. Recurrent strikes in the brickyards, lumberyards, and furniture and box factories accomplished little. Immigrant lumber shovers lost a bitter, bloody contest in 1876. One newspaper dismissed them as men but "not reasoning creatures," while another noted that one of the strikers had committed suicide for no reason "except despondency, caused by poverty." Strikers lost their jobs to the unemployed, and strike leaders usually found themselves blacklisted.[3]

Trade unions waged an uphill battle in the depression decade. Those in Illinois had to contend with an 1863 law, amended in 1873, which prohibited individuals and combinations of persons from interfering with the right to work and the right to manage one's own property. Although trade union participation declined, the typographers, iron molders, machinists and blacksmiths, tailors, and Brotherhood of Locomotive Engineers were still intact at the end of the decade, and the Seamen's Protective and Benevolent Union (1869) actually increased its membership. Moreover, Chicago carpenters, cigarmakers, coopers, brickmakers, and locomotive firemen established new organizations, and a new central body, the Council of Trade and Labor Unions, took shape in December, 1877. Buffeted by labor politics and conservative criticism, the council nonetheless played a major role in securing the Illinois Bureau of Labor Statistics and factory and tenement inspection in Chicago. Internal quarrels created a rift in 1880 between the craft unions and the socialists, but the breach was healed and the central body survived as the Trades and Labor Assembly.[4]

The prolonged depression played into the hands of labor radicals. Immigrant German socialists usually established contact with the International Workingmen's Association, headquartered in New York City after 1872. The Workingmen's party of the United States (renamed the Socialist Labor party in 1877) was a good deal more successful at winning recruits for socialist trade unionism and political action. In Chicago, German socialists dominated the tiny radical movement before the Panic of 1873, but the Workingmen's party had a solid base by the end of the 1870s, thanks to the contributions of three newcomers. Native-born Albert R. Parsons was a typesetter at the *Times* and an active member of the typographical union when he joined the socialists in 1876. Blacklisted by employers because of his radicalism, he became a full-time organizer in the late 1870s. Thomas J. Morgan, born in an Irish slum in Birmingham, England, was a machinist when he arrived in Chicago in 1869. Laid off his job in 1873, he organized other machinists and blacksmiths and converted to socialism. George A. Schilling, German-born but raised in Ohio, settled in Chicago in 1875, secured a job as a cooper, and quickly organized his fellow craftsmen. Fluent in English and German, Schilling was an effective salesman for socialism. Parsons, Morgan, and Schilling were leaders in their respective unions, active in the Council of Trade and Labor Unions, and members of the Workingmen's party.[5]

Unnoticed at the time but destined to influence the labor movement during the 1880s was the Noble Order of the Knights of Labor. Founded in Philadelphia in 1869 as a secret labor organization, it grew slowly until the railroad riots of 1877. One of its recruits during the depression years was Terence Powderly, son of Irish immigrants, member of the machinists and blacksmiths union, and jobless at the time he joined in 1874. Powderly eventually found employment in Scranton and time to organize new Knights of Labor locals and win election as mayor of Scranton in 1878 on the Greenback-Labor ticket. He also helped arrange the Knights' first two national conventions—in Reading, Pennsylvania, in 1878 and St. Louis the following year. At the latter convention Powderly was elected second-in-command of the order. He persuaded delegates to publicize the name of the order and drop secret initiation rituals to appease the Catholic Church. Members' names, however, remained secret to protect them against blacklisting and dismissal. By 1879 the Knights had approximately twenty thousand members, most of them living in Pennsylvania and other eastern states.[6]

Chicago's first local assembly was formed in August, 1877, by Richard Griffiths, a Welsh seaman and displaced Massachusetts shoemaker who had been in Chicago since the late 1860s. He was running a small tobacco and newspaper shop at the time and turned one room of his second-floor apartment into the Chicago headquarters of the Noble Order. By the close of 1878 he had enough locals to create District Assembly No. 24. Both Parsons and Schilling joined the new labor organization, drawn by its promise to unite skilled and unskilled workers in one harmonious brotherhood. Griffiths arranged for the Knights to hold their third convention in Chicago in September, 1879, and he would have accepted the top job. The delegates elected Powderly because he was younger, a Catholic, and much better known among the easterners. Chicago reporters knew the name of the new labor organization but little else. One speculated that the "secret society" had "swallowed" trade unionists, socialists, and those "Pennsylvania Mollie Maguires not yet hung."[7]

Despite this evidence of interest in labor organizing, Chicago workers' major response to the depression was a spontaneous riot in 1877 that had little to do with trade unions, socialists, or Knights of Labor. A protest against wage cuts by Baltimore and Ohio employes on July 18 quickly led to trouble at the Baltimore armory and an angry confrontation between federal troops and strikers and their sympathizers in Pittsburgh. When rioting spread to Buffalo, the eastern trunk lines closed down, and Chicago braced for trouble by stationing the Illinois militia in the city armories. On July 24 Michigan Central and Illinois Central switchmen asked in vain for restoration of wages which had been cut earlier and then walked off their jobs. Baltimore and Ohio workers joined them. In small, orderly bands, the strikers visited other railroad freight yards and carshops, asking employes to join the strike. By Wednesday, July 25, all of Chicago's freight traffic had come to a halt, and many employers, including those in the Packers' Addition, had closed their plants and sent workers home.[8]

Meantime, gangs of teenaged boys and unemployed men roamed the South Branch and the business district, forcing factories and stores to close. At Twenty-second Street, they pillaged shops and stopped the horsecars. Another gang, armed with stones, fence pickets, and revolvers, marched out Blue Island Avenue toward the McCormick Reaper Works. Reinforced by Bridgeport workers brandishing shillelaghs, this group numbered about nine hundred when it reached its destination. Armed guards at the Reaper Works called the police, and a fierce battle left many injured. Militia units arrived to guard the plant and the approach on Blue Island. That evening police used revolvers to drive a gang away from the Burlington roundhouse at Sixteenth and Halsted. Out at the Stockyards, packinghouse workers prevented Armour and Company from resuming operations and secured written pledges from some plant managers that laborers would be paid $2 a day "and butchers in proportion" for the next eighteen months. In the city, hundreds of citizens enlisted at City Hall as special police, and armed members of the Board of Trade offered their services to the mayor. Chicagoans not occupied with civil defense turned out to cheer the arrival of two companies of federal troops.[9]

The worst disorders occurred on Thursday, July 26. Throughout most of that day a huge crowd of men, women, and children battled police and militia on Halsted between Sixteenth Street and Archer Avenue. Several thousand gathered at the Halsted viaduct over the Chicago, Burlington and Quincy yards. Some wanted revenge against the police because of the McCormick Reaper Works battle; others were extending a long night of pillaging and drinking; still others turned up because they were infuriated by the appearance of federal troops in Chicago. About one-fifth of the demonstrators were women, "excessively abusive" and often armed with rocks, "pans of mud," and pistols. The police forced rioters to scatter into familiar alleys, back yards, and open lots, but they soon regrouped elsewhere on Halsted. Persistent rumors that "a mob from the Stock Yards and Bridgeport" was on the way caused the police to call for the militia and cavalry units. By mid-afternoon there were 750 law-enforcement officials on Halsted between Maxwell and Eighteenth streets.

Hearing about the disorders along Halsted, packinghouse workers gathered that morning at the Stockyards, armed with wooden gambrels and butcher knives. They walked north on Halsted, picked up lumber workers at Archer Avenue, and numbered about five hundred by the time they reached Sixteenth Street. They were no match for mounted police eager to use clubs and sometimes revolvers to subdue the "Bridgeport bruisers" and "Stock-Yards bull whackers." Reporters estimated 20 to 30 deaths, 150 injuries, and more than 300 arrests. That night militia guarded the scene of the battle and the Transit House, while special policemen patrolled the Stockyards and packing plants. Police had taken the men under arrest to the Twelfth Street station where a hostile, jeering crowd gathered. Unnerved by this opposition and thinking that a subversive meeting was being held nearby in the Bohemian Turner Hall, police barged into a peaceful cabinetmakers' discussion of hours and wages in their trade. They tossed some of the startled trade unionists down the stairs, clubbed or shot others, and killed one. Reporters accepted without question the police version of this final act of violence that long tense day: they were quelling a "communistic" cabal composed of "the lowest class of Poles and Bohemians." Fortunately, July 26 was the turning point. Militia and police cavalry watched the "infected areas" for several more days, but trains arrived without incident, not "a solitary blow" was struck on the twenty-eighth, and Bridgeport was "as quiet as the prairie." The only thing out of the ordinary was the large number of funeral processions along Archer and Halsted.[10]

Stunned by the sudden wave of violence which swept across the country from Baltimore to San Francisco, conservatives clamored for more effective law enforcement. Chicago businessmen asked for more police, militia, and armories, while the Board of Trade petitioned Congress to enlarge the army. Most employers agreed with these measures, resented workers' wage demands, and were determined to make clear "who is running their houses, the mob or themselves." They agreed with Allan Pinkerton, founder of Chicago's famous detective agency, that "vicious and unruly" characters from that "infamous locality . . . 'Bridgeport'" were at the root of the trouble. Yet when "Buck" McCarthy was mistakenly identified as a rioter, Nelson Morris, Samuel Allerton, and John Sherman testified that he had done "all in his power to allay the turbulent spirit of the mob" and deserved thanks. Louis Wahl and Benjamin Peters Hutchinson, convinced that persistent unemployment had caused the outburst, put up their own money to hire the jobless as street cleaners.[11]

Wage-earner reactions to the violence were as varied as those of employers. Socialists thought the "great railroad strike of 1877 secured us the public ear." Their Cook County ticket drew eight thousand votes in the fall, and the following spring socialists elected their first alderman and Parsons launched the first English-language newspaper, *Socialist*. It probably helped mayoral candidate Dr. Ernst Schmidt collect twelve thousand votes, but that was the high point. Internal quarreling and the return of prosperity stymied the radical movement and voters put the socialists "on the shelf" in November, 1880. This still left the vast majority of Chicago workers deeply troubled about the use of Pinkerton guards, militia, federal troops, and armed policemen against strikers. The Bohemian trade unionists filed charges of police brutality and were pleased by a court ruling that the attack was an indefensible act of "criminal riot." The only penalties, however, were six-cent fines for two police officers. Fearful and resentful of the police, foreign-born workers took a much greater interest in their quasi-social, quasi-military organizations—Lehr and Wehr Verein, Bohemian Sharpshooters, Hibernian Rifles, and Fifth Ward Irish Labor Guards. With increasing frequency, these uniformed drill corps appeared at labor meetings, picnics, church dedications, and holiday parades. But conservatives had the final word. An 1879 state law prohibited these ethnic groups from displaying their bayonets unless licensed by the governor.[12]

The Packinghouse Employes' Situation

In the aftermath of the railroad disorders, packinghouse workers shared the wholesale condemnation heaped upon strikers by nervous conservatives. They were "pig-stickers" and "bull-whackers" to *Tribune* reporters; "ignorant" men drawn to one of Chicago's "grosser industries," according to Allan Pinkerton. Traveler C. B. Berry picked up the same view: "men employed in the slaughter-houses are the most noted rough, or, as the Chicago people say, 'the hardest characters', in the city; and no respectable person goes near the Stock Yards after dark if he can help it." This, of course, was nonsense. A *Times* reporter described the packinghouse workers asking for wage increases on July 25, 1877, as eminently "respectable" men who wished it "distinctly understood that they were not ordinary railroad or city strikers."[13]

Wages and working conditions did, in fact, set packinghouse employes apart from "ordinary" workers. Their industry was expanding rapidly, the plants in Town of Lake needed "new hands," and there were unusual promotion opportunities for "old hands." Refrigeration in the pork houses reduced seasonal employment, a serious problem for packinghouse workers prior to the 1870s and for many other workers during that decade. The development of dressed beef at the end of the '70s created many new jobs for skilled cattle butchers and hide strippers. All workers received relatively good wages, and they were paid in cash on a regular schedule. Whereas trade unionists estimated that skilled wages in Chicago declined by 50 percent between 1873 and 1878, packinghouse wages remained stationary. A butchers' organization in Bridgeport tried to recruit employes at the Turner and the Reid and Sherwin plants in 1873, but police turned the organizers away and that fledgling association disappeared, and nothing more was heard from the delegation asking for wage increases in July, 1877.[14]

According to the 1880 census, the average annual wage of employes in slaughtering and meat-packing was $454, approximately the same as foundry and machine-shop workers. Employes in agricultural equipment factories and those in printing and publishing averaged about $550. Earning less than the packinghouse employes were copper and sheet-iron workers, cigarmakers, boot and shoe workers, distillery and brewery employes, and lumber and clothing workers. More precise, however, was the *Tribune*'s survey of the Chicago labor market in October, 1878. Coopers earned from $2 to $3 per day; brickmasons from $1.75 to $2.25; mechanics from $2 to $7. The range for unskilled laborers was $1 to $2 per day. At the packing plants, common laborers were paid $1.50 to $2, and skilled workers $3.50 to $4 per day; during the winter months packers customarily increased skilled wages by 25¢. In between the laborers and skilled butchers were gutters, choppers, scrapers, and trimmers whose pay varied from $2.25 to $3.50 per day. When pressed to increase packinghouse wages in 1879, one packer responded, "We pay our men better wages than are given to any other class of workmen." This was not true, but packinghouse workers were relatively well paid. An 1879 Illinois legislative committee investigating wages and working conditions toured the plants at the Stockyards, and although critical of many Chicago trades, its report made no mention of the packinghouses. Presumably they passed muster.[15]

Detailed information about working conditions inside the plants in the

1870s is hard to come by—and sometimes contradictory. Reporters wrote about "stickers" covered with "coagulated blood" and "enveloped in a heavy cloud of steam arising from the flowing blood and the scalding-vat." Steam never obscured the vision of pork plant visitors, and many of them commented on the efficient collection of blood and the cleanliness of the slaughtering operation. There was no disagreement about the speed and skill of the men wielding the knives; their performances were marvelous, fabulous, amazing. Nor was there disagreement about the presence of young boys herding animals, picking up scraps at the cutting benches, running errands in the Exchange and the Transit House. James MacDonald saw some girls, age unspecified, working at the Libby, McNeill and Libby canning factory. Of the 5,673 children under sixteen working in Chicago in 1880, only 298 of them were employed in packing plants. Contemporaries noted but did not pass judgment upon the employment of youth because it was not illegal and nearly all adults had started working before the age of sixteen.[16]

In the absence of statistics on industrial accidents, it is impossible to say how packinghouse workers fared compared to others. Judging from Chicago newspaper accounts, they faced fewer hazards than railroad workers or those employed in iron and steel mills and the small machine and tooi shops. Yet there were serious accidents, some of them due to defective machinery or plant structure. The owner of the former Kent house on the South Branch installed a steam-hoist on the third floor. In 1878 that entire floor gave way and catapulted men and machinery onto the second floor, killing one worker and injuring many others. A boiler explosion in the Wahls' glue factory claimed the lives of three men. When a rendering tank exploded at Schoenemanns' in 1873 it killed three employes and a twelve-year-old boy, who had been sent by his mother to beg for a heart or liver. Other accidents may have been the result of carelessness by workers or perhaps excessive holiday drinking. On the day before Christmas, 1879, Fred Prill caught his left hand in the guarded rollers feeding the sausage machine at Schoenemanns' plant. His arm was drawn in and so severely crushed that it had to be amputated. Just after New Year's someone on the third floor of the Anglo-American plant shoved an empty tierce into the elevator shaft, and it crushed the skull of a worker loading the open cage. John White, a laborer who was employed at hauling offal in wheelbarrows to the rendering tanks, was found "boiled almost to jelly in one of the large vats." The coroner ruled that "the deceased came to his death by accidentally falling into the vat."[17]

Neither plant safety nor working conditions served as catalysts for the first packinghouse workers' strike. It was, rather, the rising cost of living that accompanied economic recovery and the desire of all employes, not just the most highly skilled, to receive the winter wage increase. The packers were sole arbiters of wages, and they paid their "hands" according to "worth" or skill. Only the men who slit the hog throats and sectioned the carcasses and those who cleaved beef carcasses and removed hides were granted the 25¢ daily winter bonus. Other knifemen felt that they were equally essential to the smooth operation of the packinghouses, and they wanted the same financial recognition. Publicity about the prosperity of the Chicago packing industry convinced them that their employers could afford it. There was uncertainty, however, about how to proceed.

An Experimental Strike

The first attempt was a direct request by gutters and scrapers in three Town of Lake pork plants for the 25¢ increase in December, 1878. Although the hog scrapers must have been worried about the new hog-scraping machine, they did not mention job security. Higgins, Murphy, and the Chicago Packing and Provision Company refused to raise their wages from $2.75 to $3 per day, and about two hundred men walked off their jobs, forcing another one thousand hands into idleness. A dozen or so Armour employes joined them and were promptly fired. Before the three other packers could follow suit, the protestors went back to work and withdrew their wage demands. However, they continued to meet informally in December and January and to invite others to join their Butchers' Protective and Benevolent Association. Daniel O'Connell, a skilfull "old hand" on the trimming bench at Chicago Packing and Provision Company, emerged as the leader and the one who turned the ad hoc organization into a trade union. To widen its appeal and attract unskilled workers, O'Connell changed the name to Butchers' and Packing-House Men's Protective Union and Benevolent Association and promised $6 per week to sick or disabled members plus burial costs and a benefit fund to help dependents. Members had to be male, eighteen years or older, packinghouse employes, and free of taint as drunkards, politicians, or office-seekers. The initiation fee was $1 and monthly dues 25¢. When hog prices fell and living costs soared, O'Connell decided that the customary November increase would not be enough. The packers should give skilled workers 50¢ and all others 25¢. By the fall of 1879 enthusiastic crowds attended weekly meetings at a Fifth Ward saloon and trade union hall near the Stockyards. "As near as can be learned," said a reporter, the association wants "to fix the wages of every class of employes" so that "every man shall receive what he is worth."[18]

When the packers followed their usual procedure on November 1,

O'Connell called a mass rally to seek approval for the same 25¢ increase for *all* packinghouse workers and a strike against those employers refusing to comply by November 5. A "Union Butcher" justified the decisions for *Tribune* readers: "Our labor has made capital for the packers; has enabled them to build monster packing houses . . . ; has enabled their wives and children to roll in luxuries while [ours often go] in tatters and rags. . . . When their profits increase, why not increase our wages?" Philip Armour told a reporter that he would be "more than willing" to have a strike, but when the pork packers met they quickly decided to grant the union demand by the November 5 deadline. The larger houses, however, announced a cutback in production and some small plants said they would close down for a time.[19]

The packers could easily afford the winter wage increase, but they were deeply concerned about rumors that O'Connell would soon ask for a union shop. It was known that the butchers' organization had secured a promise from Richard Powers's seamen's union to support a packinghouse strike. Twenty pork packers jointly resolved to defend their "right to hire or discharge . . . without regard to any Union or Association." O'Connell backed off, assuring the employers that his members would settle for the wage increase, and they held a big celebration at the Church of the Nativity. But Hutchinson of Chicago Packing and Provision Company was disgruntled about the packers' surrender. The union "must not think we have put energy, experience, and capital into building up a big business to be rode over by any mushroom crowd." The next week he closed the Irish-cut ham and bacon bench, thereby eliminating O'Connell's job. Hutchinson feigned innocence: "We employ about 1,000 men, and it is utterly impossible for us to know anything about them personally." The plant manager quietly reversed the decision a few days later, and the "agitator of Packers' Alley" went back to work.[20]

Meantime the union increased its membership to about nine thousand and stashed $5,000 in its treasury. On December 14 officers and members decided that they were strong enough to renew the demand for a closed shop. They posted notices at the plants and informed the managers that union members would refuse to work with nonunion men after December 17. Higgins, Allerton, Tobey and Booth, Jones and Stiles, and Moran and Healy were already union shops and owners did not want a strike, but Armour, Anglo-American, and Chicago Packing and Provision welcomed a showdown. "As long as we are heads of our own houses," blustered Armour, "we shall employ what men we choose, and when we can't, why, we'll nail up our doors—that's all."[21] The three largest pork houses suspended operations until the union withdrew its demand. Chicago newspapers applauded the lockout, the *Staats-Zeitung* saying the strikers' attempts to discharge nonunion men "cannot be tolerated." How could so many men shut themselves out of employment "at good wages in the very middle of winter," asked the *Tribune*, "By what right, human or divine does a clique . . . prevent other workingmen from earning their bread and butter?"[22]

Union officials talked with packers on December 20 but got nothing except free cigars. The Town of Lake was hiring additional policemen to guard the closed plants, and Armour and Anglo-American announced that they would open after Christmas with private armed guards. Interpreting this to mean an invasion of Pinkertons, city and county officials quickly arranged for deputy sheriffs and constables; the militia was ordered to the armories on Christmas Day. Father Joseph Cartan of the Church of the Nativity tried to head off a confrontation by releasing a letter to Daniel O'Connell: "It is my earnest desire that the Union recede from their last position—that is to say, let the packers employ whom they wish. I want this to go on record as my deliberate decision. Public opinion is not in favor of anything else." Although many union members lived in Nativity parish, Cartan's letter did not undermine their determination. Nor did they budge when Armour and Anglo-American reopened on December 26 with nonunion workers and the Fowler brothers claimed to have recruited one thousand men willing to sign a pledge promising "not to join any Union inimical to the interests of . . . the Anglo-American Packing and Provision Company, while in their employment."[23]

Packinghouse strikers and their friends gathered at the Twelfth Street Turner Hall on Sunday, December 28, to protest the presence of the militia in the armories. The Lehr and Wehr Verein and Irish Labor Guard appeared, as well as representatives of the Trades and Labor Council, Seamen's Union, and socialist Workingmen's party. Daniel O'Connell assured the large crowd that packinghouse workers in Milwaukee, St. Louis, Kansas City, and elsewhere were so solidly organized that none would turn up as strikebreakers in Chicago. He also promised strike benefits in lieu of wages, to be financed by a proferred gift of $100,000 from Denis Kearney and West Coast workingmen. Richard Powers vowed the undying support of the seamen, and John McAuliffe of the Workingmen's party won wild applause for comparing the plight of Irish laborers to "the butchers in Anglo-American packing-house, who toiled for a mere pittance so that the hogs of America might be sent to England to fatten the British soldiers, who would be employed in shooting down the Irish farmers." A weary reporter listening to this windy oratory was reminded of equally extravagant packers' claims—we are going to hire "black or white, Christian or Pagan . . . without interference from anybody. . . . We are going to have the men we want . . . if we have to send to China for them." He asked himself, "What can it be in the pork-killing business which so strengthens the imagination of all who engage in it, from the highest to the lowest?"[24]

Despite the platform bravado, dissension was growing in the Butchers' and Packing-House Men's Union. The double name was not enough to bridge the differences between skilled and unskilled once the houses reopened. A formerly well paid "Disaffected Unionist" asked, "Shall we let our families want for the necessaries of life when work, honorable work, is offered us at liberal wages? . . . if we do not resume work soon our places will be filled by strangers." Another man admitted:

> There are a good many causes of jealousy. . . . I'm only a $1.75 man, and we are hearing strange things about . . . paying extravagant sums to expert men who are anxious to go back to work, and are only restrained from so doing by having it made profitable for them to remain idle. . . . We cheap men, who would really form the bone and sinew of the Union if we were only smart enough to combine, cannot get any relief to speak of, while the stickers and gutters and other high-paid workmen are many of them getting their full wages paid them by the Union to hinder their going to work.

Confidence in the union officers eroded as rumors circulated about the large salaries they were drawing from the relief fund. In an interview with the *Drovers Journal* in mid-December, Hutchinson had asked all union members "if they didn't suppose there were chiefs among them who were carrying on the thing to make money." By early January quite a few unionists did think so. A young Irishman who had signed the Anglo-American pledge and returned to work accused Daniel O'Connell of keeping "this thing up just as long as it gives him good wages. This is all he cares for. The moment the Union stops, his salary stops, and he has to go to work again like any of the rest of us."[25]

Union officials tried to devise a compromise with the packers, and when that failed they accused Michael Cudahy of bribing Father Cartan to write O'Connell. Finally, on January 11 they told the remnant of the Butchers' and Packing-House Men's Protective Union and Benevolent Association to try and retrieve their jobs, "a virtual acknowledgement that the Union had met the packers and were theirs," remarked an observer. Of the fifteen hundred former strikers who turned up at the gates of Armour, Anglo-American, and Chicago Packing and Provision Company, only three hundred were hired on Monday, January 12. Yet within a fortnight the others were back, and all of them received 25¢ more per day in wages. The packers needed their skills and therefore looked the other way as the former strikers "persuaded" nonunion workers to depart. Not even Town of Lake and Chicago police on Halsted and Laurel streets and Pinkerton guards at the plant gates could prevent assaults on strikebreakers or threats to cut their hamstrings. A Negro employe of Chicago Packing and Provision Company was surrounded and pelted with chunks of frozen meat until rescued by police. Inside the plants defeated union men brawled with the "obnoxious anti-unionists," stole their knives and cleavers, and engaged in a "favorite sport"—pelting victims with pigs' hearts, lumps of fat, and entrails. The tierce that mysteriously fell down the elevator shaft at Anglo-American on January 2 may not have been an accident.[26]

Although the butchers soon resumed the "old-time lightning rush" on the cutting benches, they resented the "iron-clad" pledges the packers made them sign and watched in dismay as their organization crumbled. Union officials quarreled with the relief committee, and before any funds were accounted for Frank O'Meara absconded with the books and $700. Unskilled members of the union scheduled a meeting with the press in February to air their grievances, but "expert hands" turned up and prevented the "cheap men" from speaking. This was the point at which Michael J. Butler arrived in Town of Lake and took a job at Botsford's pork house. Destined to lead the Knights of Labor movement in the 1880s, Butler would later write to Powderly about the aftermath of the strike: "when i came to Lake or better known as the stock yards there was not a labor organized of any kind here. the Butchers union gone to pieces and that was nothing more than its just Deserts for i believe it was a curse to all concerned."[27]

Thanks to the expansive nature of meat-packing in the 1870s, packinghouse workers fared better than many others. They had steady work at relatively good wages, yet they were not insensitive to the grievances of less fortunate employes or to the intrusion of state militia and federal troops in strikes. Thus, during the 1877 railroad strike, packinghouse workers and Bridgeport wage earners joined in the disorders that wracked Chicago. Two years later, the rising cost of living and determination of all packinghouse "hands" to receive the winter bonus reserved for the highly skilled prompted packinghouse workers to establish their first labor organization. A combination of skilled and unskilled employes, it won the wage increase without opposition, but packers drew the line at recognition and a union shop. During the ensuing strike employers defended their right to hire and fire, and all men returning to work promised to eschew labor organizations. Yet strikers got their jobs back, a wage increase, and tacit permission to get rid of the strikebreakers. In view of this split decision and the disagreements between skilled and unskilled workers, strikers and union officials, large and small packers, even plant owners and managers, the 1879 conflict was a preliminary experiment. The union was a "new thing" for everyone, and no one knew how to treat it.

NOTES

1. *Trib.*, Dec. 16, 1879.

2. Samuel Bernstein, "American Labor in the Long Depression, 1873–1878," *Science and Society*, 20 (Winter, 1956), 59–72, 81–82; John A. Garraty, *The New Commonwealth, 1877–1890* (New York, 1968), 78–79, 128–30; *Bulletin of the American Iron and Steel Association*, 8 (May 14, 1874), 154; Edward C. Kirkland, *Industry Comes of Age: Business, Labor, and Public Policy, 1860–1897* (New York, 1961), chap. 1; Samuel Rezneck, "Distress, Relief and Discontent in the United States during the Depression of 1873–1878," *Journal of Political Economy*, 58 (1950), 494–512; Bessie Louise Pierce, *A History of Chicago*, vol. 3, *The Rise of a Modern City, 1871–1893* (New York, 1957), 241–42; James Brown, *The History of Public Assistance in Chicago, 1833 to 1893* (Chicago, 1941), 118–19; *Times*, Nov. 3, 1873.

3. Pierce, *Chicago*, 3:242–43; Z. E. Jeffreys, "The Attitude of the Chicago Press toward the Local Labor Movement, 1873 to 1879" (M.A. thesis, University of Chicago, 1936), 77–84; Herbert G. Gutman, *Work, Culture, and Society in Industrializing America: Essays in American Working-Class and Social History* (New York, 1977), 72; *Trib.*, Mar. 20, 1877; *Chicago Evening Journal*, May 9, 1876.

4. Earl R. Beckner, *A History of Labor Legislation in Illinois* (Chicago, 1929), 9–10; Pierce, *Chicago*, 3:242–43, 266–67; Illinois Bureau of Labor Statistics, *Fourth Biennial Report, 1886* (Springfield, 1887), 195–96; Norman J. Ware, *The Labor Movement in the United States, 1860–1895* (New York, 1929), 305–10; Charles B. Spahr, *America's Working People* (New York, 1900), 172–73; *Trib.*, Jan. 30, May 7, 1880.

5. William M. Dick, *Labor and Socialism in America: The Gompers Era* (Port Washington, N.Y., 1972), 12–13; *Times*, Feb. 9, 1874; *Trib.*, May 10, 1876; Albert R. Parsons, "The Story of His Life," in [Lucy E. Parsons], *Life of Albert R. Parsons, with Brief History of the Labor Movement in America* (Chicago, 1889), 10–14; Paul Avrich, *The Haymarket Tragedy* (Princeton, N.J., 1984), 21–24; Ralph W. Scharnau, "Thomas J. Morgan and the Chicago Socialist Movement, 1876–1901" (Ph.D. diss., Northern Illinois University, 1969), 1–25; George A. Schilling, "History of the Labor Movement in Chicago," in *Life of Albert R. Parsons*, xiv–xxviii.

6. Vincent Joseph Falzone, "Terence V. Powderly, Mayor and Labor Leader, 1849–1893" (Ph.D. diss., University of Maryland, 1970), 14–54; Terence V. Powderly, *The Path I Trod: The Autobiography of Terence V. Powderly*, ed. H. J. Carman et al. (New York, 1940), 1–61; Terence V. Powderly, *Thirty Years of Labor, 1859 to 1889* (Columbus, Ohio, 1890), 182–237, 628–29; Knights of Labor, *Proceedings of the General Assembly of the Knights of Labor, Reading, Pennsylvania, 1878*, 75, 89.

7. *Journal of United Labor,* 4 (May, 1883), 457–58; [Chicago] *Knights of Labor,* Dec. 23, 1886; Jan. 29, 1887; Falzone, "Powderly," 55–57; Powderly, *Thirty Years of Labor,* 237–40; *Times,* June 20, 1879; *Tribune,* May 11, 1878.

8. Philip Taft, *Organized Labor in American History* (New York, 1964), 76–81; John R. Commons et al., *History of Labour in the United States,* 4 vols. (New York, 1935–36), 2:185–88; Robert V. Bruce, *1877: Year of Violence* (Indianapolis, 1959), chap. 11; John Joseph Flinn, *History of the Chicago Police from the Settlement of the Community to the Present Time* (Chicago, 1887), 163–65; Joseph A. Dacus, *Annals of the Great Strikes in the United States . . . and Riots of 1877* (Chicago, 1877), 310–11; *Trib.,* July 20–25, 1877; *Times,* July 20, 22, 23, 25, 1877; Avrich, *Haymarket Tragedy,* chap. 3.

9. *Trib.,* July 26, 1877; *Chicago Evening Post,* July 26, 1877; *Times,* July 26, 1877; Flinn, *History of the Chicago Police,* 170–71, 179–86; Howard Barton Myers, "The Policing of Labor Disputes in Chicago: A Case Study" (Ph.D. diss., University of Chicago, 1929), 119–32.

10. Flinn, *History of the Chicago Police,* 192–201; Dacus, *Annals of the Great Strikes,* 337–40; Bruce, *1877,* 230–60; *Griffiths Annual Review of the Live Stock Trade at Chicago, 1877* (Chicago, 1878), 55; Richard Schneirov, "Chicago's Great Upheaval of 1877," *Chicago History,* 9 (Spring, 1980), 3–17; Richard C. Marohn, "The Arming of the Chicago Police in the Nineteenth Century," *Chicago History,* 11 (Spring, 1982), 43–44; *Times,* July 26–28, 1877; *Trib.,* July 27–29, 1877.

11. *Trib.,* July 28, Aug. 7, 11, 1877; Alfred T. Andreas, *History of Chicago,* 3 vols. (Chicago, 1886), 3:586–89; *Griffiths Annual Review, 1877,* 55–56; Frank Morn, *"The Eye That Never Sleeps": A History of the Pinkerton National Detective Agency* (Bloomington, Ind., 1982), chap. 4; Allan Pinkerton, *Strikers, Communists, Tramps, and Detectives* (New York, 1878), 404, 388, 390; Morris, Allerton, and Sherman to editor, *Trib.,* July 29, 1877.

12. Avrich, *Haymarket Tragedy,* 39–46; Schilling, "History of Labor Movement in Chicago," xviii–xxii; Scharnau, "Thomas J. Morgan," 30–52; Edward B. Mittelman, "Chicago Labor in Politics, 1877–96," *Journal of Political Economy,* 28 (May, 1920), 409–15; Dorothy Culp, "The Radical Labor Movement, 1873–1895," *Transactions of the Illinois State Historical Society,* 44 (1937), 92–96; Myers, *Policing Labor Disputes,* 125–26; Pierce, *Chicago,* 3:253–54; Beckner, *Labor Legislation in Illinois,* 11–12; *Times,* June 20, 1879; *Trib.,* Feb. 19, Apr. 21, 24, 1879.

13. *Trib.,* Feb. 6, 1875; Pinkerton, *Strikers, Communists, Tramps, and Detectives,* 391; C. B. Berry, *The Other Side, How It Struck Us* (London, 1880), 130–31; *Times,* July 26, 1877.

14. *Trib.,* Mar. 9, 1873; Jan. 1, 1877; Oct. 11, 1878; Jan. 12, 1880;

Charles Henry Taylor, ed., *History of the Board of Trade of the City of Chicago*, 3 vols. (Chicago, 1917), 1:551–52; "Report of Special [House] Committee on Labor, March, 1879," Illinois 31st General Assembly (Springfield, 1879), 35–37.

15. *Tenth Census, 1880*, vol. 2, "Manufactures," 391–93; *Trib.*, Oct. 11, 1878; Oct. 27, 1879; *Daily News*, Nov. 7, 1879.

16. *Trib.*, Feb. 6, 1875; James MacDonald, *Food from the Far West* (London, 1878), 187–88; *Tenth Census, 1880*, vol. 1, "Population," 870; vol. 19, "Report on the Social Statistics of Cities," 511; Department of Health, *Report of the Chicago Department of Health for 1879 and 1880*, 40. The 1880 census does not give age, sex, or nativity of those employed in slaughtering and meat-packing, although it does provide these statistics for "butchers," that is, those working in retail meat markets.

17. *Trib.*, Feb. 18, 1878; *Times*, Dec. 18, 1871; *Trib.*, May 7, 1873; Dec. 25, 1879; Jan. 3, 1880; Jan. 12, 1876. On factory safety in the latter part of the nineteenth century, see Daniel Nelson, *Managers and Workers: Origins of the New Factory System in the United States, 1880–1920* (Madison, Wis., 1975), 26–28.

18. *Trib.*, Dec. 6, 7, 1878; Jan. 13, Aug. 28, Sept. 25, Oct. 25, 27, Nov. 15, 1879; *Times*, Dec. 19, 20, 1879.

19. *Trib.*, Nov. 3, 7, 1879; *Times*, Nov. 3, 1879; "Union Butcher" to editor, *Trib.*, Nov. 9, 1879; *Daily News*, Nov. 6, 1879.

20. *Daily News*, Nov. 8, 1879; *Times*, Nov. 10, 11, 1879; *Trib.*, Nov. 8–10, 15–17, 1879.

21. *Trib.*, Dec. 18, 1879.

22. *Trib.*, Dec. 15–19, 21, 1879; *Daily News*, Dec. 17, 18, 1879; *Illinois Staats-Zeitung*, Dec. 29, 1879 (CFLPS, Roll 14).

23. *Daily News*, Dec. 24, 1879; *Times*, Dec. 21, 24, 26, 1879; *Trib.*, Dec. 21, 23, 24, 25, 27, 28, 1879.

24. *Trib.*, Dec. 29, 19, 30, 1879; *Times*, Dec. 30, 1879.

25. "Disaffected Unionist" to editor, *Trib.*, Dec. 31, 1879; *Trib.*, Jan. 1, 2, 3, 1880; Hutchinson interview in *Drovers Journal* quoted in *Trib.*, Dec. 18, 1879.

26. *Daily News*, Jan. 3, 1880; *Times*, Dec. 31, 1879; Jan. 2, 13, 1880; *Trib.*, Dec. 19, 1879; Jan. 2–4, 7, 8, 9–12, 14, 15, 1880. The only other newspaper reference to blacks during the strike was Armour's threat to divert business to Kansas City where his employes were "principally negroes . . . members of no Union" and willing to "stick by the company through thick and thin." *Trib.*, Dec. 23, 1879.

27. *Trib.*, Jan. 14, 15, 25, 26, 30, Feb. 10, 12, 1880; Michael J. Butler to Terence V. Powderly, Jan. 1, 1886 (Box A1-15, Powderly Papers, Catholic University, Washington).

CHAPTER 8

Regulating the Nuisance Industries

The rapid expansion of meat-packing in the 1870s provoked a showdown on air and water pollution. Until 1876 the Board of Health had to rely on publicity and persuasion. If renderers, packers, or local slaughterers chose to ignore the "teasing attacks," they could be reasonably certain that courts would uphold their right to conduct their businesses as they saw fit. This changed when a new city charter permitted Chicago to create a strong Department of Health headed by a determined Dr. Oscar C. DeWolf. A no-nonsense ordinance passed in 1877 required licenses for these businessmen, compliance with city sanitary regulations, and fines or jail sentences for violators. Equally important, the ordinance applied to renderers, packers, and slaughterers within one mile of the city limits. The following year the Illinois Supreme Court upheld this ordinance, and Chicagoans noticed a big improvement in air quality. On the other hand, Hyde Park lost its court battle for the right to ban offal transport over the Union Stock Yard Company connecting track and the lakefront railroads. It raised such a fuss, however, that by the end of the decade offending fertilizer companies had moved down into Indiana and the Chicago and Western Indiana Railway had been chartered to convey offal through the Town of Lake.

The Causes of Water and Air Pollution

Chicagoans entered the 1870s believing that city engineer Ellis Sylvester Chesbrough and sanitary superintendent John Rauch had pollution under control. The Board of Health was publicizing sanitary regulations, making inspections, and using its limited powers to enforce the 1865 ordinance and state law prohibiting dumping in the river or its branches. The two-mile water tunnel was spectacularly successful, and the city boasted 150 miles of sewers. Best of all, Chesbrough had given them a clear "flowing stream" from Lake Michigan into the Illinois and Michigan Canal. "Had it not been for the fire," said the city engineer, reversing the flow of the Chicago River would have been the "great event" of 1871. "At all ordinary times, now," the river flows to the canal, "thus completely deodorizing what was so offensive and unbearable a year ago." Since the Bridgeport pumps were idle, the city sold them in 1873 for $2,500 and leased the land. Chicago would have industry on its river banks, a modern sewerage system, *and* pure drinking water, thanks to the genius of the city engineer.[1]

Alas, however, the South Branch was soon in worse condition than ever before. One reason was the South Fork, a slender stream that originated beyond Western Avenue, wandered east through the Packers' Addition, and joined the Stockyards Canal just above Thirty-ninth Street. From there it flowed north to the South Branch at Bridgeport near the beginning of the Illinois and Michigan Canal. (See Map 3, p. 36.) Since there was little current in the twisting West Fork and none in the Stockyards Canal, the South Fork filled up with stockyard and packinghouse wastes. Close by one rendering company, a reporter discovered, some people placed boards across the sewer to "catch the grease which collects on the surface, put it in holes in the clay till the water evaporates, and then sell it." Dr. Rauch knew by the end of 1872 that the South Fork had the potential to become "a Healy Slough on a grander scale." Two years later the Board of Health described the fork as "a stagnant pool of abominations," and Rauch's successor warned in 1876 that, although the city had no jurisdiction over Town of Lake packinghouses, they were a "serious cause of offense."[2]

Healy Slough and Ogden Slip hastened the deterioration of the South Branch. Though Chicago could rise from its ashes, it could not "drain, fill up, disinfect, deodorize, or molest the Healy Slough," remarked a weary editor. While the Healy heirs pressed their claim that the waterway was navigable, the city could not act. The heirs lost in 1877, won in the Appellate Court, lost in the Illinois Supreme Court, and then appealed to the United States Supreme Court. Meanwhile, the city did charge Reid and Sherwin with careless operation on the banks of Ogden Slip. Their wooden refuse enclosure oozed "a dark putrid fluid" and attracted "millions of flies." Reid and Sherwin managed to shift the blame on city scavengers who admitted dumping dead cats, dogs, and occasionally horses in the slip. Finally, in 1878 the troublesome area was declared public rather than private property, and Chicago immediately dredged and disinfected it.[3]

Yet another source of trouble for the South Branch was the Ogden-Wentworth Ditch between Mud Lake and the West Fork of the branch. The ditch drained Ogden's and Wentworth's property but also conveyed the spring runoff from the lake into the West Fork. Realizing that the mud and silt in the South Branch and the canal came from the ditch, Chesbrough suggested a dam with sluice gates near the Des Plaines River. The prominent owners balked until 1877 when they built a flimsy earthen dam which did little good. Mud and silt still washed into the South Fork, South Branch, and Illinois and Michigan Canal.[4]

Finally, there was the matter of human and industrial wastes emptying into the North and South branches. As Chicago's population climbed from three hundred thousand to five hundred thousand during the 1870s, Chesbrough made strenuous efforts to extend the household sewerage system. He added another 170 miles, bringing Chicago's total sewerage network to 320 miles in 1880. Some of the sewers emptied into the lake, but the city engineer was certain that lake currents would disperse the offensive material. Most of his sewers drained into the river and its branches, and these wastes were supposed to flow with the river directly into the Illinois and Michigan Canal. Dr. Rauch argued that the slow decomposition of human wastes in the still sluggish river created "carburetted and sulphuretted hydrogen." It was a health hazard, and he recommended dry earth-closets. Since neither Rauch nor Chesbrough could back their convictions with scientific proof, the city engineer ignored the sanitary superintendent and kept increasing the number of sewers that emptied into the river and its branches. Meantime, tanneries and distilleries were making the North Branch nearly as foul as the South Branch.[5]

Spring "freshets" in 1877 brought matters to a head. South Branch water forced out into the lake, health officers warned the city engineer, carried "the sewage of the city . . . [and] vast quantities of putrid animal matter from the South Fork of the South Branch." Chesbrough was sufficiently alarmed to revive his earlier proposal of conduits to flush the river branches, and he secured funds for a North Branch conduit along Fullerton Avenue. It was tested in 1880, first by pumping lake water into the North Branch and driving its contents into the main river. This made the city so unbearable that the pumps were reversed and the North Branch was "cleansed" by delivering its filth to Lake Michigan. No one, not even Chesbrough, pushed for a conduit to the South Fork or the South Branch.[6]

Towns along the banks of the Illinois River complained about the quality of the water coming to them from the Illinois and Michigan Canal. "Ever since the water from the Chicago River was let down into the Illinois River, the stench has been almost unendurable," exclaimed a resident of Morris in 1879. "What right has Chicago to pour its filth down into what was before a sweet and clean river, pollute its waters, and materially reduce the value of property on both sides of the river and canal, and bring sickness and death to the citizens?" Businessmen in Joliet threatened to shovel dirt into the canal at Summit to block it and make Chicago "stink herself to death." The *Tribune* thought these outbursts were examples of small-town Illinois "doing anything to annoy Chicago." Peoria, Joliet, Ottawa, Peru, LaSalle, and Morris had a combined population of less than one hundred thousand; Chicago with five hundred thousand residents was "entitled to the 'right of way' by the wishes of a majority." More sympathetic was the Citizens' Association of Chicago which held that deepening the canal had been a mistake. It spread pollution while failing to cleanse the Chicago River, a fact "well known to both officials and private citizens—to none better than those . . . subjected to the stenches."[7]

Chesbrough's unheralded retirement in 1879 gave the city an opportunity to rethink his policies. The *Tribune* called for "remedial action" to rid both branches of sewage and filth but did not specify the course of action. Chicagoans were similarly uncertain. A South Branch conduit was out because the North Branch one did not work. The Citizens' Association proposed intercepting sewers that would carry waste materials to an irrigation farm; politicians and taxpayers felt this would cost too much. The best remedy was finding a way to *make* the South Branch keep emptying into the canal and that meant new pumps at Bridgeport. The city council finally appropriated $100,000, and the state legislature ordered Chicago to begin construction in 1881. The city did not obey because it was hoping that either the federal government would turn the canal into a "national waterway" or that the Stockyards company, the packers, and the Town of Lake would build their own pumping station at Thirty-ninth and the South Fork. Neither of these solutions materialized, and so the aldermen parted with another $150,000 for four engines and eight pumps. Ten years after the original pumps were dismantled and sold, Chicago dedicated a new Bridgeport pumping station and prayed it would save the South Branch.[8]

Air pollution—or the smoke and stench nuisance, as it was called—was attributed to Bridgeport and the Stockyards. Chicago's prevailing southwesterly winds carried factory smoke from the South Branch industrial district and the packinghouses as well as odors from the rendering, glue, and fertilizer establishments and the aroma of the Stockyards. Reporters accused Bridgeport chimneys of belching enough smoke to turn the city into a "Stygian pit" and "begrime" even the new structures erected after the fire. The "air-bath" from the Town of Lake was "a stench abnormal," a rich compound of livestock, manure, drying hides, and the "insufferable stinks" of the rendering plants. One Chicago reporter thoughtfully described the smoke and odor wafting over the city from the southwest as something that "folds and unfolds like the coils of a snake. Its waves lap over each other like the waves of the ocean."[9] Perhaps because the sources of air pollution were more obvious and the solutions simpler, Chicago had better luck combatting the stench nuisance in the 1870s than it did with water pollution.

Chicago's Stench Ordinance

Progress was limited during the first half of the decade. The superintendent and Board of Health could issue sanitary regulations; enforcement was up to the police and the corporation counsel, who hesitated to prosecute violators in courts which favored property rights over municipal rights. Dr. Rauch, for example, banned construction of new distilleries, slaughterhouses, and rendering plants within Chicago and one mile outside city limits. Owners fought back, and in 1875 the Illinois Supreme Court rejected the Board of Health regulation. Meantime, the regulation had been widely ignored because people assumed the courts would find it illegal. Another Rauch edict requiring lard and fertilizer manufacturers to install condensers, use airtight covers on rendering tanks, and adopt James Turner's invention for burning the dry gases emitted during rendering was also ignored until the city cracked down on Reid and Sherwin. The Board of Health won that case, and as a result renderers grudgingly complied.[10]

The sanitary superintendent declined reappointment in 1873, but he did not withdraw from the arena. As president of the American Public Health Association in 1876, founder of the Illinois State Board of Health, and executive secretary of that board from 1879 until 1891, Dr. Rauch kept close ties with Chicago's sanitary reformers. When Board of Health funds were cut after his departure, he suggested the use of volunteer investigators. Diligent Citizens' Association members and newspaper reporters found wide variations in the rendering, packing, and slaughtering houses they inspected for the board. High marks for compliance with health regulations consistently went to Tobey and Booth, James Turner, Chicago Packing and Provision Company, and Allerton's plant. The chronic violators were Reid and Sherwin, Mitchell, and some Town of Lake slaughtering sheds which dumped offal in the Stockyards Canal and vacant fields southwest of the Stockyards.[11]

Citizen impatience with authorities was obvious by mid-decade. Fire destroyed the Wahl Glue Works in Bridgeport early in 1875, and the owners vowed to rebuild at the same location. They resented having "to shoulder every smell in this city, no matter where it came from" and reminded Chicagoans that "not once in nineteen years have we been before a magistrate for violating city ordinances, or have we been cited before the Board of Health." Vigilantes had probably set that fire and they penned the letter to the editor explaining why. Louis and Christian Wahl were "good men and neighbors," but the time had come to "get rid of these stink-factories, one and all." Since municipal officials were "not disposed to do anything, . . . we have taken the matter in our own hands."[12]

Relief was on the way. Later that same year Chicago voters approved a new city charter which significantly enlarged municipal power. The city council could reorganize the administrative branches, and it acquired extensive powers to regulate and license. Aldermen revamped the police and fire departments first. In July, 1876, they abolished the Boards of Public

Works and Health and transferred the powers and duties of board members to executive departments headed by commissioners. Each commissioner, named by the mayor with the advice and consent of the aldermen, was the chief executive of his department. Selected to head the Department of Health in January, 1877, was Dr. Oscar C. DeWolf, who held that position until 1889. Trained in Massachusetts and France, DeWolf was a surgeon in the Civil War and a private practitioner before coming to Chicago in 1873. Strongly interested in sanitary reform, he found time in the 1880s to offer courses at Chicago Medical College on State Medicine and Public Hygiene. The mayor asked Commissioner DeWolf to give top priority to slaughterhouses and rendering plants and relieve "the citizens of our city of the great nuisance which has afflicted them for many years."[13]

The Health Department staff of thirty-six was twice as large as the Board of Health staff, yet Dr. DeWolf hired extra investigators whose salaries were paid by the Citizens' Association. Their survey of Town of Lake found forty-four pork- and beef-packing companies, thirteen fertilizer factories, three glue works, and two blood-drying operations. These companies ran 292 rendering tanks, only eleven of which were capable of eliminating all odors. The others emitted "pungent, acrid" fumes, and if the fumes were conducted back into the furnace, "the combustion was so imperfect that . . . large volumes of noxious gases" escaped through the chimney. The health commissioner talked with packers and renderers, many of whom "good naturedly acknowledged the errors of their way." But DeWolf soon realized that "*all* had become entirely indifferent to the teasing attacks of sanitary authorities." He therefore singled out Joseph Sherwin's fertilizer factory and filed charges under existing sanitary ordinances. A police court jury refused to convict; Sherwin called Dr. DeWolf "a quack" and struck him over the head with a hickory cane in the courtroom. Sherwin's only penalty was a $5 fine.[14]

It was obvious to the commissioner and the city attorney that police court juries drawn from neighborhood saloons were not going to cooperate with the Department of Health crackdown. But under the new charter the council had authority to license packers and renderers within one mile of Chicago's boundaries, and an ordinance to this effect was submitted to the aldermen in August, 1877. It provided that anyone engaging in slaughtering, packing, rendering, or the manufacture of glue or fertilizer "within the City of Chicago, or within one mile of the limits thereof" must obtain a license from the mayor and pay a fee of $100 per year. Licenses could be revoked if the packers or renderers "violated any provision of any ordinance of the Common Council, or any statute law of the State of Illinois." Any person so convicted would lose his license immediately and if he operated without a license, he could be fined $100 a day or imprisoned for ninety days. The ordinance also stated that sanitary officers must be granted free entrance "at all hours of the day or night, to all buildings" and must be permitted to examine utensils, apparatus, and machinery.[15]

The "new stink ordinance" cleared the council without amendments and went into effect immediately. Benjamin Peters Hutchinson of Chicago Packing and Provision Company refused as a matter of principle to apply for a city license, was arrested for violating the new law, and confidently went to court to prove that the measure was unconstitutional. His lawyers argued that the Illinois general incorporation act of 1872 did not authorize any city to regulate beyond its own boundaries; Hutchinson had a license from the Town of Lake to transact business and thus the Chicago City Council had no right to interfere. The lower court ruled against Hutchinson and fined him $25 for operating without a city license, but he appealed to the Illinois Supreme Court. On June 25, 1878, that court handed down an opinion written by Justice Pinkney H. Walker. The 1872 act did bestow general powers on cities; it allowed municipal governments to require licenses and to regulate both the management and location of businesses noxious to health and comfort. There was no difficulty with the one-mile extension, said the Illinois Supreme Court, "even if that should lap over and embrace a portion of territory included in the boundaries of another municipality. Each, to that extent, has the right to protect its inhabitants, and such establishments [as Chicago Packing and Provision Company] . . . are subject to the police power of both corporate bodies." This sweeping vindication of Chicago's 1877 ordinance meant, in the words of one jubilant editor, that "The City Can Now Deal with Stench Factories."[16]

Health Commissioner DeWolf was ready to proceed. He asked members of the Citizens' Association to identify offending companies, witness the violations, and be prepared to testify in court. Ferdinand W. Peck headed a special committee of business and professional men who visited the plants by day and by night and familiarized themselves with the machinery and its operation. Their tutor was Louis Merki, a Health Department inspector and a Town of Lake resident since 1871. Incensed by pollution of the South Fork and the escalation of offensive odors in the township, Merki searched for culprits with greater zeal than the civic-minded businessmen. Early in 1878 they turned their evidence over to a grand jury which indicted twenty-seven companies, including Chicago Packing and Provision, Armour, Murphy, Higgins, Wahl Glue Works, and Sherwin's fertilizer firm. These "stink cases" came to trial in Criminal Court in June, 1878, and they were closely watched by eager newspaper readers.[17]

The first cases were those against fertilizer manufacturers Mortimer Scanlon and Joseph Sherwin. Their lawyers insisted that their equipment was efficient and there were no offensive smells. John Marshall testified that although he lived near Sherwin's plant his eleven children were healthy; saloonkeeper Frank Eddy said he and his eight children were flourishing in the shadow of Scanlon's place. George Muirhead, Town of Lake assessor and resident of Englewood, said he had never detected any smells around the Sherwin factory. The prosecution called prominent residents of Prairie, Wabash, Indiana, and Michigan avenues to explain what it was like to live downwind of the Stockyards. Louis Merki and members of the Citizens' Association committee described conditions inside the two fertilizer factories. DeWolf testified that the odors at Sherwin's place caused the city attorney to vomit; a battery of doctors confirmed that smells from the Stockyards were "depressing on the weak and convalescent and produced nausea." The city's star witness, however, was an obscure, elderly man who, thinking the "stink cases" would never come to trial, fired off this letter to Health Commissioner DeWolf: "Damn your skill, idleness, neglect and supineness in neglecting to prevent the terrible stenches that prevail nightly, caused by a few rendering places. . . . I dare not go outside the door lest I should be stunk to death. My little wife is vomiting from the foul air. . . . If you are powerless, resign. Cease to fatten at the public crib until you are able to repay those whose taxes go to fatten you."[18]

The jury found Scanlon and Sherwin guilty, and DeWolf hoped that Judge William H. Moore would impose the maximum fine and close the two plants until new machinery was installed. Before sentencing, however, the Illinois Supreme Court handed down its decision in *The Chicago Packing and Provision Company* v. *The City of Chicago*. Seeing the handwriting on the wall, remaining defendants in the "stink cases" pleaded guilty and appealed for leniency. The judge imposed fines of $25 and court costs and refused to send the sheriff to close any of the offending plants. This was, nonetheless, an important victory for the Health Commissioner. "Not a dryer could be turned, nor a fire lighted under a tank," without a city license, he rejoiced. And if a packer or renderer tried to operate without a license in the future, he "could be arrested without warrant and confined in the nearest station house." Once the city had established its authority, manufacturers scurried to install new condensing machinery and dryers. This would not increase profits, but it was essential if they wanted to stay in business. By 1880 DeWolf was praising "proprietors, superintendents, and workmen" who "cheerfully" obeyed his regulations, and Mayor Carter Harrison was praising the health commissioner. Thanks to him, "people are absolutely forgetting there ever was a Bridgeport stink."[19]

In an 1893 article in *Forum*, a prominent sanitary reformer claimed that the "great majority of the dwellers in our cities have not, heretofore, taken any active personal interest in the sanitary condition of their respective towns." Chicago was an exception. Her environmental crusaders won significant victories in the 1870s and could trace their roots back to Edwin

C. Larned, who had proclaimed in 1864 that "the air and the water . . . are the common property of all."[20]

The Suburban Perfumery War

If Town of Lake's northern neighbor could regulate the stench industries, why couldn't its eastern neighbor do the same? So reasoned the lakefront residents of Hyde Park. They disliked the livestock trains on their lakefront and the Union Stock Yard connecting track across Forty-first Street. And to control the fertilizer factories in the southern part of the township, Hyde Park had extended its boundary to the Indiana state line in 1867 and annexed land along the Calumet River in the 1870s. Residents of the northern part of Hyde Park and especially those in Paul Cornell's settlement felt that the transportation of livestock and offal threatened to turn their suburb into a "Stock-Yards sewer on wheels." Their attempt to regulate, and if possible abolish, this traffic in the 1870s was called the Perfumery War.[21]

At the opening of the decade, both Town of Lake and Chicago required slaughterers and packers either to use their offal promptly or to remove it from their premises. Some offal went directly to nearby fertilizer factories, but much of it traveled by rail through Hyde Park to the Union Rendering Company or the Northwestern Fertilizing Company in Ainsworth. In 1871 the Union Rendering Company was declared a public nuisance by court action, and it soon moved outside the jurisdiction of Hyde Park. But people living in the Ninety-fifth Street settlement complained about odors from the remaining "Monster," and so did other Hyde Parkers when the wind carried the stench to their homes. Far more annoying to the wealthy dwellers along the lakefront was the constant traffic of freight trains conveying offal in open cars. By 1872 the Northwestern Fertilizing Company was receiving two hundred tons of this raw material per day. Township trustees decided to intervene by passing an ordinance in 1872 which forbade transportation of offal, dead animals, or other unwholesome matter through Hyde Park by railroad or wagon team. The railroads ignored the ordinance, and so early in January, 1873, Hyde Park police stopped a Pittsburgh, Fort Wayne and Chicago train and jailed its conductor, engineer, and brakeman. About the same time a fire of undetermined origin completely destroyed the fertilizer plant in Ainsworth.[22]

Hyde Park's 1872 ordinance brought Chicago officialdom to the defense of South Branch and Town of Lake packers and renderers. Abolish meatpacking or even "suppress the business," warned Mayor Joseph Medill, "and you reduce the population . . . by at least one-fourth" and lose $100,000,000 a year. The townships around Chicago "must not be permitted to deprive the city of some place to deposit the offal from the slaughterhouses, for it must be dumped somewhere." Pork-packing is to Chicago, chimed in the *Tribune*, "what the iron manufacture and trade is to Pittsburgh." Hyde Park was merely an "appanage of this city," a "diminutive burg" that would "dry up and blow away in six months but for the business of Chicago." The Hyde Park board of trustees replied, "It is not the chief end of man to kill hogs and pack pork . . . and diffuse offensive odors." If Chicago could drive the fertilizer company to Ainsworth, Hyde Park could drive it out on the prairie or perhaps the Indiana dunes. Mixing offal into "the sand hills" would give them "fertility."[23]

The next round in the Perfumery War was a temporary injunction prohibiting Hyde Park from interfering with the business of the Northwestern Fertilizing Company. Since the fire, "business" meant stockpiling offal on the frozen prairie and seeking a permanent injunction so the company could rebuild in the spring. Hyde Park vowed to prevent this. The company argued in U.S. Circuit Court that it had not violated its state charter and therefore Hyde Park had no right to interfere with its operation. Hyde Park lawyers argued that the company was both a nuisance and health menace, and it depreciated property values and hindered the growth of the suburb. Under the general incorporation act of 1872 Hyde Park had secured the right to regulate and control such companies. On February 11, 1873, Judge William Washington Farwell ruled:

> On the one hand, one of our most prosperous and promising suburban towns is contending for its right to drive away a nuisance. . . . On the other hand, we see the complainant having obtained their charter, and having invested their money and established their business; and back of them the packers, looking to the works of the complainant as the only practicable outlet and means of relief which will enable them to carry on their business here; and back of all, the City of Chicago, at a loss to know what else can be done with the offal of the slaughter-houses and other refuse animal matter, already so large, and constantly increasing. . . .
>
> I am of the opinion that this charter secures to the complainant the right to carry on the business at the points and in the manner specified.

The Northwestern Fertilizing Company, he continued, "is as truly a public enterprise as the building of a railroad, or the supply of a town with water or gas, or providing its sewerage." Hyde Park officials cannot "break up its business . . . under pretense of abating a nuisance," for that would "throw back upon the city this vast mass of animal matter." The legislation of 1872 was never intended "to place a great city at the mercy of its suburbs."[24]

Hyde Park trustees thought they could at least define the manner in which offal passed through their community, and an ordinance requiring covered railroad cars and limiting the amount of offal that could be stored by any company to one hundred tons was approved by Judge Farwell as a reasonable exercise of Hyde Park's police powers. As more packers rendered their own offal, however, Northwestern and Union Rendering had to import from surrounding states. By the end of the decade there were nine companies in this business, two over the state line in Indiana* and seven at the Stockyards. Some of the latter piled offal on the prairie beyond Commissioner DeWolf's one-mile reach. He prodded Town of Lake to prohibit this "vile scavengering," and in 1879 the township did ban importation of outside offal (except from Chicago) and require the use of tightly sealed boxes so that it "not be dropped" or "scattered along the railroad tracks." Five Chicago sanitary inspectors helped Town of Lake police enforce this ordinance.[25]

Hyde Park was still unhappy. Its attorneys tried to buy the Union Stock Yard Company's Forty-first Street right-of-way, and then, emboldened by the 1878 Illinois Supreme Court decision upholding Chicago's right to regulate packers and renderers, suggested another stab at prohibition. Hyde Park no sooner passed the ordinance banning transport of offal within its boundaries than the City of Chicago sought an injunction. Before the case was argued in court, a shaky truce emerged. It rested upon two developments. One was the chartering in 1879 of a Chicago and Western Indiana Railway which would convey offal from the Stockyards to the state line fertilizer companies through Town of Lake, not Hyde Park. The other was a new airtight, leakproof, smellproof refrigerator car. The Michigan Central put one on display at the Hyde Park Fifty-third Street siding, and township officials relented. Those new cars could carry offal through Hyde Park until March, 1880, after which the traffic had to be switched to the Chicago and Western Indiana line. In the interim, Hyde Park promised not to enforce its ordinance, but it refused to repeal the measure.[26]

The livestock trade, meat-packing, slaughtering, rendering, and the manufacture of glue and fertilizer contributed to air pollution and the persistent problems of the South Branch. Other industries on the river banks, Chesbrough's expanding sewer network, and Chicago's prevailing southwesterly winds aggravated the situation. Until 1875, health officials lacked authority to do much about the stench industries, but Chicago's new charter led to the creation of a vigorous Department of Health headed by a determined commissioner. Armed with a "new stink ordinance," Dr. DeWolf licensed manufacturers within Chicago and one mile beyond, and

* Union Rendering Company and the Chicago Rendering and Drying Company, an 1878 merger of Joseph Sherwin's Company and Northwestern Fertilizing.

those who violated Chicago sanitary regulations could be fined, imprisoned, or put out of business. Of course this tough law was contested, but the city won critical cases against Chicago Packing and Provision Company and fertilizer manufacturers at the Stockyards. In his decision upholding the legality of the ordinance, Justice Walker of the Illinois Supreme Court said Chicagoans should not expect "air as pure and invigorating as in the open country; but they do have the right to be protected against . . . intolerable nuisances."[27] Hyde Parkers were not so lucky. The courts would not allow them to obstruct the livestock or offal trade, but they did impose regulations which drove the fertilizing companies to Indiana and diverted the Stockyards offal traffic to the Chicago and Western Indiana Railway.

NOTES

1. James C. O'Connell, "Technology and Pollution: Chicago's Water Policy, 1833–1930" (Ph.D. diss., University of Chicago, 1980), 45–48, 68–69; "Report of Chief Engineer E. S. Chesbrough," Board of Public Works, *Annual Report of the Board of Public Works, 1872*, 100; Louis P. Cain, "Raising and Watering a City, Chesbrough and Chicago's First Sanitary System," *Technology and Culture*, 13 (July, 1972), 369–72; George P. Brown, *Drainage Channel and Waterway: A History of the Effort to Secure . . . Disposal of the Sewage of the City of Chicago* (Chicago, 1894), 91–92, 307–8.

2. "Bridgeport vs. Stock Yards—Which Is the Best Locality for the Slaughter-Houses and Rendering Establishments?" *Trib.*, Dec. 16, 1872; Board of Health, *Report of the Board of Health of the City of Chicago for the Years 1870, 1871, 1872 and 1873*, 12–14, 160–61; Board of Health, *Report of the Board of Health of the City of Chicago for the Years 1874 and 1875*, 12–15; *Trib.*, Dec. 11, 18, 1872; June 14, 1874; Aug. 20, 1876.

3. *Trib.*, July 12, 20, Sept. 13, 17, Oct. 12, 1872; June 29, 1873; Aug. 14, 1884; Dec. 15, 1885.

4. James W. Putnam, *The Illinois and Michigan Canal: A Study in Economic History* (Chicago, 1918), 143; George P. Brown, *Drainage Channel and Waterway*, 320–25; Don E. Fehrenbacher, *Chicago Giant: A Biography of "Long John" Wentworth* (Madison, Wis., 1957), 212–14; *Trib.*, July 10, Dec. 23, 1877.

5. Louis P. Cain, *Sanitation Strategy for a Lakefront Metropolis: The Case of Chicago* (DeKalb, Ill., 1978), 34, 61–63; O'Connell, "Technology and Pollution," 55, 71–72; Board of Health, *Report of the Board of Health of the City of Chicago for 1867, 1868, and 1869; and a Sanitary History of Chicago from 1833 to 1870*, 299, 306.

6. F. Garvin Davenport, "Sanitation Revolution in Illinois, 1870–1900," *JISHS*, 66 (1973), 310; George P. Brown, *Drainage Channel and Waterway*, 329, 334; O'Connell, "Technology and Pollution," 55–57; "Report on Lake Water," Department of Health, *Report of the Department of Health of the City of Chicago for the Years 1876–1877*, 34–35, 45; "South Fork of the South Branch," Department of Public Works, *Annual Report of the Department of Public Works for 1878*, 91–92; *Trib.*, June 3, July 17, 1877; Apr. 6, 1878.

7. *Trib.*, Jan. 26, Feb. 8, 9, 26, 1879; Citizens' Association, *Annual Report of the Citizens' Association of Chicago, 1879* (Chicago, 1879), 16–17.

8. *Trib.*, Jan. 30, 1880; Citizens' Association, *Report of the Main Drainage Committee* (Chicago, 1880), 9, 14–19; George P. Brown, *Drainage Channel and Waterway*, 19–20, 311, 314–17, 326; Frank J. Piehl, "Chicago's Early Fight to 'Save Our Lake,'" *Chicago History*, 5 (Winter, 1976–77), 226, 230–31; Cain, *Sanitation Strategy*, 59–61.

9. *Trib.*, June 30, July 20, Sept. 8, 13, 17, Oct. 12, 1872; July 8, 1874; Jan. 19, Aug. 20, 1876.

10. Faith Fitzgerald, "Growth of Municipal Activities in Chicago, 1833–1875" (M.A. thesis, University of Chicago, 1933), 149–50; John R. Rauch, *The Sanitary Problems of Chicago* (Cambridge, Mass., 1879), 6; Citizens' Association, *Annual Report of the Citizens' Association of Chicago, 1878* (Chicago, 1878), 6–7; Board of Health, *Health Ordinances and Sanitary Regulations of the City of Chicago, 1874*, 6, 23–24.

11. F. Garvin Davenport, "John Henry Rauch and Public Health in Illinois, 1877–1891," *JISHS*, 50 (Autumn, 1957), 278–79; O'Connell, "Technology and Pollution," 77; C. J. M., "The Stench Nuisance," *Trib.*, Dec. 27, 1874; Board of Health, *Report for 1874 and 1875*, 12–15; *Trib.*, Jan. 3, 10, 24, 1875; July 30, 1876.

12. *Trib.*, Feb. 23, Mar. 12, 1875; "A Looker-on for Several Years" to editor, Mar. 17, 1875.

13. Bessie Louise Pierce, *A History of Chicago*, vol. 3, *The Rise of a Modern City, 1871–1893* (New York, 1957), 300–302, 320; *The Biographical Dictionary and Portrait Gallery of Representative Men of Chicago* (Chicago, 1892), 159–60; O'Connell, "Technology and Pollution," 72–73; *Trib.*, Jan. 30, 1877; Department of Health, *Report for 1878*, 13.

14. Dr. Oscar C. DeWolf, "Regulating Offensive Trades," Department of Health, *Report for 1878*, 14–16; *Trib.*, Apr. 22, Aug. 12, 1877.

15. *Times*, Aug. 14, 28, 1877; City of Chicago, *Council Proceedings, 1877–78*, 155; Department of Health, *Report for 1878*, 17–18. For a discussion of slaughterhouse control by other cities and states, see Charles V. Chapin, *Municipal Sanitation in the United States* (Providence, R.I., 1901), 199–214.

16. *Times*, Aug. 28, 1877; June 26, 1878; The Chicago Packing and Provision Company v. The City of Chicago, *Reports of Cases . . . in the Supreme Court of Illinois*, vol. 88 (Springfield, 1879), 228–29; *Trib.*, June 26, 1878.

17. Department of Health, *Report for 1878*, 15–16; Citizens' Association, *Annual Report, 1878*, 6–7; Alfred T. Andreas, *History of Cook County, Illinois* (Chicago, 1884), 665; *Trib.*, June 7, 8, 1878.

18. *Times*, June 7, 8, 11, 1878; *Trib.*, June 7, 9, 11, 12, 13, 1878.

19. Department of Health, *Report for 1878*, 16–19; *Trib.*, June 14, 19, 30, 1878; Department of Health, *Report of the Chicago Department of Health for 1879 and 1880*, 13; "Annual Message of the Honorable Carter H. Harrison to the City Council, May 9, 1881," Department of Public Works, *Annual Report of the Department of Public Works of the City of Chicago, 1881*, xi.

20. John S. Billings, "Municipal Sanitation: Defects in American Cities," quoted in Martin V. Melosi, ed., *Pollution and Reform in American Cities, 1870–1930* (Austin, 1980), 18; E. C. L. to editor, *Trib.*, Dec. 18, 1864.

21. *Trib.*, Aug. 3, 1874; A. J. Grover to editor, Aug. 22, 1879.

22. *Trib.*, Jan. 3, 6, 11, 1873; May 23, 1875.

23. *Trib.*, Jan. 7, 11–14, 1873.

24. *Trib.*, Feb. 2, 12, 1873; *Times*, Feb. 12, 1873.

25. Department of Health, *Report . . . for 1878*, 14–15, 19–20; *Report . . . for 1879 and 1880*, 100, 110–11; *Trib.*, Feb. 17, Mar. 27, Apr. 3, 1873; May 23, 1875; Feb. 15, Apr. 23, July 13, Dec. 14, 1879; Jan. 8, 1880; Town of Lake Records, Doc. 8, Apr. 22, 1879 (City Hall Archives, Chicago).

26. *Trib.*, Aug. 11, 1873; July 13, 18, 19, 26, Sept. 22, Oct. 25, 1879; Nov. 7, 1880.

27. *Reports of Cases . . . in the Supreme Court of Illinois*, vol. 88, 228.

CHAPTER 9

Neighborhood Expansion in the Town of Lake

With nearly a 600 percent increase in population during the 1870s, Town of Lake was Cook County's fastest growing township. People came because of the close proximity to the South Branch industrial wards, because of the available land and acceptance of frame houses, and because there were so many job opportunities at the Stockyards, packinghouses, new factories, and railroad yards. The Chicago fire was no sooner extinguished than Englewood began advertising its suburban charms, and it attracted the type of commuters it wanted. The jump from roughly three thousand to eighteen thousand residents within ten years brought rapid expansion in the four existing neighborhoods—Stockyards, Northeast Corners, Car-Shops, and Englewood. The basic character of these neighborhoods did not change. As they acquired more dwellings and stores, they generated more voluntary associations, started new churches, and bid for more public schools. A variety of ethnic organizations, some of them nurtured by parent associations in Chicago, helped newcomers establish contact with those who shared their cultural heritage. The one new settlement was spawned by the packinghouses and located near the Ashland Avenue and Forty-seventh Street intersection. The census enumerator counted about one thousand people, and a startled reporter who discovered the instant village on the prairie christened it "New City." The mushroomlike appearance of packinghouses and residences convinced the latter that "the Growth of Chicago" could be "Illustrated at the Stock-Yards."[1]

Chicago's Southwestern Wards

Just as Chicago's manufacturing base shifted to the southwest after the 1871 fire, so did its working-class population. The two large wards on either side of the South Branch—bounded by Sixteenth Street on the north, Clark Street on the east, and the southern and western* city limits—were major beneficiaries of the shift. The wards were numbered Fifth and

* Moved from Western to Crawford Avenue in 1869.

Sixth until 1869, then Sixth and Seventh until 1876 when they recovered their "correct" designations. Immediately after the fire, they attracted people who wanted to escape the "fire limits"; job seekers joined them when the South Branch industrial district boomed. New Irish and German immigrants reinforced the groups already established in the Fifth and Sixth wards, but Bohemians and Poles added ethnic diversity in the 1870s. As a result, the Fifth Ward, positioned between the South Branch and the Town of Lake, grew from approximately 20,000 residents in 1870 to 47,500 a decade later. The Sixth Ward had almost as many residents. Together, the South Branch wards held nearly 18 percent of Chicago's half-million people in 1880.[2]

They filled up much the same way the Town of Lake would do in the following decade. Reporters noted workers' settlements around the factories, the "busiest" of which they often called "citylets." Wooden cottages were "the favorite style" in spite of the fact that Chicago in 1874 extended its ban on frame construction to include the Fifth and Sixth wards. Enforcement was impossible, and few workers could afford brick or stone. By the time horsecars reached Ashland, Blue Island, Twenty-second and Thirty-first streets, those arteries already had a broad array of service establishments. While the influx of so many newcomers diluted the Irish flavor of Bridgeport and German dominance in Hamburg, it did not undermine the coherence of those ethnic groups. Working with people of a different nationality and living on the same block with them was a common experience for all South Branch residents. Only the newest immigrant groups strove to establish homogeneous "colonies" and they did not always succeed. Each ethnic group, however, could preserve its identity and unity through fraternal and benevolent associations, nationalist societies, the military drill corps, cultural organizations, and, most important, their churches and parochial schools. It is interesting that while reporters in the 1870s generally took a dim view of the "Sclavonians," Bohemians and Poles, they praised their churches and many of their associational activities. From the standpoint of the ethnic groups, the voluntary associations put them in touch with "their own kind," proclaimed their presence in the South Branch wards, and enabled them to help others who moved down into the Town of Lake.[3]

The South Branch Irish were enthusiastic joiners of the Ancient Order of Hibernians, the Hibernian Rifles, and nationalist groups like Clan na Gael and the Irish National Land League. Chicago's first Clan "camp" was the Bridgeport chapter, established in 1869. The South Branch Irish were also staunch supporters of the annual picnics sponsored after 1876 by the United Irish Societies of Chicago. Catholicism was the strongest bond for the Irish. Despite the 1870s depression, their generous contributions permitted St. Bridget's parish to develop a parochial school for nine hundred

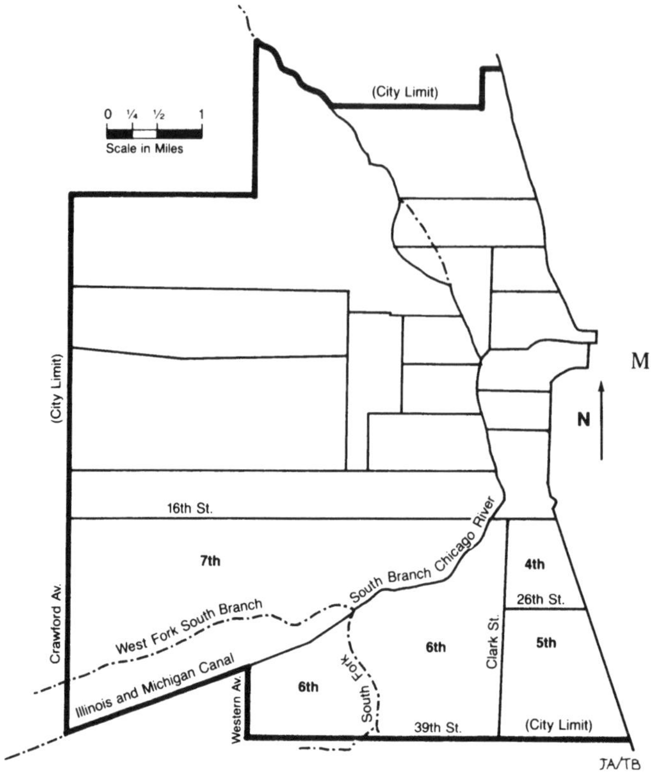

Map 4. Chicago ward boundaries, 1869–Mar., 1876

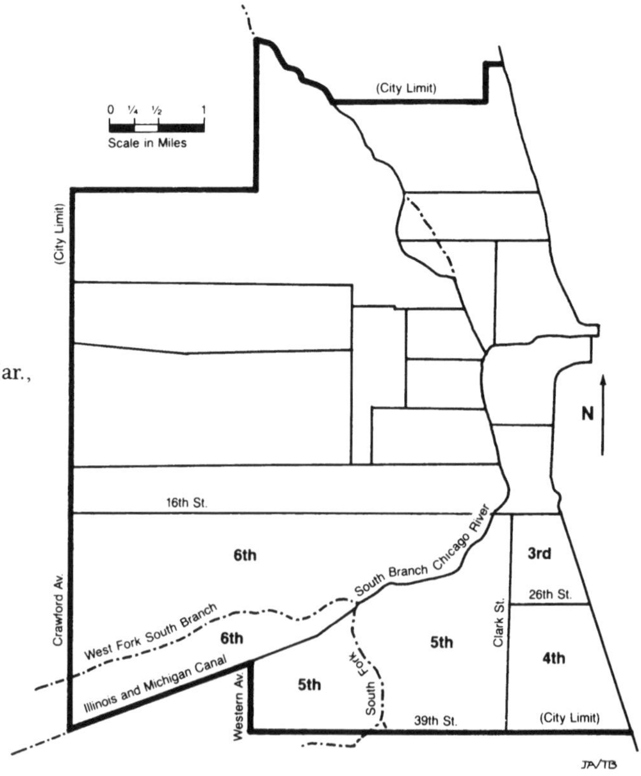

Map 5. Chicago ward boundaries, Mar., 1876–87

children and turn the Industrial School into Chicago's foremost vocational training center. That Bridgeport parish, moreover, helped Irish families east of Halsted start All Saints' parish in Hamburg. And it assisted Nativity of Our Lord parish in the southeastern corner of the Fifth Ward. From 1874 until his death in 1907 Father Joseph M. Cartan was in charge of that parish. He wasted no time starting a school and construction of a permanent church at Thirty-seventh and Winter (Union). Michael Cudahy, a homeowner on Wentworth near Thirty-seventh, was an active fund raiser for the parish. The new church was ready by the end of 1879, so Father Cartan let the Irish-dominated packinghouse union use the frame structure on Thirty-ninth street as its strike headquarters. When the union crumbled, the old church was recycled as the parish school. In 1881 Nativity of Our Lord land and buildings were worth approximately $100,000.[4]

South Branch Germans were divided into Protestant, Catholic, and socialist factions, but they all pulled together to preserve their language and cultural heritage. The Chicago public schools began hiring German language teachers in the 1870s, and German newspapers as well as musical and theatrical groups flourished. Most of those who lost their homes in the fire rebuilt on the north side of the city, as the *Staats-Zeitung* urged them to do. But some started anew in the South Branch wards and they were joined by new immigrants, many of them Catholic. The Hamburg section had a branch school for German Catholic children before the fire, but it was not until 1873 that there were enough families to create St. Anthony of Padua parish. Within seven years Father Peter Fischer had a permanent church and a school for seven hundred children. In addition, he had played a key role in founding Town of Lake's first German parish.[5]

Chicago's 1870 count of six thousand Bohemians, six thousand Swedes, and one thousand Poles was insignificant compared to the large number of first- and second-generation Germans and Irish. But these three new groups enlarged their beachhead in the 1870s, and the Bohemians showed a marked preference for the South Branch wards. Their earliest settlement around St. Wenceslaus Church on DeKoven Street had been destroyed in 1871. Some survivors moved to the Fifth Ward and started St. John Nepomucene parish, while others chose Center (Racine) in the Sixth Ward and developed St. Procopius Church, Bethlehem Congregational, and freethought societies in what was called the Pilsen colony. The Bohemians launched a newspaper in 1875, opened a cemetery two years later, and had so many voluntary associations by 1878 that the editor of *Svornost* feared Chicago Bohemians had "nothing in mind except the organization of benevolent societies." These newcomers had their troubles with the Germans and the Irish. German members of the Chicago School Board blocked Bohemian language classes in the Pilsen school, and Irish-dominated trade unions refused to let them join, which meant that Bohemians often worked alongside Irish on the same job but at substantially lower pay. Worst of all was the "American" press. During the lumberyard and railroad strikes, the newspapers heaped "calumnies . . . upon us." The *Post-Mail* described Bohemians as "depraved beasts, harpies, decayed physically and spiritually, mentally and morally, thievish and licentious." The *Tribune* ridiculed them for squandering money and time on their military drill organizations: they were in no danger of losing any property because they did not "own any worth speaking of, and as invariably the musket-carrier is a socialist."[6]

Most of the Swedes and Poles who came to Chicago in the 1870s settled on the north side. Like the Irish, the Poles were overwhelmingly Catholic and their anchor was St. Stanislaus Kostka Church. While the attraction of that Polish settlement was strong, some members of the group ventured into the Sixth Ward in search of laborers' jobs and a place to build frame houses. The fifty or so Polish Catholic families living near the intersection of Ashland, Blue Island, and Twenty-second Street formed the Society of St. Adalbert Bishop and Martyr in 1874. They laid the cornerstone for a small church at Seventeenth and Paulina streets, but the depression interfered with their building plans and they had difficulty securing a Polish pastor. All they had to show at the end of the decade was a roofed basement and tiny school, yet St. Adalbert's parish would grow rapidly in the 1880s and the Sixth Ward Polish pioneers would guide the establishment of Bridgeport's first Polish Catholic church and the first Polish parish in Town of Lake.[7]

All of the townships surrounding Chicago registered population gains in the 1870s, though none did as well as Hyde Park and Town of Lake. On the north, Lake View tripled its population, thanks to the migration of Germans and the development of the commuter settlement at Ravenswood. Jefferson township, lying northwest of Chicago, was slightly smaller with a population of about five thousand in 1880, half of them farmers and the others commuters. The western township of Cicero, which included the village of Oak Park, was approximately the same size. Town of Lake's western neighbor, Lyons township, had only 3,000 people at the end of the decade. Hyde Park, however, increased from 3,600 residents in 1870 to 15,700 ten years later. The horsecar lines brought working-class families to the northern part of the township, and Charles Cleaver's subdivision, renamed Oakland, attracted middle-class families. Hyde Park Center and Kenwood on the lakefront and Forrestville in the northwestern corner were the wealthy enclaves, while the sparsely settled southern half of the forty-eight-square-mile township had an uneasy mix of farmers, railroad and factory workers at Grand Crossing and Ainsworth (South Chicago), and iron and steel workers on the Calumet River. Hyde Park's railroad commuters, fearing an invasion by low-income Chicagoans after the fire limits were extended in 1874, favored a ban on wooden construction so that "the character of Hyde Park as the most desirable portion of suburban Chicago will be definitely fixed." The poor would still have access to Town of Lake "where property is much cheaper" and nobody objects to "tinder boxes set up on wooden pins." These were the same people who led the Perfumery War against Stockyards railroad traffic in Hyde Park, though they did not object to wealthy residents whose money came from the Stockyards or meat-packing. Livestock dealer John Bensley and packer Samuel Schoenemann lived in the northwestern corner; John R. Hoxie of the Stockyards bank and Irus Coy, attorney for the Union Stock Yard Company, were Hyde Park officeholders in the 1870s.[8]

Town of Lake outstripped Hyde Park, soaring from 3,360 in the 1870 census to 18,380 in 1880. Job opportunities, cheap land, and transit arteries from the Fifth and Sixth wards—the railroads, plus State and Halsted streets and Ashland and Western avenues—account for the demographic changes. But how did the newcomers affect the existing settlements?

The Northeast Corners, Car-Shops, and Englewood

With the exception of one new settlement near the packinghouses, the 1870s influx expanded or augmented the four neighborhoods that had emerged by the end of the 1860s. It did not alter their character, for it was a quantitative not a qualitative change. And since the Town of Lake still had relatively few horsecars at the end of the 1870s, the five neighborhoods were self-contained, walking "citylets." The closest contacts were between the Stockyards neighborhood and the Northeast Corners, the latter and the Car-Shops. But the Stewart Avenue railroad complex and Forty-seventh Street functioned as geographical boundaries, and the very different sources of employment in the three neighborhoods reinforced the distinctive characteristics of the Car-Shops, the Stockyards, and the Northeast Corners.

The unofficial western boundary of both the Northeast Corners and the Car-Shops grew ever wider during the decade. Originally, only the Pittsburgh, Fort Wayne tracks followed Stewart Avenue, but the addition of the Wabash, Grand Trunk, and Chicago and Western Indiana created a formidable barrier. In addition, both neighborhoods had Rock Island and Lake Shore and Michigan Southern tracks passing through along Clark Street. During the 1870s, the Lake Shore and the Wabash developed roundhouses and maintenance yards in the Northeast Corners and the Pittsburgh, Fort Wayne built similar facilities at the Car-Shops. In the wake of the railroads came smelting works, ironwork factories, foundries, a furniture factory, and a glass factory. Because of the horsecar line on

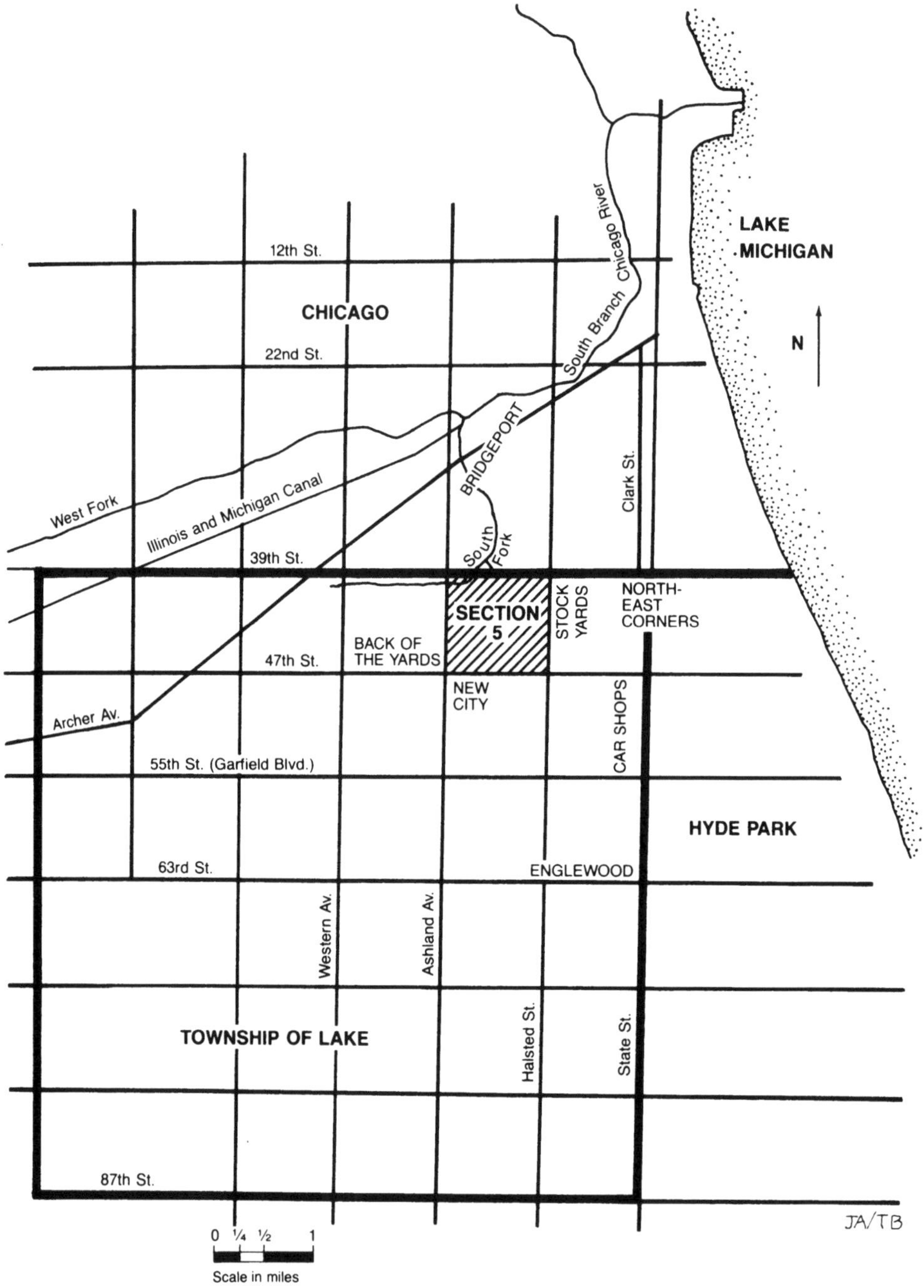

Map 6. Neighborhoods in the Town of Lake

State Street and heavy vehicular traffic, that was also the major commercial artery for both neighborhoods. Traffic was especially heavy at Thirty-ninth and State, a transfer point for Hyde Park and the Root Street horsecars to the Stockyards. It was also the most cosmopolitan spot in the Town of Lake. The 1880 census taker found in the 3900 block of State Street two large saloon-restaurant-meeting halls, one run by Italian-born Anthony Sivora and the other by German-born Conrad Walther. Also residing on that Town of Lake block were a Prussian shoemaker, English storekeeper, Michigan jeweler, Pennsylvania physician, New York milliner, Bavarian druggist, Irish horsecar driver, Hungarian liquor-store manager, Wisconsin railroad conductor, Swiss barber, German meat-market proprietor, Canadian engineer, German tailor, Illinois wagonmaker, Irish harnessmaker, German cooper, and assorted laborers.[9]

The factories and railroad yards employed about two thousand people by the end of the decade, and the Rock Island needed another one thousand in its carshops. Skilled workers in the Northeast Corners were usually machinists and iron molders, either native-born or immigrants from Canada, England, Scotland, and Germany. Irish residents, outnumbered by the Germans, worked as teamsters, carpenters, railroad employes, stockyard and packinghouse workers, and laborers. Many homeowners in the Northeast Corners had relatives living with them. Peter McGurk, for example, was a weighmaster at the Stockyards, and he sheltered a sister who did housework and a brother who worked at the Yards as well as his wife and child. The boardinghouses were usually small. Margaret Hanley's in the 3900 block of Wentworth had four Irishmen, one Canadian, and one Swede. A railroad brakeman born in Scotland lived on one side of Mrs. Hanley; on the other side was Louis Oppenheimer, an Alsatian-born saloonkeeper. Skilled workers in the Car-Shops, still predominantly English, Scotch, German, and Swedish, were machinists, blacksmiths, boilermakers, cabinetmakers, painters, and upholsterers. There were very few Irish living at the Car-Shops and they were usually laborers who boarded rather than heads of households. Horsecar service on Wentworth after 1877 made it easier to travel from the Northeast Corners to either the Car-Shops or down into Englewood; it also gave rise to many more stores on that route. By 1880, there were approximately sixty-five hundred people living between State Street and the Stewart Avenue tracks, from Thirty-Ninth Street to Fifty-fifth. The Northeast Corners and the Car-Shops neighborhoods constituted one-third of the township population.[10]

During the 1870s Englewood was eminently successful in attracting the type of people it wanted. The first published map appeared in 1872 and was designed to alert Chicagoans and others to a fine suburban opportunity. The railroad connections with Chicago were highlighted, and the map showed the shopping district at Sixty-third and Wentworth near the depot, the brick schoolhouse, Cook County Normal School, and the new First Presbyterian Church, though not the struggling Catholic church well beyond the northern fringe of settlement. Englewood's population increased from about 350 at the time the map appeared to 3,500 in 1880. Among the newcomers who promoted further development were lawyers Albert H. Veeder and Elmer A. Adkinson, both of whom left small midwestern towns to practice in Chicago and live in Englewood. Robert A. McClellan moved from Peoria to cultivate the greener fields of Englewood real estate, while Chandler S. Redfield arrived in 1873 to combine insurance and real estate. There were businessmen like Edward Kirk, who had an iron factory in the Northeast Corners, and Chicago hide dealer C. T. Northrop. Civil engineers J. T. Foster and his son, J. Frank Foster, helped build the waterworks and both became Englewood residents.[11]

In the wake of business and professional people came contractors, shopkeepers, and clerks. The commercial district spread north on Wentworth and then east on Sixty-third to State Street in anticipation of extension of the horsecar line. Englewood's first three-story brick commercial building, the Tillotson Block, contained stores, offices, meeting halls, and the first small hotel. The Masonic Hall on Wentworth sheltered the Englewood Masons, Odd Fellows, and after 1880 the Ancient Order United Workmen. In the mid-1870s, "not withstanding the hard times," brick houses sold for $2,500 to $3,000 and homes costing $10,000 or more were not uncommon. Albert Veeder maintained one of the latter, complete with a fish pond stocked with California salmon and New York shad. There were so many new people by 1878 that a sprightly paper, the *Englewood Eye,* started identifying residents, carrying advertisements and announcements, and explaining the differences between Englewood and the rest of the Town of Lake.[12]

Englewood was proud of its many fine Protestant churches, and members of those congregations viewed them as a barometer of neighborhood spirit. Although the First Presbyterian Church welcomed worshippers from other denominations when it opened in 1870, there were few takers because each group wanted its own house of worship. Lawyer Ira J. Nichols rallied the Baptists to construct a $7,000 church on School Street. Elmer Adkinson and C. T. Northrop were stalwarts in the Methodist Episcopal Church which used the Tillotson Block until 1874, when it built at Sixty-fourth and Stewart. That same year the Universalists started a Sunday school, but their experimental "Christian Union" with the Unitarian Society foundered in 1878. They hired Reverend Florence Kollock and within three years had a small but handsome First Universalist Church of Englewood. Albert H. Veeder then prodded the Congregationalists to exert themselves, and that group produced an imposing First Congregational Church of Englewood on Harvard Street, not far from Veeder's own residence. The Episcopalians and Unitarians, handicapped by doctrinal disputes within their ranks and still relatively small in numbers, did not build until the following decade. Less affluent Swedish Lutherans joined forces with those at the Car-Shops to finance a modest frame church on LaSalle.[13]

Catholics in Englewood and the Car-Shops were a tiny minority and a great distance from Nativity of our Lord Church. Grocer Patrick Fagan arranged for missionary priests and early in 1870 he and a few others purchased an empty synagogue in Chicago and moved it to the corner of Wentworth and Fifty-fifth. It became the church of St. Ann's parish in 1870 when Father Thomas Leydon was assigned to the territory south of Forty-seventh Street. A gale demolished the structure in 1871, but the pastor bought more land and started construction of a spacious permanent church. Like the publishers of the 1872 Englewood map, he knew that migration into the Town of Lake after the fire would help his parish. Peter T. Barry, who sold newspaper advertising in Chicago, came to live in Englewood, and so did John Byrne, a teacher at the Normal School. Peter McGurn, manager of a grain commission firm in Chicago, moved into the parish after the fire. Largely on the assurance of these three parishioners that money would be forthcoming, Father Leydon finished the basement of the permanent church in 1877, the year he was replaced by Reverend Peter M. Flannigan. The new pastor added an "e" to the parish name, for he was, after all, in Englewood. He regimented parishioners to raise funds through bazaars, suppers, and festivals; Nativity and St. Bridget's parishes gave money; and John R. Hoxie and John B. Sherman, neither of whom was Catholic, made generous contributions. As a result of these strenuous efforts, the body of the $28,000 church was finished in time for Christmas services in 1879. St. Anne's, the largest and most expensive church in the township, served a mere 350 families, but those who had a hand in its creation never doubted its psychological and social value for the outnumbered Catholics at the Car-Shops and in Englewood.[14]

Because of its prestige, Englewood wielded an extraordinary amount of influence within School District No. 2. Henry B. Lewis and Dr. Alfred H. Champlin were experienced school politicians, and in the 1870s they trained C. S. Brownell, a commission merchant and a Methodist who arrived after the Chicago fire. Although the district included the Stockyards settlement, Northeast Corners, Car-Shops, and a strip of Hyde Park, it was Englewood that reaped the benefits. On Normal School land at Sixty-eighth and Stewart, they built the district's first and only high school, and three new primary schools in Englewood were appropriately named Lewis, Champlin, and Brownell. The five thousand residents at the Stockyards got only one new school, and children in the Northeast Corners had to cross busy State Street to reach a school in Hyde Park. Protests to the Cook

County Board of Education did little good because Henry B. Lewis was president in the late 1870s.[15]

Englewood's western border was Halsted Street, still a farmer's highway in the 1870s though it acquired a small commercial district at Sixty-third Street. Christopher Thilmont opened a provision store there in 1871, and a half-dozen other merchants and service establishments appeared during the course of the decade. At Sixty-second and Halsted, William Bromstedt managed the Farmers' Home and Tavern, a popular way station for German and Dutch farmers delivering hay to the Stockyards and hauling manure back to their truck gardens. Fearful that taverns and saloons might invade Englewood from either Halsted or State Street, some residents advocated a ban on the sale of liquor south of Fifty-fifth Street. There was little support for such a measure elsewhere in the township, so Englewood settled for an 1879 ordinance making it unlawful for "cows, horses, swine, sheep, or goats" to roam at large in the Town of Lake.[16]

The Stockyards and New City

With a population of about five thousand in 1880, the Stockyards was the largest and liveliest neighborhood in the township. It stretched from the Stewart Avenue tracks to the Union Stock Yard, and from Thirty-ninth to Forty-seventh streets. Except for the eighty acres which were still kept off the market by obdurate owners, the district filled rapidly. Stores, saloons, hotels, and boardinghouses lined Halsted down to about Forty-fifth, and proprietors were almost as diverse as those on State Street in the Northeast Corners. There were Irish, German, and "American" saloonkeepers; Anthony Cella kept an Italian kitchen as well as a saloon; German-born Philip Kern operated the largest dry-goods store; and Irish nationalist Matthew Fleming had a funeral parlor and livery business. Charles Kotzenberg, a German immigrant who had learned pharmacy in the Army and had been stationed in Chicago after the fire, returned to open the first drugstore across from the Transit House. As the residential blocks pushed further east, there were opportunities for storekeepers and boardinghouses on the south side of Forty-third Street, land on the north side being unavailable even for short-term leases.[17]

Most residents had some connection with either the Union Stock Yards or the packinghouses. The census taker found livestock dealers, clerks, bookkeepers, drovers, butchers, teamsters, carpenters, railroad operatives, or, simply "works for Stock Yard Co." or "works in Packinghouse." The "laborers" were no doubt similarly employed, most of them being young Irish males who boarded or lived with relatives. Packinghouse engineer John Bouchard lived in the Stockyards neighborhood, and so did police captain Thomas Gahan and livestock dealer "Buck" McCarthy. Michael F. McInerney came from Ireland in 1872 at the age of seventeen, boarded on Halsted and filled a variety of jobs in the yards before selling livestock, marrying, and becoming a homeowner. Bachelor publisher Harvey L. Goodall was a permanent resident of the Transit House. Emerald Avenue and Winter (Union) Street were the "best" addresses, and livestock dealers, important Stockyards employes like Melchior Hoerner, packing managers Oswin Mayo and Robert Neill, and the Protestant doctor, English-born William Parsons, chose to build on these lots. Their substantial frame houses had well-tended yards, many trees, and usually one live-in servant.[18]

Gustavus Swift's residence was the finest of all. When he first arrived, he rented a house on Emerald next door to Philip Kern. Young Helen Swift liked the German immigrant couple, though she remembered that their broken English often made them "the butt of other young folks' jokes." Soon after the sixth Swift child was born in 1875, the parents purchased four lots at Forty-fifth and Emerald and built a frame house that attracted a good deal of attention because of its size, its numerous bathrooms, central heating, and a unique home refrigerator, five feet high and five feet wide. "Here, at last," said Helen, "we had room enough for a growing family." Four more Swift children would be born on Emerald Avenue, but in 1880 the household consisted of two adults, seven children, two nephews employed by Swift as bookkeepers, and two Irish immigrant servants. This was the only single-family home in Town of Lake with two live-in servants.[19]

The neighborhood's first church was the Winter Street Methodist Episcopal Church, built in 1877. Itinerant Methodist ministers had conducted services in the Town Hall as early as 1873, but it was only after the Swifts arrived that the group started a Sunday school, hired a minister, and built a one-story place of worship. Swift paid for a second floor in 1878. The ladies of Winter Street Methodist Episcopal Church organized a Mite Society and a Foreign Missionary Society, and they sponsored literary and musical programs for the entire neighborhood. The one new public school in the Stockyards settlement was at Forty-fifth and Winter. It was built in 1873 and named for Alexander Graham, a clerk at the Union Stock Yards and school board member who moved to Englewood at the end of the decade. The teachers at the Graham School and the badly overcrowded Brown School were nearly all Protestant female graduates of the Normal School in Englewood. Members of District No. 2 school board thought this only proper.[20]

The board finally agreed in 1880 to get rid of the old frame school and build a new brick structure at Forty-second and Wallace. Anticipating the appointment of still more Englewood ladies, parents demanded that a local

Catholic teacher be appointed principal of the Fallon School. Their candidate was Patrick H. Keenan of 4414 Winter Street, a teacher at the Car-Shops. Keenan got the job, but only after the Stockyards Irish surprised everyone by waging a fiercely contested campaign and electing young Michael F. McInerney to the school board. There were other signs of growing Catholic numerical strength and determination. The first Irish organization, Ancient Order of Hibernians, Division No. 6, was established in 1876 with Edward Byrne, a packinghouse shipping clerk, as president. Three years later Byrne won election to the post of town clerk. Most important of all was Father Cartan's decision in 1880 to give his Stockyards parishioners their own St. Gabriel's parish.[21]

Halsted Street between Forty-seventh and Fifty-fifth streets had more vegetable farms and cabbage fields than residences. The one landmark was Oswald's Hall at Fifty-second, a popular tavern, meeting hall, and beer garden established by Bavarian-born Joseph Oswald in 1875. He had a dance pavilion and bandstand in the beer garden, a flying dutchman or merry-go-round in the picnic grove, and a shooting range for the Southwestern Sharpshooters' Association. There were a few modest cottages and boardinghouses at the intersection of Halsted and Forty-seventh, and some shanties further south on Halsted. One of these was occupied by the Patrick O'Leary family of Chicago fire fame. They sold their DeKoven Street house to Bohemians and moved to Town of Lake in 1879 to escape prying reporters and give their youngest child, ten-year-old James Patrick O'Leary, a normal childhood. The father, an unskilled laborer, soon became a fixture in the Irish-owned saloons at the Stockyards, but he refused to talk about the Chicago fire.[22]

The one new settlement in the township was southwest of the packinghouses. It apparently originated in the late 1860s when Hutchinson provided housing for the construction workers building his new Chicago Packing and Provision Company plant. He may also have built a few houses for his foremen and chief engineer, Fountain W. Young, and he permitted other employes to erect cottages on company land. The cluster was soon known as the New Patch. A few years later, Armour employes started an Armour Patch on Forty-third Street in the Packers' Addition. The O'Toole family, for example, arrived in November, 1872, when their son James was twelve years old. Years later, after working in packinghouses, earning a law degree, and serving as municipal court judge, James J. O'Toole recorded his recollections of these early packinghouse workers' colonies. There were sixteen other families in the New Patch, including engineer Young, carpenter Wilmott, and Henry Friedricks, a German immigrant who lost his Chicago meat market in the fire and came to work for Hutchinson. The Armour settlement was larger. It too had an O'Toole—Luke, born in 1850 in Ireland and an Armour employe from 1868 until

1876, when he opened a saloon on Ashland. There was a Scholl family, probably headed by German-born Edward Scholl, who later bought hair from the packinghouses, dried it on the prairie, and shipped it to a brush manufacturer in Baltimore. James O'Toole recalled another small clump of settlers south of Forty-seventh and Center (Racine), but these people probably owned their lots.[23]

As more packers built in Town of Lake and the existing companies expanded, the pioneers had to vacate the patches. Armour, for example, needed his land for the cold-storage warehouse. Fortunately, William Sampson and Samuel Beers's family, unlike the owners of the eighty acres in the Stockyards settlement, were willing to sell their land west of Ashland at reasonable prices. Occupants of the more substantial houses in the patches moved them to Ashland Avenue lots; others purchased 25- by 125-foot lots for about $100 and, with the help of friends, erected new cottages. When Hoyt and Alsip, brick manufacturers on the South Branch, opened a second brickyard near Forty-third and Wood, some of their employes joined the settlement. James O'Toole remembered the small frame school which opened in 1873 and his after-school expeditions to the meandering western branch of the South Fork, at that time a clean little creek with "apple trees and hazel nut bushes along its banks." The boys also played at the edge of the drainage ditches on either side of Ashland. These "twin canals," flushed by spring thaws and freshets, emptied into the South Fork.[24]

By the end of the decade, the settlement west of Ashland Avenue had about one thousand residents. The Irish slightly outnumbered the Germans, and there were only a few Bohemians and Poles. However, at Thirty-ninth and Ashland a small enclave of Polish laborers and their families, scouts from the Sixth Ward Polish colony, established homes near their jobs in the brickyards. Ashland Avenue, from about Forty-first Street down to Forty-seventh, was filled with residences, boardinghouses, stores, saloons, and taverns. Fountain Young abandoned packinghouse engineering to open a boardinghouse and saloon, while Luke O'Toole ran the largest Irish saloon. In 1877, Henry Friedricks built a large frame boardinghouse and tavern at Forty-second and Ashland which he called Butchers' Home; everyone else called it Frederick's Hall and the census taker recorded his name as "Fredrick." Frederick's wife was Irish, as were more than half of his twenty packinghouse boarders. On Forty-seventh Street near the Ashland intersection there was a similar mix of stores, saloons, houses, and places to board. This Ashland Avenue settlement had no name at the end of the decade, but newspaper reporters would soon be identifying its residents as those who lived "back of the Yards."[25]

Chicago realtor Edward S. Dreyer realized that in spite of the depression workers were buying inexpensive, small lots at the edges of the city and in the outlying townships and building their own cottages. The *Tribune* financial editor, noting the same phenomenon, thought it would be a while before any developers took the "plunge." The growth of the Packers' Addition and the workers' impromptu solution of the housing problem convinced the German-born Dreyer that 1877 was the time to act. That winter he acquired sixty acres of land south of Forty-seventh and east of Ashland; during the summer and fall of 1878 he graded Justine, Laflin, Bishop, and Loomis streets, installed water mains, and laid plank sidewalks. When "all the preparations for a new community" had been "perfected," E. S. Dreyer and Company began selling 25- by 125-foot lots for $150, corner ones for $200, and making construction loans to purchasers. Buyers took sixty lots in nine months, and new houses averaging $500 covered two-thirds of these lots. Owners of more substantial "patch" houses had moved them into Dreyer's subdivision.[26]

Realizing that many of the purchasers of Dreyer's property and some of the Ashland Avenue settlers were migrants from St. Anthony of Padua parish, Edward Koch of Dreyer's firm decided to give them a hand. He purchased four lots at Forty-ninth and Laflin and presented the deeds to Father Peter Fischer. German Catholics living southwest of the packinghouses were, of course, desperately eager to secure a parish church. So too were the Germans in St. Anne's parish who resented Father Flannigan's pressure on them to help erase the "Irish debt." Bishop Thomas Foley was eager to accommodate non-English-speaking Catholics, and thus Father Fischer got permission to create St. Augustine's German Catholic parish. The grateful Germans purchased two more lots and constructed a 25- by 60-foot frame church and school. Conrad Weimann began teaching there in September, 1879, but the parish was unable to secure a German-speaking priest until 1881. Still, just the existence of St. Augustine's Church and the little parochial school pleased all the German Catholics in the township. It also spurred sales in Dreyer's subdivision and assured German dominance within that settlement.[27]

Since Dreyer had graded the streets and put in sidewalks and owners had landscaped their lots, the subdivision offered a sharp contrast to the older, larger, sprawling Ashland Avenue settlement. A *Tribune* reporter who discovered the tidy German settlement in the summer of 1879 dramatically announced, "A NEW CITY is springing up," Cook County's "First and Only Successful Subdivision since the Panic." Musing on the potential housing market for Stockyards and packinghouse workers, he went on to say, here is "a working population of 18,000 . . . the largest industrial population gathered in any single industry in any one square mile in the world. It is larger than that at Krupp, in Essen [Germany], where the celebrated iron-worker . . . employs 14,000 people." The reporter overestimated the number of people actually employed by the packinghouses and Stockyards in 1879, but he was absolutely right that even without horsecar service on Ashland or Forty-seventh, "the child seems likely to become a man." Home sites "southwest of the Stock-Yards" and thus free of "smoke and smells," with streets, water, sidewalks, stores on Ashland and Forty-seventh, a church, and a school were a sure bet.[28]

The only things he missed were the nuances of ethnic rivalry. Residents of the German subdivision quickly adopted the name New City and retained it long after the two settlements had grown together. New City and those living west of Ashland found themselves in the same school district. No. 6 was created in 1873 for the territory bounded by Thirty-ninth, Center, Forty-fifth, and Western Avenue. In 1879 the three-member board replaced the little frame school at Forty-third and Wood streets with a $23,000 brick structure named after Jeremiah Buckley, an Ashland Avenue saloonkeeper who was president of the board. Buckley and board member Luke O'Toole hired Irish teachers, appointed Thomas Byrne district clerk, and gave Irish nationalist George D. Plant the title of "district superintendent." The unhappy Germans demanded a public school in New City, and the board tried to quiet them by buying the discarded, decrepit Brown School at the Stockyards and moving it to Forty-eighth and Bishop. But Edward Scholl campaigned for a seat on the school board on a one-issue platform: Germans were entitled to a public school as spacious and as costly as the Buckley School. Scholl won election in 1881 and the following year New City got its "German" schoolhouse. It was, however, officially named the O'Toole School in honor of then-president Luke O'Toole.[29]

Although there are no extant copies of the Stockyards *Sun* for the 1870s, with the exception of the 1871 fire extra, it is safe to assume that Harvey Goodall chronicled many of the changes taking place in the burgeoning township. From his publishing headquarters at the Stockyards he had telegraph lines to the Northeast Corners, Car-Shops, and Englewood, and his reporters no doubt kept readers abreast of home building, new service establishments, church construction, the formation of new voluntary associations, and perhaps even employment opportunities. Goodall's two-page weekly did for the township what the *Englewood Eye* did for that neighborhood and what a good local newspaper should do—orient readers "in time and space in the local community" and "democratize prestige."[30] Since each neighborhood absorbed hundreds of newcomers yet remained relatively self-contained, the *Sun* filled an important need. Melding those neighborhoods into a larger entity, the integrated community, did not occur, however, until the 1880s.

The arrival of all those newcomers who helped boost Town of Lake's 1880 population to 18,380 altered the appearance of the township, but the influx did not affect the distinctive characteristics of existing neighborhoods. In the northeastern sector a small army of workers sought dwellings within walking distance of the Stockyards, packinghouses, factories, railroad maintenance facilities, and service establishments. By the end of the decade there were about five thousand residents in the Stockyards neighborhood; the Northeast Corners and Car-Shops had sixty-five hundred. Englewood's excellent commuting arrangements, public schools, and Protestant churches attracted the type of newcomers the suburb wanted and swelled its population to thirty-five hundred. The township's one new settlement, numbering about one thousand in 1880, lay southwest of the packinghouses where the breadwinners were employed. In all the neighborhoods voluntary associations proliferated. They were social anchors for old-timers and newcomers alike, essential mechanisms for sorting people out according to religion, ethnicity, values, and beliefs. The underlying tensions both within and between the neighborhoods were visible in school board elections of the late 1870s. Those tensions were also major forces in township politics.

NOTES

1. *Trib.*, Aug. 3, 1879.

2. *Tenth Census, 1880*, vol. 1, "Population," 132. The wards will be called Fifth and Sixth throughout this chapter despite the 1869–76 deviation.

3. "City of Chicago," *Inland Monthly Magazine*, 10 (Mar., 1877), 1198, 1207; *Trib.*, May 18, 25, 1873; Feb. 28, 1874; Apr. 6, 1878; Nov. 16, 1879; Kathleen Neils Conzen, "Immigrants, Immigrant Neighborhoods, and Ethnic Identity: Historical Issues," *Journal of American History*, 66 (Dec., 1979), 603–15.

4. Michael F. Funchion, "Irish Chicago: Church, Homeland, Politics, and Class—The Shaping of an Ethnic Group, 1870–1900," in Peter d'A. Jones and Melvin G. Holli, eds., *Ethnic Chicago* (Grand Rapids, Mich., 1981), 11–17; Thomas N. Brown, *Irish-American Nationalism, 1870–1890* (Philadelphia, 1966), 65–73, 89–104; St. Bridget Parish Report, 1879 (St. Mary of the Lake Seminary, Mundelein, Ill.); Joseph James Thompson, ed., *The Archdiocese of Chicago, Antecedents and Development* (Des Plaines, Ill., 1920), 273, 447, 399, 401; Board of Education, *School Census, 1880*, 7; *New World*, 2 (Oct. 7, 1893), 7; 8 (Aug. 25, 1900), 4; 4 (Dec. 21, 1895), 7; 15 (Nov. 10, 1906), 31; *Sun*, Feb. 1, 1891; *Trib.*, Oct. 23, 1876; Dec. 12, 13, 1877; Nativity of Our Lord Parish Report, 1881 (St. Mary of the Lake Seminary).

5. Rudolf A. Hofmeister, *The Germans of Chicago* (Champaign, Ill., 1976), 49; Andrew Jacke Townsend, *The Germans in Chicago* (Chicago, 1932), 6, 15; Henry L. Schroeder and C. W. Forbrich, *Men Who Have Made the Fifth Ward* (Chicago, 1895), 25–31; Thompson, *Archdiocese of Chicago,* 237, 239, 431, 433; *Illinois Staats-Zeitung,* May 18, 1874 (CFLPS, Roll 13).

6. *Ninth Census, 1870,* vol. 1, "Population," 598; *Tenth Census, 1880,* vol. 1, "Population," 538–41; Gustav E. Johnson, "The Swedes of Chicago" (Ph.D. diss., University of Chicago, 1940), 11–13; John J. Reichman, *Czechoslovaks of Chicago: Contributions to a History of a National Group* (Chicago, 1937), 6–12; Eugene Ray McCarthy, "The Bohemians in Chicago and Their Benevolent Societies, 1875–1946" (M.A. thesis, University of Chicago, 1950), chaps. 1–3, quoted 48; *Svornost,* Feb. 27, 1880 (CFLPS, Roll 1); *Times,* June 23, 28, 1879; quoted in Herbert G. Gutman, *Work, Culture and Society in Industrializing America: Essays in American Working-Class and Social History* (New York, 1977), 72; *Trib.,* Aug. 8, 1877; Apr. 27, 1878; June 23, 24, 1879.

7. St. Adalbert Parish Report, 1879, 1880 (St. Mary of the Lake Seminary); Thompson, *Archdiocese of Chicago,* 433, 435; *Trib.,* Mar. 14, 1886; Polish Pageant Inc., *Poles of Chicago, 1837–1937: A History of One Century of Polish Contribution to the City of Chicago* (Chicago, 1937), 95–96; Victor Greene, *For God and Country: The Rise of Polish and Lithuanian Ethnic Consciousness in America, 1860–1910* (Madison, Wis., 1975), 48–49, 62–63.

8. *Tenth Census, 1880,* vol. 1, "Population," 132; Harold M. Mayer and Richard C. Wade, *Chicago: Growth of a Metropolis* (Chicago, 1969), 154–60, 172; Barbara M. Posadas, "Community Structures of Chicago's Northwest Side: The Transition from Rural to Urban, 1830–1889" (Ph.D. diss., Northwestern University, 1976), chap. 4; Glen E. Holt and Dominic A. Pacyga, *Chicago: A Historical Guide to the Neighborhoods,* vol. 1, *The Loop and South Side* (Chicago, 1979), 59–60, 67–68, 77–78; Everett Chamberlin, *Chicago and Its Suburbs* (Chicago, 1874), 352–56; Jean F. Block, *Hyde Park Houses: An Informal History, 1856–1910* (Chicago, 1978), 10–12, 17; *Trib.,* Aug. 3, 1874.

9. *Tenth Census, 1880,* Town of Lake Census Schedule, Enumeration District no. 195, 1–3; Alfred T. Andreas, *History of Cook County, Illinois* (Chicago, 1884), 661; *Sun,* Aug. 31, 1889.

10. *Tenth Census, 1880,* Town of Lake Census Schedule, Enumeration District no. 195, 4, 20, 39, 60–128; *Sun,* Sept. 10, 1892; Greeley, Carlson and Company, *Atlas of the Town of Lake* (Chicago, 1883), 21.

11. Gerald E. Sullivan, ed., *The Story of Englewood, 1835–1923* (Chicago, 1924), 11–19; Chicago Times, *Our Suburbs: A Resume of the Ori-*

gins, Progress, and Present Status of Chicago's Environs (Chicago, 1873), 44–45; Andreas, *Cook County,* 695, 697–98, 700, 701, 703; *Tenth Census, 1880,* Town of Lake Census Schedule, Enumeration District No. 198, 5–68.

12. Sullivan, *Englewood,* 18–21, 43–46; Chamberlin, *Chicago and Its Suburbs,* 401; Andreas, *Cook County,* 692–93; *Trib.*, Sept. 17, Nov. 19, 1876.

13. *Sun,* Jan. 25, 1890; Sullivan, *Englewood,* 107–26; Andreas, *Cook County,* 688–91.

14. Thompson, *Archdiocese of Chicago,* 365, 367; Gilbert J. Garraghan, *The Catholic Church in Chicago, 1673–1871* (Chicago, 1921), 199; *New World,* 4 (Mar. 21, 1896), 5; St. Ann Parish Report, 1873, 1874, 1879, 1880 (St. Mary of the Lake Seminary); Andreas, *Cook County,* 695, 696, 700; *Trib.*, Apr. 29, 1877; Sept. 29, Aug. 3, Nov. 24, 1879.

15. Sullivan, *Englewood,* chaps. 8–11; *Trib.*, Nov. 12, 1876; June 18, 1877; "Exhibit of School District No. 2, Towns of Lake and Hyde Park" (pamphlet, n.d., Chicago Historical Society); Cook County Superintendent of Schools, *Annual Report, 1872* (Aurora, Ill., 1872), 54–60; *Annual Report 1878,* 16; *Annual Report, 1880,* 50–51.

16. *Tenth Census, 1880,* Town of Lake Census Schedule, Enumeration District no. 198, 69–87; Sullivan, *Englewood,* 23–28; Town of Lake Records, Doc. 2, Apr. 29, 1879 (City Hall Archives, Chicago); *Sun,* July 20, 1889; *Southtown Economist,* Nov. 10, 1940; *Trib.*, Feb. 16, 1879.

17. *Tenth Census, 1880,* Town of Lake Census Schedule, Enumeration District no. 196, 9–10, 17–19, 34–38, 73–84; *Sun,* Aug. 31, Sept. 14, 1889; Apr. 26, 1890; Oct. 8, 1892.

18. *Tenth Census, 1880,* Town of Lake Census Schedule, Enumeration District no. 196, 7–8, 11–16, 85–90; Charles Ffrench, ed., *Biographical History of the American Irish in Chicago* (Chicago, 1897), 605–6.

19. Helen Swift, *My Father and My Mother* (Chicago, 1937), 28–32; *Sun,* Aug. 27, 1892; *Tenth Census, 1880,* Town of Lake Census Schedule, Enumeration District no. 196, 8.

20. Andreas, *Cook County,* 656, 698; Helen Swift, *My Father and My Mother,* 45; *Trib.*, Apr. 1, 1877; *Sun,* Jan. 18, 1890; Mar. 14, 1894.

21. Andreas, *Cook County,* 656, 657, 659; *Sun,* Aug. 31, 1889; Cook County Superintendent of Schools, *Annual Report, 1879,* 49; *Annual Report, 1881,* 46.

22. Andreas, *Cook County,* 683; *Tenth Census, 1880,* Town of Lake Census Schedule, Enumeration District no. 197, 1–5, 22–39; *Trib.*, May 21, 1877; Oct. 10, 1880; Sept. 17, 1894; Mar. 31, 1935; *Drovers Journal,* Oct. 8, 1889.

23. James J. O'Toole, "Back o' the Yards, 1870 to 1890" (typescript pamphlet, 1938, Chicago Historical Society), 2, 5, 8, 9; *Ninth Census,*

1870, Manuscript Schedule for Town of Lake, 11; Andreas, *Cook County,* 665, 685, 677, 687.

24. O'Toole, "Back o' the Yards," 6, 4.

25. *Tenth Census, 1880*, Town of Lake Census Schedule, Enumeration District no. 196, 90–116; no. 197, 1–6; Andreas, *Cook County,* 677.

26. *Trib.*, Sept. 9, 16, 1877; Oct. 13, 27, Nov. 24, 1878; June 1, 15, Aug. 15, Sept. 28, 1879; John Joseph Flinn, *The Hand-Book of Chicago Biography* (Chicago, 1893), 130.

27. *Trib.*, Sept. 29, 1879; *Illinois Staats-Zeitung,* Aug. 4, 1879 (CFLPS, Roll 20); Funchion, "Irish Chicago," 12; Thompson, *Archdiocese of Chicago,* 473; St. Augustine's Parish, *Golden Jubilee and Chronological History of St. Augustine's Parish* (Chicago, 1936), 19–27; *Tenth Census, 1880*, Town of Lake Census Schedule, Enumeration District no. 197, 1–20; *Sun,* Aug. 31, 1889; O'Toole, "Back o' the Yards," 6.

28. *Trib.*, Aug. 3, 1879.

29. Ibid.; Andreas, *Cook County,* 656, 665, 685; Cook County Superintendent of Schools, *Annual Report, 1873*, 40; *Annual Report, 1879*, 49; *Annual Report, 1880*, 51.

30. Morris Janowitz, *The Community Press in an Urban Setting* (Glencoe, Ill., 1952), 73, 154.

CHAPTER 10

Governing the Township

The residents of Cook County's fastest growing township chose to govern themselves through a five-member town board. It consisted of the supervisor, assessor, collector, and two trustees, and it was responsible for levying property taxes and license fees, passing ordinances, and making improvements in the township. During the 1870s the various town boards opened new streets, cindered main arteries, enlarged the police force, started a water distribution system with Hyde Park, and put in the first household sewers. Voters judged their officials in part upon these improvements and in part upon how well the board represented the various geographic, ethnic, and economic interests of the township. In the first half of the decade, board members came from the Car-Shops, Stockyards, Englewood, and the farm district and there was little turnover. The scramble began when the popular supervisor Zenas Colman retired in 1875. The growing population needed additional services and provided eager aspirants for office. It was a Scottish engineer from Englewood, George Muirhead, who devised the winning technique of a nonpartisan coalition backing a carefully balanced slate of candidates. Since most of the neighborhoods and groups within the township had some type of representation in Muirhead's Citizens' party, it was firmly ensconced by the end of the decade. And since the neighborhoods made the township political system work, they had little interest in trying in any other form of government.

Options

During the 1870s the residents of Town of Lake could have joined Chicago and participated in the city's mayor-council form of government, or they could have emulated Hyde Park and experimented with a village form of government. However, they did not like what was happening in either jurisdiction, and the vast majority had no desire to merge with the big city or to abandon township for village governance.

Newspapers and the grapevine kept them apprised of developments in Chicago. After the fire, the Republican editor of the *Tribune,* Joseph Medill, was swept into the mayor's office on a Citizens' Union ticket. The state legislature endowed him with special emergency powers for a two-year period. Reconstruction of the burned district was Medill's primary objective, but "Law and Order" backers and Police Superintendent Elmer Washburn badgered him into strict enforcement of a Sunday closing regulation for saloons and beer gardens. Washburn, a former warden of the state penitentiary at Joliet, relished the ensuing battle with outraged Irish and German residents. This controversy helped the People's party elect a Democratic mayor in 1875, and it probably strengthened support for the 1875 city charter. That document not only confirmed the traditional powers of the council but bestowed new powers as well. The council was composed of two aldermen from each of the city's eighteen wards; they were elected in alternate years for two-year terms. Since Medill's successors were colorless men who had little authority in any event, power gravitated to local politicians who ran under regular party labels and controlled ward elections. If they stayed in the council for a number of years, they usually accrued power and influence beyond their own bailiwicks.[1]

Edward F. Cullerton was the undisputed leader of the Sixth Ward. The son of an Irish immigrant canal worker, Cullerton left school for a brickyard job when he was twelve years old. He progressed to packinghouse teamster, canal and tow boat operator, and a seat on the city council in 1871. He held onto this post until 1892, serving part of that time as chairman of the finance committee and earning a reputation as a skilfull parliamentarian. Cullerton kept close contact with packinghouse workers in the South Branch wards and the Town of Lake. His Fifth Ward protégé was Edward F. Burke, an employe and later a foreman at the Fowler brothers' plant. Burke lived on Thirty-fifth Street, was active in Nativity of Our Lord parish, and, like Cullerton, owned a saloon and meeting hall which doubled as a political headquarters. Elected Fifth Ward alderman in 1880, Burke was so immersed in politics that he resigned his packinghouse post three years later. These Irish Democrats let the American, Bohemian, and German voters in the Fifth and Sixth Wards fight among themselves for the second aldermanic seats. Divided by religion as well as party allegiance, the dissidents were no match for Cullerton and Burke. The socialist candidate for mayor in 1879 polled about one-fifth of the total vote in Chicago and helped elect a socialist alderman in the Sixth Ward. But Thomas Morgan lost his aldermanic bid in the Fifth Ward that year and again in 1881, whereupon he moved to Hyde Park.[2]

The big event in Chicago politics in 1879 was the election of Carter Henry Harrison, the first Democratic mayor since the Civil War. A Kentucky planter and lawyer turned realtor after moving to Chicago in 1856, Harrison displayed no special political skills during two terms in Congress. He came into his own in City Hall, displaying what one contemporary called "marked individuality" and "political acumen." Sympathetic to the working classes and the ethnic groups in the metropolis, Mayor Harrison soon was being hailed as "Our Carter" by an extraordinary coalition of interests. In the 1881 election, he swamped the other contenders, including socialist George Schilling, and the voters returned him to office in 1883 and again in 1885. Cullerton and Burke were ardent Harrison supporters and recipients of his patronage.[3]

During the 1860s, Hyde Park had a township government like that in the Town of Lake. But in 1872, when the Illinois legislature approved village government as a township option, Hyde Park voted to try it. Residents still elected the usual township officials, but in addition they could have six trustees who named their own president. This board appointed a treasurer, constable, and other officers as needed. Starting in 1873, Hyde Park's village government moved ahead on an ambitious program of improvements. Heavy assessments for street surfacing, gas lamps, sewers, and public schools kept property values high and low-income residents out. The Perfumery War drove the fertilizer companies into Indiana and the offal traffic into the Town of Lake. But Hyde Park's greatest achievement was the huge South Park, over one thousand acres and all of it within the township. Four times the size of Lincoln Park on the north side of Chicago, the South Park consisted of two parks joined by a midway. Title to the land was acquired in 1874, and the South Park Commission promptly hired Frederick Law Olmsted to landscape one of the parks. By the end of the 1870s, it was clear that Washington Park and the fine north-south boulevard leading to it would do more for Hyde Park's future than the shift to village government. Working-class voters in the southern part of the township had an opposition Citizen's party, and nearly everyone was disillusioned when the village treasurer, a Kenwood stalwart, could not explain the loss of over $100,000 in Hyde Park funds.[4]

At any time after 1872, Town of Lake could have tried village government. When the question was put before voters in 1879, turnout was low and the verdict decisive—921 against, 13 in favor. Residents did not vote on annexation in the 1870s, but that option apparently was even less attractive. City newspapers kept them abreast of successful annexations in Cleveland, Buffalo, Boston, and New York, and it was obvious that Chicago was not content with pushing its southern boundary to Thirty-ninth Street and its western limits to Crawford Avenue in the 1860s. Recurrent editorials in the 1870s advocated incorporation of those townships "already closely connected with the city," and the *Illinois Staats-Zeitung* thought the metropolis was entitled to Town of Lake, Hyde Park, Lake View, and Jefferson as part of its "rightful heritage." Until Chicago's 1877 ordinance was upheld in court, some Chicagoans argued that annexation of the Stockyards and packinghouses in the Town of Lake was the only way to control them. None of the townships, however, showed any desire to join the big city in the 1870s. It would constitute surrender to a gaggle of ward politicians. "Suburban," for instance, informed *Tribune* readers than annexationists wanted to "gobble up the adjoining towns" in order to secure more revenue. They failed to understand that "the growth of a city depends largely upon whether people can be of it and not in it."[5]

Town of Lake retained its charter as amended in 1867. Every spring voters chose a supervisor, assessor, collector, clerk, justices of the peace, and one trustee (who served a two-year term). The three top officers and the two trustees constituted the town board, and they had power to pass ordinances, let contracts, issue licenses, and levy special assessments. The supervisor was the chief administrator, the dispenser of patronage, and the township treasurer. He wielded considerable authority, but voters could continue or dismiss the supervisor each year. Township revenue came from property taxes, the $50 licenses for packers and renderers, and liquor licenses which climbed from $25 to $50 during the decade. Voters expected the town board to use this money for "improvements," and most of them were satisfied with what they got.[6]

Achievements

Road improvements had high priority with the 1870s town boards. Graveling the main thoroughfares and repairing their drainage ditches was sufficient in the early years, but as traffic and population increased officials did more. Halsted and Forty-third Street were widened to sixteen feet and surfaced with cinders, which were more durable than gravel. Englewood residents secured the same improvements for Sixty-fifth and Sixty-ninth streets. All the neighborhoods needed new streets, and this meant surveying the route, grading the dirt surface, and digging parallel ditches on either side. Harvey Goodall wanted street paving and lighting on Halsted at the Stockyards entrance, but New City and the Car-Shops insisted that Forty-seventh Street deserved attention first and the town board yielded to them in 1880. Since township residents paid a small "park benefits" tax to the South Park Commission, they felt justified in asking for improvements on Fifty-fifth Street east of State. Already designated Pavilion Parkway because it led to Washington Park, the road was supposed to be part of the boulevard system. Commissioners ignored the request until Town of Lake officials finally recommended that residents stop paying the park tax. The South Park Commission responded by cindering and landscaping not only Fifty-fifth Street but parts of Western Avenue as well, and it purchased twenty-one acres for a small park at the intersection of the two boulevards. No landscaping was undertaken in the "scrubby little patch," however, and Town of Lake taxpayers still felt that they were footing the bill for Hyde Park's bonanza.[7]

The town board met the expectations of residents in regard to police and fire protection. Captain Thomas Gahan expanded his force from four to twenty-five officers, and he had a "calaboose" directly behind police headquarters at the Town Hall. A second police station was built in Englewood to serve the territory south of Fifty-fifth Street and double as a hose house for volunteer fire fighters. Since the township could rely on the Stockyard company's first-rate equipment and expert firemen, it did not follow Chicago's precedent with a professional fire department. But the town did purchase equipment for the volunteers, build the hose houses, and install a telegraphic fire alarm system. And volunteers who damaged their clothing while fighting a blaze or were docked by employers for leaving work could collect from the town treasury.[8]

In the early 1870s, residents of both Hyde Park and Town of Lake had to dig their own wells, fetch water from the lake, or purchase it at 10¢ a barrel. When Hyde Park proposed a lakefront water-pumping station, Lake asked to join and pay half the cost. Each township would lay its own water mains, and they would split the operating costs of the station and the superintendent's salary. The Joint Water Works, completed in the summer of 1874, could pump three million gallons every twenty-four hours. Both communities congratulated themselves on having an adequate water supply for years to come. Within a matter of months, however, they were quarreling over mechanical defects and the allocation of costs. The pump alternately sent sand and small fish into the water mains, and ice clogged the intake pipe in the winter. When repairs on the boiler, the pump, and the suction pipe failed to solve the problem, officials reluctantly agreed to purchase new machinery. Spiraling costs made taxpayers in both townships angry. Hyde Parkers claimed that "more water is consumed by the cattle, hogs, sheep and [packing] houses of the Stock-Yards than by all the inhabitants of the Town of Hyde Park." Taxpayers in Lake were convinced that Hyde Park was squandering water on shrubbery and gardens in Washington Park. A peacekeeping committee decided in 1877 that Town of Lake should pay 60 percent of the cost of the Joint Water Works for the next two years.[9]

Before this agreement came up for renewal, Hyde Park asked for a scientific survey of water use in the townships. Meters showed that Town of Lake consumed approximately half of the water for its factories, railroad facilities, packinghouses, and the Stockyards; Hyde Park used only 5 percent for its factories and South Park maintenance. Stores and houses in both townships took the remaining 45 percent, but none of them had meters. The committee realized that counting the number of houses with running water would be unfair because some were narrow one-story cottages while others were spacious four-story mansions. They settled upon an "equivalent" number of houses—1,637 in Town of Lake and 992 in

Hyde Park. In Town of Lake houses connected to water mains there were only 55 bath tubs and 28 water closets. In the Hyde Park houses there were 376 bathtubs and 384 water closets. The committee found twenty-five stores and sixty-six saloons with running water in Town of Lake, thirty-nine stores and only twenty saloons in Hyde Park. The town boards received these statistics in November, 1879. Three months and many arguments later, they decided that Hyde Park should pay one-third and Town of Lake two-thirds of the cost. As an economy measure, they discharged the superintendent of their Joint Water Works.[10]

Hyde Park started Town of Lake thinking about sewers when it announced plans for a Forty-first Street sewer in 1876. The line would extend from State Street to Lake Michigan and drain the northern part of Hyde Park. Town of Lake officials asked for a larger sewer so that they could use it also. There were arguments about costs and complaints from Hyde Parkers who objected to sharing a sewer with "the Stock-Yards, slaughter-houses, and property owners of wet land in the Town of Lake." Yet Hyde Park finally agreed to accommodate the Northeast Corners, and the sewer was built in 1878. It made such a difference that Town of Lake planned an eight-block sewer line for the Stockyards district—four on Halsted and two blocks each on Forty-third and Emerald. Financed by special assessments on property owners, this 1879 sewer emptied into the Stockyards slip at Halsted and Thirty-ninth. Homeowners and storekeepers with sewer connections raved to their neighbors and requests for this latest improvement escalated. The town board, meantime, had the foresight to make the Chicago and Western Indiana Railway Company build a sewer in Wallace Street in return for the right to lay tracks through the township. Property owners on Wentworth agreed to an assessment that would give them a main drain from Englewood to the Northeast Corners where it would tie into Hyde Park's Forty-first Street sewer.[11]

While there was no street paving or lighting in the 1870s, township officials improved the roads, enlarged the police force and volunteer fire brigades, started a water distribution system, and built some sewers. Population had increased sixfold, but the town budget, which was $54,000 in 1871, had only doubled. Taxpayers were satisfied with these accomplishments.

Politics

Voters also judged the town board on how well it reflected the various neighborhood, ethnic, religious, and economic interests in the township. It was widely assumed that equitable representation would result in a fair distribution of both improvements and patronage in the form of town employment. The problem of balancing local interests in the larger corporate body had been on "Suburban"'s mind. "If the towns should be incorporated with the city," he warned, "their citizens would soon be represented by another class of men sitting in a body as irresponsible to them as the Government of Pekin[sic]."[12] During the first half of the decade, there was little turnover in Town of Lake offices because the board was representative—a supervisor from the Car-Shops, a farmer assessor, an Englewood collector, an Irish immigrant clerk from the Stockyards, and a Protestant livestock dealer trustee, also from the Stockyards neighborhood. When supervisor Colman retired in 1875, however, there were plenty of old-timers and newcomers ready to enter the fray. They chose to do so as nonpartisan coalitions presenting a balanced slate of candidates to the voters.

Township politicians did not disguise their partisan preferences in county, state, or federal elections. Among the most vocal Republicans were the Englewood trio, Arthur B. Condit, Albert H. Veeder, and Chandler S. Redfield, along with German-born Rudolph Biester, a draftsman who lived at the Car-Shops. Active Democrats included Peter Caldwell, Matthew Fleming, and Edward O'Grady of the Stockyards, William Brinkman of the Car-Shops, and Peter McGurn of Englewood. The most popular Democrat was John R. Hoxie, head of the Union Stock Yard National Bank and a resident of Hyde Park. The two townships were in the same congressional district, and Hoxie was the Democratic candidate in 1876. John B. Sherman managed his campaign, and although they won 60 percent of the Lake vote, Hyde Park Republicans carried the election. In the 1880 presidential contest, the Stockyards precinct voted 73 percent Democratic like the Fifth and Sixth wards, while Englewood like Hyde Park supported the Republican winner, James A. Garfield. Overall, about 57 percent of the Town of Lake voters in 1880 supported the Democratic presidential candidate.[13]

The tentative nature of the earliest township coalitions is well illustrated by the 1875 election. Englewood lawyer and school board member Arthur Condit announced his intention to run for supervisor, and clerk Matthew Fleming volunteered to oppose him. Both Condit and Fleming endorsed Peter Caldwell of the Stockyards for collector and incumbent assessor George Muirhead, the engineer at the Cook County Normal School. Realizing that the Car-Shops had no representation, Condit persuaded Biester to run for clerk. Condit, Muirhead, and Biester, all victorious in 1875, won easy reelection the following year. But in 1877, amidst grumbling about rising town expenditures and unfair distribution of patronage, Peter McGurn of Englewood decided to challenge the "Condit Ring." Supporters of his "Taxpayers' Ticket" included representatives of the Northeast Corners and Fountain Young of the Ashland Avenue settlement. They collected an impressive vote for McGurn but failed to unseat Supervisor Condit.[14]

A Town of Lake Taxpayers' Association was formed in 1878, and members began attending town board meetings and speaking at rallies. They issued a pamphlet accusing Condit of paying himself for his duties as treasurer, squandering money on town attorney Albert Veeder, and granting the township printing contract to Harvey Goodall. Assessor Muirhead supposedly underassessed the Stockyards and packinghouses, the "*favorites* of this ring." As a result, tax rates per $100 valuation had risen from 70¢ in 1874 to $1.83 in 1877. Had McGurn run again in 1878, he might well have become the supervisor. He chose not to run because his labor supporters wanted to put up socialist George Plant. An Englewood grocer headed the taxpayers' coalition. Even though Condit faced two challengers in 1878, he won a fourth term by a narrow margin. Clerk Biester went down to defeat before Edward Byrne of the Stockyards. That fall the Irish scored again by sending Peter T. Barry of Englewood to the state legislature. As for the Taxpayers' Association, it took legal action against Condit, forced him out of town politics in 1879, and four years later recovered the money which the supervisor had misappropriated.[15]

Assessor Muirhead entered this political vacuum with a clarion call for a new "Citizens' Party." He would run for supervisor and retain Collector Murphy and Clerk Byrne to satisfy the Stockyards neighborhood. Residents of the Car-Shops and Germans throughout the township were pleased by the resurrection of Rudolph Biester as trustee. The only newcomer on the ticket was Chandler Redfield for assesssor, and this met with Englewood's approval. Peter T. Barry went through the motions of running against the Muirhead coalition in 1879, but he got less than 40 percent of the vote, and a hapless Englewood grain merchant who ran in 1880 simply did not have a chance. Muirhead pared the town budget to $110,000, yet managed to keep cindering roads, laying water mains, and improving police and fire protection. He used Albert Veeder as town attorney, to the delight of Englewood, and gave the Halsted Street sewer contract to Edward O'Grady, the Stockyards contractor who laid the town's first water pipes in 1874. Muirhead, of course, had critics who accused him of robbing landowners in order to let the "great corporations go scot free." Socialist George Plant complained bitterly about the use of town police during the 1879–80 strike. Muirhead replied that Mayor Carter Harrison could not send Chicago police into the township and therefore his choices were Town of Lake police or the Pinkertons.[16]

Unlike the voluntary associations which drew like-minded people together, township and school board politics were likely to pit ethnic groups and neighborhoods against each other. They could be a source of divisiveness, but the nonpartisan, carefully balanced coalitions which emerged in the late 1870s in the Town of Lake avoided the pitfalls. A wide variety of groups were eager to participate in local politics because they knew there were openings and they had a chance to shape the future of the township. Political conflict, as Thomas Bender has pointed out, need not be "destructive of strong primary identifications" between the contestants and their community. It could, in fact, "enhance this identification simply because the local community, by providing an arena for conflict, can strengthen the sense of local boundedness." In the early 1880s, Alfred T. Andreas's observations proved that this was happening. The Town of Lake "is all one corporation," he explained, but "includes within its limits a number of villages [neighborhoods]," each of which is "as much a part of the town of Lake as the West Division of the city is a part of Chicago."[17]

In order to survive the annual evaluation by voters, township officials had to meet two different sets of expectations. They had to make improvements while holding property taxes at acceptable levels; and collectively they had to represent, and be responsive to, as many neighborhoods and ethnic and economic groups as possible. Supervisors Colman, Condit, and Muirhead met the first test: they delivered better roads, piped water and a few sewers, more efficient police and fire fighters, and even a small park. Meeting the second test was not difficult in the early 1870s, but rapid growth thereafter and the eagerness of people to participate in township government resulted in some spirited contests. Few politicians were reticent about their party preferences, yet they found that in township affairs it was best to bury partisan, religious, economic, and geographical difference. These broadly based, nonpartisan coalitions gave voters what they wanted, so there was virtually no interest in trading township for village government or surrendering to Chicago's mayor-council system of governance.

NOTES

1. Bessie Louise Pierce, *A History of Chicago,* vol. 3, *The Rise of a Modern City, 1871–1893* (New York, 1957), 300–302, 340–44; Fremont O. Bennett, comp., *Politics and Politicians of Chicago, Cook County, and Illinois* (Chicago, 1886), 137–52.

2. Charles Ffrench, ed., *Biographical History of American Irish in Chicago* (Chicago, 1897), 553–56; Bennett, *Politics and Politicians,* 508–9, 541; Edward B. Mittelman, "Chicago Labor in Politics, 1877–96," *Journal of Political Economy,* 28 (May, 1920), 409–15; *Trib.*, Mar. 24, 29, Apr. 3, 1879; Mar. 27, Apr. 7, 1880; Apr. 6, 1881; July 2, 1892.

3. Bennett, *Politics and Politicians,* 210; Pierce, *Chicago,* 3:351–52; Paul Michael Green, "Irish Chicago: The Multiethnic Road to Machine Success," in Peter d'A. Jones and Melvin G. Holli, eds., *Ethnic Chicago* (Grand Rapids, Mich., 1981), 221–22; Claudius O. Johnson, *Carter Henry Harrison I, Political Leader* (Chicago, 1928), 3–29, 68–69; Willis John Abbot, *Carter Henry Harrison, a Memoir* (New York, 1895), 93–110.

4. Jean F. Block, *Hyde Park Houses: An Informal History, 1856–1910* (Chicago, 1978), 19–20, 23–24; Laura Willard, "Local Government in Illinois as Illustrated by the Municipal Development of Hyde Park" (M.A. thesis, University of Chicago, 1895), 21, 34–41; Pierce, *Chicago,* 3:316–17; Glen E. Holt and Dominic A. Pacyga, *Chicago: A Historical Guide to the Neighborhoods,* vol. 1, *The Loop and South Side* (Chicago, 1979), 76.

5. *Trib.*, Jan. 21, 1877; Mar. 5, 14, 1879; "Suburban" to editor, Dec. 14, 1873; *Illinois Staats-Zeitung,* Feb. 10, 1879 (CFLPS, Roll 17); Jon C. Teaford, *City and Suburb: The Political Fragmentation of Metropolitan America, 1850–1970* (Baltimore, 1979), chap. 3.

6. *The Revised Ordinances of the Town of Lake, Comprising the Laws of Illinois Relating to the Town of Lake, and the Ordinances of the Board of Trustees* (Chicago, 1882), 82–128; Ann Durkin Keating, "Governing the New Metropolis: The Development of Urban and Suburban Governments in Cook County, Illinois, 1831 to 1902" (Ph.D. diss., University of Chicago, 1984), 150–51.

7. "Annual Report of the Board of Trustees of the Town of Lake, for the Year Ending Mar. 31, 1872," Town of Lake Records, Doc. 2016 (City Hall Archives, Chicago); Docs. 890, 891, June 7, 1878; 894, Oct. 22, 1880; Alfred T. Andreas, *History of Cook County, Illinois* (Chicago, 1884), 557–60; *Trib.*, May 12, 1872; Nov. 12, Dec. 17, 1876; Feb. 22, Mar. 7, 1877; Sept. 15, 1879; *Drovers Journal,* May 8, 1879.

8. *Times,* July 22, 1877; *Trib.*, Jan. 29, Aug. 29, Sept. 3, 1877; Apr. 19, May 8, 1879; Town of Lake Records, Doc. 151, July 21, 1877; "Annual Appropriations for Year Commencing Apr. 1, 1878," unnumbered doc.

9. Town of Lake Records, Doc. 1, July 13, 1874; Doc. 2060, Aug. 16, 1873; Dec. 6, 1875; July 21, 1876; May 12, 26, June 7, 1877; Dec. 23, 1878; Apr. 24, 1879; Jan. 9, 1880; *Trib.*, Sept. 3, 1874; Jan. 21, May 17, June 12, Aug. 19, 1877; Apr. 25, 1879.

10. Town of Lake Records, Doc. 2060, Nov. 21, 1879; Jan. 9, 1880; *Trib.*, Dec. 5, 1879; Jan. 10, 1880.

11. *Trib.*, Aug. 10, 15, 19, 1877; June 7, 1879; Town of Lake Records, Docs. 1814–18, Mar. 19, 1880; no. 65, Oct. 10, 1879.

12. "Suburban" to editor, *Trib.*, Dec. 14, 1873.

13. *Trib.*, Sept. 18, 25, Oct. 1, 2, 22, Nov. 8, 9, 1876; Oct. 2, 1878; Nov. 4, 1880.

14. Andreas, *Cook County,* 663, 701; *Times*, Apr. 3, 1875; *Trib.*, Apr. 9, Nov. 28, 1875; Mar. 16, 24, 25, 31, Apr. 4, 6, 1877; Jan. 26, 1878.

15. *Times,* July 22, 1877; *Trib.*, Aug. 4, 5, 11, 12, 19, 29, 1877; Feb. 8, Mar. 14–31, Apr. 4, June 18, Aug. 16, 28, 1878; Aug. 3, 10, 29, 1879; Nov. 6, 1883; "To the Voters and Citizens of the Town of Lake" (Mar., 1878, pamphlet, Chicago Historical Society); Town of Lake Records, Doc. 2060, "Circuit Court Opinion in States' Attorney v. Condit, Mar. 27, 1883."

16. *Times,* Nov. 3, 1879; Jan. 2, 1880; *Trib.*, Mar. 20, 30, Apr. 2, 19, May 8, Aug. 3, 10, Dec. 18, 1879; Jan. 2, Feb. 7, 16, Mar. 26, Apr. 5, 27, 1880.

17. Thomas Bender, *Community and Social Change in America* (New Brunswick, N.J., 1978), 100; Andreas, *Cook County,* 654.

PART THREE—BOOM YEARS IN THE INDUSTRY

CHAPTER 11

Coping with Success at the Yards

Chicagoans were aware in the late 1870s of the close relationship between the Stockyards and those packinghouses which had moved to the Town of Lake. As the "Packers' Town" filled up during the 1880s, contemporaries began to speak of the two industries as if they were Siamese twins. The *Tribune*, for instance, claimed in 1889 that the "Stock-Yards are the eighth wonder of the world. Sufficient meats are there packed to feed the standing armies of Europe."[1] The interdependence was clear, yet the Stockyards company and livestock dealers had separate roles to play. The extension of railroads, especially into the northern plains, increased Chicago livestock receipts by 50 percent between 1880 and 1892. In the latter year 13.5 million animals were delivered, and the 3.5 million cattle set a record that stood until World War I. The Stockyards company purchased more land in order to provide additional pens, railroad tracks, switching facilities, and office space. It even built two elevated roadways over the yards to relieve congestion and assumed responsibility for directing train traffic in Section 5. The middlemen who served—or were caught between—livestock sellers and buyers were the dealers. They felt it necessary to form their own organization in 1884, the Chicago Live Stock Exchange. Although most of the dealers in the early 1880s opposed federal intervention via the Bureau of Animal Industry or certification of livestock for export, they had reconciled themselves to the federal presence by the early 1890s.

Accommodating More Livestock

Railroads were the key to the prosperity of Section 5 in the boom years. They delivered just under 9 million animals in 1880, 12 million a decade later, and just over 13.5 million the year before the Columbian Exposition. Since packers were purchasing more of the livestock and shipping it out as dressed beef, packaged, canned, and processed meat, the railroads leading east from Chicago had to adapt to a shift in their carrying trade during the 1880s. Meantime, the new lines tapping "cow country" and feeder lines

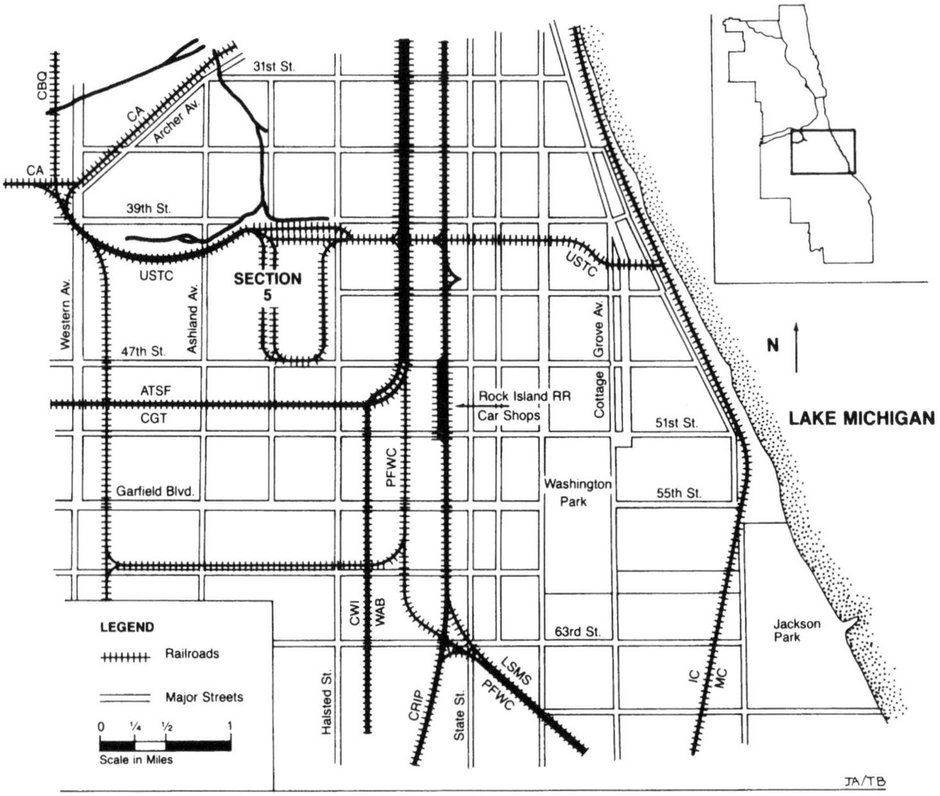

KEY TO RAILROAD ABBREVIATIONS

ATSF – Atchison, Topeka, and Santa Fe
CA – Chicago and Alton
CBQ – Chicago, Burlington and Quincy
CGT – Chicago and Grand Trunk
CRIP – Chicago, Rock Island, and Pacific
CWI – Chicago and Western Indiana
IC – Illinois Central
LSMS – Lake Shore and Michigan Southern
MC – Michigan Central
PFWC – Pittsburgh, Ft. Wayne, and Chicago
WAB – Wabash
USTC – Union Stockyards Transit Co.

Map 7. Railroads in the townships of Lake and Hyde Park in the 1880s throughout the plains made possible the increase in livestock deliveries. Chicago's twenty-three thousand miles of track in 1880 appeared insignificant compared to the two dozen railroads "radiating . . . to every point on the compass" and resembling by the early 1890s "a gigantic cobweb" with the city in its center. Within the Stockyards the original fifteen miles of track in 1865 grew to over one hundred miles, and the packers had another network in the western half of Section 5. As early as 1883, a mapmaker, hard pressed to show what happened to all the railroads entering the Stockyards and Packingtown, simply printed across them: "All Rail Roads to Chicago have Tracks to the Union Stock Yards."[2] (See Fig. 17.)

Just as the Union Pacific had lured stock growers into the Colorado and Wyoming territories, so the Northern Pacific stimulated settlement in the Dakota and Montana territories. That railroad encouraged farmers to raise livestock as well as grain, and Chicago knew that the animals were destined for the Stockyards "as naturally . . . as the devotee of Islam . . . turns his face toward Mecca." And the editor of the Chicago-based *Breeder's Gazette* explained how cattle could be fed on the public domain "with scarcely any expense." Since a thousand could be kept "as cheaply as a single one," a $5,000 investment could be parlayed into a $45,000 profit in four years. Texas cattle and "natives" were shipped into "cow country" and investors scrambled to get aboard. Livestock banks and dealers augmented the flow of British capital into the new cattle companies, while individuals settled for small ranches. John Clay, Jr., a Scottish immigrant who toured the northern plains with his father in the late 1870s, stayed on to manage British cattle companies in Montana and Wyoming. He marketed those animals in Chicago, established a livestock commission firm at the Stockyards, and left an interesting memoir of the cattle boom.[3]

Even before the disastrous winters of 1885–86 and 1886–87, the range cattle industry had problems. Rather than purchase and fence land and feed the cattle, the buccaneers turned to organizations like the Wyoming Stock Growers' Association to defend their "rights" against farmers and sheep growers. These associations blamed livestock commission firms and packers, particularly those in Chicago, for forcing cattle prices downward. The *Drovers Journal* responded with articles on "Forage and Water" and "Overstocking the Ranches" and warnings that no buyers wanted "thin, unfinished cattle" hustled off the public domain before they starved to death. When Theodore Roosevelt, the most famous rancher of them all, passed through Chicago in 1886, the *Drovers Journal* quoted him as saying, "At present the branding-iron and the cowboy are the fences, but they must go." The blizzards ended the argument. When stockmen shipped emaciated survivors to Chicago, cattle prices plummeted to half their 1882 peak.[4]

The Chicago, Burlington and Quincy and the Chicago and North Western delivered two-fifths of Chicago's livestock. They both tapped Omaha and St. Paul, major points of deposit for the Union Pacific and Northern Pacific railroads. While the North Western was building into the Dakotas, the Burlington put a line into Denver and tried to acquire the Atchison, Topeka, and Santa Fe. That railroad, however, wanted its own right-of-way into Chicago and got it by buying the Chicago and St. Louis Railroad. The new stockyards in Omaha, Denver, and St. Paul hoped to dent Chicago's trade, but the voracious appetite of Packingtown assured quicker sales at generally higher prices than in any other railroad stockyard. And so, as the *Tribune* gloated, "Chicago Draws the Beef." The declining transshipment trade was dominated by the Lake Shore and Michigan Southern Railroad, but that line was competing for the all-important refrigerator cars by the end of the decade. The livestock-carrying trade from Chicago was a victim of the changes taking place in Packingtown and the reason why older livestock dealers at the Stockyards grumbled about the tail wagging the dog.[5]

The 50 percent increase in business at the Yards between 1880 and 1892 required a larger banking capacity. Livestock dealers paid cash for the animals they received, and purchasers shipping animals east paid for them in Chicago in cash. Only the packers had accounts with dealers, and some of them preferred to settle their daily purchases in cash. At the opening of the decade the Union Stock Yard National Bank handled all this money. In the early 1880s, when Hoxie got into Texas ranching, the presidency went to Elmer Washburn. He had been a United States bank examiner after his stint as Chicago police superintendent. Serving on the bank's board of directors were Chicago banker Lyman J. Gage, a livestock dealer, a Stockyards company official, and Halsted Street storekeeper Charles Kotzenberg. When the bank's twenty-year charter expired in March, 1888, it was reorganized as the National Live Stock Bank of Chicago, and President Washburn decided to invest in a proper bank building. Daniel Burnham and John W. Root gave him a $50,000 three-story, red brick structure more elegant, many people said, than the Transit House. The bank's entrance had a terra cotta frieze featuring a cowboy, livestock grower, and steer's head, and when customers entered in January, 1889, they found Italian mosaic floors, Belgian marble counter tops, French plate-glass windows, and electric lights throughout. It was possible, however, for a second bank to flourish on the east side of Halsted, just north of Forty-second Street. The Drovers' National Bank was started in 1883 by a former Chicago hardware dealer. Fortunately, he brought along a twenty-eight-year-old bookkeeper, Edward Tilden, who soon won the respect of livestock dealers, packers, and residents of the Stockyards and Northeast Corners neighborhoods. It was Tilden who molded Drovers' National Bank into a community institution during the 1880s.[6]

The Union Stock Yard and Transit Company leaned more heavily than ever upon John B. Sherman—because of his competency and because Bostonian Nathaniel Thayer, Jr., became president after Walker's death in 1881. Thayer had a decade of experience on the Burlington board of directors and intimate knowledge of the Union Stock Yards, but unlike Walker he did not live in Chicago. The directors, therefore, made Sherman a vice-president and asked him, Thayer, and Chicagoan John Newell of the Lake Shore and Michigan Southern to form an executive committee. Assisting Sherman in the supervision of the yards were George Titus Williams, a Dutchess County friend, and James H. Ashby, Sherman's brother-in-law, who also hailed from Dutchess County. With the help of these two "foremen," Sherman directed an impressive expansion program in the 1880s.[7]

New animal pens and renovation of existing ones gave the company 280 acres for holding cattle, sheep, and hogs. The Dexter Park racetrack gave way to a livestock sale hall in 1884. And for the livestock dealers, the Exchange acquired a third wing in 1885 and a fourth in 1888, which the bank occupied while its new building was being constructed. The *Drovers Journal* calculated that the amount of office space in the Exchange had increased eightfold since 1865, "a perfect barometer of the growth of the livestock trade here." Since more and more animals went directly from the pens to Packingtown and more workers cut through the yards to reach the packinghouses and more trains serviced Section 5, there were monumental traffic snarls. Sherman sought to alleviate the crunch with a covered bridge that would span the yards. The company accepted the idea, and the packers agreed to pay half the costs. This elevated roadway started west of the Stone Gate and ended in the Packers' Addition with branches to the Armour, Swift, and Morris-Fairbank plants. Pedestrians were urged to use the bridge when crossing the yards, and tourists loved it because the viaduct windows gave them a panoramic view. Cattle deliveries went so smoothly that a lower level was added for hogs. Sherman never let the expansion program or his responsibilities to the company interfere with his annual party for Stockyards workers. Every September all employes were invited to his farm to feast on steamed New York clams and roasted chicken—never beef, lamb, or pork—and lager beer.[8]

After twenty years of service and only one vacation, "John B." asked for a year's leave of absence in 1888. The board of directors granted it and then named Elmer Washburn temporary manager of the yards. Since Washburn was president of the bank, head of the livestock dealers' organization, and supervisor of the Town of Lake, he had to delegate authority.

Instead of using Sherman's "foremen," Washburn turned to master carpenter John Hough. He rebuilt hay barns, laid out another railroad switching facility on the last piece of vacant land in the southwest corner of the yards, and then pondered the problem of packinghouse workers who preferred to walk along Exchange Avenue rather than take the elevated roadway. Hough built them a raised sidewalk from the Stone Gate to the western exit of the yards and ordered the butchers to stay on it. Everywhere one looked in the summer of 1888 there was new construction and clutter, yet Washburn chose that moment to tidy up the Transit House barn by evicting Sherman's menagerie and the aged caretaker. A perfect firestorm of abuse from Sherman's multitude of fans forced Washburn to rescind that command.[9]

Washburn's most important improvement was the installation of electric lights in the yards. With all livestock trains loading and unloading during daylight, railroad congestion had become a serious bottleneck and directors agreed that only electricity could emancipate them from the dawn-to-dusk schedule. Since the power provided by electrical companies was unreliable, Washburn placed two dynamos at the base of the water tower; one hundred poles throughout the yards carried another aerial network above the telegraph and telephone wires. Electricians wired the Transit House and Exchange and even encircled the top of the water tower. The lights went on in August, and Washburn's enemies had to admit that the effect was "superb."[10] (See Fig. 19.)

Sherman's return to duty in January, 1889, signaled "A New Deal" for the Stockyards, said Harvey Goodall. Company directors expressed themselves by naming Sherman vice-president, general manager, *and* general superintendent until he could appoint someone to the latter post. The company asked Town of Lake officials to vacate the frame building at Forty-first and Halsted which housed municipal offices and the town hall. When the "Steal Works" came down, the land was leased to Goodall's publishing company. By fall he and his 150 employes were in a three-story brick office and printing plant designed by Burnham and Root. On the site of the old publishing building the architects gave the Stockyards an attractive railroad passenger depot at long last, and later they built a large office structure to relieve crowding in the Exchange. Since it was certain that Chicago would host the World's Fair, a second viaduct for pedestrians and vehicles only spanned the yards at Forty-fifth Street, and a new lounge and restaurant adorned the trolley station. Destruction of Chicago's lakefront Exposition Building to make way for a World's Fair meeting hall left the Fat Stock Show homeless. The Stockyards company and Daniel Burnham (Root had died) came to the rescue with a $125,000 domed amphitheater. It had a seating capacity of three thousand, which was more than Chicago's Auditorium. Extending some five hundred feet along Halsted between

Forty-second and Forty-third streets, the amphitheater was finished in time to dazzle fair visitors. It was Burnham's crowning gift to the Stockyards.[11] (See Fig. 18.)

New Solutions

I'd heard all about the Stock Yards,
  'Fore ever I went to town;
And things that I had heard tell on,
  I scarcely could swaller down;
So I said, there is one thing sartin',
  Before I am laid on the shelf;
The whole of that Stock Yards business
  I'm goin' to see for myself.

"L. E. A." spoke for thousands of people—sophisticates as well as rustics, native-born as well as foreign visitors—who wanted to see for themselves "the whole of that Stock Yards business." Ever since 1865 the Stockyards had been a drawing card, but as its fame spread the number of visitors increased. From his ringside seat at the Halsted Street entrance, Goodall watched families carrying picnic lunches, convention delegates with badges, "timid and spooney" newlyweds on their honeymoon trip, "Indians, cow-boys, English swells, Chinamen, and people from almost every clime under the sun . . . all bound to see one of the biggest wonders of the world." Quite a few recorded their impressions. John Campbell of Scotland remembered "thousands of cattle bellowing . . . hogs squealing, and so many men roaring." An English swell, Rudyard Kipling, claimed he would never forget the view from the viaduct windows: a "township of cattle-pens" stretching "as far as the eye can reach." William Hardman was uncertain whether "the Union Stock Yards and their adjuncts [belonged] among the sights of Chicago" or "the smells."[12]

During the 1880s it became necessary to devise a guide service for the growing number of visitors. In earlier years young boys had charged a quarter to show people around and sometimes to rob unwary tourists of their watches. Most people wanted to see a packinghouse as well as the Stockyards, and this meant crossing railroad tracks and standing near machinery. The Stockyards company and the packers solved this problem by hiring and training guides who would answer questions and keep visitors out of harm's way. Tourists saw the elegant parlors, dining room, and billiard room at the Transit House, admired the Stone Gate, and learned that the Exchange was larger and busier than most downtown office buildings. They heard that the company employed one thousand people in 1889 and the livestock commission firms another one thousand. They listened to dealers shout instructions, while buyers and sellers hollered offers and counteroffers. In the packinghouses they watched "the Judas ox" lead cattle to the slaughtering bed and followed the progress of a carcass to the cooling room or accompanied a hog to the point where it was ham, bacon, and sausage. During the course of these tours, guides reeled off facts and figures—so many that William Howard Russell, the English war correspondent, exclaimed, "And how those statistics did reign upon us! . . . What human brain could bear the weight of that multiplication table gone mad?"[13]

Prior to the 1893 Columbian Exposition, the highest-ranking tour group consisted of delegates to the first Pan-American Conference. One of them told a Chicago reporter, "A straw for your art and that, but we must see your stock-yards and packing-houses. If we get from them new ideas we will have filled our mission." The sixty Spanish-speaking delegates, secretaries, and attachés were escorted by thirty Chicago civic and business leaders and thirty livestock dealers, packers, and Stockyards officials. From the Exchange they went to Swift's dressed-beef house, Libby, McNeill and Libby's canning establishment, Armour's pork house, and, of course, Sherman's animal collection in the Transit House barn. The only hitches on this extraordinary tour were a livestock dealer addressing the visitors in Spanish which they could not understand and a Libby employe delivering a greeting in perfect Spanish to, alas, a Chicago banker who comprehended none of it.[14]

Tourists contributed to the growing congestion in Section 5, but railroads were a far greater problem. Engineers expected pedestrians to stay out of their way, tolerated but grumbled about drovers and livestock, and fought each other for the right-of-way into, through, and out of the Stockyards and Packingtown. The heavy refrigerated meat cars, loaded during the day, were pulled out just as workers, vehicles, and commuter trains from Chicago clogged the north-south arteries. Those trains could not be stopped quickly, and if engineers missed warning whistles or failed to see oncoming lights because of fog, snow, or smoke, disaster resulted.[15]

Railroad switchmen were both referees and guards, and nobody underestimated their importance in the safe, efficient operation of train traffic. A strike by Rock Island and Lake Shore switchmen in 1881 for shorter hours caused alarm but no violence. Five years later the Switchmen's Mutual Aid Association asked the Lake Shore to fire eight nonunion employes, and the railroad refused. Union men walked off their jobs in April, 1886, and the Lake Shore retaliated with an injunction preventing strikers from interfering with company operations. Beef luggers in Packingtown refused to load refrigerator cars destined for the Lake Shore, and they harassed workers sent by the railroad to load the cars. Armour, Morris, and Fairbank resolved this dispute by persuading the railroad to dismiss the eight men, which ended the strike, so that they could hire them. When the Lake Shore switchmen turned on both the Switchmen's Mutual Association and the Knights of Labor in late June, the packers, railroad managers, and Stockyards company decided to nip the latest strike in the bud. They announced that as of September, 1886, the Stockyards company would haul the meat cars from Packingtown and deliver them to the railroads. The railroads would furnish the engines and personnel, while the Stockyards company paid wages and rent on the engines.[16]

At the suggestion of E. T. Jeffrey, chairman of the railroad General Managers' Association and a director of the Stockyards company, this arrangement was altered in 1887. John B. Sherman and the company should manage *all* switching in Packingtown, not just the meat cars. Thus the Railway Switching Association came into existence with the Stockyards company secretary in charge and Trainmaster John H. Martin supervising operations. An Irish immigrant in 1865, Martin's first job had been with the construction crew building the Union Stock Yard. He later drove livestock, counted railroad cars, and became chief car accountant for the company. Residing in the shadow of Nativity of Our Lord Church, Martin knew most of the three hundred men who would work for the Railway Switching Association and his appointment pleased them.

There already were extensive railroad switching facilities in the southeastern and southwestern corners of the Stockyards, but the association needed additional space for its thirty-five locomotives. They got it in the winter of 1889–90. The Stockyards company spent $500,000 to purchase acreage west of Ashland, north of the packing district, and adjacent to the company's western connecting tracks. The Railway Switching Association covered its costs by collecting 75¢ on loaded meat cars until 1888 and then 40¢ on all cars carried into and out of Packingtown. Railroad traffic in Section 5 constituted one-quarter of Chicago's total freight traffic in 1889, and it was Sherman's heaviest responsibility.[17]

Until the summer of 1890, the Railway Switching Association paid prevailing railroad wages, which were 28¢ an hour to the engineers and 25¢ to 29¢ to switchmen depending upon their shift of duty. In August the engineers demanded 2¢ more an hour, and packers urged the association to pay it; the stiff switching charge on their refrigerator cars ought to cover it, insisted Armour, Swift, and Morris. Railroad companies advised against it because their engineers would ask for the same increase, and so the association finally settled with its engineers for 29¢ and no Sunday work. Switchmen then demanded a pay boost to stay ahead of the engineers. When the association refused, the switchmen struck and traffic came to a halt. The association then voted itself out of existence, terminating the jobs of all employes. At the urging of the packers, the separate railroads picked up all the engineers, firemen, and clerical workers and then hired members of the Switchmen's Mutual Aid Association to replace the striking nonunion switchmen. This new arrangement was formalized in September with the creation of a Chicago Railway Transfer Association under the direction of an experienced railroad manager.[18]

Sherman and the packers had insisted all along that the Stockyards company rather than the railroads ought to run the switching operation. In the fall of 1892, after the company had been reorganized and packers had a voice on the board, the directors agreed that Sherman should have a transit department. That winter the company built a roundhouse west of Halsted between Forty-eighth and Forty-ninth streets and placed an order for new switching engines. The Chicago Railway Transfer Association sold its land and equipment to the Stockyards company, and the new system went into operation in June, 1893. Sherman reduced the switching charge on refrigerator cars from $2 to 80¢, and he appointed the popular, competent Richard Fitzgerald to head the Transit Department. Finally, everyone was satisfied. During the year ending June, 1894, the Transit Department handled 1,005,947 cars, a hefty 45 percent of them entering or leaving Packingtown. This was another reminder that the tail was wagging the dog.[19]

During the prolonged negotiations on switching, the packers must have rued the fact that they surrendered their seats on the Union Stock Yard and Transit Company board back in 1866. For they now had a large stake in the operation of the yards but no voice on its board and no share in its profits. The packers wanted to be let in, and so too did British investors. Chicago lawyer Levy Mayer was helping the latter group buy into grain elevators and breweries, and he passed on the information that President Thayer of the Union Stock Yard and Transit Company would listen to their offer. This set in motion a complicated chain of events which, in the end, let both British investors and Chicago packers into the Stockyards company.

During 1890 an English syndicate chaired by Henry Osborne O'Hagan talked with Thayer and representatives of the New York Central and Pennsylvania railroads. O'Hagan would buy their stock at $150 (the market price was $125), pay one-third of it in twenty-five-year bonds, and stay out of the Stockyards company management until those bonds were paid off. What this meant, said John B. Sherman, was that the Stockyards would not change hands for twenty-five years and meantime no one would have "to wear eye-glasses and mutton-chop whiskers." With possession of 95 percent of the stock, the English investors secured a New Jersey charter in July, 1890, for the Chicago Junction Railways and Union Stock Yards Company. Four of the ten directors were British; the only Chicagoan was Frederick H. Winston and he succeeded Nathaniel Thayer as president in the summer of 1891. Both Thayer and Winston retained their Union Stock Yard Company ties, and John B. Sherman continued as vice-president and general manager of the Chicago company.[20]

The new company's first two years of existence were marred by bitter quarrels with Chicago packers. Denied an opportunity to purchase stock or have a representative on the boards, the three dressed beef packers, Armour, Swift, and Morris, demanded concessions on yardage fees and the charge for handling refrigerator cars; if their demands were not met, they would set up their own livestock operation and leave English shareholders "with a playground on their hands in the Town of Lake." Armour, Swift, and Morris actually opened a tiny stockyard on land purchased from James D. Lehmer and serviced by the Stockyard company tracks. More ominous, however, was their purchase of four thousand acres in Lake County, Indiana, and incorporation of the Tolleston Stock-Yard Company. Their lawyer, Albert H. Veeder, said they were "crowded" in Packingtown, eager to be free of "exorbitant" charges, and looking forward to developing a new stockyard and packing center in Indiana. Following negotiations in Chicago, New York, and London, a settlement called for the Chicago Junction Railways Company to buy the small Town of Lake stockyard and one-quarter of the Tolleston land, adjust fees, give the Big Three representation on the boards of both companies, and pay them $3 million in cash, mortgages, and stock. In return, Armour, Swift, and Morris promised to stay in Chicago for fifteen years. The New Jersey company could not implement this one-sided agreement until early 1892 because its hands were tied by the smaller pork-packing firms.[21]

Throughout their negotiations, the two stockyard companies and the Big Three ignored the other Chicago packers, most of whom dealt in hogs rather than cattle. But these firms wanted concessions too, and Samuel Allerton and Henry Botsford helped them form the Chicago National Stock-Yards Company. It purchased land in neighboring Lyons Township, said the Belt Line Railroad would enable it to open a Stickney stockyard, and then the pork packers could leave Packingtown. The company asked Elmer Washburn to superintend the proposed stockyard and instructed lawyer Levy Mayer to hold up the settlement with Armour, Swift, and Morris. Mayer went to court to prove that the $3 million payment was an illegal "rebate." This quarrel was resolved when the Chicago Junction Railways agreed to pay nearly $1 million in cash, mortgages, and stock to the small packers, and they promised to stay in Chicago for five years and leave the Stickney property undeveloped. Henry Botsford joined the board of the Union Stock Yard and Transit Company in 1892, and peace prevailed. Dividends of 8 percent in 1892–93 and again in the panic year pleased stockholders of the parent company, Chicago Junction Railways, and helped heal the wounds. O'Hagan later admitted that "it was unfortunate" none of the Chicago packers was "offered a closer co-operation" in the first place.[22]

The Livestock Dealers

The middlemen at the Stockyards were the livestock commission firms. Their dealers walked a tightrope between important shippers, who wanted quick sales at high prices, and the large packers, who wanted a steady supply of quality animals at low prices. It was well known that Armour's hog and cattle buyers were as sharp as the dealers and that no one could deceive the shrewd Gustavus Swift; if packers could not find what they wanted at the Stockyards, they could establish their own procurement departments. The dealers usually had closer personal ties to livestock growers than to the packers, but as the proportion of livestock shipped east from Chicago continued to decline in the 1880s, they had to cater to the needs of the packing firms. Buffeted by frequent complaints from all their clients, dealers remained firmly convinced that their middleman role was essential to the smooth functioning of the Union Stock Yards. In March, 1884, they formed their own trade association, the Chicago Live Stock Exchange, and chose the president of the Union Stock Yard National Bank as their first chief executive. The company gave its blessing by providing a meeting hall for the Chicago Live Stock Exchange in 1885.[23]

The livestock dealers' day began when the Stone Gate opened, and many worked into the evening on accounts and records. Dealers paid the railroad freight charges on stock consigned to them and yardage fees to the company. They supervised the unloading and inspection of the animals and negotiated the sales, weighing, and head counts. The commission firms kept track of railroad charges by weight per carload, yardage fees by head, and sales at price per pound. From the proceeds of a sale, the dealer deducted freight charges, yardage fees, and his commission, usually 50¢ per head of cattle. The remainder went to the shipper and was paid in cash if he were present. The dealer, meantime, paid office rent to the Stockyards company and the wages of his clerks, bookkeepers, and salesmen. To stay ahead in this game, he had to anticipate the demand for hogs, sheep, and the various types of cattle—"exporters," "natives," "dressed-beef," "canners," and "butcher-stock."[24]

Dealing in livestock was a demanding occupation, but it provided quick recognition and rewards for skillful, energetic practitioners. The four Wood brothers had the largest commission firm in the 1880s, yet they felt the competition of younger dealers like Wilson T. Keenan, Robert Strahorn, and John Stafford. The aging John Adams and "Hank" and "Hub" Mallory stayed in business by taking their sons into partnership. W. H. Thompson, an employe of livestock dealers since 1873, became an important figure in his own right when he secured the Libby, McNeill and Libby cattle-buying account. In 1886 John Clay, Jr., and Charles Robinson formed a new firm which flourished despite the natural disasters that struck Clay's suppliers on the northern ranges. Their competent office manager was Sylvester Gaunt, former telegrapher for the Union Stock Yard Company. Opportunities in the livestock trade attracted a growing number of foreign-born dealers in the 1880s. Charles and Henry Ingwersen, "solid German businessmen," knew as much about Chicago's Sunday night German theater as they did about running a successful livestock firm. Once Simon O'Donnell, a former employe of Nelson Morris and Samuel Allerton, succeeded with his own company, he insisted that cattle buyer Patrick Byrnes stop spelling his name "Burns." Tobey and Booth sent George A. Pienkowsky to the yards to buy hogs, and Bohemian-born Joseph Wilimovsky operated a boot and shoe shop in the Exchange. In addition, many firms hired German and Scandinavian-born clerks to correspond with livestock growers using those languages.[25]

There was a strong feeling of camaraderie among the dealers, buyers, and sellers. A few were left out—a fancy dan who modeled "the latest kinks of the tailor's art" and proper John Adams because he "acts and rides like a typical Englishman, and his appearance does not belie the fact." But the others, "the boys," spun elaborate yarns, swapped jokes, whittled pine blocks, chain-smoked cigars, and drank copiously at the Exchange bar. Dealers pressed free cigars, drinks, dinners, and tours of Chicago's night life on visiting stockmen and often the railroad passes that got them to the city. At several points in the 1880s, livestock growers' associations threatened to boycott the Chicago yards because of low cattle prices, but members might well have ignored the ban. As "L. E. A." found out when he arrived in Mecca,

Live Stock Commission merchants
A hundred and fifty or more,
Had signs a tellin' their business
Tacked up over every door.
I thought of the hogs and the cattle
I'm feeding to ship by and by,
So I said I will watch these fellers
A little bit now on the sly. . . .

But to sum up the business, Mister,
In a short and sensible way,
If a man ever had a picnic,
I've sartin had one to-day.

I've been invited to dinner
By ninety fellers or more,
Been asked to drink by full fifty
I never had seen before.[26]

Goodall's *Drovers Journal* encouraged the camaraderie. With sixty thousand subscribers by the end of the decade, it was the country's leading livestock publication.[27] It carried Union Stock Yard receipts, sales, prices, and shipments, as well as brief summaries of foreign, national, and local news. The staff prepared articles on breeding, raising, and marketing livestock, and the journal reprinted some pieces from other publications. A chatty column devoted to the arrival and departure of growers and sellers vied in popularity with "Amusements and Sporting News." Advertisers like Montgomery Ward and Inman Steamship Line appealed to subscribing families far removed from Chicago. Realtors touted bargain ranches; growers advertised special breeds of livestock; manufacturers peddled wagons, carriages, boots, harness, scales, butcher frocks, meat-cutting tools, and sausage casings. Chicago theaters, hotels, clothing stores, and jewelers beckoned to "the boys" for patronage. Medicinal advertising ran the gamut from Dr. Haas' Hog and Poultry Remedy to Sassaparilla and Ayer's Cherry Pectoral. Males were urged to disguise "prematurely gray and faded hair" with walnut oil and, for one dollar, to receive in the mail, "concealed in a plain wrapper," a treatise on "Exhausted Vitality, Lost Manhood, Impaired Vigor." Although Goodall occasionally poked fun at "Hoosiers" and "grangers" looking for the "Transient House," he also took a fatherly interest in warning visitors about "runners," "drummers," and con artists. Embarrassed stockmen who drank too much and lost their money and trousers knew they had discreet friends at the *Drovers Journal* office.

The cozy male bonding of livestock afficionados in Chicago and other parts of the country helped them survive some abrasive quarrels in the 1880s. They had to contend with the Illinois Humane Society, whose president, John G. Shortall, had a flair for publicizing his objectives. Packers thought he composed the letters to the newspaper describing the piteous steers rolling their eyes as butchers skinned them alive, and livestock dealers resented his relentless search for whip and prod marks on their animals. When the reformers secured an 1885 state law turning animal abuse fines back to the society, dealers were sure that Shortall's agents would frame them. "*He* is cruel," they complained to the society. Yet all of them agreed that range cattle were being overcrowded in ancient railroad cars and that the practice was costly to shippers and dealers as well as cruel to the animals. The railroads balked at buying new stock cars, and some growers' associations threatened to buy their own as the packers were doing with refrigerator cars. The carriers finally invested in "stable cars" with hay racks and water troughs and then "palace cars" with air brakes, automatic couplers, springs to prevent jarring, a double roof and fans to prevent overheating within. Livestock crossed the northern plains in greater style than ordinary passengers.[28]

An upsurge in hog cholera, pleuropneumonia, and Texas cattle fever in the early 1880s heightened fears that defective animals would somehow get from the Stockyards to Chicago markets. Illinois and the Town of Lake prohibited the shipment of diseased animals, and the state, city, and township banned the sale of meat from diseased animals. The laws were adequate, but enforcement was up to a handful of "health policemen." The Stockyards company, therefore, welcomed a new state livestock inspector and urged Health Commissioner DeWolf to increase the number of city inspectors. Several packers asked health department agents in 1883 to inspect animals before and after slaughter and all meat products on their premises. This calmed Chicagoans, but it did not satisfy European governments, which followed Britain's lead in slaughtering American cattle at the port of debarkation. American cattle exporters complained to Congress, and it referred the matter to a Treasury Department Cattle Commission. The latter reported in 1882 that no foreign government would accept American municipal or state certification and that any federal certification program must include regulations on the quarantine of sick cattle in both states and territories.[29]

Meantime, advocates of state control secured laws providing for veterinary inspectors, quarantine of diseased animals, and bans on livestock importation from infected regions. Illinois excluded eastern cattle, then Missouri cattle, and in 1885 created a State Board of Live Stock Commissioners to enforce these laws. Advocates of federal action called livestock growers, veterinarians, academics, scientists, and government officials to a conference held in conjunction with the 1883 Fat Stock Show in Chicago. Dominated by midwestern livestock growers who favored federal action, this conference appointed a committee to work with the Treasury Cattle Commission on suitable legislation. Their bill, submitted to the House Committee on Agriculture in January, 1884, would create a special bureau with authority to declare states or parts of states in quarantine if the governor consented and to fine railroads and steamship companies transporting diseased livestock.[30]

The proposal split both livestock growers and dealers. Stockmen in the Northwest wanted to protect their herds from Texas cattle fever and pleuropneumonia spread by midwestern "natives," so these growers and their organizations backed the bill. Cattlemen in the Southwest opposed it. So too did a majority of the livestock dealers in Chicago. They objected to government interference with the free flow of livestock into and out of the Stockyards. The "obnoxious" quarantine would "harass the industry . . .

without any corresponding benefit." Veterinarians were "peripatetic cow doctors" and "unprincipled quacks." "Kill the bill!" cried the *Drovers Journal*. Forty-eight dealers, including Nelson Morris and Samuel Allerton, petitioned Congress and took the initiative in forming the Chicago Live Stock Exchange, which also denounced the bill. Proponents of a federal bureau were fewer in number but just as noisy. John Clay, Charles Culbertson, Nathaniel K. Fairbank, and the *Breeder's Gazette* said veterinarians were more knowledgeable than the "ignorant," self-serving cattle "salesmen." There were diseased livestock in Illinois in spite of state regulations; only the federal government could protect growers. The *Tribune* agreed that Allerton's "crochets" and the Texas cattle investments of the "Stock-Yard Ring" should not be allowed to stand in the way of eliminating livestock disease.[31]

Congress approved an amended bill in May, 1884. The Bureau of Animal Industry could formulate rules and regulations for quarantining diseased animals, but it could not make any state or territory comply. It could merely "invite" them to cooperate and offer them federal funds to enforce a quarantine. The law did prohibit the transfer of diseased animals across state lines, and, in spite of bitter opposition from the railroads, managers of offending lines could be fined up to $5,000 and imprisoned for one year. Sponsors of the original measure disliked the amendments but nonetheless considered the "emasculated" bureau "the first step in the right direction." Their hopes, however, that the 1883 conference would lead to a national organization of dealers and growers were shattered by the bitter quarrel over the Bureau of Animal Industry. A National Consolidated Cattle Growers' Association was formed in 1885 but slumping cattle prices soon pitted it against the Chicago packers, livestock dealers, and Stockyards company.[32]

The idea of federal inspection and certification of livestock for export did not die, though it lay dormant until the packers had also come around to acceptance of federal inspection. By 1890 it was clear that federal certification was the only way to get American livestock and meat products into European markets. Chicagoans approved the 1890 law which authorized the Bureau of Animal Industry to inspect livestock for export and certify pork products at the request of either shippers or European governments. Germany and several other countries held out for microscopic inspection of hog tissue, and so the law was amended in 1891. Livestock exporters, however, asked for federal inspection at the earliest possible date which was November, 1890.[33]

In view of the Chicago Stockyards' extensive business and rising national concern about size and monopoly, it was inevitable that charges would be leveled in the 1890s. The livestock dealers' organization touched off a controversy when it required all sellers in the yards to join the Chicago

Live Stock Exchange and observe its minimum commission fee. One group of opponents went to court to prove that the organization was a monopoly and therefore illegal. They lost because, as the court pointed out, anyone could join the Exchange. Another group sought to kill the minimum fee requirement, but it also lost. Those who disliked or worried about the sheer size of the Chicago Stockyards revived the idea of state regulation. In 1891 when several of these bills were under consideration, the company and the Exchange invited legislators to pay a visit. The Senate Agriculture Committee accepted, and John B. Sherman convinced them that Chicago stockyard fees were the same as those in Peoria and East St. Louis and that Illinois charges were lower than those in the East. The senators told the legislature that they saw no point in "adverse legislation . . . until better reason is given than has been advanced," and the regulatory bills died.[34]

The Stockyards company and livestock commission firms turned in a good performance. John B. Sherman oversaw a costly expansion of animal pens, barns, and chutes, of office space and the new amphitheater, and of railroad tracks and switching facilities. Elmer Washburn contributed a new bank building and modernized the yards with electricity. British investors and Chicago packers got a piece of the action through the formation of the Chicago Junction Railways and Union Stock Yards Company. But they were wise enough to leave Sherman in charge and give him the additional responsibility of controlling train traffic into and out of Section 5. Chicago's livestock dealers formed a trade association in 1884, the Chicago Live Stock Exchange. Challenged at times by packers, stock growers, the Humane Society, political "grangers," and city, state, and federal livestock inspectors, they nonetheless provided an essential service to sellers and buyers. Irus Coy of Chicago told a stock growers' convention in 1887 that, far from being a "necessary evil," the dealers were "legitimate and beneficial" middlemen in the livestock trade.[35] No one who worked in the eastern half of Section 5 would deny that much of their success rested upon the achievements of those who built Packingtown in the boom years.

NOTES

1. *Trib.*, Jan. 1, 1889.

2. Chicago Times, *Chicago and Its Resources Twenty Years After, 1871–1891* (Chicago, 1892), 139–40; *Trib.*, Nov. 19, 1881; Jan. 1, 1893; Board of Trade, *Annual Report, 1892*, 50–51; L. M. Snyder and Company, "Map of Hyde Park, Lyons, and Town of Lake, Cook County, Illinois" (Chicago, 1883).

3. Edward Everett Dale, *The Range Cattle Industry* (Norman, Okla., 1930), 93–104; Ernest Staples Osgood, *The Day of the Cattleman* (1929; rpt. Chicago, 1970), chaps. 2–4; Alvin Howard Sanders, *At the Sign of the Stock Yard Inn* (Chicago, 1915), 275–92; Joseph Nimmo, *The Range and Cattle Ranch Business of the United States* (Washington, 1885), 182; John Clay, *My Life on the Range* (Chicago, 1924; rpt. Norman, Okla., 1962); *Trib.*, Jan. 2, 1881; *Drovers Journal*, Jan. 25, 1883; Jan. 3, 1888; May 31, Oct. 11, 1889; *Breeder's Gazette*, 4 (Sept. 27, 1883), 421.

4. Rudolph A. Clemen, *The American Livestock and Meat Industry* (New York, 1923), 182–87; Osgood, *Day of the Cattleman*, 142–62, 216–27; *Drovers Journal*, Oct. 27, 1885; Mar. 6, July 12, 1886.

5. Richard C. Overton, *Burlington Route: A History of the Burlington Lines* (New York, 1965), 173–98; Robert J. Casey and W. A. S. Douglas, *Pioneer Railroad: The Story of the Chicago and North Western System* (New York, 1948), chap. 20; Clemen, *Livestock and Meat Industry*, 203–5; Bessie Louise Pierce, *A History of Chicago*, vol. 3, *The Rise of a Modern City, 1871–1893* (New York, 1957), 528–29; *Drovers Journal*, Jan. 2, 1890; *Trib.*, Sept. 23, 1885.

6. *Drovers Journal*, Dec. 2, 1882; Jan. 13, 1885; July 1, 1887; Feb. 24, Apr. 7, 10, 1888; Jan. 29, 1889; *Trib.*, Jan. 29, 1889; Alvin Howard Sanders, *At the Sign of the Stock Yard Inn*, 30; [Frank Gilbert], *A History of the City of Chicago, Its Men and Institutions* (Chicago, 1900), 157–59; Edward N. Wentworth, *A Biographical Catalog of the Portrait Gallery of the Saddle and Sirloin Club* (Chicago, 1920), 164–65.

7. Joseph G. Knapp, "A Review of Chicago Stock Yards History," *University [of Chicago] Journal of Business*, 2 (June, 1924), 338; *Trib.*, Feb. 3, 1887; *Sun*, Sept. 29, 1891; Alfred T. Andreas, *History of Cook County, Illinois* (Chicago, 1884), 669–70, 687; [Gilbert], *History of Chicago*, 192–93; Union Stock Yard and Transit Company (USYTC), *Minute Book*, Feb. 18, 1881; Feb. 14, 1882; Jan. 19, 1884 (Chicago Historical Society, Chicago).

8. USYTC, *Minute Book*, Nov. 15, 16, 22, 1881; *Trib.*, July 24, Aug. 23, Sept. 8, 9, 16, 1882; July 8, 1885; *Drovers Journal*, Mar. 24, 28, 1884; Sept. 23, Oct. 22, Dec. 14, 24, 1885; July 9, 1886; Dec. 27, 1888.

9. USYTC, *Minute Book*, Jan. 26, June 7, 1888; *Drovers Journal*, Jan. 24, May 25, June 5, July 3, Sept. 3, 13, Dec. 27, 1888; *Trib.*, Jan. 27, Dec. 27, 1888; Jan. 1, 1889.

10. *Drovers Journal*, Mar. 16, May 25, Aug. 11, Sept. 3, Dec. 27, 1888; June 1, 1889.

11. USYTC, *Minute Book*, Jan. 17, 1889; Apr. 3, 1893; *Drovers Journal*, Jan. 18, 19, 22, Apr. 17, May 18, Aug. 17, 24, Sept. 21, 28, 1889; *Sun*, Jan. 17, 18, 28, 1889; May 24, Sept. 23, 1890; Mar. 7, Apr. 13, 16, Oct. 15,

1892; May 20, 1893; *Trib.*, Mar. 26, Oct. 7, 1892; *Inland Architect*, 13 (Apr., 1889), 61.

12. L. E. A., "The Farmer's Story," *Drovers Journal*, Jan. 9, 1889; *Drovers Journal*, June 15, 1889; John Kerr Campbell, *Through the United States of America and Canada* (London, 1886), 209; Rudyard Kipling, *From Sea to Sea: Letters of Travel*, 2 vols. (New York, 1899), 2:148; William Hardman, *A Trip to America* (London, 1884), 92.

13. *Drovers Journal*, July 15, Aug. 6, 1889; John Clay, Jr., "How It Is Done at 'the Yards,'" *Breeder's Gazette*, 15 (June 19, 1889), 645; William Howard Russell, *Hesperothen: Notes from . . . a Rambler in the United States and Canada*, 2 vols. (London, 1882), 1:179. Few people left the pork houses without hearing that the packers used everything except the squeal. An Armour foreman once interrupted a guide to tell the visitors, "we now have a man experimenting with a view to catching the squeal in bladders to send to Germany to utilize in the manufacture of music boxes." *Drovers Journal*, Mar. 17, 1883.

14. *Trib.*, Oct. 20, 1889; *Drovers Journal*, Oct. 21, 1889.

15. *Drovers Journal*, Sept. 23, Dec. 24, 1885; Kipling, *From Sea to Sea*, 2:148–49; *Trib.*, Aug. 6, 1881; July 24, Sept. 16, 1882; Oct. 29, Dec. 21, 1887.

16. *Trib.*, May 11, 16, 19, 20, 1881; Apr. 24, July 21, 23, Oct. 16, 1886; *Drovers Journal*, July 8, Aug. 12, Sept. 13, 1886.

17. USYTC, *Minute Book*, Jan. 19, Sept. 17, 1887; Sept. 24, 1888; Nov. 23, 1889; Jan. 28, 1890; *Sun*, Dec. 6, 1887; Apr. 21, Oct. 15, 1890; *Drovers Journal*, Feb. 9, Nov. 27, 1888; Sept. 19, 1889; *Trib.*, Jan. 1, 1889; July 19, 1890.

18. *Trib.*, Aug. 12, 23–29, 1890; *Drovers Journal*, Aug. 11, 22, 26–30, Sept. 9, 19, 20, 26, 1890; *Sun*, Aug. 25, 26, 28, 29, 1890.

19. *Drovers Journal*, June 1, 1893; July 13, 1894; *Sun*, Dec. 8, 1892; May 3, 30, 1893; USYTC, *Minute Book*, Feb. 10, 1891; Nov. 26, 1892; May 29, June 12, 1893.

20. Edgar Lee Masters, *Levy Mayer and the New Industrial Era* (New Haven, Conn., 1927), 46; Henry Osborne O'Hagan, *Leaves from My Life*, 2 vols., (London, 1929), 1:306–12; *The Economist*, 3 (May 24, 1890), 647; (June 21, 1890), 800; 4 (July 5, 1890), 12; *Trib.*, June 7, 9, 10, 13–15, 19, Sept. 23, 1890; Jan. 1, 1891; *Drovers Journal*, Nov. 19, 1889; June 13, 14, 17, 28, July 1–3, 1890; Aug. 13, 1892; USYTC, *Minute Book*, Dec. 27, 1890; Feb. 2, 1891.

21. *Drovers Journal*, Jan. 15, Nov. 1, 10, 24, 1890; Feb. 3, Apr. 27, 28, May 1, Aug. 1, 1891; *Trib.*, June 13, Nov. 9, 22, 1890; Jan. 9, May 1, July 28, Aug. 1, 1891; Jan. 1, Mar. 8, Apr. 1, 1892; *The Economist*, 4 (Nov. 1, 1890), 698, 701–4; Harper Leech and John Charles Carroll, *Armour and*

His Times (New York, 1938), 202; O'Hagan, *Leaves from My Life,* 1:314–17; Pierce, *Chicago,* 3:141–42.

22. *Sun,* July 8, 1892; *Drovers Journal,* May 24, June 23, 1890; Aug. 15, Oct. 10, Dec. 21, 22, 1891; Mar. 7, 10, 23, May 25, 26, Aug. 13, 1892; July 13, 1894; *Trib.,* Aug. 1, 16, 18, 19, 23, Sept. 5, Oct. 1, 6, 1891; Mar. 7, 8, Apr. 1, Aug. 31, Dec. 4, 1892; Pierce, *Chicago,* 3:143; O'Hagan, *Leaves from My Life,* 1:313.

23. Granville L. Howe and O. M. Powers, *The Secrets of Success in Business* (Chicago, 1883), 527; Jimmy Skaggs, *The Cattle-Trailing Industry between Supply and Demand, 1866–1890* (Manhattan, Kans., 1973), 78–83; *Trib.,* Mar. 18, 1884.

24. BAI, *First Annual Report, 1884,* 260–62; Clay, "How It Is Done at 'the Yards,'" 645.

25. *Chicago Stockman,* Dec. 28, 1893; *Graphic News,* 7 (Mar. 5, 1887), 151; *Trib.,* Nov. 19, 1881; Jan. 1, 1884; Jan. 2, 1888; Jan. 1, 1891; *Drovers Journal,* Sept. 25, 1882; Aug. 14, 1884; May 28, 31, 1889; Andreas, *Cook County,* 677, 687.

26. *Drovers Journal,* May 28, 31, 1889; L. E. A., "Farmers's Story."

27. *Drovers Journal,* Jan. 11, 1888.

28. Illinois Humane Society, *Twentieth Annual Report, 1889* (Chicago, 1889), 9; *Trib.,* Mar. 6, 7, 1880; May 20, 30, 1882; *Drovers Journal,* Jan. 22, 1884; Jan. 12, 17, Apr. 15, 1885; July 6, 1886; Jan. 29, 1887; Jan. 17, July 2, 1888; Feb. 16, 1889; Clemen, *Livestock and Meat Industry,* 199–200.

29. BAI, *First Annual Report, 1884,* 251, 267–69; Town of Lake Records, Doc. 13, Nov. 28, 1879 (City Hall Archives, Chicago); Osgood, *Day of the Cattleman,* 165–69; James W. Whitaker, *Feedlot Empire: Beef Cattle Feeding in Illinois and Iowa, 1840–1900* (Ames, Iowa, 1975), 108–9; *Report of the Treasury Cattle Commission,* Sen. Exec. Doc. no. 106, 47th Congress, 1st sess., 1882; *Trib.,* Jan. 1, Sept. 10, 1881; July 4, Oct. 22, 1882; Jan. 1, Aug. 26, 1883; Jan. 1, Aug. 13, 1884; *Drovers Journal,* June 16, Oct. 24, 1883.

30. Clay, *My Life on the Range,* 115, 239–41; Osgood, *Day of the Cattleman,* 164, 169–70; BAI, *First Annual Report, 1884,* 251; *Trib.,* May 8, 1885; *National Live Stock Journal,* 14 (Oct., 1883), 448; *Drovers Journal,* Nov. 16, 1883; Jan. 14, 1884.

31. Osgood, *Day of the Cattleman,* 162–66, 176–78; Clay, *My Life on the Range,* 118, 239–41; *Breeder's Gazette,* 5 (Feb. 14, 1884), 223–24; *Trib.,* Feb. 10, 17, 19, 23–26, Mar. 22, 1884; *Drovers Journal,* Feb. 11, 19, 26, Mar. 1, 7, 31, Apr. 3, 1884.

32. BAI, *First Annual Report, 1884,* 473–74; Osgood, *Day of the Cattleman,* 172–73; *Drovers Journal,* Mar. 7, Nov. 21, 1884; Nov. 30, Dec. 8, 1885; *Trib.,* May 1, 27, Sept. 26, 29, Nov. 14, 15, 25, 1884; Nov. 2, 1887.

33. *Drovers Journal,* Mar. 20, May 19, June 18, 1890; Sept. 4, 1891; *Trib.*, Jan. 8, 15, Mar. 18, 20, June 16, 17, Dec. 21, 1890; BAI, *Sixth and Seventh Annual Reports, 1889 and 1890*, 71–78.

34. *Chicago Stockman*, Dec. 28, 1893; *Trib.*, June 10, 12, Dec. 11, 1890; Jan. 1, 26, Feb. 7, June 23, 1891; Mar. 24, 1894; *Drovers Journal,* Nov. 12, 1890; Feb. 3, Mar. 23, May 5, 7, 1891; Whitaker, *Feedlot Empire,* 42–43.

35. *Trib.*, Nov. 2, 1887.

CHAPTER 12

Packingtown—The Backbone of the Stockyards

The packers were already using so many animals in 1880 that a reporter decided they might well be considered "the backbone" of Section 5, the livestock dealers "playing but a comparatively insignificant part . . . not more than a finger." The dressed beef industry strengthened the backbone during the boom years. Large investments in artificial refrigerating machinery by the "Big Four" beef packers and steady expansion in canning, lard, margarine, and other by-products boosted the value of packinghouse goods to nearly $200 million by 1890. While consumers and most meat-market owners welcomed Chicago's cheaper beef, and eastern municipal officials dreamed of being slaughterhouse-free, there were others who hoped to thwart the "beef barons." Livestock shippers and railroads tried to raise freight rates on refrigerator cars; western livestock growers instigated a Senate inquiry into cattle prices at the Stockyards; and some market butchers questioned the safety of "embalmed beef." When the *Butchers Advocate* finally conceded defeat, it acknowledged "the commercial genius of the men who can kill cattle in far western points, lay the cattle down at the most remote New England crossroads and sell at prices lower than the bare costs of raising and killing native animals." Not content with their dominant position in American markets, the aggressive Chicagoans hoped to sell in Europe as well. Through the 1880s their pork products were shut out by foreign governments which insisted upon inspection for trichinae. The only out for the packers was submission to federal meat inspection.[1]

From Packers' Addition to Packingtown

Changes in the western half of Section 5 during the boom years were even more dramatic than those at the Stockyards. Companies already established in the Packers' Addition added new plants, dressed beef houses with the requisite railroad tracks, warehouses, glue and fertilizer works, canning factories, and their own maintenance facilities. South Branch packers who wanted space in the 1880s had to compete with outsiders who were trying to get a foothold in the same location. Land prices per front foot climbed from $80 in the early 1870s to $333 in 1890, when it was virtually impossible to find vacant land. Railroad tracks ran down the narrow, privately owned streets and gave the appearance of lacing the district together. Overhead were the livestock delivery viaducts, telephone and telegraph wires, and, after 1885 when an electrical generating plant was built at Forty-sixth and Packers' Avenue, thousands of electrical lines. The 320 acres were already so crowded by mid-decade that referring to them as an "addition" to the Stockyards was ridiculous. Contemporaries used "Packers' Town" and then the more convenient "Packingtown."[2]

Tremendous economic changes accompanied the physical alterations. The shift from natural to artificial refrigeration made possible the dramatic increase in chilled beef shipments—from 60 to 964 million pounds during the 1880s. Gustavus Swift initiated the change, but all the large companies plunged into the dressed meat sweepstakes and Swift took them on in pork-packing. The entrepreneurs of Packingtown "raced" each other to increase canning capacity and develop their by-products divisions. As John Clay observed, "The waste of yesterday is the fortune of today." The result in terms of capital investment was an increase from $8.5 million in 1880 to $39 million by 1890. And during this same interval, the value of Chicago area packinghouse products rose from $85 to $194 million.[3]

Chilled, fresh meat accounted for 30 percent of the 1890 total. Through the decade packers invested large sums of money in expensive, artificial cooling machinery. Early-nineteenth-century refrigerating machines had been unreliable and dangerous because they used ether. But Europeans Ferdinand Carré and Carl Line substituted ammonia for flammable ether as the cooling liquid, and in 1872 a Scottish immigrant secured an American patent for an ammonia-compression machine. Ice plants, breweries, and cold-storage warehouses soon put the machines to work, and Chicagoans were manufacturing them by the end of the 1870s. The packers were tight-lipped about their first experiments with the new "ice machines," but Nathaniel Fairbank cooled lard mechanically in 1880 and Armour had tested them before investing $25,000 in two cooling machines for his new beef house in 1883. That structure burned four years later, but the cooling machinery was saved by sturdy fire walls. Swift put refrigerating machinery in his 1887 pork house, and it is likely that soaring ice prices in the late 1880s resulting from unusually warm winters forced many packers to switch from natural to artificial refrigeration. Even a Halsted saloonkeeper proudly displayed an "Iceless Refrigerator" in 1889.[4]

Starting in 1891 the Chicago-based trade journal *Ice and Refrigeration* kept readers abreast of new technology, and a New York publication for packers and provision dealers, the *National Provisioner,* featured practical applications. Packinghouses, warehouses, and retail meat markets could now have cool, dry air by pumping brine through coils; hog carcasses could be chilled in fourteen hours instead of sixty. Armour, Swift, and Morris, said the *National Provisioner* in 1892, built "stupendous businesses" by utilizing "the processes of mechanical refrigeration," and "all those who wish to prosper in the meat business must . . . follow suit." This was conventional wisdom in Packingtown, but a few retail market owners insisted that the "new" ice melted faster and smelled of ammonia.[5]

Once packers broke their "bondage to natural ice," as Swift's son put it, they could send more animals through the killing beds, coolers, and into refrigerator cars or smokehouses in a given span of time, and land occupied by bulky icehouses could be utilized for new slaughtering facilities and chill rooms. As a result, packers increased their cattle kill from about four hundred thousand in 1880 to over two million in 1890; and they employed approximately five thousand skilled cattle butchers in the latter year. These men constituted one-fifth of the total number of people employed in the packinghouses and allied by-product industries in 1890. Refrigeration brought changes in the relative status of workers; cattle butchers acquired more clout than pork workers, and Packingtown engineers who tended "ice machines" had more prestige and higher pay than those who dealt with boilers, steam hoists, and rendering machinery.[6]

The strategies of Armour and Swift, the two largest packers in the world by the early 1890s, illustrate the transformation. Armour and Company entered the decade as a pork-packing operation spread over half of its twenty-one-acre plot. Ten years later, it occupied thirty acres and was a strong competitor in dressed beef, canned meats, lard, and margarine while maintaining its lead in pork. Purchase of the Wahls' Bridgeport glue works in 1884 enabled the Armour Auxiliary Works to expand into fertilizer, bone meal, gelatin, neats-foot oil, and isinglass. In the southern portion of its Packingtown land, Armour built more pork, sausage, lard, and margarine facilities and a second canning plant. Four acres in the middle of the "village" became a huge stone warehouse for pork products and canned meat in 1883. Simeon B. Armour's experiment with an "amoniatic gas" cooling machine in Kansas City prompted Philip Armour to build his first mechanically cooled beef chill room and order his first refrigerated railroad cars. These had galvanized iron ice bins at either end and were painted the Armour bright yellow, but did not yet bear the motto, "We Feed the World." While Armour's initial shipment of dressed beef arrived safely, workers had to saw the eaves off the cars to get them through a tight railroad tunnel. Early in 1883 the company started construction of Packingtown's largest dressed beef house, two stories and eighty thousand square feet of work space. The critically important refrigerating machines were enclosed in brick fire walls, and they alone survived the 1887 blaze. Armour quickly rebuilt on a larger scale and entirely of brick; this new plant opened with six hundred skilled butchers instead of four hundred.

Reporters estimated the number of company refrigerator cars at fifteen hundred, and an 1891 inventory valued them at $1,128,611. They were serviced in an Armour carshop adjoining the railroad switching facility in the southeastern corner of the Stockyards.[7]

The Armours, observed the *Drovers Journal,* are "constantly taking new departures in the conduct of their business." Their innovations included electricity in all their buildings, a foundry to build rendering tanks to specification, and, in 1885, Packingtown's first chemical laboratory and retail meat store. The chemists enabled Armour to put pepsin, pancreatin, and beef extract on the market, while the retail market served neighborhood people, restaurant and hotel managers, and Chicagoans who sometimes arrived in fine carriages accompanied by servants. For a time, railroad cars fitted out as butcher shops serviced the Chicago hinterland. In 1888 the company opened a medical station, or "hospital" as the *Sun* called it, with an attending physician, the first such facility in the Town of Lake. And Armour was the first employer to take advantage of Elmer Washburn's offer to cash employes' time checks at the Stockyards bank on payday.[8]

There were striking changes in the administrative side of the company. By 1890 it had forty-two branch sales offices, half of them equipped with cold-storage space. Employment in the Chicago Armour office jumped from one hundred to one thousand during the 1880s, and Armour added a livestock buying office in the Exchange and a management office for Michael Cudahy in Packingtown. Even so, the crowding was so severe that in the early 1890s Armour built a luxurious new office building in Packingtown and moved about half of the staff from the Home Insurance Building offices near the Board of Trade. Telephones kept these administrative headquarters in close touch. In 1882, the year Armour entered dressed beef, he sold his interest in the Milwaukee firm and John Plankinton withdrew from the Kansas City plant. Simeon Armour and his son Kirkland managed the operation under "P. D."'s close scrutiny. Armour brought one son, Jonathan Ogden, into partnership in 1884, the other, Philip, Jr., in 1889. Michael Cudahy's younger brother Edward worked with him in Packingtown and became so interested in the foreign-born employes that he learned how to converse with Bohemians and Poles. Both Cudahys were uncomfortable with Armour's unyielding stance in the 1886 strikes, and so a new arrangement was worked out in 1887. Armour and the two Cudahys formed the Armour-Cudahy Packing Company, purchased a pork plant in South Omaha, and Edward moved west to manage it and to add a dressed beef plant the following year. Michael Cudahy, meantime, joined Armour in the administrative headquarters, and George Sunderland was left in charge of the Packingtown operation. Late in 1890 the Cudahys and Philip Armour cordially parted ways. The former took control of the Cudahy Packing Company in Omaha, and Armour diverted his Omaha investment into the Kansas City plant. Armour and Company made over $14 million in net profits in the 1880s, plowed $8 million of that back into the plants, and thereby quadrupled net worth.[9]

Contemporaries took a keen interest in the competition between Armour and Swift. Although the former's department heads kept repeating "They are Swift, but we Armour," they could not dethrone the dressed beef king or keep him from entering pork-packing and carrying off a gold medal for a Premium Ham at the Paris Exposition in 1889. Gustavus Swift ran almost as fast as Philip Armour. When the decade opened, he had his original frame packinghouse, a large brick beef house, and, in partnership with the Darlings, a fertilizer company. In 1881 he built a lard factory and three years later started manufacturing margarine and butterine. Those profits went into a second beef house and in 1887 Swift's first pork plant. That required a second lard refinery. In 1888 he tore down the frame packinghouse and built a third dressed beef plant on the site. The following year he purchased property from Chicago Packing and Provision Company for a $250,000 glue works which also housed a chemical laboratory. Rather than open a canning division, Swift bought into Libby, McNeill and Libby, and though he tried a retail market on Halsted, he soon leased it to a neighborhood butcher and started a wholesale market in Chicago. Swift solved the problem of office space by leaving only his livestock buyers in the Exchange and moving other workers to the top floors of a Packingtown building and then in 1892 constructing a steel skeleton office tower. Its "high speed" steam elevators, hardwood floors, and "artistic" appointments throughout, including the "toilet rooms," were a big hit with World's Fair visitors in 1893, something they never expected to see in Packingtown.[10]

Like Armour, Swift established branch plants outside Chicago. His first was in Kansas City in 1888 and was managed by his son Louis. Next he opened a plant in South Omaha on the same terms offered to Armour, and in the early 1890s he entered East St. Louis. His marketing network expanded from New England down the East Coast and included sales offices in Europe, often in the same cities as Armour's. Along the Grand Trunk railroad, which carried most of his refrigerator cars, Swift replaced four icehouses with mechanical refrigeration. In Packingtown in the early 1890s Swift nearly doubled his work space by adding floors to existing buildings and utilizing land he acquired from a small packer who retired. Swift and Company incorporated in 1885, and over the next eight years increased its capitalization from $3 to $15 million. The Swift family controlled two-thirds of the stock; the rest belonged to New England associates, Emerald Avenue neighbors, Rudolph Biester of the Car-Shops, Englewood professional people, and a few others. It was characteristic of Swift to maintain both a company and a personal account in the neighborhood Drovers' National Bank.[11]

Nelson Morris and George Hammond completed the roster of the so-called Big Four beef barons. Morris teamed up with Nathaniel Fairbank to establish a firm in 1883 which shipped dressed beef, canned meats, and butterine. Morris also started a dressed beef house in East St. Louis. By 1890 Fairbank and Morris handled nearly as many cattle as Armour and Swift, who were neck and neck. But in overall sales Armour and Company was first, claiming $110 million in 1893, Swift and Company was second with $90 million for 1892, and Morris was third. In last place was Hammond and Company in Indiana. It had expanded into margarine, glue, and fertilizer and established a branch plant in Omaha, but George H. Hammond's death in 1886 and several serious fires held the company back until it was reorganized by British investors.[12]

Although no other companies were serious competitors in dressed beef, smaller firms in Packingtown did quite well in their specialties. Anglo-American Packing and Provision Company acquired more space by tearing down older structures and putting up four-story plants. Chicago Packing and Provision Company lost both Benjamin Peters Hutchinson and his son Charles, but Henry Botsford took over and arranged an infusion of British money. This helped the reorganized firm cope with a spectacular loss. In 1887 "Old Hutch House," Packingtown's first plant, caught fire and smoldered for an entire week. Among the newcomers who managed to get into the western half of Section 5 were John Morrell of Iowa, who took over Henry Botsford's vacant plant, and the Silberhorns of New York City. Chicagoans Tobey and Booth were not so lucky. After thirty-five years on the South Branch, they closed their doors in 1887, sold their valuable land to the railroads, and, unable to find enough space in Packingtown, went to Hutchinson, Kansas, and built the first dressed beef house in that community.[13] (See Fig. 18.)

Canned meats made impressive gains, though William J. Wilson gave up in 1882, convinced that the future belonged to chilled fresh meat. Safer cans soldered on the outside, a larger supply of cattle parts, and growing American and European markets helped Chicago boost its canned meat shipments to eight hundred million pounds in 1890. Libby, McNeill and Libby, the Morris-Fairbank operation, and Armour were the three largest canners. Cattle drives from the Stockyards to Libby's plant in the city created so much hostility that the company rented slaughtering facilities in Packingtown and, with Swift's help, managed to get enough land for a tall, modern canning facility in 1888. Its city buildings became a warehouse for goods conveyed by rail from Packingtown. Brisk competition among Chicago, St. Louis, and Kansas City canners kept prices and profits low until the contestants adopted a uniform price list. Nelson Morris secured the first American contract with the French government by agreeing in 1885 to pack in kilogram cans and let the product be inspected. The British government fed Armour and Libby products to its soldiers and sailors, and Philip Armour was inordinately proud of the fact that British troops in the Sudan ate 2 million pounds of his canned meat.[14]

The Railroad Rate Dispute

The rise of the dressed beef trade triggered an acrimonious debate on railroad carrying charges for livestock and refrigerator cars. Armour, Swift, and Hammond knew that a preferential rate for livestock to the East Coast would be damaging to them, so they fought hard to prevent it. Allied with them were stock growers who sold to dressed beef houses and eastern consumers who wanted the cheaper, superior Chicago beef. Supporting a preferential livestock rate were livestock growers and shippers who had eastern markets, some packers, and retail market butchers who feared the Chicago "monopolists." The railroads preferred the livestock carrying trade at the opening of the decade and the dressed meat trade at the close; they shifted because the growing volume of chilled meat meant larger profits for them in refrigerator cars. This free-for-all quarrel climaxed in the mid-1880s and was perfectly, though unintentionally, timed to rally support for federal regulation of railroad rate-making.

After the "Eveners" pool dissolved in the early 1880s, the railroads did not want to outbid each other for the livestock carrying trade. To avoid a rate-cutting scramble, they turned to commissioner Albert Fink of the Eastern Trunk Line Association and asked him to work out an equitable formula that would bind all roads carrying livestock east from Chicago. He established a base rate of 50¢ per hundred pounds of livestock between Chicago and New York; if the shipper allowed the trunk line to even up the traffic by using whatever railroad Fink assigned, he would be charged only 40¢ per hundred pounds. This was more generous than the rebate given by the "Eveners" and more democratic since any livestock shipper could qualify. As William Vanderbilt said, now "every man could be his own evener." Commissioner Fink let the railroads charge packers 64¢ per hundred pounds on dressed beef shipments from Chicago to New York. This base rate reflected the fact that refrigerator cars were heavier than livestock cars, and they often came back empty, depriving the carrier of any profits on the return trip.[15]

Chicago livestock shippers and railroad managers, still worried about future expansion of the dressed beef trade, urged Fink to increase the refrigerator car rate. Swift, Armour, and Hammond, meanwhile, called the 64¢ per hundred pounds exorbitant and pressed Fink for rebates or a lower rate. The commissioner invited both groups to a conference in New York in April, 1883. The packers plus representatives of the Grand Trunk and the Baltimore and Ohio squared off against livestock shippers Samuel Allerton and Nelson Morris, four eastern livestock dealers, and the other railroads. At the conclusion of this turbulent meeting, angry participants talked to the press. The *New York Times* accused livestock shippers of using "unsound and vicious" arguments to kill a packinghouse "innovation that would give the consumers of the large eastern cities cheaper and better beef." "All nonsense!" retorted Allerton. Once the packers build their monopoly, "the consumer will find out to a cent how much he is benefitted by the business." Railroad representatives claimed they would lose money on refrigerator cars if forced to haul them; packers scoffed because the railroads had not invested a penny in the cars.[16]

Commissioner Fink studied the statistics and weighed the arguments before ruling in June, 1883, that the livestock rate should be 40¢ per hundred pounds and the dressed beef rate 77¢ per hundred pounds. This outraged the packers, who were willing to pay 75 percent more than the live cattle rate but no more than that. If the base livestock rate were 40¢, the dressed beef rate should not exceed 70¢. Midwestern cattle growers and those on the range who sold to dressed beef houses in Chicago and Kansas City supported the 70-40 ratio and used the Fat Stock Shows in 1883 and 1884 to discuss "discriminatory" railroad rates and the need for "a national law that will so control inter-state commerce as to give us our just rights and demands." A *Chicago Tribune* editorial (possibly written by Henry Demarest Lloyd), entitled "Killing the Dressed Beef Trade," argued that the railroads should "carry for all men at reasonable and relatively equal rates." The eastern trunk line "usurpations" proved that it was time to "corral these corporations and harness them again with the old common-law restraints of the common carrier which they have thrown off."[17]

The dressed beef men gave as much business to the maverick Grand Trunk line as it could handle and badgered other railroad managers for private deals. Livestock shippers did likewise, and railroad rates declined. Annoyed by these "extortions," the railroads suggested that an arbitration committee settle the quarrel. In June, 1884, Gustavus Swift and Samuel Allerton agreed to serve on such a panel with Thomas McIntyre Cooley, a Michigan Supreme Court justice and law professor at the University of Michigan. Six months later chairman Cooley upheld the 70-40 ratio and went on to say that dressed beef rates should never exceed live cattle rates by more than 75 percent. During 1885 the Chicago dressed beef men bargained their rate down to about 43¢, and the railroads carried livestock for 25¢ per hundred pounds. Railroad managers complained to Fink that those rates were ruinously low, and, in February, 1886, the commissioner announced that both dressed beef and livestock shippers were going to have to pay higher rates. He set dressed beef at 65¢ and livestock at 35¢, a differential of 85 percent. Fink knew that dressed beef men would object, but gambled on livestock shippers supporting the increase because the differential also went up.[18]

As expected, the packers took their case to the newspapers. Their argument began with rates and ended with free enterprise. In 1878, they pointed out, the first refrigerator car rate was 50 percent above the livestock rate. They had accepted every increase since then and were willing to abide by the 75 percent differential endorsed by Judge Cooley's arbitration panel. Fink's arbitrary jump to 85 percent constituted "discrimination and distortion." He was waging a "relentless war" against dressed beef, aided and abetted by "the railroads and their co-partners, the stock yards." Armour, Swift, and Hammond insisted that Fink had no right to overrule the arbitrators and implied that the railroads should be punished for such dictatorial behavior. Picturing themselves as honest, hardworking suppliers seeking fair play and no favors, they asked American consumers: "How does it strike the general public to see a legitimate industry so betrayed and robbed because the bringing of dressed beef into New York City hurts the abattoir and stock yard rings, and makes them sell meat at a reasonable price instead of at the extortionate figures demanded and obtained before Western dressed beef came upon the market?"[19]

Armour's prose "reads very nicely," replied Allerton, but his facts were wrong. Dressed beef men took secret rebates from the railroads, they worked together to suppress Chicago cattle prices, and thus they exploited all cattle growers, not just those shipping east. The packers have devised an "exceedingly clever but highly monopolistic trade," charged Allerton, and unless their devious "ring" were broken by higher transportation charges, "all competitive buying would cease at the Union Stock-Yards, and the seller of cattle be left entirely at the mercy of the dressed-beef men." Already alarmed by sagging cattle prices and increased railroad rates, livestock growers in many parts of the country took up the cry against Chicago monopolists. The *Drovers Journal* refused to get involved in the rate dispute, but Goodall let it be known that whatever the outcome the Chicago Stockyards would forever remain "the best live-stock market on the globe for producers, consumers, and everybody." A violent, disorderly meeting of the Chicago Live Stock Exchange refused to criticize Fink's 85 percent differential, though it condemned the rate increases.[20]

So livestock growers and dealers, dressed beef men and packers, eastern buyers of livestock and consumers of Chicago chilled meat agreed that commissioner Fink's rate increases were unfair. "The attitude of the railroads," said the *Drovers Journal*, "is like the big boy who settled the dispute of the two small boys over the nut. One saw it, and the other picked it up. The big boy settled the dispute by taking the meat of the nut himself, and dividing the shell between the two." The 1886 convention of the National (Consolidated) Cattle Growers' Association passed a resolution urging

Congress to end railroad "oppression" with "suitable legislation." Two bills were under consideration: Texas Congressman John Reagan's measure forbade rebates and pools; Illinois Senator Shelby M. Cullom sponsored a more comprehensive bill which drew upon his committee investigation of railroad practices and his consultation with Judge Thomas M. Cooley. While Congress considered the Reagan and Cullom bills, livestock shippers, staunch allies of the railroads in the early 1880s, came out in favor of government regulation. Dressed beef men announced that they would rather take their chances with a federal railroad commission than submit to the dictates of commissioner Albert Fink.[21]

The Interstate Commerce Act, signed early in 1887, was supposed to prevent railroad pooling and rate discrimination against shippers, commodities, and localities. The law, as Swift's son noted later, did close the "long argument between father and Fink." Dressed beef producers, reassured about equal railroad rates, established new plants in Omaha, Kansas City, and East St. Louis and their own cold-storage facilities in many eastern and southern cities. Armour told a Senate investigating committee in 1889: "Since the interstate law went into effect there has been less and less cutting of rates to cattle shippers . . . consequently, one embarrassing feature of the dressed beef business has been removed, namely, that of seeking out the cut rates on the cattle business for the purpose of getting the proper equalization of the dressed beef rate." However, the new Interstate Commerce Commission, chaired for a time by Thomas M. Cooley, was less than a perfect tool for the packers. It backed railroad officials who used the new law to cancel rebates and other refrigerator car privileges. Packers still considered their carrying charge of 65¢ per hundred pounds excessive in view of a general provision rate of 30¢. When Albert Fink retired from his thankless post in 1889, the railroads, as he had predicted, stumbled into a rate-cutting contest. Refrigerator car charges plunged to 27¢ before the instigator, the Chicago and Grand Trunk, called a halt to this suicidal policy. By that time, Packingtown had won a resounding victory: two-thirds of the cattle arriving at the Stockyards left Chicago in cans or refrigerator cars.[22]

The struggle over railroad rates, coinciding as it did with the collapse of the cattle boom and declining livestock prices, encouraged stock growers to vent their anger on the Stockyards and Chicago dealers. The *Denver News*, for example, said the dealers were puppets of the Union Stock Yard Company, which was in the vest pocket of the packers. Every session of the Illinois legislature in the 1880s entertained at least one bill to regulate the Stockyards. The company's clinching argument against these "come-and-see-me-with-your-granger-suit-on" bills was the fact that their charges were exactly the same as those in western yards. The Chicago Live Stock Exchange had to answer for the sins of both the company and the packers, though they controlled neither, and contend with internal differences over railroad rates. President Elmer Washburn sided with Allerton, but during 1888 he was too busy running the bank, managing the Stockyards, and being Town of Lake supervisor to give the Exchange much attention. Gustavus Swift, still angry about Washburn's refusal to denounce the 85 percent differential, used this opportunity to rally support for new leadership. He persuaded dealer William H. Thompson and packer-dealer Levi B. Doud to run for president and vice-president. In March, 1889, this slate won an upset victory. Members of the Chicago Live Stock Exchange knew by then that Packingtown was the backbone of their trade.[23]

Other Confrontations

The livestock-dressed beef railroad rate quarrel was the most important controversy and roused the deepest passions in the 1880s, but it was not the only one. Dairy interests tried to stymie margarine and butterine sales, retail meat market owners organized to fight Chicago chilled beef, and European governments refused to accept uninspected American pork products. The packers, of course, fought back and won their battle with the opponents of chilled beef, but in the other two contests they had to compromise and accept federal intervention.

The oleomargarine imbroglio was the least serious and easiest to resolve. It stemmed from the discovery of packinghouse chemists that small amounts of cottonseed oil improved the consistency of lard and butter substitutes. Those who believed cottonseed oil unfit to eat cried adulteration. The manufacturers insisted that it was both safe and nutritious and invited people to visit their plants or watch demonstrations at the Fat Stock Shows. Dairymen were already concerned about the competition of "bogus butter" and the grocers who passed it off as the real thing, making 20¢ a pound on the deceit. Illinois in 1881 and then Ohio, New York, Massachusetts, and other states passed laws requiring producers to list all ingredients on the package and prohibiting retailers from altering labels or changing package contents. This was difficult to enforce, so the packers suggested federal regulation of retailers while dairymen lined up behind a federal tax on butter substitutes to equalize costs. A federal packaging and labeling bill with a 10¢ a pound tax on margarine and butterine pleased dairymen, but packers called the proposed tax both "ruinous" and unconstitutional. Congress slashed the tax to 2¢ before passing the Oleomargarine Law in 1886. Butter substitute sales doubled during the next five years because the debate had legitimized cottonseed oil as a food and alerted consumers to the cheap alternatives to the dairymen's expensive "choice creamery butter."[24]

Much harder to handle was the opposition of those market owners who felt threatened by the instant success of Chicago's dressed beef. Consumers liked its high quality, low price, and ability to force local meat prices down. Many eastern retail butchers welcomed it because it attracted customers, enabled them to buy only the cuts they could sell, and relieved them of peddling tallow and hides. An enthusiastic endorsement of the "Cheaper Beef" in *Harper's Weekly* in 1882 converted even the most "fastidious" restaurants and hotels. But eastern cattle growers and dealers, slaughterers for the city trade, and market owners who dressed their own beef rose to the defense of the "old-time" local butchers whose livelihood was threatened by "mere cutters of meat" in Chicago. Some market owners posted signs reading "Positively no Chicago meat sold here," and others referred to the rival product as "frozen," "stale," "embalmed," or "dead meat." The carcasses were either poisoned by ammonia in the chilling process, or else they had previously been condemned as "maimed and sick." Whatever its cheaper price, opponents contended, Chicago's "embalmed beef" was dangerous.[25]

Anti-dressed beef butchers and market owners organized in 1884, the year the Bureau of Animal Industry reported that nine-tenths of the beef sold in Boston, New York, and Philadelphia came from Chicago. New Yorkers started the Eastern Butchers' Protective Society, and its journal, the *Butchers Advocate,* encouraged butchers in other cities to do likewise. About one-quarter of the Chicago retailers, resentful of the packers' retail stores in Town of Lake and Libby's hotel and restaurant trade, organized and selected a wholesale meat dealer named Thomas Armour as their spokesman. In 1886 he founded the Butchers' National Protective Association, became its first president, and used the new *Butchers National Journal* to warn that "this is an age of organization and all who fail to adopt the methods of the times will fall far behind in the race for business success." Moreover, Thomas Armour courted the National Cattle Growers' Association because "stockmen and butchers" were "natural allies" with "a common enemy in the gigantic monopoly."[26]

The dressed beef interests in Chicago knew a good deal about "the race for business success," and at first they attributed Thomas Armour's attack to "jealousy" and recalled that "Arkwright was mobbed when he invented . . . the spinning jenny." But they had to get involved when cattle growers and the Butchers' National Protective Association lobbied for state laws protecting "home industries" and public health. Starting in 1887, Minnesota, Indiana, Colorado, and New Mexico banned out-of-state dressed beef by requiring that state agents inspect before slaughter all cattle whose meat was to be sold within state boundaries. The Chicago packers initiated test cases and all the laws were declared unconstitutional. The Minnesota court said that transportation of fresh meat in refrigerator cars across state lines was "one of the greatest and most important articles in interstate commerce" and the meat arrived "as fresh and wholesome as when placed in the car." The United States Supreme Court agreed in 1891. Thomas Armour's second strategy to get the "big fellows" was a boycott of Armour products in the aftermath of the 1886 strikes. Conducted by the Knights of Labor, it alienated some members of the Butchers' Protective Association and accomplished little, though in Chicago the packers closed their Halsted Street retail stores and discontinued the suburban "market trains."[27]

The final assault was waged by butchers, growers, dealers, some railroads, and quite a few angry ranchers on the northern plains, and it was directed against the dressed beef packers rather than their product. The Big Four, according to the opponents, constituted a monopoly, conspiracy, ring, trust, combine, or syndicate ruthlessly exploiting cattle growers, dealers, meat-market owners, and consumers. Senator George Vest of Missouri agreed in 1888 that "the cattle pool of Chicago is the most infamous tyranny that ever existed in the United States." In May of that year the Senate put Vest in charge of a special investigation of the Big Four, cattle prices, and, at Senator Shelby Cullom's insistence, railroad rates on livestock and dressed beef. In addition to Vest and Cullom of Illinois, members of the Select Committee came from the livestock growing states of Kansas, Nebraska, and Texas. "The cow has entered the arena of Politics," remarked the *Breeder's Gazette*.[28]

The committee began its hearings in St. Louis in November of 1888 when the National Cattle Growers' Association and the Butchers' National Protective Association just happened to be meeting. A St. Louis livestock dealer recalled the time "before the dressed-beef monopoly," when the St. Louis stockyard "had hundreds of buyers . . . from all points in the East, buying and shipping beef on the hoof." Now, however, it "goes to the dressed-beef concerns." The only way to turn the clock back was local inspection of livestock before slaughter in "every town and city in the United States." Another witness explained that growers preferred to ship and sell in Chicago because it handled "all classes of cattle in unlimited quantities" and had "facilities for dressing and canning the beef and utilizing everything of every character than can be shipped from the range." Simeon Armour assured the committee when it came to Kansas City that packers "have the biggest time in cutting each other's throats of any class of business that is done in America, and it is done even right against my own brother's house." In Chicago, witnesses confirmed the obvious: Armour, Swift, Hammond, Morris, and Libby bought the vast majority of the cattle. A livestock dealer likened the results to "the old expression, that 'the big fish are eating up the little ones.'" John B. Sherman explained the fee structure at the Stockyards but would not release a list of company stockholders. Armour, Swift, and Morris refused to testify, apparently feeling, as Armour put it, that Senator Vest was "notoriously on record as opposed to the dressed beef interests." As the committee chairman left Chicago, he vowed to "fetch" Philip Armour.[29]

"King Philip" bowed to a subpoena delivered in November, 1889, but he took to Washington a carefully prepared 5,000-word statement about cattle prices and beef packer profits. His statistics came from published government, Board of Trade, and railroad reports; Chicago butchers provided his meat price chart. Declining cattle prices, Armour started out, affected range cattle and were due to "overmarketing . . . brought about by reckless investment and speculations in ranch properties," overcrowding on the ranges, short pasture, droughts, and severe winters. Obviously, lightweight western cattle were not as desirable as mature midwestern natives. Complaints were coming from the shippers of inferior westerns, he noted, "and only rarely from the owners of first class stock."[30]

Since the price of a chilled beef carcass did not cover the cost of the animal, Armour continued, packers had to make use of "hides, horns, hoofs, tongue, liver, heart, tallow, oleo, fat, intestines, blood and offal." They spent large sums for their plant, equipment, and refrigerator cars and paid excessively high railroad carrying fees. Chicago packers *had* passed lower cattle prices along to consumers: corned beef sold for $2.45 a dozen one-pound cans in 1883 and $1.15 in 1889, while tenderloin declined from 25¢ per pound to 17¢. Armour then summarized his dressed beef business in 1888. He paid $15.4 million for 340,649 cattle and cleared $418,104. A profit of $1.22 per head was, he "respectfully" submitted, not "excessive." Finally, he denied that the dressed beef industry was a monopoly. "The methods employed in slaughtering the animal and preparing its products for the market are well known and open to anyone who wishes to engage in it." There are no patents "to prevent any other parties from engaging in this business. The field is and always has been open." During the questioning that followed, Armour said that the Chicago packers were always competing—"like two flints rubbing together all the while." Cattle growers, he suggested, would be in real trouble without the dressed beef industry. He even found an opportunity to say that packers could afford to pay more for cattle if Congress abolished the oleomargarine tax.[31]

The Vest committee's May, 1890, report charged the packers' agents, though not the packers themselves, with cooperating to keep cattle prices down. The Interstate Commerce Commission should do something about discriminatory railroad rates for cattle shippers, and larger foreign markets for both live cattle and beef products would help increase cattle prices. The livestock growers and market butchers who had instigated the investigation were disappointed with the results: the packers got off the hook. An 1889 St. Louis conference on the "Beef and Pork Trust" which had recommended a federal ban on combinations fixing pork, beef, and grain prices was a good deal more to their liking than the Select Committee report.[32]

No one disagreed with the Vest committee that larger European markets for American meat products would be beneficial. Pork packers were suffering under bans imposed first by Italy and then by France, Germany, Belgium, Austria-Hungary, Spain, Denmark, and Switzerland. Their exports, excluding lard, fell from $70 million to $43 million during the 1880s. Some Chicago pork packers compensated by pushing sales in the South, but specialty houses like Tobey and Booth or Moran and Healy were hard pressed. What to do about it was the question. During 1883 Philip Armour had a Department of Agriculture scientist conduct microscopic inspection of hogs at his Chicago plant, and it went so smoothly that the following year he threw his support behind a bill calling for federal inspection of livestock and meat products intended for export. Armour said the inspections did not cause spoilage, and he felt that other countries had the right to make sure imported food was safe. "Our own interest as well as common commercial honesty would cause us to see that no diseased meat should be exported from our place." At mid-decade Nelson Morris began letting the French inspect his canned meat. Yet many Chicagoans still felt that federal intervention would be tantamount to admitting the existence of diseased livestock and "embalmed" meat. The tide had turned by the time witnesses before the Vest committee supported federal inspection and certification, as did the committee report. Even the Chicago Board of Trade asked the federal government to help lift "the stigma of false and injurious accusations."[33]

The 1890 legislation, as we have seen, charged the Bureau of Animal Industry with the inspection and certification of livestock for export and the certification of pork products for export at the request of either shippers or European governments. Livestock inspection began that same year, but certification of pork products was delayed by the insistence of Germany and several other countries that hog tissues be inspected under a microscope. Congress amended the law in 1891 by providing for inspection of all cattle, sheep, and hogs sold to packing, canning, and curing establishments, plus microscopic examination of hog flesh after slaughter and again before certification. The federal government would pay for this program, and it was understood that the bureau would inaugurate the program with pork products destined for export. The first microscopic examinations were made in Chicago in June, 1891, with the secretary of agriculture and other dignitaries in attendance. The "microscopists," half of whom were women, worked in the former Town of Lake offices on Halsted. Chicago packers were so enthusiastic about the program that the number of inspectors, technicians, and clerks had doubled by 1893. The

European bans were lifted—"Uncle Sam's Pig Wins," said the *Tribune*—and by 1894 the Bureau of Animal Industry was checking thirteen million animals for forty-six firms in seventeen different cities. Expanding the program to include all livestock sold to meat processors for interstate as well as export trade would be costly, and President Cleveland's secretary of agriculture proposed that packers, canners, and curers bear part of the expense. The suggestion fell on deaf ears.[34]

"Anyone who has observed the trade," said canner William J. Wilson in 1882, "will remember that every eight or ten years there is a revolution in it, and one is now coming over it." The revolution was the result of mechanical refrigeration. Although the "ice machines" were costly, they made it possible for packers to develop the chilled fresh meat trade, speed up the carcass cooling process, and build new plants on land previously occupied by icehouses. As productivity and profits increased, the western half of Section 5 was fully occupied and substantially rebuilt. Packingtown's revolution had adverse effects on livestock shipments to eastern cities and on the trade of local slaughterers and market butchers. The number of cattle sold at Boston's Brighton market, for example, was cut in half between 1880 and 1886. The Chicago market flourished, said the packers and the *Tribune*, because the men in Section 5 could sell anything "from a spike-tailed, crumpled-horned, straw-fed cow up to a thoroughbred Hereford or Durham" and utilize "hides, hoofs, hair, horns, bristles, bones, blood, and offal of every kind." This did not console the cattle growers, dealers, and market butchers who considered themselves victims of the dressed beef revolution. Charging monopoly and exploitation, they sought to frustrate the Stockyards and Packingtown by manipulating railroad rates and securing state laws and a Senate investigation. The entrepreneurs in Section 5 turned to the federal government for assistance, endorsing both the Interstate Commerce Commission and the Bureau of Animal Industry's certification of livestock and meat products for export.[35]

NOTES

1. *Trib.*, Mar. 14, 1880; "The Trade in New England," *Butchers Advocate*, 17 (Nov. 21, 1894), 1.

2. *Drovers Journal*, Mar. 31, 1883; Jan. 2, 1890; *Trib.*, Mar. 14, 1880; June 10, 1883; Sept. 23, Oct. 4, 1885; *The Graphic*, 3 (Nov. 1, 1890), 887.

3. John Clay, *My Life on the Range* (Chicago, 1924; rpt. Norman, Okla., 1962), 188–89; *Tenth Census, 1880*, vol. 2, "Manufactures," 391, 393; *Eleventh Census, 1890*, vol. 6, "Manufacturing Industries," part 2, "Statistics of Cities," 142, 145; BAI, *Third Annual Report, 1886*, 278.

4. Oscar E. Anderson, Jr., *Refrigeration in America: A History of a New Technology and Its Impact* (Princeton, N.J., 1953), 71–91; "Artificial Ice and Refrigeration," *Nat. Prov.*, 3 (Nov. 14, 1891), 10–11; 3 (Nov. 28, 1891), 11–12; Edward A. Duddy, *The Cold Storage Industry in the United States* (Chicago, 1929), 6; for investments by other industries, see W. Paul Strassmann, *Risk and Technological Innovation: American Manufacturing Methods during the Nineteenth Century* (Ithaca, N.Y., 1959); *Trib.*, Feb. 1, 1885; July 28, 1887; Jan. 1, 1891; *Sun*, Apr. 12, 26, 1890.

5. Alexandra Oleson and John Voss, eds., *The Organization of Knowledge in Modern America, 1860–1920* (Baltimore, 1979), 431; *Nat. Prov.*, 1 (May 30, 1891), 11; 1 (June 6, 1891), 5; 1 (June 13, 1891), 5–6; 4 (Feb. 20, 1892), 11.

6. Louis F. Swift and Arthur Van Vlissingen, *The Yankee of the Yards: The Biography of Gustavus Franklin Swift* (Chicago, 1927), 200–201; *Trib.*, Jan. 2, 1888; Jan. 1, 1891; *Eleventh Census, 1890*, vol. 6, "Manufacturing Industries," part 2, 143.

7. "Sixtieth Anniversary Number," *Armour Magazine*, 16 (Apr., 1927), 7, 25; "Developing Packinghouse By-Products," *Nat. Prov.*, 52 (Jan. 23, 1915), 17, 41; Harper Leech and John Charles Carroll, *Armour and His Times* (New York, 1938), 48, 67; *Armour Magazine*, 9 (Mar., 1920), 9; Cuthbert Powell, *Twenty Years of Kansas City's Live Stock Trade and Traders* (Kansas City, Mo., 1893), 89–91; Armour and Company, "Financial Statement and Inventory Journal for Fiscal Year Ending Oct. 24, 1891" (Armour and Company Archives, Greyhound Corporation, Phoenix); *Trib.*, Oct. 12, 14, 20, 1882; Jan. 1, 1890; *Drovers Journal*, Mar. 17, June 30, 1883; Jan. 4, May 8, 1886; Dec. 30, 1887; *Sun*, Jan. 11, Oct. 26, Dec. 3, 1886.

8. *Drovers Journal*, Mar. 17, 1883; Dec. 24, 1885; Oct. 8, Nov. 23, 1889; *Sun*, Jan. 11, 1886; Mar. 21, 1888.

9. Leech and Carroll, *Armour*, 83–84; "Sixtieth Anniversary Number," 7, 17; William Terence Kane, *The Education of Edward Cudahy* (Chicago, 1941), chaps. 2–6; Federal Trade Commission, *Report on the Meat-Packing Industry, 1919* (Washington, 1919), summary and part 1, 153, 239; part 5, 21; *Drovers Journal*, July 9, Dec. 31, 1887; Mar. 23, 28, 1888; *Trib.*, Sept. 26, 1886; Nov. 14, 1890; Oct. 22, 1892; *Sun*, May 9, 1891.

10. Swift and Company, *About Swift and Company, Jan. 1, 1900* (Chicago, 1900), 20; Swift and Company, Minutes of Annual Meeting, Jan. 3, 1889 (Swift and Company Archives, Chicago); *Trib.*, Nov. 19, 1881; Dec. 19, 1885; Nov. 7, 1886; Jan. 1, 1887; *Drovers Journal*, June 19, Sept. 19, 1883; Nov. 18, 1884; Dec. 24, 1885; Dec. 20, 31, 1886; Dec. 30, 1887; June 13, 1888; Mar. 22, 1889; *Sun*, Mar. 23, 1889; Apr. 19, 1892; May 27, Aug. 12, 1893.

11. *Trib.*, Mar. 29, 1893; *Chicago Stockman*, Dec. 28, 1893; Swift and

Vlissingen, *Yankee of the Yards,* 132, 200–201; Mary Yeager, *Competition and Regulation: The Development of Oligopoly in the Meat Packing Industry* (Greenwich, Conn., 1981), 63–73; Louis Unfer, "Swift and Company: The Development of the Packing Industry, 1875 to 1912" (Ph.D. diss., University of Illinois, 1951), chap. 3; Alfred D. Chandler, Jr., "Beginnings of 'Big Business' in American Industry," *Business History Review,* 33 (1959), 6–8; Alfred D. Chandler, Jr., *The Visible Hand: The Managerial Revolution in American Business* (Cambridge, Mass., 1977), 299–301; Swift and Company, Minutes of Annual Meeting, Jan. 7, 1886; Jan. 2, 1890; "List of First One Hundred Stockholders" (Swift and Company Archives).

12. *Drovers Journal,* Sept. 8, 1883; Dec. 27, 1888; Aug. 12, 1889; Mar. 20, 1890; *Trib.,* Jan. 1, 1883; Oct. 1, 1884; Dec. 31, 1886; Jan. 1, 1887; Mar. 29, 1893; *Chicago Record-Herald,* Aug. 28, 1907; Nelson Morris, "Personal Reminiscences of the Chicago Market," *Breeder's Gazette,* 46 (Dec. 2, 1904), 1156; [Frank Gilbert], *A History of the City of Chicago, Its Men and Institutions* (Chicago, 1900), 197–98; Yeager, *Competition and Regulation,* 67, 76–77. For the comparative standing of packing companies at the end of the century, see Chandler, *Visible Hand,* 391–402.

13. *The Economist,* 9 (Oct. 22, 1892), 579–80; (May 6, 1893), 631; Kane, *Education of Edward Cudahy,* chap. 6; *Trib.,* Aug. 31, Sept. 1, Nov. 19, 1881; Oct. 8, 1882; Mar. 4, 1883; Jan. 2, 1888; June 9, 1890; *Drovers Journal,* Oct. 21, 1882; Apr. 7, July 2, 1883; Sept. 24, Nov. 20, 1885; June 27, 28, July 19, Oct. 14, Dec. 30, 1887; Apr. 23, 1888.

14. *Drovers Journal,* Sept. 15, 1884; Mar. 23–26, Apr. 17, Dec. 24, 1885; May 8, June 26, Oct. 2, 1888; *Trib.,* Nov. 18, 1882; Jan. 1, 1883; Jan. 1, 1884; Jan. 1, 1891; [Gilbert], *History of Chicago,* 196–97; BAI, *First Annual Report, 1884,* 262–65; Daniel J. Boorstin, *The Americans: The Democratic Experience* (New York, 1973), chaps. 36, 37.

15. Edward C. Kirkland, *Industry Comes of Age: Business, Labor, and Public Policy, 1860–1897* (New York, 1961), 86–87; J. W. Midgeley, "Private Cars," *Railway Age,* 34 (Nov. 7, 1902), 494; Saul Engelbourg, *Power and Morality: American Business Ethics, 1840–1914* (Westport, Conn., 1980), 25–34; Yeager, *Competition and Regulation,* 87–93.

16. David Gilchrist, "Albert Fink and the Pooling System," *Business History Review,* 34 (Spring, 1960), 24–36; *New York Times,* Aug. 21, 1883; *Trib.,* Apr. 12, 17, 19, 1883.

17. *Drovers Journal,* Aug. 21, 1883; *Trib.,* June 29, 1883; Nov. 15, 1884; Thomas C. Cochran, *Railroad Leaders, 1845–1890: The Business Mind in Action* (New York, 1965), 154–56, 391; William Z. Ripley, *Railroads, Rates and Regulations* (New York, 1913), 139–40; "Killing the Dressed Beef Trade," *Trib.,* Aug. 24, 1883; Mary Yeager Kujovich, "The

Refrigerator Car and the Growth of the American Dressed Beef Industry," *Business History Review,* 44 (Winter, 1970), 470–76.

18. Midgeley, "Private Cars," 494–95; Ripley, *Railroads,* 140–41; Yeager, *Competition and Regulation,* 93–98; *Trib.*, Feb. 19, 20, 1886; *Drovers Journal,* Feb. 20, 22, 26, 1886.

19. *Trib.*, Feb. 28, Mar. 3, and editorials of Feb. 21, 22, 26, 1886; *Times* editorial, Feb. 22, 1886; G. F. Swift to editor, *Trib.*, Feb. 20, 23, Mar. 4, 1886; Armour and Co. to editor, *Trib.*, Feb. 19, 20, 1886; *Plain Facts Regarding the Attempted Destruction of the Dressed Beef Industry* (Chicago, 1886), 2, 3, 7, 8.

20. *Drovers Journal,* Feb. 26, Mar. 11, 27, 1886; S. W. Allerton to editor, *Trib.*, Feb. 20, Mar. 4, 1886; *Times,* Mar. 2, 1886.

21. *Drovers Journal,* Feb. 27, Nov. 19, Dec. 29, 1886; Kirkland, *Industry Comes of Age,* 126–29; Ripley, *Railroads,* chap. 13; James W. Neilson, *Shelby M. Cullom: Prairie State Republican* (Urbana, Ill., 1962), 93–108; Elizabeth C. Brook, "The Struggle for the Adoption of the Interstate Commerce Commission, 1872–1887" (Ph.D. diss., University of Chicago, 1925), chaps. 3–6; Gabriel Kolko, *Railroads and Regulation, 1877–1916* (Princeton, N.J., 1965), chap. 2; Ari Hoogenboom and Olive Hoogenboom, *A History of the Interstate Commerce Commission: From Panacea to Palliative* (New York, 1976), chap. 1.

22. Swift and Vlissingen, *Yankee of the Yards,* 184–85; Senate Select Committee, *Testimony . . . on the Transportation and Sale of Meat Products* (Washington, 1889), 430; Board of Trade, *Annual Report, 1890,* 52, 54; *Trib.*, Jan. 6, 1888, Jan. 3, May 9, 1889; June 11, 19, July 1, 1890; Cochran, *Railroad Leaders,* 197–99; Gilchrist, "Fink," 39–49; Midgeley, "Private Cars," 495, 497–98; Yeager, *Competition and Regulation,* 100–105; Kujovich, "Refrigerator Car," 477–81; Kolko, *Railroads and Regulations,* chap. 3; Engelbourg, *Power and Morality,* 61–62, 66–67.

23. *Denver News,* May 31, 1887, quoted in *Trib.*, June 3, 1887; *Drovers Journal,* Apr. 2, 1886; Feb. 19, Apr. 10, Dec. 26, 1889; *Trib.*, Feb. 8, Mar. 12, 28, 1889; *Chicago Stockman,* Dec. 28, 1893; W. H. Thompson, Jr., "Live Stock Exchanges," *Nat. Prov.*, 22 (Feb. 3, 1900), 22.

24. *Trib.*, Oct. 7, Nov. 27, 1880; Dec. 17, 18, 1881; June 4, July 21, 1886; Feb. 18, Mar. 19, 1888; *Drovers Journal,* Nov. 12, 1885; May 11, 22, Nov. 20, 1886; Mar. 31, 1888; Henry Bannard, "The Oleomargarine Law," *Political Science Quarterly,* 2 (Dec., 1887), 545–57; *Nat. Prov.*, 1 (June 13, 1891), 6.

25. Inter-Ocean, *Chicago's First Half-Century* (Chicago, 1883), 134–35; *Breeder's Gazette,* 16 (July 3, 1889), 5–6; "Cheaper Beef," *Harper's Weekly,* 26 (Oct. 21, 1882), 663; *Trib.*, Aug. 25, Sept. 24, 1882; Aug. 4, 1883; Mar. 22, 26, 28, June 29, 1884; *Drovers Journal,* May 7, 1884; May 13, 1885; *Butchers National Journal,* 1 (June 11, 1886), 3.

26. BAI, *First Annual Report, 1884*, 267; Rudolf A. Clemen, *The American Livestock and Meat Industry* (New York, 1923), 242–43; *Trib.*, Mar. 24, 1884; Dec. 19, 1885; Jan. 26, 28, 1886; Jan. 26, 1887; *Drovers Journal*, May 26, 27, 1887; Aug. 24, 1888; *Butchers National Journal*, 1 (Mar. 29, 1886), 1; (May 28, 1886), 1.

27. *Trib.*, Jan. 28, 1886; Mar. 16, Apr. 1, 1887; Dec. 3, 1889; Jan. 20, 1891; *Drovers Journal*, May 7, 1884; May 5, 1886; Apr. 16, 1887; May 24, 1888; Feb. 8, Sept. 13, 14, Oct. 8, Dec. 7, 1889; Yeager, *Competition and Regulation*, 99; *Breeder's Gazette*, 15 (Mar. 20, 1889), 314–15; 16 (Aug. 7, 1889), 122; Clemen, *Livestock and Meat Industry*, 245–47.

28. *Drovers Journal*, June 11, 1888; *Trib.*, May 4, 18, 1888; *Breeder's Gazette*, 16 (Sept. 11, 1889), 243. Louis Galambos maintains that midwestern farmers, worried about economic concentration and the lure of the city in the 1880s, made "big business . . . a focal point for animosity it had not really earned." *The Public Image of Big Business in America, 1880–1940: A Quantitative Study* (Baltimore, 1975), 65–66.

29. *Trib.*, Nov. 19, 21, 1888; Sept. 3–5, 1889; *Drovers Journal*, Sept. 3, 5, 6, 1889; Senate Select Committee, *Testimony . . . on the Transportation and Sale of Meat Products*, 3, 180, 182, 23, 352, 359–60, 212–13, 243–44.

30. Senate Select Committee, *Testimony . . . on the Transportation and Sale of Meat Products*, 414, 419–21.

31. Ibid., 424, 429, 417, 427–28, 426, 430, 453, 456, 473, 477, 479.

32. Senate Select Committee, *Report . . . on Transportation and Sale of Meat Products* (Washington, 1890), 1–16; *Drovers Journal*, May 1, 2, 6, 1890; *Trib.*, Mar. 13, 1889; May 2, 5, 1890; *Breeder's Gazette*, 15 (Mar. 20, 1889), 314–15; 16 (Dec. 4, 1889), 530–31.

33. Bessie Louise Pierce, *A History of Chicago*, vol. 3, *The Rise of a Modern City, 1871–1893* (New York, 1957), 132–33; BAI, *Eighth and Ninth Annual Reports, 1891 and 1892*, 40; Leech and Carroll, *Armour*, 176–88; Board of Trade, *Annual Report, 1883*, 11–12; *1889*, 165; *Trib.*, Jan. 13, 1884; Dec. 5, 1889; *Drovers Journal*, Feb. 20, 1883; Feb. 10, 18, Mar. 7, 1884.

34. Board of Trade, *Annual Report, 1892*, xxxiii; BAI, *Eighth and Ninth Annual Reports, 1891 and 1892*, 36–41; *Tenth and Eleventh Annual Reports, 1893 and 1894*, 19–29; *Trib.*, Feb. 12, May 2, June 16, 23, 28, Sept. 4, 5, Nov. 17, Dec. 29, 1891; July 14, 1893; *Drovers Journal*, June 23, Sept. 4, 1891; *Sun*, June 23, Aug. 15, 1891; May 26, July 12, 13, 1893.

35. *Trib.*, Nov. 18, 1882; Jan. 1, 1881; Sept. 23, 1885; David C. Smith and Anne Bridges, "The Brighton Market: Feeding Nineteenth-Century Boston," *Agricultural History*, 56 (Jan., 1982), 21.

CHAPTER 13

Packers and Packinghouse Workers

The interdependence of employers and employes in Packingtown was as close as the relationship between the eastern and western halves of Section 5. The packers chose to emphasize, however, the enormous amount of good they were doing by providing jobs and food for the world. Staunch believers in the work ethic, they practiced what they preached and rewarded those managers and workers who were diligent, dedicated, and reliable. Like their counterparts elsewhere in the country, the packers shared their wealth with charitable, religious, cultural, and educational institutions. They were among the "public-spirited rich men in this city of pork barrels and grain elevators," acknowledged one editor.[1] At the opening of the decade, the hard-driving packers had little sympathy for labor's traditional saying, "eight hours for work, eight hours for sleep, and eight hours for God and Brethren." Packinghouse workers did. Their wages were comparatively good; they had steady employment and opportunities for advancement thanks to the rapid expansion of their industry; and physical conditions in the plants were improving. Yet workers in Packingtown were aware of the new organizations formed by other wage earners, livestock dealers, cattle growers, and even the market butchers resisting dressed beef. Since they too desired a reduction in the ten-hour day, they responded to Knights of Labor organizers and a group of skilled cattle butchers in the Armour, Swift, and Morris plants. Taking advantage of the labor movement's May 1, 1886, deadline for achieving the eight-hour day, packinghouse workers maneuvered their employers into accepting that popular reform.

The Priorities of the Packers

The civic-minded big businessmen who made their fortunes at the Stockyards and in Packingtown fit the mold of what historians now call the "business elite" and "urban establishment." They were self-made men from modest backgrounds, with little formal training but extensive educations in the proverbial school of hard knocks. If they could succeed, they reasoned, so could persistent hard workers in the next generation. "Always keep at it. Don't let up," Armour advised one youth, "pound away at whatever you want—and sooner or later you'll make good." Though few were born in Chicago or Illinois, they grew up with the city and honored the obligation to share their largess with less fortunate individuals and with those institutions and organizations which were "uplifting" the community. Philip Armour's 1893 gift of a technical training institute made him Chicago's most generous nineteenth-century philanthropist. Yet for Armour, Swift, and Morris, their businesses were their first loves. The economic challenges and intricate complexities excited them. "You see, we are something more than packers," Armour lectured a reporter in 1886. "We are merchants and manufacturers." He could, of course, have added large employers and important benefactors. At the time of Armour's death, Nelson Morris summed up the reasons why his friend was so widely admired. Armour "started in life as a farm boy" and "was a hard worker and a bright, smart businessman" who "did a great deal of good for this country." "He was benevolent and was willing to help all those who help themselves." Thus, he said, the accomplishments of Chicago's leading packer constitute "a fine example for all young men in this world."[2]

On the basis of personal wealth, one criterion for entry into the business elite, a surprising number of men in the livestock trade and meat-packing qualified in the early 1880s. An 1882 newspaper list of sixty-four purported local millionaires included Philip Armour, Nelson Morris, Benjamin P. Hutchinson, Sidney Kent, Robert Fowler, Samuel Allerton, Nathaniel Fairbank, John R. Hoxie, and John B. Sherman, ranked according to the alleged size of their fortunes. By 1890 the fortunes were much larger, and the *Tribune* estimated that Armour and Marshall Field were worth $25 million each; George Pullman $15 million; Potter Palmer $10 million; Swift and Morris $8 million each; Fairbank, Kent, Allerton, and "Old Hutch" about $5 million each; John and Michael Cudahy, Charles Hutchinson, Louis F. Swift, Robert Fowler, and packer Charles Counselman in the $2 to $3 million category. Most of these men had other investments which augmented their income. They owned ranches, cattle companies, shares in western stockyards, railroad securities, and urban real estate. Allerton and the younger Hutchinson were investors in the Chicago City Railway, while Kent was in on the ground floor of gas and electric utilities. Armour had interests in the Continental and Commercial Banks, Allerton and Morris in First National, and the two Hutchinsons and Kent owned the Corn Exchange Bank. Thus their businesses at the Stockyards and Packingtown were not their only source of income, but they were probably the major source.[3]

The economic power and influence of the packers grew steadily in the 1880s as the value of their product rose and the size of their work force expanded. By 1890 their manufactures accounted for 30 percent of Chicago's total. While there had been a few textile mills, iron works, and a locomotive plant in Pennsylvania that needed more workers than Armour's Town of Lake operation at the beginning of the decade, he pulled far ahead during the boom years and was, in fact, employing twice as many people in 1890 as Carnegie did at the Homestead Steel Works. Packingtown employment stood at 25,000; some 17,500 were beef and pork workers, while the remainder were in canning, lard, margarine, glue, soap, fertilizer, and closely allied industries. Harvey Goodall calculated that those 25,000 workers in turn supported "somewhere in the vicinity of one hundred thousand persons. No pigmy this." The packers were credited with creating these jobs, and they were proud of the economic contribution their enterprises made to the community. Few contemporaries laughed at Armour's oft-quoted claim, "Through the wages I disburse and the provisions I supply, I give more people food than any other man alive."[4]

Chicago's three "beef barons" were strikingly different in personality and physical appearance, but they saw eye to eye on the work ethic. Creative, productive labor, not the acquisition of dollars, was their goal and their measurement of their own success. "Ambition and pride keep a man at work when money is merely a by-product," thought Armour, and Morris told his son that wealth was "a secondary consideration." "You can be of the greatest benefit by employing lots of labor and helping to maintain thousands of people." These men were sticklers for quality, especially in their products. Louis Swift heard "hundreds" of lectures on the theme that "sixteen ounces is a Swift pound." Armour warned his managers that he could "forgive a mistake, but there is no excuse for carelessness." Swift's employes knew that he checked the most minute details and had a mania for inspecting sewer catch basins. They also knew that there was no point in "trying to wriggle out" of a mistake because only the Lord could save a worker who tried "short weight or lower quality."[5]

Armour was a human dynamo who worked from 7 A.M. to 6 P.M. with a "full head of steam" and loved the myriad strands of packinghouse administration. "Give me plenty of work, and it is about all the tonic I want. . . . I feel thankful for it every day of my life." Armour built a house on fashionable Prairie Avenue (see Fig. 9) and often walked to his downtown office with neighbors Marshall Field and George Pullman. The Armours did little entertaining or even traveling until the late 1880s when rheumatism drove him to European spas and finally to a winter home in Pasadena. Having struggled as a young man to master the two "cyclones within"—temper and a taste for strong drink—Armour often discoursed on the importance of self-discipline and teetotalism. He was willing to chat with reporters, which is something Swift and Morris never did, and if he did not like their questions, he would shrug and end the interview with the remark, "I am just a butcher trying to go to heaven." Paradoxically, Armour had no butchering skills. He told the Vest committee he never had a knife in his hand and "if you showed me a piece of meat I could not tell you what part of the bullock it came from."[6]

Both Swift and Morris were expert butchers and experienced cattle buyers. Their offices were in Section 5 so they entered the Stone Gate with hundreds of others at 6 A.M. when the yards opened. Both were better known by their employes than was Armour, and the large Swift family played an active role in the Stockyards neighborhood. Morris lived "a buggy ride away" in a large frame house at Twenty-fifth and Indiana which he built in the 1860s for his bride. Their five children were born in that house and Morris died there in 1907. He loved the place, said a son "as he loved no other spot on earth, save possibly a pen filled with milling cattle." Morris was "diminutive in size" and painfully shy, due perhaps to his size, his heavy German accent, and his high-pitched, thin, tenor voice. He constantly whittled white pine sticks, kept changing his socks during the day, and favored cheap cigars and a "rough-and-ready sack suit of clothes" that could only "impress grangers." The exceptionally tall, taciturn Swift was Morris's friend in spite of their disagreement on railroad rates. Swift's thrifty "Cape Cod ways" matched Morris's frugality, and both millionaires raised their children on the maxim, "Wasters, Wanters."[7]

These packers drove their managers and department heads as hard as they drove themselves. Anyone who failed to keep on top of facts and figures, lost the respect of those underneath him, or got caught in a shady deal was summarily dismissed. It was "always understood by my head men," said Armour, "that if any of them were let out . . . they never would be taken back again." If they could get at his "soft side," the employer reasoned, he would lose the "respect and authority that is necessary to conduct a large business." Although Swift paid comparatively small salaries in the early 1880s, he kept the men he wanted "by the force of his character and the high standards he set for them," observed his son. Everyone in the Swift organization knew that "the best a man ever did shouldn't be his yardstick for the rest of his life."[8]

Ernest Poole's remark that Armour was "a keen picker of young men" was true of Swift and Morris as well. They believed in their young men. "Take youth and train it," said Armour, while Swift claimed, "I can raise better men than I can hire." His packinghouse manager, Albert C. Foster, worked in the Clinton meat market and the Fall River slaughterhouse before coming to Chicago with Swift. The man in charge of Armour's retail market had started as a messenger boy, while John Kenny rose from green hand to trusted foreman of the cattle-killing division. Occasionally packers hired from outside; Armour chose a French margarine factory manager to head his oleomargarine department, Swift's chief engineer was lured away from a smaller packinghouse, and one of Armour's branch managers became Swift's assistant general superintendent. But training and promoting from within was the norm. Arthur Meeker began as an Armour billing clerk, then went to the lard department in Packingtown, opened sales offices in the southern states, and finally started the London office before he turned thirty.[9]

In an era when brothers often worked together and sons followed in their fathers' footsteps, the packers took it for granted that their sons would enter the packing business. Swift was the most successful. Louis, Edward, Charles, Herbert, George, Gustavus, Jr., and Harold joined the company, and daughter Helen married Nelson Morris's son Edward in 1890. "Father," she later wrote, "was very happy and, I think, proud that the boys all loved the business and had no leaning toward any other." Although the parents encouraged the sons to continue their education beyond high school, only Harold went to college, the others preferring to start their apprenticeships as soon as possible. "Old Hutch" and Philip Armour had to use different tactics. Charles Lawrence Hutchinson was an honors student who longed to attend college, but his father forced him to learn meatpacking and grain speculation instead. Hutchinson eventually rejected both careers and turned to the more congenial combination of banking and philanthropy. Philip Armour shared the senior Hutchinson's contempt for the liberal arts, but he felt that technical education was important. "If there were fewer theorists in the world," he said, "there would be more successes. Facts can be discounted at any bank, but a theory is rarely worth par. Stick to facts." Philip Danforth, Jr., had his father's stocky build and temperament. He spent one year at Yale's Sheffield Scientific School, toured Europe with a tutor, and then went to work for Armour and Company in 1888. He was an instant success and a joy to "the old man" because, among other things, he gave Armour two grandsons to carry on the enterprise. Jonathan Ogden, the quiet, introspective, older Armour son, liked architecture and begged to complete the Yale college course. He had only two years and a trip to Europe before being saddled with "business cares," as he put it. The father allegedly told John B. Sherman that Ogden "thought there would be something he would like to do instead of grubbing for money, when we already had more than enough. . . . I told him to be at the Yards in his working clothes at seven on Monday morning." Ogden complied in 1884, but he never liked the packing business and he and his wife disappointed Philip Armour with only one child, a girl.[10]

Edward, Herbert, and Ira Nelson Morris knew from infancy that they were destined for meat-packing and the livestock business. Father "could imagine no better future for any of us," wrote the youngest son in his autobiography. Edward and Herbert were content with their destinies, but Ira shared his mother's interest in art and literature and wanted a college education. Nelson Morris was opposed on the grounds that four years of high school had been enough for Ira; his boys needed "good common sense and practicality in active business life." His "dominating personality, his feeling of his own rightness, pervaded every relationship," lamented Ira, "and naturally encouraged a passive role for mother, which she accepted without question." Ira asked a family friend, banker Lyman J. Gage, to intercede with his father. He entered Yale in the fall of 1892, but the contest of wills continued. A steady stream of letters admonished Ira to be economical, to avoid French because "your time is too dear and valuable for this nonsense," to remember that "you are needed in the business," to "come here and work for me and pretty soon you can hire all those college fellows for fifteen dollars a week." Nelson Morris "won" in 1893. Ira returned to the "muddy ground of the stock pens," "mournful bellows of steers," and "thick, heavy, nauseating odor of the stock yards." He felt "barred from life" by the "ceaseless" round of buying, slaughtering, packing, and shipping, and he "longed for something besides talk of weights and prices." Yet he could not summon the courage to quit until his father died.[11]

George Horace Lorimer was made of sterner stuff. Son of a Baptist minister who knew Philip Armour, this young man left college in 1885 to decode telegraph messages in Armour's downtown office at $10 per week. After a two-year clerical apprenticeship, he was shifted to the canning department. In 1895 Lorimer was earning $5,000 a year as head of this division, but he decided to strike out on his own in the wholesale grocery business. When this venture failed, he went to work for Cyrus H. K. Curtis and in 1899 became editor of the *Saturday Evening Post.* Shortly after Armour's death in 1901, Lorimer began publishing unsigned "Letters from a Self-Made Merchant to His Son," a parody of the packers' relationships with their sons. Blunt, amiable John Graham, the self-made packer, informed his Harvard-student son, "You're not going to be a poet or a professor, but a packer," and "we don't use much poetry here except in our street-car ads." The son ought to be bracing for cranky customers who ask "how we manage to pack solid gristle in two-pound cans without leaving a little meat hanging to it" and mastering the range of packinghouse products "from A to Izzard, from snout to tail, on the hoof and in the can." One has to "eat hog, think hog, dream hog" to succeed in pork-packing, he lectured. Other letters probed the extensive dealings of packers and provision merchants with the Board of Trade and warned the son to pay attention to "this matter of speculation because you've got to live next door to the Board of Trade all your life, and it's a safe thing to know something about a neighbor's dogs before you try to pat them." As for the wheat pit, "it is only thirty feet across, but it reaches clear down to Hell."[12]

Most of Chicago's business leaders honored the obligation to share a part of their wealth with the community, and they favored those organizations and institutions which enabled less fortunate people to improve and uplift themselves. The McCormick family endowed a seminary, Walter Newberry started a library, Marshall Field founded a natural history museum, and scores of them helped the orchestra, the art museum, the new University of Chicago, hospitals, charity organizations, and social settlements. The men who made their fortunes at the Stockyards and in Packingtown were at the forefront of Chicago philanthropy. They spent varying amounts of time at it, and few could give as generously as Philip Armour, but they heeded Emery A. Storrs's plea: "I am in favor of the steers and the pork, but I believe that out of them both . . . shall grow a culture as grand . . . as that great material and physical prosperity."[13]

Nathaniel K. Fairbank, said the *Tribune* in 1885, is our "'general utility man' of philanthropic projects." He has "circulated more subscription lists in aid of plans for the public good than any contemporaneous wealthy businessman of the city." Fairbank began with the Chicago Relief and Aid Society in the 1870s, and he went on to assist Central Music-Hall, Newsboys Home, St. Luke's Hospital, and the Manual Training School, as well as musical and artistic organizations and his own Fourth Presbyterian Church. His protégé, Charles Lawrence Hutchinson, cut his teeth on the Academy of Fine Arts and in the 1880s transformed it into the Art Institute. President of that important cultural institution from 1881 until his death in 1924, Hutchinson secured a permanent building for the museum and school, guided fund-raising, and influenced acquisitions. He made time in his busy schedule for the Field Columbian Museum, the University of Chicago, Hull-House, the Chicago Peace Society, Young Men's Christian Association, and St. Paul's Universalist Church.[14]

Few members of the Chicago business elite matched the dedication or versatility of Fairbank and Hutchinson. Armour, Swift, and Morris, due to their pressing business obligations, gave considerably less time. But Morris was treasurer of the United Hebrew Relief Association in the 1870s, and as active as his wife and sons in United Hebrew Charities, established in 1888. The family contributed to Michael Reese Hospital, belonged to Sinai Congregation, and gave generously to eastern European Jewish refugees, not all of whom found a welcome mat in Chicago. Gustavus Swift was the financial angel of his local Methodist Church, an ardent supporter of Methodist missionary work and the Young Men's Christian Association. He was among the first to respond to Charles Hutchinson's call for money to establish the University of Chicago, and after the death of his daughter Annie May, a student at Northwestern University when she contracted typhoid fever, he financed a memorial hall at that institution. The entire Swift family was known in the Stockyards neighborhood for its generosity to employes and to strangers coping with death, illness, and economic pressures.[15]

Whenever possible, the restless Armour avoided board meetings and left "culture . . . mostly in my wife's name." He was a soft touch for the Citizens' Association and causes promoted by the Commercial Club and his Prairie Avenue friends. Moreover, he drew some of them into the Illinois Humane Society, temperance groups, St. Mary's Training School for Boys, Chicago Manual Training School, and the Training School for Nurses. It was characteristic of Armour, who liked to run his own show, that he personally planned and supervised the two major gifts to his city. The Armour Mission was a memorial to his brother Joseph, an advocate of city missionary work. Philip Armour made a thorough study of that movement before purchasing land on Thirty-third Street west of State where black families were beginning to settle. He added $150,000 to Joseph's $100,000 bequest, and asked Burnham and Root for a structure housing a kindergarten, day nursery, kitchen, library and class rooms, two auditoriums, and medical dispensary. Armour Mission opened in December, 1886, and its community-oriented program gave Jane Addams some suggestions for Hull-House, which she started three years later. The Armour Flats, middle-income apartments surrounding the mission, generated income to pay staff salaries and stabilized the neighborhood. The popular industrial classes appealed to so many youngsters that Armour added a vocational training building to the complex in 1889.[16]

Advanced technical training of the sort offered at Philadelphia's Drexel Institute, the Pratt Institute in Brooklyn, and London's Polytechnic Institute strongly interested Armour. He found an ally in Reverend Frank W. Gunsaulus who came to Armour's church, Plymouth Congregational, in 1887. Assured that Gunsaulus would head such a school, Armour quietly bought more land on Thirty-third Street and started building. Armour Institute opened in the fall of 1893 to about one thousand students. They took high school and college level courses in mechanical, electrical, and chemical engineering, architecture taught in conjunction with the Art Institute, and the Midwest's first library science program. Armour's $2 million gift included a generous endowment so that tuition would not exceed $60 a year. Chicago's "second new university" was viewed by many Chicagoans as more important than the liberal arts college on the Midway, for it would teach young men and women from low-income families how to "reach a self-respecting independence that need be overshadowed by no man's wealth." Armour considered the institute the best investment he ever made, and the *New England Magazine* thought no captain of industry could "rear for himself a more fitting monument."[17]

Packinghouse Work and Wages

Technical training could help wage earners move into skilled jobs or perhaps even white-collar work, but it could not resolve the difficult problems confronting many factory employes in the 1880s. Periodic "hard times" between 1882 and 1886 brought wage cuts and layoffs to some groups of workers and some areas of the country. Many others were alienated by the increasing size of their industrial plants and worried that laborsaving machinery would eliminate their jobs and relegate their skills to the scrap heap. Newcomers, often foreign-born and unable to speak English, threatened the job security of those who survived the laborsaving machines. And finally, workers were increasingly aware that no possible combination of thrift and hard labor on their part would yield the necessary capital to launch their own factories. Chicago area wage earners wrestled with all of these troubles at one time or another during the decade. The city factory inspector noted the "almost universal practice of subdividing the labor in factories" so that many operatives were "skilled only in the manipulation of a piece of *machinery*." And Thomas J. Morgan declared that it was "utterly impossible for a wage-worker to become an employer in the packinghouse business." They were mere cogs in a great machine, "stopped or set going like so many pack-mules at the pleasure of the driver."[18]

In trying to reconstruct the position of packinghouse workers in the industry's boom years, the historian must rely on newspaper coverage, the reports of the Illinois Bureau of Labor Statistics, trade union statements and records, and the observations of visitors to the plants. Chicago factory inspection began in 1880 but did not cover the Town of Lake prior to annexation, and the state of Illinois waited until 1893 to launch factory inspection. The information that is available leaves many questions unanswered. Yet it is apparent that while packinghouse employes shared some of the frustrations and anxieties of other workers, they also had some things going for them—steady employment, opportunities for promotion in an expanding industry, some machine-proof skills, and relatively good wages. They also had a good deal of spunk, which helped.

Physical conditions in the plants improved during the 1880s. The new plants were better ventilated, and electricity revolutionized lighting. Employes came to and from work in street clothes by the end of the decade because plants had washrooms and places to change and leave the working garb. They wore overalls on the job and used smocks or aprons provided by employers. The Libby, McNeill and Libby plant had a lunchroom for wage earners, a striking contrast to one old plant where a reporter spotted men "utilizing the corpse of a gigantic porker as a table." It is likely that Chicago's 1879 law setting minimum standards of factory ventilation and sanitation influenced the packers when they constructed their new plants in the Town of Lake. And the sharp decline in child labor throughout the Chicago area may have been the result of city and township bans in 1881 and state laws in 1889 and 1891. The 1890 census covered a larger territory due to annexation and boys aged sixteen were counted as children, yet the number of child laborers was only half the 1880 figure.[19]

Visitors to the packing plants often commented on the variety and sophistication of packinghouse machinery. An English tourist in 1887 saw "an army of men standing alongside the machinery." The hog scraping machines did reduce the number of men working at that task: one plant that needed twelve men to clean fifteen hundred hogs per day by hand installed machines which handled three thousand hogs per day and required only eight men to scrape the ears and occasional flesh folds. That same plant, however, was then able to hire twice as many slitters, gutters, and trimmers. Packinghouse machinery which lifted, hauled, ground, and mixed did reduce laborers' jobs; at the same time, by speeding the process, they created new jobs for skilled and semiskilled workers. Since there were no robots which could gut, carve, trim, or slit an animal's throat, the packinghouse knifemen were secure in their jobs.[20] (See Fig. 20.)

Machines, especially the hoists and overhead rails, did set the pace of work for the knifemen. One visitor said the hog sticker's right elbow resembled "the piston-rod of a steam engine," while others noted that gutters and trimmers finished their tasks "in a twinkling." Departures from the cutting bench caused problems. When an Armour employe left his post to sharpen a knife and stayed away for ten minutes, his bench was piled high with meat. The other trimmers refused to help him clear the backlog, and he turned on them with his newly sharpened knife. This was rare, but the "celerity" and "rapidity" of the work required steady concentration and, no doubt, led to tension and fatigue at the end of a ten-hour day. Those paying their first visit to a packinghouse often commented on the "nonchalance" of the knifemen, the fact that they tended "strictly to business," or, in the case of a French tourist, that they paid "no attention whatsoever" to him. They were probably too busy to divert their gaze.[21]

Many of the jobs demanded a high degree of skill, and there can be no doubt that those knifemen were proud of their expertise. The "beheader" of hogs made three precise cuts to sever the head without touching the shoulder; those who quartered the carcass had to land their cleavers "at just the right spot between the shoulder and the side, and the space is only about as thick as a pencil." Cattle butchers needed strength as well as muscular coordination to split their carcasses; skinners had to exercise great caution to avoid damaging the hide with their knives. With these men it was "a matter of pride as to who shall have the best record." Butchers in the dressed beef houses arranged tests of speed, strength, endurance, and skillful handling of knives and cleavers. Ambitious young men challenged older butchers; the "king" of one house baited butchers in other establishments. An 1883 exhibition between Chicago market butchers and packinghouse butchers ended in victory for the latter. Relations between the two groups deteriorated because of the fight over dressed beef, and in 1886 packinghouse butchers decided to hold their own contest at the Fat Stock Show. The winner was Michael F. Mullins, a twenty-three-year-old Swift employe, who was six feet tall, weighed 175 pounds, and already had a dozen years of meat-cutting experience. In 1888 Mullins took on challengers from outside Chicago, and a huge crowd watched him dress a steer in eight minutes, four seconds. His arms, knives, and cleavers were in constant motion, and when he had finished, "he stepped back, gracefully shook some gore from his arm, kicked a lobe of liver across the stage, and bowed. . . . Mullins is undoubtedly the king of butchers," said an admirer.[22]

Understandably, the skilled butchers were the highest paid knifemen in the plants. From 1882 until the end of the decade, they earned $4 a day in summer and $4.50 in winter, with the exception of 1884–85, when packers did not grant the customary November increases. Packers in St. Louis, Kansas City, and Omaha paid less and expected their skilled butchers to fill in on other jobs if necessary. A surprised migrant exclaimed, "In Chicago a beef butcher is not required to even report at the house when there are no cattle to kill, and his pay goes on the same at $4 per day." Surveying wages in a dozen different occupations in 1887, the Chicago Department of Health found that only lithographers could earn up to $5 a day, and electricians, plumbers, and gasfitters came next at a top of $4 per day. The most highly skilled butchers had annual incomes of $1,200 to $1,500, a figure that was higher than the average annual wage of male clerical, sales, and office workers in Packingtown.

Less highly skilled knifemen—the gutters, choppers, and trimmers—earned from $2.25 to $3.75 per day. The cellar men and tank men ranged from $1.75 to $2.50, and laborers drew $1.25 in summer, $1.75 in winter. What we do not know is the proportion of men in these different pay categories. It is likely that skilled cattle butchers by the end of the decade outnumbered the other workers in dressed beef houses, while gutters, choppers, and trimmers were the largest block in the pork plants. As for regularity of employment, the Knights of Labor reported that two-thirds of their packinghouse members at mid-decade worked a six-day week for eleven or more months. A surprising 98 percent had full-time work for at least ten months of the year. The range of packinghouse wages in 1890,

$1.50 to $4.50, compared favorably with the Rock Island Car-Shops ($1.25 to $3) and McCormick Reaper Works ($1.50 to $2.50). The average annual income of Chicago factory workers in 1890 was $589; the average for the 17,500 people in slaughtering and meat-packing was $615. The national average annual income of factory workers was only $427 in 1890.[23]

Women and children were a tiny component of the Packingtown work force and the low people on the wage totem pole. The 1890 census reported 405 children, sixteen or under, working in the plants and averaging $187 per year. The 487 packinghouse women averaged $299, while 26 female clerical workers averaged $423 per year. Male counterparts of the clerks earned approximately $1,100 annually. Packers hired women to sew bags around hams and sides of bacon, a task which had been performed in 1880 "by men who manage the needle with a cleverness that a seamstress might emulate," said a reporter. Unfortunately, we do not know what male ham sewers were paid in 1880. Many packers also put widows of former employes on the payroll making and laundering smocks and aprons for the butchers. The majority of female employes worked at piece rates filling and labeling jars and cans. Two Chicago reporters, inspired by Helen Campbell's New York City investigations, took jobs in Packingtown canneries. Nora Marks fumbled at the labeling table in the new Libby plant with Irish girls who dispatched the cans "like lightning." Then she went upstairs to chop cooked meat, stuff cans, and guide them into the soldering machine. Soon "splattered" with beef fat, she understood why the Irish labelers said "nobody but Poles and Bohemian girls" worked upstairs. Nell Nelson found that Fairbank and Armour paid the same rate as Libby, 5¢ for each 100 cans. The girls could earn from $6 to $9 per week if they glued two to three thousand labels each day, six days a week. Armour's employes ate their lunches while perched on window sills, so Nelson wrote that it was "certainly very good of Mr. Armour to build Sunday-schools, educate struggling artists, buy pictures, and patronize music," but "a clean sitting-room . . . and chairs in which to rest at noon . . . would not be wasted charity."[24]

There was never a shortage of applicants for these jobs, and Harvey Goodall noted the "merry" dispositions of cannery workers, even after a day "of toil pasting labels." A survey of Chicago's working women conducted by the Illinois Bureau of Labor Statistics in 1892 sheds light on this paradox. Statisticians gathered information on 5,011 women in forty-three different occupations. Three packing companies employing 270 women were included. The average weekly wage for Chicago female office workers was $9.54; packinghouse office women averaged $11.68. Factory women in the survey averaged $5.93 per week; female packinghouse blue-collar workers earned $6.78. The women in the survey received an average annual wage of $317, while packinghouse women took home $404. Bureau statisticians did not explore the differential between male and female wages, but they did note that the vast majority of the women were "securely sheltered within the home circle" and were practising the "cardinal virtue" of "filial piety" by augmenting family income. Packinghouse women, like others in the survey, averaged twenty-one years of age and only 6 percent were married. But half rather than one-third of them were foreign-born. The stenographers, clerks, and "typewriters" worked six days a week from 8 A.M. to 5:30 P.M. with an hour for lunch. Women in the plants worked ten hours at the traditional female jobs. Only one firm in Packingtown allowed women to do any knife work, and that was merely "light" trimming of meat, according to a *Sun* reporter.[25]

In view of the rapid increase in employment and the sweeping changes in production during the boom years, packinghouse managers shouldered heavy responsibilities. There were two layers of supervisory personnel between the factory hands at the bottom and the general superintendent at the top. These foremen and department heads had to move animals into and finished products out of the plants as quickly as possible, yet maintain high quality at all times. They were in charge of, and at the same time dependent upon, the men underneath them. These middlemen in the managerial chain of command knew full well that either factory hands or the plant superintendent could bring about their downfall. Identifying, training, and getting the results from foremen and department supervisors was critical to the successful operation of a packinghouse.[26]

Foremen in the large houses "bossed"—hired, fired, promoted, and demoted—anywhere from seventy-five to two hundred men. They had to weed out those who were incompetent, careless or lazy, quarrelsome, light-fingered, or habitually tardy, as well as those who drank on the job. Foremen sometimes hired from another division in the plant and occasionally from outside, but normally they took "green" hands and taught them what to do. The foreman set daily work schedules, watched the pace and performance of his men, and tried to prevent the formation of cliques, harassment of unpopular workers, and disruptive arguments. The best of them were blind to ethnic distinctions in hiring and promoting. Although sausage departments were usually dominated by Germans, and the newly arrived, unskilled Bohemians and Poles started in lower-paying jobs, there was a mix elsewhere of Americans, Irish, Germans, and a lesser number of skilled Swedes and Bohemians. An effective foreman could perform any task he assigned, teach others how to do it, assess their work fairly, and reward on the basis of merit. In his memoir of Packingtown, cattle butcher John T. Joyce said there was a surprisingly large number of highly respected managers, "the kindly good kind of foreman and superintendents, men who understood their business and the ability of the men that worked under them and . . . were also broadminded in regards to racial makeup of the employes."[27]

Department supervisors needed all of these qualities plus some business skills, for they submitted reports to the plant superintendent on the work of their division. They appointed and watched the foremen and did their best to prevent bottlenecks in production or slackening of standards. Delays and defective goods inevitably spelled trouble for department supervisors. The general plant superintendent was the key man at the packinghouse. He chose the division heads, usually from among the ranks of foremen; he was the final arbitrator of departmental disputes; he was director-in-chief of the ceaseless traffic of animals in, finished goods out. Swift's plant superintendent, Albert C. Foster, left in 1886 with the highest accolade possible: engraved resolutions from all thirty-eight foremen praising his fairness and impartiality in dealing with subordinates. Michael Cudahy's departure from Packingtown in 1887 caused unrest in the Armour plant. His replacement, George Sunderland, had been the chief lifestock buyer, not a packinghouse department head, and Armour had to intervene in order to give Sunderland a chance to establish his credentials with supervisors, foremen, and factory hands. Stepping into the shoes of the legendary Cudahy, the man who built the "village and could perform any job in it," was a tough assignment.[28]

Armour's managerial salaries "Make the Average Man's Eyes Bulge Out," said the *Drovers Journal* in 1889. Sunderland received $10,000 a year; John Bouchard, superintendent of machinery, and Watt Conway, in charge of curing hams and pickling meats, each got $4,000. The superintendent of the dressed beef houses earned $5,000. John Kenny, foreman of the cattle-killing beds, earned $2,000 for supervising one hundred expert butchers, and his counterpart, the foreman of the pork-cutting benches, drew the same salary. Managerial styles differed. "Big Watt" was outgoing and jovial, while Michael Conway in the pork house was tagged "old sober sides" because he seldom laughed. Bouchard was as taciturn as Swift. Not all the managers were gems. A canning foreman skipped town with a winsome labeler, leaving his family to fend for itself. Others played favorites, were vindictive, or goaded their men with remarks like "Hurry up; there is a man at the gate waiting for your job; get your roller skates on, etc." Workers called them "long-eared skunks," or just "Long Ears," and said they were bucking for office jobs in the "Frock Section." Employes retaliated by synchronizing slowdowns, botching cuts of meat, damaging hides, and creating inventory shortages. They also complained as a group to the foreman's supervisor. Their favorite revenge was a noisy Saturday morning walkout and rendezvous with one of Goodall's reporters. Provided they showed up on time Monday morning, they kept their jobs and the foreman had a "black eye." If this happened often enough, the foreman would either be reassigned or demoted. Most packinghouse managers used their authority judiciously, for they knew workers could take care of "Long Ears."[29]

Packinghouse work was inherently dangerous because of the tools and the machinery. Defective equipment caused some of the accidents in Packingtown. Elevator cables snapped, and men stepped into open elevator shafts. An exploding lard tank at Armour's killed one and burned three others. On at least a dozen occasions in the 1880s newspapers reported deaths due to "getting in some machinery." Louis Schlovsk, for example, got tangled in a fertilizer dryer shaft, and the son of a packinghouse owner caught his untied apron in the revolving wheel of the pig-hoist and was dashed against the ceiling. Few workers could afford to sue for damages, and on the rare occasions when they did and won awards, there was no guarantee that the employer would pay. A man whose hand was damaged in a Fowler sausage machine never received the $7,500 court judgment. At the other extreme, Swift, Armour, and Morris were known to pay medical expenses of workers injured by their equipment and to compensate families whose breadwinners were either disabled or killed on the job.[30]

While newspaper accounts do not spell out the causes of other accidents, they do imply carelessness and drinking, which is why managers were so strict about these matters. At Chicago Packing and Provision Company, a reckless employe decided to take a walk on the rim of the scalding tub while holding on to an overhead water pipe. The pipe broke, he fell into the tub and died an hour later. An Armour worker took a short cut across a slippery cutting table, lost his footing, and slid into a hog scraping machine. Another man lost his hand as a result of trying to clean a can-stuffing machine without turning it off. Drinking probably explains a ham trimmer's fate on Saturday, December 30: he cut himself and the foreman reassigned him to picking up meat from the cutting table where he somehow got his other hand directly under a worker's cleaver. And there was Charles Duffy, a teamster reprimanded for drinking, who drowned in a cistern while trying to water his horse. An additional hazard was quarreling, which could end in serious injuries if one or both workers resorted to knives and cleavers, and drinking often contributed to these tragedies.[31]

At the request of the packers and the Stockyards company, the Town of Lake in 1881 prohibited the sale of intoxicating beverages in Section 5 with two exceptions, the Exchange bar and Transit House and a 150-foot strip of land on the east side of Ashland Avenue. Packinghouse workers patronized the Ashland establishments at noon or bought and carried beer to the packinghouses to have with their lunches. Managers never objected to this. It was workers clearly under the influence of intoxicants who were fired for their own good and the safety of others. Observing that there were approximately six serious accidents in the township each month and that most of them occurred on the railroads or in the packinghouses, Goodall suggested in 1885 that Lake needed a small emergency hospital. Philip Armour had one in operation before the year was out.[32]

The Demand for Shorter Hours

Packinghouse workers were ripe for organization in the 1880s, not because of low wages or irregular employment, but for other reasons. It was "an age of organization," as Thomas Armour had said, and all around them they saw wage earners forming labor organizations, dealers at the Yards starting the Chicago Live Stock Exchange, cattle growers organizing, and market butchers forming a national association. If these people could come together, why not packinghouse workers? Their employers may have "created" their jobs, but those same employers were dependent upon the workers' skills. Few were foolish enough to think their ten-hour day "worth" as much as Armour's or Sunderland's ten-hour day, yet they did long for some tangible recognition of their contribution. Shorter hours without pay cuts would fill the bill. And certainly an eight- or nine-hour day would help to alleviate fatigue, which must have been a factor in many packinghouse accidents and quarrels.

The trade union movement revived as soon as the 1870s depression lifted. In 1881, a Federation of Organized Trades and Labor Unions appeared; five years later it became the American Federation of Labor, headed by Samuel Gompers and representing fifty thousand trade unionists. Meantime, Terence Powderly was recruiting unskilled as well as skilled workers into the Knights of Labor, and he too claimed fifty thousand members in 1884. An unexpected victory over railroad magnate Jay Gould and recognition of the Knights sent membership soaring to seven hundred thousand in 1886. Still another triumph for wage earners was the proliferation of state bureaus of labor statistics and the establishment of a federal Bureau of Labor the same year the Bureau of Animal Industry was approved. Chicago area workers joined labor organizations in the hope that united action could reduce working days that sometimes stretched to fourteen and fifteen hours. The Chicago Trades and Labor Assembly, headed by iron molder George Rodgers, went on record in favor of an eight-hour day in 1882, and two years later the new Illinois State Federation of Labor endorsed the same proposal. The national Federation of Organized Trades held its 1884 convention in Chicago and set May 1, 1886, as the deadline for winning the eight-hour day.[33]

Roughly seventy-five thousand Chicago area workers were unionized by 1886, half in trade associations, one-quarter in the Knights of Labor, and some seven thousand with dual memberships. The latter was not unusual because trade unionists and Knights had many common objectives; they differed on strikes, the unions approving of them and Powderly preferring arbitration because strikes gave "temporary relief at best." The Knights endorsed such other reforms as consumer and producer cooperatives, graduated income taxes, and a ban on child labor, but when 90 percent of the members worked ten hours or longer, the shorter workday was the most powerful drawing card. In Cook County the number of Knights of Labor locals increased fivefold between 1880 and 1886, and Richard Griffiths persuaded Powderly to create District Assembly 57 for the South Branch locals and those in southern townships. One of the organizers was Michael J. Butler, who had started working in a Pennsylvania mine when he was nine years old. He arrived in the Town of Lake in 1880, and spent a year in a packinghouse before securing a blacksmith job with the Stockyards company. Starting in 1885, District Assembly 57 paid Butler $18 a week plus expenses. One of his new locals was 1597, for workers living "back of the yards." It met at the Buckley School and consisted primarily of packinghouse employes. Butler wrote Powderly that all his locals were "doing pretty well but there is no reason why they might not do better." He invited the General Master Workman to visit the Town of Lake early in 1886.[34]

Chicago area socialists were split on the eight-hour day. The more radical, revolutionary faction headed by Albert Parsons and August Spies at first scorned the reform as irrelevant to their campaign against capitalism, private property, wage slavery, and the ballot box. The moderates like Thomas Morgan and George Schilling held firm to their Marxian, evolutionary philosophy, but without a newspaper to combat Parsons's *Alarm*, they were at a disadvantage. The moderate socialists were members of the Knights, the trade unions, and the Chicago Trades and Labor Assembly; they supported shorter hours and liked the idea of a united labor front enforcing the May 1, 1886, deadline. In October, 1885, the radicals suddenly realized that a general strike might lead to wider disorders and so they too endorsed the deadline for shorter hours. The next month their Central Labor Union joined the Chicago Trades and Labor Assembly and the Knights of Labor in a Chicago Eight-Hour Association. As the Citizens' Association would later say, the anarchist "enemies" of organized labor "seized upon the eight hours movement as pirates would upon a peaceful trading vessel temporarily separated from her convoy."[35]

Although Powderly refused to endorse the May 1 deadline and the Eight-Hour Association said nothing about a general strike, wage earners responded as if there might be one. During the winter of 1885–86 they attended mass rallies, distributed literature, and canvassed employers, clergymen, editors, judges, and other civic leaders. Alderman Cullerton got an eight-hour day for city workers beginning May 1, and many employers promised to try the reform. The *Tribune* thought it "practically certain" that all employers would go along, and Harvey Goodall reported that in the Town of Lake "even the steady old family clocks, which for years have yielded implicit obedience to the requirements of their owners, are now inclined to strike." Tension mounted as Saturday, May 1, approached. Radical socialist speakers in Haymarket Square and on the lakefront urged listeners to take up arms, while moderates tried to disassociate themselves from these clamorous meetings. Schilling, in fact, headed the Trades Assembly's Eight-Hour Committee and conducted successful negotiations with many employers. Some brickmakers, lumber- and ironworkers, and freight handlers stayed away from work the last days in April because employers had not declared themselves. However, the weekend was peaceful. Reporters estimated another fifty thousand joined the strikers on Monday, but, with the exception of a clash outside the gates of the McCormick plant, there was comparatively little violence.[36]

At the Stockyards, John B. Sherman announced that he would go along with shorter hours. Schilling talked with a number of packers, but only Sidney Kent, partner in Chicago Packing and Provision Company, had promised an eight-hour day before May 1 and that plant was the only one to open at 8 A.M. instead of 7 A.M. on Saturday. Swift told Schilling that he would agree to shorter hours but the request must come from his employes. No doubt he expected to hear from cattle butcher John T. Joyce. The latter had joined the Knights in Kansas City in 1881 and when he came to Packingtown three years later he joined forces with two other young cattle butchers, Edward Condon at Swift's and George Schick at Armour's. They could have taken cattle butchers into Michael Butler's miscellaneous packinghouse workers' local, but they wanted their own charter and Powderly was not granting any during the eight-hour-day excitement. The packers held a meeting Saturday afternoon but adjourned without announcing their plans for Monday. The small plants soon posted 8 A.M. notices for May 3, but Armour, Swift, and Morris employes turned up at 7 A.M. as usual. Then Joyce, Condon, and Schick sent small delegations to talk to plant supervisors. Albert Foster and Michael Cudahy promised an eight-hour day with nine hours' pay, while Nelson Morris said he would give the full ten hours' pay to those earning $2 a day or less. Insisting upon "full pay" for all hands, the cattle butchers and their supporters, numbering about three thousand, left their posts. The leaders went to Frederick's Hall on Ashland to set up strike committees. Meantime, some laborers walked in to see Swift and he promptly granted their request for ten hours' pay. Word spread that the "Big Three" would give everyone "full pay" for an eight-hour day, and by noon the packinghouses were back to normal.[37]

Joyce would later claim that the "extraordinary efforts" of his cattle butchers overcame the "stubborn attitude of the packers" and sent the ten-hour day to "its Waterloo." It is likely, however, that before the cattle butchers acted, the packers knew that with the Stockyards on shorter hours and so many of their workers in the Knights of Labor they would have to accept the reform.[38]

The men who made their fortunes in Packingtown contributed so generously to charitable and cultural projects that a foreign visitor exclaimed, Chicago's "great butchers . . . are also the greatest of all philanthropists."[39] In the conduct of their businesses, those same men drove themselves hard and held managers and employes to the same rigorous standards. Since the packers were expanding rapidly and believed in promotion from within, there were unusual opportunities for advancement in the boom years. Employers were proud of the number of jobs they offered and the money they pumped into the community. Employes, including packinghouse women, received good wages in comparison with other Chicago area workers. Yet packinghouse labor was fast-paced, and six ten-hour days per week was an arduous schedule. When other wage earners organized and asked for shorter hours, packinghouse workers quickly fell in line. A few small plants and the Stockyards company had used occasional eight-hour shifts prior to 1886, but most of the employers waited to see how strong the demand would actually be. When they realized that the eight-hour day was at full tide in Packingtown, they acknowledged their dependence upon employes by blowing plant whistles at 8 A.M. and 4:30 P.M.

NOTES

1. *Trib.*, Oct. 25, 1887.

2. Ernest Poole, *Giants Gone: Men Who Made Chicago* (New York, 1943), 156; Frederic Cople Jaher, *The Urban Establishment: Upper Strata in Boston, New York, Charleston, Chicago, and Los Angeles* (Urbana, Ill., 1982), 8, 491–92, 495–98; *Trib.*, Oct. 12, 1886; *Chicago Times-Herald*, Jan. 7, 1901. See also, Jocelyn Maynard Ghent and Frederic Cople Jaher, "The Chicago Business Elite: 1830–1930. A Collective Biography," *Business History Review*, 50 (Autumn, 1976), 294–309; Kathleen D. McCarthy, *Noblesse Oblige: Charity and Cultural Philanthropy in Chicago, 1849–1929* (Chicago, 1982), chap. 4; Helen Lefkowitz Horowitz, *Culture and the City: Cultural Philanthropy in Chicago from the 1880s to 1917* (Lexington, Ky., 1976), chap. 2; Edward Chase Kirkland, *Dream and Thought in the Business Community, 1860–1900* (Ithaca, N.Y., 1956), chaps. 1, 6.

3. *Trib.*, Oct. 1, 1882; "The Men of Millions," *Trib.*, Apr. 6, 1890; Thomas W. Goodspeed, *The University of Chicago Biographical Sketches*, 2 vols. (Chicago, 1922), 1:88; 2:30–31; Harper Leech and John Charles Carroll, *Armour and His Times* (New York, 1938), 113–14; Bessie Louise Pierce, *A History of Chicago*, vol. 3, *The Rise of a Modern City, 1871–1893* (New York, 1957), 220–21, 224–27.

4. *Eleventh Census, 1890*, vol. 6, "Manufacturing Industries," part 2, 143; *Trib.*, Jan. 2, 1891; *Sun*, Jan. 18, 1891; Daniel Nelson, *Managers and Workers: Origins of the New Factory System in the United States, 1880–1920* (Madison, Wis., 1975), 6–8; Poole, *Giants Gone*, 139.

5. Daniel T. Rodgers, *The Work Ethic in Industrial America, 1850–1920* (Chicago, 1978), chap. 1; Leech and Carroll, *Armour*, 123, 54; Merle Crowell, "'P.D.' and 'J.O.'—Personal Stories and Business Wisdom of the Two Armours," *American Magazine*, 83 (Feb., 1917), 83; Louis F. Swift and Arthur Van Vlissingen, *The Yankee of the Yards: The Biography of Gustavus Franklin Swift* (Chicago, 1927), 98, 99, 96, 168; Ira Nelson Morris, *Heritage from My Father: An Autobiography* (New York, 1947), 13.

6. Leech and Carroll, *Armour*, 40, 75, 88; Charles Beadle, *A Trip to the United States in 1887* (Oxford, 1887), 167; H. I. Cleveland, "Philip Armour—Merchant," *World's Work*, 1 (Mar., 1901), 540; *Drovers Journal*, Sept. 13, 1884; May 20, 1889; Oct. 3, 1891; *Trib.*, Feb. 19, 1888; Mar. 23, 1890; Senate Select Committee, *Testimony . . . on Transportation and Sale of Meat Products* (Washington, 1889), 457.

7. Swift and Vlissingen, *Yankee of the Yards*, 100; Ira Nelson Morris, *Heritage from My Father*, 4, 8–9, 14–15; *Drovers Journal*, July 12, 1887; John Joseph Flinn, *Chicago, the Marvelous City of the West* (Chicago, 1890), 293.

8. Leech and Carroll, *Armour*, 220; Swift and Vlissingen, *Yankee of the Yards*, 111, 112, 159; Thomas W. Goodspeed, "Gustavus Franklin Swift, 1839–1903," *University [of Chicago] Record*, 7 (Apr., 1921), 112.

9. Poole, *Giants Gone*, 146; Arthur Warren, "Philip D. Armour," *McClure's*, 2 (Feb., 1894), 275, 279; Swift and Vlissingen, *Yankee of the Yards*, 141; *Drovers Journal*, June 26, 1889; Alfred T. Andreas, *History of Cook County, Illinois* (Chicago, 1884), 677, 678, 684–86; Arthur Meeker, *Chicago, with Love: A Polite and Personal History* (New York, 1955), 195–99.

10. Swift and Vlissingen, *Yankee of the Yards*, 91; Helen Swift, *My Father and My Mother* (Chicago, 1937), 58; Goodspeed, *Biographical Sketches*, 2:27–31; Cleveland, "Philip Armour—Merchant," 547; Edward N. Wentworth, *A Biographical Catalog of the Portrait Gallery of the Saddle and Sirloin Club* (Chicago, 1920), 176–77, 316; Leech and Carroll, *Armour*, 79–83, 85, 88; *Trib.*, Jan. 28, 1900.

11. Ira Nelson Morris, *Heritage from My Father*, 5, 12, 14, 18, 20–24, 30–32, 42–44, 45.

12. John Tebble, *George Horace Lorimer and the Saturday Evening Post* (New York, 1948), 6–10, 15, 27–30; [George Horace Lorimer], *Letters from a Self-Made Merchant to His Son* (Boston, 1902), 29, 133, 142–43, 192, 196; Carl S. Smith, *Chicago and the American Literary Imagination, 1880–1920* (Chicago, 1984), 161–64. Lorimer's popular satires boosted *Post* circulation and sold well in book form until the 1930s.

13. Kathleen D. McCarthy, *Noblesse Oblige*, 75–78; *Trib.*, Mar. 28, 1881.

14. *Trib.*, Dec. 20, 1885; Horowitz, *Culture and the City*, 50–57, 231–32; John J. Glessner, *The Commercial Club of Chicago* (Chicago, 1910), 13; Goodspeed, *Biographical Sketches*, 2:34–44.

15. George Upton, *Biographical Sketches of the Leading Men of Chicago* (Chicago, 1876), 216; Helen Swift, *My Father and My Mother*, passim; Goodspeed, *Biographical Sketches*, 1:190–97.

16. John J. Glessner, *Should Auld Acquaintance Be Forgot?* (privately printed, 1924), 20–21; Louise C. Wade, "Something More than Packers," *Chicago History*, 2 (Fall–Winter, 1973), 225, 230; Leech and Carroll, *Armour*, 209–12; *Inland Architect*, 8 (Jan., 1887), 106–7; *Trib.*, Jan. 6, 8, 15, 1881; Dec. 5, 1886; Oct. 17, 1887; June 1, Aug. 25, Oct. 19, 1889; Flinn, *Chicago*, 160–61.

17. James Clinton Peebles, *A History of Armour Institute of Technology* (typescript, 1955, Chicago Historical Society), 1–14; Leech and Carroll, *Armour*, 207 9, 212–16; Willis John Abbot, "The Armour Institute," *Outlook*, 48 (Dec., 1893), 993–94; Clifford L. Snowden, "The Armour Institute of Technology," *New England Magazine*, 16 (May, 1897), 354–72; Kathleen D. McCarthy, *Noblesse Oblige*, 93–95; *Trib.*, Oct. 15, 1893; *Chicago Evening Post*, July 7, 1894; *Chicago Times-Herald*, Jan. 7, 1901.

18. Department of Health, *Report of the Department of Health of the City of Chicago for 1888*, Report of Chief Tenement and Factory Inspector, 67–68; *Trib.*, Jan. 31, 1881; Irwin Yellowitz, *Industrialization and the American Labor Movement, 1850–1900* (Port Washington, N.Y., 1977), 21–46; Melvyn Dubofsky, *Industrialism and the American Worker, 1865–1920* (Arlington Heights, Ill., 1975), chaps. 1, 2; Nelson, *Managers and Workers*, 3–17; James B. Gilbert, *Work without Salvation: America's Intellectuals and Industrial Alienation* (Baltimore, Md., 1977), chap. 5; Edward Peters, "Some Economic and Social Effects of Machinery," American Association for the Advancement of Science, *Proceedings* (1884), 638–42.

19. *Trib.*, Feb. 20, 1881; Mar. 7, 1886; Nov. 25, 1888; *Drovers Journal*, Feb. 22, 1886; [Chicago] *Knights of Labor*, Jan. 22, 1887; *Eleventh Census, 1890*, vol. 6, "Manufacturing Industries," part 2, "Statistics of Cities," 144; Lynn Gordon, "Women and the Anti-Child Labor Movement in Illi-

nois, 1890–1920," *Social Service Review,* 51 (June, 1977), 228–30; Town of Lake Records, Doc. 2060, Dec. 23, 1881 (City Hall Archives, Chicago).

20. "A Visit to the States," *The Times* (London), Oct. 21, 1887; *Trib.,* Jan. 1, 1881.

21. *Trib.,* Oct. 12, Feb. 24, 1883; *Drovers Journal,* Feb. 22, 1886; "A Visit to the States," *The Times* (London), Oct. 21, 1887; Beadle, *Trip to the United States,* 169; L. de Cotton, "A Frenchman's Visit to Chicago in 1886," *JISHS,* 47 (Spring, 1954), 52.

22. *Drovers Journal,* Feb. 22, 1886; Apr. 10, 1885; Aug. 20, 1883; Nov. 8, 1886; June 14, Nov. 20, 1888; *Sun,* Oct. 13, Nov. 13, 15, 1888.

23. *Drovers Journal,* Mar. 11, Oct. 19, Nov. 10, 1886; *Trib.,* Nov. 14, 1886; *Sun,* Apr. 28, 1890; Department of Health, *Report of the Department of Health of the City of Chicago for 1887,* 82–83; Illinois Bureau of Labor Statistics, *Fourth Biennial Report, 1886* (Springfield, 1887), 280, 312, 353, 356; Knights of Labor, *Proceedings of General Assembly, 1887,* 1491–92; *Eleventh Census, 1890,* vol. 6, "Manufacturing Industries," part 2, "Statistics of Cities," 143, 144, 3–5; Clarence D. Long, *Wages and Earnings in the United States, 1860–1890* (Princeton, N.J., 1960), 42.

24. *Eleventh Census, 1890,* vol. 6, "Manufacturing Industries," part 2, "Statistics of Cities," 143, 144; *Trib.,* June 12, 1880; "Nora's Stock-Yards Fun," *Trib.,* Nov. 25, 1888; Francis L. Lederer, "Nora Marks, Investigative Reporter," *JISHS,* 68 (Sept., 1975), 306–18; "City Slave Girls," *Times,* Aug. 12, 1888.

25. *Sun,* Jan. 18, 1891; "Women in Packingtown," May 9, 1891; Oct. 22, 1892; Illinois Bureau of Labor Statistics, *Seventh Biennial Report, 1892,* part 1, xv, xliii, 5, 39, 64–65, 67, 82–83, 160–61, 168–71, 211, 213–15, 304–5, 312–13, 329, 338, 340–41; *Times,* Dec. 2, 1894; Elizabeth Jeanne Humphreys, "Working Women in Chicago Factories and Department Stores, 1870–1895" (M.A. thesis, University of Chicago, 1943), 25–26.

26. Nelson, *Managers and Workers,* 35–48; Alfred D. Chandler, Jr., *The Visible Hand: The Managerial Revolution in American Business* (Cambridge, Mass., 1977), 240–53.

27. Amalgamated Meat Cutters and Butcher Workmen, *Butcher Workman,* Dec., 1932, 2.

28. *Sun,* Oct. 12, 1886; *Trib.,* Jan. 3, 1888; *Drovers Journal,* June 26, 1889.

29. *Drovers Journal,* Oct. 29, 30, 1888; June 26, 1889; *Sun,* June 22, 1887; *Trib.,* Mar. 11, 26, 1883; *Butcher Workman,* Dec., 1932, 2.

30. *Trib.,* Dec. 12, 1882; Jan. 31, 1883; Dec. 6, 1884; May 10, Sept. 8, 1886; Jan. 17, Nov. 3, 1888; *Drovers Journal,* Feb. 1, 1883; July 26, 1886; June 19, 1888; *Sun,* Sept. 8, 1886; Mar. 10, 1890.

31. *Trib.,* Dec. 20, 30, 1882; Apr. 6, 1883; Feb. 4, 1887; *Drovers Journal,* Jan. 6, 1883; Apr. 11, 1888; *Sun,* Oct. 20, 1887.

32. Town of Lake Records, Doc. 61½, July 1, 1881; *Sun,* Sept. 24, 1885.

33. Pierce, *History of Chicago,* 3:261–63, 271; Terence V. Powderly, *Thirty Years of Labor, 1859 to 1889* (Columbus, Ohio, 1890), chaps. 11, 12; Norman J. Ware, *The Labor Movement in the United States, 1860–1895* (New York, 1929), chaps. 7–10; James Leiby, *Carroll Wright and Labor Reform: The Origin of Labor Statistics* (Cambridge, Mass., 1960), 69–75; John Lombardi, *Labor's Voice in the Cabinet: A History of the Department of Labor, from Its Origin to 1921* (New York, 1942), 18–35; Vincent Joseph Falzone, "Terence V. Powderly, Mayor and Labor Leader, 1849–1893" (Ph.D. diss., University of Maryland, 1970), 158–62.

34. Illinois Bureau of Labor Statistics, *Fourth Biennial Report, 1886,* 215, 168–69; Falzone, "Powderly," 171–96, 214–16; Powderly, *Thirty Years of Labor,* 493, 634–37; Donald L. Kemmerer and E. D. Wickersham, "Reasons for the Growth of the Knights of Labor in 1885–6," *Industrial and Labor Relations Review,* 3 (Jan., 1950), 213–20; [Chicago] *Knights of Labor,* Aug. 14, Oct. 30, 1886; *Trib.,* July 13, 1884; Feb. 18, 23, July 19, Oct. 4, 1885; Michael J. Butler to Terence V. Powderly, Jan. 1, 1886 (Box A1-15, Powderly Papers, Catholic University, Washington).

35. Paul Avrich, *The Haymarket Tragedy* (Princeton, N.J., 1984), 85–91, 181–84; Henry David, *The History of the Haymarket Affair* (New York, 1963), chap. 7; Ralph W. Scharnau, "Thomas J. Morgan and the Chicago Socialist Movement 1876–1901" (Ph.D. diss., Northern Illinois University, 1970), chaps. 2, 3; George A. Schilling, "History of the Labor Movement in Chicago," in [Lucy E. Parsons], *Life of Albert R. Parsons, with Brief History of the Labor Movement in America* (Chicago, 1889), xx–xxv; Chicago Citizens Association, *Annual Report, 1886* (Chicago, 1887), 35; Ware, *Labor Movement,* chap. 13; Powderly, *Thirty Years of Labor,* chaps. 12, 13; Pierce, *History of Chicago,* 3:265–68, 271–73.

36. *Trib.,* Mar. 16, 30, Apr. 9–11, 23, 26, May 1–4, 1886; *Times,* May 1–4, 1886; *Daily News,* May 4, 1886; *Drovers Journal,* Apr. 26, 1886; *Journal of United Labor,* 6 (Feb. 10, 1886), 1195; [Chicago] *Knights of Labor,* May 15, Aug. 14, 1886; Powderly, *Thirty Years of Labor,* 495–97; David, *Haymarket Affair,* 158–64; Pierce, *History of Chicago,* 3:274–75; Avrich, *Haymarket Tragedy,* 185–87.

37. *Trib.,* Apr. 19, 30, May 1–4, 16, 23, 1886; *Sun,* Apr. 29, 30, May 1, 3, 4, 1886; *Chicago Sun,* May 4, 5, 1886; *Drovers Journal,* May 5, 1886; *Butcher Workman,* Feb., 1932, 2; Mar., 1932, 3; Apr., 1932, 6; June, 1932, 2; Goodspeed, *Biographical Sketches,* 1:89; Helen Swift, *My Father and My Mother,* 121.

38. John T. Joyce, "One-Hour Strike Brings Eight-Hour Day," *Butcher Workman,* Apr., 1932, 3.

39. Marie T. Blanc, *The Conditions of Woman in the United States, a Traveller's Notes* (Boston, 1895), 59.

CHAPTER 14

Showdown on the Eight-Hour Day

The May 4 tragedy in Chicago's Haymarket Square turned out to be the Waterloo of the eight-hour day. Public fear and fury were aimed primarily at radicals, but labor organizations and labor reform took a beating in the conservative backlash. Many employers reneged immediately on the shorter workday; packers held on until fall but they complained about competition from ten-hour packing centers. Packinghouse workers felt that the best way to protect the shorter day was through organization, and during the tense summer of 1886 they flocked into new Knights of Labor locals. There was friction between skilled and unskilled workers from the beginning, but none between pork workers and beef workers until the pork plants returned to a ten-hour day in October. Then, without consulting any Knights of Labor leaders, the pork workers walked off their jobs. They were stunned to discover that the beef workers had a contract guaranteeing them the eight-hour day. An attempt to broaden the strike by pulling Armour beef workers out was doomed when Powderly ordered the strikers back to work. A second strike involving all packinghouse employes erupted when the beef houses went to a ten-hour day in November. Their local leader's involvement in a political campaign, more internal quarrels, and Powderly's rigid insistence that the strike was "illegal" were damaging, but when the packers brought in "scabs," Pinkertons, the National Guard, and deputy sheriffs, the workers' cause was hopeless. The eight-hour day went down to defeat, and strike repercussions helped the American Federation of Labor bring down the Knights of Labor.

Repercussions of the Haymarket Bomb

One holdout against the eight-hour day was Cyrus McCormick, Jr., who had recently replaced his deceased father. Well-known for his opposition to labor unions, young McCormick in 1885 had ignored both Mayor Carter Harrison and Philip Armour when they urged him to be more conciliatory toward his employes. Since the McCormick plant did not get shorter hours by the 1886 deadline and in fact kept operating with nonunion workers, it was understandable that striking South Branch factory, lumber, and brick workers gathered around that factory on Monday, May 3. Strikers and their sympathizers listened to August Spies before moving to the gates to taunt nonunion workers as they left for the day. The police were already there, and Spies arrived in time to see officers escorting "scabs" and protestors aiding wounded comrades. He responded by getting handbills on the street the next morning inviting workmen to Haymarket Square that evening to hear "Good speakers . . . denounce the latest atrocious act of the police." Another confrontation occurred on Monday evening when a small band of Bohemian packinghouse workers marched down Ashland Avenue shouting antipolice slogans and carrying a red flag. They were attacked by angry onlookers, and Town of Lake police had to separate the brawlers. One person was killed at the McCormick plant and one Bohemian shot to death in the Ashland Avenue melee. Otherwise the city was calm, and some 200,000 workers retired on May 3 knowing that they had won shorter hours, three-quarters of them by quiet negotiations with their employers.[1]

A small crowd gathered in Haymarket Square the next evening to hear Spies, Albert Parsons, and others deliver restrained speeches. The mayor stopped by, decided there would be no trouble, and departed before it started to rain. Listeners were heading for shelter when 180 policemen, some armed with two revolvers, entered the square and ordered the meeting adjourned. A moment later a dynamite bomb landed in the police column, injuring about seventy officers. The others, said the commanding officer, "recovered, instantly, and returned the fire of the mob." That meant turning on the stunned spectators, clubbing and shooting at random. Seven policemen and at least four civilians died; scores sustained serious injuries. Chicago newspapers held the radical orators and their audience—"serpents," "vipers," and immigrant "desperadoes"—responsible for the "Hellish Deed." One prominent clergyman said the anarchists had talked about heads falling and now it was their turn to provide "a few heads for the basket." While the police arrested Spies, Parsons, and other known radicals, vigilantes besieged city hall with offers to help, and the Citizens' Association named a law and order committee consisting of Armour, Field, McCormick, Pullman, and five other prominent citizens. Nobody paid attention to the Trades and Labor Assembly, which insisted there was a vast difference between "law-abiding, organized labor" and "reckless, law-defying men." Workers quietly speculated about the possibility that Pinkerton detectives had thrown the fatal bomb.[2]

Seven men, including Spies and Parsons, were sentenced to hang for the crime, and when four of the seven were executed in November, 1887, most Americans probably felt as did the *Illinois Staats-Zietung,* "The bloodshed of May 4, 1886, is now atoned." Samuel Gompers, president of the new American Federation of Labor, had asked the Illinois governor for clemency, and George Schilling had organized a defense fund to help the men appeal. The Knights of Labor, embarrassed by the membership of Parsons, Spies, and Schilling, thought the defendants had a fair trial and got what they deserved. Powderly asked the 1886 and 1887 General Assemblies to repudiate anarchy and eschew resolutions of sympathy for the condemned men. "Better that seven times seven men hang," he said in a moment of anger, "than to hang the millstone of odium around the standard of this Order." The Chicago District Assembly 24 suspended Parson's and Schilling's locals, and Richard Griffiths informed Powderly that reinstatement "would be fatal to the future success of the order in Chicago."[3]

The Haymarket tragedy caught Powderly in a tug of war with local assemblies on railroads in the Southwest. They had launched another strike in March without informing him and in violation of the agreement worked out in 1885 with Jay Gould. Powderly ordered the Knights to return to work; they ignored him until early May. Meantime, the forty-day freeze on new locals had expired, and members were once again pouring into the order. A special session of the General Assembly adopted stringent new strike rules: two-thirds of the unit wishing to strike must agree; the General Executive Board must have an opportunity to negotiate a settlement; strikers then needed specific approval from the board if they expected the order to back them up. The General Assembly also tightened the reins on organizers and selected Joseph Buchanan, of the Denver District Assembly and a member of the General Executive Board, and Albert Carlton, a New England organizer and lecturer, to help Powderly enforce the new rules. That same General Assembly told Chicago's south side District Assembly 57 to solve its internal disputes by electing new officers. In July members chose Michael J. Butler as their new Master Workman.[4]

Wage earners knew instinctively that the horrendous backlash to the Haymarket affair could sweep away their eight-hour day. Two of the locals in District 57, for example, passed resolutions denouncing the perpetrators, "whether Anarchists, Socialists, or Nihilists," reaffirming their preference for "peaceful discussion" of grievances, and thanking their "humane and magnanimous employers—the packers and the Stock Yards Company—for their readiness in acceding to . . . the Eight-Hours' System." The cattle butchers met the day after the bombing to regularize their loose organization. They elected Armour employe Granville Sawyer president and Joyce secretary. These two and Edward Condon persuaded about six hundred cattle butchers that affiliation with the Knights was the best way to protect shorter hours. By the end of June they had a charter for Cattle Butchers' Local Assembly 7802, and Sawyer now became Master Workman. Packinghouse managers were already sounding out foremen and workers about longer hours in return for higher wages, something the cattle butchers resisted because they were handling as many animals on the shorter shift as they had previously killed in ten hours. Packers told reporters that competition from Milwaukee, Kansas City, Omaha, and St. Louis, where wages were lower and the ten-hour day prevailed, left them in an "unfair position."[5]

Convinced that solid organization of the packinghouses was the only answer, Michael Butler and John Joyce bent every effort to establish new locals during the tense summer of 1886. Sheep and hog butchers signed up when they were promised separate locals like the cattle butchers. Casing cleaners, teamsters, carpenters, coopers, and freight handlers in Packingtown got separate craft locals. Four new mixed locals took in cellar workers, smokehouse gangs, beef boners, pork trimmers, margarine workers, and employes in the fertilizer departments. The Ashland Avenue mixed local was working so well that Butler set up another regional local, the Halsted Assembly of Packinghouse Workers. Germans, Bohemians, Poles, and Swedes could either join the appropriate existing local or, if they preferred, an ethnic mixed local. The latter had proved in the vicinity of St. Adalbert's Church to be "the track by which we will . . . get in all the Poles." Butler helped workers organize in other parts of Lake and in Hyde Park's industrial district. By September he had more than fifty locals with a total of eight thousand members.[6]

Butler shared the concern of Joyce, Condon, and Sawyer about unskilled packinghouse workers. Ineligible for membership in the twelve skilled and semiskilled locals, they could, but were reluctant to, join mixed locals. One possible lure was wages. The highest unskilled wage in Packingtown was $1.75 per day, and only Armour's laborers received that; if the Knights persuaded the other packers to match it, the unskilled would probably join. Butler made the mistake of airing the strategy first and finding later that the packers would only move from $1.50 to $1.65. Nonetheless he called a "convention" of delegates from each local in the district and asked them to ratify the $1.65 offer. Skilled workers approved, Joyce later wrote, but "the inevitable came." An Armour elevator operator talked the mixed locals into holding out for $1.75, saying that was modest compared to the wages of those in "the trades." Following an acrimonious debate, Butler's proposition failed. The troublemaker, grumbled Joyce, "was playing to the gallery as he had political ambitions." It was "the tail trying to swing the animal," the laborers wanting "to run the whole proceedings." Butler hoped to bury this fiasco with a Labor Day parade that would convince employers that the Knights of Labor was a solid organization. Over five thousand beef workers, led by the cattle butchers with their own fife and drum corps, and fifteen thousand pork workers put on a colorful show and then went to Ogden's Grove to hear Albert Carlton and others talk about labor solidarity.[7]

The cattle butchers felt that the importance of dressed beef gave them extra leverage, and they were determined to keep their eight hours and full pay no matter what happened to other packinghouse workers. When their president Granville Sawyer joined the district executive board, they elected Sylvester Gaunt, bookkeeper for a livestock firm and trusted counselor of the cattle butchers. Then they sent a delegation to confer with Michael Cudahy, Gustavus Swift, and Nelson Morris. What they got was the first written contract in the industry. It guaranteed the eight-hour day; set a schedule for beef-house wages that ranged from $24 per week for the skilled to $1.75 per day for front-feet skinners; and included the provision that any worker temporarily assigned to a lower grade job would keep his regular pay. The contract could be amended if both parties agreed; neither could act unilaterally without giving three days' notice. These "Articles of Agreement" were signed on October 4 by Swift, Cudahy, Morris, Gaunt, Sawyer, Condon, Thomas Dolan, Edwin Harper, and William Brooks. The signers were so quiet that other locals and reporters knew nothing about the contract. Even Michael Butler was in the dark until Gaunt "explained the situation of the beef men" in mid-October. Understandably, Joyce chose not to mention the agreement in his 1930s memoir.[8]

Butler, like Powderly and scores of other Knights in 1886 and 1887, had a strong interest in political reform. He agreed with Chicago's moderate socialists that a new labor party, "independent" of the Democratic, Republican, and discredited Socialist Labor parties, had a chance. In September, 1886, a United Labor party called for a national eight-hour day, a ban on private detective agencies, government ownership of all means of transportation and communication, state inspection of factories and penal and charitable institutions, compulsory school attendance, and an employers' liability law. The party nominated candidates for the state legislature and the offices in Cook County. Michael J. Butler, head of District Assembly 57 and guardian of the eight-hour day in Packingtown, agreed to run for sheriff in the November election. This was a controversial step because many workers were opposed to an independent labor party and others shared Griffiths's fear that "County politics" would invade "the Sanctuary of Local Assemblys." Butler was not a socialist, yet one Town of Lake Knight complained to Powderly that honest workingmen were being duped by "the Socialists in Chicago."[9]

Powderly was too busy preparing for the Richmond, Virginia, convention to get involved. It would have nearly four times as many delegates as the last General Assembly, and the General Master Workman was determined to achieve four objectives. He asked the delegates to denounce anarchism, endorse the new rules governing strikes and boycotts, and approve National Trade Districts which would help the Knights counter the appeal of Gompers' national trade associations. Powderly's fourth goal was a two-year term at $5,000 instead of $2,000 per year: he had just moved into a new residence in Scranton and heavy loans were pressing. The delegates complied and left for home October 20. Powderly assured his friend Henry George, a reform candidate for mayor of New York City, that he would help him campaign before the November 2 election. Packingtown was not on Powderly's fall agenda.[10]

Two Strikes in Packingtown

Getting rid of the eight-hour day before they went into the heavier winter season definitely *was* on the agenda of pork packers. The twenty-one firms had many more competitors outside Chicago than did the three dressed beef companies, and they insisted that comparable workdays was the only way to remain competitive. Said one, it's "die in our boots here, or go West. Armour has already gone West," but we "prefer to fight it out here and do not care to move." After informal discussions during the summer, the pork packers, including Armour, issued an October 7 statement announcing the return to the ten-hour day on Monday, October 11. Some fifteen thousand pork, lard, margarine, canning, and fertilizer workers would be affected, though not the sixty-five hundred hands in the beef houses. Swift did not sign the announcement because his first hog house was still on the drawing boards and Nelson Morris did not pack hogs. Anticipating trouble, the pork packers, calling themselves the Packers' Association, asked dealers to head off Chicago market hogs for a few days.[11]

Skilled hog butchers of local 7654 walked out of Chicago Packing and Provision Company on Friday, and the next day twelve thousand pork workers were out. They left their houses in "good shape," clean and ready for a lengthy shutdown. Butler was at the Richmond convention, and the first news he and Powderly received came as a surprise. The latter sent Butler home immediately and, for good measure, added Thomas Barry of the General Executive Board. Barry's experience had been in textile mills, lumber camps, and sawmills, yet Powderly hoped he could negotiate with the meat packers. Both men were warned that should talks fail, the Knights of Labor would not take responsibility for the unauthorized walkout or provide financial assistance. Butler and Barry arrived to find the pork houses locked, the beef houses operating normally, and 150 Pinkertons setting up camp in a small plant that had closed during the summer. Butler now learned about the eight-hour agreement in the dressed beef plants, but he assured strikers that Thomas Barry, "an angel of peace," would soon recover the eight-hour day for them. Barry had to talk to the packers individually because they denied there was an organization. They were not interested in an eight-hour plus overtime proposal, and the position of strikers was "Hours first, wages afterwards." Sympathetic Stockyards company employes backed the strikers and switchmen scrambled railroad traffic. Hoping to throw a monkey wrench into the dressed beef operation, strikers derailed a Rock Island cattle train at the crucial Halsted Street entrance to the Stockyards. Barry was furious at the strikers for disobeying his explicit orders to leave the beef workers alone and discouraged because the violence made his task more difficult.[12]

The executive board of District Assembly 57 added to his woes. Since Armour was the only pork packer who could balance his strike losses with dressed beef profits, the men assumed that he was holding small pork packers in line for the ten-hour day. They also accused Armour of bringing in the Pinkertons, though Allerton later claimed credit for that development. Convinced that Armour was "at the top and bottom of the trouble," the executive board voted to pull Armour's beef workers out on Friday, October 15. Butler signed the order in the belief that the cattle butchers' local supported the move. Three members were vehemently opposed; Gaunt, Dolan, and Harper, all signers of the October 4 contract, said the action violated the union promise to give three days' notice. When Barry learned the bad news, he fumed to a reporter that packinghouse workers were "thick-headed" and should be ordered back to work. "There is no discipline amongst them. They are a howling mob." Fortunately, the newspaper did not print the tirade, and Barry tersely wired Powderly the same day, "Negotiations ended. Neither side will yield."[13]

About one thousand Armour butchers heeded the strike call and took with them most of the carpenters, refrigerator car repairmen, mechanics, and even the firemen when they were asked to load refrigerator cars. Clerical and office people held the fort over the weekend, and Armour prepared to bring in cattle butchers from Milwaukee, Kansas City, and Omaha. He lashed out at local 7802 for welching on the contract and welcomed a statement signed by all the other pork packers and influential John B. Sherman accusing the Knights of Labor of "unjust and unreasonable" discrimination against Armour and Company. Father Flannigan of St. Anne's Church wired Powderly that the strikers were apt to be "replaced by others and never taken back." From a wealthy northern suburb, Henry Demarest Lloyd counseled tough action against the odious packer who manufactured "bogus butter to cheat peoples' pockets and ruin their health." He wanted the Knights General Assembly to endorse the strike before it adjourned in Richmond.[14]

Without seeing either of these recommendations, Powderly told Barry to end the strike, and the latter, as a spokesman for the General Executive Board, prepared an order "To the Locked out employes of the Union Stock Yards." They were to accept the ten-hour day and return to work at 7 A.M., Tuesday, October 19. Arguing that the order came from above, Butler forced Barry to break the bad news to the strikers. Some two thousand men came to the Germania Turner Hall to hear Barry discourse on the "hungry army" of unemployed waiting for their jobs, the impossibility of retaining an eight-hour day, and the simple truth that "honorable retreat is better than a complete defeat." Barry then read his order, and, according to reporters outside, "Bedlam was turned loose." After two hours of bitter argument, during which Barry yelled himself hoarse, he emerged claiming victory. "The men had their hearts set on eight hours . . . but I gave them the medicine and they had to swallow it." After stopping at Armour's downtown office to tell him that the strike was off and wiring the same to Powderly, Barrry left Chicago. Goodall's *Sun* commended the strikers on their "bearing and conduct," adding that "whatever the future may bring forth, their good behavior will always be scored to their credit."[15]

The Pinkertons, by contrast, offended just about everyone—Harvey Goodall, pedestrians and shoppers on Halsted, Forty-seventh, and Ashland, Town of Lake policemen, and striking switchmen and packinghouse workers. They were overbearing, insulting, often intoxicated, and quick to threaten angry citizens with their Winchesters. The end of the strike, noted the *Tribune,* means that the troublesome Pinkertons "can now draw their pay and go home." Sullen strikers, disgusted with Barry and worried about retrieving their jobs, vented their anger on unarmed Pinkertons preparing to depart from Packingtown. Discovering one guard in a drunken stupor in an empty railroad car, they stripped his uniform off and beat him severely. On the afternoon of October 19, a train carrying nonunion workers from Armour's plant and about one hundred departing Pinkertons left the Stockyards amidst hoots and jeers from bystanders at Fortieth and Halsted. The train backed up to collect two more passenger cars, and when it crossed Halsted the Pinkertons had their Winchesters leveled at pedestrians. Some people threw stones; the Pinkerton commander on a rear platform fired a warning shot over their heads; his men thought they had been fired at and so they opened fire on the crowd. Miraculously only one man was killed. He was Terrence Begley, a self-employed teamster recently arrived from Ireland, who left a wife and four children in a squatter's shack on the eighty acres. Charges against four Pinkertons were dropped after two grand juries refused to indict them. The *Knights of Labor* probably spoke for a sizeable number of strikers when it said "Phil Armour's hired bandits murdered a man at last."[16]

The strikers got their jobs back and a 50¢ winter wage increase, but all of them worked a ten-hour day. Employes in the Swift and Morris beef houses, numbering about thirty-five hundred, worked eight hours at the wage scale established by the October 4 contract. Michael Butler, George Schilling, Edwin Harper, and two other cattle butchers continued to talk with employers in late October about hours and wages. Cudahy refused to put the Armour cattle butchers on eight hours but he guaranteed their

$4.50 daily wage. Before leaving Chicago, Thomas Barry had hinted that Sidney Kent and Robert Fowler would accept an eight-hour day at nine hours' pay, and if Swift, Morris, Anglo-American, and Chicago Packing and Provision adhered to an eight-hour day, other houses presumably would fall in line. No such agreement was nailed down, however, and Barry, Butler, and Gaunt gave conflicting accounts of it later on. Some Packingtown workers hoped Michael Butler would call another strike after the election. Others were grateful to have their jobs back and steady winter wages to clear debts from the first strike.[17]

The eight-hour beef workers in the Swift and Morris plants faced an uncertain future. They knew that most Chicago area employers had reneged on shorter hours in the aftermath of the Haymarket bomb and at the Rock Island carshops the last group of eight-hour workers were going to the longer day on November 1. They could not talk to Michael Butler because he was in the final throes of the United Labor party campaign. So a delegation from the cattle butchers' local went directly to Swift and Morris. These packers considered the first contract null and void because of local 7802's action against Armour, and thus they were free to switch to the ten-hour day on November 1. They offered, however, to advance skilled wages by 50¢ and all others by 25¢ per day. And they were willing to try another contract provided it had a seven-day ban on unilateral action and specified the longer workday. The men accepted these terms, and Swift, Morris, Gaunt, Condon, Harper, and six others from local 7802 signed the agreement October 28. The very day it went into effect, two butchers, one of them a signer of the agreement, asked Swift superintendent Fred Wilder for still higher wages. Wilder had just stepped into Albert Foster's job, and he apparently lost his temper and fired the signer on the spot. The rest of Swift's skilled butchers walked out, whereupon Swift ordered Wilder to rehire the man and consented to wage increases on the lower levels only. November 1 ended in a fog of confusion and rumor.[18]

It was impossible to verify strike plans the next day because the "leading spirits among the workingmen were busy with the election, and could not be found about the yards." They captured 60 percent of the Town of Lake vote for Butler, but he lost to the incumbent Republican sheriff. The United Labor party elected some candidates to the state legislature and predicted a much stronger showing in the spring municipal elections. Allerton, meantime, had convened the pork packers plus Swift and Morris. This group resolved to keep the ten-hour day, guard their property at any and all costs, and take whatever steps were necessary to protect new employes should they choose to hire them. Cornered by reporters after this meeting, Swift confirmed that he and Morris would "stand together" with the others and that he was "about disgusted with Knights of Labor and consultations." The packers must have noticed a *Tribune* article that same day about striking pork workers in East St. Louis who took possession of a plant in order to keep nonunion men out. Powderly was in New York City with Henry George and did not catch up on the first round of Chicago letters and telegrams until Thanksgiving. Thus he missed Richard Powers's warning that District Assembly 57 was "unsettled" and in a "bad state" and Barry's query, "Trouble in Chicago; they wire for me to come; shall I go?" The head of the Knights of Labor read in the newspaper that Barry was enroute to another strike in Packingtown.[19]

Meanwhile, the "leading spirits" in District Assembly 57 had taken the opportunity to flex their muscle as Knights of Labor at the time Powderly, the General Executive Board, and Thomas Barry were looking in another direction. They created an ad hoc strike committee composed of twenty-three representatives; the latter were appointed, not elected, because the leaders did not want to risk another fiasco like their earlier "convention." The strike committee knew that no matter what Swift and Morris did about wages, their beef workers wanted to keep the eight-hour day. They also knew that many skilled cattle butchers, including Armour's men, were itching to strike. Condon, Joyce, and others, therefore, proposed this strategy to local 7802 on November 4. Gaunt, Harper, and Dolan were opposed to a beef workers' strike because it would violate the terms of the second contract. A large majority of those attending the meeting, however, voted in favor of the scheme, and instructions went out under Michael Butler's name. Fewer than half of Armour's beef workers heeded the strike call. Thomas Dolan fired off a letter to a Chicago newspaper saying a member of the Knights' General Executive Board had sent him back to work, he needed the $27 weekly wage, and he would fight any many man who stood in his way. When reporters asked why District 57 pulled the Armour workers out too, Butler said it was local 7802's decision. Sylvester Gaunt then accused Butler of trying "to crawl out from under a mistake by prevarication at my expense," and a few days later he resigned as president of the local. Annoyed by the unexpected opposition and attendant publicity, the strike committee called an irregular session of local 7802 and expelled Gaunt, Harper, and Dolan. Those three pointed out to reporters that even their expulsion was illegal.[20]

"Everybody at the Stock-Yards is waiting for something to drop," said the *Tribune* on November 4. They did not have long to wait. The Pinkertons returned to their former barracks on Friday, armed with revolvers and clubs instead of Winchesters. That evening the strike committee held a mass rally which shouted approval of a general strike by all Packingtown employes. Michael Butler issued the order and later told Powderly, "it was decided that the present was the most available time to secure a return to the eight-hour system." The packers closed their houses for the duration. Over the weekend, the recently reelected Republican sheriff of Cook

County sent 150 deputy sheriffs to Packingtown. Then he traveled to Springfield to ask the governor for four regiments of National Guardsmen. Governor Richard Oglesby thought two would be sufficient and ordered the First and Second Regiments to their Chicago armories. The militia marched to the railroad depot Monday morning, receiving a rousing cheer from members crowding the balcony of the Board of Trade. The Second Regiment went by rail directly to Packingtown; the First Regiment, pulling its Gatling gun, marched from the Forty-third Street station to the Stone Gate and through the Stockyards on Exchange Avenue to the J. C. Ferguson and Company warehouse. Six hundred and fifty soldiers set up headquarters at "Fort Ferguson," while Pinkertons and deputy sheriffs shared the Washington Butchers' Sons plant. The soldiers would guard the plants and approaches to Packingtown during daylight hours, the Pinkertons and deputy sheriffs at night.[21]

Thomas Barry arrived after the Pinkertons but before the militia. He conferred with Michael Butler, George Schilling, the various factions of cattle butchers, and a few packers. On Sunday evening he told strikers to stay away from the packinghouses, shun the saloons, and "conduct yourself orderly." The next day he sounded out the packers on an eight-hour day and 10 percent wage cut; they were adamant about maintaining the ten-hour day. "Send instructions what I shall do," Barry wrote Powderly; "packers still refuse arbitration, and the men are firm for eight hours. Both sides are unwillng to yield." Powderly and the General Executive Board reinforced Barry with another member of the board, Albert Carlton. Years later, Powderly would express regret that he did not follow his "first impulse" and go to Chicago himself. Carlton arrived on November 11 and learned from Butler, Condon, Sawyer, and John T. Joyce that "the strike would be won." It looked otherwise to the public. Reporters covering the arival of Pinkertons, deputy sheriffs, and militia units got wind of the bitter quarrel among the cattle butchers and pieced together the earlier scheme to sever Kent and Fowler from the packers' organization. Barry foolishly discussed these matters with them and went on to accuse Butler of playing politics with the District Assembly during his absence. A *Tribune* editorial entitled "Barry Accuses Butler of Treachery" concluded that the "upshot of the whole affair will doubtless be the dissolution of the Stock-Yards Assembly of Knights."[22]

On Monday, November 8, the packers met at the Board of Trade and decided that resignation from "the labor organization" was essential to reinstatement of the strikers. "It is plain that we must fight the organization and not the men," said Charles Counselman. They resolved to hire "only such men as recognize the fact that their first allegiance is to us, their employers, and not to any system of tyranny in the guise of a labor organization." Armour, grumbling about a new strike every Monday morning, advertised in Chicago papers for laborers, carpenters, coopers, and butchers, all of whom were promised "steady work, good wages, and protection." Swift and Morris signed the resolution requiring "ironclad" renunciation of the Knights of Labor, but they soon had second thoughts. It would generate sympathy for the strikers, increase the effectiveness of any labor boycott against Chicago meat, and inflict "unintentional injustice" on loyal employes. They requested another meeting which lasted a record-breaking three and one-half hours and rescinded the earlier resolution. Armour, Swift, Morris, and the Union Stock Yard and Transit Company headed the list of twenty-three firms which signed this November 10 resolve: "while we will not exclude from employment the members of such organizations, we will exercise the right to employ and discharge whom we please, and conduct the business on the ten-hour plan, and according to our best interests."[23]

The packers were serious about hiring and protecting nonunion men. They drew on their "defense fund" to purchase cots, blankets, and stoves, bring new workers in by train and house them in the plants and warehouses. During the October strike, there had been fewer than five hundred strikebreakers in Packingtown. By Friday, November 12, however, there were approximately seventy-five hundred men working in defiance of Butler's strike order. Some were neighborhood people who disliked the Knights of Labor or desperately needed the wages. Harvey Goodall estimated that about three thousand strikers returned to work. Others came from Baltimore, Philadelphia, New York, East St. Louis, Milwaukee, Kansas City, and Omaha to collect high hourly pay while the strike lasted. There were enough skilled butchers in the lot to keep the houses running and teach novices the bare essentials. Guarding these strikebreakers were about one thousand law enforcement agents—the two National Guard regiments reinforced by a cavalry unit, Pinkertons, deputy sheriffs, and forty-two special Town of Lake policemen. While strikers had left the packinghouses in disarray when the second conflict began, they did not attempt to damage or reoccupy the plants.[24]

Although militia guarded the four main entrances—Forty-third and Ashland, Forty-seventh and Center Avenue, Halsted and Exchange, and the Ullman Avenue bridge over the Stockyards Canal, strikers could identify "scabs" by their lunch pails and the hours they kept. Unwary Poles, Bohemians, and some new German immigrants were beaten, knifed, and shoved into the canal. Stones with messages attached came through their windows, and family members were harassed. The strikers also taunted soldiers from the east side of Halsted. The militia finally called on a cavalry unit to guard the bridges, keep Halsted Street clear, and make occasional forays into the district southwest of Packingtown to prove that they were not "afraid to go out in those directions." Some southern black strikebreakers brought in by train caused "vicious comment," and one of Goodall's reporters heard a strike leader remind an angry crowd that the Knights of Labor believed in racial equality. Someone retorted, "if we are not permitted to wallop them because they are niggers, there is nothing to prevent us ('except the soldiers,' interjected another) from knocking h—— out of them because they are not Knights."[25]

Barry still thought an "honorable settlement" could be worked out, but Powderly and the General Executive Board reviewed his earlier assessment of the "losing fight," examined the "fusillade of letters and telegrams" from dissidents, considered newspaper predictions that the strike would fail, and reminded each other that few of the strikers were dues-paying Knights. On November 10 Powderly wired Barry and Carlton "to settle by putting men back at old hours until the Order . . . takes definite action on eight-hour plan. If men refuse, take their charters. We must have obedience and discipline." By the time Powderly's agents received these instructions, the Board of Trade had already posted a copy and reporters were preparing their stories. Since the wire was not in code, Barry and Carlton sought confirmation and then asked, "Should we obey in opposition to our judgment?" Powderly's answer was a cryptic comment one year later, "To this message no reply was necessary."[26]

The strikers wanted to hold out even though their families were suffering and most were in debt to local storekeepers. They thought the Board of Trade surrender notice was a ruse to demoralize them. When Barry summoned them to the Germania Turner Hall on Saturday, November 13, and told them the strike was off, shouts of "No, never" reverberated throughout the building. Barry, Carlton, and Michael Butler managed to divert the strikers' anger from themselves to Powderly and the General Executive Board which had "obliged" them to take that action. The next day local assemblies grudgingly voted to return to work "under protest." Elsewhere the National Guard celebrated its final day of Stockyards duty. Some two thousand friends and relatives came to Packingtown to watch the cavalry drill and have a look at "Fort Ferguson." There was a religious service with the chaplain preaching from wooden planks laid atop empty packing barrels, and many guardsmen proudly displayed the cattle horns presented to them as mementoes by Philip Armour. "More disastrous strikes have been ordered," wrote Harvey Goodall, "but not one that ever had a more humiliating ending."[27]

The Aftermath

After the strike collapsed, conservatives rewarded the National Guard with a new Chicago armory, secured a state law permitting city police to assist suburban officers in mass disorders, and began lobbying for an army base on the outskirts of the city. The packers' main concern was getting their skilled hands back to work and simultaneously demonstrating that employers, not employes, had won the showdown. They accomplished this by asking the Cook County sheriff to post notices on Halsted, Forty-seventh, and Ashland instructing men to assemble at designated entrances to Packingtown if they wanted work. While militiamen guarded those entrances, managers and foremen read the list of men to be rehired and gave them passes to enter Packingtown. Of the many thousands seeking reinstatement on Monday, November 15, only 1,356 secured passes. However, as supplies of livestock increased and strikebreakers dropped out, more strikers were taken back. Within two weeks, nearly 14,000 were working at their former jobs. They had signed contracts renouncing all labor organizations, promising two weeks' notice before quitting the job, and agreeing to deposit two weeks' wages as a guarantee of good faith. Employers paid 5 percent interest on the deposit and allowed workers to accumulate the money by forfeiting one day's pay every two weeks for six months. Cattle butchers signed the ironclad like everyone else and were further chastened by getting hourly instead of weekly wages. Strike leaders were left out in the cold for several months. But during 1887 Joyce got his job back at Armour's beef house, and Anglo-American hired Edward Condon. The latter was arrested in September for dropping a heavy ham on a "scab" and then assaulting the man. Granville Sawyer started his own meat market but ran afoul of the law when he failed to pay his supplier, Nelson Morris. Gaunt stayed on with John Clay's livestock firm, and Michael Butler had snagged an $1,800-a-year Town of Lake job in May, 1886.[28]

District Assembly 57 was in deep trouble. The cattle butchers' once-proud local 7802 "dwindled down to a few of us," admitted Joyce, and the "general condemnation against the Knights of Labor" boded ill for the other locals. Before the year was out, one settled for "a lecture, recitation, songs, etc." at meetings and found that "so far all have been pleased with it." Of course there was spirited discussion of responsibility for the strike loss. Joyce blamed "stool pigeons" who lied to "our far-off 'Leaders.'" Gaunt blamed Thomas Barry and warned Powderly if the need arose to send anyone else "for pity sake . . . give us a man that has some brain and able to cope with any trouble he may find." Others blamed Butler's fling with the United Labor party. The Master Workman of District Assembly 57 said it was not a strike but rather "a lock-out manipulated by P. D. Armour (who organized the packers into an association) in order to force a return to the ten hour day." The packinghouse workers wanted "to be left alone to fight their battle. They felt they held a winning hand & only asked to be left to play it successfully." Butler presided over the assembly until January, 1889, but he could not arrest its steady decline. A boycott against Armour products was taken up by Knights of Labor in other parts of the country, and Butler tried to keep it alive by holding Armour "morally responsible" for "pools and rings" which hurt consumers and competitors, for using Pinkertons during the strike, and for employing "both black and white" strikebreakers. He also promoted a cooperative packinghouse and tannery until its directors made it clear that employes would have no say in determining hours or wages. Both the boycott and the cooperative had failed by the time Butler pulled out, and District Assembly 57 expired unnoticed in September, 1891.[29]

The Stockyards strikes split District Assembly 24 and poisoned the atmosphere of the General Assemblies for several years. Richard Griffiths, Richard Powers, and George and Elizabeth Rodgers sided with Powderly, while George Schilling staunchly defended Michael Butler and rattled Powderly by continuing to refer to the condemned Haymarket anarchists as "my friends—my brothers." Aiding the Schilling-Butler faction was Joseph R. Buchanan, who had used the Denver *Labor Enquirer* during the strikes to criticize Powderly. Schilling and Thomas Morgan invited Buchanan to establish a socialist labor paper in Chicago; he accepted and got the first issue out in February, 1887, just in time to help the United Labor party in the spring elections. Buchanan's Chicago *Labor Enquirer* articles rehashing the 1886 strikes appeared in many other labor newspapers and forced Powderly to make a detailed report at the 1887 Knights of Labor convention. The head of the order documented his position paper with letters, telegrams, and the instructions he had sent to Chicago. The delegates gave Powderly a vote of confidence and expelled Buchanan. During 1888 Schilling, Buchanan, Butler, and Thomas Barry tried to create a National District of Packinghouse Workers centered in Chicago but embracing Kansas City, Omaha, East St. Louis, and Milwaukee. They failed, Buchanan's Chicago paper folded in the summer of 1888, and when the Socialist Labor party expelled him, he moved to New Jersey to work for the American Press Association. At the 1889 General Assembly, Powderly engineered the expulsion of George Schilling, the last of the "kickers."[30]

Some observers found a moral in the catastrophic decline of Knights of Labor membership while the American Federation of Labor was growing. Trade unionists clubbed the Knights with the Stockyards fiasco. An officer of the Chicago bricklayers' association, for example, charged Powderly with ordering the strikers "back on worse terms than those they struck against" yet expecting them to go on paying dues "just the same. What for? . . . The unions teach benevolence and protection, which is good enough education for me." Gompers slyly observed that the Knights' General Executive Board had "acceded to the demands of the employers" in Packingtown and Powderly "could do the work of the [packers] no better." When the federation voted in 1890 to revive the eight-hour campaign, delegates were reminded that it could have been preserved in the Stockyards if "the great stultifier" had not issued his "traitorous manifesto."[31]

Powderly, however, refused to acknowledge mistakes on his part. The Chicago storm came out of the blue, he told the General Assembly, was aggravated by disobedient strikers, and "enlarged upon and scattered to the world by enemies from within and from without." The subsequent membership decline of the Knights was due to other unauthorized strikes which "swept thousands . . . into poverty and forced them from the Order." This version of events appeared in *Thirty Years of Labor, 1859 to 1889*, but the autobiography, written nearly three decades later, took greater liberty with the facts. "It was my duty to know the real situation in Chicago and I did know it." Powderly's most trusted informant was the ailing Richard Griffiths, who admitted confusion about "this Stock Yard Affair" and said, "I do not know who to believe . . . I do not know what advice to give." Copies of Powderly's letters to Griffiths were presumably removed while he was working on the autobiography. They must have contained dark thoughts, for Griffiths hoped his friend would never again ask, "did I do wrong in declaring the strike off at Chicago?"[32]

In the aftermath of the 1886 strikes there was no feasible way to rebuild a packinghouse workers' organization. Powderly knew from his correspondence that the men in 1888 were still "too bitter toward me to give heed to anything I may say to them." When the American Federation of Labor set May 1, 1890, as the new eight-hour deadline, George Schilling tried in vain to arouse interest in one large union which could not only recapture the eight-hour day but also get rid of the embarrassing ironclad agreement. A former ham sewer, Frank O'Neill, did put together a Packing-House Laborers' Union of about four thousand Bohemians, Poles, and Germans. He claimed that if they struck on May 1 for shorter hours and a 25¢ pay increase, the semiskilled and skilled workers would have no choice except to join them. O'Neill riled the cattle butchers, who felt the packers would not grant shorter hours and who did not want to be manipulated by laborers. Edward Condon and Patrick Mulcahy urged the cattle and hog butchers to sabotage the Packing-House Laborers' Union. They did by announcing their intention to ignore any action O'Neill's group might take on May 1. O'Neill caved in and his organization crumbled immediately. Mulcahy praised the skilled knifemen for having the "intelligence . . . to manage their own affairs." The laborers could find other jobs, but butchers "work here or nowhere at our trade."[33]

Mulcahy and Condon did not include the sheep butchers, perhaps because so few of them had been through the 1886 strikes and perhaps because they, unlike cattle and hog butchers, both killed and dressed and were paid by the carcass. Late in 1890 the packers tried to put the sheep butchers on the "ring system," assigning each a specific task and paying them a daily wage. The men objected, and John T. Joyce counseled them to walk out. Assured of a patronage job, Joyce quit his beef butchering job at Armour's and tried valiantly to organize a sheep butcher's union. In January, 1891, Armour agreed to restore the old system, but Joyce kept the Armour strikers out until Swift and Morris also abandoned the sheep "ring." Unfortunately for Joyce, those packers did not follow the scenario, Armour withdrew his offer, and disillusioned sheep butchers ended their resistance in February. One final effort to organize cattle butchers was just as fruitless. In the summer of 1892 Joyce and Condon excoriated the packers for promoting from within rather than hiring experienced butchers who came to Chicago from other packing centers. Irish butchers were worried about the advance of other nationalities from the trimming benches to the killing beds; one exclaimed to a reporter in 1894 that "Polacks . . . are actually butchering beef . . . now." But Joyce made no headway with the issue in 1892, either because experienced butchers did not consider it a major grievance or because they lacked confidence in the leadership of Joyce, Condon, and Mulcahy. At any rate, Joyce noted in his memoir that the "packers didn't have any trouble with the butchers in Chicago for the time being."[34]

In retrospect it is clear that the Haymarket bomb caused heavy damage to packinghouse workers. The public recoiled against labor organizations and labor reforms and even Mayor Harrison for tolerating the radical socialists in Chicago. During the conservative backlash employers retreated on the eight-hour reform, and packers found themselves tempted to return to the longer workday. But rather than risk a dressed beef strike, three of them experimented with a written contract, a "new thing" in 1886 for both sides. Worker violations of that agreement and their vindictive actions against Armour actually pulled pork and beef packers together and convinced them to use all resources at their command to win the test of wills. Being a labor leader in the wake of Haymarket was a thankless task, but trying to build a "solid" organization of packinghouse workers was even more difficult. There was a wide gulf of distrust separating skilled and unskilled workers, and the maneuvering of the cattle butchers' local made matters worse. Moreover, Irish dominance in skilled jobs and union leadership positions did not sit well with workers belonging to other ethnic groups. A *Tribune* reporter explained the 1890 disarray solely in terms of ethnic friction. Most of the butchers in 1886 had been Irish and "agreed well together," but as soon as "different nationalities" outnumbered them, "a concerted movement" became "more difficult." Michael Butler made mistakes, but his record looks good compared to Powderly's inept delegation of responsibility to agents who knew nothing about meat-packing. As John R. Commons said, "Powderly did not possess the aggressive qualifications required for a successful leader in strikes."[35]

The packinghouse strikes were precursors of Homestead and Pullman, and they ought to have taught some lessons. The civility of the contest in Packingtown was a distinct advance over the 1877 railroad strikes. The two sides talked to each other and even tried to codify points of agreement; in addition, injuries, loss of life, and property damage were held to a minimum and the strikers as well as their leaders got their jobs back. The strikes were, as Henry Demarest Lloyd put it, a "*private war* between two great classes," yet both sides recognized their dependence upon each other and they therefore waged a comparatively civilized contest. Unfortunately, these lessons were lost sight of by other employers and other strikers in the 1890s.[36]

During the summer of 1886 Knights of Labor leaders in Packingtown tried valiantly to build an organization that could withstand employer pressures to return to the ten-hour day. The packers' decision to shift pork workers first caught Michael Butler by surprise and he apparently knew nothing of the contract worked out by the cattle butchers and Armour, Swift, and Morris. Since the wildcat pork workers' strike was in violation of Knights of Labor rules and regulations, Powderly sent a member of the General Executive Board, who soon ordered the men back to work. But local leaders had called Armour's beef workers out, in violation of their contract, so employers felt free to restore the ten-hour day in the beef houses. A second unauthorized strike pitted all packinghouse workers against their employers on the one hand and against Powderly's agent Thomas Barry on the other. Barry described the strikers as "a determined, headstrong set," "the hardest body of people I have ever tried to control."[37] In the end, the packinghouse workers lost because nonunion workers, protected by militia, deputy sheriffs, and Pinkertons, enabled packers to start up operations without them. Powderly's brusque return-to-work order merely won their enmity. Although the strikers and even the strike leaders got their jobs back, the Knights of Labor locals disappeared and nothing arose in their place. Skilled and unskilled workers went their own ways, while market butchers, the Chicago Trades and Labor Assembly, and the American Federation of Labor kept their distance from the "headstrong" packinghouse workers.

NOTES

1. Stella Virginia Roderick, *Nettie Fowler McCormick* (Rindge, N.H., 1956), 146–48; Paul Avrich, *The Haymarket Tragedy* (Princeton, N. J.,

1984), 187–91; Henry David, *The History of the Haymarket Affair* (New York, 1963), 164–69; Paul C. Hull, *The Chicago Riot: A Record of the Terrible Scenes of May 4, 1886* (Chicago, 1886), 38–58; John Joseph Flinn, *History of the Chicago Police from the Settlement of the Community to the Present Time* (Chicago, 1887), 269–87; Bessie Louise Pierce, *A History of Chicago*, vol. 3, *The Rise of a Modern City, 1871–1893* (New York, 1957), 275–78; Illinois Bureau of Labor Statistics, *Fourth Biennial Report, 1886* (Springfield, 1887), 479; *Trib.*, May 4–6, 1886; *Daily News*, May 4, 5, 1886; *Sun*, May 4, 5, 1886.

2. Avrich, *Haymarket Tragedy*, chaps. 14, 15; David, *Haymarket Affair*, chaps. 9, 10; Hull, *Chicago Riot*, 58–97; Charles Edward Russell, "The Haymarket and Afterwards," *Appleton's Magazine*, 10 (Oct., 1907), 399–405; Francis X. Busch, "The Haymarket Riot and the Trial of the Anarchists," *JISHS*, 48 (Autumn, 1955), 247–70; Richard C. Marohn, "The Arming of the Chicago Police in the Nineteenth Century," *Chicago History*, 11 (Spring, 1982), 44–46; Pierce, *History of Chicago*, 3:280–81; Reverend Frederick A. Noble, "Christianity and the Red Flag," May 9, 1886 (pamphlet at Chicago Historical Society); Frank Morn, *"The Eye That Never Sleeps": A History of the Pinkerton National Detective Agency* (Bloomington, Ind., 1982), 99; *Times*, May 5, 6, 1886; *Trib.*, May 5, 7, 11, 16, 1886; *Chicago Sun*, May 11, 1886.

3. Avrich, *Haymarket Tragedy*, chaps. 17–19; David, *Haymarket Affair*, chaps. 12–20; Norman J. Ware, *The Labor Movement in the United States, 1860–1895* (New York, 1929), 315–19; Pierce, *History of Chicago*, 3:281–89; Alan Dawley, "Anarchists, Knights of Labor and Class Consciousness in the 1880s" (Paper delivered at Knights of Labor Centennial Symposium, Chicago, May, 1979); *Illinois Staats-Zeitung*, Nov. 12, 1887; *Trib.*, Aug. 21, 1886; Nov. 12, 1887; Knights of Labor, *Proceedings of the General Assembly, 1887*, 1499–1513; Richard Griffiths to Terence Powderly, July 6, 1886 (Box A1–22, Powderly Papers, Catholic University of America, Washington); C. D. Wheeler to Powderly, Aug, 21, 1886 (Box A1–23).

4. Knights of Labor, *Proceedings of Special Session, 1886*, 20, 69; Terence V. Powderly, *Thirty Years of Labor, 1859 to 1889* (Columbus, Ohio, 1890), 639–41; Terence V. Powderly, *The Path I Trod: The Autobiography of Terence V. Powderly*, ed. H. J. Carman et al. (New York, 1940), 119–21; Vincent Joseph Falzone, "Terence V. Powderly, Mayor and Labor Leader, 1849–1893" (Ph.D. diss., University of Maryland, 1970), 198–220.

5. *Sun*, May 6, 22, 1886; *Drovers Journal*, Aug. 5, 1886; *Trib.*, May 18, 23, 27, July 24, Aug. 21, 28, Sept. 1, 22, 29, 1886; *Butcher Workman*, Apr. 1932, 3, 6; June, 1932, 2.

6. *Butcher Workman*, June, 1932, 2; Aug., 1932, 5; Powderly, *Path I*

Trod, 145; Knights of Labor, *Proceedings, 1886,* 326; [Chicago] *Knights of Labor,* Aug. 28, Sept. 25, 1886; Joseph G. O'Kelly to Powderly, Feb. 12, 1886 (Box A1–16); *Sun,* July 21, Aug. 6, 27, 1886.

7. *Butcher Workman,* Aug., 1932, 5; *Sun,* Sept. 6, 1886; *Trib.,* Sept. 7, 1886; [Chicago] *Knights of Labor,* Sept. 11, 1886.

8. *Butcher Workman,* Sept., 1932, 2; Gaunt to Powderly, Nov. 25, 1886 (Box A1–26); Knights of Labor, *Proceedings, 1887,* 1490–91, 1486.

9. Leon Fink, "The Uses of Political Power: Toward a Theory of the Labor Movement in the Era of the Knights of Labor," in Michael H. Frisch and Daniel J. Walkowitz, eds., *Working-Class America: Essays on Labor, Community, and American Society* (Urbana, Ill., 1983), 110–15; Edward B. Mittelman, "Chicago Labor in Politics, 1877–96," *Journal of Political Economy,* 28 (May, 1920), 418–21; Ralph W. Scharnau, "Thomas J. Morgan and the United Labor Party of Chicago," *JISHS,* 66 (Spring, 1973), 42–48; R. W. Wright to Powderly, Sept. 2, 1886; Patrick Caldwell to Powderly, Sept. 25, 1886 (Box A1–24).

10. Falzone, "Powderly," 218, 237–47, 256–58; Knights of Labor, *Proceedings, 1886,* 39–40, 260, 265, 287–88, 314–26; Powderly, *Thirty Years of Labor,* 544–45, 639–44; Powderly to Bob, Oct. 25, 1886 (Letter Press Book 23).

11. *Trib.,* Oct. 8, 15, 1886; *Sun,* Oct, 8, 9, 1886; Clarence E. Bonnett, *History of Employers' Associations in the United States* (New York, 1956), 279–80.

12. *Trib.,* Oct, 9, 10, 12, 13–16, 1886; [Chicago] *Knights of Labor,* Oct. 16, 1886; *Drovers Journal,* Oct. 11, 14, 1886; *Sun,* Oct, 11, 12, 14, 15, 1886; Powderly, *Path I Trod,* 145–46; Knights of Labor, *Proceedings, 1886,* 174–75; Gaunt to Powderly, Oct. 15, 1886 (Box A1–25).

13. Barry to Powderly, Oct. 15, 1886 (Box A1–25); Gaunt to Powderly, Oct. 15, Nov. 25, 1886 (Boxes A1–25, A1–26); Powderly, *Path I Trod,* 146–47; *Sun,* Oct. 14–16, 1886; *Times,* Oct. 15, 1886; *Drovers Journal,* Oct. 14, 15, 1886; *Trib.,* Oct. 10, 13, 15, 19, 1886.

14. *Drovers Journal,* Oct. 15, 16, 1886; *Trib.,* Oct. 16, 18, 1886; *Daily News,* Oct. 16, 1886; Powderly, *Path I Trod,* 147–48; P. M. Flannigan to Powderly, Oct. 16, 1886 (Box A1–25); Henry Demarest Lloyd to Thomas Barry, Oct. 15, 1886 (Henry Demarest Lloyd Papers, State Historical Society of Wisconsin, Madison).

15. *Trib.,* Oct. 18, 19, 1886; *Sun,* Oct. 19, 1886; *Times,* Oct, 18, 19, 1886; *Drovers Journal,* Oct. 20, 1886; Barry to Powderly, Oct. 18, 19, 1886; "T. B. Barry to Knights of Labor in Stockyards Lockout," Oct. 19, 1886 (Box A1–25).

16. Morn, *"Eye That Never Sleeps,"* 100; *Trib.,* July 21, Oct. 19, 20, 22–24, Nov. 5, 19, 1886; *Drovers Journal,* Oct. 18, 19, 1886; *Times,* Oct. 20, 1886; *Sun,* July 21, Oct. 18, 19, 21, 1886; [Chicago] *Knights of Labor,* Oct.

23, 1886. Father Dorney of St. Gabriel's Church started a fund for the Begley family, but Philip Armour quietly provided the money to buy the widow a boardinghouse and take care of the children's education. *Labor Enquirer,* June 4, 11, 1887.

17. *Trib.,* Oct. 20, 22, Nov. 18, 1886; *Drovers Journal,* Oct. 20, 1886; Barry to Powderly, Nov. 7, 1886 (Box A1–26); Butler to Powderly, Dec. 27, 1886 (Box A1–27); Gaunt to Powderly, Nov. 25, 1886 (Box A1–26).

18. *Trib.* Oct. 30, Nov. 2, 1886; *Sun,* Oct. 30, 1886; *Drovers Journal,* Nov. 1, 3, 1886; *Butcher Workman,* Sept., 1932, 2; Knights of Labor, *Proceedings, 1887,* 1491–92.

19. *Times,* Nov. 4, 1886; *Trib.,* Nov. 2, 3, 4, 1886; *Sun,* Nov. 3, 4, 1886; Scharnau, "Morgan and the United Labor Party," 48–49; Powderly, *Path I Trod,* 150–53; Richard Powers to Powderly, Oct. 24, 1886 (Box A1–25); Gaunt to Powderly, Nov. 25, 1886 (Box A1–26); Knights of Labor, *Proceedings, 1887,* 1480.

20. Gaunt to Powderly, Nov. 25, 1886 (Box A1–26); *Butcher Workman,* Sept., 1932, 2; *Trib.,* Nov. 4–6, 9–11, 1886; *Times,* Nov. 5, 6, 10, 11, 1886; *Sun,* Nov. 5, 6, 1886; *Drovers Journal,* Nov. 10, 11, 1886.

21. *Trib.,* Nov. 4, 6, 8, 9, 1886; Butler to Powderly, Dec. 27, 1886 (Box A1–27); *Sun,* Nov. 6, 8, 9, 1886; *Daily News,* Nov. 8, 9, 1886; *Drovers Journal,* Nov. 9, 1886.

22. Barry to Powderly, Nov. 6, 7, 10, 1886 (Box A1–25); Gaunt to Powderly, Nov. 25, 1886 (Box A1–26); *Butcher Workman,* Sept., 1932, 2; Powderly, *Path I Trod,* 152; Knights of Labor, *Proceedings, 1887,* 1481; *Trib.,* Nov. 8, 9, 10, 11, 1886.

23. *Drovers Journal,* Nov, 5, 8, 10, 1886; *Sun,* Nov. 10, 1886; *Trib.,* Nov. 8, 9, 10, 11, 13, 1886; *Times,* Nov. 11, 1886. Three small firms that slaughtered for the city trade signed an agreement to reestablish the eight-hour day. Armour suddenly dropped the price of his pork loins to disrupt their trade. *Trib.,* Nov. 13, 1886; Barry to Powderly, Nov. 10, 1886 (Box A1–26).

24. *Trib.,* Nov. 8, 10, 13, 1886; *Sun,* Nov. 11, 1886; *Drovers Journal,* Nov. 9, 11, 15, 1886; Barry to Powderly, Nov. 10, 1886 (Box A1–26).

25. *Trib.,* Nov, 6, 8, 11, 13, 14, 1886; *Drovers Journal,* Nov. 9, 11, 1886; Howard Barton Myers, "The Policing of Labor Disputes in Chicago: A Case Study" (Ph.D. diss, University of Chicago, 1929), 178–97.

26. Barry's Nov. 10 letter was incorrectly dated Nov. 16 when reproduced in the *Proceedings* of the 1887 General Assembly. Powderly, *Path I Trod,* 150–55; Knights of Labor, *Proceedings, 1887,* 1481–83; *Sun,* Nov. 11, 1886, *Trib.,* Nov. 12, 13, 1886; Barry and Carlton to Powderly, Nov. 12, 1886 (Box A1–25).

27. Barry and Carlton to Powderly, Nov. 12, 1886 (Box A1–25); Barry to Powderly, Nov. 16, 1886 (Box A1–26); *Butcher Workman,* Sept., 1932, 2;

Oct., 1932, 2; *Times*, Nov. 15, 1886; *Trib.*, Nov. 12, 13, 14, 15, 1886; *Sun*, Nov. 12, 1886; *Drovers Journal*, Nov. 15, 1886.

28. Pierce, *History of Chicago*, 3:289–90, 297–99; *Trib.*, Nov. 11, 15–18, 21, 24, 1886; Jan. 29, Feb. 4, 24, Sept. 25, 1887; *Times*, Nov. 16, 17, 1886; *Drovers Journal*, Dec. 17, 19, 1886; *Sun*, Nov. 18, 1886; *Labor Enquirer*, Mar. 9, 1887; [Chicago] *Knights of Labor*, Oct. 30, 1886; Jan. 8, 1887; *Butcher Workman*, Oct., 1932, 2.

29. *Butcher Workman*, Sept., 1932, 2; P. L. Caldwell to Powderly, Dec. 7, 1886; Gaunt to Powderly, Nov. 25, 1886 (Box A1–26); Butler to Powderly, Dec. 27, 1886 (Box A1–27); *Sun*, Jan. 21, 1889; Sept. 11, 1891; *Trib.*, Nov. 13, 23, Dec. 12, 1886; Jan. 3, 5, 21, 1887; *Drovers Journal*, Nov. 22, 29, 1886; Jan. 5, Feb. 14, 1887; [Chicago] *Knights of Labor*, Dec. 23, 28, 1886; Jan. 8, 1887; *Labor Enquirer*, Jan. 7, Feb. 23, 1887; *Journal of United Labor*, 7 (June 4, 1887), 2415.

30. *Trib.*, Dec. 19, 22, 1886; Oct. 3, Nov. 26, 1887; July 24, 29, Oct. 18, 21, 28, 1888; June 15, 1889; *Labor Enquirer*, Oct. 29, Nov. 26, Dec. 3, 1887; Mar. 10, Apr. 7, 14, 1888; Knights of Labor, *Proceedings, 1887*, 1477–1513, 1774–76, 1699; *Proceedings, 1888*, 36–37; *Proceedings, 1889*, 1, 3; Joseph R. Buchanan, *The Story of a Labor Agitator* (New York, 1903), 319–43, 347–65, 441–56; Avrich, *Haymarket Tragedy*, 308–10, 432; Gerald N. Grob, "Terence V. Powderly and the Knights of Labor," *Mid-America*, 39 (Jan., 1957), 49–50; Falzone, "Powderly," 265–87; Powderly, *Thirty Years of Labor*, chap. 14; *Path I Trod*, 158–59.

31. *Trib.*, Dec. 13, 14, 15, 19, 26, 1886; Dec. 15, 1888; Falzone, "Powderly," 234–37, 270–71; *New York Times*, Dec. 25, 1886; Ware, *Labor Movement*, chaps. 12, 18.

32. Knights of Labor, *Proceedings, 1887*, 1477; Powderly, *Path I Trod*, 154, 140, chap. 12; Griffiths to Powderly, Dec. 6, 26, 29, 1886 (Boxes A1–26, A1–27). For other assessments of Powderly, the Chicago strikes, and the Knights' internal problems, see: Harry J. Carman, "Terence Vincent Powderly—An Appraisal," *Journal of Economic History*, 1 (May, 1941); Carroll D. Wright, "An Historical Sketch of the Knights of Labor," *Quarterly Journal of Economics*, 1 (Jan., 1887); William Birdsall, "The Problem of Structure in the Knights of Labor," *Industrial and Labor Relations Review*, 6 (July, 1953); Gerald N. Grob, *Workers and Utopia: A Study of Ideological Conflict in the American Labor Movement, 1865–1900* (Evanston, Ill., 1961), chap. 4; Edna Clark, "History of the Controversy between Labor and Capital in the Slaughtering and Meat Packing Industries in Chicago" (M. A. thesis, University of Chicago, 1922) chap. 2; Stuart Bruce Kaufman, *Samuel Gompers and the Origins of the American Federation of Labor, 1848–1896* (Westport, Conn., 1973), chap. 9.

33. Powderly to R. D. Townsend, Aug. 28, 1888 (Letter Press Book 36); *Sun*, Jan. 6, 17, Feb. 15, Mar. 31, Apr. 14, 17, 28, 30, May 1, 2, 13, 1890;

Trib., Mar. 5, Apr. 1, 11, 20, 23, 29, 30, May 1, 3–7, 1890; Sidney Fine, "The Eight-Hour Day Movement in the United States, 1888–1891." *MVHR*, 40 (Dec. 1953), 441–62.

34. *Drovers Journal*, Jan. 27, 1891; *Times*, June 18, 1894; *Butcher Workman*, Dec., 1932, 2; Jan., 1933, 2.

35. *Trib.*, Apr. 29, 1890; John R. Commons et al., *History of Labour in the United States*, 4 vols. (New York, 1935–36), 2:419.

36. Henry Demarest Lloyd to Henry C. Adams, Dec. 6, 1886 (Henry Demarest Lloyd Papers).

37. Knights of Labor, *Proceedings, 1887*, 1481, 1480.

PART FOUR—FORGING A COMMUNITY

CHAPTER 15

The Township's "Wonderful Growth"

In view of the tremendous expansion in packinghouse employment, it is not surprising that Town of Lake's population increased sharply in the 1880s. That it soared from eighteen thousand to eighty-five thousand in just nine years was "wonderful growth" indeed. It put Town of Lake well ahead of the other townships and prompted Chicago to hint at merger. Town of Lake ignored these overtures because it was able to absorb the newcomers, encourage the formation of voluntary associations, meet the demand for improvements, and accomplish all this through the five-member town board form of government. When residents first voted on annexation, an overwhelming majority registered satisfaction with the community they had created in the Town of Lake. That process began with physical accommodation of the burgeoning population. Each of the existing neighborhoods expanded under the impact, and horsecars opened new subdivisions and provided ties between the neighborhoods. The Stockyards, Northeast Corners, and Car-Shops melted into "the north end of town"; "New City at the back of the Yards" conveyed the coming together of the two settlements southwest of Section 5. New stores and multistoried brick blocks and halls appeared along all the horsecar lines. Public transit and commercial development so altered the Englewood hub that realtors were able to push "additions," or suburbs of the suburb. Church building kept pace with residential and commercial construction. The township had eight houses of worship in 1880, fifty-nine by 1889. The proliferation of churches was, in the opinion of contemporaries, the strongest indication of the town's progress toward a mature community.[1] (See Map 6, p. 150, and Map 7, p. 178.)

City and Township Population Changes

Between 1880 and 1889 Chicago's population climbed from 500,000 to slightly over 800,000. Only the massive 1889 annexation enabled it to claim 1,100,000 people in the 1890 census and to narrowly edge out Philadelphia as the country's second largest city. The townships of Lake and

Hyde Park contributed over 150,000 residents to Chicago; Lake View, Jefferson, and the Cicero annexation yielded less than half that number. During the 1880s both of the southern townships fattened on Chicagoans seeking more desirable places to live and work. The Town of Lake was a veritable magnet for residents of the triangular Fifth Ward lying between the South Branch and Thirty-ninth Street. That territory held approximately 47,000 people in 1880 and 84,000 ten years later. In 1887 it had been divided at Halsted Street into the Fifth Ward on the east and the Sixth Ward lying west of Halsted. Horsecar lines on State, Wentworth, Halsted, and Ashland augmented the ties of kinship and employment between the South Branch wards and the Town of Lake.[2]

Despite the relocation of packinghouses and the departure of some heavy industry to southern Hyde Park, factory jobs remained plentiful in the Fifth and Sixth wards. Many of the people who settled near Thirty-ninth Street worked across the city-township boundary at the Stockyards, packinghouses, brickyards, and railroads. The most noticeable change was the growing number of Bohemians and Poles. Bohemian men worked in cabinet and upholstery shops and packinghouse sausage departments, while women found openings in commercial laundries and as domestics. The Catholic families reinforced St. Procopius parish; Bohemian Protestants started Bethlehem Congregational Church, and their assistant pastor, Josef Jelinek, counseled those who were moving into the Town of Lake. The ten thousand Poles at mid-decade were mostly unskilled laborers drawing low wages, but since nearly all were Catholic, they enabled St. Adalbert's Church to fund a building program equal to that of St. Procopius. Moreover, Father John Radziejewski helped the Poles in Bridgeport launch St. Mary of Perpetual Help parish in 1885. Under the guidance of Reverend John Zilla, that parish had a frame church and school by the end of the decade and was lending help to Catholic Poles in the Town of Lake. Furthermore, it was poised to dig the foundation of a permanent church that would rival the Irish Catholic landmark in Bridgeport, St. Bridget's Church.[3]

Blacks constituted only 1.1 percent of Chicago's total population in 1880 and 1.3 percent in 1890, yet the numerical increase from approximately 6,500 to 14,300 and the easy identification of these people convinced some Chicagoans that the proportion was much larger. Although Negroes could be found in many areas of the city and suburbs, the majority of them lived south of the business district in a corridor surrounding State Street. Sixteenth Street, the northern boundary of the Fifth and Sixth wards in 1880, was also the southern edge of the Negro settlement. Two new railroads sliced through this district during the 1880s. First the Chicago and Western Indiana and then the Santa Fe tracks forced Negroes, Italians, Poles, and Russian Jews to find new living quarters. The blacks pressed further south on Wabash, State, and Dearborn, and they were reinforced by new southern migrants. At the end of the decade there were Negro families as far south as Thirty-fifth Street. White families lived in this corridor too, but social contacts were limited to the public schools and the Armour Mission. Most of the black men worked in hotels and restaurants and as laborers in freight and railroad yards, and on lake vessels, while the women were domestics and laundresses. Their residential corridor was defined by the same railroad tracks that came through the eastern strip of Town of Lake. Chicago's 1887 ward remap left the Fifth Ward adjacent to the corridor, and thus the census enumerator in 1890 found 401 Negroes among the 41,000 residents. The Sixth Ward, lying west of Halsted, had only 33 blacks among its 43,000 people.[4]

Annexation of the northern townships netted Chicago some fifty-two thousand people in Lake View and ten thousand in Jefferson, though some sections of the latter had already split away to merge with the city. Hyde Park was the only suburban unit whose growth rate in the 1880s came close to Town of Lake's. The southeastern township boosted its population from just under sixteen thousand in 1880 to seventy-two thousand at the time of annexation. Its three distinct zones—the northern district tied by horsecars to Chicago, the suburban Kenwood and Hyde Park Center, and the industrial Calumet basin region—quarreled over allocation of taxes, distribution of services, and the type of government best suited to the township. Tax-consious residents in the first two zones balked at paying for drainage in the third zone, and siding with them was George M. Pullman, who financed his own improvements. On four thousand acres between the Illinois Central tracks and Lake Calumet, he built a self-sufficient company town and new plant. By the mid-1880s Pullman employed four thousand and the model town had a population of eight thousand. It was "the regular thing," said the *Times*, to show distinguished visitors the new Board of Trade, the Stockyards and Packingtown, the Chicago park system, and the town of Pullman, for all of them were Chicago "institutions."[5]

Town of Lake avoided the bitter wrangling that plagued Hyde Park in the 1880s. And it managed to do so despite the fact that it too had a major industrial district and Englewood, which, like Hyde Park Center, aspired to elite suburban status. Town of Lake residents, no doubt, would have agreed with a *Tribune* reporter who noted quite matter-of-factly in 1887 that Fifty-fifth Street was the natural "dividing line": those living north of it scoffed at the "colonels," while some people to the south wished that Garfield Boulevard (as Fifty-fifth was called after 1881), were thrice as wide.[6] Differences did exist, and the possibility of warring zones was ever present. But the Town of Lake avoided polarization in part because there was so much motion within. Stockyards and packinghouse workers and managers whose first homes were close to their jobs took advantage of horsecars to move south, and since they were good neighbors and concerned citizens, they helped mute distinctions and erode earlier prejudices. Another reason for Town of Lake's success was the willingness of the industrialists to pay their own way and to get along with elected township officials. Channels of communication remained open and it was possible to form new coalitions, even as thousands of people moved into the township.

Employment opportunities drew most of the newcomers. But for the Stockyards and packinghouses, a correspondent wrote the *Sun*, "our town would be a hamlet still, and our most beautiful districts would be unadulterated marshes." That assessment overlooked the many factories already located along the railroads and the addition of two companies building railroad cars, a boot and shoe factory, a lumber company, and a buggy factory, plus a second Lake Shore and Michigan Southern railroad yard, this one in Englewood. Construction workers were in constant demand, and the relentless growth meant openings for service establishments.

The opportunity to acquire land and build a home was part of Town of Lake's attraction in the 1880s. Three-quarters of the new construction was residential, and Chicago realtors attributed the "brisk investment" to the price of the land, township acceptance of frame buildings, and exemption from city taxes. Starting in 1882, Town of Lake required building permits and by mid-decade it was issuing about seven hundred annually. The vast majority of the houses were wooden, evenly divided between one- and two-story structures averaging twenty-two feet in width. Home ownership was both the realization of the newcomer's dream and an announcement that he too had a stake in the future of the community.[7] (See Figs. 12 and 13.)

Horsecars lured Chicagoans, encouraged relocation within the township, and spurred new settlements. The first track was laid in 1881 on State Street from the city limits to Fifty-fifth Street; the Wentworth line reached Englewood; and the Halsted cars traveled from Thirty-ninth to Forty-third in 1883, then on down to Sixty-third Street, and by 1885 they were double-tracked "to accommodate parties residing in Englewood and doing business at the Stock-yards." Meantime, tracks across Root, Forty-seventh, and Sixty-third streets linked the State, Wentworth, and Halsted lines, and the Archer Avenue line reached Brighton on the township's western edge. People living south and west of Packingtown complained that they were "the only ones" lacking "convenient communication with other parts of the Town, or City." Tracks finally were laid on Ashland in 1887 and, as anticipated, they opened new markets for "cheap lots and moderate priced houses." When the first horsecars traversed Halsted, Goodall predicted that "the whole space between the city limits and Englewood, will, in a comparatively short time, be filled compactly with business establishments and dwellings." He was right. Public transit made Wentworth, Ashland, Forty-seventh, Sixty-third, and Halsted prime locations for grocery, dry goods, hardware, paint, furniture, and clothing stores, pharmacies, restaurants, and saloons. These businesses were located in two- and three-story frame structures with living quarters or offices above. The so-called blocks were brick buildings catering to realtors and building and loan associations, lawyers, and insurance agencies. The multipurpose "halls" combined saloons and restaurants on the ground floor with meeting rooms, dance halls, and living quarters, and these buildings usually were located on the major transit arteries.[8]

Harvey Goodall was the unofficial accountant of this "wonderful growth" and "progress." He had a full-time reporter in each of the four outlying news offices—Englewood, the Car-Shops, Northeast Corners, and the Ashland-Forty-seventh intersection—and two men covering the Stockyards district. The editor celebrated the town's fifty thousand population mark by expanding the *Sun* to four pages; when he took possession of the new printing plant in 1889, he went to six pages. Goodall cheered the horsecar lines, waxed enthusiastic over the "veritable boom" of new houses and churches, and commended owners of the blocks and halls. Local merchants initiated the township's first directory. Following the format of an 1883 Hyde Park publication, the sponsors started canvassing in 1886. Unnumbered houses and the labor strife caused delays, but that winter residents could purchase copies of the first *Town of Lake Directory, Embracing a Complete List of the Residents and Business Houses, with Miscellaneous Information*. Annual revisions, it was assumed, would be necessary to keep pace with the town's rapid expansion.[9]

"The North End" of Lake

A closer look at the physical changes in the neighborhoods is necessary in order to understand how township residents forged the larger community in the 1880s, and the best place to start the tour is the northeastern sector. At the opening of the 1880s, there were approximately twelve thousand people living in the Stockyards neighborhood, the Northeast Corners, and the Car-Shops. By 1889 there were thirty-seven thousand residents in the district bounded by Thirty-ninth, State Street, Fifty-fifth, and Halsted; the cabbage fields were gone; and it was difficult to find a vacant lot. The Stewart Avenue railroad tracks were still a formidable barrier and people used the three neighborhoods' names, but as new construction and horsecar lines obliterated old boundaries, the walking neighborhoods meshed in reality and in peoples' minds. The northeastern sector became simply "the north end" of town.

The Northeast Corners became an even more important transfer point after Chicago's cable cars terminated at Thirty-ninth and State Street. Original frame structures gave way to high-rent commercial blocks, and homeowners on Wentworth and Root turned front rooms into stores and enlarged their cottages into small boardinghouses. Tosetti's brewery opened in 1886, new factories appeared on the north-south railroads, and a few packers and slaughterers who could not afford Packingtown settled for the narrow strip of land between Thirty-ninth and the Stockyards company tracks on Forty-first Street. Many more livestock and refrigerator cars rolled down those tracks, and the manufacturing along the other rail lines increased smoke and soot. Older residents petitioned the town government to do something about air pollution, noise, street congestion, and filthy alleys which depreciated the "properties of parties whose savings of a lifetime have been invested therein." Realtors had no trouble selling standard-sized lots on Root and Forty-second for $150 to $200, but families building on them usually shared occupancy with others. Packinghouse worker Patrick Cuddy, for example, lived with his wife and five children in half of his modest Forty-second Street home and rented the remainder to a railroad section boss with a wife and three children.[10]

Gamblers had a field day at the Northeast Corners because it was easy for them to escape the uncoordinated raids of Town of Lake, Hyde Park, and Chicago police. The same was true for gangs of rowdy, hard-drinking young Irishmen, addicted to brawling and drunken serenading, threatening pedestrians and merchants, and stealing from grocers and peddlers. Since many of them came from Canaryville, an Irish neighborhood just north of the township-city boundary, they called themselves "wild canaries" and everyone else referred to them as "Canaryville toughs."* Their bravado, bullying, and crime distressed residents and convinced the *Sun* that the Northeast Corners was "unfit to live in." By mid-decade those who

* The origin of "Canaryville" is unclear, but it is probably related to the abundant English sparrows which plagued many cities in the 1880s and '90s. They fed on grain and manure at the Stockyards, spillage along all the railroad tracks, and debris in alleys. "Canary" was a derogatory term for the troublesome, noisy sparrow in the 1880s, and it may well have been applied to the Fifth Ward railroad corridor and then to the rowdy Irish teenagers. After annexation, "Canaryville" was used to describe all the Irish in the Sixth and Twenty-ninth Wards, and by the time automobiles reduced the sparrow population the term had lost its derogatory connotation. That Hyde Park shared the sparrow nuisance is clear from an old-timer's 1892 lament that all the good birds—"sparrows don't count"—had disappeared.(*Drovers Journal*, Feb. 12, 1886; Mar. 23, 1888; *Trib.*, May 15, 1892; Eugene Kinkead, *Wilderness Is All around Us: Notes of an Urban Naturalist*, New York, 1978, 89–178.)

could afford it were moving to safer, quieter, cleaner spots. Soon after the collapse of the 1886 strike, Michael J. Butler left for a new house at Fifty-first and Emerald.[11]

The Car-Shops experienced additional commercial development on State and Wentworth and the spread of boardinghouses on Forty-seventh, a major crosstown artery by the late 1880s. However, Fifty-fifth Street was park property exempt from commercial development, and St. Anne's Church and quality housing kept property values high. Skilled workers bought lots in the southern part of the neighborhood from E. S. Dreyer at prices ranging from $500 to $1,000. Those with lower incomes settled for cheaper land close to the railroad tracks or else lived in the boardinghouses. There was so much new construction that Father Flannigan lost his unobstructed view from St. Anne's to the Transit House. All he could see by the end of the decade was the hotel cupola.[12]

In the 1880s as in the previous decade, the Stockyards neighborhood had more excitement, more esprit de corps, than either the Northeast Corners or the Car-Shops. A ceaseless flow of businessmen and visitors patronized the Halsted hostelries, restaurants, and saloons. If the Transit House was too expensive, they had a wide choice of medium-priced establishments and a bargain-basement frame hotel and saloon called "The Rookeries." Bateman's Exchange advertised "first-class meals . . . any hour day or night"; scores of restaurants offered "a fair meal served in pretty good style" for a quarter; and it was simple to find a ten-cent meal or "free" lunch with the purchase of a beer. The saloons ranged from high-toned places for livestock growers with fat bankrolls to Dutchy Keefe's watering hole, where the owner once chewed off a patron's nose. Halsted and Exchange was the liveliest intersection in the township, a swirl of livestock buyers and sellers, "dressy clerks and bookkeepers," packinghouse workers, retail meat-market customers, and bewildered tourists. Brassy "runners" hustled "grangers," promising to lead them to hotels, clothing and jewelry stores, saloons, and even Chicago "after nightfall to see the tiger."[13]

Owners of the eighty acres east of Halsted still refused to sell and squatters' shacks were an eyesore and a surprise to visitors approaching on the Root Street cars. But long-term leases on property facing Halsted and Forty-third were available, and this led to new construction. Drovers National Bank obtained the first such lease; John Christman built a large block for his clothing and jewelry store; pharmacist Charles Kotzenberg put up a two-story brick paint and hardware store. The finest building was the three-story Gahan Block at Forty-second and Halsted, built in 1886 by retired town supervisor Thomas Gahan. (See Fig. 16.) That office had "placed many a good dollar into Captain Gahan's purse," noted Goodall, and he wisely invested them in a way that benefited the town. "Bully for

Captain Gahan." The importance of the structure was further enhanced when the Stockyards Post Office moved into the ground floor. Two other officeholders, Michael McInerney and Michael J. Tearney, built a block at Forty-eighth and Halsted in 1889 for their real estate, insurance, and brick company business.[14]

"The outside world little thinks . . . that nestling close to the borders of the stock yards is a nook of sylvan quietness and verdant beauty," wrote a *Sun* reporter in 1889. He was referring to the three streets that paralleled Halsted—Emerald, Winter, and Sherman. Gustavus Swift's house on the corner of Emerald and Forty-Fifth marked the southern edge of the enclave in the 1870s. In the mid-80s, however, his married sons Louis and Edward built in the 4600 block of Emerald. The gregarious Edward Swift had parquet floors in his spacious double parlors and dining room, electric lights (which his father staunchly refused to accept), and an impressive library. By the end of the decade, "the head" or "upper end" of Emerald was at Garfield Boulevard. Oswald's Hall, an 1870s Halsted Street landmark between Englewood and the Stockyards, was surrounded by residences, including those of Charles Kotzenberg and Michael J. Butler. Lots on Winter and Sherman Streets, almost as desirable as those on Emerald, commanded $2,500 at the end of the decade. Livestock dealers, Stockyards managers, packinghouse department heads, Thomas Gahan, Sylvester Gaunt, and Peter Caldwell's son, Dr. Charles P. Caldwell, resided on these streets. Between Sherman and the Stewart Avenue railroad tracks were modest frame houses, boarding establishments, small stores, and workshops. Standard 25- by 125-foot lots sold for approximately $700 at mid-decade. This district was cleaner than the Northeast Corners but lacked the shade trees and handsome gardens that graced the larger lots on Emerald, Winter, and Sherman Streets.[15]

Church construction was an integral part of the township's "wonderful growth," and the north end celebrated its contributions to this visible progress. The Winter Street Methodists spent $8,000 to redouble the size of their house of worship, and in 1883 the First Presbyterian Church of Lake erected a $10,000 building on Winter between Forty-second and Forty-third streets. Baptists were fewer in number and although they purchased two lots on Emerald in 1889, they could not finance construction until the 1890s. At the Car-Shops, Swedish Lutherans and German Evangelicals, reinforced by believers in Hyde Park, built modest frame churches costing about $3,000 each and operated small schools. Charles Kotzenberg arranged for Jews to hold Passover services at the Masonic Hall on Halsted, but they were too small a group and too widely scattered to establish a synagogue in the 1880s.[16]

The achievement of St. Gabriel's parish dwarfed Protestant efforts, thanks in large part to the charismatic Father Maurice J. Dorney. The parish was established in the spring of 1880 with boundaries at Fortieth Street, State, Fifty-first, and no western limit. The twenty-nine-year-old pastor arrived in April; the love match with his parishioners would last until his death in 1914. Dorney grew up in Chicago, where his immigrant father was a lumber buyer for the Illinois Central Railroad; he attended both public and parochial schools, completed his religious training in 1874, and had served in Chicago and Lockport, Illinois, before coming to St. Gabriel's. The pastor offered his first services at the Transit House where he boarded. Then he used Walsh's Hall at Forty-fourth and Halsted, the bandstand serving as an altar. Dorney soon contracted for twenty lots on the north side of Forty-fifth Street between Sherman and Wallace, and Patrick Hennesey had a temporary frame hall ready by the end of the summer. Since the pastor liked Burnham and Root's work at the Stockyards and knew John Root through musical circles, he chose them as parish architects. In 1881 they built the first permanent structure, a combination church and school. Then came a brick rectory for Dorney and his assistant, the finest residence in the township according to Goodall. Fund-raising was a year-round activity in the parish. The lots cost $600 each, the two brick structures came to about $10,000, and the frame hall plus a temporary convent for the teaching sisters cost $3,500. They had yet to tackle the centerpiece, the permanent church.[17]

Dorney wanted an honest parish church, not a fussy diminutive cathedral, and John Root gave him the first set of plans in June, 1886. The strikes delayed construction and prompted Dorney to ask for slight revisions which would lower costs. What he got in the end was a Romanesque church, 100 by 190 feet at the transept, with a low body, a bold tower, and large stained-glass windows. Both church and spire were constructed of reddish-brown pressed brick. Some parishioners worried that it was not as grand as Nativity's traditional church in the Fifth Ward, but they took Dorney's word for it that they had a masterpiece. Archbishop Patrick Feehan presided at both the cornerstone-laying ceremony in 1887 and the dedication one year later. The church was no sooner finished than Father Dorney built a permanent brick convent for the teaching sisters. Thus the "populous but not wealthy" parish ended the decade with what Goodall called a "magnificent pile of buildings." Father Dorney's 1889 parish report valued the land and structures at $135,000, only one-quarter of which remained to be paid. St. Gabriel's achievement was all the more remarkable because three new Irish parishes had been carved out of its domain. Catholics at the Northeast Corners and the northwestern sector of Hyde Park started St. Elizabeth's parish; Visitation parish served the district south of the Stockyards and west of Halsted; and St. Rose of Lima was launched southwest of the packinghouses. In addition, German-speaking Catholics in the north end of town, many of them migrants from St. Anthony of

Padua, got their own parish in 1883 and promptly built a modest church and school at Thirty-ninth and Wentworth. In the eyes of contemporaries, however, it was St. Gabriel's parishioners who made the most significant contribution to the township's "progress."[18]

New City and Back of the Yards

When Town of Lake joined Chicago, ten thousand people lived in the broad crescent surrounding the intersection of Ashland Avenue and Forty-seventh Street. No one was sure what to call it—"Beyond the Packers' Town," "back of the Stock-Yards," "New City, in the district known as 'back of the yards'" and "New City at the back of the Yards"—but everyone was amazed at the tenfold increase in population during the 1880s.[19] The *Drovers Journal* had noted as early as 1883 that the prairie was "dotted all over with new buildings," a "veritable 'boom' . . . of frame houses." Sales were "flat" during the 1886 strikes, but activity resumed the following spring and continued "with great persistence" to the end of the decade.[20]

New settlers in the first half of the decade were still within walking distance of the packinghouses, and thus the delay in getting an Ashland Avenue horsecar line did not hold back growth. The City Railway Company waited for the town government to build an Ashland Avenue sewer; by 1887 it was able to extend its tracks from Thirty-ninth to Fifty-fifth and two years later the line reached Sixty-third Street. "Many people employed in the Yards can go further south now and secure homes," rejoiced the *Sun*. Just the talk of horsecars and sewers prompted potato farmer Hugh Chittick to sell his land at Ashland and Fifty-ninth to a developer in 1886 and move to Englewood. So great was the demand for housing that it was not unusual for lot owners to build and occupy dwellngs before town officials extended the streets. Realtor B. F. Jacobs's improved lots sold for $300 each, and building permits indicate that his purchasers spent from $600 to $1,000 on their houses. Most of the new residences in this district were one-story wooden cottages with English basements; a two-story house with a mansard roof was unusual enough to merit newspaper comment.[21]

New City-Back of the Yards' best-planned subdivision was in the heart of the settlement, not on the periphery, and it was designed by an expert in working-class housing—Samuel Eberly Gross. A former lawyer who thought there had to be a better solution to factory-worker housing than George Pullman had devised, Gross began experimenting. He discovered that it was possible to put in sewers, water, sidewalks, and some landscaping, sell at reasonable prices on easy terms and still make a profit. In 1889, he served six thousand customers, transacted over $2 million worth of business, and won the nomination of the United Workingmen's Societies for mayor of Chicago. The challenge of housing packinghouse workers was one he could not ignore. During the 1886 lull, he purchased eight square blocks bounded by Forty-fifth, Loomis, Forty-seventh, and Ashland. He kept Forty-sixth and Laflin plus one block of Justine and one of Bishop as the town had laid them out, but he altered the grid plan on the rest of his property by running a broad diagonal street between the southwest and northeast corners. Thus half of his lots were the traditional size and shape while the others were pleasingly irregular. He put in sewer and water lines, paved the streets, and built sidewalks at the same time the Chicago City Railway Company laid horsecar tracks on Ashland and double-tracked Forty-seventh. In the fall of 1887, Gross opened a branch office in his subdivision and began selling the four hundred lots.[22]

"Homes for Workingmen, Corners for Business Men, Investments for Everybody," he advertised in the *Sun*. The cheapest lots were $400, those fronting on Ashland and Forty-seventh cost $700, and buyers put one-tenth down and paid the rest in monthly installments over a four-year period. The Gross firm offered twenty-five free house plans and would "make you a loan or build . . . on your own plans." Cheaper models had a parlor, two bedrooms, kitchen, small entry hall, and pantry on the main floor and two more rooms with seven-foot ceilings and a total of four windows in the English basement. Price tags on a Gross house and lot ranged from $975 to $1,500. Purchasers put $100 down and paid $8 to $12 monthly, "the same as rent." "*Think of a New, Comfortable, Well-Built Cottage, and Large Lot That $100 and your rent will buy.*" The subdivision was a two-minute walk from the packinghouses, eight minutes from the Stockyards, two blocks from the Grand Trunk commuter railroad stop, and on two horsecar lines. Understandably, it sold out by the end of the decade. There were more people in Gross's 350 houses than there had been in the Ashland Avenue-Forty-seventh Street settlement at the beginning of the decade.[23]

The horsecar lines augmented the importance of Ashland and Forty-seventh as commercial arteries. Stores, offices, meeting halls, saloons and eating places, and boardinghouses vied for space. (See Fig. 11.) Henry Frederick, whose boardinghouse fronted on Ashland near the western entrance to the packinghouses, added a 25- by 75-foot meeting hall and then a dance hall to accommodate large parties and wedding receptions. Henry Schumacher, the proprietor of Ashland House near the Forty-seventh Street intersection, purchased two additional lots for a much larger two-story hall. Bishop's Hall was just one block south, and the newest gathering place, Columbia Hall, was at Forty-eighth and Paulina. The first floor of Frank Bischoff's brick structure on Forty-seventh Street was rented to shopkeepers; the owner lived with his family on the upper floor. The proliferation of saloons and quick-eating places on Ashland between Forty-first and Forty-fourth corresponded to the number of men employed in Packingtown. Called "Whiskey Row" by the end of the decade, these noisy, sometimes rowdy, blocks bore little resemblance to the thriving commercial center at Forty-seventh and Ashland.[24]

No single ethnic group dominated church construction as did the Irish at the Stockyards, but the rivalry produced striking results in New City and Back of the Yards. At the opening of the decade, St. Augustine's parish had the only church, a small frame building where priests from St. Anthony of Padua occasionally said mass and Margaret Oswald taught an ungraded school for about two dozen youngsters. Father Denis Thiele arrived in May, 1882, and found about seventy families. With the help of carpenter John Kirschen, pharmacist John Masquelet, and the proprietor of Oswald Gardens, he raised the money to enlarge the school and build a rectory and then a convent for the Poor Maidens of Jesus Christ who took charge of the school in 1884. Thiele was reassigned the following summer, and the parish had to accept an elderly Irish cleric in poor health and unable to speak or understand German. But Chicago Franciscans visited the parish and reported to their superior in St. Louis that "everything, though small and of frame," is "in excellent condition." If the order could not spare a priest, it would be "better to quit [Chicago] and begin here, for a promising future awaits us in this place." John Masquelet assured the Franciscans that they were looking at "a bargain . . . the cream of the pick. The people are all steady working people . . . earning good wages. They are of good Catholic stock . . . better than you will find elsewhere!" Archbishop Feehan turned the parish over to the Franciscans in July, 1886, and the next month Reverend Symphorian Forstmann began a tenure that would last until the end of the century.[25]

The Franciscans purchased an entire block of land from realtor B. F. Jacobs through his German-speaking agent. The forty-eight lots fronted on Laflin, Fiftieth, Bishop, and Fifty-first Streets, and because of heavy expenditures on the building program, the mortgage was not paid off until 1902. Meantime, the Franciscans helped scores of German Catholic families buy lots from Jacobs in the blocks adjoining the church property, and they in turn helped the parish erect a $6,000 combination church and hall in the winter of 1887–88. The old church was moved to the new property and enlarged to accommodate 350 students. Dwellings for the teaching sisters and the priests completed the building program in the 1880s, but Father Forstmann had a Building Society canvassing for money to construct a permanent church for St. Augustine's parish.[26]

The Irish were not to be outdone. With Father Dorney's help, they started St. Rose of Lima parish and used the Buckley school for services until they could build a frame church and hall at Forty-eighth and Ashland in 1882. Their first parish fair raised the $7,000 to pay for the structure, and Luke O'Toole later donated stained-glass windows. A bell tower was added in 1887 and used for the first time on St. Patrick's Day. The parish's second pastor, Father Denis Hayes, turned his attention to school and convent construction, and he reported at the end of the decade that there were 350 families in his charge.[27] Polish settlers longed to do as well as the Irish and the Germans, but their numbers were too small. They did, however, form an independent St. Joseph Society, purchase land at Forty-eighth and Paulina from Jacobs, and start to build a small frame church before the 1886 strikes drained their financial resources and brought the project to a halt. Father Radziejewski of St. Adalbert's came at Christmastime and saw no reason to disagree with heady predictions that there would soon be five or six hundred "Polanders" in the vicinity. By the end of the decade St. Joseph's Polish Catholic Church had a building and a priest, Reverend Stanislaus Nawrocki, and about two hundred families in the large parish which stretched from the city limits to South Chicago.[28]

Protestants were also-rans in this heavily Catholic district. German Lutherans had a church and school at Fifty-second and Justine, and Josef Jelinek came down from Bridgeport to hold services for Bohemians from time to time. English-speaking Protestants gathered at the O'Toole school to hear Methodist missionary preachers sent to them by the Winter Street church. In 1882 Gustavus Swift and other benefactors built them a small frame church at Dreyer and Forty-seventh. Despite its optimistic name, the First Methodist Episcopal Church of New City had a hard time holding its own. To prevent Catholic children from throwing stones through the windows, the church built a high board fence on Forty-seventh Street. This barrier plus the short tenure of the pastors contributed to the slow growth of the congregation. Reverend William H. Carwardine coped for two years before seeking greener pastures in the predominantly Protestant town of Pullman. In the brick and mortar contest, the Protestants could not match the German, Irish, and Polish Catholic houses of worship lying within a three-block radius.[29]

Just as new construction destroyed Father Flannigan's vista at St. Anne's, so the horsecars, houses, stores, and churches in New City and Back of the Yards played havoc with Andrew Vogler's childhood haunts. He was eight years old in 1881 when his father built a house in Edward Dreyer's subdivision. "Back of the yards," he remembered, was "mostly prairie with plenty of wild flowers and cabbage fields." He and his friends searched the drainage ditches on either side of Ashland for frogs, crabs and snakes and ogled Stockyards cowboys pursuing stray cattle on the prairie. Progress in the form of urban improvements and ten times as many people had transformed the territory by the time it joined Chicago.[30]

"Englewood and Its Additions"

The editor of Englewood's 1882 *Directory* emphasized the suburb's seven commuter rail lines, superior schools, abundant churches, and easy access to Washington Park. He could not forsee that horsecar lines in the Town of Lake would bring new residents from the north end or that Englewood's relentless advertising would attract thousands of newcomers from outside Cook County. By 1889 the population had climbed to nearly thirty thousand, and the new stores and businesses, greater ethnic diversity, and public transit had changed the village into a bustling center with "city airs." Those in search of rustic tranquillity moved to new subdivisions south and west of the hub, and by 1889 the editor was talking about "Englewood and its additions."[31] (See Fig. 15.)

Garfield Boulevard and the two South Parks aided Englewood as well as Hyde Park. When they were officially named in 1881, there were some fears that Jackson, whether Andrew or "Stonewall," might hurt real estate prices. But the beauty and fame of Washington Park assuaged the residents. Carriages and bicycles carried Englewood residents directly into the gardens, meadows, small zoo, and many fine drives. Moreover, South Park Commissioners had landscaped Fifty-fifth to Ashland, and in the 1880s they continued on to Western Avenue and began improvements on Western. But if the parks and boulevard enhanced Englewood's suburban image, the advent of public transit undermined it. By 1885 horsecars plied State, Wentworth, Halsted, and Sixty-third; the heavily traveled Halsted line was double-tracked to Sixty-ninth; and at the end of the decade horsecars were coming down Ashland as well. Homeowners on Wentworth south of Sixty-third tried in vain to fight off the horsecars, but in the end they not only accepted an extension of the Wentworth line but a crosstown route on Sixty-ninth Street. In addition, the Chicago and Western Indiana Railroad came through Englewood and opened another passenger depot on Sixty-third. Older residents knew without being told by the *Real Estate and Building Journal* that horsecars meant more retail establishments, conversion of small houses to commercial use, "an end to seclusion and quiet," and the migration of "the wealthier class to other quarters."[32]

Commercial development was most pronounced on Sixty-third Street. When the decade opened, the Tillotson Block on Sixty-first near Wentworth was the only brick building of its kind in Town of Lake. Englewood acquired six more blocks in the 1880s, five of them on Sixty-third Street. Central Block at Yale Street housed the Masonic Hall, and Christian Vehmeyer's Block rented space to the Englewood Building and Loan Association and Englewood's first bank. The Englewood Opera House, the veterans' Memorial Hall, and the Young Men's Christian Association

Building also were constructed on Sixty-third. The "infectious fever" spread west to Halsted where William Bromstedt replaced his Farmer's Home and Tavern with a multipurpose brick structure in 1885. Wentworth Avenue shared in the boom with the First National Bank of Englewood, Arcade Hall, Music Hall, and the Ingram Block.[33]

Despite their proximity to the commercial core, residents of Yale, Harvard, and Stewart between Sixty-third and Sixty-sixth tried hard to preserve the elite residential status. (See Fig. 10.) Harvard and Yale were the first streets in the township to be macadamized and curbed, and the expensive gabled and turreted houses surrounded by "noble shade trees" were widely admired. The owners, noted Goodall, were "wealthy lumbermen, rich contractors, prosperous merchants, thrifty politicians, and men with stockyards interests." John Hough, an assistant to Elmer Washburn the year he supervised the yards, sold his house on Yale for $14,000 in 1888. Politician, realtor and insurance agent Chandler Redfield and the prestigious First Presbyterian Church anchored Yale, while lawyer Albert H. Veeder and the First Congregational Church did the same for Harvard. In addition, the township's first private club was formed in 1889 and took its name, the Harvard Club, from the street. The two hundred male members could play cards six days a week in the luxurious $40,000 clubhouse, but they could not drink, gamble, or discuss politics and business on the premises. Directly south was a new settlement called Normal Park after the Cook County Normal School. With service by a Rock Island commuter station at Seventy-first and Stewart, the founders (including lawyer Charles S. Thornton) hoped to replicate the Yale and Harvard Street enclave. Their new houses, however, were not as expensive, and their Home Club was a less exclusive version of the Harvard Club.[34]

Vacant land south of Garfield Boulevard and west of Halsted was ripe for development, and the horsecars on Halsted, Ashland, and Sixty-third eventually pushed Englewood's boundary one mile west. Lots in these new subdivisions were usually smaller and houses less costly than in Normal Park. B. F. Jacobs, for example, priced his homesites on Racine at $250, and August Jernberg, a Swedish contractor and realtor, promoted comparable tracts occupied primarily by Scandinavian immigrants. While Germans could be found throughout this district, their numbers were largest around Bromstedt's Hall, which served as their community center. Anticipating settlement west of Ashland, Town of Lake opened both Sixty-ninth and Seventy-first to Western Avenue at the end of the 1880s. The Stetson family, manufacturers of hats in New York City and owners of forty acres west of Ashland between Seventy-first and Seventy-third, knew that the value of their property would soon increase and they turned down an offer of $2,500 per acre. In the southwestern corner of the township, one lucky developer persuaded John B. Sherman to sell 320 acres of his Forest Hill farm for $1,000 an acre in 1889. There were already enough people living around Western and Seventy-ninth to justify a Forest Hill schoolhouse. At the rate Town of Lake and Chicago were growing, reflected James J. O'Toole in 1890, it was "only a matter of time until Forest Hill would be the site of the National Capitol with a new Pennsylvania Avenue, Western Boulevard, leading to the center of the greatest city" in the United States.[35]

In Englewood and its additions, as elsewhere in Town of Lake, church building kept pace with residential and commercial construction. There had been six churches south of Fifty-fifth at the opening of the decade, but there were three dozen by 1889. Swedes in the northern part of Englewood enlarged the existing Swedish Lutheran Church and started three new Methodist and Congregational churches. The people who settled west of Halsted established Presbyterian, Congregational, Swedish Lutheran, German Lutheran, and Dutch Reformed churches. And in Normal Park residents put up Presbyterian, Congregational, Baptist, and Methodist churches plus Town of Lake's first Episcopalian church. The Englewood and Normal Park Christian Church was another new entry. The fine structures in Normal Park made Englewood's 1870s churches look shabby by comparison, and rather than remodel and enlarge, these five churches decided to rebuild. The Presbyterians and Congregationalists kept their sites on Yale and Harvard, while the Methodists, Baptists, and Universalists moved to Stewart Avenue. At $60,000 the First Baptist Church of Englewood claimed to be the finest Protestant structure in the Town of Lake.[36]

Though Englewood Protestants showed little interest in the Catholic building program, it made surprising headway. Father Flannigan had only 350 families, counting "those who live 6 and 8 miles away" and "come once or twice a year," at the beginning of the decade, but by 1889 there were over five hundred families in his smaller parish and St. Anne's had a finished church and rectory. St. Bernard's parish to the southwest was established in 1887 despite the grumbling of some that they were severed as soon as St. Anne's church debt was cleared. Non-Catholics in Normal Park and Englewood insisted that a Catholic church at Sixty-sixth and Stewart would encourage smaller lots and cheaper houses thereby damaging their property. Ignoring the high price he had to pay for the land, Father Bernard Murray managed to erect not only a church but Englewood's first Catholic grammar school. Moreover, he purchased the abandoned First Baptist frame church and moved it to Bishop and Sixty-seventh where it served as a mission for yet another Irish parish, St. Brendan's. German-speaking Catholics secured permission in 1886 to start St. Martin's parish, and they promptly spent $10,000 for thirteen lots near Fifty-ninth and School (Princeton) Street. The following year they erected a $12,000 combination brick church and school. It was not the structure but rather its location in the heart of Protestant Englewood that brought the archbishop to the dedication ceremonies.[37]

Relentless construction enabled the Town of Lake to accommodate those newcomers who boosted population from eighteen thousand to eighty-five thousand in just nine years. The north end held three times as many people in 1889 as it had in 1880, and Englewood and the districts southwest of the packinghouses each held ten times as many. Available land and the advent of horsecars kept housing costs within the grasp of workers, and thousands of families fulfilled their dreams of home ownership. The population increase spelled opportunity for storekeepers, managers of halls, and owners of commercial blocks. These people vied for land along the horsecar lines and in the process turned Wentworth, Ashland, Forty-seventh, and Sixty-third into commercial arteries resembling Halsted and State streets. In the eyes of newcomers and old-timers, church formation and construction were significant measurements of growth and progress. The fifty thousand people living north of Garfield Boulevard, most of them Catholic, maintained twenty-one churches by 1889. The thirty-five thousand residents south of the boulevard, most of them Protestant, had thirty-eight houses of worship. Since the "colonels" were responsible for two-thirds of the churches, Goodall referred to Englewood as "the Brooklyn of Chicago."[38] The personal commitment and financial sacrifice that lay behind church construction illustrate the importance of voluntary associations in building the social fabric of the community.

NOTES

1. *Sun*, May 25, 1889; *Englewood Eye*, Jan. 12, 1884.

2. *Eleventh Census, 1890*, vol. 1, "Population," 454–55; City of Chicago, *School Census of the City of Chicago, Taken May, 1888* (Chicago, 1888), 1, 3; *Trib.*, July 16, 1888; June 30, 1889. On the ability of horsecars to disperse urban populations, see Sam B. Warner, Jr., *Streetcar Suburbs: The Process of Growth in Boston, 1870–1900* (Cambridge, Mass., 1962), 21–29; and Roger D. Simon, "The City-Building Process: Housing and Services in New Milwaukee Neighborhoods, 1880–1910," *Transactions of the American Philosophical Society*, 68 (July, 1978), 7, 48, 54; James Everett Clark, "The Impact of Transportation Technology on Suburbanization in the Chicago Region, 1830–1920" (Ph.D. diss., Northwestern University, 1977), chaps. 4, 5; Clay McShane, *Technology and Reform: Street Railways and the Growth of Milwaukee, 1887–1900* (Madison, Wis., 1974), chap. 4.

3. [Albert Nelson Marquis], *Marquis' Hand-Book of Chicago: A Com-*

plete History, Reference Book, and Guide to the City (Chicago, 1885), 33; Joseph James Thompson, ed., *The Archdiocese of Chicago, Antecedents and Development* (Des Plaines, Ill., 1920), 455, 457, 435; "Special Report of Bohemian Work in Connection with Bethlehem [Congregational] Church, Apr. 1, 1889 to Aug. 1, 1890" (pamphlet, Chicago Historical Society); "Our Polish Citizens," *Trib.*, Mar. 14, 1886; June 12, 1892; Victor Greene, *For God and Country: The Rise of Polish and Lithuanian Ethnic Consciousness in America, 1860–1910* (Madison, Wis., 1975), 48–49; Joseph John Parot, *Polish Catholics in Chicago, 1850–1920: A Religious History* (DeKalb, Ill., 1981), chap. 4. See also, M. Haiman, "The Poles in Chicago," in Polish Pageant, Inc., *Poles of Chicago, 1837–1937* (Chicago, 1937); A. G. Tomczak, "The Poles in Chicago," in Polish Day Association, *Poles in America* (Chicago, 1937).

4. *Trib.*, Aug. 21, 1887; May 26, 1889; Allan H. Spear, *Black Chicago: The Making of Negro Ghetto, 1890–1920* (Chicago, 1967), 11–12; Thomas Lee Philpott, *The Slum and the Ghetto: Neighborhood Deterioration and Middle-Class Reform, Chicago, 1880–1930* (New York, 1978), chap. 5; Glen E. Holt and Dominic A. Pacyga, *Chicago: A Historical Guide to the Neighborhoods*, vol. 1, *The Loop and South Side* (Chicago, 1979), 52; *Eleventh Census, 1890*, vol. 1, "Population," 454.

5. *Trib.*, June 30, 1889; *Chicago, Illustrated and Descriptive* (Chicago, 1882), 92; Alfred T. Andreas, *History of Cook County, Illinois* (Chicago, 1884), 662; Jean F. Block, *Hyde Park Houses: An Informal History, 1856–1910* (Chicago, 1978), 17–35; Stanley Buder, *Pullman: An Experiment in Industrial Order and Community Planning, 1880–1930* (New York, 1967), 41–74, 109–11; *Times*, July 26, 1886.

6. *Trib.*, July 29, 1887.

7. *Sun*, Jan. 5, 1887; Sept, 7, 1889; *Trib.*, June 12, 1880; Dec. 17, 1882; Jan. 27, 1884; *Drovers Journal*, July 31, 1889; Town of Lake Records, Doc. 2017, Mar. 1, 1882; Doc. 2012, Mar. 24, 1886 (City Hall Archives, Chicago); Andreas, *Cook County*, 661–62; Sam Bass Warner, Jr., "Introduction," in *The Zone of Emergence*, by Robert A. Woods and Albert Kennedy (Cambridge, Mass., 1969), 39.

8. The Economist, *History and Statistics of Chicago Street Railway Corporations with Maps* (Chicago, 1896), 19–20; Inter-Ocean, *Chicago's First Half-Century* (Chicago, 1883), 174; Town of Lake Records, Doc. 362, Sept. 14, 1885; *Sun*, Sept. 7, 1889; *Drovers Journal*, Sept. 2, 16, 1882; Sept. 11, Oct. 2, 1884; *Trib.*, Sept. 10, 11, 1881; Feb. 10, Apr. 13, 1883; Jan. 1, Oct. 26, 1884; Feb. 3, 1887.

9. *Sun*, May 15, 1886; Nov. 11, 1887; Sept. 29, 1888; Preface to *Town of Lake Directory, 1886* (Chicago, 1886).

10. *Sun*, Oct. 6, 1886; Sept. 21, 22, Oct. 27, 1887; Town of Lake Rec-

ords, Doc. 524, Feb. 21, Mar. 27, 1888; Doc. 507, June 21, 1887; *Trib.*, Sept. 19, 1883.

11. *Sun,* June 10, 1884; Sept. 3, 30, 1886; Sept. 22, Dec. 6, 1887.

12. *Sun,* Nov. 17, 1886; Aug. 24, 1889; *Trib.*, Apr. 9, 1882.

13. *Drovers Journal,* Jan. 7, 1885; Mar. 3, 1885; July 17, Oct. 22, 1889; *Trib.*, Mar. 3, 1887; July 21, 1889; Town of Lake Records, Doc. 803, May 16, 1887.

14. *Sun,* June 14, July 21, 24, Sept. 3, 1886; Aug. 9, Sept. 14, 1889.

15. *Sun,* July 12, 1884; Aug. 14, Nov. 20, 24, 1886; May 18, 25, 1889; *Drovers Journal,* Mar. 17, 19, July 9, 1883; Helen Swift, *My Father and My Mother* (Chicago, 1937), 81, 87–88, 92. After 1889, Winter and Sherman streets took the names of the Chicago streets leading to them. Winter became Union, and Sherman was renamed Lowe.

16. [Englewood] *Eye,* Dec. 1, 1883; *Trib.*, Dec. 17, 1883; *Drovers Journal,* June 2, 1883; Sept. 26, 29, 1884; Sept. 10, 1885; *Sun,* July 24, Oct. 5, 14, 1889; Andreas, *Cook County,* 657–58.

17. Charles F. Ffrench, ed., *Biographical History of the American Irish in Chicago* (Chicago, 1897), 796–801; Saint Gabriel's Church, *Diamond Jubilee Souvenir Program, 1880–1955* (Chicago, 1955), 2, 7, 14, 17; St. Gabriel's Parish Report, 1881 (St. Mary of the Lake Seminary, Mundelein, Ill.); Sisters of Mercy, *Reminiscences of Seventy Years, 1846–1916* (Chicago, 1916), 252–53; Harriet Monroe, *John Wellborn Root: A Study of His Life and Work* (Boston, 1896), 149–52; *Sun,* May 25, 1889; Nov. 26, 1894.

18. *Inland Architect,* 7 (June, 1886), 85; Donald Hoffmann, *The Architecture of John Wellborn Root* (Baltimore, 1973), 99, 102; Saint Gabriel's Church, *Diamond Jubilee,* 2, 14; St. Gabriel's Parish Report, 1889 (St. Mary of the Lake Seminary); Thompson, *Archdiocese of Chicago,* 483, 485, 507, 509; *Trib.*, Jan. 15, 1883; July 10, 1886; May 16, 1887; Nov. 30, 1890; *Sun,* Aug. 20, 1885; May 25, 1887; May 25, 1889.

19. *Drovers Journal,* Sept. 18, 1884; *Trib.*, Mar. 5, 1885; [Englewood] *Eye,* Jan. 12, 1884.

20. *Drovers Journal,* Apr. 7, 1883; *Trib.*, May 13, 21, June 10, 1883; *Sun,* Mar. 25, 1887; *Trib.*, Sept. 23, 188; July 14, 1889.

21. *Trib.*, Oct. 19, 1882; *Drovers Journal,* Apr. 9, 1883; Sept. 18, 1884; *Sun,* Mar. 17, Aug. 5, Nov. 2, 1886; June 14, 1889; Inter-Ocean, *Chicago's First Half-Century,* 174, 183–84.

22. John Joseph Flinn, *The Hand-Book of Chicago Biography* (Chicago, 1893), 171; Chicago Times, *Chicago and Its Resources Twenty Years After, 1871–1891* (Chicago, 1892), 62; *Trib.*, Oct. 9, 1881, Mar. 18, 1888; Jan. 5, 1890.

23. *Sun,* Oct. 28, 1887; *Trib.*, Sept. 6, Oct. 9, Nov. 23, 1887; Mar. 18,

May 19, 1888; Jan. 5, 1890; *Tenth Annual Illustrated Catalogue of S. E. Gross' Famous City Subdivisions and Suburban Towns* (Chicago, 1891), 60–63.

24. *Sun.*, Sept. 3, 17, 1886; *Trib.*, Dec. 29, 1888; *Drovers Journal*, Sept. 11, 1884.

25. St. Augustine's Parish, *Golden Jubilee and Chronological History of St. Augustine's Parish* (Chicago, 1936), 25–49; Marion A. Habig, *The Fransciscans at St. Augustine's and in Chicagoland* (Chicago, 1961), 25–28, 34; Vivien M. Palmer, "History of New City," Doc. 13, interview with Reverend Denis Thiele (Mary McDowell Papers, Chicago Historical Society); St. Augustine's Parish Report, 1884 (St. Mary of the Lake Seminary).

26. *Sun*, Aug. 2, 1886; St. Augustine's Parish, *Chronological History*, 53, 59, 63–65, 67, 69; Habig, *Franciscans at St. Augustine's*, 32–33, 42–43; St. Augustine's Parish Report, 1889 (St. Mary of the Lake Seminary).

27. *Drovers Journal*, Nov. 18, 1882; Mar. 17, 1883; *Sun*, Dec. 10, 1885; Mar. 17, 1887; *Trib.*, July 9, 1883; Thompson, *Archdiocese of Chicago*, 487; St. Rose of Lima Parish Reports, 1884, 1885, 1887, 1889 (St. Mary of the Lake Seminary).

28. *Trib.*, May 5, 6, 11, Sept. 9, 1885; *Drovers Journal*, Jan. 11, Feb. 17, 1886; *Sun*, Oct. 5, Dec. 17, 20, 1886; William Kucinski, "Polish People in Town of Lake," Golden Jubilee Edition, *Journal of Town of Lake*, Sept. 14, 1939; Thompson, *Archdiocese of Chicago*, 525–26; St. Joseph's Parish Report, 1889 (St. Mary of the Lake Seminary).

29. *Trib.*, Dec. 31, 1884; May 17, 1885; *Sun*, Sept. 30, Nov. 12, 1886; Mar. 8, 1890.

30. Andrew Vogler, "From an Old Timer Back of the Yards" (typescript, n.d., Mary McDowell Papers).

31. J. H. Brayton, *Englewood Directory for 1882* (Englewood, Ill., 1882), 8, 10; Preface to *Englewood Directory, 1890* (Chicago, 1890); *Trib.*, July 21, Sept. 15, 1889.

32. *Trib.*, Oct. 2, 6, Dec. 15, 29, 1881; July 5, 6, 1884; Apr. 16, 1885; Feb. 3, 1887; Nov. 14, 1888; *Sun*, Aug. 16, 1884; June 7, Nov. 23, 1889; Town of Lake Records, Doc. 562, July to Dec., 1888; *Real Estate and Building Journal*, Aug. 28, 1880, 120.

33. *Southtown Economist*, Englewood Golden Jubilee Edition, Nov. 10, 1940, 10; *Sun*, July 31, 1886; Aug. 3, Sept. 7, Nov. 16, 1889; *Trib.*, July 14, 1884; July 21, 1889; Apr. 9, 1893; *The Town of Lake Directory, 1889* (Chicago, 1889), 44–46; Gerald E. Sullivan, ed., *The Story of Englewood, 1835–1923* (Chicago, 1924), 49, 157.

34. *Drovers Journal*, Jan. 13, Mar. 16, 1888; *Sun*, Aug. 5, 1885; June 22, 1886; Aug. 3, 1889; *Trib.*, Apr. 9, 1882; Nov. 14, 1888; June 30, Oct. 11, 1889.

35. *Trib.*, June 12, 15, Sept. 6, 1887; *Sun,* June 7, 14, 1889; Sept. 10, 1892; *Drovers Journal,* Oct. 15, 1889; James J. O'Toole, "Back o' the Yards, 1870 to 1890" (typescript pamphlet, 1938, Chicago Historical Society), 8.

36. *Trib.*, Aug. 20, 21, 1887; May 5, June 24, Aug. 5, Oct. 5, 1888; *Sun,* Oct. 13, 1887; July 20, 27, Aug. 10, 31, Dec. 16, 1889; Jan. 25, 1890; Sullivan, *Englewood,* 107–8, 123–24, 128; *Town of Lake Directory, 1889,* 38–40.

37. St. Anne's Parish Reports, 1879, 1889 (St. Mary of the Lake Seminary); Sullivan, *Englewood,* 112–14; *New World,* 4, Nov. 9, 1895; *Trib.*, May 29, 30, July 29, 1887; *Sun,* June 19, 1884; Nov. 3, 23, 1886; July 27, 1889; May 12, 1890.

38. *Town of Lake Directory, 1889,* 37–40; *Sun,* July 20, 1889.

CHAPTER 16

The Social Anchors

Town of Lake's mushroom growth in the 1880s forced old-timers and newcomers alike to seek contacts with those who shared their values, interests, commitments, and native tongue. The voluntary associations helped people make these selective connections. The variety of nonprofit organizations was formidable—churches and religious societies, political parties and pressure groups, trade unions, secret societies, moral reform groups, social clubs, and athletic, literary, dramatic, and musical associations. Membership required little time or money but provided contacts with like-minded people, opportunities for service and leadership, and sometimes ties to Chicago or national parent organizations. In addition to the voluntary associations, there were broader group loyalties binding residents of the township. The Protestant and Catholic camps constituted one such division; language and culture bound all Germans or Bohemians regardless of religious affiliations; for a brief time the Knights of Labor united packinghouse workers. Group consciousness, of course, increased the likelihood of conflict. Spirited contests over school board elections and township drinking regulations pitted ethnic and religious and reform groups against each other. Yet the voluntary associations and the larger groups were evidence of a healthy community. They were social anchors for people who had made their commitment to Town of Lake and wanted a voice in molding its future.

Churches and Other Voluntary Associations

The quest for social anchors is deeply rooted in human nature. People in the Town of Lake, like those everywhere else, needed to find compatible associates, and they made their selection on the basis of occupation, age, religion, politics, gender, income, education, and many other criteria. Voluntary associations facilitated the process. They enabled joiners to say who they were and what they believed in. Participation provided friendly forums for the exchange of views and fellowship with a preselected group of manageable size. Many of the voluntary associations offered opportunities to assist others, and they were vehicles for learning organizational and leadership skills which members could transfer to other arenas. If the association were part of a larger national group, then members had instant connection with more powerful factions such as, for example, the Knights of Labor, the Salvation Army, the Young Men's Christian Association, the Masons, or the Ancient Order of Hibernians. Every successful community had its network of voluntary associations. They were as important in the social fabric of the small town as they were in the industrial metropolis.[1]

Since the Town of Lake was a veritable patchwork of subcultures, it generated a large number of voluntary associations. Irish Catholics dominated the Stockyards neighborhood and native-born Protestants set the tone of Englewood, but neither group lived in seclusion. The mix of ethnic, religious, and economic groups within each of the neighborhoods created the need for many social anchors. They were the prerequisites of ethnic working-class culture—friendly and benevolent societies, sympathetic politicians, churches, sports, saloons and beer gardens, music, labor organizations, reformers, and radicals. Yet similar voluntary associations met the needs of middle- and upper-class residents of the township—social clubs, sympathetic politicians, churches, sports, music, reformers, and conservatives. Englewood's Music Hall and Opera House drew a different clientele than Joseph Oswald's beer garden or the performances of the Irish fife and drum corps, but they all satisfied the same cravings. Town of Lake's 1870s associations included the earliest churches and branches of the Masons, Odd Fellows, and Ancient Order of Hibernians. The surge of newcomers in the next decade led to the founding of many more organizations, and the 1889 *Directory* listed 215, fifty-nine of them churches and ninety-one secret societies. The editor, however, missed a number of religious societies based in the churches and quite a few ethnic organizations. In addition, many of the trade unions active in the middle of the decade had disappeared by 1889. The *Sun* carried date, time, and place of voluntary association meetings, and Goodall was evenhanded about reporting their achievements. A sokol exhibition in Back of the Yards was as worthy of note as the dedication of a Normal Park church. Like many other contemporaries, Harvey Goodall viewed the voluntary associations as the social counterpart of new construction. Both were forms of commitment to the new community taking shape before their eyes.[2]

Some of the voluntary associations had their own buildings. The churches, of course, sheltered their religious societies; St. Gabriel's parish welcomed the Irish nationalist organizations; and the First Universalist Church served as headquarters for the Englewood Woman's Club. There were Masonic halls at the Stockyards and in Englewood, two temperance halls, the veteran's Memorial Hall, and a Foresters' Hall in the southern part of the township. The Commercial Club, Home Club, and Harvard

Club had their own buildings. Some voluntary associations maintained permanent rented headquarters: the Odd Fellows in the Englewood Opera House, the Salvation Army in the Tillotson Block, and the Englewood Social Club in Vehmeyer's Block. Most groups, however, rented meeting rooms, auditoriums, and offices in the various halls. Proprietors catered to them and often specialized in particular ethnic groups. Thus the German societies favored Bromstedt's Hall in Englewood, Henry Schumacher's Ashland House, and Conrad Walther's establishment in the Northeast Corners. Swedes at the Car-Shops preferred Dahlgren's and Werkmeister's Halls, while the Irish headed for Walsh's or Ryan's in the north end and Kelly's or Morony's in Englewood. Goodall rejoiced that the town had a "superabundance" of these adaptable halls.[3]

Of all the voluntary associations, the churches were the most successful at stressing "the unifying values" shared by their members.[4] They were the first associations in Town of Lake—the small brick building erected in 1862 at The Junction served as a nondenominational church, and within three years of the opening of the Stockyards Irish Catholics had Nativity of Our Lord parish. The five dozen religious organizations present in 1889 involved more people and elicited stronger commitments than did any other cluster of associations. In addition to meeting the spiritual needs of members, they served a wide variety of social purposes. By institutionalizing cultural heritages, they provided friendly receptions for both native and foreign-born newcomers. All of the churches helped train the young, either through Sunday schools, elementary schools, or youth organizations, and for many parents this alone was worth the price of admission. Active participation in church affairs gave laymen the chance to become leaders, and many of them parlayed their church reputations into political careers. In an era when women were excluded from public life and few worked outside the home, the socially commendable church activities were important outlets. They could win acclaim as musicians, fund-raisers, planners of bazaars, activists in missionary work, and helpers of families in distress.

The proliferation of religious societies within St. Augustine's parish in the 1880s illustrates the widening opportunity for social involvement. Starting with an Altar Society in 1881, the parish added a choir, a benevolent society, St. Anthony's Fraternity, the Young Men's Society, the Young Ladies' Society, male and female courts of the Catholic Order of Foresters, and a branch of the Catholic Knights of America. In the township Protestant churches, there were lecture series, musical programs, missionary societies, reading rooms, and many young people's groups in addition to the Sunday school classes. Catholic parishioners planned and staffed the fund-raising bazaars or festivals, some of which lasted as long as two weeks. St. Gabriel's were famous for their door prizes, wheels of fortune, shooting galleries, popularity contests, display booths run by parish societies, and the sale of food and handicrafts. One such bazaar raised $10,000 for the new church.[5]

Many of the churches were allied with secular voluntary associations whose membership closely overlapped that of the religious organization. The thousands of spectators who turned out for St. Gabriel's cornerstone-laying ceremony knew that they could enjoy the smartly uniformed bands of the Clan na Gael Guards, Hibernian Rifles, Catholic Order of Foresters, and Catholic Knights of America. St. Rose of Lima Church dedicated its new bells with the help of the Ancient Order of Hibernians and the New City Fife and Drum Corps. The Winter Street Methodists provided a hall for temperance lecturers and encouraged the Citizens' League to hold its meetings in their church. The Englewood Protestant churches made it possible for the Young Men's Christian Association to build a $15,000 gymnasium and headquarters on Sixty-third Street. They also participated in the Englewood Church Union, a Protestant temperance forum established in 1885. The First Universalist Church was the unofficial headquarters for several women's groups, thanks to the broad interests of its pastor, Florence Kollock. A University of Wisconsin graduate and former schoolteacher, Reverend Kollock was the township's only female pastor, and her relationships with male colleagues in the Englewood Church Union were often unpleasant. But she built her church from fifteen members to over two hundred and maintained close ties with the Englewood Kindergarten Association, Illinois Woman's Suffrage Association, Woman's Christian Temperance Union, and World's Council of Women. Kollock attracted local women from these organizations to the First Universalist Church and introduced church members to the other voluntary associations.[6]

Well over half of the associations in Town of Lake had no religious ties or orientation. These included the dozen building and loan associations, the trade unions, and the secret fraternal societies such as the Masons, Odd Fellows, United Workmen, Knights of Pythias, and others. The social dimension of these organizations was clear. Long after the Knights of Labor had crumbled as a trade union, locals gathered former members to enjoy each other's company. The expressed goal of the Union Veteran Club of Englewood was to strengthen "the social ties that bind together the veteran survivors." Two-thirds of its members had served in regiments raised outside Illinois, and participation in the Englewood veterans' organization was a way to establish friendships with natives of the state. Members of the several citizens' associations found people who agreed with their economic and political views and were good companions as well. The social clubs picked their members on the basis of compatibility, the Harvard Club of Englewood and the Home Club of Normal Park being the most exclusive. However, people could always turn to the Big Four, the

Acorn, the Olympian, and many other just-for-fun clubs that were not so persnickety.[7]

"One of the signs of prosperity and advancement of a community," declared the *Sun*, "is the character and style of its amusements." By the end of the 1880s, Town of Lake had three dozen associations promoting drama, literature, music, and sports. Local thespians and musicians competed with imported talent, and there were so many plays, concerts, readings, and lectures that scheduling was often a problem. One could join or listen to choral groups, brass bands, and fife and drum corps. Dancing enthusiasts twirled at the Transit House and the many neighborhood halls with dance floors. There were two roller-skating rinks in the town and hundreds of bicycle riders, some of them organized like the Englewood Bicycle Club. Athletic clubs flourished, and their gymnastic exhibitions drew large crowds. As for baseball, there were packinghouse teams, a post office team, and scores of neighborhood nines with names like the "Limekilns" and "Haymakers." New construction in the 1880s obliterated many of their playing fields, but the Town of Lake Base Ball Association came to the rescue. It purchased five acres at Forty-eighth and Halsted, fenced a first-class diamond, and built a grandstand for fifteen hundred spectators. By 1889, Henry Werkmeister, owner of Werkmeister Hall at the Car-Shops, was managing a town team—christened "The Lakes," of course.[8]

Ethnic voluntary associations displayed the same range of purpose—religious, benevolent, cultural, economic, and athletic—and served the same social functions. Yet it is likely that they held greater significance for their members than did most of the other associations. The ethnic groups were minorities within the township, and none of them had separate compounds. Their voluntary associations provided unity for the group within the township and often linked them with the larger group in Chicago which shared their language and culture. For newly arrived immigrants, the ethnic societies were lifesavers; for those who were eager to break into public life, leadership credentials in the ethnic voluntary associations were essential prerequisites. And finally, all of the ethnic groups used their voluntary associations, particularly their churches, as a basis of comparison with other foreign-born groups and with "the Americans."[9]

The Ethnic Blocs

Town of Lake residents perceived themselves and others as members not only of voluntary associations but of larger groups as well. In the 1880s the ethnic blocs were the most important. Gender obviously counted for some Englewood women, but they did not reach out to other women in the north end of town. In the spring of 1887, "The Working Man's Wife" told the *Labor Enquirer* that the eight-hour-day controversy reminded her of "a class of laborers who . . . get up at 5 o'clock in the morning and never go to bed until 10 or 11 o'clock at night. They work without ceasing, . . . are harassed by a hundred responsibilities," receive no emolument, and "cannot organize for their own protection." A male Irish correspondent from Back of the Yards agreed that his sex was responsible for turning the wives into "bitter brooding mothers, neglected and frowned down" upon when their "bloom is over." We have, he continued, "a holy horror of women in politics and society. . . . In public we admire women's progress; in private we wet blanket the feeblest gleam of ambition." He hoped the Knights of Labor would be able to protect the rights of working women, but his communication to the *Labor Enquirer* reveals why that campaign was doomed to failure: "We never dream of lifting women to an equality with ourselves." Thus the workingmen's wives and daughters were swallowed up in the ethnic group to which they belonged, and, with only a few exceptions, women in the Town of Lake did not think of themselves or act as a distinct social group.[10]

Members of the foreign-born blocs, however, did take concerted action to help their groups make economic gains and win political recognition. It was a highly competitive atmosphere in which all the ethnic groups struggled for the same reward—"coming to the front," as Irish-American congressman John Finerty put it. The Irish had the advantage of understanding the English language, being unified by Catholicism and concern about their homeland, and voting solidly for Irish candidates. The other ethnic groups struggled with religious differences and the language barrier. They, along with "the Americans," could only look with envy upon the rapid proliferation of Irish parishes and church construction, Irish domination of the labor movement, and Thomas Gahan's upset victory as supervisor of the Town of Lake. Throughout the 1880s, the commitment to Irish nationalism helped upwardly mobile Irish-Americans make an impression upon their local communities. Their fight for a free homeland was simultaneously "an identity badge and pathway to respectability." The Town of Lake Irish are perfect illustrations of this phenomenon.[11]

Irish hopes were pinned on Charles Stewart Parnell, who turned from economic reform through the Land Leagues to political reform and a self-governing Irish nation. The long-deferred dream of Home Rule excited the American Irish, and in 1883 they established an umbrella organization called the Irish National League. It pulled together the Clan na Gael, Ancient Order of Hibernians, Irish Catholic Benevolent Union, Catholic Total Abstinence Union, and eventually the Land Leagues. The fever peaked in 1885, the year Parnell's Irish party held the balance of power in Parliament and Prime Minister Gladstone was believed to be a convert to the cause. In the summer of 1886, however, British voters defeated both Gladstone and Home Rule. The Irish National League was soon torn by internal quarrels, and the Clan na Gael reverted to its original creed of physical force. Parnell's disgrace in the O'Shea divorce case in 1890 ended the Home Rule debate and devastated the Irish National League.[12]

Irish-American leaders were deeply involved in the struggle. Henry George argued from countless public platforms and in *The Irish Land Question* (1881) that British exploitation of Ireland was comparable to capitalist exploitation of wage earners in the United States. Terence Powderly was vice-president of the Irish National Land and Industrial League when it joined the Irish National League in 1883, and he was a national leader of the Clan na Gael. Delegates to the 1886 Irish National League convention in Chicago heard that city's leading nationalists, John Finerty and Alexander Sullivan. Finerty, the first Irish congressman from Chicago, founded the *Citizen* in 1882 and used it to promote nationalism and ethnic pride in equal portions. He belonged to the Clan, the Land League, and the Irish National League. Sullivan, a reporter who had turned to law and politics, was national chairman of the Clan in 1881 and first president of the Irish National League.[13]

Nationalist enthusiam was also strong among the Irish in Town of Lake. The Stockyards branch of the Ancient Order of Hibernians used Home Rule to build new branches in the Northeast Corners and Back of the Yards. There were Land Leagues on both sides of Section 5, and a Town of Lake Irish-American Literary Club may have been a female nationalist organization. A branch of the Clan na Gael, established in 1871 but somnolent, came to life when Father Dorney arrived and took an active interest in it; he had the explicit approval of Archbishop Feehan, an open sympathizer with Irish nationalism. Thus Irish societies met at St. Gabriel's Hall; every March Father Dorney hosted a celebration of Robert Emmet's birth; he was usually on the speakers' platform at the annual Irish picnic; and Dorney presided in 1886 when Michael Davitt was the United Irish Societies' guest of honor. Town of Lake sent three delegates to the founding convention of the Irish National League—Father Dorney for the Clan na Gael, Michael McInerney for the Land Leagues, and Dr. Charles P. Caldwell for the Ancient Order of Hibernians. A personal friend and close associate of Alexander Sullivan, Dorney was temporary chairman of that convention, and he later chaired the Illinois State Irish National League.[14]

Aspiring politicians in the township recognized the importance of the Irish nationalist organizations as vehicles for establishing leadership credentials. Michael McInerney, for example, ran a saloon and then a funeral parlor and livery business in his spare time; his major commitments were to St. Gabriel's parish, the Ancient Order of Hibernians, the Hibernian Rifles, the Stockyards Land League, the Michael Davitt branch of the Irish National League, and the Clan na Gael. He parlayed these contacts into seven years on the local school board, one term as township trustee, two terms in the state legislature, and a postmastership at the Stockyards. Michael J. Butler drew upon his base of support in the Ancient Order of Hibernians and the Irish National League to build the Knights of Labor organization and run for county sheriff. Thomas Gahan, a member of almost as many Irish organizations as McInerney plus many other voluntary associations, counted on the support of these groups when he ran for supervisor of the township. The vanquished candidate sourly attributed Gahan's election to the machinations of the numerous Irish societies and the cohesion of Irish voters. Newspaperman Finley Peter Dunne pinpointed the connection between Irish Home Rule and local politics when he let Mr. Dooley ask, "Did ye iver see a man that wanted to free Ireland th' day afther to-morrah that didn't run f'r aldherman soon or late?"[15]

Irish-American nationalists faced hard times after 1886. Henry George's defeat in the New York mayoralty race and Powderly's problems with the Knights of Labor dampened spirits. Parnell kept his distance from the quarreling factions in the Irish National League and the Clan na Gael. Seeking to disprove that Parnell had anything to do with Clan violence, Alexander Sullivan chose Father Dorney to deliver the evidence to London in 1888. The larger than usual St. Patrick's Day parade in Town of Lake that spring was both a tribute to Dorney and a demonstration of Irish unity in the face of mounting criticism, according to Goodall. Charges that Alexander Sullivan had mishandled Clan funds and behaved arbitrarily as one of the Irish National League's ruling "Triangle" poisoned the atmosphere in Chicago. Dr. Patrick Henry Cronin, a relentless critic of Sullivan, disappeared in May, 1889, and his battered body was later found in a Lake View sewer. Cronin's allies accused Sullivan of masterminding the murder. Father Dorney indignantly denied that Irish nationalists had committed the crime, and John Finerty said such behavior was "foreign to the national character and religious disposition of the Irish people." He hoped the "bitter cup of possible disgrace" would "pass away from the lips of Ireland." It did not. Three members of Sullivan's north-side Clan went to the penitentiary, and for a full six months newspaper readers feasted on Clan secrets, Triangle feuds, and the bloody Irish revolutionary record. The Chicago Irish ended the decade disgraced and sorely divided.[16]

Fair or not, the whole group had to answer for the sins of a few. The *Illinois Staats-Zeitung* said the Cronin murder proved that Irishmen could be far more brutal than German-Americans, who were held accountable for the Haymarket bomb. The "obstreperous" rhetoric of "professional Irish patriots" got under the skin of others who thought the nationalists ought to pay attention to Irish troublemakers in their own localities, such as Town of Lake's "champion bad man," a former prizefighter who went on rampages of "mayhem, rape and . . . other kinds of viciousness" when drunk, which was often. Even more deserving of restraint was the township's most notorious criminal, Cornelius O'Leary. His father, "old man" O'Leary, was a quiet drinker who spent his days in the Halsted Street saloons, willing to talk about anything except the Chicago fire, a topic which turned him into "a sphinx." But Cornelius, nicknamed Puggy, was an "uncouth ruffian" in chronic trouble with the police. One hot August night in 1885, he staggered out of a saloon, encountered his mistress and his sister, recently widowed by a barroom brawl, and continued drinking with them. When the trio ran out of beer, Puggy asked his mistress for money to buy more. She refused, and he shot and killed both women. Cornelius O'Leary was already behind bars in Joliet when Cronin's murderers—Burke, Coughlin, and O'Sullivan—entered the penitentiary.[17]

Germans, Bohemians, and Poles tried just as hard as the Irish to present a positive image, ward off criticism, encourage unity, and impress upon "the Americans" that they too were "coming to the front." They had the problem of mastering the language of employment and politics while at the same time preserving the native tongue and culture for their children. Getting a church school in operation was tremendously important to these parents. St. Augustine's was not the only ethnic church that had a teacher before it acquired a pastor. The Germans, however, rarely voted as a bloc because the Protestant, Catholic, and socialist contingents could seldom agree upon candidates. This allowed slate-makers in the Town of Lake and Democrats and Republicans in Chicago to bait German voters with token recognition. Germans, of course, complained about this shabby treatment and demanded a larger share of patronage jobs. In the immediate aftermath of Haymarket, all Germans had to contend with slurs and innuendoes concerning their supposed penchant for radicalism and anarchism. After the hysteria died down, they decided to "be more combative," as one ward leader put it, and make the point that Germans were more "numerous, more respectable, and much better educated than the Irish."[18] In the Town of Lake, the catalysts for change were Supervisor Gahan's Irish favoritism and Irish arrogance in the Knights of Labor. German votes helped bring Gahan down, and few Germans mourned when Michael Butler and Terence Powderly crash-landed. Thereafter, they did not hesitate to demand a fair share of town jobs and chances to run for office.

German-Americans were not above boosting their own image by denigrating others. Pork packer Samuel Schoenemann blamed the loss of French and German markets on American Irish demagogues who monopolized the newspapers defending their "murderers" and thereby preventing the public from learning about the European restrictions on pork products. The *Illinois Staats-Zeitung* was deeply suspicious of the Irish nationalist societies; they were run by "demagogues" fishing for Irish votes at home. That newspaper also took a dim view of the "half-civilized" laborers from Italy and the "lamentably ignorant and superstitious" Jewish refugees from eastern Europe. The latter bore so little resemblance to German Jews that it was like comparing "the Voodoo worshippers of Dark Africa . . . with a professor of philosophy in Berlin."[19]

Poles and Bohemians were convinced that everyone looked down upon them, and derogatory statements certainly were plentiful in the 1880s. Charles Dudley Warner sang Chicago's praises in 1888 but fretted about the clannish Bohemians and Poles who were unable to use English and were "mentally and morally brutal." A *Tribune* reporter accused Polish and Bohemian families of "living in indescribable filth" and settling for wages that "would be scorned by any Irish, German, or American laborer." The Chicago City Missionary Society infuriated Bohemians by calling them so "earthy that spiritual ideas scarcely find a lodgment in their hearts. . . . Truth dawns upon them very slowly." "We are not ashamed that we are Bohemians," retorted the editor of *Svornost*. Three out of five Bohemians were buying lots or houses and doing it through their own building and loan associations; they had Catholic and Protestant churches, the Bohemian cemetery, a dozen Bohemian halls, one bank, scores of athletic organizations, English classes for adults, and Bohemian classes for children. Moreover, there were branches of the Czecho-Slovak Benevolent Society and the Bohemian Roman Catholic Central Union, both of which established national headquarters in Chicago in the 1880s. Like the Germans, they were angry about "minor places" on Irish-dominated political tickets and patronage scraps. The Irish paid no heed, but Mayor Carter Harrison appointed lawyer Adolf Kraus to the Chicago Board of Education, and all Bohemians rejoiced when the board later chose him as president.[20]

Since the vast majority of Poles were Catholic, their world centered on the north-side St. Stanislaus Kostka parish, headed by Father Vincent Barzynski until his death in 1899. He was unstintingly helpful to the South Branch parishes, St. Adalbert's and St. Mary of Perpetual Help, and to St. Joseph's parish in the Town of Lake. Nearly all Poles strove for homeownership, even though this meant crowding and taking in boarders. Like the Bohemians, they had their own building and loan association, banks, cemeteries, and benevolent and fraternal organizations. The Polish Roman Catholic Union and the Polish National Alliance, Polonia's two largest national voluntary associations, had headquarters in Chicago and both published newspapers. In addition, the first Polish language daily in Chicago began publication in 1890. Poles wavered between local Democrats and Republicans and thus had cause to grumble about lack of recognition from either party. But their interest in local politics picked up after the election in 1888 of the first Polish alderman and Peter Kiolbassa's upset victory three years later in the contest for city treasurer. Polish hostility to Chicago area Germans stemmed from German domination of western Poland and German socialist attacks on religion. Their "very bitter feelings" toward Polish Jews, however, puzzled reporters. In 1888 the secretary of the Polish National Alliance tried to explain: "The Poles are one thing and the Polish Jews another—that is what the people in America ought to know."[21]

Town of Lake had a "Polackville" at Ashland and the city-township boundary where close to one thousand Poles and Bohemians were living by mid-decade. The men were considered "faithful" laborers in the brick-yards and packinghouses, but Irish organizers ignored them because of language barriers and lack of skills. When the *Sun* noted cases of infant cholera in the settlement, it omitted family names because they were "un-pronounceable" and presumably impossible to spell. An 1888 encounter between Irish baseball players and residents illustrates how vulnerable "Polackville" really was. Two stockyard-packinghouse teams were playing near a Bohemian house where a dozen families had gathered on a Sunday afternoon to visit and drink beer. The Irish players tried to cadge some beer and a fight broke out. August Detlauf, fresh from Bohemia, compre-hending no English, and thinking his house and family were under siege, grabbed a revolver and killed the two men who started the trouble. Only the timely arrival of the police saved the Bohemians from retaliation and the house from total destruction.[22]

Polish and Bohemian families buying lots and constructing houses southwest of Ashland and Forty-seventh had an easier time of it. Whether they came from the Thirty-ninth Street colony or the South Branch wards, they had better paying jobs, some knowledge of English, and a cluster of voluntary associations. Columbia Hall at Forty-eighth and Paulina shel-tered Sokol Prahn, Kralovic Lodge, a branch of the Czecho-Slovak Benev-olent Union, and the New City Athletic Club. Poles and Bohemians socialized with each other more often than they did with Germans or Irish; they were like the Croats and Slovenes in Steelton, Pennsylvania: "Stran-gers amidst strangers, we lived in harmony . . . consoling one another." Reporters tried to spell their names and politicians attempted to pronounce them because these people were making progress toward homeownership and associational activities. Although the four ethnic groups sharing New City and Back of the Yards were pursuing the same goals, their differences with each other were never far from the surface. Father Thiele of St. Au-gustine's remembered that the Irish "seemed to live apart from the Ger-mans." And since many of the Poles had come from Prussia, they were "expected to attend St. Augustine's although we did not have Polish ser-vices for them." Once the Poles had their own Catholic church, Bohemians preferred that parish to St. Augustine's. Father Nawrocki, however, could report in 1889 that he had baptised "100 of my own people" and sixty Bohemians. The only solution for Catholic Bohemians was a parish of their own as soon as possible.[23]

Chicago's black residents, like the various ethnic groups, utilized voluntary associations to knit their people together. Whereas the Poles and Bohemians were nearing 5 percent of the city's total population by the end of the 1880s, the Negroes constituted just over 1 percent throughout the decade. Small clusters of blacks were scattered in many areas of the city, but the largest concentration was south of the business district. This is where most of the black churches were located and where the weekly newspaper, *Chicago Conservator*, was published. The Negroes also had musical and dramatic groups, a Colored Men's Library Association, Colored Masons, and a benevolent organization, the Knights of Tabor. At mid-decade black business and professional men published a directory, and five years later the *Tribune* profiled those Negroes who were making their mark in wealth and fame. But skin color made a tremendous difference. So many black workers were confined to menial jobs at low pay that only 2 percent could afford home ownership, compared to 29 percent for the city as a whole. Politicians and the press constantly reminded them of their lowly status. Republicans in search of Irish votes in 1880 pointed out that Negroes were competent workers who could "underbid" the Irish and "crowd them out," and that blacks had as much right "to come North as the Irish have to come here from Ireland," and the only way to keep them in the South was to vote Republican. Newspapers assumed their readers shared the "natural abhorrence against mixed living between whites and colored" in the same locality, and a reporter seeking to describe the South Fork aroma said it was "worse than a 10-cent lodging-house for negroes."[24]

Of the 14,271 Chicago blacks in 1890, 434 (3 percent) lived in the Fifth and Sixth wards and 557 (3.9 percent) lived in the three wards carved out of the Town of Lake. The school census, taken in May, 1890, found 621 blacks in the former Town of Lake. Since the total population of the former township had risen to 99,723 by 1890, the blacks constituted only .5 percent or at most .6 percent of the total. Their increase in numbers from 26 in 1880 to approximately 600 by 1890 did not cause much of a stir. With the exception of a cluster of black families on Sixty-third Street near Ashland Avenue, they stayed close to State Street. There were blacks in the Northeast Corners and a sizeable group in Englewood around the Sixty-third and State Street intersection. The sale of a house at the Car-Shops to a black family in 1885 caused some objections but no trouble. Although blacks had established two small churches in Englewood by the end of the decade, few white residents considered them social equals or thought of them as a cohesive group striving to come to the front.[25]

Saloon and School Board Conflicts

"Coming to the front" meant having a voice in the formulation of public policy, and each of the ethnic groups plus many of the voluntary associations fought for this "right." When they did not agree on what the policy should be, and this was often the case, sparks flew. During the 1880s the two most controversial issues were drinking regulations and equitable representation on public school boards. An examination of these two problems will reveal why the groups collided and how they put together some highly unlikely coalitions to carry the day.

Illinois permitted local communities to regulate the sale and consumption of liquor within their boundaries provided they adhered to state law. An 1874 statute banning sales to minors and drunkards was incorporated in Town of Lake's first saloon ordinance, which also prohibited gambling on the premises and required people selling beer, wine, ale, or liquor to purchase $50 licenses and post $500 bonds. Aside from sporadic meetings sponsored by the Chicago Woman's Christian Temperance Union, there was no organized temperance activity until the end of the decade. Then an Englewood Citizens Temperance League appeared, and Robert Neill started a Stockyards branch of the Sons of Temperance. In 1880 these two groups merged and elected Neill president of the Citizens' League of the Town of Lake for the Suppression of the Sale of Liquor to Minors and Drunkards. Patterning their organization on the Chicago Citizens' League, they soon hired Captain A. R. Palmer as a full-time agent to ferret out unlicensed saloonkeepers and anyone selling illegally. The reformers also pressured the town board to establish prohibited districts within the township. Between 1881 and 1883, saloons were barred within 150 feet of public parks, boulevards, schools, and churches; Section 5 was declared off limits for saloons except for the narrow strip of Ashland, the Exchange, and the Transit House; and then Englewood went dry from Fifty-fifth to Seventy-first, State to Halsted with the exception of 125-foot strips on the latter two thoroughfares. These restrictions caused little controversy because they inconvenienced few saloonkeepers or patrons.[26]

When the Citizens' League of Illinois advocated $500 liquor licenses, there was an outcry. The reformers promised that the tenfold increase in the cost of licenses would drive some saloonkeepers out of business, raise the price of all intoxicating beverages, and reduce the number of customers. Irish and German spokesmen said it was an attack on their businessmen and their customs. Chicago liquor dealers organized in 1882, those in Town of Lake the following year, and they blamed the minors and drunkards for violating the 1874 law. Chicago aldermen decided that fines on these people would solve the problem. Nonetheless the state legislature mandated $500 licenses in 1883. Chicago dragged its feet, but Town of

Lake complied when the new regulation went into effect. Captain Palmer was in his element: many saloonkeepers protected by friendly policemen tried to operate without the expensive licenses. Infuriated by Palmer's meddling, proprietors assaulted him and some even tossed the Citizens' League agent out on the sidewalk. The league retaliated by pressuring the town board to give Palmer special policeman status. It finally did so when it realized that Father Dorney, Harvey Goodall, John B. Sherman, Philip Armour, Gustavus Swift, Nelson Morris, Sidney Kent, Michael Cudahy, Eneas Wood, Elmer Washburn, Reverend Florence Kollock, and scores of other Protestant ministers, livestock dealers, and Englewood businessmen supported the league. And so Captain Palmer pressed on, nabbing Joseph Oswald for selling to minors at the beer garden when they came with their parents on Sunday and picking up the boys who fetched beer for the packinghouse workers at noon.[27]

The Englewood Church Union, headed by Reverend H. S. Taylor of Normal Park Baptist Church, who was the Prohibition party's candidate for Congress in 1888, came up with two other proposals. It wanted Sunday closing and annual review of licenses which would force saloonkeepers to gather signatures of voters living within one-eighth of a mile of their establishments every year. Opponents had no trouble scotching these suggestions, but they could not stave off yet another increase in license fees to $1,000 at the end of the decade. The Citizens' League and Englewood Church Union took pride in the fact that the number of saloons in the township had only increased from 265 in 1881 to about 300 in 1889 and that arrests for drunkenness had actually declined. They did not cite statistics for disorderly conduct or resisting arrest while under the influence of alcohol, for those figures belied the reformers' claim that they had Demon Rum under control in the Town of Lake.[28]

While the battle over license fees was raging, Father Dorney won a stunning victory for property owners and residents of the Stockyards neighborhood. In June, 1886, James Lynch quietly circulated petitions seeking permision to open a grocery and saloon in the 4500 block of Wallace, provocatively close to St. Gabriel's Church but outside the 150-foot limit. Dorney alerted parishioners, and Goodall threatened to publish the names of signers; both men argued that there were plenty of places to drink on Halsted and if a saloon slipped into the residential blocks, others would soon occupy "every corner in the district." But Lynch presented the necessary number of signatures, and so the town board had to grant his license. Dorney then teamed up with Robert Neill to convene a citizens' meeting at St. Gabriel's Hall on Sunday evening, July 11. An enormous crowd from the parish, the Methodist Episcopal Church, and the Citizens League endorsed a resolution condemning saloons; they "poison the life springs of our people" and "bring crime and vice into the sanctuary of our homes." Dorney, Neill, and Gustavus Swift circulated a new petition asking for a prohibition district bounded by Forty-third, Stewart Avenue, Forty-ninth, and the alley between Halsted and Emerald. Within a few weeks they collected over 450 signatures, including those of Thomas Gahan and James J. "Buck" McCarthy. Thomas Cleary, confused by the petition battle, penned a note to Dorney which ended up in the town board's files: "Father you will please have my name taken off of that saloon list and have it on to yours." By the end of August, the Town of Lake had a new dry district, one that was zealously guarded by foreign-born and native-born, Protestant and Catholic homeowners.[29]

The struggle to control public policy put the town board in an uncomfortable position, but its records show that members tried to be reasonable about enforcement. On hundreds of occasions they allowed halls to remain open beyond midnight for weddings, anniversary celebrations, and benefits. Friends of ailing, destitute Michael O'Meara convinced them that festivities at Schumacher's Hall were "a fitting way to relieve his wants." August Loula got permission to keep Columbia Hall open for a Kralovic Lodge fund-raiser, and both Protestant and Catholic German churches routinely sold beer at their bazaars. The board quietly persuaded two legal saloons to relocate at greater distances from St. Augustine's Church when the priest complained that they were "not nurseries of morality and decency." And finally, saloonkeepers who fell behind in quarterly installment payments on their licenses could expect reprimands, not prosecution, if they were obeying all other regulations. The town board could not satisfy everybody, but it could and did minimize offense.[30]

There was less room for compromise in the school board quarrels because candidates either won or lost their elections. Aspirants hoped to gain recognition for the group they represented, build reputations for themselves, and participate in one of the township's growth industries. Although there were six Catholic and five Protestant grammar schools by 1889, most of the soaring school-age population attended public institutions. The number of teachers quadrupled during the decade, and forty-five elected school board members were administering twenty-five elementary and two high schools at the time of annexation. The district school boards had the power to enlarge existing structures, build new schools, let maintenance and construction contracts, and hire, fire, promote, and set salaries of the principals and some two hundred teachers. This part of the job held far greater appeal than the pedagogical responsibilities of the board. When population in a school district exceeded two thousand, the board went from three to six members, and for every ten thousand more people, three more members joined the board. Incumbents guarded their perquisites by obstructing enlargement, and County Superintendent of Schools Albert G. Lane thought one district per township would eliminate the bickering. Town of Lake, however, liked its school board politics so much that it increased the number of districts from two to five during the 1880s.[31]

District No. 6 included New City and Back of the Yards, each of which had a public school in the early 1880s, and it was run by two Irishmen and one German. German parents wanted German language instruction in their school, and they asked the directors to establish a six-member board. Both requests were turned down by a two to one vote. In 1886, when the school district population exceeded five thousand the Germans turned to the county superintendent for help. He ordered the election of a six-member board in April, 1887. The six winners mirrored the voting strength of the Irish and the Germans in School District No. 6—James J. O'Toole, Richard Bergen, Edward Ring, Anton Koehler, Phillip Pfiel, and Jacob Hansen. When Frank Bischoff won election the following year, the board hired a German language teacher. This prompted John Quinn, Back of the Yard's self-appointed poet laureate, to start his own class in Gaelic.[32]

An 1883 school census found thirty thousand people in the huge District No. 2, making it one of the largest in the state and a certain candidate for division. Residents of northwestern Hyde Park feared a Fifty-fifth Street boundary which would put them at the mercy of the Irish nationalists elected from the Stockyards neighborhood. Moreover, an 1883 law requiring all children in Illinois to attend school at least twelve weeks out of the year could force their new Springer school to accommodate disruptive "street urchins" from the Northeast Corners. So the Hyde Park territory asked for a "divorce" from District No. 2. Parents in the Northeast Corners preferred to have their children cross State Street to reach the spacious new Springer school than walk west across the dangerous railroad tracks to attend the crowded Stockyards schools. Their views were ignored, and the county superintendent liberated the Hyde Park strip. That did not end the tumult because District No. 2 still embraced the north end of town and Englewood. When the latter's Dr. Alfred H. Champlin was ousted from the presidency of the board, Englewood voters circulated petitions asking for their own school district. The north end majority, they charged, was shortchanging Englewood on new schools, putting "the good of their friends" ahead of their duty as "public servants," and dragging their feet on a census which would enlarge the board. As pressure mounted, the board grudgingly agreed to add three new members. In spite of this, 1200 of the eligible 1439 voters in Englewood signed separation petitions, and Superintendent Lane created Englewood School District No. 10.[33]

Englewood used its independence to fashion a school district worthy of Cook County Normal School and attractive enough to employ its strongest graduates. The district built six new elementary schools, two of them in Normal Park, plus a new high school and turned the former high school into yet another grammar school. This kept Englewood schools at half the size of those in the Stockyards neighborhood. Approximately two-thirds of the teachers were "Americans," the remainder Irish or German. Until 1889, when the first Swede was elected to the board, all members were native-born Protestants. Catholics ran for school board seats but none were elected. Yet the Englewood board appointed a German principal to the new Kershaw school at Halsted and Sixty-second, and it employed three female principals. In 1886 Dr, Champlin joined Dr. Francis Parker of the Normal School and Reverend Florence Kollock in establishing a Kindergarten Association. This group soon persuaded the Englewood school board to open Town of Lake's first public kindergartens. Dr. Champlin brought further recognition to Englewood by winning election to the Cook County Board of Education and serving as the president of that body. Englewood had no regrets about cutting out of District No. 2.[34]

That district, the north end of town, had to compensate for loss of the Springer school and the township high school at the same time that enrollments were rising. A crash construction program, costing about $100,000 per year, produced four elementary schools and a Town of Lake High School on Forty-third Street midway between State and Halsted. William Fallon, Michael McInerney, and "Buck" McCarthy wielded greater influence on the board than did livestock dealer Eneas A. Wood or Rudolph Biester of the Car-Shops. The Irish triumvirate controlled the Standing Committee on Teachers as well as the committees dealing with finance, buildings, supplies, and janitors. All of the eleven principals were Irish, as were two-thirds of the one-hundred-odd teachers. One principal, John McCarthy, was an active nationalist who often invited Father Dorney to speak at public school commencements. There were wage discrepancies as well. Elementary teachers, all of them female in District No. 2, earned from $40 to $65 per month; Englewood paid $60 to $75. Ten male principals in District No. 2 averaged $180, while Englewood principals got only $125. Kate Kellogg was the highest paid Englewood principal at $160 per month. John McCarthy drew $200, the top figure for elementary principals in District No. 2; the lowest compensation, $80 per month, went to the lone female principal in District No. 2. Both districts paid the high school principals $300 per month.[35]

At $70 to $85 per month the male janitors in District No. 2 fared better than the female teachers. By 1886 Irishmen held all the school janitor positions with the exception of two jobs in the Car-Shops neighborhood. That summer the school board sacked the offending Swedish and German janitors, and the action caused such a furor that the board scheduled a public hearing. Swedes explained that their man had fallen ill, they had raised money to send him back to his homeland to recuperate, and meanwhile his wife and children performed his duties. He had returned to Town of Lake in good health, only to find that the Irish had stolen his job. Friends of Adam Sturkle, the longtime janitor at the Pullman school, complained that "the Germans in the Town had very little, if any, representation in any branch of the Town affairs, and now Sturkle has been slaughtered." Michael McInerney denied that the dismissals had anything to do with national origin. Sturkle, he said, was reputedly worth $30,000 and did not need the job. The Germans retorted that he did need the job, he had been a model janitor, and no charges ever had been or ever could be made against him. Sturkle was a "faithful servant of the Board." When the acrimonious debate finally ended, board members voted to sustain the firings and to appoint two new Irish janitors.[36]

The clean sweep philosophy eventually backfired. Saloonkeeper John Nugent, angry about the $1000 license fee, decided to go public in 1889 with a school board slate of liquor dealers and a campaign managed by Edward Condon, former Knights of Labor leader. McInerney and McCarthy had the gall to accuse Nugent and Condon of lusting after patronage. Name-calling led to fistfighting, and Goodall abandoned his usual neutrality to create a last-minute slate of "respectables"—Thomas Gahan, Dr. Charles P. Caldwell, and Armour foreman John Kenny. These men won and promptly elected the long-suffering Protestant Eneas A. Wood president of District No. 2. Few things were predictable in Town of Lake group conflicts.[37]

On the heels of a job and a place to live came the need for social ties with people who shared similar values, beliefs, and interests. Voluntary associations provided this "human surround."[38] They offered fellowship, opportunities for service and leadership, and contacts with like-minded residents of the township. Church affiliation was attractive because the religious organizations sponsored so many social activities. Ethnic bonding reinforced immigrant minorities and helped them measure their achievements against those of other groups, including "the Americans." The challenge of influencing township drinking policies and controlling local school boards heightened group consciousness and inevitably led to clashes. The stakes were high because contestants cared about group prestige and the future of their community. The same type of jousting accompanied the wild scramble for township improvements in the 1880s.

NOTES

1. For discussions of the importance of these social groups, see Don Harrison Doyle, *The Social Order of a Frontier Community: Jacksonville, Illinois, 1825–70* (Urbana, Ill., 1978), 156–93; Olivier J. Zunz, *The*

Changing Face of Inequality: Urbanization, Industrial Development, and Immigrants in Detroit, 1880–1920 (Chicago, 1982), 177–95; John Bodnar, *Immigration and Industrialization: Ethnicity in an American Mill Town, 1870–1940* (Pittsburgh, 1977), 3–21; Daniel J. Walkowitz, *Worker City, Company Town: Iron and Cotton-Worker Protest in Troy and Cohoes, New York, 1855–84* (Urbana, Ill., 1978), 101–42; and Thomas Bender, *Community and Social Change in America* (New Brunswick, N.J., 1978), 61–120.

2. Herbert G. Gutman, *Work, Culture, and Society in Industrializing America: Essays in American Working-Class and Social History* (New York, 1977), 44–45; *The Town of Lake Directory, 1889* (Chicago, 1889), 41–46; Morris Janowitz, *The Community Press in an Urban Setting* (Glencoe, Ill., 1952), 14, 21–26, 73, 154.

3. *Sun,* Sept. 7, 1889; *Town of Lake Directory, 1889,* 44–46.

4. Doyle, *Frontier Community,* 157. T. Scott Miyakawa found that the churches "were at once centers of religious and social life, advocates of public order, and schools for group and community leadership" (*Protestants and Pioneers: Individualism and Conformity on the American Frontier* [Chicago, 1964], 3). Detroit "Poles focused their energy on the church," says Zunz (*Changing Face of Inequality,* 188). "Most important in maintaining a separate Irish identity was their Catholicism," writes Michael F. Funchion. "Clearly, the local parish, with its school and various societies, was the most important institution in Irish Chicago" ("Irish Chicago: Church, Homeland, Politics, and Class—The Shaping of an Ethnic Group, 1870–1900," in Peter d'A. Jones and Melvin G. Holli, eds., *Ethnic Chicago* [Grand Rapids, Mich., 1981], 11, 16). See also, Walkowitz, *Worker City, Company Town,* 121–28; Stuart Blumin, "Church and Community: A Case Study of Lay Leadership in Nineteenth Century America," *New York History,* 56 (1975), 393–408.

5. St. Augustine's Parish, *Golden Jubilee and Chronological History of St. Augustine's Parish* (Chicago, 1936), 31, 55, 57; Marion A. Habig, *The Franciscans at St. Augustine's and in Chicagoland* (Chicago, 1961), 54–57; *Town of Lake Directory, 1889,* 45–46; *Sun,* Dec. 30, 1887; Jan. 30, 1888.

6. Alfred T. Andreas, *History of Cook County, Illinois* (Chicago, 1884), 691; *Trib.,* Dec. 7, 1883; Feb. 5, 6, Mar. 18, 1888; *Sun,* May 4, 25, 1887; July 20, 27, Nov. 16, Dec. 23, 1889; Mar. 31, 1890.

7. *Town of Lake Directory, 1889,* 44–45; Andreas, *Cook County,* 658–61, 692–94.

8. *Sun,* Aug. 10, 1889; *Town of Lake Directory, 1889,* 41–46; *Sun,* Sept. 4, 1886; Feb. 12, June 1, Aug. 9, 1889; *Drovers Journal,* Oct. 20, 1888; Feb. 23, 1889.

9. Kathleen Neils Conzen, "Immigrants, Immigrant Neighborhoods, and Ethnic Identity: Historical Issues," *Journal of American History,* 66 (Dec., 1979), 603–15; Bodnar, *Immigration and Industrialization,* chap. 6; Josef J. Barton, *Peasants and Strangers: Italians, Rumanians and Slovaks in an American City, 1890–1950* (Cambridge, Mass., 1975), chap. 4.

10. *Labor Enquirer,* Mar. 2, Apr. 9, 1887.

11. *Trib.,* Aug. 16, 1889; Thomas N. Brown, *Irish-American Nationalism, 1870–1890* (Philadelphia, 1966), 164; Lawrence J. McCaffrey, "A Profile of Irish America," in David Noel Doyle and Owen Dudley Edwards, eds., *America and Ireland, 1776–1976: The American Identity and the Irish Connection* (Westport, Conn., 1980), 87.

12. Thomas N. Brown, *Irish-American Nationalism,* chaps. 4–9; Michael F. Funchion, *Chicago's Irish Nationalists, 1881–1890* (New York, 1976), 26–28, 59–60, 93–96, 120–22.

13. Thomas N. Brown, *Irish-American Nationalism,* xv, xvi, 118–20, 155–64; David Montgomery, "The Irish and the American Labor Movement," in Doyle and Edwards, eds., *America and Ireland,* 216–17; Funchion, *Chicago's Irish Nationalists,* 29–41, 124; Funchion, "Irish Chicago," 16–21; Charles Shanabruch, *Chicago's Catholics: The Evolution of an American Identity* (Notre Dame, Ind., 1981), 41–43.

14. Funchion, *Chicago's Irish Nationalists,* 28, 38–40; Thomas N. Brown, *Irish-American Nationalism,* 155–56; *Trib.,* Mar. 14, Aug. 16, 1881; Aug. 16, 1882; Apr. 24, May 25, Sept. 10, Nov. 8, 26, 1883; Mar. 3, July 19, 1884; Feb. 9, Mar. 18, May 7, 25, June 23, Nov. 28, 1885; *Sun,* Aug. 18, 19, 1886; Feb. 28, 1889; *Drovers Journal,* Aug. 7, 1885; Aug. 10, 19, 21, 1886.

15. [Chicago] *Knights of Labor,* Oct. 30, 1886; *Trib.,* June 13, 1885; Mar. 16, 1914; Thomas N. Brown, *Irish-American Nationalism,* 173–74; Funchion, "Irish Chicago," 24; quoted in Charles Fanning, "Mr. Dooley in Chicago: Finley Peter Dunne as Historian of the Irish in America," in Doyle and Edwards, eds., *America and Ireland,* 162.

16. *Trib.,* May 6, 23, June 2–12, 30, Aug. 16, 17, 1889; *Sun,* Feb. 28, Mar. 4, May 23, June 3, 11, 1889; *Drovers Journal,* Feb. 27, June 15, Aug. 16, 1889; Thomas N. Brown, *Irish-American Nationalism,* 174–76; Funchion, *Chicago's Irish Nationalists,* 98–114. For contemporary accounts, see Henry M. Hunt, *The Crime of the Century or the Assassination of Dr. Patrick Henry Cronin* (Chicago, 1889) and John T. McEnnis, *The Clan-na-Gael and the Murder of Dr. Patrick Henry Cronin* (Chicago, 1889).

17. *Illinois Staats-Zeitung,* May 28, 1889, quoted in *Trib.,* June 1, 1889; *Sun,* Aug. 25, 1885; Jan. 2, 1886; Aug. 14, 31, 1889; *Trib.,* Aug. 11, 1881; Jan. 21, 1883; Aug. 24, 26, Sept. 24, Dec. 25, 1885.

18. *Trib.,* Sept. 25, 1887.

19. *Trib.*, Jan. 9, 1884; *Illinois Staats-Zeitung*, May 11, Aug. 11, Oct. 15, 1888 (CFLPS, Roll 13).

20. Charles Dudley Warner, "Studies of the Great West—III Chicago," *Harper's New Monthly Magazine*, 76 (May, 1888), 876; Chicago City Missionary Society, *Third Annual Report, 1886* (Chicago, 1886), 14; *Svornost*, Aug. 23, 1884 (CFLPS, Roll 6); Feb. 8, 1882; Apr. 2, 1884 (CFLPS, Roll 2); *Trib.*, Jan. 18, June 20, 22, 1885; Mar. 7, Oct. 17, 1886; Jan. 24, 1888; Eugene Ray McCarthy, "The Bohemians in Chicago and Their Benevolent Societies, 1875–1946" (M. A. thesis, University of Chicago, 1950), 26–66; Shanabruch, *Chicago's Catholics*, 47–49.

21. *Trib.*, Mar. 14, 1886; Sept. 5, 1888; June 12, 1892; Victor Greene, *For God and Country: The Rise of Polish and Lithuanian Ethnic Consciousness in America, 1860—1910* (Madison, Wis., 1975), 85–90; Edward R. Kantowicz, *Polish-American Politics in Chicago, 1888–1940* (Chicago, 1975), 12–53; Dominic A. Pacyga, "Packingtown Polonia: The Polish Worker and the Development of Community in Chicago's Stock Yard District" (unpublished paper, Oct., 1981), 1–6; Shanabruch, *Chicago's Catholics*, 44–47; Joseph John Parot, *Polish Catholics in Chicago, 1850–1920: A Religious History* (DeKalb, Ill., 1981), chap. 4.

22. *Sun*, Aug. 27, 1885; *Trib.*, Mar. 14, 1886; July 30, 1888.

23. Quoted in Bodnar, *Immigration and Industrialization*, 103; Vivien M. Palmer, "History of New City," Doc. 13, interview with Reverend Denis Thiele (Mary McDowell Papers, Chicago Historical Society); St. Joseph's Parish Report, 1889 (St. Mary of the Lake Seminary, Mundelein, Ill.).

24. Bessie Louise Pierce, *A History of Chicago*, vol. 3, *The Rise of a Modern City, 1871–1893* (New York, 1957), 48–50; St. Clair Drake and Horace R. Cayton, *Black Metropolis: A Study of Negro Life in a Northern City* (New York, 1945), 47–53; Thomas Lee Philpott, *The Slum and the Ghetto: Neighborhood Deterioration and Middle-Class Reform, Chicago, 1880–1930* (New York, 1978), 115–19; Monroe N. Work, "Negro Real Estate Holders of Chicago" (M. A. thesis, University of Chicago, 1903), 14, 19; *Trib.*, Oct. 31, 1880; Aug. 21, Sept. 4, 1887; "Chicago Colored People," *Trib.*, May 4, 1890.

25. *Eleventh Census, 1890*, vol. 1, "Population," 454–55; City of Chicago, *School Census of the City of Chicago, Taken May, 1890* (Chicago, 1890), 1; Charles Branham, "Black Chicago: Accommodationist Politics before the Great Migration," in Melvin C. Holli and Peter d'A. Jones, eds., *The Ethnic Frontier: Essays in the History of Group Survival in Chicago and the Midwest* (Grand Rapids, Mich., 1977), 214–15; *Trib.*, May 26, 1889.

26. Town of Lake Records, Doc. 1, July 13, 1874; Doc. 61½, July 1, 1881; Doc. 166, Feb. 17, 1882; Doc. 167, June 30, 1882; Doc. 19½, May 28, 1883 (City Hall Archives, Chicago); *Trib.*, Sept. 25, Oct. 2, 1880; Oct.

11, Nov. 15, Dec. 6, 1882; Pierce, *History of Chicago,* 3:455–60; Perry R. Duis, *The Saloon: Public Drinking in Chicago and Boston, 1880–1920* (Urbana, Ill., 1983), 97–99.

27. *Trib.*, Oct. 11, 16, 1882; Mar. 17, May 25, June 3, 1883; Aug. 10, 13, 1885; Jan. 24, 1886; *Sun,* Oct. 23, 1884; Sept. 21, 1886; Dec. 21, 1889; Town of Lake Records, Doc. 170, July 9, 1883; Doc. 868, Dec. 9, 1885; Doc. 591, Sept. 10, 1886; Duis, *Saloon,* 26–27, 99–103; *History of Chicago and Souvenir of the Liquor Interest* (Chicago, 1891), 112–30, 147–48, 201.

28. Town of Lake Records, Doc. 835, May 7, 1889; Doc. 871, Sept. 20, 1887; Doc. 213, Dec. 26, 1888; *Trib.*, Apr. 21, 1887; July 15, Dec. 9, 1888; Sept. 23, 1889; *Sun,* Jan. 28, 1887; Oct. 19, 1889.

29. Town of Lake Records, Doc. 830, July 1, 1886; Doc. 363, July 14, 1886; Doc. 819, Aug. 9, 1886; Doc. 38½, Aug. 25, 1886; *Sun,* June 26, July 12, 1886.

30. Town of Lake Records, Doc. 871, June 11, 1888; Doc. 833, May 22, 1888; Doc. 861, Jan. 8, 1889; Doc. 833, Apr. 5, 1888.

31. *Town of Lake Directory, 1889,* 40–41; Albert G. Lane, Cook County Superintendent of Schools, *Annual Report . . . Year Ending July 1, 1880* (Chicago, 1880), 50–51; *Biennial Report . . . July 1, 1886, to June 30, 1888* (Chicago, 1888), 70–75; *Biennial Report . . . July 1, 1884 to June 30, 1886* (Chicago, 1886), 19–21.

32. Lane, Superintendent of Schools, *Biennial Report . . . 1884–1886,* 20; *Sun,* Aug. 27, 1885; Apr. 17, 18, 1887; *Trib.*, July 25, 1888; Apr. 7, 1889.

33. *Trib.*, Apr. 9, July 9, Aug. 11, Sept. 12, 1883; Apr. 15, May 10, 1884; [Englewood] *Eye,* Mar. 10, 17, Apr. 7, 1883; Mar. 8, 29, Apr. 5, 19, 1884; Hannah B. Clark, *Public Schools of Chicago* (Chicago, 1897), 44–45.

34. *Trib.*, July 3, 16, 1884; July 12, 1886; Aug. 24, 1887; Apr. 7, 1889; *Sun,* Oct. 18, Nov. 2, 1886; Lane, Superintendent of Schools, *Biennial Report . . . 1886–1888,* 74–75.

35. Lane, Superintendent of Schools, *Biennial Report, 1884–1886,* 66; *Biennial Report, 1886–1888,* 68, 70–75; *Town of Lake Directory, 1889,* 40; *Trib.*, July 16, 1884; Feb. 20, Aug. 25, 1885; July 8, 1888; *Sun,* Apr. 9, 1885; Jan. 12, 16, May 13, June 25, 1886; Jan. 5, May 13, 1887; Jan. 12, May 11, 18, June 1, Oct. 19, 1889.

36. *Sun,* June 26, July 20, 1886.

37. *Sun,* Apr. 5, 8, 1889; *Drovers Journal,* Apr. 22, 1889; *Trib.*, Apr. 7, 1889.

38. Bender, *Community and Social Change,* 98.

CHAPTER 17

Providing "City Improvements"

Technological advances in street paving and lighting, sewering, and public transit brought striking changes to many American municipalities in the 1880s. Since the Town of Lake was actually a medium-sized city by the latter part of the decade, its residents naturally expected local government to give them some or all of these urban amenities. As one town official acknowledged in 1886, both old-timers and newcomers now "entertain metropolitan ideas and demand city improvements." The records of the town board document the delivery of macadam street surfaces, electric streetlights, more piped water and a complex sewer system, scavenger service, a larger police force, and full-time firemen. Although never providing these things as quickly as petitioners demanded, local government did modernize the township in the 1880s. It meant hiring a fire marshal, sanitary superintendent, and town engineer, creating many more jobs in the public works, fire, and police departments, and balancing patronage among the various competing groups. Taxpayers were anything but shy about communicating with elected officials. The "Skandinavian [*sic*] Citizens Club," for example, insisted that "any changes in the police, fire and other departments . . . be selected from the same Nationality. . . . We were promised that as many should be employed under the present administration as under the former." The ability of township leaders to meet the expectations of residents is one reason why Town of Lake preferred autonomy to merger with Chicago.[1]

Streets and Railroad Crossings

In view of the township's nearly fivefold population increase in the 1880s and the relentless home construction boom, it is not surprising that new roads and improvements on existing streets had top priority. Park commissioners took care of Garfield and Western boulevards, Cook County contributed small sums to the upkeep of the main north-south arteries, and Hyde Park shared the costs of State Street, but Town of Lake had to spend approximately 10 percent of its revenue on roads. It widened and cindered Halsted, Ashland, and Forty-seventh in the early 1880s, yet traffic was so heavy that the surfaces soon deteriorated. Users and residents then pestered the town board to "fill the worst places in said street with slag and cinders" or complained that "no team can pass this way in safety." In the new subdivisions the town government surveyed and graded dirt roadbeds and dug the drainage ditches; property owners paid for cinder or gravel surfaces through assessments. By the latter half of the decade, the government was so busy opening new roads that maintenance of existing ones suffered. Realtor B. F. Jacobs informed the board in 1887 that Paulina Street was so bad that "parties who wish to build find great difficulty in getting their lumber onto their grounds." A "Bohemian Politican [*sic*] Independent Club of Town Lake" reported "the ditches . . . filled and stopped with stagnated water" in the blocks west of Ashland.[2]

Meantime, the settled areas in the township were clamoring for street lighting and the newest paving which promised redemption from dust and mud. Technological advances in stonecutting enabled engineers to pave with slabs of granite, and macadam surfaces of sand and gravel in a bituminous binder were proving satisfactory in many communities. While both would later give way to asphalt and cement, they were nonetheless a vast improvement over gravel and cinders. Town of Lake contracted with private paving firms whenever a majority of property owners abutting residential streets agreed to the assessment. The timing of street improvements, however, "perplexed" the board. In some neighborhoods there were property owners who said they could not afford the tax or who preferred sewers to macadam streets. Homeowners on Emerald and Winter resisted street improvements because they feared it would attract traffic from Halsted and jeopardize their quiet enclave. The board saw no point in paving streets that would later be dug up for a new or a larger sewer, and if they anticipated a second horsecar track, they waited until it was laid so that the street railway company paid for paving between the two tracks. The scores of petitions made it clear that most residents wanted "speedy relief" immediately, and if the superintendent of public works did not respond, they would retaliate at the polls.[3]

In the spring of 1883 Town of Lake experimented with macadam on one block of Wentworth. Residents of Harvard and Yale then asked to have their streets paved, and by the end of that year the entire length of Wentworth had a macadam surface. This touched off the stampede. Halsted at the Stockyards needed a sturdier surface, and as soon as the horsecar tracks were down, property owners agreed to granite block paving and wide limestone curbs. These new street surfaces intensified demands for better lighting. Between 1881 and 1885 the town installed over five hundred gas street-lights; many of them burned unevenly and some were "as useless as a sign-post." When the packers used their new electric generator to illuminate the north side of Forty-seventh from Halsted to Ashland in 1885, the improvement was so dramatic that the town board contracted with Chicago Arc and Light Power Company to supply electricity to the rest of the township. Electric streetlights quickly replaced gas lamps. Spiraling rates led to a quarrel between the township and the electric company, and in January, 1889, the latter cut off the current. A citizen protest rally forced the town board to back down and pay its overdue bills. Delays in placing streetlights on Garfield Boulevard gave rise to the first improvement associations, the Northern Englewood Improvement Club in 1886 and the Garfield Improvement Club three years later.[4]

The eagerness and impatience which citizens displayed for street paving and lighting did not extend to systematizing street names and numbering buildings. Nonetheless, the public works department prepared a report on this matter in 1883. It recommended continuity with Chicago street names for continuous roads and elimination of duplicate names within the Town of Lake. Then the town board required property owners to find the number of their home or store and post it in plain view. "I find that but *very* few people avail themselves of this provision," complained the town engineer in 1884. "The charge for issuing a certificate is 50¢ and the public would rather *guess* at the correct number from some established house, than pay the fee." The town board finally decided to issue the number free of charge. It could then fine violators $5. Implementing this "improvement" took several years, but it was the necessary first step toward publication of a town directory.[5]

With two hundred miles of railroad track (excluding Section 5) in the township at the opening of the decade and all street crossings at grade level, there were dangers for vehicles and pedestrians. The railroad flagmen were often "superannuated, semi-demented, one-legged, one-eyed, listless, and utterly incompetent," residents informed the town board, and engineers ignored the 1885 ordinance limiting passenger trains to ten miles per hour and freight trains to six miles. Freight trains blocked intersections near the Stockyards for "upwards of an hour," and angry pedestrians sometimes risked their lives climbing through. Electric warning lights and gates installed during the last half of the decade made some intersections safer, but they were not the best answer for the wide stretch of tracks at Stewart and Forty-third. When the town board gave the Chicago and Western Indiana Railway permission to join this complex, it made the railroad build a sewer under Wallace Street and provide "free and easy passage of vehicles" over its tracks at Forty-third. Everyone assumed that the railroad would join with the Pittsburgh, Fort Wayne which, in 1880, promised to build a viaduct over Forty-third. In 1884 a new public school opened on that busy street and concerned parents who inquired about the viaduct discovered that town politicians had surrendered it in return for a longer sewer. The town had, however, shared expenses with the Rock Island and Lake Shore railroads for a viaduct at Sixty-first Street. This Englewood improvement whetted the appetite of people in the north end for an overhead crossing at Forty-third and the Stewart Avenue tracks.[6]

Supervisor Thomas Gahan tried hard to resolve the impasse. In 1885 he asked Samuel Allerton, John B. Sherman, Gustavus Swift, Philip Armour, and Irus Coy to meet with Chicago and Western Indiana officials. They failed to shake the railroad's claim "that by some mysterious, and to outsiders inscrutable legerdemain, it has been relieved from all its obligations." In the fall of 1886, Gahan's successor plus a committee of sixteen packers and stockyards officials negotiated with the six railroads occupying the Stewart Avenue right-of-way. Those talks deadlocked when the Chicago and Western Indiana refused to contribute unless the Pittsburgh, Fort Wayne did, and that railroad insisted that the Town of Lake become a partner in the venture. Finally, in 1888 the Pittsburgh, Fort Wayne surrendered because it wanted permission to double the number of its tracks. The town board granted permission the following year on a firm contractual agreement that the railroad build the viaduct over Forty-third. Having learned the hard way, Town of Lake officials extracted a much better deal from the Santa Fe. That railroad promised to place no more than four tracks across Forty-seventh, to build viaducts upon request, and to post a $100,000 compliance bond.[7]

Water and Sewers

Distributing pure water under sufficient pressure and devising a system of drainage and sewerage required more money and greater technical skill than street paving. Yet piped water, household sewers, and properly drained streets were among the "metropolitan ideas" entertained by nearly all Chicago area townships. Lake View never mastered water distribution and its sewers emptied into the lake endangering the water supply. Despite this, Jefferson begged for Lake View water and offered in return to let the lakefront township's sewerage pass through Jefferson to the North Branch of the Chicago River. Hyde Park developed its own waterworks in 1882, but low pressure and sewage pollution caused serious problems toward the end of the decade. By comparison, Town of Lake fared much better.[8]

It entered the 1880s as joint owner with Hyde Park of a waterworks that, with luck, could pump five million gallons per day. Aware that it soon had to be expanded and distrustful of each other's water use, the two townships decided to end joint ownership in 1881. Lake bought Hyde Park's interest and agreed to sell water for one year while Hyde Park built a new station.

Hyde Park and Englewood had plenty of water in the hot summer of 1881, but there was a "famine" in Section 5 and the residential district to the southwest. Stockyards officials and packers resorted to artesian wells; residents paid $1 a barrel for peddled lake water and grumbled that "water goes where it will pay officials the most." By the time the separation actually took place, Town of Lake had purchased two new pumps and extended the intake pipe, and the packers had financed their own twenty-four-inch water main so their use would not deprive New City and Back of the Yards. The superintendent of the waterworks confidently reported in July, 1882, that the fifteen million gallons per day were "enough to supply bountifully" the township's homeowners, manufacturers, stockyard and packinghouses, and the fire pumps. The town board was so grateful to the packers for their assistance that it reimbursed them with certificates worth $80 per one million gallons. However, winter ice still clogged the inlet pipe and severe wave action sent sand into the pumps and "fish chowder" into the faucets. Englewood engineer Ralph E. Brownell was hired to investigate, and he found that the 1870s pumps were virtually useless, the two new $45,000 Gaskill engines endangered by "gravel, sand, mud, fish etc.," and the engine house in need of repairs and a new water closet. The board extended the intake pipe again and installed strainers to save the pumps.[9]

The next problem was the population buildup in New City and Back of the Yards. It strained the capacity of the supply main and the 1870s four-inch pipes; there were so many requests for six-inch lines that the town board had to let some homeowners and developers hire private contractors. In the summer of 1886, when some residents had trouble getting water even at night, they staged a protest at Ashland and Forty-third. Equipped with a keg of beer, they shut off the valve to the packinghouse district and settled down to await the police. The demonstrators refused to disband until the officers promised to convey to the town board their demand for a separate residential supply main. Board members bought water from Hyde Park that summer, but another "water famine" two years later forced them to build a twenty-four-inch main for New City and Back of the Yards. The contract went to Thomas Gahan and Thomas Byrne, who employed four hundred laborers at eight hours per day and completed the job in three months. There was no "feast" of water in the north end of town or southwest of Section 5, due to the many small pipes that needed replacing, but the water department did end the "famine."[10]

Household water exacerbated the problem of household waste disposal, as Town of Lake and all other municipalities discovered. New sinks, bathtubs, and water closets drained into basement or outdoor privy vaults and cesspools. Some people emptied buckets in the street ditches. Piped water without household sewers caused overflowing privies and cesspools, contaminated ground water, and less effective surface drainage. With the exception of the eight-block sewer line in the Stockyards neighborhood, Town of Lake's sewers were for storm water only. The best solution was main sewers capable of carrying surface water and industrial and household wastes, such as Chicago and Hyde Park were building. Engineering, financing, and constructing these drains took time and money. Meanwhile impatient residents lectured the town board that sewers were "a necessity not only for the improvement and progress of our neighborhood but also for the preservation of our health."[11]

The township's first two combined sewers were north-south lines which emptied into Hyde Park's massive Forty-first Street drain. Property owners on Wentworth agreed to pay for a brick sewer, four feet in diameter, that would extend from Thirty-ninth to Sixty-third, and construction started in the spring of 1880. The second sewer, under Wallace Street, was financed by the Chicago and Western Indiana Railway Company in return for the right to lay its tracks in Town of Lake. During 1882–83 sewer contractors were at work on Center Avenue; packers and the Stockyard company paid for the segment between Thirty-ninth and Forty-seventh, which was five feet in diameter. Property owners footed the bill for a smaller line that extended to Garfield Boulevard. Anticipating future needs of the packinghouse district and the residential area to the southwest, the town board approved an Ashland Avenue sewer that would be five feet in diameter at Garfield Boulevard and six feet across at the northern outlet, the South Fork of the Chicago River's South Branch. Objections to the necessarily heavy assessments delayed construction from 1884 until 1887. But the Wentworth, Wallace, and Center Avenue projects enabled eager property owners to secure lateral lines on their streets and household connections to those sewers. In March of 1886 the town engineer proudly announced that 2,555 dwellings had tied into the township's thirty-one miles of sewers. This, incidentally, put Town of Lake ahead of Hyde Park.[12]

Township officials, meantime, had commissioned the engineering firm of Benezette Williams and Ralph E. Brownell to prepare a comprehensive long-range drainage and sewerage plan. (Williams, a former Chicago assistant city engineer, had designed the water and sewerage system for Pullman.) Their 1885 report recomended relatively inexpensive storm water drains for swampy areas in the western and southwestern parts of the township. These would discharge by gravity into the Illinois and Michigan Canal and Lake Calumet. The engineers approved the Ashland Avenue combined sewer plan and said it should be built as quickly as possible. "The lateral sewers that will follow the construction of this important outlet will, no doubt, give a new impetus to New City," making it "second to no section in the Town." Their recommendation for a massive sewer under Halsted Street from Thirty-ninth to Sixty-ninth did not come as a surprise.

Englewood residents were pressing for this improvement, and people in the Stockyards neighborhood were complaining about "overflows" and "backwater in the cellars." The only remedy was a huge combined sewer emptying into the Stockyards Canal. And finally, to prevent overloading that ditch and the South Fork, Williams and Brownell recommended a conduit "from the west end of the Stock Yards slip to the [Illinois and Michigan] Canal, with pumping works at the Canal."[13]

Since implementation of this plan would adversely affect the South Fork and South Branch, Town of Lake delayed endorsement until Chicago resolved its drainage dilemma. The new Bridgeport pumps helped, but certainly did not cure, the sluggish river or its "rotten" Fifth Ward fork. The Chicago city engineer insisted that "the South Fork is polluted entirely by the Stock-Yards. No city sewers run into it." John B. Sherman and the packers were willing to shoulder part of the cost of a pumping station at Thirth-ninth and the South Fork but felt that the Town of Lake should also contribute because its sewage took the same route to the South Branch. Torrential rains in August, 1885, sent the contents of the fork and the branch surging into Lake Michigan; city officials found an unmistakable stain of "raw, unoxidized sewage" and filth at the water crib. Angrily denouncing Chicago's "sanitary history of . . . makeshifts and expedients," the Citizens' Association demanded that "all sewerage whatsoever" be diverted from the lake. Since Evanston, Lake View, Chicago southeast of State Street, and Hyde Park sewered into the Lake at all times, the only way to accomplish this was to redesign the entire Chicago area drainage. The Citizens' Association Main Drainage and Water Supply Committee urged reconsideration of a proposal it had made in 1880: a new drainage channel from Bridgeport to Joliet to convey the wastes of Chicago and adjoining townships "for all time to come." This "New River" or "independent cut" would cost approximately $12 million, but the expense would be shared by everyone in the huge drainage district.[14]

At the urging of Mayor Harrison, Dr. Rauch, Dr. DeWolf, the Citizens' Association, and newspaper editors, the city council agreed in January, 1886, to appoint a commission to determine the route and estimate the cost of a new sanitary channel. A well-known Philadelphia sanitary engineer, Rudolph Hering, headed the commission and one of his assistants was Benezette Williams. The council accepted the preliminary report of these experts one year later, and Town of Lake, assured that a final solution to metropolitan drainage was in sight, began planning the Halsted Street main sewer. Chicago needed permission, however, from the state legislature to create a 185-square-mile sanitary district with taxing powers. The legislature made its own study of the proposed sewage waterway and altered it to accommodate steamboats before passing the Sanitary District Enabling Act in May, 1889. Voters within the drainage district then had to register their approval or disapproval. In November, 1889, they cast 242 votes against and 70,958 in favor of the Chicago Sanitary and Ship Canal. The "New River" was not finished until 1900, but realization that a channel ten times the size of the Illinois and Michigan Canal was actually underway improved the city's battered sanitary reputation.[15]

Town of Lake, meanwhile, had levied assessments for its badly needed Ashland Avenue sewer. Ditches on either side of Ashland were filthy, odorous, and cleansed only by spring thaws and heavy rains; the public works department warned that residents were "without any drainage whatever for their sewage." Yet a disgruntled coterie of landowners went to court to contest the sewer tax. When they lost, the town board was finally able to let the contract in 1887. It was then besieged by eager residents demanding the right to install lateral and household lines immediately. Forty-seventh Street property owners wanted their sewer before the Chicago Street Railway Company laid a second track. Morris and Swift sought permission to connect new buildings at the western edge of Packingtown, and they assured the board they would use "the best hard sewer brick and hydraulic cement." Developer S. E. Gross wanted to install sewers by private contract "as the season is already late." In the frantic scramble, contractors put fifteen-inch mains in blocks assessed for twenty-four inch lines, and vice versa. Homeowners on Dreyer, aware that small mains quickly became overloaded, petitioned for a thirty-inch brick sewer "or nothing at all."[16]

People on Halsted were as eager as those on Ashland for their main sewer, and the delay worried them. Those south of Forty-seventh had been denied permision to hook into the overloaded existing line. Since the Halsted sewer would be the township's largest and most expensive, board members were wary about legal protests and the added cost of a conduit and pumping station to save the Stockyards Canal. However, Chicago's progress toward the "New River" allowed Town of Lake to endorse the Williams-Brownell report officially and start planning the Halsted sewer in January, 1888. It would originate at Sixty-ninth Street with a five-foot diameter and terminate at Thirty-ninth with a seven-foot opening, large enough for a very tall man walking erect, marveled a reporter. Creating a Town of Lake drainage and sewerage district and assessing all who would benefit from either sewers or surface drainage consumed another year. But construction was underway when the township joined the city, and completion of the Halsted Street project gave Lake an impressive seventy miles of sewers.[17]

The frenzied demand for water and sewers created golden opportunities for local contractors, as township records reveal. Ambitious men acquired skills as employes of a contractor, then gained experience on small jobs of their own, and worked up to the large projects which required bonding.

Most of the street sewers and all north-south trunkline contracts came from the town board, and political connections helped. Upon completion of a term of service, officeholders sometimes turned to water and sewer contracting; and those who had established reputations as reliable contractors sometimes counted upon satisfied customers and employes to vote them into office. In the early 1880s, the leading town contractors were the Kelly brothers, Thomas, John, and Philip. Thomas Gahan worked with them for a brief time in 1883 and mastered the essentials. During his supervisorship, Gahan let contracts to the Kellys and to Thomas Byrne, a former packinghouse employe who was edging into street paving and water and sewer contracting. Byrne's other assets were membership on the New City-Back of the Yards school board, participation in Irish nationalist affairs, and political loyalty to Gahan. When Gahan left office, he and Byrne formed a partnership which landed lucrative town contracts in the latter third of the decade. Although contractors and politicians fought among themselves, they agreed that town contracts must go to town contractors. Thus an 1886 ordinance banned Chicago sewer builders from working in the Town of Lake, and an 1889 regulation restricted bidding to contractors whose headquarters were in the township.[18]

The Kellys, Byrne, and Gahan were reliable, often designated the "lowest *responsible* bidder" in town memos. Officials did meet irresponsible contractors. For example, residents of Normal Parkway objected to the sewer and water contractors sent to them. "On account of an excess of scientific Engineering," they wrote, "the water pipe main was put in too high which brings the water pipe directly opposite the outlets of the sewer pipe and causes . . . a back pressure and at times makes all filth and sewer gas flow back into the Basements of the houses." Bonding requirements protected the town board from such incompetence, but angered many contractors. Michael Fitzsimons let officials know that "remarkes in the board meeting and outside the board" had "ingered me virry much. . . . I am froze out." Gahan's successor rejected bids from the Kellys and "the two Toms" on the $80,000 Ashland Avenue sewer job, but later rued the selection of William O'Brien. He substituted a cheap grade of brick and had to redo two-thirds of the sewer. The contractor collected $8,315 in "extras" but neglected to pay the manhole cover subcontractor. Fourteen months after the sewer went into use, the outlet arch at the South Fork collapsed.[19]

Health and Safety

Township residents expected their local government to stay abreast of the promising public health movement and to guard their safety with well-trained, well-equipped fire and policemen. The improvements in Chicago's health, fire, and police departments provided models for the Town of Lake. Discovery of the bacterial origin of many diseases revolutionized the concept and practice of public health in the 1880s. Scientists still could not explain how disease spread, but their advocacy of municipal cleanliness and many other reforms captured attention. Dr. John Rauch and the Illinois State Board of Health attacked sanitary nuisances, and promoted stricter medical school standards and licensing of physicians, new controls on epidemic diseases, and collection of vital statistics. Dr. DeWolf and the Chicago Department of Health cooperated with these reforms and instituted others. They began making sanitary inspections of dwellings and places of employment and secured an antismoke ordinance. Refuse collection and disposal took on new importance since garbage and manure nurtured flies, mosquitoes, and sparrows, and these creatures might be carriers of bacteria. Dr. DeWolf inherited the costly, inefficient scavenger system whereby aldermen appointed the scavengers; he replaced it with a contract system which gave him control over the performance of the scavengers. Moreover, DeWolf was in the vanguard of municipal sanitarians experimenting with "garbage crematories" until Chicago's model plant incinerated itself in 1889.[20]

By the end of the decade the Chicago Department of Health had approximately fifty sanitary police and inspectors plus two smoke watchers. Some of DeWolf's sleuths were at the Stockyards, and he reacted angrily to the charges that diseased animals went to the packinghouses. Three of his agents checked livestock alongside two state inspectors, the Humane Society agent, and a state veterinary surgeon; he thought it unlikely that "any large meat supply in the world is more carefully inspected and supervised than that from the stock yards of Chicago." The health commissioner could do little except collect statistics when cholera and typhoid increased sharply after the 1885 flooding. But during his twelve years in office, there was an encouraging decline in the death rate. In 1877 it had been 26 deaths per 1,000 people; in 1889 it was 19. The one disappointment was the increase in Chicago's typhoid fever mortality rate.[21]

Determined to keep pace with the city sanitarians, Town of Lake established a health department which usually was headed by local physicians. The town board in 1879 authorized the position of "sanitary superintendent" and the appointment of "health policemen" charged with condemning diseased livestock. Under the leadership of Dr. Alphonso L. Cory the department began collecting vital statistics, inspecting factories, and enforcing alley, privy, and water closet regulations. The sanitary superintendent had the assistance of regular policemen in 1880 and two full-time inspectors the following year. Dr. Cory believed that the extension of Chicago's "jurisdiction in nuisances for one mile outside her limits" was "unfortunate," but his tiny staff could not cover Section 5 and he did not want to "clash" with Commissioner DeWolf. Thus the township sanitary police watched the small packinghouses east of Halsted and stood ready to assist city agents if needed, an arrangement continued by his successors.[22]

Town of Lake entered the decade with the requirement that residents take care of their own trash, garbage, and waste material. The town government licensed teamsters, but it was up to homeowners, storekeepers, and manufacturers to make their own arrangements with the teamsters. There were many problems with this system. Scavengers refused to enter alleys clogged with snow or spongy with mud and manure; some people dumped their own wastes in cabbage fields, vacant lots, or street ditches. The town's first sanitary inspection in May, 1881, resulted in five hundred notices to clean up premises. Festering privy vaults were the most common violation, so the health superintendent hired a scavenger to clean the vaults and deliver the contents to farmers who wanted it as fertilizer. Cory's successor, Dr. Charles P. Caldwell, was a Harvard Medical College graduate, resident of the Stockyards neighborhood, and public health ally of DeWolf and Rauch. Alarmed by the increase in disease after the 1885 rains and by the deteriorating condition of alleys in the Northeast Corners, Caldwell recommended that the town provide scavenger service every summer. The five teams that scoured the town in August and September made such a difference that the health superintendent pressed for year-round garbage collection at public expense. He did not get it, but the spring cleanup in 1887 was so costly that the town board finally relented and agreed to provide regular scavenger service.[23]

Township sanitary superintendents also dealt with public health issues. Officials cracked down on the few recalcitrants who refused to hook into available sewer lines, and, after a small child drowned in an uncovered privy, they paid close attention to the filling of abandoned vaults. The department was less successful in remedying the smoke and soot nuisance in the Northeast Corners. They could not patrol all the railroads or make factory owners install smoke abatement equipment. Housewives near Stewart Avenue were "an afflicted community," they told the town board in 1887, for "we have to wait some times a week or more for favorable winds to hang out clothes so that they won't be covered with cinders and smoke . . . it is not alone that it covers everything around your house with a black dirt coating." Local health officials were more successful in carrying out Rauch's orders concerning smallpox vaccinations for school children and quarantine of people with infectious diseases. A smallpox hospital south of Englewood operated until mid-decade, when encroaching homeowners complained that the "Pest House" tended "to impair the value of said lots and prevent the increase of population." Town of Lake then arranged with Dr. DeWolf to place its patients in Chicago's facility at the cost of $1 per day.[24]

The township's three medical superintendents reflected the prevailing uncertainty about how people contracted dysentery, cholera, tuberculosis, scarlet fever, typhoid, and pneumonia. Dr. Cory blamed "upward currents of ground air carrying . . . these disease germs." Dr. Caldwell and his successor leaned toward "bad house drainage and street sewage." They agreed that excessive rain "intensifies and spreads" disease, while gentle showers absorb "imperfections" in the air. Moreover, the distinctive Stockyards odor was "not deleterious to health." Declining mortality rates proved that. Diphtheria, scarlet fever, and typhoid were the major killers in 1885 and 1886; they carried off three of Thomas Gahan's children. A reduction in the first two of these diseases plus fewer railroad accidents helped bring the death rate from 19 per 1,000 in 1882 down to 16 per 1,000 in 1889. Behind these statistics, of course, were Town of Lake's sanitary improvements, especially sewers and scavenger service.[25]

The township and Cook County shared responsibility for the indigent and "sick poor" in the 1880s. The county maintained a poorhouse, hospital, and insane asylum, and it helped with outdoor relief and medical care for individuals certified as eligible by city and suburban health departments. Church societies and fraternal and benevolent organizations aided many more people than did the public program, which was a last resort. During 1882–83, the Town of Lake health department spent about $3,000 for supplies, medicine and vaccine, funerals and burials, and transportation of the poor to Cook County Hospital; and Dr. Caldwell saw 166 indigent patients. These welfare activities caused nary a ripple. In April, 1886, however, layman George Chatfield became commissioner of health, and he hired Michael J. Butler, Knights of Labor organizer, as a sanitary inspector. During June, Butler authorized $850 in relief supplies and services, approximately twice the normal monthly expenditure. His authorizations increased in the fall and averaged $5,000 per month in the first quarter of 1887. Butler swore that the 695 families on relief were packinghouse blacklist victims and that he was merely fulfilling his obligation to see that no deserving family in the Town of Lake lacked food or fuel. Chatfield, Butler, and welfare expenses helped defeat the incumbents in April, 1887; their successors fired Butler, placed the health department under the jurisdiction of the police department, and appointed Dr. J. H. Eskridge the chief health official.[26]

The tremendous population increase and residential expansion during the 1880s made larger fire and police forces inevitable. But Town of Lake professionalized as well as expanded these services. The first "modern" fire station was built in 1881 at the southern edge of the Stockyards to house the steam Liberty Engine. Anticipating the purchase of similar machines, the town board voted to establish a full-time, paid fire department, and on May 1, 1882, a marshal and eighteen trained fire fighters officially took over from the volunteers. The marshal and two-thirds of the men were native-born; three Irish immigrants, two Canadians, and one Swede completed the roster. Eight men served the Stockyards firehouse, while the others went to the hose houses at the Northeast Corners, the Car-Shops, and Englewood. A watchman atop the Stockyards water tower had telephone connections to the station and hose houses as well as to the Transit House stables, where one recalcitrant volunteer brigade was holed up. These "Minute Men" came from the Stockyards neighborhood, refused to don uniforms or obey the marshal, but nonetheless were called Company No. 1 and charged with protecting their own turf.[27]

Frank T. Sweenie (also Swenie), the town's third fire marshal, shaped the department. Born in Scotland of Irish parents, Frank and Denis Sweenie were Chicago volunteer fire fighters who turned professional in 1859; twenty years later Denis became Chicago's fire marshal. When Frank accepted the Town of Lake job in 1883 and moved his large family to the Stockyards neighborhood, he took an active part in St. Gabriel's parish affairs and soon won over the "Minute Men." Then he purchased a Silsby steam engine, more powerful than the Liberty and superior to any Chicago steamer, christened it "Town of Lake, No. 1," and placed it in Company No. 1's new station at Forty-third and Wallace. Next he built proper fire stations at the Car-Shops and in New City-Back of the Yards and bought steamers for them as well as for Englewood. By 1888 Sweenie had increased the force to sixty-four men whose salaries ranged from $840 to $1,200. He earned $1,800. While responding to an alarm in June of that year, he was accidentally pitched from the fire wagon, suffered head injuries, and six months later ended his own life. Stunned firemen and town officials rallied around George Byrne, a charter member of the force, and he carried on his former boss's expansion program. Thus the department at the time of annexation consisted of eighty-five firemen, seven steam engines, three trucks, two hose cars, and forty horses—a commendable seven-year achievement.[28] (See Fig. 14.)

The police department, like the fire department, changed in size and complexity. Its twenty-four-man force in 1880 grew to eighty-two by 1889, and expenditures rose from $20,000 to $50,000. The police captain earned as much as the fire marshal; lieutenants and sergeants received about $1,200 and patrolmen $900. But there the similarity ends. The firemen were heroic; the policemen roused strong feelings when they restrained strikers, charged people with disorderly conduct, and either enforced or failed to enforce saloon ordinances. Mr. Dooley noted that "whin a fireman dies th' whole city mourns an' whin a polisman dies all annywan says is:

'Who's th' first illigible on th' list?' How is it? . . . I think th' reason is we're bumpin' too much into th' polis. . . . He mixes in with th' populace an' familyarity breeds contempt." None of the police chiefs—Thomas Gahan, John William Sweeney, Michael Markey, and S. A. Danforth—commanded the respect or admiration that residents felt for Fire Marshal Sweenie.[29]

In 1882, the year the fire department was created, the town board endorsed Gahan's "Rules and Regulations Governing the Police Department." Members of the force had to be at least 5′8″ and twenty years of age; they could not hold a second job and were subject to dismissal if they drank or "loitered" while on duty or connived with anyone to break the law; they had to display their star when on duty and give their name and number if asked. They must swear that they had not "Paid or promised to pay Anything to secure . . . appointment on the Police Force." While they could use "sufficient firmness" to perform their tasks, they had to "refrain from harsh, violent, coarse, profane or insolent Language." They enforced all state laws governing criminal conduct and township ordinances concerning robbery, burglary, drunkenness, and disorderly behavior. Moreover, town officials expected them to report bridges, streets, and alleys that needed attention and to keep an eye on houses of ill repute and those who entered. They enforced state and township liquor license and saloon laws. They were supposed to turn up at fires and assist if necessary, and, for a time, they doubled as sanitary inspectors.[30]

Numerous petitions to the town board make it clear that credentials other than those set forth in Gahan's "Rules and Regulations" carried weight in the selection of policemen. Thomas Tobin's application had this note from his sponsor on the bottom: "Mr. Tobin was secretary of the People's Club. . . . We had 50 working members all of whome took an active part in the campagne from the very first until the close on election day." Patrick Touhey personally informed the board that his political services qualified him for "a situation on the Police Force or anney other situation which your Honerable Board may think fit." Ethnic groups also applied pressure. A dozen Poles plus a handful of Germans and Bohemians sought the appointment of Paul Sulaski: "he speaks beside his Mother languishe, the english language pretty fairly and is also able to help himself along in the german languishe. . . . The reason we do recommand is this, that bak at the Yards . . . a population is growing up rapidly, commonly known under the 'polish settlement.' we therefore think it as a success of the administration of our Town if [you] would grant this our prayer." Sulaski did become the first Polish policeman in 1887. Two years later, upon the recommendation of Dr. Champlin and an Englewood school superintendent, Enos Bond, a black, joined the force.[31]

Requests for special policemen whose salaries were paid by private employers needed approval by the town board and the police chief. Permission was granted to businessmen who wanted a guard at busy commercial intersections and to developers who hired night watchmen for construction sites. Englewood had a special patrolman on the high school grounds; residents of the Northeast Corners paid 25¢ per dwelling for a night patrolman to deal with the Canaryville toughs. Managers of the railroads, packinghouses, and Stockyards hired by far the largest number of special policemen, most of them assigned to guard duties. The town board and chief Michael Markey readily granted the packers' requests for special patrolmen in 1886 and the early months of 1887. As a result, noted Markey, the strikes did not "cost the tax payers one dollar, the railroads and packers paying for any special protection that they desired to throw around their property." Since most of these guards lived in the Town of Lake and were often known to the policemen, there was little friction. When some packers tried to hire Pinkertons as Town of Lake special policemen, Markey and the board said no.[32]

Between 1882 and 1889 the number of arrests doubled, reaching thirty-six hundred during the township's final year. Throughout the decade, drunkenness, disorderly conduct, and resisting a policeman accounted for two-thirds of the apprehensions. The total number of burglary, robbery, assault, and manslaughter charges just about equaled the number of saloonkeepers charged with licensing violations. Four elected justices of the peace and one police magistrate heard the cases involving licensing, drunk and disorderly behavior, and resisting arrest. They imposed fines and court costs and were supposed to turn that money over to the town treasurer, who was also the supervisor. In practice, the justices and magistrate often kept court costs in lieu of pay for their time on the bench. The clustering of saloons on Halsted and Ashland and the heavy traffic to and from the Stockyards and packinghouses meant that most of the liquor-related cases originated in the jurisdiction of the police magistrate's court at the Town Hall. From 1879 until 1884, lawyer J. B. Thomas presided over a scrupulously honest magistrate's court. He was succeeded by Michael J. Tearney, a former justice of the peace in Brighton and a well-known Irish nationalist. His ethnic bias was obvious. In 1885, Irish youths pelted Joseph Schwartz with snowballs and he returned one which hit the son of police chief John William Sweeney. The chief himself appeared at Schwartz's door and marched him to Tearney's court, where the magistrate obligingly fined Schwartz for disorderly conduct.[33]

Manipulation of money as well as Irish favoritism got Tearney into trouble. He increased court costs by raising fees for subpoenas and warrants, charging for services not performed, and imposing costs on guilty and innocent alike. He also split one offense into three or more cases so he could levy multiple fines on the guilty party. Visiting livestock growers usually paid on the spot to avoid further embarrassment. Others promised to pay within a reasonable time, and Tearney considered this money "owed" to him. The jobless went to the County House of Correction to work off fines and court costs, money which Tearney arranged to collect. Arguing that court costs were in fact his, Tearney held back enough money from fines to cover his "earnings." Thus in 1886, he imposed $13,000 in fines and kept $5,500. (The justices of the peace stationed elsewhere in the township seldom collected as much as $100 a year in court costs.) Irate victims of Tearney's justice prodded the town board to "correct this damnable abuse" and stop the magistrate's "official plunder." The Town Hall was "the Steal Works." Tearney was an issue in the 1888 election, and the new administration launched an investigation. They found that the Englewood justice had paid all fines and costs to the treasurer; three other justices kept "sloppy dockets" and may have used some fines to cover court costs due them; only Tearney had an illegible docket, thanks to his "abbreviations and arbitrary characters" and "peculiar system of shorthand writing." In what the investigators called a "beautiful adaptation of means to ends," Tearney heard ninety-four hundred cases over a four-year period, imposed $75,000 in fines and costs, and kept $20,785. The board charged Tearney with imposing $12,775 in illegal court costs, and the magistrate resigned. In 1889 the township created two police courts with salaried magistrates required to file daily reports, but the suit to recover the $12,775 from Tearney was still pending at the time of annexation. Since the money would then go into Chicago's coffers, Michael McInerney suggested amnesty for his friend and a majority of board members concurred.[34]

Town of Lake entered the 1880s with a few cindered thoroughfares, a small police force, volunteer fire brigades, a start on piped water, and a few blocks of sewers. As population increased and residents asked for "city improvements," town officials responded with street paving and lighting, a professional fire department, a much larger police force, and regular scavenger service. The town board hired sanitary engineers to design a drainage system for the township, and four of the five major trunkline sewers had been built by 1889. These municipal services never came fast enough to satisfy taxpayers, as their petitions to the town board make clear. But township officials did modernize the community and in the process avoided fragmenting it into "a welter of competing needs," as happened in Jefferson.[35] Just as town politicians displayed great sensitivity to the various groups interested in saloon policy, so they paid close attention to neighborhood and ethnic demands for improvements and a fair share of patronage. Equitable hiring policies in the public works, police, and fire departments and evenhanded delivery of services were the keys to Town of Lake's successful modernization—and one reason why annexation was soundly defeated in 1887.

NOTES

1. Town of Lake Records, Doc. 2012, Annual Reports of Town Officers for the year Mar. 25, 1885 to Mar. 24, 1886; Doc. 818, May 6, 1889 (City Hall Archives, Chicago). On the efforts of other Cook County townships to provide services in the 1880s, see Jean F. Block, *Hyde Park Houses: An Informal History, 1856–1910* (Chicago, 1978), 19–23; Barbara M. Posadas, "Community Structures of Chicago's Northwest Side: The Transition from Rural to Urban, 1830–1889" (Ph.D. diss., Northwestern University, 1976), 143–63; and Ann Durkin Keating, "Governing the New Metropolis: The Development of Urban and Suburban Governments in Cook County, Illinois, 1831 to 1902" (Ph.D. diss., University of Chicago, 1984), 242–78. For a discussion of services in Detroit's newly developing areas in this same period, see Olivier J. Zunz, *The Changing Face of Inequality: Urbanization, Industrial Development, and Immigrants in Detroit, 1880–1920* (Chicago, 1982), 113–28.

2. Town of Lake Records, Doc. 2017, Report of Chief Engineer and Superintendent of Public Works for Year Ending Mar., 1883; Doc. 374, Oct. 29, 1883; Doc. 797, Apr. 24, 1888; Doc. 801, July 15, 1887; Doc. 797, May 15, 1888; *Sun*, Apr. 30, 1886.

3. Clay McShane, "Transforming the Use of Urban Space: A Look at the Revolution in Street Pavements, 1880–1924," *Journal of Urban History*, 5 (May, 1979), 279–90; Town of Lake Records, Doc. 2012, Annual Reports of Town Officers for the Year Mar. 25, 1885, to Mar. 24, 1886; Doc. 2018, Annual Report of Department of Public Works for Year Ending Mar. 31, 1884; Doc. 799, Sept. 23, 1885; Doc. 802, Apr. 24, 1888.

4. Town of Lake Records, Docs. 900–903, Apr. 10, 1883; Docs. 904–5, Nov. 12, 20, 1883; Doc. 2018, Annual Report of Department of Public Works for Year Ending Mar. 31, 1884; Doc. 2012, Annual Report of Engineer for Year Mar. 25, 1885 to Mar. 24, 1886; Doc. 803, June 25, 1889; *Trib.*, Jan. 2, Feb. 25, Mar. 8, Apr. 9, Sept. 24, 1883; Apr. 1, 1884; July 3, Aug. 13, 1885; June 2, Aug. 31, 1887; Oct. 24, 1888; Feb. 4, 1889; *Sun*, Oct. 6, 1886; Aug. 3, 1889; Amalie Hofer, *Neighborhood Improvement in and about Chicago* (Chicago, 1909), 31–32. Residents of Woodlawn in Hyde Park established the first such organization in 1882 in order to secure better services from local government.

5. Town of Lake Records, Doc. 2018, Annual Report of the Department

of Public Works for the Year Ending Mar. 31, 1884; Doc. 361, Sept. 10, 1884.

6. Town of Lake Records, Doc. 2019, Report of Superintendent of Public Works for the Year Ending Mar. 31, 1883; Doc. 79, Aug. 5, 1885; Doc. 560, June 27, 1887, Doc. 560, Oct. 10, 1885; Doc. 63, Sept. 5, Oct. 10, 1879; Doc. 66, Nov. 7, 1879; Doc. 75, Apr. 4, 1884; Doc. 26, Jan. 14, 1895; *Dollar Weekly Sun,* May 10, 31, 1884; *Trib.,* July 25, Dec. 7, 1883; Nov. 25, 30, 1884; Nov. 25, 1887.

7. Town of Lake Records, Doc. 2060, July 15, 1885; Nov. 24, 1886; Doc. 111, May 18, 1888; July 5, 1889; Doc. 93, Aug. 16, 1887; Doc. 97, Aug. 21, 1888; Doc. 98, June 28, 1889; *Trib.,* Oct. 5, 1884; Aug. 6, 1885; Sept. 17, 1887.

8. On the technological challenge, see Stanley K. Schultz and Clay McShane, "To Engineer the Metropolis: Sewers, Sanitation, and City Planning in Late-Nineteenth-Century America," *JAH,* 65 (Sept., 1978), 395–96; Block, *Hyde Park,* 20; Posadas, "Chicago's Northwest Side," 146, 158–63.

9. Town of Lake Records, Doc. 2060, July 8, Oct. 22, 25, Dec. 21, 1880; Doc. 2017, Report of the Superintendent of Public Works for the Year Ending Mar. 1, 1882; Doc. 20, Jan. 7, 1884; Doc. 2017, Report of the Superintendent of Public Works for the Year Ending Mar. 1, 1882; Doc. 2060, Report on Town of Lake Water Works, June 11, 1883; Engineer R. E. Brownell to Board of Trustees, Sept. 3, 1883; *Trib.,* Jan. 1, Sept. 15, 25, Oct. 5, 26, 1880; July 13, 23, Aug. 6, 12, 19, Sept. 23, Oct. 4, 9, 1881; July 3, 18, Dec. 17, 1882; July 25, 1883.

10. Town of Lake Records, Doc. 810, Sept. 8, 1885; Doc. 811, June 2, Aug. 4, Sept. 7, 1886; Doc. 813, May 15, 1888; Doc. 814, May 21, 1889; Doc. 865, July 3, Sept. 25, 1888; *Trib.,* July 8, Aug. 8, 1886; Mar. 7, July 10, 1888; *Sun,* Mar. 12, 1888; Sept. 6, 1889.

11. Martin V. Melosi, ed., *Pollution and Reform in American Cities, 1870–1930* (Austin, 1980), 59–69; Joel A. Tarr, "The Separate vs. Combined Sewer Problem: A Case Study in Urban Technology Design Choice," *Journal of Urban History,* 5 (May, 1979), 308–18; Town of Lake Records, Doc. 805, July 31, 1884.

12. Town of Lake Records, Docs. 1814–17, Mar. 19, 1880; Doc. 1824, June 23, 1882; Doc. 66, Nov. 7, 1879; Doc. 75, Apr. 4, 1884; Doc. 2012, Engineer's Report for Year Ending Mar. 1886; *Drovers Journal,* Sept. 19, Nov. 11, 1882; *Trib.,* Dec. 13, 1884.

13. James C. O'Connell, "Technology and Pollution: Chicago's Water Policy, 1833–1930" (Ph.D. diss., University of Chicago, 1980), 88–90; Town of Lake Records, Doc. 2012, Town Engineer R. E. Brownell's Report for Year Mar. 25, 1885, to Mar. 24, 1886.

14. "Chicago Sewers," *Trib.*, June 15, 1884; Aug. 3, 1885; *Daily News*, Aug. 28, 1885; *Times*, Aug. 17, 1884; *Sun*, July 23, 1884; Citizens' Association, *Report of the Committee on the Main Drainage and Water Supply of Chicago, Sept., 1885* (Chicago, 1885), 3, 5, 9, 12, 16; Citizens' Association, *Report of the Main Drainage Committee* (Chicago, 1880), 8–9, 13–20; George P. Brown, *Drainage Channel and Waterway: A History of the Effort to Secure . . . Disposal of the Sewage of the City of Chicago* (Chicago, 1894), 19–20; Frank J. Piehl, "Chicago's Early Fight to 'Save Our Lake,'" *Chicago History*, 5 (Winter, 1976–77), 231–32; Louis P. Cain, *Sanitation Strategy for a Lakefront Metropolis: The Case of Chicago* (De Kalb, Ill., 1978), 59–61, 63–64; O'Connell, "Technology and Pollution," 86–89.

15. *Trib.*, Jan. 24, 20, 1887; Dec. 13, 14, 1889; O'Connell, "Technology and Pollution," 89–98; Cain, *Sanitation Strategy*, 64–70; George P. Brown, *Drainage Channel and Waterway*, 345–76, 392–96; F. Garvin Davenport, "Sanitation Revolution in Illinois, 1870–1900," *JISHS*, 66 (Autumn, 1973), 310–13.

16. *Trib.*, June 17, 1886; *Sun*, Apr. 13, 1887; Town of Lake Records, Doc. 2018, Annual Report of the Department of Public Works for Year Ending Mar. 31, 1884; Doc. 805, July 31, 1884; Feb. 21, 1885; Doc. 806, June 30, 1886; Doc. 807, Apr. 12, July 14, 15, 1887; Doc. 808, July 10, Nov. 19, 1888; Doc. 809, June 11, 1889.

17. Town of Lake Records, Doc. 806, July 14, 1886; Doc. 2013, Report on Sewerage, Jan. 17, 1888; Doc. 1967, Jan. 17, 1888; Doc. 1969, Feb. 14, 1888; *Sun*, June 27, 1889; *Trib.*, Oct. 13, 1889.

18. Town of Lake Records, Doc. 379, Apr. 4, Dec. 10, 1884; Doc. 639, July 7, 1886; Doc. 642, Apr. 16, 1889; Alfred T. Andreas, *History of Cook County, Illinois* (Chicago, 1884), 673; *Trib.*, July 24, 1883; July 8, 27, Sept. 10, 12, 1886.

19. Town of Lake Records, Doc. 806, May 3, 1886; Doc. 872, Feb. 7, 1888; Doc. 807, Nov. 26, 1886; Doc. 2053, June 9, 1886; Doc. 2020, Feb. 28, 1888; *Trib.*, Dec. 1, 16, 1886; Mar. 7, 1888; *Sun*, Dec. 29, 1886.

20. F. Garvin Davenport, "John Henry Rauch and Public Health in Illinois, 1877–1891," *JISHS*, 50 (Autumn, 1957), 277–93; Department of Health, *Annual Report of the Chicago Department of Health for 1888*, 9, 11, 15; Martin V. Melosi, "Refuse Pollution and Municipal Reform," in Melosi, ed., *Pollution and Reform*, 105–15; *Trib.*, Sept. 6, 1889.

21. Department of Health, *Annual Report of the Chicago Department of Health for 1881 and 1882*, 32–33; *Annual Report, 1887*, 3; *Annual Report, 1888*, 12–13; *Trib.*, July 23, 1889; Melosi, ed., *Pollution and Reform*, 66.

22. Town of Lake Records, Doc. 13, Nov. 28, 1879; Doc. 2060, Dec. 23,

1881; Doc. 2021, Annual Report of the Health Department for the Year Ending Feb. 28, 1882.

23. Town of Lake Records, Doc. 2021, Annual Report of the Health Department for the Year Ending Feb. 28, 1882; Doc. 2022, Annual Report of the Health Department for the Year Ending Feb. 28, 1884; Doc. 2012, Annual Report of the Health Department for the Year Ending Mar., 1886; Doc. 862, May 6, 1885; Doc. 656, Apr. 16, 1886; Doc. 2023, Monthly Report for Sept., 1885; Monthly Report for June, 1886; Doc. 45, July 26, 1887.

24. *Sun,* June 8, 1886; Dec. 13, 1887; Town of Lake Records, Doc. 2024, Annual Report of the Health Department for the Year Ending Feb. 28, 1887; Miscellaneous Report, May 12, 1888; Annual Report of the Health Department for the Year Ending Mar. 31, 1889; Doc. 651, Jan. 26, 1887; Doc. 2021, Annual Report of the Health Department for the Year Ending Feb. 28, 1882; Doc. 651, Apr. 10, 11, 15, 22, 1885; Doc. 871, Apr. 28, 1886.

25. *Sun,* July 23, 1884; Aug. 3, 1885; Aug. 9, 1889; *Drovers Journal,* Aug. 19, 1884; Town of Lake Records, Doc. 2021, Annual Report of the Health Department for the Year Ending Feb. 28, 1882; Doc. 2022, Annual Report of the Health Department for the Year Ending Feb. 28, 1884; Doc. 2023, Annual Report of the Health Department for the Year Ending Feb. 28, 1886; Doc. 2024, Annual Report of the Health Department for the Year Ending Feb. 28, 1887; Miscellaneous Report for Mar., 1888; Annual Report of the Health Department, for the Year Ending Mar. 31, 1889.

26. James Brown, *The History of Public Assistance in Chicago, 1833 to 1893* (Chicago, 1941), 81–112; Joseph Van Hise, "Cook County Outdoor Poor Relief, 1893–1907" (M.A. thesis, University of Chicago, 1948), chaps. 2, 3; Town of Lake Records, Doc. 2022, Annual Report of the Health Department for the Year Ending Feb. 28, 1883; Doc. 648, June 9, 1886; Doc. 2024, Annual Report of the Health Department for the Year Ending Apr. 22, 1887; *Trib.,* Apr. 17, 21, May 16, 1887.

27. *Trib.,* Oct. 22, 1881; Town of Lake Records, Doc. 154, Apr. 28, 1880; Doc. 155, Apr. 29, 1881; Doc. 2028, Report of Fire Marshal for 1882 to Mar., 1883.

28. Andreas, *Cook County,* 655–56; *Trib.,* Feb. 5, 1884; June 1, 1887; Dec. 18, 1888; Jan. 9, 1889; Town of Lake Records, Doc. 884, Mar. 31, 1884; Doc. 362, Jan. 13, 1886; Doc. 384, May 31, 1887; Doc. 2028, Fire Marshal's Report for Year Ending Mar., 1886; Fire Marshal's Report for Year Ending Mar., 1888; Annual Report of Fire Department for Year Ending Apr., 1889.

29. Town of Lake Records, Doc. 154, Apr. 28, 1880; Doc. 164, May 3, 1889; Doc. 384, May 31, 1887; Doc. 2027, Annual Report of the Police

Department for the Year Ending Mar., 1889; quoted in Charles Fanning, *Finley Peter Dunne and Mr. Dooley: The Chicago Years* (Lexington, Ky., 1978), 58. On the status of firemen and policemen in the 1880s and 1890s, see Fanning, op. cit., 56–65, and Robert M. Fogelson, *Big-City Police* (Cambridge, Mass., 1977), 13–39.

30. Town of Lake Records, Doc. 883, June 9, 1882.

31. Town of Lake Records, Doc, 658, Apr. 19, 1886; Doc. 816, Apr. 16, 21, 1886; Doc. 817, Apr. 16, 1887; Doc. 869, Sept. 27, 1887; *Sun,* May 15, 1889.

32. Town of Lake Records, Doc. 815, July 15, 1885; Doc. 816, Apr. 14, June 15, 1886; Doc. 659, Sept. 20, 1888; Doc. 2025, Annual Report of the Police Department for the Year Ending Mar. 30, 1887.

33. Town of Lake Records, Doc. 2025, Reports of the Police Department for the Years Ending Mar., 1882; Mar., 1883; Mar., 1887; Mar., 1889; Doc. 165, July 5, 1878; Doc. 2026, Report on Police Court Dockets, Aug. 28, 1888; Doc. 2030, Report on Police Magistrate Tearney's Dockets for 1886; *Trib.,* Mar. 3, 1885.

34. Town of Lake Records, Doc. 2030, Report on Police Magistrate Tearney's Dockets for 1886; Doc. 661, July 26, 1887; Doc. 365, Apr. 17, July 10, 1888; Doc. 2030, Report on Books of M. J. Tearney, July 10, 1888; Report on Dockets of Justices of the Peace, Aug. 7, 1888; Doc. 219, May 28, 1889; Doc. 366, July 1, 1889; *Trib.,* Jan. 14, 1887.

35. Posadas, "Chicago's Northwest Side," 146.

CHAPTER 18

The Political Challenge

In the face of a soaring population and thus an ever-changing electorate, town board members had to grapple with the demands of ethnic, religious, economic, and neighborhood groups for recognition. Petitioners wanted not only their fair share of improvements but patronage jobs and chances to run for office as well. Officials walked a tightrope because disappointed voters could join or, if need be, form an opposing coalition, and they could cozy up to "soreheads" who were encouraging merger with Chicago. The old system of nonpartisan coalitions accommodated a major shift in the locus of power from Englewood to the north end. Thomas Gahan won the "top spot" in 1884 and brought a number of Germans into local government along with his Irish supporters, but excessive favoritism to Irish job seekers brought him down two years later. The Haymarket trauma and the strikes in Town of Lake led to formation of a socialist labor party which propelled others into a law and order movement that swept Chicago and the Town of Lake. Thereafter, township elections were fought on more partisan lines, with Irish Democrats winning a clean sweep in the final spring contest. Annexation held few attractions in 1887, when two-thirds of the voters registered satisfaction with Town of Lake's noisy style of politics. By June, 1889, Chicago had made major concessions to the townships, and a slim majority approved merger. They were not seeking services, as were voters in Jefferson, Lake View, and southern Hyde Park, but rather expressing doubt that township officials elected in April of that year could cope successfully with the political challenge.[1]

The Rise and Fall of Gahan

The township entered the volatile 1880s wedded to its nonpartisan political coalitions. Democrats and Republicans "ran together," Goodall pointed out, in township affairs, and the system continued to work until mid-decade. The Citizens' coalition, headed by Supervisor George Muirhead of Englewood, stayed in power from 1879 until 1883 because it was representative and it delivered improvements. The supervisor and assessor came from the Republican south end of town; the town clerk and police chief were Stockyards Irish Democrats; and the Car-Shops provided the trustees. That town board created an independent waterworks, three main line sewers, macadam streets and gaslights, a larger police force, and a full-time fire department. Critics grumbled about rising expenditures, but they had little chance of unseating the Muirhead group until it made a mistake.[2]

Compensation for town board members proved to be the Achilles heel. Illinois law permitted the supervisor (who was also the treasurer) to keep 2 percent of all money collected through taxes, license fees, and special assessments. Other board members received $3 per day for attendance at meetings. Muirhead began paying them $3 "for each day's service in the necessary business of the town" and helped himself to 2 percent of the surplus carried over from the previous year. The Taxpayers' Association uncovered these changes, blamed them for the sharp increase in town expenses, and hinted that Supervisor Muirhead was earning more than the governor of Illinois. People in the north end of town also believed that the "Englewood ring" had been bribed by the Chicago and Western Indiana railroad. That was the only logical explanation for giving the railroad permission to abandon the Forty-third Street viaduct. The meetings "to lay pipe" for the 1883 election brought together workingmen's advocate Peter T. Barry, the Taxpayers' Association, some temperance spokesmen, and concerned packers and livestock dealers. Calling themselves the People's party, they chose a livestock dealer for supervisor, an Englewood businessman for assessor, a Back of the Yards Irish packinghouse foreman for clerk, and a German-American from the Northeast Corners for trustee. Gustavus Swift and Englewood attorney Charles Thornton managed the campaign. The People's party won the 1883 election by carrying the Stockyards, Northeast Corners, and Car-Shops.[3]

Their supervisor, Wilson Darlington, was an inept leader who demoted police chief Thomas Gahan in favor of a roundsman named Michael Markey. When Gahan and other experienced officers resigned, public criticism forced Darlington to dismiss Markey and rehire Gahan. A quarrel with saloonkeepers who wanted delayed enforcement of the $500 license law and the disclosure that the clerk had dipped into license funds made Darlington a tempting target in the next election. The *Englewood Eye*, a supporter of Darlington and the People's party, rejected the concept that the "Irish must be represented, and that the Germans must be acknowledged, by having a man of their nativity put in office." But that concept gave the Citizens' party a new lease on life and a chance to offer voters "a new deal." It nominated Gahan for supervisor, an Englewood Protestant realtor for assessor, and three German-Americans from Englewood, the Stockyards, and New City. Of course Joseph Oswald's German Independent Club was overjoyed with this ticket; the Irish celebrated because they now moved from "end spot" to head of the ticket and Michael Tearney was slated for police magistrate. The Gahan ticket won endorsement from Gustavus Swift, John B. Sherman, Philip Armour, and Emerald Avenue friends of Darlington who agreed that he was an "indecisive" supervisor. Seeing the handwriting on the wall, the *Eye* acknowledged that "new factions . . . coming up" would shift power from Englewood to the Stockyards. Gahan swamped Darlington, 4578 to 1088 votes. The Englewood editor attributed the outcome to solid ethnic bloc voting; the only consolation he could find was the fact that Gahan had the backing of "the best element at the north end of town."[4]

The new supervisor made some excellent appointments. He named Ralph Brownell the town engineer and put Dr. Charles P. Caldwell in charge of the health department. John William Sweeney succeeded Gahan as police chief, and Muirhead, an engineer, took charge of public works. Increased assessments on Packingtown, the Stockyards, and the national bank yielded enough revenue to enlarge the police and fire departments and appoint six sanitary inspectors. The town board commissioned the drainage report and moved both street paving and lateral sewer construction into high gear. Expenditures rose to $235,626, and a larger sum raised through special assessments paid for improvements. No one wanted to run against Gahan in 1885, and the People's party had trouble persuading Sylvester Gaunt to give it a whirl. The supervisor demolished the challenger, but the Citizens' ticket contained the seeds of the party's destruction. Two of the German-American officeholders chose not to run again; rather than replacing them with another German and perhaps a Scandinavian, the Irish strategists chose two of their own. This came at the same time the Irish were flexing their muscle in School District No. 2, Tom Byrne was getting the most lucrative town contracts, Michael McInerney snagged a postmastership, and Michael Tearney was revealing his bias in the police magistrate's court. In the spring of 1886, the Citizens' party once again nominated three Irishmen including Gahan as supervisor, Edward Scholl of New City in an "end spot," and Alexander Graham for collector. Their overweighted Irish ticket was the kiss of death.[5]

A new coalition, calling itself the People's Reform party, resolved to bring the Irish down. It consisted of disgruntled Germans and Scandinavians, Knights of Labor organizers Michael J. Butler and Sylvester Gaunt, banker Edward Tilden, Peter McGurn and Charles Thornton of Englewood, and Gustavus Swift and Wilson Darlington of Emerald Avenue, the Stockyards. Their slate was a masterful balance of two "Americans," two "nonprofessional" Irishmen, and one German, the popular John Kirschen of New City. The campaign focused on unfair patronage policies and soaring town expenses. The Citizens' party was distracted by an internal Irish revolt: hotheads wanted four out of five spots on the ticket. Gahan asked Michael

McInerney to read them the riot act. According to the *Sun*, McInerney warned the Irish to leave some flesh on the bones for the other nationalities. He reminded them of Irish gains in the police and fire departments, among contractors and town laborers, and in School District No. 2, where eighty-six of the ninety-eight teachers were Irish. Newspaper versions of this speech brought a deluge of angry letters. "A German Citizen" deplored the party's cavalier dismissal of other ethnic voters who had supported the Citizens' party in past elections. Letting one nationality take control was always a mistake because it wound up "talking and working" for its "own benefits and pockets." An Englewood correspondent accused McInerney, Gahan, and Tom Byrne of acting like "they were the universe . . . entirely independent of the public." Charles Thornton called it "Irish Know-Nothingism."[6]

The township followed new election procedures in the spring of 1886, for it was experimenting with advance registration and new ballot boxes. Moreover the town board increased the number of polling places from ten to twenty-six and agreed to keep them open from 6 A.M. to 4 P.M. This would make it easier for wage earners to vote and presumably keep Chicago "floaters" from invading the north end of town. Seventy-five hundred people registered and nine-tenths of them voted. Only 45 percent of them cast ballots for Gahan. "We met the enemy and they gobbled us," admitted Goodall, a Gahan supporter. The *Tribune* called it a "political cyclone" and a lesson to politicians who pandered to the "bigotries of the untutored naturalized citizens." The People's Reform party supervisor, livestock dealer John Stafford, expected to hear from his diverse coalition of supporters. They did not disappoint him. Charles Thornton recommended a Swede for the fire department: "Without making any individual promises of positions, it was agreed that your Board would properly recognize the *Swedish population*, if they would not insist on having a representative on the Board." Michael J. Butler pushed a loyal party worker for a patrolman's job and got himself appointed to the health department. The supervisor rewarded Michael Markey by making him police chief and gave the Ashland Avenue sewer contract to another ally of the People's Reform party. The town board cut expenditures by about one-third, bringing the budget back to $240,000, and Stafford was happy to abide by a state law setting township supervisors' compensation at a maximum of $5,000. Assessments on railroads and manufacturers went up to match those on the packinghouses and Stockyards. By 1886–87 these large employers were paying approximately one-half of the taxes collected in the township.[7]

Until the Haymarket bomb and the eight-hour strikes reshaped city and township politics, the shifting, nonpartisan coalitions dominated Town of Lake contests. In state and federal elections, however, Town of Lake voters expected to be Democratic or Republican partisans. The November, 1884, battle between Cleveland and Blaine and Democratic challenger Mayor Carter Harrison and Republican Governor Richard Oglesby is a good example. Among the Republican stalwarts were Gustavus Swift, Nelson Morris, Wilson Darlington, George Muirhead, Michael Markey, Rudolph Biester, Christian Vehmeyer, and John Bartlett. Working the Democratic side were Thomas Gahan, Michael McInerney, Michael Tearney, Jesse Sherwood and Charles Thornton of Englewood, and Thomas Byrne of Back of the Yards. Township voters cast a bare majority of their ballots for Cleveland and Mayor Harrison, though the latter was beaten by Governor Oglesby. This meant that Supervisor Gahan and Magistrate Tearney got their Democratic president, while Assessor Bartlett, Collector Vehmeyer, and Trustee Scholl got their Republican governor. When the election was over, there were no hard feelings and town officials went back to work. Democrats and Republicans, as Goodall noted, were accustomed to working together in township affairs.[8]

Labor versus Law and Order

The creation of a United Labor party in Cook County just four months after Haymarket threw old certainties to the winds. The party's chief architects were George Schilling and Thomas J. Morgan, both members of the Knights of Labor, both socialists, and both disgusted with the Democratic and Republican parties. It was their expectation that Democrats, Republicans, and anyone else favorably disposed to the working class would vote for candidates of the independent labor party. The United Labor party tried its wings in November, 1886, by running the first socialist alderman for Cook County treasurer, Michael J. Butler for county sheriff, and John Peter Altgeld for judge of the Superior Court. Only Altgeld, who also had the Democratic nomination, won, but the party carried Town of Lake and the Fifth and Sixth wards, collected one-quarter of the votes cast, and helped send seven men to the state legislature. Schilling and Morgan vowed to enter the Chicago mayorality race in the spring of 1887 and possibly run a labor ticket in the Town of Lake. "No party ever polled so large a vote nor made itself so generally felt at so young an age," exulted the editor of the Chicago *Knights of Labor*.[9]

The thought of a three-man race was unsettling to Carter Harrison, already vulnerable to charges that he had given the radicals too much leeway and thereby encouraged the Haymarket tragedy. The mayor tried to persuade Schilling and Morgan to fuse with the Democrats; they would not budge, and the United Labor party nominated iron molder Robert Nelson, head of Knights of Labor District Assembly 24. Though not a socialist himself, he endorsed the party's call for municipal ownership of transit and utilities, an end to patronage appointments, heavier taxation of capitalists, and an eight-hour day for city workers. Realizing that the labor vote could throw the election to the Republicans, Mayor Harrison withdrew from the race. "The fight is between the classes—the rich and the poor," said the jubilant Schilling. "Only the silk stockings and boodlers will vote the Republican ticket. . . . The workingmen can't be misled this time."[10]

Realists knew that the outcome hinged upon the selection of a Republican candidate. Silk stockings, boodlers, and capitalists were out of the running. Samuel Allerton lobbied for Louis Wahl on the grounds that he could appeal to Germans, Bohemians, and Scandinavians. But the Republicans chose a self-made mechanical engineer who had risen from working-class ranks. Even the Democratic *Times* urged voters to support John P. Roche. So too did Alderman Cullerton because a socialist labor party victory would mean dismemberment of the police force, confiscatory taxes, the flight of capital from Chicago, "cancellation of orders to our shops and factories . . . stagnation and paralysis." The *Herald* charged that the United Labor party was infected with the "virus of anarchism," and the *Tribune* told Democrats and Republicans they were "in the same canoe" and if they failed to paddle in unison they would "go over the cataract together."[11]

A similar contest took shape in the Town of Lake. Joseph Buchanan's *Labor Enquirer* encouraged Butler, "Buck" McCarthy, Peter McGurn, and Peter T. Barry to enter the fray. A small faction of the Citizens' party joined them, and the labor party slate, headed by McGurn for supervisor, included an "American" assessor, Irishmen for collector and clerk, and a German trustee. The latter was known as "a Dutch-Irishman" among other German voters in the township. The new party promised to erase patronage, equalize tax assessments, abolish the contractors' "ring," and restore fiscal accountability. Buchanan accused the existing coalitions of playing footsie with "packers and other freebooters"; only the labor party represented "the mind and muscle of the Town." Just as Democrats and Republicans coalesced in the face of danger in Chicago, so the Citizens' and People's Reform parties favored joint action. Germans promised to cooperate if they had two people on the town board. The negotiators finally settled on Elmer Washburn for supervisor; they were impressed by his background in Chicago police work and his performance at the Stockyards bank and as president of the Chicago Live Stock Exchange. The incumbent supervisor agreed to run for collector; the Citizens' group retained their incumbent clerk and got the assessor's post for Luke O'Toole of Back of the Yards. The carry-over trustee was John Kirschen and the nomination of Christian Vehmeyer as the other trustee gave Germans two seats. The rest was easy. They took the name Citizens' and Law and Order party, and promised equal treatment for all groups, no antagonism between economic interests, secure conditions for industries in the township, and steady employment for wage earners, uninterrupted by strikes.[12]

The township campaign was spirited. Goodall supported the Washburn slate because he feared radicals could manipulate McGurn and their threat to quadruple corporation taxes was the talk of "blatant madmen." Voters in Englewood were uneasy about the assessor, a candidate whose only apparent qualification was his background as a Back of the Yards saloonkeeper. To calm their fears, Charles Thornton started the *Englewood Call.* Not all the candidates, admitted the newssheet, are men "of refinement and culture; but [we Englewood residents] being greatly in the minority . . . cannot have everything." The township faced a "grave crisis." A labor victory would "rob the industrious for the benefit of the improvident"—a jab at Butler's manipulation of relief rolls—and bring "nothing more or less than the triumph of socialism." Meanwhile, the *Labor Enquirer* dubbed Washburn, a Transit House boarder, a carpetbagger in the township, "a tool of Armour and the other blood-suckers at the Stock Yards." Victory for the workingmen's ticket would mean an end to "king rule, bulldozing and King Hog." Buchanan thought the growing strength of the labor party ticket caused opponents to "shriek 'comunists and anarchists' in order that they may retain their clutch upon the throat of labor and their grip on the money bags."[13]

Using similar arguments and waging complimentary campaigns, "law and order" forces triumphed in Chicago and in the Town of Lake. John P. Roche carried every ward except the Fifth and Sixth and won two-thirds of the city vote. Chicago "cleaned out the whole house and put the Star-Spangled Banner on the roof," rejoiced the *Tribune*. Of the 7,224 ballots cast in the Town of Lake, 58.5 percent went to Washburn. Goodall thought labor radicals "killed" Peter McGurn's chances and Luke O'Toole's strength in Back of the Yards helped the Washburn ticket. Given the intensity of the campaign and the strong feelings of voters, the *Sun* editor was pleasantly surprised that "no racketing or slugging" occurred in any precinct. James S. Quinn, the self-styled "Stock Yards Rake," explained labor's defeat this way: "Money was spent like water; threats, bribes, promises and patronage were cunningly thrown into the meshes . . . subsidized press, subsidized pulpits, subsidized saloons. The ministers, God and the devil were employed to work against the cause of honesty." Ruminating a short time later about citizen participation in local government, Goodall commented: "It strikes us that if politics were religion, nine-tenths of the Town of Lake people would be saved."[14]

In spite of the defeats in the spring of 1887, Morgan remained upbeat about the labor party's future. "We've done wonders in nine months. We've smashed up one party and scared the other almost to death." He neither foresaw the unraveling of the Knights of Labor nor comprehended the desire of many United Labor party supporters to eliminate "red-flagism." When an antisocialist faction broke away, Morgan's followers regrouped as the Radical Labor party. In the next Chicago municipal election their ticket attracted a mere thirty-six hundred votes. That fall the editor of the *Knights of Labor* admitted that "the time has not yet arrived when anything can be accomplished by independent political action of the labor party." In the Town of Lake, the United Labor party expired quietly. Butler lost his town job in April, 1887, and appealed to the Democrats for a patronage niche. "Buck" McCarthy was implicated in a financial scandal and forced to resign his county post. Labor spokesmen asked Gahan to be their congressional candidate in 1888; he advised them to join the Democrats. Buchanan's loss of the *Labor Enquirer* scarcely compared to his "bitter surprise" and "sore disappointment" at the political failure. While "we have quarreled and squabbled," he confessed, "the thieves have robbed us and the voters have left. . . . It is not a very handsome picture; but the likeness is good."[15]

Speeding the labor party's demise was Town of Lake's first crisp, businesslike administration. Supervisor Washburn secured tight control by making himself ex officio police chief, fire marshal, health and water commissioner, and superintendent of public works. He could suspend any town employe until the next board meeting, whereupon members voted on the dismissal. Michael Butler was the first to go, and the health department was placed under the police chief. Washburn launched the long overdue investigation of Magistrate Tearney, and he reduced the wages of town laborers from $2 to $1.75 per day and increased their hours from eight to ten, bringing them in line with the private sector. The trustees, assessor, and collector, chafing over their political isolation, tried to stay busy overseeing streets, water, and sewers. When the Illinois legislature added an elected president to all village and township boards, Town of Lake's majority chose the collector rather than the supervisor as president until the next election.[16]

The First Chance to Merge

The increase in population and services created political strain in all the townships surrounding Chicago. The 1887 state law adding presidents to the local boards was intended to broaden representation, but the townships were also considering adoption of city government, which would give them a mayor and aldermen elected from wards. Lake View decided to try this; Paul Cornell in Hyde Park and "Buck" McCarthy in Town of Lake were advocates of mayor-council government. Some residents agreed that it was the best method of holding off Chicago annexationists: if Brooklyn could preserve its independence from New York City, so could Cook County residents with a ring of cities surrounding the metropolis. At the same time, there were people favoring annexation as the best solution. A section of Jefferson joined Chicago in order to get municipal services; residents of northern Hyde Park already had services, but expected merger with the city to relieve them of the burden of improvements in Hyde Park's southern industrial district. The spectre of being outnumbered and thus outvoted by wage earners prompted other Hyde Parkers to contemplate merger. Chicago newspapers, of course, encouraged the suburban annexationists. The ring of parks and boulevards, said the *Tribune,* should be part of Chicago; city tax rates were lower than those in Hyde Park or Lake; mayor-council government was more efficient and more representative than township "rings" and "cliques." "The suburbs should come in out of the cold," argued an 1886 editorial, and they would if state law permitted Chicago to annex "by degrees" those suburban districts that were "ripe for it."[17]

The legislature obliged with an 1887 Chicago Consolidation and Annexation Act. Actually an amendment to the 1872 Township Organization Act, it permitted any contiguous township or part of it to petition for a referendum on joining the city. Parts of Lake View, Jefferson, Cicero, and the northern third of Hyde Park secured permission to vote on merger with the three townships that constituted Chicago. In Town of Lake, the strongest advocates of annexation were members of the Citizens' Association. Armed with verbal assurances from Mayor Roche and Chicago's corporation counsel that the city would not ban frame construction or interfere with local prohibition districts, these Englewood residents arranged several forums in the summer of 1887 to test public opinion. Convinced that there was enough interest to merit a referendum, they circulated petitions in the eastern half of the township and arranged for those districts to vote on the question in November, 1887.[18]

Proponents of merger took it for granted that Chicago would respect the dry districts and would not extend the fire limits. They went on to argue that schools and police and fire departments would benefit from joining those in the city. Mayor Roche assured the suburbs that their teachers, firemen, and police officers would keep their jobs. In addition, annexationists predicted a decline in political strife and perhaps a reduction in taxes. Those who believed suburbs destined to enhance the glory of central cities were coached by Chicago editors. American cities "have grown as much by annexation as through all other causes combined," the *Tribune* pointed out, and Chicago could be number two in 1890 and number one by 1900 "if the interests of the suburbs are not subordinated to the greed of a horde of petty office-seekers and officeholders." For this reason the *Hyde Park Herald,* a strong advocate of annexation, wanted the merger to take place before the 1890 census. Harvey Goodall, an opponent of annexation, was skeptical of the claims of proponents. He suggested a few more benefits they might explore: "the Englewood women suffragists [would win] the right to vote" and there would be "no more stench from the river."[19]

Anti-annexationists in the Town of Lake minced no words in expressing their views. They doubted that Chicago would abide by the fire limits promise. Chicago newspapers were sure to nag about "kindling wood in the suburbs" and the ban would "kill the building interests . . . for at least ten years," said Peter McGurn and Charles S. Thornton. The president of the Citizens' League considered annexation the "worst thing" for the temperance movement: we "would soon be overrun with low doggeries, and the prohibitory districts would be a thing of the past." Sylvester Gaunt was certain voters would "put annexation away in a large coffin" because it was "conceived by . . . disappointed politicians." An Englewood lawyer conceded that township elections were "somewhat noisy," but he preferred them to Chicago's machine politics. Michael McInerney and scores of others warned that Town of Lake aldermen would be "jeered at and ignored" in the Chicago council; already the city neglected the "deplorable" streets and sidewalks in the Fifth and Sixth wards. Former supervisors Gahan and Darlington demanded proof that Chicago could "govern properly" the territory it already had. "When the people in the city are better off than we are, then it will be time to talk of annexation." Gustavus Swift was "decidedly opposed" because it would destroy the wage earners' dream of home ownership. Furthermore, a "Board of our people are better able to look after the interests of the town generally than a council of men who, in a local sense, would be foreigners."[20]

"We are our own masters yet," said the *Sun* on election eve, "let us remain so." Two out of every three voters agreed. The only pockets of support for annexation were in the Northeast Corners, the Car-Shops, and Englewood, but the referendum lost in those districts. Opposition was overwhelming in Normal Park, New City, Back of the Yards, and the Stockyards. Of the 4,171 people who voted, 65.5 percent turned down the first invitation to join Chicago. Residents of Lake View, content with their city government, were just as decisive. Cicero, Jefferson, and the northern part of Hyde Park voted to join the adjacent Chicago townships. Questions about the constitutionality of the crudely drafted annexation law soon put the Hyde Park results in court, but the *Tribune* meantime rejoiced that a sizeable portion of the lakefront suburb, which was "far more desirable" than "the whole of Lake," had given Chicago a vote of confidence. Goodall retorted that "respectable" Englewood and Normal Park had been as eager to stay out of Chicago's "clutches" as the allegedly "ring-ridden," "disreputable" north end. This was why local autonomy triumphed and the Town of Lake escaped the city's "Avaricious Grasp."[21]

Dr. Alfred H. Champlin of Englewood offered readers of the Chicago *Tribune* a different explanation. Opponents had carried the election because they focused their "missionary work" on the "saloon element" in the north end of town and the Prohibitionists in the south. Their "oratory was fervid. Money was freely spent, and the measure was defeated." He predicted, however, that the next time around voters living east of Halsted Street would agree to join the city because "it is whispered that the packers favor this proposition." Of course, township officials and the local press would try to prevent it: "The Town of Lake is a well squeezed orange, and so long as there is any juice in its 'chartered privileges' it will not be forsaken by the politicians and demagogs, nor will their undying love for the people cease to reverberate in our ears," he wrote.[22]

The postmortem on the first annexation referendum was still underway when President John Stafford's sudden death disrupted the balance of power in the town board. Supervisor Washburn pressed for the election of an Englewood Republican; but Assessor O'Toole and the German trustees chose Michael McInerney, prominent Democrat and Citizens' party stalwart. Hoping to eliminate Washburn in the April, 1888, election, the Citizens' group and a faction of the People's Reform coalition settled on Peter McGurn for president and an eight-hour-day Englewood manufacturer for supervisor. Their carefully balanced slate had German, Irish, and "American" candidates hailing from Englewood, the Car-Shops, Stockyards, and Back of the Yards. Michael McInerney, Michael J. Butler, and Thomas Gahan were in charge of selling it to the voters. The remainder of the People's Reform party and their "law and order" allies reconstituted themselves as the United People's party. Since Elmer Washburn had replaced Sherman at the Stockyards for the year, he agreed to run for president and let Jesse Sherwood, a Democratic livestock dealer who lived in Englewood, run for supervisor. Another Englewood resident was selected as trustee, but Germans and Irish divided the remaining slots. Charles Thornton agreed to manage the campaign in the south end and Sylvester Gaunt in the north end of town. McGurn's group promised to restore the eight-hour day to the Town of Lake and rid it of "the autocrat." Elmer Washburn vowed to continue his economical administration of township affairs. By a very close margin, the candidates of the United People's party won the 1888 elections. The *Labor Enquirer* had no interest in the outcome, for "the thread of spoils . . . runs through the fabric of local politics."[23]

The Rocky Road to Annexation

Washburn's second year in office was clouded by the knowledge that there would be a second referendum on annexation. In March of 1888 the Illinois Supreme Court upheld Hyde Park's contention that the 1887 results were invalid because the law was unconstitutional. It was obvious that annexationists would secure another measure in the next session of the legislature. They used that opportunity to clarify the promises to suburbanites: prohibition districts could only be altered by voters living within the boundaries; all policemen and firemen would automatically be transferred to the city departments; sewerage taxes levied in the annexed territories could be spent only in those districts; and the annexed territories could continue to elect their own assessors. These provisions removed fears that suburbanites would end up financing Chicago sewers and that Chicago assessors would exploit the former suburbs. The new annexation measure became law in April, 1889, and people in Jefferson, Lake View, Hyde Park, and the Town of Lake would have a second chance to join Chicago in June of that year. Since the timing of the second referendum was not immediately known, the townships had no choice except to proceed with business as usual.[24]

The aggressive Elmer Washburn was ready to do just that when he moved from supervisor to president of the town board. His reorganization ordinance created five departments—law, public works, water, police, and fire—and gave the president supervisory powers over all five. With the consent of the board, he appointed the men who actually administered the departments and reported to him, not the board. Seven committees handled patronage matters with the help of ex officio member Washburn. Only Supervisor Sherwood fought these changes. Washburn, overburdened with work because he would not delegate authority, became ever more brusque in his dealings with associates. People called him "God," and there was applause when the Stockyards company relieved him of managerial duties and cheers when Swift masterminded Washburn's defeat in the Chicago Live Stock Exchange. The autocrat's fall from grace was complete when the Stockyards company told him to vacate the Town Hall property by April 1, 1889. Elmer Washburn was finished, but the township's future was so uncertain that precinct hustlers in the spring election were muddled as to "which party they are with." The slates mirrored that confusion. The United People's party chose as president a Stockyards railroad agent related by marriage to Gustavus Swift and as supervisor a former Citizens' party candidate. Charles Kotzenberg, Peter Caldwell, Englewood businessman E. J. Noble, and, of course, Swift worked for this slate. The Citizens' coalition nominated two men who had bolted from the Washburn administration, the clerk and Supervisor Jesse Sherwood. Their presidential candidate was the livestock dealer who had beaten Washburn in the Exchange, William H. Thompson; and Michael McInerney was slated for collector.[25]

Although both coalitions had ethnic, geographical, and political balance, the prominence of Swift and Noble gave a Republican tinge to the People's group, and the Citizens' had the Democratic stamp of Gahan, McInerney, and Sherwood. The latter group had a field day with Washburn's unattractive personality and his cowardly refusal to build a new town hall. Neither camp talked about tax rates or assessments, for a change. Those had been increased for "the corporations" in the mid-1880s and for owners of undeveloped property in 1888; homeowners' rates had steadily declined. During 1888 the township collected $270,000 in taxes and license fees, $100,000 of it from the Union Stock Yard and Transit Company and $53,000 from Packingtown. Armour and Company, which had paid $1,231 in taxes in 1876, was paying $23,000 in 1888. Large employers did not complain about these taxes, and since the demise of the labor party no one campaigned on the issue of higher corporate taxes. Unlike Hyde Park, where tax rates were a chronic sore point, voters in Town of Lake made their decisions in April, 1889, on the basis of candidates' reputations. Thompson won a resounding victory and all the other candidates on the Citizens' slate won their races. The new town board scrapped Washburn's reorganization and took charge once again of departmental administration. Collector McInerney got the patronage-rich department of public works, and at his behest the board raised the wages of town laborers to $2 per day.[26]

Attention by then was riveted on the annexation debate and the June 29 referendum. Proponents of merger convened a meeting in Chicago of some three hundred volunteers. They created a metropolitan committee in charge of campaign literature and solicitation of letters to Chicago newspapers. Town of Lake activists included Gustavus Swift, Charles Kotzenberg, Dr. Alfred H. Champlin, Father Flannigan, Elmer Adkinson, Patrick Phelan, Rudolph Biester, Luke O'Toole, Joseph Oswald, and Albert Veeder. They circulated brochures explaining that they were proud to consider themselves part of Chicago's "overflow," and they maintained that "the prosperity and welfare of the Town of Lake and Chicago are identical." Englewood minister Henry C. Kinney was impressed by the differences between the various neighborhoods within each township; he concluded that the towns needed to be united with the metropolis. "Englewood has little in common with the Stock-Yards. . . . What is common to all these places? Chicago, Chicago, Chicago alone." The contribution that citizens in the Town of Lake and other suburbs could make to Chicago was another popular theme. An Englewood commuter said he looked forward to helping maintain city streets which he was using for free. Reverend Kinney was convinced that the "conservative influence" of commuters would promote "good government in Chicago." Another Town of Lake correspondent worried about Chicago's business center having fallen into "the hands of an unintelligent voting population." This "increasing evil . . . can only be countered by bringing in the suburbs."[27]

In return, the annexationists pointed out, residents of Lake would get more reliable water distribution and purer water because the Chicago intake crib, unlike Town of Lake's, was not threatened by Hyde Park sewage, plus access to the city's public library and superior fire and police protection. Moreover, merger with Chicago would cure the inadequacies of township government. Lake had "outgrown" its town board, and a mayor-council arrangement would "still leave us in about the same condition we are in now," so why not "go at once to the place where we properly belong?" Annexationists loathed the "ringsters" who were chronically in search of contracts, patronage, and favors; they put taxpayers at the mercy of "petty office-holders, each of whom has brothers, uncles, brothers-in-law, sons, and cousins already provided for, and others growing up to the officeholding age for whom provision must be made." Lawyer Elmer Adkinson opposed annexation in 1887 but changed his mind because joining Chicago was a way to even the score with "town rings, officials, and contractors." A mailing to voters said the quickest way "to free ourselves from dictatorial and corrupt ring rule" and "to break up this system of public plunder . . . is to vote for annexation." Many speakers saw the demolition of Town Hall, "the Steal Works," as symbolic of Town of Lake's future. German-Americans, however, were more concerned about unfair representation than they were about corruption. They blamed the Irish for the fact that they had "end spots" on the party tickets and often had to choose between German candidates slated for the same position by both parties. Needless to say, the *Illinois Staats-Zeitung* vigorously urged all suburban Germans to join the city.[28]

Opponents of annexation realized that Chicago's guarantees, its "sweeteners" or "bait" for suburban voters, had undermined their position. They also knew that many suburbanites believed it was Chicago's "destiny" to absorb her suburbs eventually. Yet the *Sun* urged "timid voters" to take heart and follow the example of Brooklyn, which refused to be "swallowed up" by New York City. The Anti-Annexation Club of Englewood finally took the initiative in June to form a townwide campaign organization. It included livestock dealers Wilson and Henry Darlington, banker Edward Tilden, and magistrate Peter Caldwell; New City-Back of the Yards residents James J. O'Toole, Thomas Byrne, Jacob Hansen, and Henry Schumacher; Marshall Hughson, the president of the Citizens' League, and prohibitionist Reverend H. S. Taylor; labor sympathizers Michael J. Butler, Edward Condon, Joseph Gallagher, and Peter McGurn; Thomas Gahan and "Buck" McCarthy; Englewood businessmen E. J. Noble and P. S. Hudson and lawyers Edward Maher and Charles S. Thornton. Officeholders agreed to stay off the committee and public platforms lest their participation in the campaign lend credence to the charge that the antis were after political spoils. This meant that Sherwood and McInerney stayed on the sidelines, but anti-annexationists discovered an effective speaker in E. J. Noble, a convert since the first referendum.[29]

The antis made headway with the fire limits issue until mid-June, when Chicago passed an ordinance specifically exempting annexed territories. If the guarantee was extended by an ordinance, it could be taken away again, said the opponents. How long would Chicago tolerate brick on one side of Thirty-ninth Street and frame on the other? Temperance spokesmen conceded that the prohibited districts would be autonomous, but if so, asked Noble, why surrender the township to a council one-fifth of whom were habitual drunkards and one-half were blackmailers? Those same aldermen could sell railroad rights-of-way down the best streets in Lake, send in Italian street sweepers who were paid 90¢ a day, and give all future improvements in the township to Chicago contractors. Local schools might well become as overcrowded as those in Chicago, and Town of Lake would have no voice on the appointive school board. Opponents of annexation denied that taxpayers would save money by merging with the metropolis. Lake's water rates were lower, and if differences in calculating assessed valuation were taken into account, property taxes were lower too. The antis were also fond of pointing out that Town of Lake's indebtedness averaged $3.56 per person, while Chicago's debt amounted to $16 per head. The metropolis was "graciously" offering to assume Lake's debt and simultaneously giving township taxpayers the "privilege" of sharing Chicago's "enormous debt." Members of the town board, local chauvinists insisted, had done an excellent job delivering services. They were "neighbors and friends," known to all and responsive to voters. "Shall we abandon these advantages?"[30]

In a moment of levity, Goodall predicted that officeholders would oppose annexation, "soreheads" would favor it, and "the corporations" would determine the outcome. Both camps worked on the packers, the Stockyard company, and livestock dealers. Each found some support but claimed much more. Gustavus Swift and Henry Botsford arranged several meetings in early June at the Transit House to stress the advantages of metropolitan water and sewerage, police and fire protection. They also insisted that tax rates would go down, not up, if the township joined the city. As a result of these meetings, Chicago newspapers cheerfully reported that all the packers and "the Stockyards interests" favored annexation. Livestock dealers and packers who opposed the merger then spoke up, and one informed the *Herald* that "everything is just as we want it" in the Town of Lake. By the end of June, the *Sun* was claiming that all except two packers had let it be known that they opposed annexation. In fact, the Stockyards company took no stand and John B. Sherman was silent; comparatively few packers played active roles in the campaign or made public commitments; and livestock dealers, like temperance spokesmen, businessmen and manufacturers, and property owners, could be found on both sides. Strategists, therefore, resorted to last-minute scare tactics. Even if "obstructionists" defeat annexation, said the *Tribune*, "the contest will be renewed again and again." And if "the corporations" assist the antis, "they will have to renew the tribute." Opponents asked what the Stockyards and Packingtown would do if Chicago made Section 5 build and maintain its own sewer conduit all the way to the Des Plaines River? And what could Hyde Park and Town of Lake do if Chicago routed its new Sanitary Channel along Forty-third Street?[31]

The June 29 referendum added 220,000 people to Chicago and boosted the population over the magic one million mark. The city annexed about 130 square miles, giving it a total of 168 square miles and making it the largest municipal area in the United States. Rivals scoffed that much of it was cow pasture or muskrat swamp, but the *Tribune* saluted "One United City, Second Only to New York." Residents of Jefferson were happy to throw in the towel; 57 percent of the voters in Lake View favored merger. Of Hyde Park's eighty-five hundred voters, 62 percent supported annexation; Pullman, Hyde Park Center, and Kenwood, however, voted against the proposition. In the Town of Lake only eighty-two hundred ballots were cast, though the April township election had drawn ninety-five hundred voters. Of those who went to the polls, 53.7 percent supported merger, 46.3 percent opposed it. The annexationists carried twenty-three of the forty-two precincts and had majorities in the Northeast Corners, the Car-Shops, and New City. Opponents of annexation prevailed in Englewood, Back of the Yards, and at the Stockyards. The Germans in Town of Lake gathered at Oswald's Gardens for a joyous election-night celebration, while Englewood annexationists staged a colorful parade and fireworks display. Harvey Goodall and the other antis were not surprised by the vote in the Northeast Corners and Car-Shops, or even in New City since the Germans "made a straight fight for annexation." What puzzled the editor of the *Sun* and what determined the outcome of this close election were the smaller than expected proportion of negative votes in Englewood and the light turnout of voters at the Stockyards and in Back of the Yards.[32]

The answer to the puzzle lies in the disarray of Irish voters in the Town of Lake and the reaction of other residents to the shocking events surrounding the murder of Dr. Cronin. The doctor disappeared May 4, his body was found May 22, the Irish policeman in charge of the investigation was himself implicated and arrested May 28, the coroner's jury decided on June 11 that Cronin had been the victim of a Clan na Gael conspiracy, Alexander Sullivan was arrested the same day, and a special grand jury indicted seven men for the murder on June 29, the day Town of Lake voted on annexation. Throughout May and June Chicago newspapers featured the Cronin-Sullivan quarrel, Triangle rule, and internal conflicts of the Irish nationalist organizations. Thus the Cronin case played havoc with "the public image of the Irishman," one scholar has argued, and shattered "the veneer of respectability that had barely begun to attach itself to the nationalist movement and the whole Irish community in Chicago."[33]

The Cronin affair was particularly devastating for the Irish in Town of Lake. Most of them were Sullivan supporters like Father Dorney, who in 1882 had helped clear Sullivan of charges that he stole nationalist funds. The accuser was expelled from the Clan, moved to Pekin, Illinois, and then in June of 1889 informed Chicago newspapers that he considered Dorney "morally responsible for the blood of poor Cronin." A tiny pro-Cronin faction tried to persuade Archbishop Feehan to remove the priest from St. Gabriel's parish, but the overwhelming reaction of the Irish was fury that their leading spokesman had been drawn into the embarassing Cronin case. Defending Father Dorney—and themselves—took precedence over the annexation referendum. Harvey Goodall knew that the matter was too painful and too sensitive to mention. His only comment was a cartoon entitled "A Merited Rebuke." It depicted one Irishman clubbing another to the ground; the caption read, "The prostrate man in the above picture . . . merely asked the other man who in his opinion killed Cronin."[34]

Non-Irish residents of Lake were shocked and disgusted by the unsavory Cronin revelations. Those who had been rubbed the wrong way by the Irish seized the opportunity to castigate the local Triangle of "Buck" McCarthy, Michael McInerney, and Thomas Gahan. All belonged to Clan na Gael, all were prominent "professional Irishmen," and all were back in the saddle as a result of the April elections. Even more significant was the fact that Town of Lake's Triangle opposed annexation. Should the township retain its autonomy, the untrustworthy Irish "Home Rulers" would run the show. Goodall alluded to this line of reasoning when he said in July that annexationists thought they were getting rid of Michael McInerney by killing off the Town of Lake. It seems likely that second thoughts about leaving the Irish in control of the town board influenced Englewood voters and explains their smaller-than-expected vote against annexation. It is certain that it strengthened the determination of German, Bohemian, and Swedish voters to get even with the Irish by eliminating the town board. It is also clear that Irish disarray accounts for the slow, fumbling start of the anti-annexation campaign and the near-paralysis of Irish voters at the Stockyards and in Back of the Yards on election day. The people who turned out in force to approve annexation had no illusions about Chicago being free of Irish influence. But as one Town of Lake correspondent put it, if the town joined the city, the local Irish "ringsters" would "sink to their proper level."[35]

The town board had two weeks to wind up its affairs and prepare for the

July 15 "surrender." Only President Thompson, Supervisor Sherwood, magistrate Peter Caldwell, some Englewood annexationists, and a small curious crowd gathered in front of the township's rented Halsted headquarters on the appointed day. The Chicago mayor, corporation counsel, and other dignitaries visited Hyde Park first; their arrival in Lake was delayed by a standing freight train and ignorance of the new location of Town Hall. When the ceremonies finally commenced, Mayor DeWitt Cregier pleaded for "good fellowship." "The Town of Lake is no more. We are here as friends and neighbors, and not as interlopers." He swore in the fire marshal and police chief; the corporation counsel accepted the town records; firemen sounded a gong in lieu of church bells, and it was all over. The next day the *Sun* had a front-page drawing of a tombstone bearing the legend, "In Memory of Town of Lake, Killed by Annexation, Age 24 Years," with the caption, "Rest in Peace."[36]

Until 1886, Town of Lake was well served by its nonpartisan coalitions. They permitted power to shift from Englewood to the north end, and Supervisor Thomas Gahan brought more workingmen and more Germans into township government. The relentless increase in voters and the lobbying of ethnic, religious, economic, and neighborhood groups posed difficulties for the politicians. As the German Club informed one supervisor, we have "a right to hold a proportionate share of the appointive positions, . . . we as Germans ask to be recognized," and the fourteenth precinct told another, it is "due us . . . to have at least one of our residents wishing employment of the town kept steadily employed."[37] Haymarket and the 1886 strikes introduced other changes: the emergence of a labor party in turn gave rise to a "law and order" coalition both in Chicago and in the Town of Lake. When the dust settled, the township's People's party had a Republican cast and the Citizens' group sheltered most of the Democrats. Finally, the political waters were muddied by the protracted debate on annexation. Two-thirds of Lake's voters turned it down in 1887; the bare majority that accepted merger in 1889 did so because the town board no longer "fit"—fairly represented—the eighty-five thousand residents. Annexation was the lesser of two evils.

NOTES

1. Michael P. McCarthy, "The New Metropolis: Chicago, the Annexation Movement, and Progressive Reform," in Michael H. Ebner and Eugene M. Tobin, eds., *The Age of Urban Reform: New Perspectives on the Progressive Era* (Port Washington, N.Y., 1977), 45–47.

2. *Sun,* Nov. 2, 1889; Mar. 21, 1890; Town of Lake Records, Doc. 155, Apr. 29, 1881; Doc. 156, May 5, 1882 (City Hall Archives, Chicago); *Trib.*, Apr. 3, 1881; Mar. 17, 1882; *Englewood Eye,* Mar. 10, 1883.

3. Town of Lake Records, Doc. 2060, Dec. 23, 1881; *Trib.*, Mar. 25, 27, 1881; Apr. 30, 1882; Mar. 1, 4–9, 14, 27–31, Apr. 5, 6, 11, 14, 1883; *Englewood Eye,* Mar. 24, 31, Apr. 7, 1883.

4. Town of Lake Records, Doc. 381, May 1, Aug. 17, 1883; Doc. 169, Apr. 23, 1883; *Englewood Eye,* June 9, 1883; Feb. 2, 16, Mar. 8, 15, 22, Apr. 5, 19, 1884; *Trib.*, May 10, July 24, Aug. 14, 17, Sept. 12, Nov. 6, 1883; Feb. 29, Mar. 1, 3, 5, 9, 16, 28, 30, Apr. 2, 1884.

5. Town of Lake Records, Doc. 383, June 3, 1885; *Trib.*, May 1, June 11, July 3, Oct. 15, Dec. 20, 1884; Jan. 3, Mar. 4, 21, 24, Apr. 1, 2, 4, 7, 9, 1885; Mar. 17, 21, Apr. 3, 7, 19, 1886; *Sun,* May 5, 17, 1884; Mar. 31, Apr. 3, 6, 8, 1885; Mar. 1, 29, 1886. On Irish political loyalty, see Thomas N. Brown, "The Political Irish: Politicians and Rebels," in David Noel Doyle and Owen Dudley Edwards, eds., *America and Ireland, 1776–1976: The American Identity and the Irish Connection* (Westport, Conn., 1980), 143–44.

6. Town of Lake Records, Doc. 2012, Annual Reports for the Year Mar. 1, 1885 to Mar. 1, 1886; *Trib.*, Feb. 7, 22, Mar. 1, 14, Apr. 7, 8, 18, 1886; Jan. 29, 1888; *Drovers Journal,* Jan. 27, Feb. 9, 1888; *Sun,* Mar. 1, 22–24, 29, 1886.

7. Town of Lake Records, Doc. 658, May 3, 1886; Doc. 816, Apr. 10, 1886; Doc. 161, May 19, 1886; Doc. 869, Jan. 12, 1887; *Sun,* Apr. 7, May 26, Sept. 15, Nov. 16, 1886; Jan. 5, Mar. 26, 1887; *Trib.*, Nov. 4, 1885; Apr. 7, 8, 18, July 13, 1886.

8. *Sun,* May 3, Aug. 8, Nov. 3, 6, 8, 1884; *Trib.*, Aug. 5, Sept. 13, Nov. 6, 23, 1884.

9. *Sun,* Nov. 3, 1886; *Trib.*, Sept. 15, 26, Nov. 4, 1886; [Chicago] *Knights of Labor,* Nov. 6, 1886; Edward B. Mittelman, "Chicago Labor in Politics, 1877–96," *Journal of Political Economy,* 28 (May, 1920), 417–21; Ralph W. Scharnau, "Thomas J. Morgan and the United Labor Party of Chicago," *JISHS,* 66 (Spring, 1973), 42–49; Harry Barnard, *Eagle Forgotten: The Life of John Peter Altgeld* (New York, 1938), 118–20.

10. *Trib.*, Feb. 26, 27, 28, Mar. 13, 30, 1887; Scharnau, "Morgan and the United Labor Party," 49–54; [Chicago] *Knights of Labor,* Jan. 8, Feb. 5, Mar. 5, 1887; Duncan Eldridge McBride, "The Chicago Labor Parties, 1886–1889" (M. A. thesis, University of Chicago, 1943), 45–56.

11. *Trib.*, Mar. 17, 18, 20, Apr. 1, 5, 1887; Cullerton to editor, Apr. 4, 1887; *Chicago Herald,* Apr. 4, 1887; *Times,* Apr. 5, 1887; Scharnau, "Morgan and the United Labor Party," 54; Bessie Louise Pierce, *A History of Chicago,* vol. 3, *The Rise of a Modern City, 1871–1893* (New York, 1957), 362–63.

12. *Sun,* Nov. 16, 1886; Mar. 3, 14, 17, 28, 30–31, 1887; *Labor Enquirer,* Mar. 12, Apr. 2, 1887; *Trib.*, Feb. 6, 14, 21, Mar. 22, Apr. 1, 4, 1887.

13. *Sun,* Mar. 26, 28, 31, 1887; *Englewood Call,* Mar. 17, 1887, reprinted in *Labor Enquirer,* Mar. 17, 1888; Mar. 31, 1887, reprinted in *Labor Enquirer,* Mar. 24, 1888; *Labor Enquirer,* Apr. 2, 6, 1887.

14. *Trib.*, Apr. 6, 7, 1887; *Sun,* Apr. 6, 1887; Jan. 21, 1888; [Chicago] *Knights of Labor,* Apr. 9, 1887; *Labor Enquirer,* Apr. 9, 1887.

15. *Labor Enquirer,* Nov. 26, 1887; Apr. 7, 14, 1888; *Trib.*, Apr. 7, 11, Aug. 8, 9, 1887; Apr. 4, 1888; *Times,* Apr. 4, 1888; [Chicago] *Knights of Labor,* Apr. 9, 1887; Nov. 10, 1888; *Sun,* Sept. 24, 1888; Scharnau, "Morgan and the United Labor Party," 56–60.

16. Town of Lake Records, Doc. 42, Apr. 16, 1887; Doc. 183, Apr. 16, 1887; Doc. 38, Apr. 16, 1887; Doc. 184, May 20, 1887; *Sun,* Apr. 7, 1888; *Trib.*, Apr. 17, 21, May 14, 16, 20, 26, 1887.

17. *Sun,* Feb. 23, Apr. 22, 1887; *Trib.*, Jan. 21, 1883; Dec. 20, 1885; Jan. 13, Sept. 29, 1886; Barbara M. Posadas, "Community Structures of Chicago's Northwest Side: The Transition from Rural to Urban, 1830–1889" (Ph.D. diss., Northwestern University, 1976), 163–64; Jean F. Block, *Hyde Park Houses: An Informal History, 1856–1910* (Chicago, 1978), 22–25; Stanley Buder, *Pullman: An Experiment in Industrial Order and Community Planning, 1880–1930* (New York, 1967), 109–11; Ann Durkin Keating, "Governing the New Metropolis: The Development of Urban and Suburban Governments in Cook County, Illinois, 1831 to 1902" (Ph.D. diss., University of Chicago, 1984), 279–306; Louis P. Cain, "To Annex or Not? A Tale of Two Towns: Evanston and Hyde Park," *Explorations in Economic History,* 20 (Jan., 1983), 58–72. On the broader problem of city-suburban relationships, see Jon C. Teaford, *City and Suburb: The Political Fragmentation of Metropolitan America, 1850–1970* (Baltimore, 1979), chaps. 2, 3; Kenneth T. Jackson, "Metropolitan Government versus Suburban Autonomy: Politics on the Crabgrass Frontier," in Kenneth T. Jackson and Stanley K. Schultz, eds., *Cities in American History* (New York, 1972), 442–62; Kenneth T. Jackson, *Crabgrass Frontier: The Suburbanization of the United States* (New York, 1985), 140–48.

18. Pierce, *Chicago,* 3:331–32; *Trib.*, Jan. 20, 30, May 26, June 1, 10, 20, Sept. 2, 14, 1887.

19. *Trib.*, Jan. 23, Oct. 16, 26, Nov. 7, 1887; *Sun,* Sept. 30, 1887; *Daily News,* Nov. 5, 1887; Teaford, *City and Suburb,* 44.

20. *Trib.*, Sept. 2, 14, 1887; *Sun,* Sept. 22–26, 30, Nov. 6, 1887.

21. *Sun,* Nov. 1, 2, 7, 9, 1887; *Trib.*, Nov. 9, 1887; Block, *Hyde Park,* 25–26; Michael P. McCarthy, "New Metropolis," 45–47.

22. A. H. Champlin to editor, *Trib.*, Jan. 1, 1888.

23. *Sun,* Jan. 28, Mar. 12, 14, 22, 26, 27, 29, 31, Apr. 2, 4, 1888; *Trib.*,

Jan. 27, 29, Feb. 29, Mar. 18, Apr. 4, 1888; *Labor Enquirer,* Mar. 17, 24, 31, 1888; "K. of L." to editor, Dec. 17, 1887.

24. *Trib.,* Mar. 17, 18, 1888; Apr. 25, May 10, 1889; *Sun,* Apr. 25, May 10, 13, 1889; Pierce, *Chicago,* 3:332–33; Teaford, *City and Suburb,* 44–45.

25. Town of Lake Records, Doc. 201, Apr. 24, 1888; *Sun,* Jan. 4, 19, Feb. 4, 6, Mar. 11, 20, 28–30, 1889; *Trib.,* Apr. 25, 1888; Feb. 4, Mar. 4, 8, 20, 31, Apr. 1, 3, 18, 1889.

26. *Sun,* Jan. 25, 30, Feb. 5, Mar. 7, Apr. 3, 1889; *Inter Ocean,* Apr. 4, 1889; *Trib.,* Mar. 30, Apr. 3, 7, 18, 1889; 1876 Collectors Warrants, Town of Lake, 1:179; 1888 Collectors Warrants, Town of Lake, 2:72–73 (Cook County Archives, Chicago); Town of Lake Records, Doc. 373, May 28, 1889.

27. *Sun,* May 11, June 28, 1889; *Trib.,* May 5, 15, June 9, 16, 1889; "R. M. M." to editor, June 26, 1889; Reverend H. C. Kinney to editor, June 23, 1889; Michael P. McCarthy, "New Metropolis," 47.

28. *Sun,* May 10, June 20, 1889; *Trib.,* June 16, 23, 25, 27, 1889; *Daily News,* June 21, 25, 1889; *Chicago Herald,* June 23, 1889.

29. *Sun,* June 7, 10, 13, 1889; *Trib.,* May 15, 17, June 9, 1889.

30. *Sun,* June 6, 11, 15, 20, 22, 27, 28, July 1, 1889; *Trib.,* June 5, 18, 19, 23, 25, 26, 28, 1889. Chicago taxed real estate at 4 percent on assessed valuation, which was one-third of the cash value; Town of Lake taxed property at 8 percent on the assessed valuation, which was calculated at one-tenth of the cash value (*Sun,* June 15, 1889).

31. *Sun,* May 10, June 7, 20, 26, 27, 1889; *Trib.,* June 2, 5–7, 27, 28, 1889; *Chicago Herald,* June 26, 1889.

32. *Trib.,* June 29, 30, 1889; *Daily News,* June 30, 1889; *Sun,* July 1, 1889; Buder, *Pullman,* 113; Michael P. McCarthy, "New Metropolis," 47; Teaford, *City and Suburb,* 46–47; Barbara M. Posadas, "Suburb into Neighborhood: The Transformation of Urban Identity on Chicago's Periphery," *JISHS,* 76 (Autumn, 1983), 170–72.

33. Charles Fanning, *Finley Peter Dunne and Mr. Dooley: The Chicago Years* (Lexington, Ky., 1978), 156; Michael F. Funchion, *Chicago's Irish Nationalists, 1881–1890* (New York, 1976), 105–9.

34. *Drovers Journal,* May 28, 1889; *Trib.,* June 2, 16, 17, 24, 1889; *Inter Ocean,* June 16, 1889; Funchion, *Chicago's Irish Nationalists,* 89.

35. *Sun,* July 17, 1889; *Trib.,* May 21, 1889.

36. *Times,* July 16, 1889; *Trib.,* July 15, 16, 1889; *Sun,* July 16, 1889.

37. Town of Lake Records, Doc. 657, May 7, 1888; Doc. 655, Dec. 23, 1887.

CHAPTER 19

The Township in the City

Early in 1890 Chicago won the honor of hosting an exposition to mark the four hundredth anniversary of Columbus's discovery of America. New Yorkers had strenuously opposed the choice of the brash young midwestern metropolis; it was merely "an inland and prosaic city."[1] Determined to prove its rivals wrong, Chicago set to work on plans for an impressive exposition and a flurry of improvement projects for the city. Because of its close proximity to the Jackson Park fair grounds, the former Town of Lake was a major beneficiary of the frenzied cleanup campaigns. Packingtown, Stockyards, and city officials solved such long-standing problems as South Fork pollution, water shortages in the northern part of the township, and convenient transportation for the large number of visitors expected to pass through the Stone Gate. Meanwhile, residents of the former township adapted quickly to Chicago's brand of politics. They already had some familiarity with partisan slates and a good deal of experience with ethnic factors. The doubling of the population within five years after annexation enhanced the importance of the three Town of Lake wards, and national publicity featuring the livestock trade and meat-packing as Chicago's premier industry drew attention to the former township. Even the "colonels" of Englewood had a change of heart about Section 5. They tried to lure Philip D. Armour into the mayor's race in 1893, and when that failed, they voted for livestock dealer and packer Samuel Allerton as the most appropriate man to preside over the World's Fair.

The Political Adjustment

The city council's first order of business in the summer of 1889 was a new ward map. The aldermen welcomed recommendations from the annexed territories, and Hyde Park had little difficulty settling the boundaries of the three wards to which it was entitled. Confusion reigned in Town of Lake. Some advocated east-west lines at Forty-third and Forty-seventh streets; others favored north-south boundaries at Stewart Avenue and Halsted Street. Both proposals would create three wards of roughly equal popula-

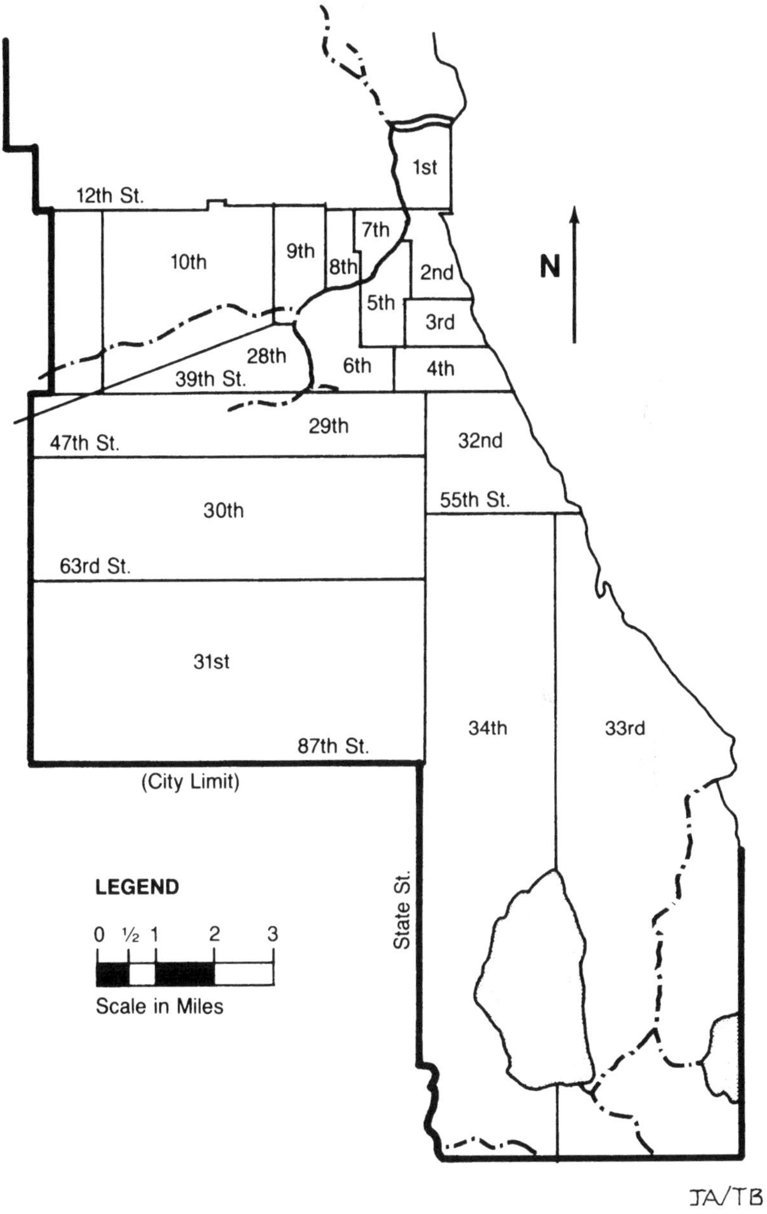

Map 8. Selected Chicago ward boundaries, 1890–1900

tion but grossly unequal size. A third group suggested two wards east of Halsted divided by Fifty-fifth and one large ward for the western part of the township. In the end, the council devised its own solution—three wards with east-west boundaries at Forty-seventh and Sixty-third streets. When a portion of Calumet Township joined Chicago in 1890, it was attached to the southernmost ward. The township had not proposed the division it ultimately received because those boundaries cut through the heart of Englewood and separated New City-Back of the Yards.[2]

Henceforth it would be up to the two aldermen from each of these wards to see that their districts got services and patronage. They soon found that the township experience in balancing competing interests and edging closer to Democratic and Republican parties stood them in good stead. In September, 1889, voters identified the aldermen who would serve until the regular spring election. Since the Twenty-ninth Ward included the Northeast Corners, the Stockyards, and Back of the Yards, the Democrats were sure to carry it and Thomas Gahan was certain to be one of the aldermen. Back of the Yards hoped to claim the other seat, but the caucus favored a second Stockyards alderman. Republicans owned the southernmost ward, the Thirty-first, and voters wanted E. J. Noble, foe of annexation and a Union Army veteran. The middle ward was an awkward amalgam of New City, the northern part of Englewood, and the Car-Shops. A *Sun* reporter thought the interests of "Scandinavians, Germans, railroad men and silk stockings" were so different that the Thirtieth Ward would always be a "hot-bed of political unpleasantness." In this first election, Republicans backed a German-American candidate and the editor of the *Western Rural;* Democrats lined up behind the popular Armour dressed beef foreman, John Kenny, and a German-American employed by a livestock commission firm. The Democratic candidates went to the city council. Aldermen Gahan, Kenny, and Noble won two-year terms in April, 1890, and voters in the three wards chose Charles Kotzenberg as their assessor. Although the ambitious young Tom Carey of Back of the Yards lost his primary fight in 1890, it was generally agreed that he had staked a claim to the Twenty-ninth Ward's two-year aldermanic seat the next time around.[3]

State and local elections were complicated for the next two years by the so-called Edwards School Law. This 1889 statute required children aged seven to fourteen to attend public or approved night or private schools for at least sixteen weeks each year. Its second requirement caused the controversy: reading, writing, arithmetic, American history, and geography must be taught in English and private schools had to submit to state inspection. Germans, Bohemians, Swedes, and Poles opposed the intrusion in their religious institutions, and Irish Catholics took up their cause. Members of the American Protective Association and professional educators who supported the Edwards law were dubbed "the little red school house" faction. Republican state superintendent of public instruction, Richard Edwards, went down to defeat in November, 1890, and the Democratic victor, Henry Raab, vowed to have the law repealed. Republican legislators blocked this until 1893, so the law remained a major irritant to ethnic voters. Michael McInerney, a manager of Raab's campaign, won a seat in the legislature in the fall of 1890. The next spring he encouraged Democrats in the Thirtieth Ward to run a German-born engineer, Adam Rauen, on an anti-Edwards law platform. He won by a whisker.[4]

Another ethnic issue, Mayor DeWitt Cregier's favoritism to the Irish, caused unrest within the Democratic party. To the chagrin of Town of Lake Democrats who had worked hard for annexation, the mayor saved his best cigars and patronage plums for the Irish antis, McInerney, Gahan, and Byrne. They made Michael J. Butler a gas inspector and Edward J. Condon a street-cleaning inspector and then built an Irish "Democracy" in the Twenty-ninth and Thirtieth wards. Former mayor Carter Harrison, desirous of hosting the World's Fair, heard the rumbles and decided to enter the mayoralty race in 1891. Charles Thornton of the Thirty-first Ward volunteered to run his campaign. After a bitter primary and raucous convention, the Democrats ended up with two candidates, Cregier for "Democracy" and Harrison for "Chicago Democracy." The Republicans nominated Hempstead Washburne, and the socialists offered Thomas J. Morgan. A Citizens' party, standing for business efficiency, Sunday closing of saloons, and the Edwards law, persuaded Elmer Washburn to enter the fray. A cynical *Tribune* reporter dismissed Morgan and Elmer Washburn as hopeless and said the only difference among the others was that silk hats, rubbers, and umbrellas cluttered Republican headquarters; cigars, Charles Thornton, and many German and Bohemian political workers characterized Harrison's campaign office; cigars, Michael McInerney, Irish pols, and an absence of Germans let him know that he was at Cregier's City Hall.[5]

In the aftermath of Hempstead Washburne's victory, the Democratic factions exchanged charges of election irregularities. Cregier's lieutenants, it was said, used strong-arm tactics in seven wards, including the "bloody Sixth," the Twenty-ninth, and Thirtieth. Tom Carey's precinct Back of the Yards, for example, reported 542 out of 543 votes for him as alderman and 502 votes for Cregier. The Republican precinct judge was frightened off at gunpoint, and Henry Frederick wanted to vote Republican but "sized up the crowd . . . and thought I had better go home and tend to my business." A German shopkeeper saw Harrison supporters crowded out of line but refused to testify for fear his "windows would be smashed by the toughs and my stock gutted." A citizens' rally at the Armory, sponsored by

Philip Armour, Charles Thornton, Samuel Allerton, Charles Hutchinson, and Father Dorney among others, demanded registration before municipal elections and a single term for mayors. The city council enacted the first reform but held off on the second in order to see how the Australian or secret ballot worked in Illinois. Observers predicted striking changes. "It will be a simon pure picnic for party bolters and kickers," chortled Harvey Goodall, "and a terror to machine managers," their "boys," and their "thumpers."[6]

The loss of city jobs as well as the new election laws convinced Irish Democrats that they would have to broaden the base of the party if they hoped to recapture City Hall in 1893. A staunch ally of McInerney, Gahan, and Carey confided to a *Sun* reporter, "Thornton can knock us silly plugging among the silk stockings, and it is they who control the party after all. When we get away from home, Thornton has us where the hair is short." Experience in the legislature widened McInerney's horizon: "there wasn't much money in it, but I learned a great deal. I didn't suppose I had so much to learn." Irish holdouts were converted in the spring of 1892 by the humiliating defeat of aldermen Burke in the Sixth Ward and Cullerton in the Ninth Ward by German-American candidates. The Irish faction in the Democratic party was ready, therefore, to support the nomination of Judge John Peter Altgeld for governor in 1892. Altgeld's vigorous campaign and the enthusiastic reponse of voters surprised seasoned reporters. Illinois Republicans hoped that national issues of tariff and currency would save the day for their incumbent governor and President Harrison, yet nothing could stop the "Democratic contagion." It was so virulent that Altgeld and Grover Cleveland collected 40 percent of the vote in the Thirty-first Ward.[7]

Altgeld's victory encouraged German Democrats in Chicago to dream about a German-American mayor in 1893. Their candidate, the publisher of the *Illinois Staats-Zeitung*, lost the primary to Carter Harrison and promised not to run as an independent. Republicans and members of the Citizens' party believed that they finally had a chance to elect "a man of stature," a businessman with a national reputation. Many felt that Philip D. Armour, the quintessential embodiment of Chicago "ingenuity," was the best choice "for Mayor of Chicago during the World's Fair." Armour brushed the idea aside, but Samuel W. Allerton was willing to give it a try. With ties to the Stockyards, Packingtown, Illinois stock growers, the trade unions, and German-Americans, Allerton secured the backing of the Citizens' party and then won the Republican nomination. During the hard-fought campaign, both Allerton and Carter Harrison appealed for "packinghouse votes." Readily admitting that he did not have an international reputation, Allerton said he would much rather shake hands with packinghouse workers than European royalty. Harrison ran on his record as mayor and left it to others to say that Allerton lacked political experience and the only Chicagoans known abroad were Philip Armour and Carter Harrison. Eyeing the potential Democratic vote in the Twenty-ninth and Thirtieth wards, the former mayor vowed that with the help of "the three Toms"—Gahan, Byrne, and Carey—"I'll carry the Town of Lake" and then not even "all creation" can stand in the way of victory.[8]

Local quarrels influenced the outcome of the 1893 election in the three Lake wards. The sudden death of Assessor Kotzenberg forced voters to choose between Republican Conrad Walther and Democrat Michael McInerney, a classic German-Irish contest. In the Twenty-ninth Ward, Alderman Tom Carey ran for reelection and urged supporters to vote for McInerney and Carter Harrison; Republican "Buck" McCarthy ran as an "independent" allied with Walther and Allerton. Since John T. Joyce, former Knights of Labor leader, now held a Republican patronage job, he worked for Walther and Allerton. When the votes were counted, Conrad Walther was the new assessor, Tom Carey had another term in the city council, Carter Harrison swept the Twenty-ninth Ward, and Allerton took the Thirtieth and Thirty-first. German support for Allerton had not been strong enough to counteract Irish, Bohemian, Polish, and other Chicago ethnic votes for Harrison. Charging that patronage promises won the election for Harrison, a Polish editor found consolation in the fact that Germans would be cut out of the spoils; they "cannot expect consideration . . . after their scurrilous attacks upon him." As for the defeated Allerton, he had no regrets about being "an independent citizen" instead of "a public official bound by a hundred pledges."[9]

Town of Lake hopefuls came out on top in the scramble for patronage. Gahan gave up his council seat when Governor Altgeld appointed him to the Illinois Railroad and Warehouse Commission and President Cleveland relied upon him to distribute federal jobs. Mayor Carter Harrison put Charles Thornton on the Chicago Board of Education and gave Alderman Carey a free hand with city jobs. Carey promoted Edward J. Condon to superintendent of street cleaning in the South Division and placed so many Twenty-ninth Ward friends on the payroll that Goodall thought he had more patronage jobs "than twenty members of the Council . . . put together." When Carey's grateful flock gave him a gold star with an interchangeable emerald and diamond center, he modestly responded, "I came here a poor man. . . . What I am [today] I owe to the Twenty-ninth Ward." John T. Joyce lost the job "Buck" McCarthy had secured for him but bounced into an even better one as Conrad Walther's deputy assessor of the Town of Lake. Understandably the new Lithuanian newspaper informed its readers, "who wants to get an easy and well paid job must take part in political action." The following month a Lithuanian Political Club sprouted in Back of the Yards.[10]

Delivery of City Services

Opponents of annexation were wrong about local politicians being powerless in the larger Chicago pond, and they were also in error about municipal services deteriorating in the former township. The police force merged with that of Hyde Park to form Chicago's Second Division with headquarters in the new station at Forty-seventh Street and Halsted. The man in charge was Hyde Parker Nicholas Hunt, an Irish immigrant whose career in law enforcement paralleled that of his good friend Thomas Gahan. Town of Lake welcomed him and applauded his decision to eliminate the police magistrate court at the Stockyards and divide its business between Englewood and the Sixth Ward. As for the firemen, they received a small wage hike upon joining the city, and they came under the jurisdiction of Marshal Denis Swenie, brother of their dead chief. The Union Stock Yard and Transit Company had enough confidence in Swenie to merge its Liberty Engine Company with the city force.[11]

Frantic preparations to ready the city for Columbian Exposition visitors yielded benefits for the Town of Lake. Concern about unpaved streets and irregular garbage collections in the crowded inner city wards prompted Charles L. Hutchinson to wonder if "perhaps . . . we had made a mistake in undertaking the 'World's Fair.'" On the other hand, the obligation just might "teach us for once to clean the City properly." Members of the Citizens' Association and residents of Hull-House badgered the city into providing more scavenger teams in the "Forgotten Region," but this soon filled the clay pits of Lake View and Town of Lake which were used as dumps. A Women's Municipal Order League and a committee of businessmen, including Gustavus Swift and Nathaniel Fairbank, finally sold the city council on garbage crematories. Two opened in 1893, and there was a demonstration garbage furnace on the fair grounds. Thanks to the crowds anticipated at the Stockyards, all the streets in the Twenty-ninth Ward east of Halsted were resurfaced and the alleys paved. As soon as the Halsted sewer was finished, Goodall wanted to see the entire length of that artery paved with granite blocks. Property owners objected to the additional cost, however, and Halsted got a macadam surface. Edward J. Condon sent four hundred scavenger teams into the township in May, 1893, and while Mayor Harrison's promise "to make the entire city as clean as a park" did not materialize, the three Lake wards were cleaner than they had ever been before.[12]

Chicago signaled its intent to reduce smoke by fining Marshall Field and Company and warning Packingtown to install condensers or else. Some packers pointed out to Alderman Gahan that Section 5 had no "public streets" and employes never had objected to smoke. Gahan relayed this message to the health department, which replied that packinghouse smoke traveled to other parts of the city and distance made it "no less offensive. . . . You . . . should set an example worthy of your wealth and position in society." Ultimately they did. Nathaniel K. Fairbank successfully tested a downdraft smokeless furnace and persuaded others to try it. He and Samuel Allerton became charter members of the Society for the Prevention of Smoke, which used volunteer spotters and hired agents to bring over six hundred prosecutions during the two years preceding the opening of the exposition. By the winter of 1893–94, however, contributions to the society and civic support for a smoke-free atmosphere had dissipated. "If 'what goes up must come down,' and 10 percent of the coal used in Chicago goes up in smoke," calculated the *Tribune*, "then something like 300,000 tons of filth and dirt fall annually on the heads of Chicago people."[13]

Chicago's plans for pure drinking water and improved drainage were linked to the Sanitary and Ship Canal approved by voters in 1889. Questions about the constitutionality of the "new river" and administrative quarrels delayed the start of construction until September, 1892, too late to be of any help during the fair year. Two of the annexed townships and part of Chicago sewered into the lake; Chicago's high typhoid fever statistics received national publicity in the early 1890s; and the city knew that it had to find a remedy before the exposition opened. It built a new four-mile water tunnel into Lake Michigan and a powerful pumping station at Fourteenth and Indiana. The new waterworks doubled the city's pumping capacity and delivered pure water, as falling typhoid rates demonstrated. The new supply mains serving the Twenty-ninth Ward, however, did not solve the occasional water shortages on either side of Section 5. Renewed grumbling about watering and washing hogs and cattle while children went thirsty prompted Stockyards officials and packers to ask Chicago for permission to build their own $500,000 water conduit, pumping station, and lake intake tunnel. Alderman Gahan introduced an enabling ordinance, but the scheme hit a snag when the council demanded the right to let the contracts. Finally, a crash program to replace the 1870s four-inch mains in the residential parts of the ward solved the entire problem.[14]

Chicago's nineteen trunk line sewers emptying into the branches of the Chicago River were as much as the drainage channel could bear, and everyone knew that South Fork and Town of Lake wastes might clog that precarious system before the new Sanitary Canal was ready. In the fall of 1890 an aldermanic committee, including Gahan, Kenny, and Burke, met with packers and Stockyards officials to explore solutions. Since annexation was behind them and the World's Fair immediately ahead of them, none of the participants engaged in the usual banter of stockyard and packinghouse waste versus Town of Lake and Sixth Ward sewage. A rare "spirit of moderation and good temper on both sides" enabled them to hammer out a three-part solution. The city installed powerful new pumps at the juncture of the South Branch, South Fork, and Illinois and Michigan Canal. It also implemented the 1885 recommendation of Benezette Williams and Ralph E. Brownell for a large conduit from the South Fork to the canal and a pumping station to guarantee a current in the conduit. The packers and Stockyards company built an intercepting sewer on the south side of their Thirty-ninth Street canal, an improvement that just might make the notorious slip "as pure as Jackson Park," joked Goodall. Having solved the crisis of the South Fork, city engineers approved plans for additional sewers in the western part of the former Town of Lake. Alderman Carey had been pressing for a north-south trunk line between Ashland and Western avenues. It would be Chicago's largest sewer, take eighteen months to build, employ five hundred men, and cost $335,000. Mayor Carter Harrison gave his consent and the council let the contract to Thomas Gahan and Thomas Byrne—a clean sweep for Lake's "three Toms."[15]

By the time the World's Fair buildings were dedicated in the fall of 1892, Chicago's frenzied cleanup was producing results. The Citizens' Association, usually at odds with City Hall, went out of its way to commend the "unusual activity" and praise the "orders, ordinances, and resolutions bearing on the sanitary condition of the city." Even the Women's Municipal Order League, which once pictured the city as "greedy for praise and flattery" while wallowing in filth, harbored hopes that Chicago would pass muster in 1893. Prospective visitors worrying about Chicago's sanitary condition learned from *Forum* magazine that Mayor Harrison had cleansed the streets and the infamous river, filtered the water in public drinking fountains, and arranged for the sale of inexpensive Wisconsin spring water at hotels, restaurants, and the fair grounds. It was, therefore, "absolutely safe" to visit Chicago and drink its water.[16]

Transit improvements between annexation and the opening of the fair impressed even New Yorkers and certainly benefited the former Town of Lake. Extension of the State Street cable line from Thirty-ninth Street to Englewood cut travel time in half to downtown Chicago and boosted property values at State and Forty-eighth to an unprecedented $180 per front foot. In both Town of Lake and Hyde Park, the older two-story frame stores gave way to four- and five-story brick structures whose first floors were occupied by merchants vying for cable car customers. It was not long, however, before an even speedier elevated train lured patrons away from the cable cars. The Chicago and South Side Rapid Transit Company started building to the city's southern limits in 1888, and since some of its track passed through downtown alleys, Chicagoans called it the "alley elevated" and eventually the "Alley L," a name adopted by the company. Following annexation, the elevated continued to Sixty-third Street, and in 1892 it built from Englewood to Jackson Park along Sixty-third.[17]

Elevated trains traveling at three times the speed of cable cars intrigued commuters, realtors, and promoters. Gahan, Byrne, John B. Sherman, and Irus Coy formed a company to provide elevated service on Thirty-ninth, Forty-third, Sixty-third, and Eighty-seventh; although they had charters from the Town of Lake and later the City of Chicago, they could not secure adequate financing. They and others tried hard to persuade the Alley L to build a spur to the Stockyards, but they did not succeed and the 1894 depression throttled further discussions. The tremendous success of "electric horse-cars" helped delay construction of more elevated lines. The electric trolleys, or streetcars, were much cheaper and more versatile than elevated lines, and they moved as fast as cable cars. Town of Lake's first trolley ran across Forty-seventh Street, and by 1893 there were streetcars on Sixty-third, Halsted, and Root Street from State to the Stockyards. The Chicago City Railway Company could not electrify its horsecar lines fast enough to meet the demand. When the city council tried to extract electric streetlights in return for permission to electrify, residents of the Lake wards staged a protest rally. They wanted trolleys immediately; streetlights could wait.[18]

Railroad tracks crossing horsecar and trolley lines at grade level troubled many parts of Chicago, but the problem was especially serious in Town of Lake due to the heavy railroad traffic at the Stockyards. In one twelve-month period, three collisions on Forty-seventh Street killed six and seriously injured thirty-six people. Father Dorney accused the railroads of causing six times as many accidents as all other employers in the Twenty-ninth Ward combined. The "47th Street murders" led to formation of an Anti-Grade Crossing Association. Its members knew that viaducts were difficult to use in winter and they had a depressing effect upon property values. In 1893 a solution appeared. Chicago required the Illinois Central to elevate its lakefront tracks prior to the opening of the fair, and the underpasses for major streets worked well. When the city council ordered all other railroads to elevate by 1899, the Pennsylvania dickered for temporary viaducts at Forty-third, Forty-seventh, and Fifty-first streets in Town of Lake. This would make the visitors' approach to the Stockyards much safer, and Carter Harrison explored the possibility. But the Anti-Grade Crossing Association stood firm for track elevation. "Temporary viaducts mean permanent viaducts" and those unsightly structures "destroy our property." The mayor backed off, and track elevation began in 1894. Stockyard visitors were urged to use the Root Street trolley, and fortunately there were no major accidents during the summer of 1893.[19]

Continuous Growth

Annexation did not stunt Town of Lake's continuous "wonderful growth." Between 1889 and 1894, the three wards doubled their population, reaching 165,576, which was slightly more than one-tenth of the total population of Chicago. The steady increase in the number of second-generation immigrant families in the Town of Lake brought down the proportion of foreign-born residents from 44 percent in 1870 to only 36 percent a quarter-century later. Jobs and reasonably priced building lots remained magnets for newcomers. The proliferation of building and loan associations encouraged home building, and Assessor Kotzenberg's relentless pressure on owners of undeveloped land forced them to put large acreages on the market. Public transportation also facilitated the 1890s building boom. While public attention focused on cable cars, elevated trains, and electric trolleys, the Chicago City Railway Company quietly "gridironed" the western districts of the township with horsecar lines "in advance of civilization." As in the 1880s, noted Goodall, those lines soon became "regular colonization roads."[20]

The Twenty-ninth Ward, lying between Thirty-ninth and Forty-seventh streets, had a population of 41,041 in 1894, and two out of every five people had been born outside the United States. Because the ward's southern boundary excluded New City, Irish were nearly twice as numerous as German immigrants. Poles outnumbered Bohemians and Scandinavians, yet these three groups combined constituted fewer than one-tenth of the foreign-born in the Twenty-ninth Ward. Joseph Greenhut, a factory and tenement house inspector in the health department, surveyed industrial employment in the spring of 1893. He calculated twenty-one thousand blue-collar jobs in Packingtown, over two thousand in the Stockyards, and close to three thousand in foundries, machine shops, small factories, and the brickyards. If one adds white-collar and service jobs, Goodall may have been correct when he said there were as many jobs as people in the ward.[21]

New construction east of Halsted was possible because Kotzenberg quadrupled taxes on the eighty acres and convinced the recalcitrant owners to sell. Commercial lots on the north side of Forty-third Street commanded $2,500, while standard residential lots along the extension of Emerald brought $1,500. In the "sylvan nook" south of Forty-third Street, the oldest frame houses gave way to luxury flats featuring the latest bathroom fixtures. The township's first brownstone-front house was built at 4328 Emerald in 1891, and three years later a modern apartment building occupied the corner of Forty-fifth and Emerald. Heavier traffic in this residential enclave and trolleys on Halsted were factors in the decision of Eneas Wood, Louis Swift, and Thomas Gahan to seek quieter locations. Even Gustavus Swift bought land in Kenwood, although he continued to live on Emerald Avenue for several more years. To the west of Packingtown, residential construction extended the Back of the Yards settlement ever closer to Western Avenue. Land prices remained stable and single-family frame cottages could still be built for less than $1,000. Polish and Bohemian property owners often invested twice that amount in two-story structures. These either had a store below and flat above or two flats, one of which provided rental income for the owner.[22]

By 1894 the middle ward had nearly as many residents as the entire township at the time of annexation. The Thirtieth Ward with close to eighty-five thousand people was twice the size of either the Twenty-ninth or Thirty-first wards. Moreover, it sheltered over half of the township's foreign-born. Thanks to the inclusion of New City, Germans constituted one-third of the immigrant population; Irish accounted for 20 percent, Scandinavians 15 percent, Poles and Bohemians about 6 percent each. While some people in the southeastern corner of the ward worked in downtown Chicago and continued to think of themselves as Englewood commuters, the majority were wage earners employed at the Stockyards or in Packingtown. The Rock Island carshops, the company's major facility for building and repairing cars in the 1880s, serviced only Chicago area cars in the early 1890s. Then, in 1892, the Rock Island railroad decided to move its Chicago switchyards and Town of Lake carshops to Blue Island, Illinois; most of the employes relocated as well. They sold their houses to Chicagoans who used the State Street cable cars to reach their jobs, people who neither knew nor cared "that the Town of Lake ever had a corporate existence," groused the local editor.[23]

Prior to the Rock Island migration, the *Sun* noticed that blacks as well as whites found the eastern edges of the ward "a convenient quarter" and since "they pay good rents they experience little difficulty in getting homes." By 1894 the Twenty-ninth Ward had 418 blacks, and a similar number lived in the Thirty-first Ward, primarily along the eastern edge. But the Thirtieth Ward had sixteen hundred black residents and the *Sun* detected a corridor in which "the whites are slowly decreasing in number." The Negroes "never . . . attempt to locate west of the Rock Island tracks, looking on the streets [between the tracks and State Street] as their own ground." The black families were neat and clean, "paid higher rent than their predecessors and painted and improved the property in a striking manner." They did not "interfere" in politics or cause the police any trouble, and thus the "colored colony of the east side of Lake" was considered "superior" to most black enclaves. The township's other "Negro Settlement" won even higher praise. Three-quarters of the blacks living between Center and Ashland, from Sixtieth to Sixty-third, owned their homes, and this group built Shiloh Baptist Church and established a theatrical group under the leadership of policeman Enos Bond. The number of blacks in the three wards climbed from 557 in 1890 to 2,428 by 1894 and their proportion of the total population went from .5 to 1.5 percent; yet they experienced "little difficulty."[24]

Garfield Boulevard (Fifty-fifth Street), once the dividing line between wage earners and upper-income groups in the township, emerged as the showplace of the Thirtieth Ward. St. Anne's Church at the eastern end purchased more land and added a parochial school and residence for the teaching sisters. A Methodist Sunday school at Emerald and the boulevard blossomed into a $40,000 church when its hinterland filled up. West of Halsted the fine homes built by Thomas Byrne and Charles Kotzenberg anchored an elite colony of boulevard houses worth $12,000 to $18,000. Heartened by the influx of well-to-do Irish Catholics, Father McGuire of Visitation parish announced plans for a $60,000 edifice at Peoria and the boulevard. To the north and south of Fifty-fifth, Swedes and Germans built more modest homes and churches, sometimes of wood but usually brick. Members of B'Nai Israel Congregation erected the township's first synagogue in 1892. West of New City, residential construction was similar to that in Back of the Yards. The growing number of Polish and Bohemian families made it possible for Father Zaleski to build St. Joseph's school and for Father Thomas J. Bobal to establish the Bohemian Catholic Church of St. Cyril and St. Methodius. Ten minutes away, at Forty-eighth and Ashland, the Irish church of St. Rose of Lima added a new school building and a community hall to serve its parishioners, most of whom lived Back of the Yards in the Twenty-ninth Ward. Only a few blocks from St. Rose of Lima was New City's oldest and largest ethnic Catholic church, St. Augustine's. It claimed six hundred families in 1893 and nearly eight hundred students in its parochial school. The Franciscans planned an immense Gothic church, two hundred feet in length with towers reaching almost as high. German craftsmen supervised by John Kirschen had half of the structure completed by 1892; it could seat about 1,000 people and cost $75,000. When one of the popular assistant priests died, St. Augustine's parishioners gave him a funeral their neighbors in New City would long remember. The undertaker, "measuring up to the enthusiasm of the occasion," provided "a hearse drawn by four proud black steeds." Uniformed members of the church societies, "plumed knights with drawn swords," lined Ashland Avenue down to Garfield Boulevard, the route of the sixty-odd carriages in the magnificent funeral procession.[25]

Ethnic Catholic activities in the middle ward failed to impress residents living south of Sixty-third Street in the Thirty-first Ward. Although it doubled its population between 1890 and 1894 and had nearly as many people as the Twenty-ninth Ward, it was strikingly different. There were few industrial jobs, and only one-third of the residents were foreign-born, most of them coming from Scotland, England, Canada, and Sweden. Standard-sized lots and medium-priced houses prevailed in the Scandinavian enclave on Ashland and the Irish settlement around St. Brendan's Church, but elsewhere realtors pushed forty-foot-wide lots and boasted about stone sidewalks and curbs, "Boulevard streets" with macadam surfaces, and a border of trees. Residents worried needlessly about the impact of the Columbian Exposition. When the boundaries of their prohibited district were challenged by aspiring saloonkeepers, the Englewood Church Union, the Woman's Christian Temperance Union, the Citizens' League, Charles Thornton, Alderman Noble, and established saloonkeepers who cherished their monopoly formed an invincible defensive coalition. Since the boardinghouses on State Street for World's Fair construction crews were later dismantled and Englewood's two hotels for exposition visitors became respectable apartment houses, there was no invasion of "city people." Annexation, mused Goodall, merely intensified Englewood's desire to preserve its "rural life." The Thirty-first Ward would be the last part of the township to blend "into the great metropolis."[26]

Absorption into the metropolis was considerably less traumatic than some township residents had feared it would be. Chicago's preparations for the Columbian Exposition yielded many benefits—street and alley paving in the northeastern sector, a resolution of the South Fork drainage impasse, the new south side waterworks, and access to cable cars, the Alley L, and the first electric trolleys. The certain knowledge that thousands of World's Fair visitors would also be entering the former township to view the Stockyards and Packingtown turned out to be an asset. Ward boundaries imposed by the city council severed New City and Back of the Yards and plowed through the very heart of Englewood. Yet voters, office seekers, and aldermen adjusted to the new political districts and the two-party system in local elections. Prior to merger, the *Inter Ocean* accused township politicians of opposing annexation because they would not know how to get the "larger plums in the municipal pudding." Town of Lake did well on that score—a school board position, many patronage jobs thanks to "the three Toms," the city's largest sewer project, and a mayoral candidate in 1893. The features that had attracted newcomers in the 1880s continued to pull additional settlers after Thirty-ninth became an ordinary city street. Industrial and service jobs in the Twenty-ninth and Thirtieth wards could still be matched with reasonably priced building lots close by a horsecar line. Thus Back of the Yards and New City experienced the same "wonderful growth" that had characterized the township in the previous decade. New churches and social organizations, plus the strengthening of existing ones, proved that neither annexation nor artificial ward boundaries could unravel the social fabric of the community. Although the legal entity of Town of Lake had disappeared, township as the "container" of community life within it survived the merger.[27]

NOTES

1. William Waldorf Astor, "New York's Candidacy for the World's Fair of 1892," *Cosmopolitan*, 8 (Dec., 1889), 167.
2. *Trib.*, July 1, 2, 13–23, 1889; May 6, 1890; *Sun*, July 10, 11, 13, 17, 18, 19, 23, 1889.
3. *Sun*, July 24, 27, Sept. 3–5, 7, 11, 1889; Mar. 17, 24, 25, 29, Apr. 2, 3, 1890; *Trib.*, Sept. 4, 5, 8, 11, 15, 1889; Mar. 11, 12, Apr. 2, 1890.
4. *Daily News*, Oct. 14, 16, 21, 28, 1890; *Trib.*, Nov. 2, 6, 1890; *Sun*, Aug. 30, 1889; Sept. 5, 6, 8, 20, Nov. 3, 5, 6, 1890; Mar. 8, 15, 19, 21, 29, Apr. 8, June 15, 1891; Charles Shanabruch, *Chicago's Catholics: The Evolution of an American Identity* (Notre Dame, Ind., 1981), 59–73; James W. Sanders, *The Education of an Urban Minority: Catholics in Chicago, 1833–1965* (New York, 1977), 33–36.
5. *Sun*, May 17, 1890; Feb. 27, Mar. 7, 8, 19, 20, 23, 25, 27, 29, Apr. 2, 6, 1891; *Trib.*, Mar. 10, June 13, July 8, 1890; Mar. 16, 17, 20–22, 28, Apr. 2, 4, 1891; Claudius O. Johnson, *Carter Henry Harrison I, Political Leader* (Chicago, 1928), 142–43.
6. Citizens' Association, *Annual Report for 1891* (Chicago, 1891), 9; *Trib.*, Jan. 3, Apr. 8–11, 14, 15, 17, Sept. 4, 1891; *Sun*, Apr. 8, 11, May 28, Aug. 8, 1891.
7. *Trib.*, Mar. 13, Apr. 6, 7, Oct. 27, 28, Nov. 7, 10, 11, Dec. 18, 1892; *Chicago Herald*, Aug. 29, 1892; *Sun*, June 15, 1891; Feb. 25, Mar. 14, 22, Apr. 6, 7, Oct. 22, Nov. 4, 9, 10, Dec. 14, 1892.
8. *Trib.*, Feb. 5, 11, 16, 18, 21, 26, 28, Mar. 2, 6, 10, 12, 14–16, 21–23, Apr. 1, 3, 1893; *Nat. Prov.*, 7 (Feb. 18, 1893), 13; *Sun*, Feb. 14, 18, 21, 27, Mar. 20, 23, 25, 30, 31, Apr. 22, 1893; Paul Michael Green, "The Chicago Democratic Party, 1840–1920: From Factionalism to Political Organization" (Ph.D. diss., University of Chicago, 1975), 45–53.
9. *Sun*, Feb. 1, 4, 11, Mar. 2, 11, 15, 16, 18, 20, 30, Apr. 5, 6, 1893; *Trib.*, Mar. 2, Apr. 5, 6, 1893; *Dziennik Chicagoski*, Apr. 5, 1893 (CFLPS, Roll 50).

10. *Trib.*, Dec. 18, 1892; Apr. 9, 1893; *Sun*, Nov. 25, 28, 30, 1892; May 30, June 19, July 3, 12, 13, 21, 29, Aug. 23, 1893; Apr. 11, 1894; *Lietuva*, Dec. 17, 1892; Jan. 7, 1893 (CFLPS, Roll 41). A nasty quarrel in 1892 between Edward J. Condon and Michael J. Butler, both of whom wanted to be deputy coroner, prompted a disgusted observer to suggest that they bury the hatchet and collaborate on a book entitled *How to Hold Office Continually* (*Sun*, Nov. 30, 1892).

11. *Sun*, Jan. 21, Apr. 25, Sept. 13, 17, Oct. 9, 13, 1890.

12. Charles L. Hutchinson, Diary, Mar. 27, 1890 (Box 1, Charles L. Hutchinson Papers, Newberry Library, Chicago); *Trib.*, July 8, Dec. 12, 1890; Feb. 15, Apr. 16, 17, 1891; Mar. 19, 27, June 17, 26, 28, July 3, Sept. 16, 1892; Jan. 1, June 28, 1893; Citizens' Association, *Annual Report, 1891*, 28; *Sun*, Jan. 4, 13, 14, 31, July 24, 1890; July 29, Dec. 7, 28, 1892; Mar. 24, May 24, June 27, 1893.

13. *Times*, Jan. 3, 1892; *Trib.*, Sept. 18, 1890; Jan. 14, 15, Dec. 29, 1891; Mar. 4, May 15, 1893; May 20, 27, 1894.

14. Louis P. Cain, "The Creation of Chicago's Sanitary District and Construction of the Sanitary and Ship Canal," *Chicago History*, 8 (Summer, 1979), 102–3; James C. O'Connell, "Technology and Pollution: Chicago's Water Policy, 1833–1930" (Ph.D. diss., University of Chicago, 1890), 101; Frederick P. Kenkel, *Chicago and Its Environs: A Complete Guide to the City and the World's Fair* (Chicago, 1893), 176–77; *Trib.*, June 13, July 1, 5, Aug. 17, 19, 20, Oct. 19, Dec. 11, 1890; Dec. 13, 1891; Apr. 25, 1892; July 23, 1893; *Sun*, June 3, 30, Aug. 19, Sept. 24, Nov. 30, 1890; *Drovers Journal*, Jan. 11, June 30, July 7, 8, Sept. 17, 18, 1890.

15. Louis P. Cain, *Sanitation Strategy for a Lakefront Metropolis: The Case of Chicago* (De Kalb, Ill., 1978), 59–61; *Sun*, Oct. 25, 1890; Apr. 20, 1893; *Drovers Journal*, Jan. 18, Feb. 3, 1890; *Trib.*, Jan. 27, Feb. 6, July 1, 1890; Sept. 26, 1891; July 19, 1893.

16. Citizens' Association, *Annual Report for 1892*, 4; O'Connell, "Technology and Pollution," 104; E. Fletcher Ingals, "Chicago's Sanitary Condition," *Forum*, 15 (July, 1893), 585–93; *Trib.*, June 28, 1892.

17. Julian Ralph, *Our Great West* (New York, 1893), 4; *Trib.*, May 28, June 7, 1892; *Sun*, May 10, 24, 1890; Mar. 29, 1891; June 6, 1892; The Economist, *History and Statistics of Chicago Street Railway Corporations with Maps* (Chicago, 1896), 21; Mark H. Putney, *Real Estate Values and Historical Notes of Chicago* (Chicago, 1900), 90; Kenkel, *Chicago and Its Environs*, 52.

18. Town of Lake Records, Doc. 95, May 22, 1888; Doc. 105, Apr. 16, 1889; Doc. 112, June 11, 1889; Doc. 125, July 12, 1889 (City Hall Archives, Chicago); *Trib.*, Apr. 21, 1891; Dec. 9, 1892; *Sun*, Feb. 13, 1890; Aug. 20, 1891; June 3, 6, 11, 1892; May 16, 1893; Mar. 7, 8, 10, 30, June 18, Sept. 22, 24, Oct. 6, Dec. 4, 1894.

19. *Sun*, Apr. 19, May 5, 1890; Dec. 1, 15, 1891; Jan. 11, Mar. 5, Dec. 29, 1892; May 1, 4, 13, June 15, 1893; Feb. 13, Aug. 10, Nov. 9, 1892; *Trib.*, Jan. 15, 16, Dec. 3, 30, 31, 1892; Jan. 17, 21, 31, Feb. 2, 24, Apr. 30, May 4, July 18, 20, 1893; Jan. 30, Mar. 20, 24, July 10, Aug. 15, 1894.

20. *Ninth Census, 1870*, vol. 1, "Population," 110, 598; Board of Education, *School Census of the City of Chicago, April, 1894*, 2, 3, 9; *Sun*, Jan. 11, 1891. The census enumerators in 1890 reported a total population of 99,723 for the three wards, 38 percent of whom were foreign-born. *Eleventh Census, 1890*, vol. 1, "Population," 454–55.

21. Board of Education, *School Census, 1894*, 2, 3, 6; *Drovers Journal*, Oct. 25, 1890; *Sun*, May 26, 1893. The *Tribune*'s figure for total employment in the packinghouses was 22,400. *Trib.*, Jan. 1, 1893.

22. *Sun*, Mar. 14, Nov. 16, 1890; Jan. 18, 25, Feb. 8, May 9, June 2, July 18, Dec. 4, 1891; Apr. 22, May 3, Aug. 27, Oct. 8, Dec. 5, 1892; Jan. 6, Apr. 18, July 26, Nov. 10, 1894; *Dziennik Chicagoski*, July 6, May 18, 1892; Mar. 22, June 7, Oct. 5, 1893 (CFLPS, Roll 55).

23. Board of Education, *School Census, 1894*, 2, 3, 6; *Trib.*, Sept. 22, 1892; *Sun*, Apr. 2, Sept. 3, 22, 1892; Jan. 27, 1894.

24. *Sun*, Oct. 20, 1890; Apr. 14, 1892; May 7, Nov. 10, 1894; Board of Education, *School Census, 1894*, 2, 3; *Eleventh Census, 1890*, vol. 1, "Population," 455.

25. "What the Roman Catholics Have Done at Lake," *Trib.*, Apr. 24, 1892; *Sun*, Jan. 18, Mar. 14, July 31, Aug. 28, 1890; July 16, 23, Sept. 10, 1892; Feb. 25, Aug. 26, 1893; Feb. 10, Mar. 22, Sept. 3, 1894; *Trib.*, Nov. 30, 1890; Apr. 24, Aug. 31, 1892; Sept. 2, 3, 1894; St. Augustine's Parish, *Golden Jubilee and Chronological History of St. Augustine's Parish* (Chicago, 1936), 71–83.

26. Board of Education, *School Census, 1894*, 2, 3, 6; *Sun*, Mar. 14, May 12, Sept. 27, Oct. 14, 21, Nov. 9, 1890; Apr. 9, July 18, 1891; Sept. 10, 1892; July 8, 1893; *Trib.*, June 1, Oct. 11, 12, Nov. 9, 1890; Dec. 25, 1892.

27. *Inter Ocean*, June 28, 1889; Thomas Bender, *Community and Social Change in America* (New Brunswick, N.J., 1978), 99.

Conclusion

On Display in 1893

Although the idea of the American exposition to mark the four hundredth anniversary of Columbus' discovery had been broached as early as 1882, Chicago was not a serious contender for the honor of hosting the show until the latter part of the decade. The city had to recover its equilibrium after the Haymarket tragedy and overcome the bungled annexation effort of 1887. With the suburbs safely gathered into the metropolis, Chicago was ready to fight for the fair. What other city could match its central location, its excellent transportation network, its lakefront setting, its representative population, its stunning recovery from conflagration, or its world-renowned economic prowess?

In the eyes of many Chicagoans there was no better example of America's "lightning progress" than "the great multifarious business" transacted at the Stockyards and Packingtown. The city's name was "indissolubly associated" with that great industry, noted a proud local reporter. New York journalist Julian Ralph visited Section 5 and concluded that "America is great, and Chicago is its prophet." Livestock dealers and meat packers were among the most enthusiastic lobbyists for the fair. Their 1889 Fat Stock Show featured a life-sized statue of Christopher Columbus made of four hundred pounds of butterine. When President Harrison came to dedicate the Auditorium, Chicagoans gave him a royal welcome and an earful of reasons why it was Chicago's turn to hold an international exposition. The *Drovers Journal* was more succinct. "It would simply be fair to the world to let Chicago have the World's Fair."[1]

St. Louis, Washington, New York, and Boston disagreed. "What will Chicago do with an undertaking so various and so colossal?" asked a Boston editor. "Beef on the hoof and beef in the cans . . . sausage raw and pigs' feet cured . . . the odorous creek and antiquated bridges," the presumptuous town could not host "an adequate world's fair." According to the *New York Times*, a Chicago exposition would consist of "much machinery" and "fat cattle and prize pigs galore," "a Western show, and nothing else." Paul de Rousiers found New Yorkers so hostile to Chicago that nearly every newspaper carried "some satire . . . addressed to lard-sellers in Chicago." Just the mention of Chicago, sighed Gertrude Barnum, makes people think of "pork or anarchists."[2]

Jealousy prompted those "merry jests about the rich pork-packers," replied Chicagoans. They had something "beyond the purely material . . . to offer the world," and so they pressed their case with relentless tenacity. In April, 1890, President Harrison signed the bill which made Chicago the site of the exposition. To enable local communities to stage their own Columbus Day celebrations in 1892, the World's Columbian Exposition would open May 1, 1893. The decision was no sooner made than eastern journalists began descending on Chicago, some out of curiosity, some sent by editors who hoped to dispel the "crass ignorance of the West." Chicago's livestock and meat-packing business was carefully examined by writers for *New England Magazine* and *Scientific American*. Julian Ralph's numerous articles in *Harper's Weekly* generated so much interest that they were reissued in 1893 under the titles *Our Great West* and *Harper's Chicago and the World's Fair*. The western metropolis, predicted Ralph, "will be the main exhibit at the Columbian Exposition." The star attraction for many fair visitors was indeed the "young giant city . . . with all its feverish energy and enterprise."[3]

Mindful of the ridicule heaped upon Chicago's livestock and meat products, fair directors wisely decided to scatter those exhibits in Jackson Park. Livestock growers and dealers had a Stockmen's Assembly Hall linked by colonnades to Machinery Hall and the Agriculture Building. To the south of it were ornamental sheds for horses, cattle, sheep, and swine, easily accessible but out of the way of those who did not fancy blooded stock. Packing company exhibits appeared in Machinery Hall, the Agriculture Building, and the Manufactures and Liberal Arts Building. Swift, for example, mounted five displays, the largest being a refrigerator car with glass sides revealing the cooling equipment and beef quarters. His other exhibits featured the manufacture of butterine; the disposition of hoofs, horns, bones, and hides; and the inner workings of the pharmaceutical laboratory. The companies distributed souvenir booklets detailing the origin, growth, and present status of the firm. They also gave out invitations to visit the Stockyards and Packingtown and clear instructions on how to get there. In Section 5 there was a trained corps of uniformed guides ready to escort visitors, provide information, answer questions, and, Goodall hoped, upset some of those "popular illusions" about "darkest" Packingtown.[4]

Every weekday from early June until October some ten thousand visitors made their way to the Stockyards and Packingtown. The architectural distinction of the Transit House, amphitheater, office buildings, and bank surprised them, while Burnham and Root's massive Stone Gate and matching high water tower pleased young and old alike. Gazing down from the viaduct on the wide expanse of pens, many found it nearly impossible to comprehend the number of animals even though tour guides cheerfully repeated the statistics. Inside the packinghouses, visitors, like the journalists who had preceded them, were struck by the variety of machines. Their favorite was the sausage-stuffer which paused just long enough to permit an attendent to twist and tie the casing. Machinery obviously saved time and labor, but it had not displaced butchers. Visitors begged for more time to watch the "skilfull specialists," each "an artist in his own line." They came away convinced that there would never be a "legendary machine into which you put a pig at one end and draw forth . . . sausages at the other."[5]

Packinghouse by-products proved more interesting to some tourists than the pork and beef departments. Guides never let them forget that "not one part of an animal from horn to hoof is wasted now." Cumulative measurements of what went on in Section 5—acres of work space, numbers of animals slaughtered daily, pounds of chilled beef shipped weekly, or dozens of canned meats produced annually—may well have gone in one ear and out the other. Julian Ralph was willing to believe that the cattle, sheep, and hogs, canned meat, sides of beef, hams, and lard containers, "if piled one on the other," would stretch "from here to the moon." Those who visited the Stockyards and Packingtown in 1893, however, did relate the wonders they saw there to "western ingenuity." Chicago's livestock dealers and packers, concluded one tourist, are "enterprising in a manner at once foolish and admirable."[6]

The Industry in Retrospect

The Columbian Exposition was a memorial to America's industrial, technological, and cultural progress and at the same time a celebration of Chicago's embodiment of those accomplishments. At the close of the fair, Mayor Carter Harrison explained that "Chicago has chosen a star, has looked upward to it, and knows nothing that it will not attempt and thus far has found nothing that it cannot achieve." A mere "swamp" when he was born, the city had become the country's second largest by 1893, and he was confident there would be a time when "New York will say 'Let us go to the metropolis of America.'" There was no better illustration of Chicago's rise than the development of its leading industry and the settlement of the Town of Lake. Harvey Goodall had grudgingly added the World's Fair to "the list of Chicago attractions," but he stated categorically and unequivocally that the square mile encompassing the Stockyards and Packingtown "still holds first place."[7]

Nineteenth-century Chicagoans never ranked their city's achievements nor did anyone query exposition visitors. Many, no doubt, would have agreed with the chauvinistic editor. But even those whose work and values were light-years away from the Stockyards and packinghouses understood the economic and psychological importance of the industry. Louis Sullivan, for instance, considered it central to the city's image. The fledgling architect had arrived in 1873 when "the sense of ruin was still blended with ambition of recovery." Yet the "intoxicating rawness," "the sense of big things to be done," was already there. Two decades later he realized that those braggarts—"the greatest this, and the greatest that"—in fact "had vision. What they saw was real, they saw it as destiny." Sullivan, like so many other Chicagoans, eventually traveled to Mecca to observe the "droves of steers, hogs and sheep . . . bellowing, squealing, bleating, or silently anxious as they crowded the runways to their reward." He had watched the "endless procession of oncoming hogs" destined for delivery to "the coterie of skilled surgeons, who manipulate with amazing celerity." Fulfillment of the packers' prophecies prompted him to muse:

> Inasmuch as all distinguished strangers, upon arrival in the city, at once were taken to the Stock Yards . . . to view with salutary wonder the prodigious goings on, and to be crammed with statistics and oratory concerning how Chicago feeds the world; and inasmuch as the reporter's first query would be: "How do you like Chicago?" Next, invariably: "Have you seen the Stock Yards?" and the third, possibly: "Have you viewed our beautiful system of parks and boulevards?" it may be assumed that in the cultural system prevailing in those days . . . , the butcher stood at the peak of social eminence, while slightly below him were ranged the overlords of grain, lumber, and merchandising.[8]

As early as the Civil War, a full decade before Louis Sullivan's arrival, Chicagoans had prematurely claimed to be the "great *meat manufactory* of the world."[9] They still had midwestern competitors, and Chicago products were just beginning to penetrate eastern markets. Yet in 1865 the packers, livestock dealers, and railroad managers laid the groundwork for Chicago's future eminence. They built the first consolidated railroad stockyard and equipped it with a hotel, office building, and bank, as well as animal pens and switching facilities for the railroads. Annual livestock receipts topped two million by the end of the decade and climbed to nine million by the end of the 1870s, thanks to new settlements beyond the Mississippi and the extension of Chicago's rail network to twenty-three thousand miles of tracks. The immediate success of the new stockyard in the Town of Lake lured packers away from the South Branch of the Chicago River. Guaranteed access to the railroads serving the yards, they purchased land in the western half of Section 5 and built large, modern packinghouses. These plants had steam rendering tanks, steam hoists, and overhead rails on which the carcasses were moved; hog-scraping machines were developed in the late 1870s, and packers experimented with natural refrigeration to extend the season into the summer. During 1880 they used five million animals, produced $85 million worth of pork and beef products, and clinched the position of leading "meat manufactory" in the world.

By the time Chicago hosted the Columbian Exposition, annual livestock receipts had reached thirteen million and the value of packinghouse products approached $200 million. This economic miracle rested upon western settlement and additional railroad construction; development of ice-cooled railroad cars and mechanical refrigeration; a dramatic increase in chilled, fresh meat and packinghouse by-products; and more aggressive marketing strategies. The "Packers' Town" west of the Stockyards was crowded with large beef and pork houses and lard, sausage, canning, oleomargarine, fertilizer, and glue factories. Ruminating on "a cinchry iv pro-gress" and "an age iv wondhers," Mr. Dooley's thoughts turned quite naturally to Chicago's best illustration: "A cow goes lowin' softly in to Armours an' comes out glue, beef, gelatine, fertylizer, celooloid, joolry, sofy cushions, hair restorer, washin' sody, soap, lithrachoor an' bed springs so quick that while aft she's still cow, for'ard she may be annything fr'm buttons to Pannyma hats."[10]

Development of packinghouse by-products was a blessing for the sluggish Chicago River. In 1865 a state law and a city ordinance prohibited the practice of dumping animal wastes in the river or its branches. Compliance was minimal and enforcement lax until 1878 when the Illinois Supreme Court upheld the right of the city to license packers, slaughterers, and renderers within its limits and one mile beyond. Sewer catch basins plus utilization of blood, bones, and offal reduced the amount of packinghouse waste that found its way into the South Fork of the South Branch. Meantime, however, Chicago built more household and industrial sewers which emptied into the river, and Town of Lake's sewers terminated in that same unfortunate stream. Although city engineer Ellis Sylvester Chesbrough claimed to have reversed the flow of the Chicago River, it often emptied into Lake Michigan rather than the Illinois and Michigan Canal. The long-term solution was a new sanitary channel paralleling the old canal; approved by voters in 1889, it was not ready until 1900. A new four-mile water tunnel into the lake, more powerful pumps at the juncture of the river and the canal, and a conduit from the South Fork to the canal enabled Chicago to get through the 1890s.

As livestock trade and packing industry mushroomed, employment shot up from approximately two thousand in 1870 to twenty-five thousand by 1890. There were white-collar, blue-collar, skilled, semiskilled, and unskilled jobs in that square mile. The yards and packinghouses needed clerks, accountants, salesmen, coopers, carpenters, mechanics, railroad workers, canning operatives, and, of course, "knifemen"—stickers, beheaders, skinners, gutters, slitters, choppers, and trimmers. Contrary to Upton Sinclair's 1906 depiction of packinghouse employment, workers in the 1880s and early '90s had comparatively good wages and many opportunities for advancement in the expanding industry. The Knights of Labor statistician found that two-thirds of the men in 1886 worked a six-day week for eleven or more months and that 98 percent had full-time work for at least ten months of the year. Packinghouse employes earned as much as foundry and machine-shop workers, according to the 1880 census. Ten years later, Chicago packinghouse employes averaged $613 annually, while local factory workers received $589 and the national average wage in manufacturing was $427. Plant foremen earned $2,000 to $3,000, division superintendents $4,000 to $5,000, and Armour paid his Packingtown manager $10,000.[11]

Establishing a union in the face of steady work, good wages, and opportunities for advancement was a challenge. Yet a Butchers' and Packing-House Men's Protective Union and Benevolent Association tried its luck in 1879 and even conducted a brief, unsuccessful strike. With trade unionism on the upswing in the mid-1880s and workers demanding shorter hours, packinghouse and Stockyards employes secured the eight-hour day just before the Haymarket tragedy. During the tense summer of 1886, they flocked into the Knights of Labor, hoping the national labor organization could protect their gains. That fall the packers signed a contract with beef workers before returning pork workers to the ten-hour day. An inconclusive October strike was followed by a much larger walkout in November. With deputy sheriffs, Pinkertons, and the militia guarding Packingtown and the Stockyards, some plants reopened with nonunion workers. This setback plus indecisive leadership, ethnic cleavages, and tension between skilled and unskilled members of the Knights of Labor undermined the strike. In the end, strikers and even strike leaders got their jobs back, for the packers realized that machinery could not split, carve, skin, or trim a carcass. Foremen and managers looked the other way when former Knights of Labor harassed the "scabs" with well-aimed hearts and livers. The demise of the union diminished but did not destroy the workers' bargaining power in the packinghouses.

The pragmatic employers were prominent and highly respected members of the community. Although a French visitor was puzzled by Chicago's "strange combination of pork and Plato," packers fulfilled contemporary expectations by sharing profits with charity, culture, and education. Armour's technical institute was the city's largest local gift in the nineteenth century. Since many were self-made men, they pleased contemporaries by proving that poor farm boys and immigrants could rise to the top. George Horace Lorimer let his "Self-Made Merchant" echo the packers by criticizing those people "who think that they are all the choice cuts off the critter, and that the rest of us are only fit for sausage. . . . A man's as good as he makes himself, but no man's any good because his grandfather was." The packers also won praise for living up to the work ethic which they preached. At sixty years of age, noted an admirer in 1893, Philip Armour was still "the busiest soldier in the army," the one who put "zip and electricity into the air," the one who best exemplified "the qualities, the methods, and the ideas that have made the young Western Metropolis what it is."[12]

The Community in Retrospect

In the eyes of contemporaries, the "marvelous growth" which transformed the Town of Lake from "open prairie" to thriving community was another example of progress. When the stockyard company purchased land in 1865, there was only a small farm population in the thirty-six-square-mile township. By 1889 the Town of Lake had eighty-five thousand residents. It was the same size as New Haven, Connecticut, and approximately twice as large as Los Angeles or Seattle. Certainly it was an "instant suburb." It probably considered itself an "instant city," capable of managing its own affairs, when voters emphatically rejected the 1887 bid to join Chicago.

Census enumerators in 1870 found three thousand people—farmers, commuters at the Englewood railroad juncture, workers living close to the Rock Island carshops, and, in the northeastern sector, Stockyards employes near Halsted and settlers at Thirty-ninth and State where Town of Lake, Hyde Park, and Chicago met. These pioneers were too widely scattered to constitute a community, but Harvey Goodall's sprightly weekly and the annual township elections kept them in touch. The distinctive colorations of these early settlements were already visible. Englewood commuters were native-born Protestants who regarded the Fifty-fifth Street parkway as a buffer separating them from wage earners to the north. The Rock Island employes were skilled craftsmen and mechanics, often from Scotland, Germany, and England. The Stockyards neighborhood had a variety of shopkeepers on Halsted, livestock dealers and managers of the yards (most of them "Americans") on the three streets paralleling Halsted, and blue-collar families, often from Ireland, whose breadwinners worked in the yards, packing plants, and for the railroads.

Township population climbed to eighteen thousand during the 1870s and then soared to eighty-five thousand by 1889. Englewood attracted the type of people it wanted by stressing its rural setting, fine schools and Cook County Normal School, and its many "First" Protestant churches. Horsecar lines enabled the better-paid Stockyards and Packingtown employes to move there, but the tone was set by business and professional people who worked in Chicago and were known as "colonels" to others in the township. The neighborhood that grew up around the Rock Island carshops escaped its isolation with the advent of horsecars; in the early 1890s, however, the shops and most of the employes moved out to Blue Island and Chicagoans bought their houses. State Street cable cars increased the traffic in the Northeast Corners, while small factories along the railroads added to the congestion. By the late 1880s crowded housing, soot and smoke, and "Canaryville toughs" were causing problems for the Northeast Corners. Most of Town of Lake's small black population—not even 1 percent—lived close to State Street between the northern township border and Englewood's Sixty-third Street commercial district.

Jobs at the Stockyards and Packingtown were magnets for many of the newcomers, and they swelled the settlement east of Halsted and created new neighborhoods south and west of Section 5. The Stockyards neighborhood tripled in size during the 1880s as many more Irish workers took up residence there. Expansion of the packinghouse district forced employes off company land; some moved south of Forty-seventh Street into a subdivision developed by German-born Edward S. Dreyer and christened "New City" by a reporter who came across the project. Others built homes west of Ashland in a district called "Beyond Packers' Town" and eventually "Back of the Yards." The Forty-seventh Street and Ashland Avenue horsecar lines created a commercial center at that intersection and carried workers well beyond walking distance of their jobs. Thus it was still possible to buy a 25- by 125-foot lot for around $300 and put up a $600 frame house in the late 1880s. Since packinghouse annual wages ranged from $450 to $1,200, the cherished dream of home ownership was a realistic goal.

Accompanying the "veritable boom" of new houses in Town of Lake was the rapid proliferation of voluntary associations. These organizations gave members a "human surround," as one historian has put it.[13] They provided a friendly forum for the exchange of views, offered opportunities for service, enabled individuals to establish reputations within the group, and often linked them with a larger parent or national organization. The appeal was hard to resist, and the 1889 *Town of Lake Directory* listed 215 voluntary associations, 59 of them churches. The religious societies were of special importance to the immigrants, for they preserved linguistic and cultural heritages as well as meeting spiritual needs. The Irish proclaimed their dominance in the Stockyards neighborhood by forming St. Gabriel's parish in 1880 and completing a $200,000 building program by the end of the decade. Dreyer's gift of land to the German Catholics who launched St. Augustine's parish gave New City its German stamp. Just a few blocks away, Back of the Yards Irish built St. Rose of Lima Church, and in time Bohemian and Polish Catholics were numerous enough to do the same. Churches were undoubtedly the most important voluntary associations, and they anchored people in their neighborhoods. But other organizations attracted members from all parts of the township. The Knights of Labor accomplished this, and so did Irish nationalist organizations, ethnic fraternal societies, the Masons, and the Citizens' League of the Town of Lake for the Suppression of the Sale of Liquor to Minors and Drunkards.

The at-large elections for members of the town board drew the special interest groups into a common arena. "Americans" and ethnic voters, white-collar and blue-collar workers, Protestants and Catholics came together in nonpartisan coalitions striving to elect the supervisor, assessor, collector, clerk, trustees, and magistrates of the township. Through the 1870s, residents of Englewood, the Car-Shops, and the farmers had the upper hand. The surge of newcomers in the 1880s was quickly reflected in volatile, shifting political alliances. A livestock dealer from the Stockyards neighborhood, for example, defeated "the Englewood Ring" in 1883, only to see his coalition crumble before a workingman's slate headed by police captain Thomas Gahan. Supervisor Gahan's favoritism to the Irish enabled a People's Reform party to win in 1886 with "American," German, and Scandinavian backing. The Haymarket affair and Packingtown strikes gave law and order advocates a chance to flex their muscles in 1887. In the final township election the Irish, closely allied to city Democrats by then, staged a comeback. They opposed annexation, but when it came they knew how to play in the major leagues. Newcomers to the Town of Lake were soon drawn into its clamorous politics, for they too wanted a voice in shaping the future of the community. Participation was so widespread that Goodall once remarked, "if politics were religion, nine-tenths of the Town of Lake people would be saved."[14]

Unlike other nineteenth-century suburbs which waited for annexation to secure improvements, Town of Lake plunged ahead on its own. It had a waterworks capable of pumping fifteen million gallons per day, seventy miles of sewers, and a drainage plan devised by professional sanitary engineers. Its major thoroughfares were lighted, part of Halsted had granite paving, and many other streets had macadam surfaces. The town's police force numbered eighty-two by the time of annexation, and it came through the 1886 strikes with the respect of both sides. The eighty-five firemen and seven steam engines could be augmented by first-class fire-fighting equipment at the Stockyards and Packingtown. And the small health department supervised scavenger service, dispensed public assistance, helped with livestock inspection, and collected vital statistics. Town of Lake did much better than the other Chicago suburbs in making improvements and delivering services. Board members were always under pressure to move faster in the 1880s, but their progress convinced voters in 1887 that the township was better off than the metropolis.

After a visit to the Stockyards in 1867, Heinrich Schliemann noted in his journal, "there is no doubt that the city will reach this point within a few years." Chicago reached the township in the 1870s and coveted it in the 1880s. The *Inter Ocean* expressed the city's nervousness about the outcome of the second annexation referendum. Suburbanites who refused to look beyond their "own little garden patch" were "contemptible." In June the editor warned both urban and suburban voters against letting the sensational Cronin murder "obscure the question of annexation." Ironically, he did not realize that agitation over the Cronin crime was distracting Town of Lake Irish from the anti-annexation campaign. Nor did he connect their unusually low turnout with the narrow victory of the annexationists in Town of Lake. He was busy celebrating Chicago's suburban harvest and its overnight elevation to the country's number two city.[15]

Merger was not the inevitable destiny of the township. However, it *was* fortuitous for the metropolis because the Town of Lake helped shape Chicago's twentieth-century image. Without that industrial suburb, Carl Sandburg might not have perceived Chicago as "City of the Big Shoulders" or "Player with Railroads"—or "Hog Butcher for the World."

NOTES

1. *Trib.*, Apr. 10, 1892; Julian Ralph, "Killing Cattle for Two Continents," *Harper's Weekly*, 36 (July 9, 1892), 670; Francis Lederer, "Competition for the World's Columbian Exposition: The Chicago Campaign," *JISHS*, 65 (Winter, 1972), 382–88; Charles B. Farwell, "Chicago's Candidacy for the World's Fair of 1892," *Cosmopolitan*, 8 (Nov., 1889), 50–58; *Drovers Journal*, Sept. 10, 11, 14, Nov. 13, 1889.

2. Quoted in "Editor's Table," *New England Magazine*, 6 (May, 1892), 405; quoted in *Trib.*, Feb. 26, 1890; Paul de Rousiers, *American Life*, trans. A. J. Herbertson (New York, 1892), 57; Robert Parmet, "Competition for the World's Columbian Exposition; The New York Campaign," *JISHS*, 65 (Winter, 1972), 365–81; Gertrude Barnum, "The Chicago Woman and Her Clubs," *The Graphic*, May 27, 1893, 343.

3. *Trib.*, Oct. 25, 1887; Apr. 22, 26, June 1, 1890; Lederer, "Chicago Campaign," 388–94; "Editor's Table," 403; Julian Ralph, *Harper's Chicago and the World's Fair* (New York, 1893), preface, 1; David F. Burg, *Chicago's White City of 1893* (Lexington, Ky., 1976), 333.

4. *Drovers Journal*, May 16, 1890; Sept. 2, 1891; May 27, Aug. 23, Sept. 20, 1893; *Sun*, June 18, 1892; Apr. 27, May 27, Aug. 23, 1893; *Trib.*, Sept. 5, 1891; Apr. 30, 1893.

5. *Sun*, Aug. 23, 1893; *Drovers Journal*, Sept. 20, 1893; Rousiers, *American Life*, 65, 68; Martindale Ward, *A Trip to Chicago, What I Saw, What I Heard, What I Thought* (Glasgow, 1895), 77.

6. *Trib.*, April 10, 1892; Ralph, "Killing Cattle for Two Continents," 670; P. J. O'Keeffe, "The Chicago Stock Yards," *New England Magazine*, 6 (May, 1892), 369; "Hog Killing at the Chicago Stock Yards," *Scientific American*, 65 (Nov. 7, 1891), 291; Rousiers, *American Life*, 73; Ward, *Trip to Chicago*, 77.

7. Alan Trachtenberg, *The Incorporation of America: Culture and Society in the Gilded Age* (New York, 1982), 213–16; Jessie Heckman Hirschl, "The Great White City," *American Heritage*, 11 (Oct. 1960), 75; *Sun*, June 18, 1892.

8. Louis H. Sullivan, *The Autobiography of an Idea* (New York, 1926), 200, 201, 305, 307–8.

9. Department of Agriculture, *Annual Report for 1862* (Washington, 1863), 326.

10. Finley Peter Dunne, *Mr. Dooley on Ivrything and Ivrybody*, selected by Robert Hutchinson (New York, 1963), 196, 197, 198.

11. *Tenth Census, 1880*, vol. 2, "Manufactures," 391–93; Illinois Bureau of Labor Statistics, *Fourth Biennial Report, 1886* (Springfield, 1887), 280, 312, 314, 325, 353, 356; *Eleventh Census, 1890*, vol. 6, "Manufacturing Industries," part 2, "Statistics of Cities," 143, 144; *Drover's Journal*, Nov. 10, 1886; June 26, 1889; *Sun*, Apr. 28, 1890; *Trib.*, Apr. 30, 1890; Clarence D. Long, *Wages and Earnings in the United States, 1860–1890* (Princeton, N.J., 1960), 42.

12. [Price Collier], *America and the Americans from a French Point of View* (New York, 1897), 254; [George Horace Lorimer], *Letters from a Self-Made Merchant to His Son* (Boston, 1902), 230–31, 240; Carter H. Hepburn, "Philip D. Armour," *Munsey's Magazine*, 9 (Apr., 1893), 56–58.

13. Thomas Bender, *Community and Social Change in America* (New Brunswick, N.J., 1978), 98.

14. *Sun*, Jan. 21, 1888.

15. Donald Zochert, "Heinrich Schliemann's Chicago Journal," *Chicago History*, 2 (Spring-Summer, 1973), 173, 178–79; *Inter Ocean*, June 21, 28, 1889.

Essay on Sources

Chicago's Pride could not have been written without access to the city newspapers, especially the *Tribune, Times,* and *Daily News,* and Harvey Goodall's two Town of Lake publications. The Chicago Historical Society has the [Stockyards] *Sun* (1884 on), and the *Drovers Journal* (1882 on) is available in the Regenstein Library, University of Chicago. Other important sources are arranged under seven thematic headings to facilitate scholarly use. Readers, however, will recognize that many items serve multiple purposes.

Chicago

All students of nineteenth-century Chicago are indebted to Bessie Louise Pierce for her three-volume *History of Chicago.* Volumes 2 (*From Town to City, 1848–1871* [New York, 1940]) and 3 (*The Rise of a Modern City, 1871–1893* [New York, 1957]) are essential for this study. John S. Wright, *Chicago: Past, Present, Future* (Chicago, 1868); S. S. Schoff, *The Glory of Chicago, Her Manufactories* (Chicago, 1873); Inter-Ocean, *Chicago's First Half-Century* (Chicago, 1883); and Chicago Times, *Chicago and Its Resources Twenty Years After, 1871–1891* (Chicago, 1892) are valuable contemporary accounts. Descriptive articles include [James Parton], "Chicago," *Atlantic Monthly,* 19 (Mar., 1867); [James W. Sheahan], "Chicago," *Scribner's Monthly,* 10 (Sept., 1875); A. A. Hayes, "The Metropolis of the Prairies," *Harper's Monthly Magazine,* 61 (Oct., 1880); and those by Julian Ralph reprinted in *Our Great West* (New York, 1893) and *Harper's Chicago and the World's Fair* (New York, 1893).

For identification of Chicagoans, see George Upton, *Biographical Sketches of the Leading Men of Chicago* (Chicago, 1876); *The Biographical Dictionary and Portrait Gallery of Representative Men of Chicago,* 3 vols. (Chicago, 1892); John Joseph Flinn, *The Hand-Book of Chicago Biography* (Chicago, 1893); and Thomas W. Goodspeed, *The University of Chicago Biographical Sketches,* 2 vols. (Chicago, 1922).

Among the guidebooks mentioning the packinghouses, stockyards, and Town of Lake are Mrs. M. L. Rayne, *Chicago and One Hundred Miles Around: Being a Complete Hand-Book and Guide* (Chicago, 1865); [James B. Runnion], *Out of Town* (Chicago, 1869); Chicago Times, *Our Suburbs: A Resume of the Origins, Progress, and Present Status of Chicago's Environs* (Chicago, 1873); Everett Chamberlin, *Chicago and Its Suburbs* (Chicago, 1874); [J. M. Wing and Co.], *Seven Days in Chicago: A Complete Guide* (Chicago, 1876); *Stranger's Guide to the Garden City* (Chicago, 1883); *Marquis' Hand-Book of Chicago: A Complete History, Reference Book, and Guide to the City* (Chicago, 1885); [Elmer E. Barton], *A Business Tour of Chicago, Depicting Fifty Years' Progress* (Chicago, 1887); [Edwin Stine], *What Everybody Wants to Know about Chicago* (Chicago, 1887); and John Joseph Flinn, *Chicago, the Marvelous City of the West* (Chicago, 1890).

A baker's dozen of pertinent travel accounts: Newman Hall, *From Liverpool to St. Louis* (London, 1870); David Macrae, *The Americans at Home*, 2 vols. (Edinburgh, 1870); Grace Greenwood [Mrs. S. J. C. Lippincott], *New Life in New Lands: Notes of Travel* (New York, 1873); John Leng, *America in 1876* (Dundee, 1877); C. B. Berry, *The Other Side, How It Struck Us* (London, 1880); Walter Gore Marshall, *Through America: Nine Months in the United States* (London, 1882); William Hardman, *A Trip to America* (London, 1884); L. de Cotton, "A Frenchman's Visit to Chicago in 1886," *JISHS*, 47 (Spring, 1954); Charles Beadle, *A Trip to the United States in 1887* (Oxford, 1887); "A Visit to the States," *The Times* (London), Oct. 21, 24, 1887; Rudyard Kipling, *From Sea to Sea: Letters of Travel*, 2 vols. (New York, 1899); Paul de Rousiers, *American Life*, trans. A. J. Herbertson (New York, 1892); Martindale C. Ward, *A Trip to Chicago, What I Saw, What I Heard, What I Thought* (Glasgow, 1895).

Town of Lake

Indispensable for understanding the development of the township are the Town of Lake records (stored in the basement of Chicago City Hall when the author used them). Alfred T. Andreas, *History of Cook County, Illinois* (Chicago, 1884) contains a short history of the township and biographical information unavailable elsewhere. Population changes can be traced in the United States censuses and manuscript schedules of the 1860, 1870, and 1880 counts; the Chicago Board of Education's biennial school censuses include the former Town of Lake from 1890 on. Reports of the Cook County Department of Public Instruction note the expansion of the public schools in Lake during the 1870s and 1880s. James J. O'Toole's 1938 reminiscence, "Back o' the Yards, 1870 to 1890" (typescript pamphlet, Chicago Historical Society), and Andrew Vogler's "From an Old Timer Back of the Yards" (typescript, Mary McDowell Papers, Chicago Historical Society) are the best accounts of the origins of that neighborhood. McDowell founded the University of Chicago Settlement near Ashland and Forty-seventh Street in 1894, and her papers and the settlement records contain valuable information, including the extant portions of Vivien M. Palmer's typescript, "History of New City." Gerald E. Sullivan, ed., *The Story of Englewood, 1835–1923* (Chicago, 1924) and the editions of *The Town of Lake Directory* published between 1886 and 1889 are also important sources of information about the township.

Livestock Trade

Bessie Louise Pierce's fourth chapter in volume 3, *The Rise of a Modern City, 1871–1893,* is the best short account of Chicago's livestock and packing industries in the post-Civil War decades. She had access to the 1870s *Drovers Journal,* but these volumes can no longer be located. Additional information can be found in Rudolf A. Clemen, *The American Livestock and Meat Industry* (New York, 1923); Paul Wallace Gates, "Cattle Kings in the Prairies," *MVHR,* 35 (Dec., 1948); "Where the Beef Comes From," *Lippincott's Magazine,* 24 (Nov., 1879); and John Clay, *My Life on the Range* (Chicago, 1924; rpt. Norman, Okla., 1962). The Octave Chanute Papers (Library of Congress), the Chicago, Burlington and Quincy Railroad Archives (Newberry Library, Chicago), and Paul M. Angle, "The Union Stockyards: December 25, 1865," *Chicago History,* 7 (Winter, 1965–66) are essential for the founding of the Union Stock Yards. Although the Union Stock Yard and Transit Company lost many of its early records in a twentieth-century fire, some annual reports are available and the Chicago Historical Society has the corporate *Minute Book* for the 1865–1904 period. Joseph G. Knapp, "A Review of Chicago Stock Yards History," *University [of Chicago] Journal of Business,* 2 (June, 1924); P. J. O'Keeffe, "The Chicago Stock Yards," *New England Magazine,* 6 (May, 1892); W. H. Thompson, Jr., "Live Stock Exchanges," *Nat. Prov.,* 22 (Feb. 3, 1900); Jack Wing, *The Great Union Stock Yards of Chicago* (Chicago, 1865); W. Joseph Grand, *Illustrated History of the Union Stockyards* (Chicago, 1896); and M. S. Parkhurst's brief *History of the Yards, 1865–1953* (Chicago, 1953) cover the growth of the yards. Annual reports of the Chicago Board of Trade and *Griffiths' Annual Review of the Live Stock Trade at Chicago* (Chicago, 1869–78) carry receipts and shipments. Occasional articles in the *Breeder's Gazette,* which began publication in 1881, and the reports of the Bureau of Animal Industry (Department of Agriculture) are also informative.

Meat-packing

On development of the packing industry in Chicago, see, in addition to Pierce and Clemen, Howard C. Hill, "The Development of Chicago as a Center of the Meat Packing Industry," *MVHR,* 10 (Dec., 1923); Margaret Walsh, "Pork Packing as a Leading Edge of Midwestern Industry, 1835–1875," *Agricultural History,* 51 (1977) and *The Rise of the Midwestern Meat Packing Industry* (Lexington, Ky., 1982); "Sixtieth Anniversary Number," *Armour Magazine,* 16 (Apr., 1927); James MacDonald, *Food from the Far West, or American Agriculture with Special Reference to the Beef Production and Importation of Dead Meat from America to Great Britain* (London, 1878); Oscar E. Anderson, Jr., *Refrigeration in America: A History of a New Technology and Its Impact* (Princeton, N.J., 1953); and Rudolf A. Clemen, *By-Products in the Packing Industry* (Chicago, 1927). Internal descriptions of the packinghouses can be found in many of the travelers' accounts and *Prairie Farmer,* 8 (Nov., 1848), and 29 (Feb. 20, 1864); "Cheaper Beef," *Harper's Weekly,* 26 (Oct. 21, 1882); "Hog Killing at the Chicago Stock Yards," *Scientific American,* 65 (Nov. 7, 1891); and Julian Ralph, "Killing Cattle for Two Continents," *Harper's Weekly,* 36 (July 9, 1892).

Armour and Company records (now in the Greyhound Tower, Phoenix) are disappointingly thin for the nineteenth century. Those of Swift and Company in Chicago are more useful, as Louis Unfer, "Swift and Company: The Development of the Packing Industry, 1875 to 1912" (Ph.D. diss., University of Illinois, 1951) demonstrates. For expansion of the industry, see Alfred D. Chandler, Jr., and Louis Galambos, "The Development of Large-Scale Economic Organizations in Modern America," *Journal of Economic History,* 30 (Mar., 1970); Mary Yeager Kujovich, "The Refrigerator Car and the Growth of the American Dressed Beef Industry," *Business History Review,* 44 (Winter, 1970); and Mary Yeager, *Competition and Regulation: The Development of Oligopoly in the Meat Packing Industry* (Greenwich, Conn., 1981). Additional information on the industry can be found in articles in the *National Provisioner;* the Senate Select Committee, *Testimony . . . on the Transportation and Sale of Meat Products* (Washington, 1889) and *Report* (Washington, 1890); and Federal Trade Commission, *Report on the Meat-Packing Industry, 1919* (Washington, 1919).

The best sources on Chicago's early packers are "Archibald Clybourne: Pioneer Packer," *Chicago History,* 7 (Fall, 1963); Charles Cleaver, *Early-*

Chicago Reminiscences (Chicago, 1882); and Elizabeth T. Kent, "William Kent, Independent: A Biography" (typescript, 1950, Chicago Historical Society). For Philip Armour, see Harper Leech and John C. Carroll, *Armour and His Times* (New York, 1938); Arthur Warren, "Philip D. Armour," *McClure's* 2 (Feb., 1894); Cora Lillian Davenport, "The Rise of the Armours: An American Industrial Family" (M.A. thesis, University of Chicago, 1930); and Clifford L. Snowden, "The Armour Institute of Technology," *New England Magazine*, 16 (May, 1897). Ira Nelson Morris, *Heritage from My Father, an Autobiography* (New York, 1947) supplements Nelson Morris, "Personal Reminiscences of the Chicago Market," *Breeder's Gazette*, 46 (Dec. 2, 1904). Two of Gustavus Swift's children wrote about him: Helen Swift, *My Father and My Mother* (Chicago, 1937) and Louis F. Swift and Arthur Van Vlissingen, *The Yankee of the Yards: The Biography of Gustavus Franklin Swift* (Chicago, 1927). William Terence Kane, *The Education of Edward Cudahy* (Chicago, 1941) contains material about the older Cudahy brothers. The packers are viewed from a different perspective in Kathleen D. McCarthy, *Noblesse Oblige: Charity and Cultural Philanthropy in Chicago, 1849–1929* (Chicago, 1982); Joyce Maynard Ghent and Frederic Cople Jaher, "The Chicago Business Elite: 1830–1930. A Collective Biography," *Business History Review*, 50 (Autumn, 1976); and Frederic Cople Jaher, *The Urban Establishment* (Urbana, Ill., 1982).

Pollution

The relationship of the packinghouses to the South Branch, South Fork, and Illinois and Michigan Canal is a staple topic in city newspapers and annual reports of the Citizens' Association of Chicago, the Chicago Board (Department) of Health, and the Chicago Board (Department) of Public Works. See also Dr. John H. Rauch's *Sanitary Problems of Chicago* (Cambridge, Mass., 1879), and F. Garvin Davenport's "John Henry Rauch and Public Health in Illinois, 1877–1891," *JISHS*, 50 (Autumn, 1957). Recent studies include James C. O'Connell, "Technology and Pollution: Chicago's Water Policy, 1833–1930" (Ph.D. diss., University of Chicago, 1980); Louis P. Cain, *Sanitation Strategy for a Lakefront Metropolis: The Case of Chicago* (DeKalb, Ill., 1978); and Martin V. Melosi, ed., *Pollution and Reform in American Cities, 1870–1930* (Austin, 1980).

Labor

Chicago and Town of Lake newspaper accounts are important sources for the labor material in this book. Useful for the 1870s are Richard Schneirov,

"Chicago's Great Upheaval of 1877," *Chicago History,* 9 (Spring, 1980); Samuel Bernstein, "American Labor in the Long Depression, 1873–1878," *Science and Society,* 20 (Winter, 1956); Samuel Rezneck, "Distress, Relief and Discontent in the United States during the Depression of 1873–1878," *Journal of Political Economy,* 58 (Dec., 1950); and Robert V. Bruce, *1877: Year of Violence* (Indianapolis, 1959). Edward B. Mittelman, "Chicago Labor in Politics, 1877–96," *Journal of Political Economy,* 28 (May, 1920) and George A. Schilling, "History of the Labor Movement in Chicago" in [Lucy E. Parsons], *Life of Albert R. Parsons, with a Brief History of the Labor Movement in America* (Chicago, 1889) should be used in conjunction with Ralph W. Scharnau, "Thomas J. Morgan and the Chicago Socialist Movement, 1876–1901" (Ph.D. diss., Northern Illinois University, 1969) and "Thomas J. Morgan and the United Labor Party of Chicago," *JISHS,* 66 (Spring, 1973).

Information about stockyard and packinghouse workers in the 1880s and early 1890s can be found in the Chicago Knights of Labor journal, *Knights of Labor;* Paul C. Hull, *The Chicago Riot: A Record of the Terrible Scenes of May 4, 1886* (Chicago, 1886); Henry David, *The History of the Haymarket Affair* (New York, 1963); Paul Avrich, *The Haymarket Tragedy* (Princeton, N.J., 1984); and Howard Barton Myers, "The Policing of Labor Disputes in Chicago: A Case Study" (Ph.D. diss., University of Chicago, 1929). The Terence Powderly Papers (Catholic University of America, Washington), Henry Demarest Lloyd Papers (State Historical Society of Wisconsin, Madison), Knights of Labor General Assembly *Proceedings,* and *Journal of United Labor* are essential. So too are Powderly's views in *Thirty Years of Labor, 1859 to 1889* (Columbus, Ohio, 1890) and *The Path I Trod: The Autobiography of Terence V. Powderly,* ed. H. J. Carmen et al. (New York, 1940). Compare the latter with Vincent Joseph Falzone, "Terence V. Powderly, Mayor and Labor Leader, 1849–1893" (Ph.D. diss., University of Maryland, 1970). Other valuable sources are Joseph R. Buchanan's short-lived newspaper, *The Labor Enquirer,* and his autobiography, *The Story of a Labor Agitator* (New York, 1903). John T. Joyce's recollections appeared in the Amalgamated Meat Cutters and Butcher Workmen's journal, the *Butcher Workman,* during 1932 and 1933. The 1886 and 1892 reports of the Illinois Bureau of Labor Statistics contain information on wages and hours.

Also useful are Earl R. Beckner, *A History of Labor Legislation in Illinois* (Chicago, 1929); Sidney Fine, "The Eight-Hour Day Movement in the United States, 1888–1891," *MVHR,* 40 (Dec., 1953); and the opening chapters of Daniel Nelson, *Managers and Workers: Origins of the New Factory System in the United States, 1880–1920* (Madison, Wis., 1975) and David Brody, *The Butcher Workmen: A Study of Unionization* (Cambridge, Mass., 1964).

Ethnic Groups

The Chicago Foreign Language Press Survey, a compilation of ethnic newspaper articles translated into English, is a valuable source. Catholic parish reports and correspondence at St. Mary of the Lake Seminary, Mundelein, Illinois, augment Charles Shanabruch's *Chicago's Catholics: The Evolution of an American Identity* (Notre Dame, Ind., 1981) and Joseph James Thompson, ed., *The Archdiocese of Chicago, Antecedents and Development* (Des Plaines, Ill., 1920). See also Gustav E. Johnson, "The Swedes of Chicago" (Ph.D. diss., University of Chicago, 1940); John J. Reichman, *Czechoslovaks of Chicago: Contributions to a History of a National Group* (Chicago, 1937); and Eugene Ray McCarthy, "The Bohemians in Chicago and Their Benevolent Societies, 1875–1946" (M. A. thesis, University of Chicago, 1950).

Polish Pageant Inc., *Poles of Chicago, 1837–1937: A History of One Century of Polish Contribution to the City of Chicago* (Chicago, 1937); Edward R. Kantowicz, *Polish-American Politics in Chicago, 1888–1940* (Chicago, 1975); Victor R. Greene, *For God and Country: The Rise of Polish and Lithuanian Ethnic Consciousness in America, 1860–1910* (Madison, Wis., 1975); and Joseph John Parot, *Polish Catholics in Chicago, 1850–1920: A Religious History* (De Kalb, Ill., 1981) are important sources on that immigrant group.

On the Germans, see Andrew Jacke Townsend, *The Germans in Chicago* (Chicago, 1932); Henry L. Schroeder and C. W. Forbrich, *Men Who Have Made the Fifth Ward: Being a Collection of Biographical Sketches* (Chicago, 1895); Marion A. Habig, *The Franciscans at St. Augustine's and in Chicagoland* (Chicago, 1961); St. Augustine's Parish, *Golden Jubilee and Chronological History of St. Augustine's Parish* (Chicago, 1936).

For the Irish, see Charles Ffrench, ed., *Biographical History of the American Irish in Chicago* (Chicago, 1897); St. Gabriel's Church, *Diamond Jubilee Souvenir Program, 1880–1955* (Chicago, 1955); Michael F. Funchion, *Chicago's Irish Nationalists, 1881–1890* (New York, 1976); Thomas N. Brown, *Irish-American Nationalism, 1870–1890* (Philadelphia, 1966); and Charles Fanning, *Finley Peter Dunne and Mr. Dooley: The Chicago Years* (Lexington, Ky., 1978).

Essential for understanding the Chicago ethnic landscape are two collections of articles edited by Melvin G. Holli and Peter d'A. Jones, *The Ethnic Frontier: Essays in the History of Group Survival in Chicago and the Midwest* (Grand Rapids, Mich., 1977) and *Ethnic Chicago* (Grand Rapids, Mich., 1981).

ILLUSTRATIONS

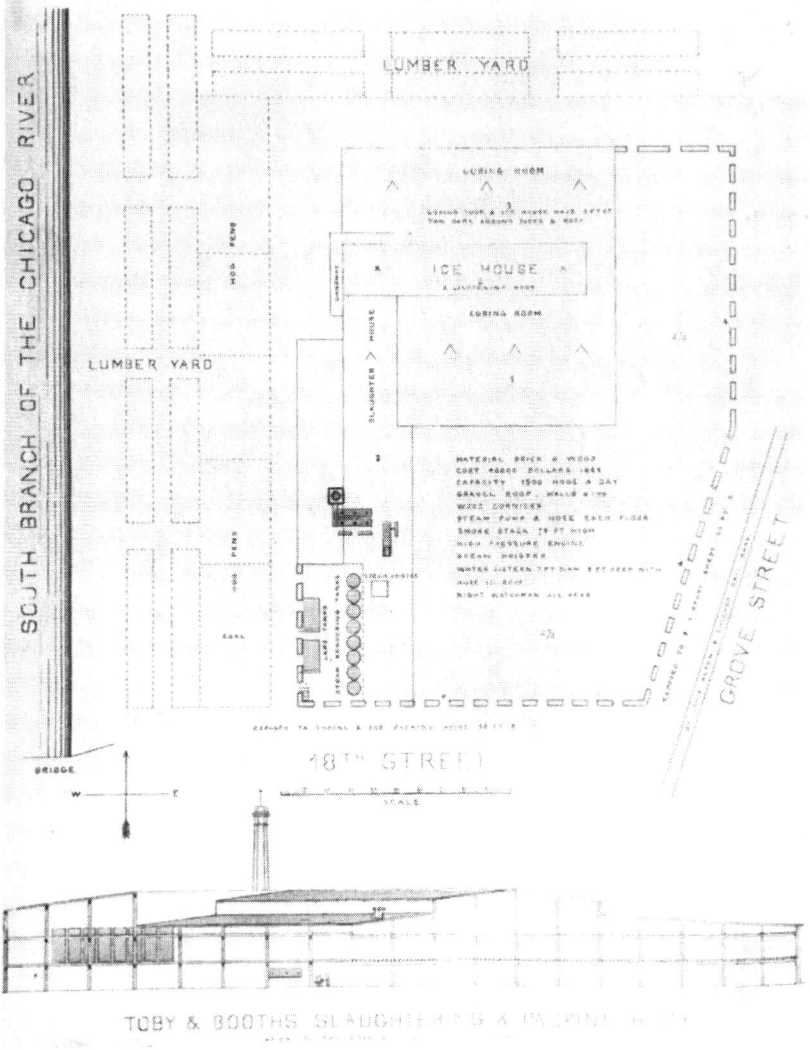

Fig. 1. Toby [*sic*] & Booth's Slaughtering & Packing House. Floor plan and elevation of the Tobey and Booth pork-packing plant, a model in the 1860s. From B. W. Phillips and Company, *Fire Insurance Maps of the City of Chicago, Illinois* (1865).

Fig. 2. Hough House in 1866, with the Exchange in the background.

Soon after the end of the Civil War, immigrants Otto Jevne, Peter Almini, and Louis Kurz pooled their talents to produce a series of tinted "Lithographic Views" of their adopted city. Of course they included the new livestock facility and its large hotel.

Fig. 3. View of the Union Stock Yard in 1866, showing the Exchange and the original wooden water tanks.

From Jevne and Almini, *Chicago Illustrated, 1866–67,* after drawings by Louis Kurz. Courtesy, Chicago Historical Society, ICHi-06873 (fig. 2) and ICHi-06898 (fig. 3).

Fig. 4. Cook County Normal School. Built in 1869 in Englewood, this academic institution became an important drawing card for the surrounding residential neighborhood. Courtesy, Special Collections, Chicago Public Library.

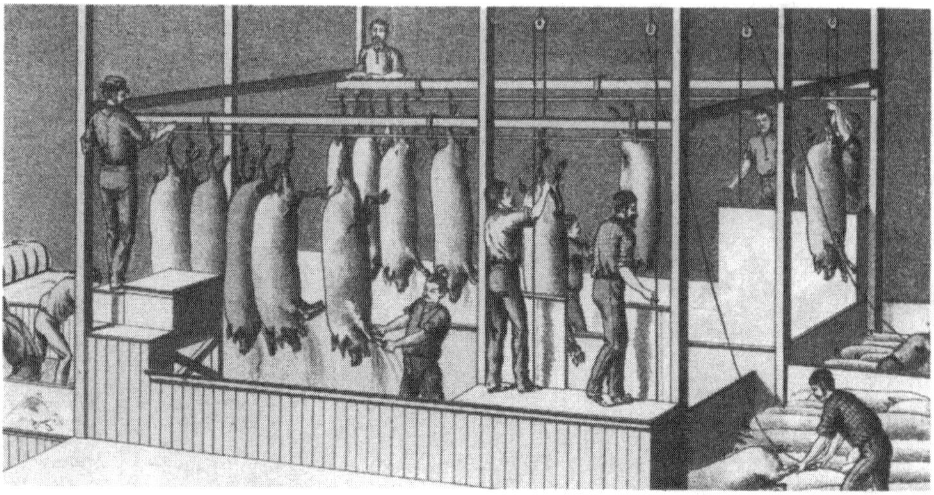

Figs. 5 and 6. Two details from an 1880 lithograph published in Chicago by James Campbell, Inspector of Provisions for the Board of Trade. He entitled it "Interior Views of A Modern First Class Pork Packing & Canning Establishment of the United States of America." The first detail shows the hoisting, slaughtering, and deposit of the carcass in the scalding vat. The second detail features the iron clamp which removed the carcass from the vat and the new hog-scraping machinery invented in the late 1870s. Courtesy, Chicago Historical Society, ICHi-04064.

Fig. 7. Chicago—entrance to the Union Stock Yards. The Stone Gate was built in 1879 by Daniel H. Burnham and John W. Root and was designated a Chicago landmark in 1972. From the *Graphic News,* Mar. 6, 1886. Courtesy, Chicago Historical Society, ICHi-28422.

Fig. 8. Bird's-eye view of the Union Stock Yards of Chicago. Depiction of the Stockyards and packing plants in G. L. Howe and O. M. Powers, *The Secrets of Success in Business* (Chicago, 1883). Courtesy, Chicago Historical Society, #0018.

Fig. 9. Philip D. Armour's home on Prairie Avenue. Courtesy, Chicago Historical Society, ICHi-28773.

Fig. 10. Englewood residence in the 6400 block of Harvard Street. Courtesy, Special Collections, Chicago Public Library.

Fig. 11. Boardinghouse and saloon on Ashland Avenue near the western entrance to Packingtown. Photo by Chicago Daily News. Courtesy, Chicago Historical Society, DN-003265.

Fig. 12. Frame houses in the 5300 block of Halsted Street, probably built in the late 1880s. Photo by Mildred Mead. Courtesy, Chicago Historical Society, ICHi-00831.

Fig. 13. Late 1890s lantern slide of houses near Ashland Avenue and Forty-seventh Street in Back of the Yards. From the University of Chicago Settlement, courtesy of Chicago Historical Society, #0292.

Fig. 14. Englewood fire and police station at Wentworth Avenue and Sixty-third Street as it appeared in 1889. Courtesy, Special Collections, Chicago Public Library.

Fig. 15. View of Englewood in 1889, looking southwest toward Sixty-third Street. Courtesy, Special Collections, Chicago Public Library.

Fig. 16. Halsted Street at Forty-second, showing from right to left Thomas Gahan's building, Drovers National Bank, and Charles Kotzenberg's pharmacy and paint store. From the *Graphic News*, Mar. 5, 1887. Courtesy, Chicago Historical Society, ICHi-18549.

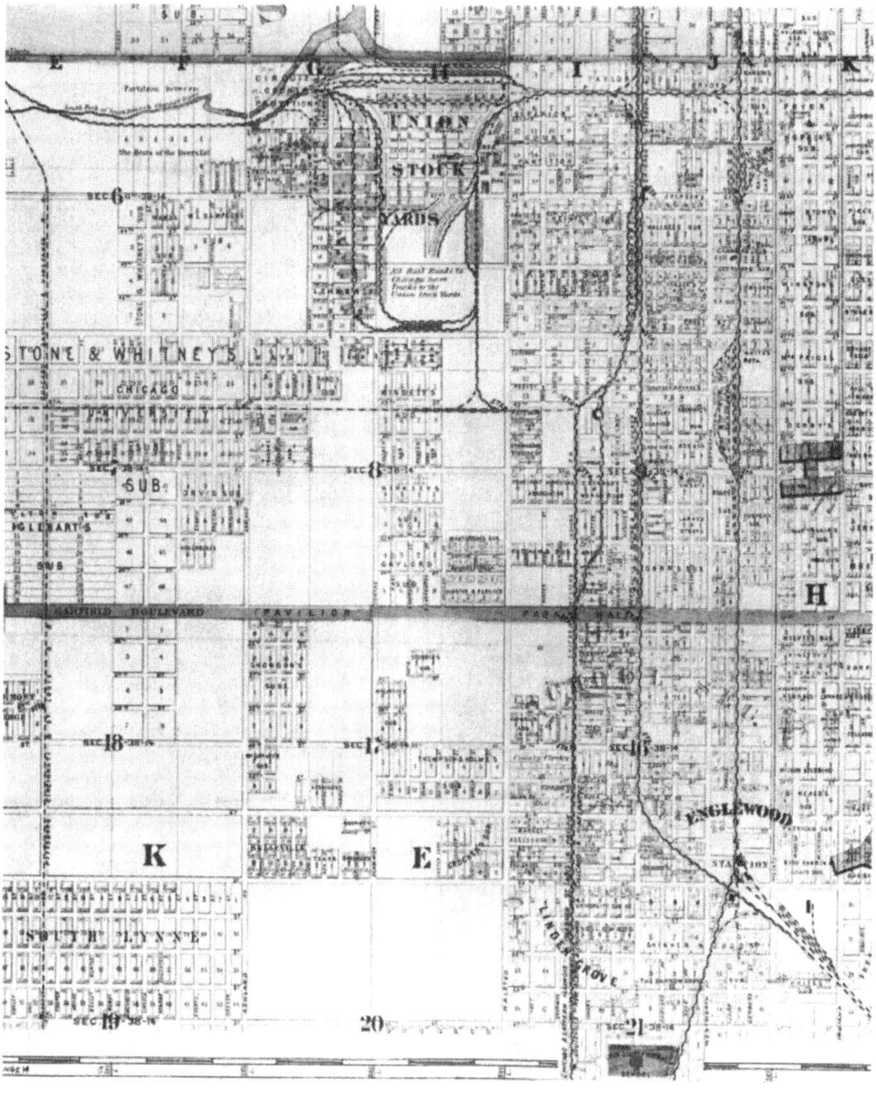

Fig. 17. Detail from an 1880s map informing users that "All Rail Roads to Chicago have Tracks to the Union Stock Yards." From Snyder's Park & Guide Map of Chicago, 1886.

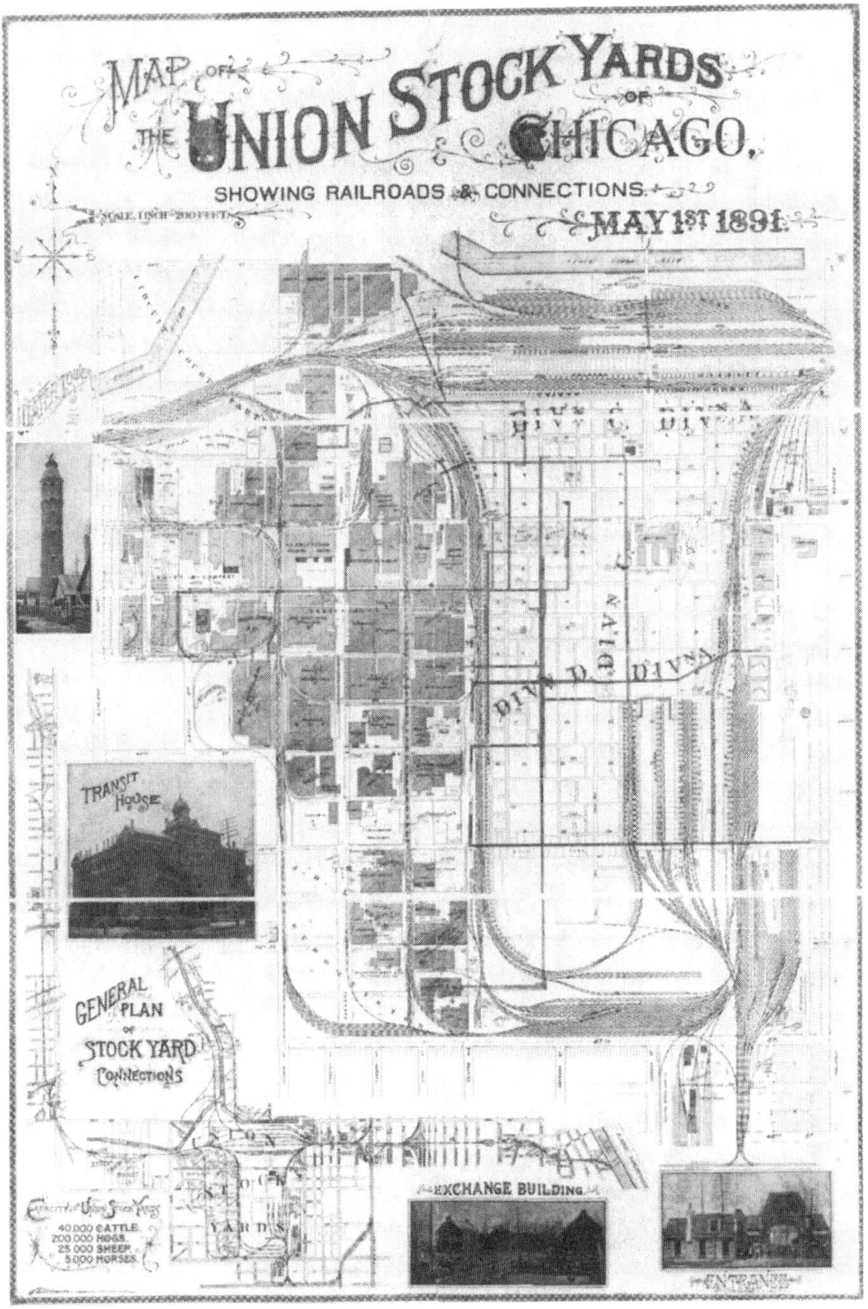

Fig. 18. Rand, McNally's 1891 map of the yards, railroad complex, and structures in Packingtown. Courtesy, Chicago Historical Society, ICHi-27741.

Fig. 19. An 1889 photo of the crowded pens at the Stockyards with the Transit House in the distance. From A. Wittemann, *Select Chicago* (New York, 1889). Courtesy, Chicago Historical Society, ICHi-24284-B.

Fig. 20. Trimming. Photograph of the knifemen at work. From A. Wittemann, *Views of the Chicago Stockyard and Packing Houses* (New York, 1892). Courtesy, Chicago Historical Society, ICHi-04076.

Index

The University of Illinois Press
is a founding member of the
Association of American University Presses.

University of Illinois Press
1325 South Oak Street
Champaign, IL 61820-6903
www.press.uillinois.edu